# THE COMPLETE GUIDE

# TAHOE

## 1995-96 Edition

## BY KEN CASTLE

ISBN 0-935701-02-8

Foghorn
Press
BOOKS BUILDING COMMUNITY™

51895 >

9 780935 701029

Foghorn Press
555 DeHaro Street #220
San Francisco, CA 94107
415-241-9550

Foghorn Press titles are distributed to the book trade by Publishers
Group West, Emeryville, California. To contact your local sales
representative, call 1-800-788-3123.

To order individual books, please call Foghorn Press at
1-800-FOGHORN (364-4676).

Library of Congress ISSN Data:
May 1995
Tahoe: The Complete Guide
ISSN 1082-2240

Printed in the United States of America

# THE COMPLETE GUIDE

# TAHOE

## 1995-96 Edition

◆

## BY KEN CASTLE

Foghorn Press

BOOKS BUILDING COMMUNITY™

## Book Credits

Editor—Howard Rabinowitz
Copyeditors—Ann-Marie Brown, Kristin Barendsen
Research Editor—Sherrie Christopher
Book and Map Design—Michele Thomas
Production—Julianne Boyajian


## Photo Credits

Cover Photo by Ken Castle
*Emerald Bay, Lake Tahoe*

All other photos by Ken Castle except:
p. 13—James Mell Photography,
courtesy of North Lake Tahoe Historical Society
p. 64—Courtesy of the *M.S. Dixie II*
p. 492—Courtesy of Cal-Neva Lodge

*For my wife, Kathy, and for our departed companions, Chapman Wentworth, Wayne Poulsen, Gary Niver and little Oskar, who will always be in our hearts.*

# **Contents**

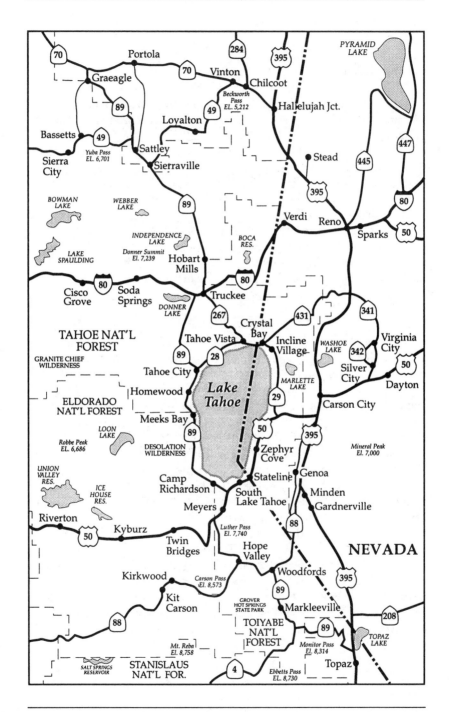

# How to Use this Book

This book includes several distinct parts: general overviews of natural and historic points of interest in the Lake Tahoe and Reno areas; chapters on summer and winter recreation, lodging and restaurants, kids' activities, wedding sites and annual events; appendices on transportation and important phone numbers in Lake Tahoe and Reno; and an index. For information on a particular activity, refer to the table of contents on page 6 and turn to the relevant chapter. If you know the name of a particular resort, trail, park, lodging or restaurant, or the general area you wish to visit, look it up in the index beginning on page 673.

You will also find a list marked "★ Author's Choice ★" at the beginning of many chapters. (For example, the chapter on alpine ski resorts features a list of the author's top resorts for beginning, intermediate and advanced skiers.) Selections that are marked with the "★" symbol within the chapter are recommended, and appear on the Author's Choice list.

# Disclaimer

Weather always plays a key role in many of the outdoor opportunities available. Rain and snow runoff can create washouts and obstructions, such as fallen trees and rockslides, on backcountry trails. It's essential for hikers to bring USGS topographic maps and trail maps in case signage and trail markers have vanished. Always consult local sources, such as government offices and outdoor outfitters, to get the latest information before setting out on any backcountry excursion.

Change is a constant at Lake Tahoe. Restaurants change ownership or even disappear with some regularity. Hotel and motel rates are always subject to change. The prices of ski lift tickets and trail passes, as well as associated services at resorts, increase a notch or two every year. While we have sought to provide the most up-to-date information for this book, you should always call ahead to confirm prices and hours of operation before leaving home.

If you discover any facts that need revising or updating, comments that need clarifying or know of another area, lodging or restaurant that should be listed, please write to Foghorn Press, 555 De Haro Street, Suite #220, San Francisco, CA 94107. We are committed to making *Tahoe: The Complete Guide* the most accurate, detailed and enjoyable guide book of its kind.

# Foreword

Some projects are hatched in relatively short order, but this one has been incubating for a quarter of a century. Granted, that's a long time to be wool-gathering for a book, but it has taken me 25 years and change to explore all of the facets of Lake Tahoe that are covered in this book. From my first experience on a ski slope to a heart-stopping descent in a small submarine 900 feet below the surface, Lake Tahoe has continually captivated me.

Over the years I have written many columns and articles on Tahoe as the outdoors editor for the *San Francisco Chronicle* and the *San Jose Mercury News*, as well as West Coast editor for *Ski Magazine*. During that time, I was always amazed at the number of new discoveries I made in the Tahoe region each year.

Tahoe has a haunting but elusive beauty. Capturing it in print, even in a book of this length, is as impossible as defining the Grand Canyon with a postcard. The Lake of the Sky has many personalities, and they are not easily absorbed in one or even 100 visits. In my case, it has taken one-third of a lifetime and a lot of globe-trotting to fully appreciate the wondrous amalgam of mountains, water, sky and desert that is Lake Tahoe.

I have traveled thousands of miles and received cooperation from scores of people to collect the information that is in this book. More than once, I have found encouragement by talking with visitors from other states and other countries, sharing with them the wonder of seeing Tahoe for the first time. I have tried to incorporate that perspective in this book.

Lake Tahoe is the centerpiece of a region that incorporates more natural treasures, human history and recreational opportunities than any other place on the West Coast. While this work is designed to be a practical user's guide, I encourage everyone to consider the lake and its wilderness areas as irreplaceable natural resources that need diligent protection. It is my fondest hope that this book will help stimulate new appreciation for this magnificent place and its heritage.

*Ken Castle*

# Chapter 1

# Introduction

Explorer John C. Fremont first saw Lake Tahoe in 1844 from the top of Red Lake Peak, which is located south of the basin at what is now Carson Pass. He named it Lake Bonpland after a botanist, but then changed it to Mountain Lake. Subsequently it was named Lake Bigler after a California governor, but the U.S. Department of Interior didn't care for that name either, and commissioned Dr. Henry Degroot, a journalist, to come up with a name. Degroot suggested "tahoe," an Indian word meaning "big water." It took decades before the name finally stuck, thanks to action in 1945 by the California State Legislature.

In the 1860s, Tahoe was the center of a lively commerce that involved the silver mines in Virginia City, where the Comstock Lode was discovered in 1859, and the Central Pacific Railroad, which was pushing over the Sierra toward the town of Truckee. To supply wood to the mines, the new boomtowns and the railroad, an extensive logging empire was established on the East Shore of the lake, from Incline Village to Glenbrook. The loggers clear-cut the entire shoreline and left scars for decades, until both the mines and the demand for timber petered out in the late 1870s and early 1880s. By then, the only business that showed promise was tourism, and thus began a new land rush to build resorts.

It is interesting to note that nearly every community around Tahoe owes its existence today to a resort or hotel. During the late 19th century and early 20th century, travelers from San Francisco would take one train to Truckee, and from there board a second train that rode on a narrow-gauge track to Tahoe City. When they got to the lake, they would have their choice of fabulous resorts such as Tahoe Tavern at Tahoe City, Brockway Springs Hotel near Crystal Bay, the Tallac House on the West Shore and the Glenbrook Inn on the East Shore. Of course, without roads the only way to reach the distant resorts was by passenger ferry, and a network of steamships developed to service the lake. A typical day outing for guests of these lavish hotels was to circumnavigate the lake, stopping at various landings to enjoy refreshments and see the sights.

None of the historic inns has survived to modern times. Most were destroyed by fire, a problem that constantly bedeviled Virginia City and Truckee, where fire-fighting methods were primitive at best. The only resort that made it to the 1960s was Tahoe Tavern, and it was demolished for environmental and commercial reasons. The Tavern was an opulent hotel, often compared to the Ahwahnee in Yosemite, that didn't seem to have any savior during the condominium-building craze. Had it been standing today, it would likely be booked 100 percent of the year. Only now, after so much of the lake's history has vanished, is there a move to preserve what's left and to promote the classic "Old Tahoe" look.

The lake is a constant swirl of controversy, a fact of life that escapes most visitors who come here to enjoy its natural wonders. Two-thirds of

*The famous steamer* Tahoe *plied the waters of the lake for nearly half a century before being scuttled in the 1940s.*

Tahoe is in California, with one-third in Nevada. There are five counties with jurisdiction in the basin, four U.S. Forest management units, two state fish and game agencies, and a myriad of cities, towns and regional agencies. The bi-state Tahoe Regional Planning Agency (TRPA), whose mission is to balance growth with the environment, is constantly under fire either by development interests or conservation groups. Everyone has a different idea of what Tahoe's future ought to be, and there is a provincialism that always seems to stand in the way of collective action.

There is no denying that unregulated growth in the late 1950s and 1960s, a lot of it stimulated by the arrival of the 1960 Winter Olympics in Squaw Valley and the development of gaming on the South Shore, added an urban blight that still remains around much of the lake. Freshwater marshes were dredged or filled for waterfront homes, thereby interrupting the natural cleansing process of the lake. Traffic has become a major problem, both from its congestion and its air pollution. The city of South Lake Tahoe is embarking on a $236-million redevelopment plan with the goal of razing dozens of tacky motels and replacing them with quality resorts, hotels, inns and open space. Many of the condominium developments, which were cheaply built to cash in on America's craving for inexpensive "second homes," still mar otherwise beautiful forests at both the north and south ends of the lake. Fortunately, a new breed of entrepre-

*Zephyr Cove*

neur is acquiring worn-out lodges and turning them into elegant cottages and bed and breakfasts, especially on the North and West shores.

Despite human tinkering with the landscape, Tahoe endures with an undiminished grandeur. Nothing can diminish the first impressions of flying over Lake Tahoe and seeing this giant pool of indigo-blue water cradled between mountain ranges. Nothing can detract from the experience of entering Emerald Bay and finding yourself surrounded by cathedrals of granite. And nothing compares to the sense of awe that comes from scrambling up the trails of Desolation Wilderness to visit pristine alpine lakes and revel in the pure glory of nature. If Tahoe had not been carved up into so many fiefdoms, it would unquestionably qualify as a national park.

After making hundreds of visits over the course of 30 years, and after traveling around the world many times to exotic destinations, I find that the magic and allure of Lake Tahoe is still as strong as the first day I saw it. The lake is one of the great marvels of our time, and it offers a lifetime of pure joy. It is, as famous American author Mark Twain wrote, "surely the fairest picture the whole earth affords."

# LAKE TAHOE FACTS & FIGURES

- Lake Tahoe is located 200 miles northeast of San Francisco, California, and 58 miles southwest of Reno, Nevada, in the Sierra Nevada mountain range.
- As the North American continent's largest alpine lake, Lake Tahoe stretches 22 miles long, 12 miles wide and covers a surface area of 191.6 square miles. It has 72 miles of shoreline.
- Lake Tahoe is two-thirds in the state of California and one-third in the state of Nevada.
- The lake's average surface is 6,226.95 feet above sea level and the natural rim is 6,223 feet above sea level, making it the highest lake of its size in the United States.
- Mount Tallac at 9,735 feet is the highest peak rising from the shoreline. The highest point in the Tahoe Basin is Freel Peak at 10,881 feet.
- Lake Tahoe is the third deepest lake in North America and 10th deepest in the world (Lake Baikal in Russia is the deepest, at over 4,600 feet). Tahoe's deepest point is 1,645 feet, near Crystal Bay, and its average depth is 989 feet.
- The estimated 39.75 trillion gallons of water contained in the lake is 99.9 percent pure, with visibility to 75 feet below the surface.
- If completely drained, the lake would cover a flat area the size of California to a depth of 14 inches, but would take over 700 years to refill.
- Lake Tahoe is, geologically, a "young lake," having been formed 10,000 to 11,000 years ago.
- Glaciers are responsible for carving out the broad, U-shaped valleys that hold Emerald Bay, Fallen Leaf Lake and Cascade Lake.
- Sixty-three streams flow into Lake Tahoe, but only one, the Truckee River, flows out past Reno and into Pyramid Lake.
- Lake Tahoe loses much of its water to evaporation. If the water that evaporates from the lake every 24 hours could be recovered, it would supply the daily requirements of a city the size of Los Angeles.
- Although the summer's heat can warm the upper 12 feet to a comfortable 68 degrees Fahrenheit, Lake Tahoe never freezes over in the winter. This is due to the constant 39 degrees Fahrenheit maintained at depths below 700 feet, largely because of the constant movement and volume of water.
- The sun shines at Lake Tahoe approximately 274 days a year. Shorts and T-shirts are typical summer day attire, but jackets and sweaters are advised during the cooler evenings. Weather in the Sierra can be unpredictable. Snowfall, for example, has been recorded in every month and averages 420 inches a year.

## Trees of the Lake Tahoe Basin

Alder
Aspen
Incense cedar
Jeffrey pine
Lodgepole pine

Ponderose pine
Sugar pine
Sierra juniper
Whitefir
Willow

## Wildflowers of the Lake Tahoe Basin

### White Flowers
California corn lily
Cow parsnip
Mariposa lily
Ranger buttons
Common yarrow

### Yellow Flowers
Buttercup
Mountain fule ears
Sulphur flowers

### Pink / Red Flowers
Thistle
Columbine
Indian paintbrush
Snow plant
Shooting star

### Blue / Purple Flowers
Dwarf alpine aster
Meadow penstemon
Lupine

## Mammals of the Lake Tahoe Basin

Yellow-bellied marmot
Douglas squirrel or chikaree
Golden-mantled ground squirrel
Mule deer
Black bear
Coyote
Pine martin

## Birds of the Lake Tahoe Basin

Western tanager
Dark-eyed junco
Yellow-headed blackbird
Mountain chickadee
California gull
Bald eagle
Red-tailed hawk

Hairy woodpecker
American robin
Dark-eyed junco
Mallard
Canada goose
Stellar's jay

# Chapter 2

# Lake Tahoe Points of Interest

## ★ Author's Choice ★

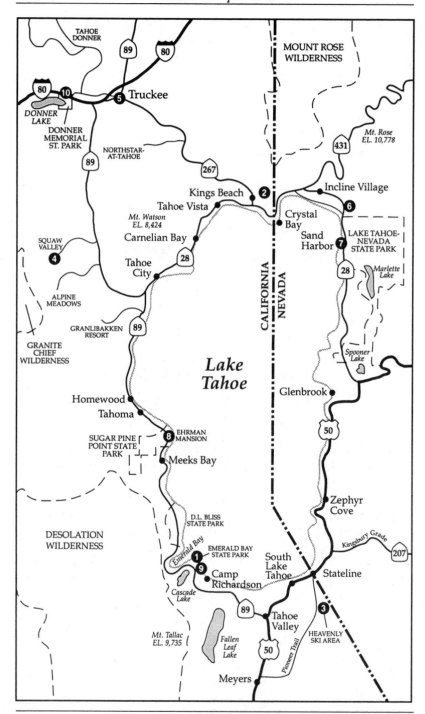

## Map References—Lake Tahoe Points of Interest

◆

When you examine the map of Lake Tahoe's 72-mile perimeter, you begin to realize the time that is needed to fully explore this mountain wonderland. And when you add in neighboring attractions, such as the vintage logging and railroad town of Truckee, you'll need to plan on a couple of days, at least, to hit the highlights. The Tahoe basin is a delightful collection of historical mansions, museums, aerial trams and parks, and every community along the shoreline has its unique charms. Some of them are not obvious, or not well marked. The following outline is designed to cover not only the "must-sees" for first-time visitors, but also some lesser-known points of interest for returning Tahoe regulars.

# TAHOE'S TOP ATTRACTIONS

## ★ Emerald Bay State Park ★

★ *notes Author's Choice*
See number 1 on map, page 18

This 593-acre state park on the southwest shore of Lake Tahoe contains three major attractions: Emerald Bay, Eagle Falls and Vikingsholm Castle.

***Emerald Bay:*** Tahoe's most photographed natural wonder, a glacier-carved blue and turquoise bay surrounded by granite peaks, is spectacular any time of the day or year. The blue-green bay is three miles long by one mile wide, with a narrow entrance from the east. Motorists can find several excellent high vantage points along Highway 89, or take one of a half-dozen tour boat excursions that circumnavigate the bay. Within the bay is Fannette Island, the only island in the lake. Rising 150 feet above the water, this rocky island, believed to be a remnant of the glacial action that created the bay, is crowned by a crumbling stone structure called the "Tea House." The house was built in 1928 by the founder of the sprawling Vikingsholm estate at the head of Emerald Bay. Using a motorboat to reach the island, residents and guests once enjoyed afternoon refreshments at a large oak table in the center of a room 16 feet square. Today, only the shell of the building remains, having been vandalized over the years. The island is available for day-use activities between 6 a.m. and 9 p.m., but camping, picnicking and pets are prohibited. From February 1 through June 15, Fannette is closed to protect nesting Canadian geese, which number as many as 100 in some years. In 1969, Emerald Bay was designated a National Natural Landmark by the U.S. Department of Interior. The park includes a campground with 100 sites and a boat camp with 20 sites.

***Eagle Falls:*** This is a series of three successive waterfalls that pour into Emerald Bay. The lower falls are in the state park, while the upper falls are on U.S. Forest Service land across the road. You can hike (very carefully—the rocks are slippery!) to the foot of the lower falls, or begin at the Eagle Falls Trailhead on the west side of Highway 89. The best view of the other falls, the largest of which is over 75 feet high, can be seen from a footbridge that crosses Eagle Creek. A brisk uphill hike to Eagle Lake, a beautiful natural impoundment accessible from a marked trail, takes you a mile from the parking lot. Beyond the lake, the trail enters Desolation Wilderness. On weekends, the lot and most of the roadside spaces fill rapidly, so it's best to go early in the morning or late in the afternoon.

***Vikingsholm Castle:*** Getting to this unique mansion requires a hike down a steep, one-mile paved trail that drops 500 feet in elevation. But it's worth the effort, because visitors will see one of the finest examples of Scandinavian architecture in the Western Hemisphere. Vikingsholm was built in 1928-29 by Mrs. Lora Josephine Knight, who spared no expense to create a replica of an 11th-century Viking castle. The granite foundation and stonework, turrets and high-pitched roofs—some of them covered by sod—were constructed out of materials found at the lake. An army of 200 workers completed the 38-room mansion in just one summer, using old-fashioned techniques of hand-hewing huge timbers and forging hinges and latches. Some sections of the home contain no nails, pegs or spikes. During the construction, Mrs. Knight prowled the cities of Norway, Finland, Sweden and Denmark for 18th- and 19th-century antique furniture, and what she couldn't buy she had duplicated, as precisely as possible, from drawings of museum pieces. Tours, offered every half hour in summer, allow visitors to see two ornately carved dragon beams, paintings on ceilings and walls, and six fireplaces of Scandinavian design. Admission: Adults, $2; children (ages 6 to 12), $1; children under 6, free. Open daily 10 a.m. through 4 p.m., mid-June through Labor Day. Parking in the lot on Highway 89 is free. Information: Eagle Point Campground, (916) 541-3030 (summer only); D.L. Bliss State Park, (916) 525-9529.

## ★ Stateline Fire Lookout ★
*See number 2 on map, page 18*

Poorly marked and generally overlooked by most visitors, this facility straddling the California/Nevada border is without a doubt the best high-elevation vantage point (7,017 feet) on the North Shore. It has spectacular vistas of Crystal Bay and Brockway beaches, as well as the entire Tahoe basin and its watershed. There's an excellent self-guided interpretive trail with detailed signposts explaining the human and natural history of the area, as well as several strategically placed picnic tables. The area has long figured in an ongoing boundary dispute between the two states. The lookout tower, infrequently used today, is the best spot for photographs. One drawback is the occasionally bothersome cloud of gnats and midges that might be encountered along the paved walkways. To reach the lookout, don't bother looking for signs. At Crystal Bay, Nevada, turn up Reservoir Road between the Tahoe Biltmore Lodge and Casino and the old Tahoe Mariner casinos, then turn right at the firehouse and continue up the hill until you reach a point where a steeper U.S. Forest Service road doubles back to the left above you. Follow this for one-quarter of a mile, beyond the green metal gate, to the parking lot. If the gate is closed, park and walk the distance. Admission is free. Information: Lake Tahoe Basin Management Unit, (916) 573-2600.

## ★ Heavenly Ski Area Tram ★
*See number 3 on map, page 18*

How's the view from the top? Just hop on Heavenly's tram for a quick lift some 2,000 feet above the lake, where you can fully appreciate the grandeur of Tahoe and its snow-capped mountains. There's a decent restaurant at Monument Peak, as well as a spacious outdoor deck. You can hang out here for the view of Stateline's high-rise casinos and the city of South Lake Tahoe, or you can scramble up a mile-long, self-guided nature trail through woods and boulder fields for more vistas. The best time to arrive is just before sunset, when the light is magical and the paddlewheel cruiseboats are chugging back and forth to Emerald Bay. Admission: Adults, $12; children 6 to 12 and seniors 65 and over, $6; children under 5, free. At the end of Ski Run Boulevard, South Lake Tahoe, CA. Information: Heavenly Ski Area, (800) 2-HEAVEN.

## ★ Squaw Valley USA ★
*See number 4 on map, page 18*

The site of the 1960 Winter Olympics has become one of the great ski destinations in the world, even though not much is left to remind anyone of the Olympic Games. Still, owner Alexander Cushing has created a unique year-round attraction with a goosebump ride on an aerial tram that soars 2,000 feet above the valley to his High Camp Bath and Tennis Club. (The tram ride is $12 for adults during daytime and $5 after 4 p.m., $5 for children 3 to 12, and free for tots under 3.) If you don't mind the thin air at elevation 8,200 feet, you can ice skate, swim in an artificial rock lagoon, mountain bike, bungee jump and, oh yes, play tennis. Just don't think of chasing a lost ball over the sheer rock face next to the courts. Instead, count your blessings and have a tall one at Alexander's, the restaurant and bar complex that is adjacent to the "club." If high places bother you, you can always plant your feet firmly on the ground (or rather, in a marsh) on the 18-hole golf course at The Resort at Squaw Creek, one of Tahoe's most lavish resorts with 405 rooms. Or you can horseback ride to the top of a ridge to view Lake Tahoe.

One famous structure is the Christy Inn, the former home of Squaw Valley founders Wayne and Sandy Poulsen, which houses Graham's, a gourmet restaurant, along with a small inn. The Poulsens, longtime residents of the valley, produced their share of talented Olympic skiing contenders, and another family, the McKinneys, contributed Olympic skier Tamara McKinney and the late Steve McKinney, who set a world speed-skiing record. Squaw Valley is an eclectic community of corporate entrepreneurs, upscale second-home owners, and an assortment of daredevils, mountaineers and adventurers. West of Highway 89 and south of Truckee, Squaw Valley boasts several excellent restaurants, overnight lodges and dramatic views of Granite Chief, the area's highest peak at 9,050 feet. Information: Squaw Valley USA, (800) 545-4350 or (916) 583-5585.

## ★ Truckee ★

*See number 5 on map, page 18*

Once a rollicking railroad and lumber town, every vice known to man (and woman) has been practiced here. Filled with rowdy saloons, gambling halls and bawdy houses, Truckee in the late 1800s had more kick than a miner's mule. The town is named after a friendly Paiute Indian who helped guide the first party of white settlers through the region in 1844. It rose quickly in population when the Central Pacific Railroad arrived in 1868 as part of the Transcontinental Railroad. This development created two major industries—logging and ice-harvesting—and attracted a resident Chinese population that reportedly numbered as high as 10,000, second in size only to that of San Francisco's Chinatown. But the hard-working Chinese, who threatened to monopolize the logging business, were driven out of town in 1886 by jealous white vigilante groups. Truckee's fortunes declined after the 1920s, and growth was stagnant until the 1960 Winter Olympics at Squaw Valley provided an economic rebirth as a ski resort destination. Today, Truckee is once again booming. The town incorporated in 1993, combining the communities of old Truckee, Tahoe Donner and Donner Lake. Burned-out city refugees looking for greener pastures have pushed the population to 10,000 and attracted new businesses.

Through all of this, however, the gritty character of the old section of Truckee has been preserved. Nearly 100 of the 300 downtown structures were built prior to the turn of the century, and most of the historic buildings are concentrated along Commercial Row, where visitors can stroll along the wooden walkways and enjoy a slice of the Old West. While the historic district has become gentrified (with gourmet restaurants and stores catering to travelers), there are rustic places as well. Among these are the Southern Pacific Railroad Depot, which has an interesting gallery of old photographs and is still an active stop for both freight and Amtrak passenger trains; the Bar of America, whose walls are adorned with pictures of famous outlaws and gunslingers; Cabona's clothing store, which always seems to have the latest in country chic; and Robert's hardware store, which has a lot more than hammers and nails. The Truckee Hotel, an institution on Bridge Street since 1873, has been restored to its former Victorian elegance and is a marvelous place to stay if you don't mind the trains tooting their way through town. Jibboom Street, once notorious as Truckee's famous red light district, has an old two-story jailhouse that is now a museum.

Other interesting places to check out include the Squeeze In, a tiny breakfast house with creative omelets; Zena's Restaurant in the vintage C.B. House (circa 1874), known for its muffins; Earthsong, whose basement is stocked with an aromatic variety of spices and coffees; Bob Roberts Jewelers, with Western silver and gold pieces and crystal geodes; Truckee Books, with a variety of local lore; Richardson House, a historic bed and breakfast above Commercial Row; and The Passage, a favorite hangout for food and drink. The century-old Masonic Building, destroyed by an explosion in 1993, has been rebuilt to house the Cafe Meridian, the first Truckee restaurant with a second-floor balcony dining area. The Capitol building, built in 1870 and the second oldest structure in town, once housed a saloon and dance hall and, later, Piper's Opera Company. Among the notables associated with Truckee is the great silent screen comedian Charlie Chaplin, who filmed *The Gold Rush* and other movies in the area. Truckee is a convenient stop along Interstate 80 and is 20 minutes north of Lake Tahoe. Information: Truckee Donner Visitors Center, (800) 548-8388 or (916) 587-2757.

## ★ Ponderosa Ranch ★
*See number 6 on map, page 18*

Anyone who grew up with *Bonanza*, the most popular Western series in television history, will enjoy a nostalgic visit to the Cartwright Ranch to commune with the ghosts of Ben, Hoss, Adam and Little Joe. This open-air museum and theme park offers guided tours of the original ranch house set where the 1960s series and two recent TV movies were filmed. Situated on a hill above Incline Village, the ranch features a complete Western town with the Silver Dollar Saloon, Ponderosa Museum and several stores, and there's an extensive collection of authentic wagons and automobiles. You won't see live horses or cattle, but there are free pony rides for the kids and a handful of animals at a petting zoo. The morning haywagon breakfast ride (wagons pulled by a tractor) offers a meal of flapjacks and bacon on a hill overlooking Lake Tahoe. There's no gourmet restaurant, but you can order a Hoss Burger in Hop Sing's Kitchen. An authentic 19th-century church is popular for weddings, and both the saloon and the barbecue area can be booked for large groups. Ponderosa Ranch isn't exactly Knott's Berry Farm in scope or activities, but you never know where or when a gunfight will break out. Open daily, 9:30 a.m. to 5:30 p.m. (May through October). Admission: Adults and seniors, $8.50; children 5 to 11, $5.50; tots under 3, free. Off Highway 28, 100 Ponderosa Ranch Road, Incline Village, NV. Information: (702) 831-0691.

## ★ Sand Harbor ★
*See number 7 on map, page 18*

With its crystalline beauty and polished circular rock formations, this mile of white sand beaches, Jeffrey pines and protected coves is a real stand out. Set in 14,000-acre Lake Tahoe-Nevada State Park (which also includes Spooner Lake and the famous Flume Trail for mountain bikes), Sand Harbor is arguably the most picturesque piece of public real estate on the lake. Fine white sand and gently sloping contours create vivid turquoise hues in the shallows, giving the area a distinctly South Pacific flavor, although the water is quite cold. Photographers, sunbathers and boaters frequent the rocky shoreline both north and south of here, and, in July and August, Sand Harbor is the site of an annual Shakespeare festival. A boat-launching area, picnic grounds, paved walkways, restrooms and a snack bar are located at the park. Because of Sand Harbor's popularity, the small parking lot is often filled between 11 a.m. and 3 p.m. on weekends. Admission: $5 per car for parking ($2 in winter), $1 for walk-ins and bicyclists, and $7 for boat-launching in summer. On Highway 28 four miles south of Incline Village. Information: Lake Tahoe-Nevada State Park, (702) 831-0494.

## ★ Ehrman Mansion ★

*See number 8 on map, page 18*

Built at the turn of the century, this Queen Anne Victorian in Sugar Pine Point State Park represents the opulent post-mining period when wealthy businessmen built elegant summer homes at Lake Tahoe. The three-story rock and wood estate, completed by West Coast financier Isaias W. Hellman in 1902, was designed by well-known architect Walter Danforth Bliss. Hellman, who later became president of Wells Fargo Nevada National Bank, called his 11,703-square-foot summer retreat "Pine Lodge." It had all of the latest comforts, including electricity supplied by a wood-burning steam generator in an adjacent tank house. Hellman even had tons of topsoil brought in to create a beautifully manicured but steeply sloping grass lawn, which today affords visitors a magnificent picnic grounds. A long pier extends from the shoreline, enabling guests to come and go from Tahoe's passenger steamers. A cadre of butlers, maids, cooks and groundskeepers constantly tended to the estate and its guests. After Hellman's death in 1920, the home was operated by his daughter, Florence Ehrman, and later by her daughter, Esther Lazard, until 1965 when it and nearly 2,000 acres in the General Creek watershed were acquired by the California State Park System.

Visitors who tour the mansion will see the spacious living and dining rooms with their oak floors, polished wood ceilings and elegant fireplaces. The dining table, 30 feet long and eight feet wide, could accommodate 30 guests at one sitting. On the second floor, circular master bedrooms anchor the north and south ends, with six guest bedrooms and eight bathrooms in between. Much of the original furniture was auctioned off in 1965, but the volunteer Tahoe Sierra State Parks Foundation has redecorated the estate with period pieces. The day-use fee for parking is $5 per car. Free tours are held every hour from 11 a.m. to 4 p.m. daily from July to early September. On August 14, the state park's Living History Day, park guides and volunteers dress in period clothing and recreate the feel of the place in its heyday. Sugar Pine Point State Park is located on Highway 89, one mile north of Meeks Bay. It also has a small beach, trails system and a large campground. Information: (916) 525-7982.

## ★ Tallac Historic Site ★

*See number 9 on map, page 18*

Three of Tahoe's grand old homes, one of them an excellent museum celebrating the "Era of Opulence," are located at this 150-acre South Lake Tahoe site managed by the U.S. Forest Service. Though it is well off Highway 89 and sequestered in tall pine trees, the site has become not only an important historic landmark at the lake but also the focal point of

*The Tahoe of yesteryear is celebrated during the annual Great Gatsby Festival at the Tallac Historic Site at South Shore.*

Tahoe's burgeoning arts and music community. As an added bonus, it adjoins some of South Tahoe's finest white sand beaches. Tallac was the location of a palatial resort built in 1880 by Elias J. "Lucky" Baldwin, a California entrepreneur who catered to the nouveau riche from San Francisco, Sacramento and Virginia City. The resort featured two lavish hotels, a massive casino (boasting "500 electric lights") and several accessory buildings, accommodating over 250 well-heeled guests with its spacious ballroom, string orchestra, croquet, tennis, steamer rides and strolls along a promenade. Seven years after Baldwin's death in 1909, his daughter Anita, bowing to the influx of automobiles and the construction of other elaborate estates around the lake, dismantled the resort. But three large summer estates and 33 other structures remain, including the following:

**Baldwin Estate:** Built in 1921, this hand-hewn log home houses the Tallac Museum, which has exhibits on local Washoe Indian culture, the significance of the Baldwin family in California history, photographs of the hotel and casino and a presentation room for a 15-minute slide show. The site was historically used by Native Americans, who migrated each summer from the Carson Valley to the area from Taylor Creek to Camp Richardson. Admission to the museum is free, and there is a small bookstore inside. The museum is open daily except Mondays from 10 a.m. to

4 p.m. from mid-June to Labor Day, with a reduced schedule through October 1.

***Pope Estate:*** Celebrating its 100th anniversary in 1994, this estate is dominated by an elegant main house, which is still in the process of being restored. From its living room windows, it has a commanding view of Lake Tahoe. Built in 1894, the estate was purchased by the George Pope family of San Francisco in 1923, and became known whimsically as the "Vatican Lodge." As a summer retreat, the home was a great place to entertain the rich and famous, from author John Steinbeck to actor Rudolph Valentino. Several adjacent cottages contained maids' and workers' quarters, laundry and children's play areas. Although visitors can stroll through the estate and look inside the cottages, guided tours of the main house, offered on Tuesdays, Fridays and Saturdays at 1 p.m. and 2:30 p.m., are by reservation only. Admission: $1.50 per person.

***Heller Estate:*** Known as Valhalla, this 1923 estate built by Walter Heller borders Camp Richardson and is the community events center for the historic site. The non-profit Tahoe Tallac Association holds a variety of jazz, bluegrass and classical music concerts on the grounds here from late June to early September, and there are periodic arts and crafts exhibits as well. The small cabins north of the estate house regular summer attractions including a cultural arts store, a photo arts gallery, fiber arts and folk crafts exhibits, a fine art gallery and a variety of workshops for children. The biggest event is the annual Great Gatsby Festival in mid-August, when association members dress in period costumes, serve gourmet food and display antique cars.

The Tallac Historic Site, which is listed on the National Register of Historic Places, is located 3.5 miles north of the city of South Lake Tahoe on Highway 89, next to Camp Richardson. Parking is free. Open daily from late May to early September. Information: Tallac Historic Site, (916) 541-5227; Lake Tahoe Basin Management Unit, (916) 573-2600.

## ★ Emigrant Trail Museum and Pioneer Monument ★
*See number 10 on map, page 18*

One of the profound tragedies of the westward migration of settlers in the 1840s is remembered at this excellent museum at Donner Memorial State Park in Truckee. Lured by tales of unlimited opportunity in California, George Donner and his brother Jacob, both farmers in Illinois, organized a wagon train of several families and, in April 1846, set out for the promised land. In Wyoming, the Donner Party heeded bad advice and took what they thought was a short cut, which proved to be a fatal mistake. The treacherous secondary route over the Wasatch Mountains and across the waterless Great Salt Lake Desert sapped their resources and put the group three weeks behind those who kept to the main trail. When they reached the base of Donner Pass in October, they were halted by early snowstorms and forced to construct emergency shelters at Donner Lake. Hampered by the most brutal winter in recorded history and by a lack of food, nearly half of the group perished. Those who survived did so largely by eating the flesh of their dead companions. The fate of the Donner Party prompted a search for a new route over the Sierra Nevada mountains, resulting in the creation of the Mormon-Emigrant Trail south of Lake Tahoe.

The museum, opened in 1962, offers a memorable 30-minute film that reconstructs the ordeal of the trek, and has several exhibits on the logging and railroad history of Truckee. The monument outside has a stone pedestal that is 22 feet high—the depth of the snow that trapped the settlers. (Another location, called the Donner Historical Site, is three miles north of Interstate 80 on Highway 89, and is the site where the Donner family camped.) Self-guided nature trails, a large campground and a beachfront picnic area are included in the park. Admission: Adults, $2; children 6-12, $1. The day-use fee for the park is $5 per car. Open daily, 10 a.m. to 5 p.m. Information: Donner Memorial State Park, 12593 Donner Pass Road, Donner, CA 96161; (916) 582-7892.

# STATE PARKS
## D.L. Bliss State Park

Named after a pioneering lumberman, railroad owner and banker, this 1,237-acre park offers one of Tahoe's most scenic beaches, a spectacular, lofty overlook at Rubicon Point, and the amazing Balancing Rock. Located on the West Shore of the lake on Highway 89 south of Tahoma, Bliss is a day hiker's paradise. Just a short walk along the 4.5-mile Rubicon Trail from Calawee Cove Beach will take you to the top of a high promontory, called Rubicon Point, where you can peer more than 100 feet down into the clear depths of Lake Tahoe. If you follow the ridgetop trail south to its terminus, you'll reach Vikingsholm Castle at adjoining Emerald Bay State Park. Shorter hikes can be made to an old lighthouse (0.75 miles one way) and to Balancing Rock (one-half mile one way). The rock, a phenomenon at Tahoe since the time of the first settlers, is all of 130 tons resting precariously on a narrow granite pedestal. Eventually, continued erosion around the waist of the rocks will cause the boulder to fall. Bliss Park encompasses 3.5 miles of shoreline, and boasts spectacular Calawee Cove Beach—a protected cove with a sandy area flanked by boulders and forested bluffs—and Lester Beach, a long, flat, white sand beach. The park also has one of Tahoe's best campgrounds with 168 sites, 15 picnic sites and four miles of trails. Admission is $5 per car, and only 25 parking permits are sold each day (they are usually gone by 10 a.m.)

Located nine miles north of South Lake Tahoe on Highway 89. Information: (916) 525-7277.

## Sugar Pine Point State Park

Named for the majestic sugar pine trees that used to be common on the West Shore of Lake Tahoe, this 2,011-acre park sits on a forested promontory 10 miles south of Tahoe City on Highway 89. Its main points of interest are the elegant Ehrman Mansion (see page 25); a 19th-century log cabin; a nature center with bird and animal exhibits; and the General Creek watershed, which creates a natural entryway into the 62,469-acre Desolation Wilderness. In the developed area of the park east of the highway, day visitors can see the mansion, the cabin and the Edwin L. Z'Berg Natural Preserve, all of which border 1.75 miles of Tahoe shoreline. The cabin was built in 1860 by former Indian fighter and trapper General William Phipps, who is believed to be the first permanent settler of record on the West Shore of Tahoe, although the presence of grinding rocks and bedrock mortars indicates that Washoe Indians inhabited the area for generations before.

An attractive small swimming beach and a vast manicured lawn shaded by tall trees offer excellent picnicking opportunities. The park is also a staging area for cyclists riding the paved West Shore Bike Path, which begins here and extends north to Tahoe City. Near the east side parking lot is the nature center, which is housed in the old water tower and generating plant once used by the Ehrman Mansion. Some 11 miles of hiking trails wind through the park, including the Dolder Nature Trail, which follows the lakeshore and passes the world's highest (in elevation) working lighthouse. On the west side of the highway, the General Creek Trail is a 6.5-mile loop, with an optional side trip to Lily Pond. Lost Lake, a spectacular alpine jewel, is a 15-mile round-trip and requires some cross-country trekking by seasoned hikers. In winter, the park offers over 20 kilometers of marked cross-country ski trail. The General Creek Campground has 175 sites and is also open year-round. Interpretive programs are conducted by ranger-naturalists throughout the year. Admission: $5 parking fee per car (or Sno-Park Permit in winter). Ten miles south of Tahoe City and one mile north of Meeks Bay on Highway 89. Information: (916) 525-7982.

## Lake Tahoe-Nevada State Park

The largest park in the Tahoe basin encompasses five management areas along the East Shore, stretching from Cave Rock on US 50 near Zephyr Cove to Sand Harbor on Highway 28 near Incline Village. The heaviest use is at Sand Harbor (see above) and Spooner Lake. Spooner has become popular with hikers, anglers (catch-and-release fishing only), picnickers, mountain bikers and cross-country skiers. In summer, several trails originate here, including side routes to the Tahoe Rim Trail, a trail around the lake, the North Canyon Road to Marlette Lake, and the famous Flume Trail, with a breathtaking single-track cycling path notched into the cliffs above Lake Tahoe. The Marlette/Hobart Backcountry Areas, which are accessible at Spooner Summit on US 50, contain 13,000 acres of forest, including three primitive "hike-in" campsites with fire pits and pit toilets.

Of the other sections in the park, Cave Rock, seven miles north of Stateline, offers one of Tahoe's most dependable public boat-launching ramps (accessible even during drought years when the lake level is low), a small beach with a fine view, a comfort station and six picnic tables. Once a sacred place for native Washoe Indians who used the waters as a burial ground, the rock is located three miles south of Glenbrook. US 50 follows a tunnel through this huge formation, which is the neck of an ancient volcano. Farther up the road, on Highway 28, Memorial Point, one mile north of Sand Harbor, is a paved parking area with a scenic vista and trails to a rocky shore. Hidden Beach, two miles north of Sand Harbor, has limited parking, but it's a great spot for sunbathing, swimming and boating. Admission: At Spooner, $4 per car, $2 per bike and $1 per hiker. At Cave Rock, $4 for parking ($2 in winter) and $7 for boat launching ($5 off-season). There is no fee for parking at Memorial Point and Hidden Beach. Information: (702) 831-0494.

## Donner Memorial State Park

Located 13 miles north of Lake Tahoe and just west of Truckee, this 353-acre park features the Emigrant Trail Museum, which is dedicated to the memory of the ill-fated Donner Party (see page 27), and offers access to sprawling Donner Lake. The lake, called "The Gem of the Sierra," is three miles long, three-quarters of a mile wide and 200 feet deep. The park, at nearly 6,000 feet, is forested with lodgepole, Jeffrey pine and white fir. It has steep granite cliffs and huge boulders, denoting the up-heavals of the earth's crust and the glacier action that scoured the land-scape thousands of years ago.

The park has an excellent picnic and day-use area, with shallow swim-ming inlets and coarse sand beaches. While there is no boat ramp (a private one is available on the northwest corner of the lake), visitors can launch cartoppers, inflatables and windsurfers from the beach. Both powerboats and sailboats are allowed on this elongated lake, which can be quite windy in the afternoons. Other amenities include a large camp-ground of 154 sites, 2.5 miles of hiking or cross-country skiing trails, 78 picnic sites and a lakeside interpretive trail that has 18 panels discussing the area's natural and human history. Admission: $5 per car in summer, with Sno-Park permit required in winter (includes free entrance to the Emigrant Trail Museum). Open year-round (except for the campground, which is open from late May to early September). Off Interstate 80, at the Truckee-Donner Lake exit. Information: (916) 587-3841.

## Grover Hot Springs State Park

Need a break to relieve aching muscles or tired feet? Skiers and hikers have made Grover Hot Springs a favorite retreat for years, but almost everyone enjoys the therapeutic value of this natural mineral springs. Located 3.5 miles west of Markleeville, about a 45-minute drive from South Lake Tahoe, the park features two concrete pools fed by runoff from six springs. The water issues from the ground at 148 degrees Fahrenheit but is cooled to between 102 and 104 degrees for the hot pool (the other pool remains cool). Unlike most mineral springs, there is very little sulphur in the water; the main ingredient is sodium carbonate. The hot pool is open daily year-round (usually until 9 p.m.) except for Christmas, New Year's and Thanksgiving holidays, and occasional cleaning days; fees are $4 for adults 18 and older and $2 for youths under 18.

Beyond the springs, the 519-acre park offers excellent hiking trails. At 5,900 feet, the meadows of Hot Springs Valley are surrounded by mountains rising abruptly on three sides. Hawkins Peak, at 10,023 feet, is three miles northwest of the valley, and Markleeville Peak, 9,417 feet, is four miles southwest. Hikers can take the Burnside Trail to Burnside Lake, which rises more than 2,000 feet in less than four miles, or make a short walk to a small waterfall. One of the Sierra's finest campgrounds, with 76 sites, is one-quarter mile from the springs, and there are 25 picnic sites nearby. Parking is $5 per car (or $3 for a Sno-Park permit) except for the hot springs, where parking is free. At the end of Hot Springs Road off Highway 4/89 in Markleeville. Information: Grover Hot Springs pool, (916) 694-2249; park headquarters, (916) 694-2248.

## Plumas Eureka State Park

When a group of nine miners discovered gold on the east side of Eureka Peak in 1851 ("Eureka! I've found it!"), they touched off a massive development that led to 62 miles of shafts in this forested region an hour's drive north of Truckee. Before the boom ended in 1943, several mining companies had extracted $25 million worth of gold. They used three water- and steam-powered stamp mills, of which the most famous, called the Mohawk, had 60 stamps, each of which could crush 2.5 tons of ore per day. The largest operators were the Sierra Buttes Mining Company, a British firm, and the Jamison Mine. Around this extensive mining district, the towns of Jamison City, Johnsville and Eureka Mills sprang up. Today, most of this once-rich mining empire is contained within the 2,000-acre state park, which adjoins the golfing Mecca of Graeagle to the east and the fabulous Lakes Basin area to the south.

The focal point of the park is the museum, which originally was constructed as a miner's bunkhouse. Here, displays chart the history of the mines and showcase the flora and fauna of the area. Outside and across the street stands the Mohawk Stamp Mill, a stable, a mine office and a blacksmith shop, all of which are maintained in a "near-restored" condition. In summer, tours of the buildings and blacksmithing demonstrations are conducted by park staff and docents, and once a month they recreate the era by dressing up in clothing of the 1890s. Historians believe that the gravity-powered tramway that brought ore from high on the mountain was used for recreation in winter and thus may have been California's first ski lift. Today, a small ski area operates on the site.

While the mining complex is reason enough to visit Plumas Eureka State Park, there is a wealth of recreation here, including a forested, well-designed campground with 67 sites (free hot showers), five picnic sites, 8.6 miles of hiking trails, two lakes and 3.5 miles of fishing along Jamison Creek. Moreover, hikers and backpackers can use the park as a staging area for extended trips into the Lakes Basin, or climb to the summit of Eureka Peak (elevation 7,447 feet), an elevation gain of 1,500 feet. Admission: $5 per car for day use; a donation is requested for the museum. Off Highway 89, five miles west of Graeagle on County Road A-14 to Johnsville. Information: (916) 836-2380.

### Burton Creek State Park

Lake Tahoe's second largest state park (2,036 acres) is largely undeveloped, except for about six miles of dirt roads, and is best accessed by hiking, mountain biking and cross-country skiing. The park lies adjacent to Tahoe State Recreation Area on the north side of Highway 28 in Tahoe City. Burton Creek, which bisects the park from the northeast corner to the southeast corner, meanders past Antone Meadows Natural Preserve and Burton Creek Natural Preserve, where black bears and other wildlife have been seen. The area is a scenic mix of meadows, forest and riparian habitat. In winter, Lakeview Cross-Country grooms trails through the park. Admission is free. Information: (916) 525-7982.

# MUSEUMS
## Western SkiSport Museum

Located at Boreal Ski Resort on the Donner Summit, this fascinating museum chronicles the history of skiing from the late 1850s to modern times. It follows the development of alpine jumping at Granlibakken, the arrival of Sugar Bowl and the ski train in the 1940s, and the 1960 Winter

Olympics at Squaw Valley. There's a pair of eight-foot-long wooden skis used by "Snowshoe" Thompson, the famous Norwegian mountaineer who hauled mail over the Sierra from the mid-1850s to the mid-1870s. Old ski movies run constantly in the theater. Admission is free. Hours: Open year-round from 11 a.m. to 5 p.m. Wednesday through Sunday. Interstate 80 at the Castle Peak exit, eight miles west of Truckee. Information: Auburn Ski Club, P.O. Box 729, Soda Springs, CA 95728; (916) 426-3313.

## Gatekeeper's Cabin and Marion Steinbach Indian Basket Museum

One of Tahoe's best collections of historic lore, including memorabilia from the passenger steamship *S.S. Tahoe* and the posh Tahoe Tavern Resort, are on display in this reconstructed log cabin (the original was destroyed by fire in 1978). From 1910 to 1968, the Tahoe City cabin was inhabited by federal employees from the Bureau of Reclamation, who manually controlled water releases from Lake Tahoe into the Truckee River by manipulating 17 gates in a dam. Water from the lake is routinely diverted to the city of Reno and Pyramid Lake, but with the advent of computer technology the gatekeeper's position was eliminated. Now, historic archives on North Tahoe are displayed here, as well as interesting photographs, old newspapers and exhibits of the lake's bygone days.

Recently, a new 2,000-square-foot wing adjoining the cabin has been opened to showcase a world-class collection of Native American baskets. Over 800 baskets from local tribes as well as from Southwestern, Northwestern, Alaskan and Plains Indians are displayed here, along with 100 dolls. The collection, from the estate of the late Marion Steinbach, was donated to the North Lake Tahoe Historical Society, which raised $375,000 in two years to build the addition. The baskets represent one of the most extensive collections on the West Coast. The museums are located at William B. Layton Park between Fanny Bridge and the Truckee River Bank, and there's room outside for picnicking next to the shoreline. Admission is free. Open 11 a.m to 5 p.m. Wednesday through Sunday. Closed in winter. Information: North Lake Tahoe Historical Society, 130 West Lake Boulevard, Tahoe City, CA 96145; (916) 583-1762.

## Watson Cabin Museum

Built in 1909 by Robert Montgomery Wilson, this honeymoon cottage with original furnishings is the oldest structure standing in Tahoe City. It also houses the city's first indoor private bathroom. During tours conducted by the North Lake Tahoe Historical Society, volunteer docents dress up as turn-of-the-century Tahoe residents. On North Lake Boulevard (Highway 28), on the lake side of the road. Open seven days a week in summer from 12 p.m. to 4 p.m. (year-round on weekends and holidays). Admission is free. Information: 560 North Lake Boulevard, Tahoe City, CA 96145; North Lake Tahoe Historical Society, (916) 583-1762; Watson Cabin Museum, (916) 583-8717 (June to September).

## Lake Tahoe Historical Society Museum

Located next to the South Lake Tahoe Chamber of Commerce, this small museum covers the development of Lake Tahoe, including the Lake Valley Railroad and the famous passenger steamers. Other displays include Native American arrowheads and dolls, a collection of ranch tools, several pairs of old skis and a 140-year-old pipe organ. A video, "Lake Tahoe: 1915-1930," features clips of films made in the area. Behind the museum is a tollhouse from 1859 and a log cabin built in the 1930s. Admission: Adults, $1; seniors (65 and older), 75 cents; children (ages 5-12), 50 cents. Open weekdays from 11 a.m. to 12:30 p.m. and 1 p.m. to 4 p.m.; weekends from 11 a.m. to 4 p.m. (June 15 to Labor Day). At 3058 US 50 (near Rufus Allen Boulevard), South Lake Tahoe, CA. Information: (916) 541-5458.

## Old Truckee Jail Museum

Built in 1875, this was the longest operating jail in California, closing only in 1964. The two-story building has four cells, two on the ground floor and two on the second floor, with the upstairs reserved for women and juvenile prisoners. Apart from the steel-lined cells with iron bars, there's a historical photo display, ice-harvesting and logging paraphernalia, skiing memorabilia, some Chinese artifacts and a few Native American baskets. The museum is operated by the Truckee-Donner Historical Society. Admission is free. Open Saturdays and Sundays from May 1 through Labor Day, 11 a.m. to 4 p.m., with special tours for groups by advance reservation. At 10142 Jibboom Street (behind Commercial Row), Truckee, CA. Information: (916) 582-0893.

## Sierra Nevada Children's Museum

Established in 1992 by volunteers, this unique museum in Truckee offers hands-on educational exhibits that run the gamut of art, science and technology, health, social development and ecology. Rotating exhibitions have featured themes such as "Jungle Impressions," "Dinosaurs in Truckee," "A Night in the Forest" (children using flashlights to find animals), and "The Truckee Model Railroad." Admission: $2 per person (free for tots under 2). Summer hours are Wednesday through Saturday, 10 a.m. to 4 p.m.; off-season hours are Wednesday, 11 a.m. to 5 p.m., and Thursday and Saturday, 10 a.m. to 4 p.m. Open Mondays and Tuesdays for groups by advance reservation. At 11400 Donner Pass Road (at the 7-11 Shopping Center), Truckee, CA. Information: (916) 587-KIDS.

## Portola Railroad Museum

Anyone who has ever loved trains, even model trains, will feel more than a twinge of excitement at this 35-acre open-air museum 45 minutes north of Truckee in the quaint hamlet of Portola. The big draw is the opportunity to operate a diesel locomotive for one hour on a 2.5-mile loop track with your own private instructor. If you can't play engineer (you'll need to schedule that kind of thing well in advance), you and the kids can climb on and through many of the 36 locomotives and 95 freight and passenger cars on the grounds and in the 220-foot shop building. Some of the largest and rarest diesel engines in the world are on display, and several are undergoing restoration. While this place is considerably less developed (and less formal) than other rail museums, it has a vibrancy that is compelling. Admission is free for the museum. Operating a diesel locomotive for one hour with an instructor is $175, and operating vintage diesel switchers or road switchers is $75. Open daily year-round from 10 a.m. to 5 p.m.; train rides are available on weekends from 11 a.m. to 4 p.m. (Memorial Day to Labor Day, weather permitting). To reach the museum, drive north of Truckee on Highway 89 to the Sattley turnoff. Follow this road to Highway 70, then turn west to Portola. Information: Feather River Rail Society, P.O. Box 608, Portola, CA 96122; (916) 832-4532 or (916) 832-4131.

## Kentucky Mine Museum

Northwest of Truckee on Highway 49, this museum offers displays of mining history in Sierra County, and has an outdoor amphitheater that features live jazz, bluegrass, country, swing, folk and classical artists in the summer. Exhibits trace the history of the Kentucky Consolidated Gold Mining Company, formed in 1853, and also showcase the lives of loggers, Native Americans, millworkers and miners. The mine had a 10-stamp mill in 1888 and was operated until 1953, though its later years involved mainly hobbyists. Each year, the Sierra County Historical Society sponsors the Kentucky Mine Summer Concert Series, with concerts held every Friday evening from July 4th until Labor Day weekend. Museum admission: Adults, $1; children 12 and under, free; tours, $4, including museum admission. Concert admission: $10 at the door, $5 for children 12 and under. Open daily from Memorial Day through early September, 11 a.m. to 4 p.m. One mile east of Sierra City on Highway 49 in Sierra County Park, Sierra City. Information: Sierra County Historical Society, (916) 862-1310.

## Old Webster School and Old Log Jail Museums

South of Lake Tahoe, in Markleeville, this complex operated by the Historical Society of Alpine County includes a one-room schoolhouse built in 1882 and an old log jail constructed in the mid-1800s. Restored in 1968, the interior of the school is adorned with original artwork by former students. The jail is believed to be the only one of its kind, with two hand-riveted iron cells, heavy iron bar doors, vertical log walls and a log foundation. Farming, mining and lumbering tools and artifacts are presently housed in the jail. Nearby, a museum contains exhibits on the county's history, including an old country store, a blacksmith shop, Washoe basketry, toys and dolls, rocks and gems, old bottles and a collection of scenic paintings by local artist Walt Monroe. Open Memorial Day through October, Wednesday to Sunday from noon to 5 p.m. Admission is free, but donations are welcome. Markleeville is located south of South Lake Tahoe on Highway 4/89. Information: Alpine County Historical Complex, P.O. Box 24, Markleeville, CA 96120; (916) 694-2317.

### Tahoe Tessie's Lake Tahoe Monster Museum

Some call it hokey, some call it mysterious. But the occasional sighting of a long-necked prehistoric creature in Lake Tahoe has spawned a local folklore and a line of cutesy souvenirs. This place, created by local entrepreneur Bob McCormick, who has trademarked the name "Tessie," is a souvenir stand thinly disguised as a museum, but the kids will probably love it, especially the green stuffed monster toys and T-shirts. Newspaper clippings of various alleged sightings are displayed. Admission is free. Open June through September. Information: 8612 North Lake Boulevard, Kings Beach, CA 96143; (916) 546-8774.

## OTHER POINTS OF INTEREST

### Lake Tahoe Visitor Center

Operated by the U.S. Forest Service, this is the best place for information on recreation in the national forests, including backcountry permits and maps for Desolation Wilderness. Beyond that, the major attraction is the Stream Profile Chamber, an underground cutaway view of Taylor Creek that allows you to see migrating kokanee salmon. The best time to view them is late summer through early fall. Admission is free. On Highway 89 north of Camp Richardson in South Lake Tahoe. Information: Lake Tahoe Basin Management Unit, (916) 573-2600.

### Carson Pass

This famous pass on Highway 88, about 20 miles southwest of South Lake Tahoe, commemorates the discovery of Lake Tahoe in 1844 by explorer John C. Fremont, who saw part of the lake when he climbed the top of Red Lake Peak (elevation 10,061 feet). A few years later, famous scout Kit Carson forged a trail near this pass that became the Mormon-Emigrant Trail, the main east-west route from Utah to California. From a marked turnoff at the Pass, visitors can see Red Lake, Hope Valley and the Carson Valley below. There's a U.S. Forest Service visitors center just west of this point.

### Cal-Neva Lodge

Once owned by singer Frank Sinatra, this historic casino straddles the California and Nevada borders on the North Shore of Tahoe. The Indian Room on the California side houses an excellent Washoe Indian historical display. Admission is free. At Crystal Bay, Nevada, on Highway 28. Information: 2 Stateline Road, P.O. Box 368, Crystal Bay, NV 89402; (702) 832-4000.

### Fanny Bridge

It's not hard to figure out how this bridge at the intersection of highways 89 and 28 in Tahoe City got its name. Most summers, when the lake is spilling into the Truckee River, sightseers peer over the bridge to see and feed—but not fish for—large rainbow trout in the waters below. There are several restaurants and bicycle and raft concessions next to the bridge.

### Dollar Point

Named after a San Francisco shipping tycoon, Robert S. Dollar, this promontory three miles northeast of Tahoe City has both public and private beaches, several condominium developments, and the lake's headquarters for the U.S. Coast Guard (one mile east in Lake Forest, CA). The area was once considered as a site for Lick Observatory, but ultimately the telescope was built 200 miles west on Mount Hamilton in the San Francisco Bay Area. Dollar Point, originally named Chinquapin by the Washoe Indians, still contains the old Wychwood Estate, consisting of a cluster of small chalets and a main house built in 1916 by Mrs. Lora Knight of St. Louis. This is the same woman who later constructed the splendid Vikingsholm Castle at Emerald Bay. Information: Tahoe City Public Utility District, (916) 583-3790.

### Martis Creek Lake Recreation Area

A wildlife refuge, campground and catch-and-release fishing are the attractions of this lake, where power boats are prohibited. South of the Truckee-Tahoe Airport on Highway 267. Information: U.S. Army Corps of Engineers, (916) 639-2342.

### Mount Rose

Wonderful vistas of Lake Tahoe are available by driving up Highway 431, known as Mount Rose Highway, from Incline Village. Designated turnouts on this sometimes winding road provide ample viewing and photography opportunities. At Mount Rose Ski Area, elevation 8,933 feet, there's a hiking trail to the summit, which reaches 10,776 feet and requires a strenuous 12-mile round-trip trek. Information: Carson Ranger District, Toiyabe National Forest, (702) 355-5302.

## Old Highway 40 Scenic Overlook, Donner Pass

You can reach this great panorama of Donner Lake by one of two ways—turning off at the Norden/Soda Springs exit of Old Highway 40 and driving beyond Sugar Bowl Ski Resort until you reach the designated turnoff, or driving up Donner Pass Road at the western end of Donner Lake. If the old bridge at the summit looks familiar, you may have seen it in the movie *True Lies*, starring Arnold Schwarzenegger. Some of the "European" winter scenes were shot here.

## Fleur du Lac (Kaiser Estate)

You can't see much of this exclusive gated residential estate from Highway 89, but several tour boats, especially from the north and west shores, regularly cruise past the lakeside entrance. The property, built in 1937 by industrialist Henry J. Kaiser, was used in the movie *The Godfather, Part II*, starring Al Pacino. Some of the structures were removed after the film was completed, but the rock boathouse and the yacht club remain. There are 22 exclusive condominiums, many of them used by corporations for executive retreats. At 4000 West Lake Boulevard in Homewood, on the West Shore.

## Eagle Rock

On Highway 89 one mile north of Homewood, this enormous rock formation is the neck of an eroded basalt volcano and is believed to have been named after bald eagles that once nested there.

## Blackwood Canyon

A paved road off Highway 89 at Kaspian on the West Shore of Lake Tahoe winds 7.5 miles to a high ridge overlooking Lake Tahoe, where it becomes a dirt road and intersects the Pacific Crest Trail at Barker Pass. A short hike on the well-marked trail provides inspiring views of Desolation Wilderness to the west and the lake to the east. Information: Lake Tahoe Basin Management Unit, (916) 573-2600.

## Angora Lakes and Lookout

An obscure road in South Lake Tahoe leads to a scenic fire lookout and two alpine lakes, one of which has a swimming beach, a rowboat rental concession and a small overnight lodge. To get here, turn south on Fallen Leaf Road from Highway 89. Drive about two miles, then take a left. Turn right after the first half mile on a dirt road labeled "1214."

Continue two miles to Angora Fire Lookout (elevation 7,290 feet) for a breathtaking view. Farther up the road is a parking lot and a trail to Angora Lakes Resort. The lot fills up fast on weekends. Information: Lake Tahoe Basin Management Unit, (916) 573-2600.

## Camp Richardson

This enclave of buildings set in heavy forest north of South Lake Tahoe on Highway 89 has been a resort since the early 1920s. The land is owned by the U.S. Forest Service, but the cabins, lodge and recreation amenities are run by private concessions. Amenities include hiking and biking trails, beaches, boat rentals, a campground, riding stables, cross-country skiing and the Beacon Restaurant. Information: Richardson's Resort, (916) 541-1801.

## Cascade Lake

Mostly in private ownership, this lake and adjoining Cascade Falls can be seen from Highway 89 or from a short Forest Service path at the Bayview Trailhead. Naturalist John Muir and author Mark Twain are among the notables who have visited here, and the lake was a popular film location in the 1930s for movies such as *Lightnin'*, with Will Rogers, and *Rose Marie* with Jeannette McDonald and Nelson Eddy.

## Fallen Leaf Lake

The largest alpine lake in the basin (outside of Tahoe) was named after a Delaware Indian chief who was a guide for Colonel Jack "Cock-Eye" Johnson during a series of Tahoe-Sierra explorations in the late 1840s and 1850s. At the head of this three-mile-long lake is a lodge and group of cabins known as the "Stanford Camp." Faculty members and graduates of Stanford University have occupied the area since the early 1900s, and continue to use it as a summer retreat and conference center. Other than the marina, there is limited public access to the lake, which is surrounded by private homes. One of them was used in the Kevin Costner/Whitney Houston movie *The Bodyguard*. The lake is on Fallen Leaf Road off Highway 89 north of Camp Richardson. Information: Lake Tahoe Basin Management Unit, (916) 573-2600; or Fallen Leaf Campground, (916) 573-2674.

## Freel Peak

At 10,881 feet, this is the tallest peak around Lake Tahoe. It is located south of Heavenly ski area in the Carson Range and can be seen from many points in the basin.

## Mount Tallac

West of Fallen Leaf Lake, this is one of Tahoe's dominant mountains, rising to 9,735 feet in elevation. There's a trail to the summit, but it's an arduous all-day hike (see page 120 in Chapter 5, "Hiking Trails").

## Tahoe Keys

This 750-acre private waterfront community in South Lake Tahoe has 11 miles of inland waterways with access to Lake Tahoe. Before the complex was built, the land was part of the Truckee Marsh, where the Upper Truckee River flows into Lake Tahoe. At times harshly criticized by environmentalists for its impact on the area, the Tahoe Keys offer Tahoe's largest inland marina, as well as a plethora of condominiums, palatial waterfront villas and private homes. There's a restaurant and launching ramp at the marina. At the end of Tahoe Keys Boulevard from US 50, South Lake Tahoe. Information: Tahoe Keys Resort, (916) 544-5397.

## Zephyr Cove

This protected and scenic cove on the east shore of Lake Tahoe, developed as a resort in the early 1900s, is owned by the U.S. Forest Service but is operated privately under a special-use permit. The constant beehive of activity results largely from the berthing of the *M.S. Dixie II*, a large sternwheel sightseeing vessel modeled after vintage Mississippi River boats. Amenities here include a beach, a campground, rustic cabins, riding stables, picnic areas, water sports rentals and tours, snowmobile tours and a marina. In Zephyr Cove, Nevada. Information: Zephyr Cove Resort, (702) 588-6644.

# Chapter 3

# Reno Area Points of Interest

## Including Carson Valley and Virginia City

### ★ Author's Choice ★

W hile Lake Tahoe has its natural beauty and high-alpine attractions, the cities and towns on the east slopes of the Sierra Nevada offer historical venues, high-desert scenery, silver mines, hot springs and big-city comforts. From the growing nest of high-rise casino hotels in Reno, to the Old West town of Virginia City, there's much to explore in day trips from Tahoe, or on separate trips of one or more nights to each of these destinations.

# Reno & Vicinity
## TOP ATTRACTIONS
### Fleischmann Planetarium
*See number 1 on Reno map, page 43*

Known as "The Space Place," this planetarium at the University of Nevada features rotating exhibits and presentations that run the gamut from dinosaurs to black holes to planetary volcanoes to international hot air balloon expeditions. There's a free astronomical museum and free public access to the observatory, which has a 12-inch telescope, every Friday night. The newly remodeled theater dome has six-channel digital sound, and features star shows and laser shows. Admission: Adults (ages 13-59), $5; children (under 13) and seniors (over 60), $3.50. Children under 6 are not admitted in the evening theater. Open daily 8 a.m. to 5 p.m. and 7 p.m. to 9 p.m. Monday through Thursday, 8 a.m. to 10 p.m. Friday, 10:30 a.m. to 10 p.m. Saturday, and 10:30 a.m. to 5 p.m. and 7 p.m. to 9 p.m. Sunday. Closed during holidays. Located 1.5 miles north of the Reno Arch on 1650 North Virginia Street at the campus. Call for recorded show times: (702) 784-4811. Reservations: (702) 784-4812.

### ★ Nevada Historical Society Museum ★
*★ notes Author's Choice*
*See number 1 on Reno map, page 43*

This is Nevada's oldest museum and research library, and its permanent and changing exhibits vividly chronicle the state's long history, from the early days of Native Americans to the casinos of the 20th century. Located next to Fleischmann Planetarium and the University of Nevada, the museum features scenes that celebrate the lives of famous people, such as Jedediah Smith, the first American explorer to enter what is now Nevada; Mark Twain, the famous newspaperman and author; and Bugsy Siegel, the man most credited with developing gaming in Nevada. There's an exhibit of priceless baskets made by the famous Washoe Indian basket weaver, Dat So La Lee. The research library houses books, maps, microfilm documents and over 350,000 photographs relating to the history of

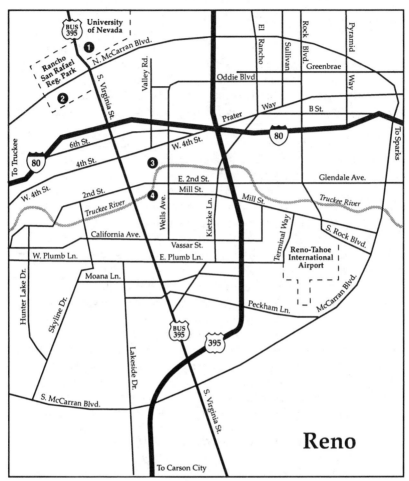

*Reno points of interest*

Nevada and the Great Basin. The museum is open Monday through Saturday, 10 a.m. to 5 p.m. The library is open Tuesday through Saturday, 12 p.m. to 4 p.m. Admission: Adults, $2; children 17 and under, free. Memberships are available. At 1650 North Virginia Street. Information: (702) 688-1190.

### ★ The Wilbur D. May Center ★
*See number 2 on Reno map, page 43*

This museum is a must-see for any visitor to Reno, and it's a great stop for families. It combines exhibits from a famous adventurer with an arboretum and botanical garden of native plants from the Great Basin. Wilbur May, who was born in 1898 with a malformed leg, was a successful businessman who founded the May Department Stores. Vowing to let no disability hamper his life, he became a pilot, musical composer, African big-game hunter, the owner of a 2,600-acre ranch, and Reno's most generous philanthropist. The museum gallery reflects his 40 trips around the world and his penchant for collecting things, such as rare Tang Dynasty pottery, Eskimo scrimshaws, Egyptian scarabs, Greek icons, Italian amulets predating the birth of Christ, and even a shrunken human head from South America.

The 10,000-square-foot museum is designed to resemble May's home, and features four large rooms, including a big-game hunting room with numerous African trophies, a ranch room with Western paraphernalia and a living room that shows a television film of May's career. Another wing of the museum contains the arboretum with lush greenery, waterfalls, rock gardens and native songbirds. Displays are changed quarterly with plants that reflect the seasons, and some of them include exotic species from around the world. The Great Basin Adventure, designed for children ages 2 to 12, is located outdoors and has a petting zoo, pony rides, an old-fashioned log flume ride, a mine replica with shaft slides and gold panning, a wetland habitat for nature walks and a few miscellaneous dinosaur replicas (one-third actual size).

The museum is open 10 a.m. to 5 p.m. Monday through Saturday, and noon to 5 p.m. on Sunday. Admission: Adults, $2.50; children (3-12), $1.50. Seasonal exhibit admission prices vary. Arboretum and park hours: 8 a.m. to sundown all year. Admission is free (donations welcome). At Rancho San Rafael Park on the hills north of downtown Reno, at 1502 Washington Street. Information: (702) 785-5961 or (702) 785-4319.

### ★ National Bowling Stadium ★
*See number 3 on Reno map, page 43*

Reno's biggest attraction is no longer gaming or automobiles; it's the world's largest and most technologically advanced bowling center. Opened in February, 1995, this massive, six-story building in the middle of downtown Reno consumes an entire square block. Its tiered roofline sports a giant silver dome, which contains a circular theater showing films on special events and attractions in the Reno and Lake Tahoe areas.

There are 80 championship lanes in a tournament room that is cavernous, with 44-foot-high ceilings (the grand opening featured fireworks indoors). The video scoring system is 450 feet long, and there's a video wall that is 16 square feet and is capable of instant replays and sponsor messages between games. Screens are eight feet high and 11 feet wide over each pair of lanes, and they can be joined to create a continuous image from one end of the stadium to the other. The computerized video BowlerVision scoring system also allows for arcade games such as "Strike

Bingo" and "Crap Shoot."

Seats are available for 1,200 spectators, media and VIPs. There's a large restaurant, Ruby's Diner, which is a 1940s-theme diner at street level, and the Stadium Sports Shop with its own bowling lane for shoppers to try before they buy. Tournament staging rooms, lockers and a three-level parking garage complete the ensemble. Built by the Reno-Sparks Convention & Visitors Authority at a cost of $45 million, the bowling center is a "look, but don't touch" facility for the general public. Only major pro and amateur tournaments and outside conventions have access to the fabled lanes, and a lot of those groups already have booked the place years in advance. Visitors, however, may tour the stadium and watch tournaments, as well as visit the restaurant, shop and theater. There is usually no charge for admission to watch tournaments; however, some tournaments may charge admission by special arrangement with the stadium. At 300 North Center Street, in downtown Reno, NV. Information: (702) 334-2600.

## ★ National Automobile Museum ★
*See number 4 on Reno map, page 43*

Detroit has nothing on Reno when it comes to celebrating the automobile. Located close to the casino district downtown, this is the city's premier museum attraction, and it is one of the finest automobile collections in the country. The displays of more than 200 classic, vintage and special interest vehicles are couched in theme "galleries," including four period street scenes that range from the turn of the century to the present.

After starting your tour with a 22-minute, high-tech multimedia theater presentation that features a moving conveyor belt of real cars, you step through a marvelously detailed service station to reach the classic machines of the 1930s and 1940s. Among the highlights of the museum are Elvis Presley's 1973 Cadillac Eldorado, the 1949 Mercury that actor James Dean drove in the movie *Rebel Without a Cause*, Al Jolson's classic 1933 Cadillac V-16, and the 1907 Thomas Flyer, the only car to win an around-the-world race. The Changing Exhibits Gallery might include items such as a rare 1930 Ruxton, a front-wheel-drive sedan that was one of only 500 cars produced, or a 1939 Bugatti Type 57C, one of a line of famous racing machines.

The museum was built in 1989, primarily to save some of the more than 1,400 cars collected by the late casino mogul Bill Harrah. When Holiday Inn bought Harrah's casinos, the new owners began dismantling the collection, selling 1,000 pieces before a local group of businessmen stepped in to establish the museum. There's a cafe and gift shop, and guided tours are given on weekends only. Most visitors use the Acousti-guide audio tour system, which allows you to tour at your own pace, with a narrator describing each exhibit. Open daily from 9:30 a.m. to 5:30 p.m. Admission: Adults, $7.50; seniors (62 and older), $6.50; children 6 to 18, $2.50; children 5 and under, free. Adopt-a-car memberships are available. At 10 Lake Street, next to the Truckee River in downtown Reno. Information: (702) 333-9300.

## ★ Pyramid Lake ★
*See number 5 on Reno/Carson Valley area map, page 47*

There is beauty in desolation, and this weird, shimmering lake 32 miles north of Sparks in the middle of the desert has a compelling allure that is uniquely its own. Named after the pointed tufa mounds on the east shore of the lake, Pyramid extends in length for 25 miles within the Pyramid Lake Paiute Indian Reservation. It is the last remnant of a prehistoric inland sea called Lake Lahontan, which once covered much of Nevada and Utah. Cradled among burnished pink and gold mountains, the lake has many moods, all of them interesting. Afternoons can bring tempestuous winds and dancing dust devils, and mornings and evenings are often hauntingly still. From various high vantage points, the lake has an eerie, photogenic quality that is more like a matte painting than reality.

Pyramid has been popular with anglers since the turn of the century. Despite its relatively shallow and alkaline depths (300 feet), it is home to the giant Lahontan cutthroat trout; the world record of this species (41 pounds) was caught here by a Paiute Indian in 1925. There's a new marina to service boaters, as well as charter boats and fishing guides (a reservation fishing license is required). The lake has two fish hatcheries, Numana and David Dunn, both operated by the tribe, and both are involved in trying to restore the endangered Lahontan fish population. The hatcheries, with net-covered holding pens, are open to the public Monday through Friday from 9 a.m. to 3 p.m.

Another facility, the Marble Bluff Dam Pyramid Lake Fishway, operated by the U.S. Fish and Wildlife Service, is located one mile north of the tribal council headquarters in Nixon on State Route 447. It has a fishway that is designed to allow the migration of the endangered cui-ui sucker and the threatened Lahontan trout from the lake to spawning areas in the Truckee River. Visitors can observe fish runs during March, April and May, as well as the sorting of the cui-ui and trout. The fishway and fish handling building are open Monday through Friday from 7 a.m. to 3:30 p.m., and there is no admission charge. For information, phone (702) 265-2425 or (702) 574-0187.

Pyramid also is home to Anaho Island National Wildlife Refuge, which has one of the largest white pelican nesting colonies in North America, as well as cormorant, great blue heron and seagull nesting colonies. Although it is closed to public access, the island can be viewed from boats. For casual visitors, the lake has sandy beaches and wading areas, some with hot springs bubbling up under the cool water.

The lake is located 32 miles north of Sparks on Highway 445. The road passes a historical marker that describes a Paiute Indian ambush of a white volunteer army led by Major William Ormsby in 1860. The conflict began after Indians raided a trading post 25 miles east of Carson City, reportedly in retaliation for the kidnapping and rape of two young Indian squaws. In an ill-advised show of bravado, Ormsby led a ragtag army of 105 settlers into a canyon along the Truckee River, where they were attacked and slaughtered. A few weeks later, the Presidio in San Francisco sent a force of Army regulars, who defeated the Indians after a three-hour battle. In 1879, President Ulysses S. Grant set aside 475,000 acres for the reservation.

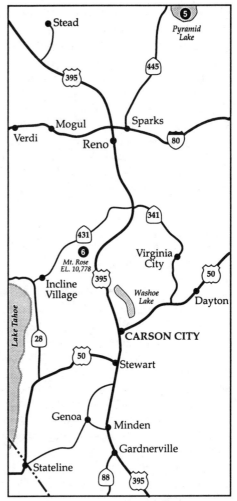

*Reno / Carson Valley area points of interest*

## ★ Bowers Mansion ★

*See number 6 on Reno / Carson Valley area map, above*

This historic two-story granite stone mansion, built in 1864 by one of the early Comstock mining entrepreneurs, is located in Washoe County 20 miles south of Reno and 10 miles north of Carson City. The building is a fine example of the extravagance that owners Sandy and Eilley Bowers lavished on their home from the riches they extracted from the mines in Virginia City. Eilley Bowers survived the death of her young husband;

after Sandy's fortune dwindled, she moved back to Virginia City and lived the remainder of her life as a fortune teller. Over the years, the home went through several owners and, unfortunately, much of the furniture was sold. But the county has faithfully restored the building and found suitable period pieces as replacements. Guided tours are offered daily from the visitor's center (located behind the mansion) from Memorial Day to Labor Day, and on weekends during spring and fall. The park next door includes amenities such as swimming pools, snack bar, volleyball court, a children's playground, horseshoe pits, and picnic and barbecue facilities. Admission: Adults, $3; seniors and children (12 and under), $2. Mansion hours: 11 a.m. to 4:30 p.m. daily from Memorial Day to Labor Day, and on weekends only from May 1 to Memorial Day weekend and Labor Day to October, with 11 half-hour tours offered daily; the mansion is closed daily from 1 p.m. to 1:30 p.m. Closed November through April. Park hours are 8 a.m. to 9 p.m. in summer and 8 a.m. to 5 p.m. in winter. Bowers Mansion Regional Park, 4005 US 395, Washoe Valley, NV. Information: (702) 849-0201 or (702) 849-1825.

## ★ Black Rock Desert ★

Though it is a two- to three-hour drive northeast of Reno, the Black Rock Desert is one of the most extraordinary regions in the western United States, and is largely unknown to the public. It is a mystical, magical place of wild mustangs galloping through chaparral, of desert hot springs suitable for swimming, of steep and twisting canyons bearing inscriptions from early pioneers, and of a vast, dry lake bed that dominates the region. The jumping-off place, literally, is the town of Gerlach, a tiny settlement 100 miles north of Sparks that is known for its public hot springs, which were originally discovered by explorer John C. Fremont in 1843. Beyond Gerlach is the vast, flat playa, which was the bottom of ancient Lake Lahontan. The plain consists of silt, with some sections as deep as 10,000 feet. On October 4, 1983, a British racing team set a world land speed record here, using a four-ton, jet-powered car that established an average speed of 633.468 miles per hour through a measured mile.

Historically, the desert was the converging point for three pioneer trails: the Fremont Trail, the Applegate-Lassen Trail and the Nobles Emigrant Trail, all of which were used by settlers on their way to California and Oregon. In the High Rock Canyon, which is a spectacular series of deep gorges, the rocks still bear the marks of wagon wheels. One interesting stop is Soldier Meadows, a historic cavalry post that is now used as a guest ranch and is probably the most idyllic piece of real estate in the desert. Throughout the ranch, wild horses, burros and antelope can be seen frequently, and natural springs, ranging from boiling to bathtub-warm, dot the landscape. During sunrises and sunsets, the hills take on vibrant hues of orange, purple and pink. And trails leading into the mountains above the desert reach lush oases of aspen forests once occupied by Basque sheepherders.

The Black Rock Desert, named after the visually distinctive Black Rock Promontory, is currently under consideration by the U.S. Bureau of Land Management as a National Conservation Area. Right now, all roads beyond Gerlach are dirt, and travel through most of the area is advisable for four-wheel-drive vehicles only, and only in groups. It's easy to get lost, disoriented or disabled in this vast wilderness. For information on the area, contact the BLM, Winnemucca District, 705 East Fourth Street, Winnemucca, NV 89445; (702) 623-3676. Information on Soldier Meadows can be obtained through Spanish Springs Guest Ranch in California, (916) 234-2064.

## OTHER POINTS OF INTEREST

***Earth Window Museum:*** Next to the Riverboat Hotel & Casino on the Truckee River in downtown Reno, in what was formerly the old Penny's building, this facility offers a collection of Native American artifacts from the Washoe and Paiute tribes, natural science displays, and live animal exhibits including iguanas, water dragons, snakes, monitor lizards, frogs and toads, turtles, chinchillas, rabbits, birds and other creatures. You have to look a bit to find the museum; it's in the basement of a shopping mall that houses a deli, a clothing store, a bar and a craft concession stand. Next to the museum is a gift shop with Native American arts and crafts. Admission: Adults, $2, and children under 12, $1. Open daily from 11 a.m. to 4 p.m. June through December, and 11 a.m. to 4 p.m. Wednesday through Sunday from January through May. At Town Center Mall, 100 North Sierra Street, Reno, NV. Information: (702) 333-2828.

***Liberty Belle Slot Machine Collection:*** Do slot machines and prime rib go together? They do in this place, which is not only a popular restaurant but also a living museum of gaming history. The restaurant owner's grandfather, Charles Fey, invented the first slot machine, called the Liberty Bell, in 1898. This was the forerunner of today's three-reel slot machine, and it was followed in 1901 by a five-card draw poker machine and in 1929 by the silver dollar machine. Fey's creations, along with those of others, surround the dining room and bar. If you visit during off-hours, you may have a chance to see the rest of the collection in a room upstairs. Some of the early slots dispensed cigarettes, candy and other items before plain ol' money became the standard. Marshall Fey, one of Fey's grandsons and co-owner of the restaurant, has authored a definitive history called *Slot Machines*, and autographed copies of this lavish coffee-table book are available at the bar for $30. Open 11 a.m. to 10 p.m. on week-days, and 11 a.m. to 11 p.m. on weekends. Admission is free. The Liberty Belle Saloon and Restaurant is located near the Reno Convention Center at 4250 South Virginia Street, Reno, NV. Information: (702) 825-1776.

*Mackay School of Mines:* Named after John Mackay, one of the mining barons of Virginia City, this exhibit features mining parapher-nalia, minerals, fossils and silver from the Mackay household. Admission is free. Open 8 a.m. to 5 p.m. Monday through Friday. At the University of Nevada, 1650 North Virginia Street, Reno, NV. Information: (702) 784-6867.

*Nevada Museum of Art:* Modern art, pop art, photography and Native American art of the 19th and 20th centuries are featured at this new museum, which contains the E.L. Wiegand Museum of Art. Well-known traveling exhibitions stop here for six-week stays throughout the year. Permanent displays include Native American baskets, sculptures, paintings, drawings and decorative pieces. The museum also has collec-tions by noted artists such as Maynard Dixon, Stuart Davis, Michael Heizer, Wayne Thiebaud, Chris Unterseher, Robert Cole Caples and others. There are educational programs and a gift shop. Open 10 a.m. to 4 p.m. Tuesday through Saturday, and noon to 4 p.m. Sunday. Admission: Adults, $3; seniors (55 and older) and students (13 to 17), $1.50; children (6 to 12), 50 cents; and children 5 and under, free. There is free admission to all on Fridays. Memberships are available. E.L. Wiegand Gallery, 160 West Liberty Street, Reno, NV. Information: (702) 329-3333.

*Sparks Heritage Foundation Museum:* This museum, a short drive from downtown Reno in neighboring Sparks, features railroad memorabilia (including a collection of lanterns) and celebrates the life of small-town America at the turn of the century. It includes milk separators, family quilts, vintage clothing and toys, photographs, farm tools, a collec-tion of law enforcement patches, and railroad and mining artifacts dating back to the early 1900s when Sparks originated as a railroad town. Open 1 p.m. to 4 p.m. Tuesday through Sunday. Admission is free. At Victorian Square, 820 Victorian Avenue, Sparks, NV. Information: (702) 355-1144.

# Carson City

Nevada's only territorial and state capital, founded in 1858, is not named after the famous scout, Christopher "Kit" Carson, though his name was attached to so many places by his friend, explorer John C. Fremont, that the town at least indirectly pays homage to him. Carson City owes its development as a lively center for commerce and industry to the Comstock mines and the Tahoe lumber companies that flanked the town to the east and west. As silver and gold poured out of Virginia City,

Gold Hill and Silver City, mills were built on the Carson River to process the ore. This activity led to the construction of the Virginia & Truckee Railroad, which connected the mines with the reduction mills. The U.S. Mint in Carson City was completed in 1869 under pressure from mine owners who wanted to save on the cost of shipping the ore to San Francisco.

With so many fortunes being made in the region, a vast residential district of stunning homes grew up on the west side of town. This district is the largest of its kind in Nevada, and today it forms the basis for walking tours. Ornate and fabulous houses dating from the early 1860s can be seen along the side streets, especially on Mountain, West Robinson, Division and West King streets. These peaceful, tree-lined avenues create a marked contrast to the traffic congestion on Carson Street (US 395). Travelers should make a point of seeing the Governor's Mansion (circa 1909), the Bliss Mansion (circa 1879), the Yerington House (circa 1863) and the Roberts House (circa 1859). Maps available from the local visitor's bureau describe these and 55 other historic sites in town, including the museums and state government buildings. Today, Carson City is still thriving as a burgeoning bedroom community for Reno, 30 miles to the north, and Lake Tahoe, 14 miles to the west. New housing subdivisions and shopping centers are popping up everywhere. Information on Carson City's attractions can be obtained from the Carson City Convention & Visitor's Bureau, 1900 South Carson Street, Suite 200, Carson City, NV 89701, or by calling (702) 687-7410 or (800)-NEVADA-1.

## POINTS OF INTEREST

***Brewery Arts Center:*** *See #7 on Carson City map, page 52.* This center has rotating exhibits, concerts, workshops and arts and crafts classes. The art center is open 9 a.m. to 5 p.m. weekdays, and the gallery is open 10 a.m. to 4 p.m. Monday through Saturday. At 449 West King Street at Division Street. Information: (702) 883-1976.

***Carson and Mills Park Narrow Gauge Railroad:*** *See #8 on Carson City map, page 52.* Visitors can ride behind a narrow-gauge, oil-fired steam locomotive, and see two- and four-axle switch engines and a rail bus. Admission: General, $1; children 2 and under, free when accompanied by an adult. Open 11 a.m. to 4 p.m. Saturday and Sunday (weather permitting), from Memorial Day to Labor Day. At Mills Park. Information: (702) 885-8578.

***The Children's Museum of Northern Nevada:*** *See #9 on Carson City map, page 52.* This museum features interactive family exhibits on the humanities, fine arts and sciences. Open 11 a.m. to 4 p.m. Tuesday through Saturday. Admission: Adults, $4; children (3-12), $2; and chil-

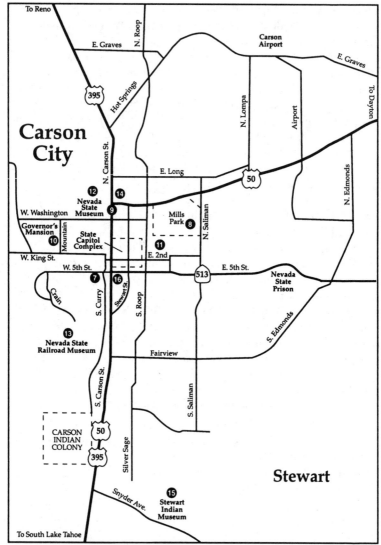

*Carson City points of interest*

dren 2 and under, free. At 813 North Carson Street. Information: (702) 884-2226.

**Governor's Mansion:** *See #10 on Carson City map, above.* Built in 1908, this colonial-style mansion can be toured only by appointment. At 606 Mountain Street. Information: (702) 882-3281 or (702) 882-2333.

**Nevada State Library and Archives:** *See #11 on Carson City map, above.* This building features a library, archives, historic preservation offices and rotating exhibits. Open 8 a.m. to 5 p.m. Monday through Friday. Admission is free. At 100 Stewart Street. Information: (702) 687-8313.

★ *Nevada State Museum: See #12 on Carson City map, page 52.* One of the finest museums on the West Coast houses a number of unique exhibits, including America's largest complete skeleton of an Imperial mammoth found in Nevada's Black Rock Desert, an amazingly realistic replica of an 1870s gold mine, and the reconstruction of a Western ghost town. The museum itself once housed a branch of the U.S. Mint, and coins were minted here from 1870 to 1893. The museum beautifully and thoroughly showcases Nevada's natural and human history, from prehistoric times (represented by a "walk-through" of the Devonian Sea) to the Lost City Indian pueblos of the Great Basin and the wildlife of Nevada. There's an exhibit by Washoe Indian basketweaver Dat So La Lee, whose works are regarded as among the finest in the world. Also, there are extensive collections of cowboy gear, firearms, arrowheads, buttons, bottles and gaming memorabilia. The museum is open 8:30 a.m. to 4:30 p.m. daily, and the bookstore and gift shop are open 9:30 a.m. to 4:30 p.m. daily. Admission: Adults, $3; seniors (55 and older), $2.50; youths 17 and under, free. At 600 North Carson Street. Information: (702) 687-4810.

★ *Nevada State Railroad Museum: See #13 on Carson City map, page 52.* Located at the south end of town, this museum houses over 25 pieces of railroad equipment from Nevada's past, with most of them coming from the Virginia & Truckee Railroad, the richest and most famous short line of the 19th century. The railroad buffs who serve as volunteer guides offer enthusiastic tours of the main building, which has steam locomotives, restored coaches and freight cars. But if you can get them to take you into the storage warehouses behind the museum, you'll find the majority of rolling stock in varying stages of decay—waiting for the funds to restore them. During the summer season through September, visitors can ride the museum's 65-year-old railbus on a short, circular track. Rail enthusiasts in the area have mounted a campaign to restore the rail line between Virginia City and Carson City, allowing vintage trains to serve these historic communities once again. The railroad museum includes a bookstore and gift shop. Open 8:30 a.m. to 4:30 a.m. Wednesday through Sunday. Admission: Adults, $2; youths under 18, free. On US 395 at 2180 South Carson Street. Information: (702) 687-6953.

*Roberts House Museum: See #14 on Carson City map, page 52.* Tours of the oldest Victorian home in Carson City are available, and Victorian-style weddings can be arranged. Open 2 p.m. to 4 p.m. weekdays and 10 a.m. to 4 p.m. weekends May through October. At Roberts House Park on 1207 Carson Street. Information: (702) 882-4133.

**Stewart Indian Museum:** *See #15 on Carson City map, page 52.* Now the museum is mainly a collection of photographs and a store selling Native American crafts, but future plans call for a major Native American Cultural Complex. The site was the former Stewart Indian Boarding School, which was closed by the U.S. Bureau of Indian Affairs in 1980. The big event here is the annual Pow Wow and Arts and Crafts Festival held during the third weekend in June. Open 9 a.m. to 4 p.m. daily. Admission is free. On the east side of Carson City at 5366 Snyder Avenue. Information: (702) 882-1808.

**Warren Fire Museum:** *See #16 on Carson City map, page 52.* This building features an old fire engine, an original fire bell and historic photographs. A new site for the museum was scheduled to reopen in June, 1995. Open 1 p.m. to 4 p.m. daily. Admission is free. At Fire Station #1, 777 South Stewart Street. Information: (702) 887-2210.

**Washoe Lake State Park:** The park features camping, boating, fishing, hiking, biking, and horseback riding trails. Day use is $3 per car from April to November, $2 during winter. The main entrance is on East Lake Boulevard, three miles east of US 395. Information: (702) 687-4319.

**Dayton State Park:** Situated next to the Carson River, this park includes camping, fishing, swimming, nature trails, the historic Rock Point Mill Site, and picnic and barbecue facilities. On US 50, 12 miles east of Carson City. Information: (702) 687-5678.

# ★ Virginia City ★

Often called "the liveliest ghost town in the West," this National Historic Landmark in a desolate canyon southeast of Reno was the birthplace of the Comstock silver bonanza of 1859, which fueled the economies of San Francisco, northern Nevada, Lake Tahoe and even the Union during the Civil War. Once occupied by 30,000 people, Virginia City yielded over $400 million in silver and gold ore before a series of fires and the demise of the mines reduced it to a hamlet of a few hundred.

Many historic buildings, including the ornate mansions of the silver barons and several unique museums, are interspersed with saloons, jewelry stores, T-shirt shops, old-fashioned casinos and food concessions. There's an operating vintage steam train, called the Virginia & Truckee Railroad, that takes passengers on a short run through the hills. And there's an underground mine tour that allows visitors to get a taste of what the miners experienced. Perhaps the best chronicle of life here is the windswept cemetery, where the epitaphs tell of hardship and heartbreak.

The town's biggest event of the year is the annual Virginia City International Camel Races in mid-September. Virginia City is 23 miles (35 minutes) from downtown Reno, via US 395 south to Highway 341.

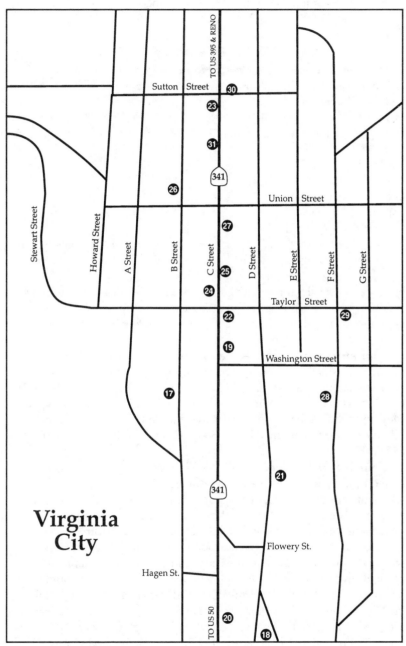

*Virginia City points of interest*

Information: Virginia City Chamber of Commerce, (702) 847-0311; Reno-Sparks Convention & Visitors Authority, (800) 367-7366.

## POINTS OF INTEREST

***The Castle:*** *See #17 on Virginia City map, page 55.* Once referred to as "the house of silver doorknobs," this grand, château-style Victorian was built in 1868 by Robert Graves, a superintendent of the Empire Mine. Its architectural style is based on a castle in Normandy, France. Sitting majestically on a hill high above the business district, the magnificent white home features richly appointed rooms, crystal chandeliers, Carrara marble fireplaces, steel engravings dating from 1852, and Italian hanging stairways. Open during the summer only. Admission: Adults, $3; children 6 to 12, 25 cents; children five and under, free. Open 11 a.m. to 5 p.m. daily from Memorial Day through early October. 70 South B Street. Information: (702) 847-0275.

***Chollar Mine:*** *See #18 on Virginia City map, page 55.* This facility offers a half-hour walking tour of a real underground mine which produced over $18 million. Gold panning is available during the summer; it's taught by an experienced panner, with gold guaranteed. Admission: Adults, $4; children (5 to 14), $1; children 4 and under, free. Panning is $5. Open noon to 5 p.m. daily in summer, 1 p.m. to 4 p.m. in spring and fall. South F Street at D Street. Information: (702) 847-0155.

***Comstock Fireman's Museum:*** *See #19 on Virginia City map, page 55.* This is a small museum with several historic fire engines, which always seemed to be in use, judging from the checkered history of Virginia City and its frequent encounters with fire. Open daily, 10 a.m. to 5 p.m. May through October. Admission is free, but donations are welcome. At Liberty Engine Company #1, 125 South C Street. Information: (702) 847-0717.

***Fourth Ward School:*** *See #20 on Virginia City map, page 55.* Walk right in and have a seat at one of the old-fashioned desks. Maybe the schoolmarm will show up, maybe not. The school was built in 1876 to accommodate 1,025 students, and it boasted the latest comforts, including modern heating, water piped to all floors, and outside bathrooms. The four-story building housed 16 classrooms with high ceilings and large windows, two study halls, a gymnasium and a vocational training area. Students from grade school to high school were educated here, and the school continued operating until 1936. Today there are rotating exhibits on Nevada's history, including occasional displays of Native American artifacts. Open 10 a.m. to 5 p.m. daily May through October. Admission is free, but donations are accepted. On South C Street at Highway 431. Information: (702) 847-0975.

*Once the home of a silver baron, the Mackay Mansion in Virginia City is now a site for history buffs and weddings.*

**The Mackay Mansion:** *See #21 on Virginia City map, page 55.* Built in 1860, this elegant mansion is the oldest home on the Comstock. It was the office for the Gould and Curry Mining Company, and the first resident was George Hearst, father of newspaper baron William Randolph Hearst. The property has the original mine office, vault, ore samples and records. An interesting footnote in history is that the building managed to escape the Great Fire of 1875 that destroyed 90 percent of the city, and ultimately became the home of John W. Mackay, the "Bonanza King" and "Boss of the Comstock" who, with a net worth of $100 million, was the richest man in town. The museum features Comstock mining artifacts, Civil War collectibles, Victorian furnishings and a well-manicured garden. It is a popular spot for weddings and special group functions. Admission: Adults, $3; children 17 and under, free. Open 11 a.m. to 5 p.m. daily in the summer. Located at 129 South D Street. Information: (702) 847-0173.

**Mark Twain's Museum of Memories:** *See #22 on Virginia City map, page 55.* Artifacts from the late 1800s include player pianos, rail/telegraph/mining equipment, trade stimulators and gaming machines. Free ore samples from the Comstock lode are available. Admission is free (donations encouraged). Open 10 a.m. to 4 p.m. daily from April through November; hours vary from December to February, weather permitting. At 109 C Street. Information: (702) 847-0454.

**Marshall Mint Gold Shop Museum:** *See #23 on Virginia City map, page 55.* Housed in the historic Assay Office, the museum features gold nuggets, gem crystals and collectible coins. Admission is free. Open 9 a.m. to 5 p.m. daily. At 96 North C Street. Information: (702) 847-0777 or (800) 321-6374.

**Mine Tours, Ponderosa Saloon:** *See #24 on Virginia City map, page 55.* This is the place where most visitors sample the life of a miner in the 1870s. Guided tours are held frequently, and provide a glimpse of what used to be over 700 miles of underground shafts. Guides describe the tools and mining processes used to extract silver, and point out tunnels, cross-cuts, drifts, stopes, raises, winzes and shafts. Admission: Adults, $3; children 12 and under, $1.50. Open 10 a.m. to 6 p.m. from Memorial Day to Labor Day, and 11 a.m. to 6 p.m. the rest of the year. On the corner of C and Taylor streets, in the main business district. Information: (702) 847-0757.

**Nevada Gambling Museum:** *See #25 on Virginia City map, page 55.* Want to know how the card sharks did it—and continue to do it? Here you can see cheating devices, guns and knives—the basic tools of the trade. The exhibits cover 150 years of gaming, with over 100 antique slot machines from the 1800s and 1900s. There's the requisite souvenir/gift shop inside. Open 10 a.m. to 6 p.m. daily from June through August, and 10 a.m. to 5 p.m. daily from September through May. Admission is free, though donations are welcome. In the Palace Emporium Hall across from the Delta Saloon parking lot, at 20 South C Street. Information:(702) 847-9022.

**Piper's Opera House:** *See #26 on Virginia City map, page 55.* The first opera house built in Nevada (the original two buildings were destroyed by fire) is still owned and operated by the Piper family. The building contains pictures, posters and artifacts of the stars who once performed here, including humorist and author Mark Twain. The tongue-and-groove maple wood dance floor was installed without nails and is supported by railroad car springs. Open 12:30 p.m. to 4:30 p.m. Saturday through Thursday, though the facility is sometimes closed unexpectedly. Admission: Adults, $1.50; children 12 and under, 50 cents. Free parking is available in the Opera House lot adjacent to the courthouse. At the corner of B and Union streets. Information: Virginia City Chamber of Commerce, (702) 847-0311.

**Territorial Enterprise:** *See #27 on Virginia City map, page 55.* It's easy to miss this fascinating museum, simply because it's in the basement of a fairly mundane T-shirt shop. But it has the real newspaper office of author and reporter Mark Twain, along with his desk and the newspaper's printing facility. The best souvenir is a reproduction of the edition of October 27, 1873, describing a devastating fire that leveled most of the business district. Next to the headline, "Virginia City in Ruins," a column reads, in part: "A breath of hell melted the main portion of town to ruins. Our eyes are still dazed by the lurid glare; our ears are still ringing with the chaos of sounds of a great city passing away on the whirlwind of a storm." Ah, what prose. Admission: Adults, $1; children 12 and under, 50 cents. Open 10:30 a.m. to 5 p.m. daily, all year. At 63 North C Street. Information: (702) 847-0525.

***Virginia & Truckee Railroad Company:*** *See #28 on Virginia City map, page 55.* Yikes! There may be gunslingers at any bend of the tracks. Or maybe they'll board the train and ask for "donations." This is a short but enjoyable ride from Virginia City through Tunnel 4 to Gold Hill, with views of the high desert mountains and mining operations. An authentic steam locomotive pulls open cars and a caboose that are over 70 years old. All 30-minute round-trip rides are narrated by the conductor. Special excursion and party rates are available. Admission: Adults, $4; children, $2; an all-day pass, $8. Open 10:30 a.m. to 5:45 p.m. daily from May through October. The station is located on F Street south of Washington Street. Information: (702) 847-0380.

***The Virginia City Radio Museum:*** *See #29 on Virginia City map, page 55.* This recent addition to town is located in the lower level of a Victorian home. The collection contains over 100 radios, accessories, tubes, vintage music and phonographs dating from 1915 to 1950, including cowboy movie star Hoot Gibson's 500-pound radio phonograph. Admission: Adults, $1.50; children, 50 cents. Open noon to 5 p.m. on weekends from Memorial Day through Labor Day, and 10 a.m. to 5 p.m. daily from July through August. At 109 South F Street. Information: Virginia City Chamber of Commerce, (702) 847-9047.

***The Way It Was Museum:*** *See #30 on Virginia City map, page 55.* For an orientation of Virginia City and its history, this should be the first stop for every visitor. The museum, on the north end of town, features a continuous video presentation on the Comstock Lode, Piper's Opera House and the life and times of Mark Twain. There's a scale model of the hundreds of miles of underground mine workings that lay beneath Virginia City. Also, there are early maps of the Comstock, the original Sutro Tunnel mule-train mine cars, a mineral collection, a collection of period costumed dolls, a fully equipped blacksmith's shop, a collection of early medicines in bottles and tins, and a large photo gallery of historic prints. Admission: Adults, $2, children 11 and under, free when accompanied by an adult. Open 10 a.m. to 5 p.m. daily Monday through Friday, and 10 a.m. to 6 p.m. Saturday and Sunday all year. At 66 North C Street. Information: (702) 847-0766.

***The Wild West Museum:*** *See #31 on Virginia City map, page 55.* Old West artifacts are on display. Admission is free, but donations are welcome. Open daily from 1 p.m. to 4 p.m. from Memorial Day weekend to Labor Day weekend. 66 North C Street. Information: (702) 847-0400.

# Genoa

Dating from an 1851 post established by Mormon traders, this is Nevada's first permanent settlement. Located on the Emigrant Trail on the eastern slope of the Sierra Nevada, it was a resting place for settlers before tackling the rugged high country for California's gold fields. The town was the seat of Carson County, Utah Territory, from 1855 until the creation of Nevada Territory in 1861. It was an important Pony Express and Stage Station. Presently, the small town has several interesting spots to visit in its historic district. Outside of the town, new subdivisions are flourishing, and the Genoa Lakes Golf Course has brought considerable business to the area. One of the popular stops is Walley's 1862 Hot Springs Resort, which is open to the public and offers a series of refreshing outdoor pools of various temperatures. Genoa is located 12 miles south of Carson City off US 395.

## POINTS OF INTEREST

*Genoa Courthouse Museum:* The original Douglas County courthouse features rotating and permanent exhibits. There is no admission, but donations are welcome. Open daily, 10 a.m. to 4:30 p.m. May through October. At Main and 5th Streets, Genoa, NV. Information: (702) 782-4325.

*Mormon Station Historic State Monument:* This is the site of Nevada's first town, which was founded by Mormon settlers. It features a restored stockade and trading post, 19th-century artifacts and other historic displays. There is no admission, but donations are welcome. Open daily from 9 a.m. to 5 p.m. May through October. At 2295 Main Street, Genoa, NV. Information: (702) 687-4379 or (702) 687-5678.

# Chapter 4

# Boating & Sightseeing Cruises

You can drive, hike, skate or cycle around Lake Tahoe, but nothing beats seeing Tahoe from the lake itself. Probably every type of watercraft known to man exists here, from polished, old-fashioned "woodies" to sleek fiberglass speedboats. It's a diverse fleet that sets out from Tahoe's marinas in the summer: large tour vessels, Hobie Cats, luxury motorcruisers, jetskis, fishing boats, rowboats, rubber rafts, paddle craft, parasailing boats, sailing yachts and waterski boats. If it floats, it's probably on the lake.

Boating on Tahoe provides a wonderful perspective; it affords a chance to see elegant estates close up, revel in the ambience of Emerald Bay and its granite peaks, view the skyline of high-rise casino hotels, and explore the rocky coves and white-sand beaches along the lake's 72-mile shoreline. Boating is the only way to see Fleur du Lac, a stone mansion that was featured in Francis Ford Coppola's *The Godfather, Part II*. While the gated compound is closed to visitors from the highway, it is quite approachable from the water, and is a primary point of interest for commercial sightseeing cruises.

The lake is the lifeblood of Tahoe's residents, and the prime attraction for some four million visitors a year. To appreciate the richness of Tahoe's nautical heritage, plan a visit in August when the Tahoe Yacht Club holds its annual Concourse d'Elegance, a three-day showcase of handcrafted wooden vessels, some of which date to the turn of the century. It's a visual feast to see 60 to 70 of these elegant boats motoring along the shoreline from Carnelian Bay to Homewood. Certainly the social elite, celebrities and business tycoons of the early 1900s made the most of their stay at this alpine wonderland.

Tahoe is a lake of many moods. In the morning, it can be calm and tranquil, so smooth that you can see the ripple of a damselfly. By early afternoon, however, it can be a raging sea of whitecaps, whipped into a frenzy by powerful winds blowing through the mountains. The lake never freezes in winter, but it stays cold year-round except in the shallows. Not surprisingly, wetsuits are a prerequisite for anyone who waterskis, sails dinghies, kayaks, swims or dives in the lake.

Water safety is paramount. All boats should be equipped with Coast Guard-approved flotation vests, ship-to-shore radio or phone and signaling devices. Small boats should avoid the middle of the lake in the afternoon and early evening, when the winds are most likely to kick up a fuss. The lake can behave like a small ocean, with rollers and waves posing hazards to the unwary. In general, sticking to the West Shore or leeward side affords some protection, since the East Shore gets the brunt of the winds.

Every boater has a favorite hangout. Emerald Bay, boasting the lake's only boat-in campground as well as its only island, is probably the top choice. On a warm summer weekend, hundreds of boats swirl in and out of the bay, some of them stopping on the beach for a picnic, others lingering around the rocks of Fannette Island, where a crumbling stone teahouse, part of Vikingsholm Castle (now a state park), offers a reminder of bygone extravagance. Sand Harbor, at Incline Village, has its charms, including a rocky promontory and pristine public beaches. At the south end of the lake, a labyrinth of waterways snakes through Tahoe Keys, a man-made waterfront residential community. Zephyr Cove and Camp Richardson, located on opposite shores close to South Lake Tahoe, offer a myriad of family recreation activities and fine beaches. And boaters can tie up for a gourmet lunch or dinner at places such as Chambers Landing, Homewood, Sunnyside, Carnelian Bay and Tahoe City, where waterfront restaurants are plentiful. Slips and mooring buoys can sometimes be in short supply, however, and you may have to wait for a spot.

Don't have a boat? No problem. You can rent or charter just about anything, from a 52-foot motor yacht to a small runabout. No matter how you choose to explore the lake, being on the water is pure bliss.

## SIGHTSEEING CRUISES

No introduction to Lake Tahoe and its history would be complete without taking a cruise. During the summer, there are regular sightseeing voyages from every corner of the lake, using motor yachts, sailing vessels and Tahoe's trademark paddlewheelers, which are replicas of vintage Mississippi riverboats. The paddlewheelers get the lion's share of attention, and represent the most popular excursion for visitors. Both the *Tahoe Queen* and the *M.S. Dixie II*, berthed at South Shore marinas, can carry over 500 passengers each. They offer narrated, two-hour cruises to Emerald Bay, serve lunches and dinners (and sometimes breakfasts), feature live entertainment in the evenings, and are virtually impervious to strong winds. The *Queen* and the *Dixie* are longtime competitors, but now there's a third "wheel"—the *Tahoe Gal*, which inaugurated cruises from the North Shore in the summer of 1994. However, the "Gal" is much smaller, has side wheels instead of stern wheels, and makes most of its runs along the West Shore. Apart from these high-profile vessels, other, more contemporary options exist for exploring the lake. There's an elegant sailing trimaran, several luxury motor yachts and a few fishing cruisers that double as sightseeing boats.

*One of Tahoe's most popular cruise boats is the new* M.S. Dixie II *out of Zephyr Cove.*

## South Shore

### ★ *M.S. Dixie II* ★

★ *notes Author's Choice*

Lake Tahoe's newest and largest cruise boat was launched at Zephyr Cove, Nevada, in May of 1994. A successor to the smaller *M.S. Dixie*, which operated on the lake for 22 years, the new paddlewheel vessel was built in La Crosse, Wisconsin, and was transported in several sections to Lake Tahoe. It is 151 feet long, has three enclosed decks, can carry 550 people, and can accommodate 200 for dinner. During 3.5-hour dinner-dance cruises, there are two seatings; while one group dines, the other group drinks and dances to live music in the upper deck lounge. The best open-air views are from the hurricane deck, next to the pilot house. The *Dixie*'s meals are generous and well prepared, demonstrating the benefits of a modern galley for chefs. The menu features charbroiled New York steak, broiled Alaskan halibut, honey-dijon chicken breast, caesar salad, dessert and unlimited California wine. The interior of the vessel, however, does not have the richness of detail that embellishes the *Tahoe Queen*. The *Dixie* leaves for cruises of Emerald Bay every day on a year-round basis, with more departures scheduled in summer. During the voyage, the *Dixie*'s exclusive underwater video, "The Sunken Treasures of Lake Tahoe," is shown at no extra charge (it is also available for sale on the boat). Those who want to have a peek directly at the netherworld of Tahoe can check out the glass-bottomed viewing window.

*Services:* Champagne brunch cruise, Glenbrook breakfast cruise, Emerald Bay shoreline cruise, Emerald Bay dinner cruise, sunset dinner-dance cruise, weddings, charters, smoke-free dining room and free shuttles between Stateline casino hotels and Zephyr Cove (four miles away).

*Fees:* The champagne brunch and Glenbrook breakfast cruises are $16.50 for adults, $8 for children 3 to 11; children 2 and under are free. Emerald Bay sightseeing cruises are $14 for adults and $5 for children. Emerald Bay sightseeing/dinner cruises (two hours) are $24 for adults, $10 for children. The sunset dinner-dance cruise (3.5 hours) is $34 for adults and is not recommended for young children. There are discounts for senior citizens. Traveler's Checks, MasterCard, Visa, Discover and American Express are accepted. Reservations are recommended.

*Information:* M.S. Dixie II, c/o Zephyr Cove Resort, P.O. Box 12309, Zephyr Cove, NV 89448; (702) 588-3508 or (702) 882-0786.

## ★ *Tahoe Queen* ★

Departing daily from Ski Run Marina in South Lake Tahoe, California, this authentic Mississippi paddlewheeler is 144 feet long and can carry 500 passengers. The *Queen* offers a unique service among Tahoe cruise boats—a morning winter cruise for skiers from South Lake Tahoe to Homewood Marina, on the North Shore, where they can take a free shuttle to the slopes of Squaw Valley or walk across the street to Homewood. The cruise leaves Monday through Friday, featuring an optional breakfast buffet and, on the return, an optional dinner or snack. Cruising time is two hours each way. Apart from the ski shuttle, the vessel has daily two-hour tours of Emerald Bay and, in summer, nightly dinner-dance cruises. The *Queen* was manufactured in 1982 in La Crosse, Wisconsin (not by the company that built the *M.S. Dixie II*). The interior of the *Queen* is luxurious and elaborate, with oak and brass accents. The vessel derives all of its thrust from its paddlewheels, making it entirely authentic. For evening cruises, a popular three-piece band plays music for dancing, and dinner entrées usually include a choice of salmon, prime rib or New Orleans-style chicken. Lunch offerings vary, with everything from burgers to salmon.

*Services:* Daily, year-round departures to Emerald Bay, with a nightly sunset dinner-dance cruise (3.5 hours) in summer, and on Saturdays only in winter. Morning ski shuttles to the North Shore (weather permitting) include an optional breakfast buffet, an après-ski party with live music on the return and an optional light dinner. The *Queen* has a glass-bottomed viewing area, a full bar, a dance floor and a restaurant. Emerald Bay cruises feature live narration, and there is free viewing of a video, "Mysteries Beneath Lake Tahoe" (it is also available for sale on the boat). Special arrangements can be made for weddings, anniversaries and groups.

*Prices:* The two-hour Emerald Bay cruise is $14 for adults and $5 for children. Dinner-dance cruises have a boarding fee of $18 for adults and $9 for children, with dinner entrées ranging from $18 to $20 extra. Ski shuttles are $18 for adults and $9 for children, with an optional breakfast at $9 and light dinners ranging from $6 to $12. Visa, Master-Card and American Express are accepted. Reservations are required for dinner cruises.

*Information:* Tahoe Queen, 970 Ski Run Boulevard, South Lake Tahoe, CA 96151; (916) 541-3364.

### ★ *Tahoe Para-Dice* ★

Operating out of Richardson's Resort in summer, this elegant, 70-foot Skipper Liner is the epitome of pampered luxury. It has a spacious, en-closed salon, with dining area, bar, galley and L-shaped couch. It has a flying bridge with more deck space—perfect for sipping wine coolers and watching the scenery go by. And it has—get this—a circular hot tub, for weddings, parties and special charters.

*Services:* When not chartered for private groups, the vessel offers daily, two-hour cruises to Emerald Bay. It can accommodate up to 49 passengers. Bar service and snacks are extra.

*Fees:* The Emerald Bay cruise is $14 for adults and $9 for children. Reservations are suggested. The boat is based out of Richardson's Resort, which is on Highway 89 four miles north of the "Y" at South Lake Tahoe.

*Information:* Tahoe Para-Dice, P.O. Box 11436, Tahoe Paradise, CA 96155; (916) 541-7499.

### *The Party Boat*

This 52-foot luxury yacht, operating out of the Tahoe Keys Marina, is specifically for chartered groups and does not run regular tours. It can accommodate 49 passengers in complete comfort. Amenities include a flying bridge, two bathrooms, conference cabins, indoor and outdoor areas, a bar, a kitchen and a salon.

*Services:* The boat is available for weddings, family reunions, parties, club events, fund-raisers and corporate meetings. It can offer scenic cruises to Emerald Bay and other parts of Lake Tahoe.

*Fees:* The fee depends on group size and services desired. Inquire at Tahoe Keys Yacht Charters.

*Information:* Tahoe Keys Yacht Charters, Tahoe Keys Marina, 2435 Venice Drive East, South Lake Tahoe, CA 96150; (916) 541-2155 or (800) 462-5397.

## ★ *Woodwind* ★

Break out the champagne and live it up on this elegant 41-foot trimaran, which has been a tradition on the lake since 1975. If you time your voyage for the afternoon, you'll almost certainly see her sails unfurled and feel the power of the winds pushing her through the waters. While the sightseeing powerboats offer mere cruises, the *Woodwind* offers an exhilarating experience, ideal for those with a yen for adventure. The three-hull design affords great stability under sail, and the spacious cockpit and wide decks provide plenty of room to stretch out. Features include glass-bottomed windows, a heated, enclosed cabin, and a bathroom. Guests do not need to have sailing experience (the crew handles all of the rigging), and no special clothing or shoes are required. The *Woodwind* berths at Zephyr Cove Resort and sails mainly along the East and South shores of the lake, although it has no particular destination. As might be expected, the craft is enormously popular and is booked well in advance. The capacity on board is 30, and the vessel sails four to six times daily.

***Services:*** Daily, 90-minute cruises set off starting in late morning from April 1 through October 31. Sunset champagne cruises generally leave at 7 p.m. It is available for weddings (averaging 100 per year), private charters, birthdays and company outings.

***Fees:*** Regular cruises are $14 for adults and $7 for children under 12. Children under 2 are free. Champagne cruises are $20 for adults. Visa and MasterCard are accepted. Reservations are recommended.

***Information:*** Zephyr Cove Resort, P.O. Box 1375, Zephyr Cove, NV 89448; (702) 588-3000.

# North Shore

### *Sierra Cloud*

This 55-foot-long, 30-foot-wide catamaran seats 49 passengers. It departs three times daily from the beach at the Hyatt Regency from May to September, and offers nightly, two-hour champagne cruises in summer evenings, weather permitting. Cruises cover the North Shore area. All cruises offer snacks and beverages, including beer, wine and sodas.

***Services:*** Daily cruises from May to September are offered from 10:30 a.m. to 12 noon, 1:30 p.m. to 3:30 p.m., and a nightly champagne cruise from 4:30 p.m. to 6:30 p.m. The boat is available for private charters and weddings.

***Fees:*** The morning cruise is $25 for adults and $15 for children 12 and under. Afternoon and champagne cruises are $35 for adults and $15 for children 12 and under. Reservations are suggested. Visa, MasterCard, American Express and Discover are accepted.

**Information:** Hyatt Regency Activity Desk, P.O. Box 3239, Incline Village, NV 89450; (702) 832-1234.

## *SunRunner II*

Departing from the Tahoe Yacht Harbor in Tahoe City, this 65-foot luxury cruise boat, which was totally rebuilt in 1994, offers tours along the West Shore, including the Fleur du Lac mansion, and longer cruises to Emerald Bay. With two outboard motors, the *SunRunner II* is one of the quietest cruise boats in Tahoe. Up to 110 passengers can be accommodated in the enclosed, air-conditioned cabin, which has large, oversized windows, or at tables on the top deck behind the bridge. The salon has a full bar, knotty-pine interior and lush carpeting. Optional drinks and snacks are available on every cruise.

**Services:** Daily departures beginning in April include two-hour West Shore cruises, three-hour Emerald Bay cruises and two-hour evening sunset cruises. It is also available for weddings, catered dinners or lunches and other special functions. The boat is located behind Roundhouse Mall at 700 North Lake Boulevard.

**Fees:** The Emerald Bay cruise is $17 for adults and $7.50 for children. The West Shore and evening sunset cruises are $14 for adults and $5 for children 12 and under.

**Information:** North Shore Cruises, P.O. Box 5697, Tahoe City, CA 96145; (916) 583-5570.

## ★ *Tahoe Gal* ★

Sure, it looks diminutive and hokey, but this newest paddlewheeler is a lot of fun. Launched in May of 1994, this 70-foot-long, 150-passenger sidewheel boat is reminiscent of the Mississippi riverboats and it came from—you guessed it—La Crosse, Wisconsin. Whereas the big paddlewheelers at the South Shore are impressive, the *Tahoe Gal* is, well, cute. There's a large, air-conditioned salon with a full galley and bar on the lower deck, and room for tables and chairs on the top deck, behind the bridge. This vessel offers two-hour cruises along the West Shore and three-hour cruises to Emerald Bay. The main points of interest are the resorts, lakeside homes and Fleur du Lac (Kaiser Estate) mansion, which was featured in the film *The Godfather, Part II*. Continental breakfast and an optional tableside lunch are served, depending on the cruise and time of year. Lunches are quite tasty and creative, and the staff is enthusiastic. Tours are narrated.

**Services:** Shoreline, Emerald Bay, continental breakfast, cocktail, sunset and dinner cruises are offered. New for 1995 is a brunch cruise along the rocky East Shore, which will be offered on Wednesdays and Sundays and visit Whittel's Castle, a private estate south of Incline Village. Apart from scheduled cruises, the *Tahoe Gal* can accommodate special functions such as weddings and catered meetings; the vessel's salon can seat 25 people. It operates June through September from Lighthouse Marina, at Lighthouse Mall in Tahoe City.

***Fees:*** Shoreline and sunset cocktail cruises are $15 for adults and $5 for children 12 and under. The Emerald Bay cruise is $18 for adults and $8 for children 12 and under. The brunch cruise is $18 for adults and $8 for children, with an additional charge for breakfast. Weddings, meetings and corporate functions can also be accommodated. Reservations are suggested.

***Information:*** North Tahoe Cruises, P.O. Box 7913, Tahoe City, CA 95730; (916) 583-0141 or (800) 218-2464.

## West Shore
### *Kingfish*

The *Kingfish*, a 43-foot vessel built in 1985, is outfitted for fishing, but it also offers 2.5-hour narrated cruises to Emerald Bay, generally in the afternoon. The boat operates out of Homewood, from the pier next to the West Shore Café. It travels along the shoreline, passing Sugar Pine Point, Fleur du Lac, Ehrman Mansion, Rubicon Point and Emerald Bay. Don't expect a lot of frills; passengers are encouraged to bring a small ice chest and picnic basket for goodies.

***Services:*** Tours, gourmet dinners, birthday cruises and weddings. Available year-round.

***Fees:*** For Emerald Bay tours, adults are $20, seniors 65 and over are $18, children 6 to 12 are $12, and children under 5 are free.

***Information:*** Kingfish Guide Service, P.O. Box 5955, Tahoe City, CA 95730; (916) 525-5360.

## RENTAL BOATS, JETSKIS & WATERSKI LESSONS
### North Shore

**Action Watersports of Tahoe:** Offering boats, jetskis, parasailing and waterskiing rentals. 967 Lakeshore Boulevard, Incline Village, NV 89451; (702) 831-4386.

**Goldcrest Water Ski School:** A waterski school for children and adults, with wetsuits, ski tows, a heated pool, a lakeside spa and a sandy beach. American Express, Visa and MasterCard are accepted. 8194 North Lake Boulevard, Kings Beach, CA 96143; (916) 546-7412.

**High Sierra Water Ski School:** A complete ski school (U.S. Coast Guard-licensed, AWSA-certified school, with everything included), with jetski rentals, powerboat charters/tours/rides, Ski Nautique powerboat rentals (hourly and daily), sailing (lessons, rentals and charters), a pro shop, sales, and equipment rentals and repairs. Visa and MasterCard are accepted. At three locations: 5000 North Lake Boulevard, Carnelian Bay, CA 96141, (916) 546-4909; Sunnyside Marina, 1850 West Lake Boulevard, Tahoe City, CA 96145, (916) 583-7417; and 5190 West Lake Boulevard, Homewood, CA, (916) 525-1214.

**Jet Ski Rentals:** Instruction and wetsuit included with jetski rentals (650 SX Jet Ski, Tandem Sports, Three-Seaters). 8290 North Lake Boulevard, Kings Beach, CA 96143; (916) 546-2419.

**Tahoe Boat Company:** Offering 21-foot powerboats, Wave Runners/jetskis, platform boat rentals and 43-foot luxury yacht charters. Roundhouse Mall, 7000 North Lake Boulevard, Tahoe City, CA 96145; (916) 583-5567.

**Tahoe Water Adventures:** Offering powerboats, jetskis, parasailing, tandem, ski boat rentals (lessons and tows), a snack bar and a full bar. Open daily in summer, dawn to dusk. Checks, American Express, Visa and MasterCard are accepted. 120 Grove Street, Tahoe City, CA 96145; (916) 583-3225.

**North Tahoe Marina:** Offering powerboats (18 to 21 feet), jetskis, rental gear (skis, inner tubes, wetsuits, Skurfers, kneeboards), waterskiing, a pro shop, a ski school, Mac-A-Tac Fishing Charters, picnic facilities and two restaurants (Sunsets on the Lake and Dockside Deli). At highways 267 and 28. 7360 North Lake Boulevard, Tahoe Vista, CA 96145; (916) 546-8248.

## Truckee/Donner

**Donner Lake Boat Rentals:** Offering jetski/Wave Runner, powerboat rentals, waterskiing and tubing. Reservations are recommended. All major credit cards are accepted. In Donner Lake Village Resort at Donner Lake Marina, 15695 Donner Pass Road, Truckee, CA 96161; (916) 587-6081.

## South Shore

**Captain Kirk's Beach Club:** Offering jetski rentals (half hour to full day, one- to three-rider models, with full instruction, wetsuit and life vest included) and parasailing (dry launch and land from boat, 500 feet above lake, any ages or dress). Reservations are accepted, as are Visa, MasterCard, American Express and Discover cards. At Zephyr Cove Marina, four miles north of Stateline. P.O. Box 481, Zephyr Cove, NV 89448; (702) 588-3530.

**Lakeside Marina:** Offering boat rentals and leasing. 4041 Lakeshore Boulevard, South Lake Tahoe, CA 96150; (916) 541-6626.

**Lake Tahoe Rentals and Thrills:** Offering jetskis/Wave Runners, mountain bikes, powerboats, and waterskiing rentals and equipment. Reservations are suggested. Across from the Bijou Safeway on US 50, South Lake Tahoe, CA 96156; (916) 542-4472 or (916) 544-2942.

**Lake Tahoe Water Ski School:** Offering waterski lessons (AWSA-certified instructors), charters, kickboards, kneeboards, and wetsuit and equipment rentals. Reservations are recommended. At Camp Richardson and Round Hill Pines Beach. P.O. Box 5298, Stateline, NV 96157; (702) 544-7747.

**Lakeview Sports:** Offering rentals (full and half day), sales, repairs, jetskis and powerboats (18 to 25 feet). Open daily from 8 a.m. to 7 p.m. American Express, Visa and MasterCard are accepted. At the Tahoe Keys Marina. 3131 US 50, South Lake Tahoe, CA 96150; (916) 544-0183.

**Paradise Watercraft Rentals:** Offering powerboats, a luxury deck, fishing, jetskis, sailing, paddle water toys (canoes, kayaks, Zodiacs), water trampoline rentals and parasailing. Reservations are accepted. 1900 Jameson Beach Road, Camp Richardson, South Lake Tahoe, CA 96157; (916) 541-7272.

**Tahoe Keys Boat Rentals and Sales:** Offering powerboats, jetskis, patio boats, windsurfing rentals, lessons, sales and free parking. Visa and MasterCard are accepted. Tahoe Keys Marina, 3131 Harrison, South Lake Tahoe, CA 96150; (916) 541-8405.

**Zephyr Cove Marina:** Offering boat (speed, fishing, waterski) and jetski rentals. Located four miles north of South Shore casinos on U.S. Forest Service lands. 760 US 50, P.O. Box 830, Zephyr Cove, NV 89448; (702) 588-3833.

# Reno

**The Boat Shop:** Offering waterskiing equipment and supplies. 95 East Glendale, Sparks, NV 89431; (702) 358-7211.

**Tropical Penguins Scuba and Water Sports:** Offering waterskiing, scuba diving, equipment and supplies. 180 West Peckham Lane, Reno, NV 89509; (702) 828-2363.

**Jones' Jet Skee Motorcycle:** Offering boat and jetski rentals. 55 North Edison Way, Reno, NV 89502; (702) 856-7533.

**Marine Specialties:** Offering Connelly waterskiing equipment and accessories. 890 Steneri Way, Sparks, NV 89431; (702) 359-2363.

**Mark-Fore & Strike Sporting Goods:** Offering Mercury outboards, boat rentals and equipment, waterskis, fishing equipment (tackle, bait, flies), camping/outing equipment (tents, stoves, sleeping bags), and backpacking equipment. Open 8 a.m. to 6 p.m. Monday through Thursday and Saturday; 8 a.m. to 7 p.m. on Friday. American Express, Visa, Discover and MasterCard are accepted. 490 Kietzke Lane, Reno, NV 89502; (702) 322-9559.

# PUBLIC LAUNCHING RAMPS
## Lake Forest, Tahoe City
*See number 1 on map, page 73*

*Hours:* Open 24 hours.

*Amenities:* A boat ramp and fishing. There is no fee for launching, but the parking fee is $5 for each visit or $55 for a season pass. It is operated by the Tahoe City Public Utility District. Located off Highway 28 north of Tahoe City, CA. Tahoe City Public Utility District, P.O. Box 33, Tahoe City, CA 96145; (916) 583-5544.

## Kings Beach, Tahoe Vista
*See number 2 on map, page 73*

*Hours:* Open 24 hours.

*Amenities:* A boat ramp, sail and non-powered rentals, restrooms and fishing. The launch fee is $6; the parking fee is $5 at Kings Beach State Recreation Area. Located at the bottom of Coon Street in Kings Beach. North Tahoe Public Utility District, P.O. Box 33, Tahoe Vista, CA 96148; (916) 546-7248.

## Sand Harbor, Lake Tahoe-Nevada State Park
*See number 3 on map, page 73*

*Hours:* 8 a.m. to 7 p.m.

*Amenities:* A boat ramp, restrooms, fishing and a telephone. Self-launching is at your own risk. The launch fee is $7. Located off Highway 28, four miles south of Incline Village, NV. Lake Tahoe-Nevada State Park, P.O. Box 8867, Incline Village, NV 89452; (702) 831-0494 or (702) 885-4384.

## South Lake Tahoe Recreation Area
*See number 4 on map, page 73*

*Hours:* Open 24 hours.

*Amenities:* Although the public boat ramp had been closed since 1989 due to drought conditions, the city has plans to re-open the ramp in summer 1995, thanks to a terrific 1994-1995 rainy season. Facilities include a boat ramp, a picnic site with benches and barbecue grills, a beach, a swimming area, a children's playground, powered and non-powered boat rentals, restrooms, telephones and limited parking. There is no fee. At US 50 and Lakeview Avenue in South Lake Tahoe, CA. South Lake Tahoe Parks and Recreation Department, (916) 542-9056.

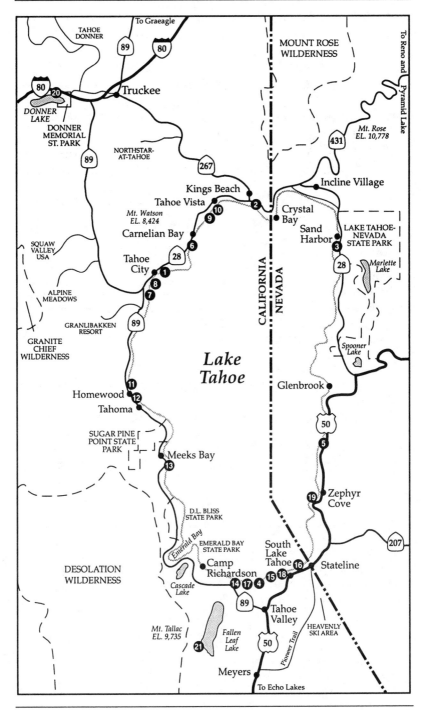

## Cave Rock
*See number 5 on map, page 73*

**Hours:** Open 24 hours.

**Amenities:** A boat ramp, restrooms, fishing and a telephone. Dredging two years ago has allowed this public ramp, operated by Nevada State Parks, to offer the most consistent public self-launch on the lake. It will accommodate boats of up to 30 feet. The launch fee is $7. Located on US 50, Lake Tahoe-Nevada State Park north of Zephyr Cove, NV. Lake Tahoe-Nevada State Park, P.O. Box 8867, Incline Village, NV 89452; (702) 831-0494.

# PRIVATE MARINAS
## North Shore
### Sierra Boat Company
*See number 6 on map, page 73*

**Hours:** 8 a.m. to 5 p.m.

**Amenities:** A boat ramp, moorings (buoys), gas, supplies, repairs and fishing. Hoist launching ranges from $25 to $35 each way; sail launching is $3 per foot. At 5146 North Lake Boulevard (Highway 28). P.O. Box 69, Carnelian Bay, CA 96140; (916) 546-2552.

### Sunnyside Marina
*See number 7 on map, page 73*

**Hours:** 8 a.m. to 6 p.m.

**Amenities:** Powered, non-powered and sail rentals, moorings (slips and buoys), food, gas, repairs, parasailing, waterskiing lessons, valet service and free parking. Launching is $35 each way, by appointment, for boats up to 21 feet. 1850 West Lake Boulevard, Tahoe City, CA 96145; (916) 583-7201.

### Tahoe Boat Company
*See number 8 on map, page 73*

**Hours:** 8 a.m. to 5:30 p.m.

**Amenities:** Powered and non-powered rentals, moorings (slips and buoys), food, gas, supplies, repairs and parasailing. Launching is $35 each way, $45 round-trip, for boats up to 20 feet. At Roundhouse Mall. P.O. Box 45, Tahoe City, CA 96145; (916) 583-5567.

### Captain Jon's
*See number 9 on map, page 73*

**Hours:** Vary. Phone ahead.

**Amenities:** A boat ramp. There is no fee. 7220 North Lake Boulevard, Tahoe Vista, CA 96148; (916) 546-4819.

### North Tahoe Marina
*See number 10 on map, page 73*

**Hours:** 8 a.m. to 6 p.m.

**Amenities:** Powered and non-powered rentals, moorings (slips and buoys), food/restaurant, gas, supplies, repairs and a fishing charter center. Launching is $22 each way for boats up to 21 feet ($1.25 per extra foot). Located in Tahoe Vista on Highway 28. 7360 North Lake Boulevard, Tahoe Vista, CA 96148; (916) 546-8248 or (800) 58-MARINA.

## West Shore

### High & Dry Marina
*See number 11 on map, page 73*

**Hours:** 8 a.m. to 5 p.m.

**Amenities:** A boat ramp, powered and non-powered rentals, moorings (buoys), food, restrooms, fishing, gas, supplies, repairs and year-round dry-rack storage. The launch operation is open May 1 through September 30. Forklift launching is $25 each way for boats up to 20 feet, $35 for boats 21 feet and over. Located on Highway 89. 5190 West Lake Boulevard, Homewood, CA 96141; (916) 525-5966.

### Obexer's
*See number 12 on map, page 73*

**Hours:** 7 a.m. to 8 p.m.

**Amenities:** Moorings (slips and buoys), a deep-water ramp, a launching trailer for deep draft sailboats, a travel lift and forklift, food, gas, supplies and repairs. The ramp launching fee is $15 for same-day round-trip (self-launching only), $10 each way if on different days. A seasonal pass is $150. Highway 89, Homewood, CA 96141; (916) 525-7962.

### Meeks Bay Marina
*See number 13 on map, page 73*

**Hours:** 8 a.m. to 6 p.m.

**Amenities:** A boat ramp, fishing, powered and non-powered boat rentals, moorings (slips), food, gas and supplies. The ramp launching fee is $5 round-trip, free for guests staying in cabins or the campground. Slips are $15 per night. Open Memorial Day through mid-October. Located on Highway 89, 10 miles south of Tahoe City, CA. P.O. Box 411, Tahoma, CA 96142; (916) 525-7242 or (702) 829-1977 (winter).

# South Shore

## Anchorage Marina
*See number 14 on map, page 73*

**Hours:** 8 a.m. to 7 p.m.

**Amenities:** A boat ramp, powered, non-powered and sail rentals, moorings (buoys), food, gas, supplies and repairs. The self-launching fee is $27 round-trip; assistance is available if needed. Parking costs $3 weekdays and $5 weekends. Located on Highway 89, 2.5 miles north of South Lake Tahoe. P.O. Box 9028, South Lake Tahoe, CA 96158; (916) 541-1777 or (916) 541-1801.

## Lakeside Marina
*See number 15 on map, page 73*

**Hours:** 8 a.m. to 7 p.m.

**Amenities:** Powered and non-powered rentals, moorings (slips and buoys), gas, supplies and repairs. The launching fee is $10 each way. Located off US 50, at the end of Park Avenue in South Lake Tahoe. 4041 Lakeshore Boulevard, South Lake Tahoe, CA 96150; (916) 541-6626.

## Ski Run Marina
*See number 16 on map, page 73*

**Hours:** 8 a.m. to 6 p.m.

**Amenities:** Powered, non-powered and sail rentals, moorings (buoys), food, gas, supplies and repairs. No launching or pump-out station is available to the public. Located off US 50 on Ski Run Boulevard in South Lake Tahoe. 900 Ski Run Boulevard, South Lake Tahoe, CA 96150; (916) 544-0200.

## Tahoe Keys Marina
*See number 17 on map, page 73*

**Hours:** 8 a.m. to 6 p.m.

**Amenities:** A boat ramp, powered and sail rentals, moorings (slips), food, restrooms, fishing, gas, supplies and repairs. Launching is $25 round-trip (forklift and travel lift available). Located off US 50 in South Lake Tahoe. 2435 Venice Drive, South Lake Tahoe, CA 96150; (916) 541-2155.

## Timber Cove Marina
*See number 18 on map, page 73*

**Hours:** 8 a.m. to 6 p.m.

**Amenities:** Powered, non-powered and sail rentals, moorings (buoys), food, gas, supplies, repairs and fish charters. Launching availability depends on the lake level. 3411 Lake Tahoe Boulevard, South Lake Tahoe, CA 96150; (916) 544-2942.

## Zephyr Cove Marina
*See number 19 on map, page 73*

*Hours:* 8 a.m. to 6 p.m.

*Amenities:* Powered, non-powered and sail rentals, moorings (buoys), food, restrooms, a telephone, camping, fishing, gas, supplies and cruises. No launching is available. Parking is $4. Located off US 50 in Zephyr Cove. P.O. Box 830, Zephyr Cove, NV 89448; (702) 588-3833.

# Donner Lake
## Donner Lake Marina
*See number 20 on map, page 73*

*Hours:* 9 a.m. to 5 p.m.

*Amenities:* Rentals—powered and non-powered boats, jetskis, inboards, and waterskiing and fishing equipment. Reservations are advised. All major credit cards are accepted. Donner Lake Village Resort, 15695 Donner Pass Road, Truckee, CA 96161; (916) 587-6081.

# Fallen Leaf Lake
## Fallen Leaf Lodge Marina
*See number 21 on map, page 73*

*Hours:* Vary. Phone ahead.

*Amenities:* A boat ramp. 400 Fallen Leaf Road, South Lake Tahoe, CA 96150; (916) 541-3366 or (916) 541-6330.

# Echo Lake
## Echo Chalet

*Hours:* Vary. Phone ahead.

*Amenities:* A boat ramp. Located on US 50 south of Meyers. 900 Echo Lake Road, Twin Bridges, CA 95735; (916) 659-7207.

# Pyramid Lake, Nevada
## Pyramid Lake Marina

*Hours:* 7 a.m. to 6 p.m.

*Amenities:* A boat ramp, restrooms, camping and fishing. Launch fee is $6 per day. Tribal permits are required. Located 30 miles north of Reno on Highway 445, in Pyramid Lake, NV. Pyramid Lake Fisheries, Star Route, Sutcliffe, NV 89510; (702) 476-1156.

## Popcorn

*Hours:* Sunrise to sunset.

*Amenities:* A boat ramp, restrooms, camping and fishing. Launch fee is $6 per day. Tribal permits are required. Located off Highway 445, 36 miles north of Reno on Highway 446, in Pyramid Lake, NV. Pyramid Lake Fisheries, Star Route, Sutcliffe, NV 89510; (702) 476-0500.

# Chapter 5

# Hiking Trails

## ★ Author's Choice ★

### Top 5 Short Hikes

Upper Echo Lake to Echo Chalet (Echo Lakes Trail)—p. 106
Barker Pass to Twin Peaks—p. 94
Eagle Falls Trail to Eagle Lake—p. 100
Alpine Meadows to Five Lakes (Five Lakes Trail)—p. 94
Horsetail Falls Trail—p. 107

### Top 10 Day Hikes

Glen Alpine Trail to Suzie and Heather Lakes—p. 104
Eagle Falls Trail to Dicks and Fontanillis Lakes—p. 100
Big Bend Trail to Loch Leven Lakes (Loch Leven Lakes Trail)—p. 116
Wrights Lake to Grouse, Hemlock and Smith Lakes—p. 109
Upper Echo Lake to Lake Aloha (Echo Lakes Trail)—p. 106
Tahoe Rim Trail, Spooner Summit North—p. 98
Rubicon Trail to Emerald Bay—p. 99
Round Lake Loop Trail—p. 117
Woods Lake to Round Top Lake Loop—p. 112
Meeks Bay to Crag Lake (Meeks Bay Trail)—p. 96

### Top 5 Peak Hikes

Sierra Buttes—p. 122
Mount Tallac—p. 120
Round Top—p. 120
Mount Rose—p. 119
Ellis Peak—p. 121

Sooner or later, almost everyone who comes to Lake Tahoe has the urge to explore the natural wonders that surround the basin. Hiking in the high country takes you to flowering meadows and indigo alpine lakes, granite peaks and volcanic buttes, verdant fir forests and towering waterfalls. Perhaps nowhere on the West Coast, with the exception of Yosemite, is there such geologic diversity and inspirational scenery. Surely, for anyone who travels the globe, there is little comparison to the hypnotic beauty of Emerald Bay. Scramble to the top of one of Tahoe's 10,000-foot mountains and the whole of creation seems to unfold below you: the Sierra in its rugged majesty, with the arid valleys of Carson and Washoe snuggling up to the eastern slopes. If you venture out on Tahoe's trails, be prepared for considerable elevation gain on some routes, where your heart and lungs will get a workout. But you can also enjoy a rewarding hike with modest effort, on routes that skirt the basin's shoreline or fan out from high-altitude trailheads reachable by car or sightseeing tram.

With few exceptions, the majority of trails are on public lands, usually those managed by the U.S. Forest Service. These are the five forest jurisdictions in the region:

- Lake Tahoe Basin Management Unit, which encompasses the Tahoe rim and the drainages that face the lake.

- Tahoe National Forest, which embraces much of the North Shore between Tahoe City and Truckee, part of the crest above the West Shore, Donner Pass, Sierra Buttes, Highway 89 north of Truckee, and most of the Lakes Basin.

- Eldorado National Forest, which includes US 50 west of South Lake Tahoe, Highway 88 from Silver Lake to Carson Pass, and Crystal Basin Recreation Area to the west of South Lake Tahoe.

- Toiyabe National Forest, which covers Mount Rose, Spooner Summit and the Carson Range on the East Shore, and most of the high country on Highway 88 from its junction with Highway 89 east toward Markleeville and Gardnerville.

- Plumas National Forest, which contains the Lakes Basin and Feather River drainage near the resort community of Graeagle and northwest of Truckee and Interstate 80.

Apart from federal lands, both California and Nevada have trail systems in their state parks. In California, these include D.L. Bliss, Sugar Pine Point, Donner Memorial, Emerald Bay, Burton Creek (undeveloped), Washoe Lake, Lake Valley State Recreation Area, Tahoe State Recreation Area, Plumas Eureka and Grover Hot Springs. In Nevada, the 14,000-acre Lake Tahoe-Nevada State Park is the largest in the region; it embraces Sand Harbor, Spooner Lake and Cave Rock. Also, there is a profusion of county, city and public utility (PG&E) recreation areas that offer trails. Throughout the region, trails can cross private lands, and hikers should respect "No Trespassing" signs.

## WILDERNESS AREAS & PERMITS

Within the national forests bordering Tahoe are four official wilderness areas: Desolation, Granite Chief, Mount Rose and Mokelumne. A wilderness designation means that access is restricted to hiking and horseback riding, and no mechanized vehicles, such as mountain bikes, four-wheel-drive vehicles and hang gliders, are allowed. Although trails are generally maintained, hiking in wilderness can be a raw, challenging experience. When you venture into one, be prepared for anything, from high-water stream crossings to sudden storms to forest fires.

## Desolation Wilderness

As the most popular hiking/backpacking destination in the region, this area has 63,475 acres of subalpine forests, granite peaks and glacially formed valleys. There are 130 reasons why so many people come here, all of them lakes—fabulous, deep-blue gems scattered across a rocky landscape. Elevations range from 6,500 feet to over 10,000 feet, and sometimes passes and saddles may be snowbound well into midsummer. Alpine timber and flora abound along most of the access routes, but thin considerably at the higher elevations. You can enter Desolation from the west out of Crystal Basin Recreation Area (the least crowded alternative), from the east out of Lake Tahoe, or from the south at Echo Lakes, on the Pacific Crest Trail. The heaviest use occurs at the Eagle Falls, Fallen Leaf, Echo and Wrights trailheads.

And, as might be expected, Desolation has the most stringent regulations. Backcountry campers, for instance, must obtain permits by advance reservation or by personally visiting a Forest Service office. From June 15 to Labor Day, there is a quota of 700 overnight users per day, with specific numbers of permits varying from one entry point to the other, although a single permit may be issued for up to 15 people. Half of the quota permits can be reserved up to 90 days in advance, by phone or in person, and half are issued on the actual day of entry on a first-come, first-served basis. The permit must specify a particular day of entry and a particular trailhead. Because of high demand, soon there may also be a quota for day hikers who, until now, have not had restrictions. All day hikers, however, must register at the trailheads for their free wilderness permit (one per party is OK) and carry a copy with them. The permit boxes are stationed at most trailheads; those without self-registration (mainly on the west

*Desolation Wilderness and Pacific Crest Trail*

entry points) require a visit to the nearest Forest Service office. Another major restriction in Desolation, which puts off a number of backcountry campers, is the unconditional ban on open campfires. *Note: Only portable gas stoves are allowed.*

**For permit, reservations and other information:** Contact the Lake Tahoe Basin Management Unit, 870 Emerald Bay Road, South Lake Tahoe, CA 96160; (916) 573-2600.

# Granite Chief Wilderness

Located on the West Shore of Lake Tahoe, this 25,700-acre area borders the back of the Alpine Meadows and Squaw Valley ski areas, then extends southward toward Twin Peaks and Barker Pass. It includes several streams and the headwaters of the American River, and the terrain varies from granite cliffs to glaciated valleys. The southern section is forested with mixed conifer, red fir and lodgepole pine at higher elevations, with deciduous and evergreen woodlands farther down. This wilderness isn't as crowded as Desolation (with the exception of the Five Lakes basin, a high-traffic area) and doesn't require a wilderness permit. However, campfire permits are required.

*For permit information:* Contact Tahoe National Forest, Highway 49 and Coyote Street, Nevada City, CA 95959; (916) 265-4531.

# Mokelumne Wilderness

Located between Highway 88 and Highway 4 south of South Lake Tahoe, the largest wilderness in the area has 100,600 acres of remote backcountry, with sections of the famous Mormon-Emigrant Trail cutting through it. The elevation ranges from 4,000 feet near Salt Springs Reservoir to over 10,000 feet at Round Top. There are many small lakes in the valleys north of Mokelumne Peak, and vistas of the deep and rugged Mokelumne River Canyon. Wilderness permits are required May 25 through September 15 for overnight users only. Campfires are allowed in many areas with a permit. However, campfires are *not* allowed at the following lakes: Frog, Winnemucca, Round Top, Fourth of July and Emigrant, which are the most heavily used destinations in the wilderness. Dogs must be on leashes.

*For permit information:* Contact the Eldorado Information Center, Eldorado National Forest, 3070 Camino Heights Drive, Camino, CA 95709; (916) 644-6048.

# Mount Rose Wilderness

Located northeast of Lake Tahoe above Incline Village on both sides of the Mount Rose Highway, this recently established, 28,000-acre wilderness area offers outstanding views of Tahoe and the Great Basin areas above Reno in Nevada. This is mostly steep, arid land with mixed conifer and red fir forests, ranging from 6,000 feet to 10,000 feet, and there are very few lakes. Mountain meadows, however, offer a profusion of wildflowers. There is access from seven trailheads, and all except the trail to Mount Rose receive light use. No wilderness permits are required at present, but overnight users must obtain a campfire permit, and portable stoves are encouraged.

*For permit information:* Contact the Carson Ranger District, Toiyabe National Forest, 1536 South Carson Street, Carson City, NV 89701; (702) 882-2766.

# Pacific Crest National Scenic Trail

Many of the day hikes and extended backcountry trips in the Lake Tahoe basin involve the famous Pacific Crest Trail (PCT), which, in its entirety, stretches 2,638 miles from Mexico to Canada. The concept of a hiking and horseback trail spanning the West Coast has been around since the 1920s, but it wasn't until passage of the National Trails System Act in 1968 that the PCT began to take shape. Under the direction of the U.S. Forest Service, trail construction was completed in May, 1990. The PCT is for humans and horses only, and all mechanized vehicles, including mountain bikes, are prohibited. The route crosses 19 major canyons, reaches 900 lakes, and climbs 57 major mountain passes as it winds through 24 national forests, seven national parks and various other public lands.

The trail enters all five forest jurisdictions in the Tahoe region, from Plumas National Forest in the north to Eldorado National Forest in the south. The largest segment is in Tahoe National Forest, where it extends for 97 miles. The majority of day hikers who enter Desolation Wilderness encounter the trail from most of the major access points on the eastern side. The PCT is easily recognizable by the uniform, triangular trail markers and its wide, well-maintained routes.

Near Lake Tahoe, access points are at the following trailheads: Highway 49 east of the Sierra Buttes, Norden at Interstate 80, Barker Pass at the end of Blackwood Canyon Road on the South Shore, Echo Lake and Little Norway on US 50, and Carson Pass on Highway 88. Perhaps the most impressive segment of the trail in this region bisects Desolation Wilderness, where it is the main north/south artery.

A permit isn't required for travel on the PCT as such, but you must obtain one to pass through wilderness and other special areas, as well as for use of portable stoves or for building campfires in the backcountry. Permits are free and can be acquired from any Forest Service office in the region. One advantage for PCT users is that if you start on the trail in Desolation Wilderness, you aren't subject to the area's quota system. However, it's advisable for all users planning multi-day trips on the PCT to check with Forest Service offices along their route for any special restrictions. For example, campfires are not allowed in any portion of Desolation Wilderness, but they are allowed in Mokelumne Wilderness and in Tahoe National Forest.

*For permit information:* Contact any of the U.S. Forest Service offices in preceding wilderness area listings.

# Mormon-Emigrant Trail

Hikers in the Carson Pass and Mokelumne Wilderness areas along Highway 88 have the opportunity to retrace the path of a pioneer trail that was carved through the Sierra in 1848. The impetus for the route began when the United States Army asked Brigham Young and the Church of Latter-Day Saints (Mormons) to recruit 500 men to fight for California in the Mexican-American War. By the time the Mormon Battalion arrived in San Diego, however, the conflict was over. So they turned, instead, to the task of finding a new trans-Sierra route as an alternative to the difficult Truckee Route, which crossed the Truckee River more than two dozen times. Starting just east of Coloma, where gold was discovered at Sutter's sawmill in 1848, the Mormons followed a ridge south of Silver Lake, descended to Twin Lakes (now known as Caples Lake), climbed over Carson Pass, and followed the Carson River through Hope Valley on a course that is now south of Highway 88. When they reached Carson Valley, they joined the Truckee Route to Salt Lake City. In the ensuing years, thousands of settlers and gold-seekers pushed their way west on this trail.

Today the trail is accessible from Caples Lake, the Kirkwood Ski Resort and Silver Lake. The most spectacular portion, one of the truly undiscovered outings in the Tahoe region, can be traveled by foot or horseback from a trailhead just behind the stables at Plasse's Resort on the west end of Silver Lake. From here, hike on steep and dusty switchbacks through canopied forest until you ascend to an open ridge. There you connect with the Mormon-Emigrant Trail—now a wide road occasionally used by motorized dirt bikes—next to the site of an old general store and supply post. At this point, head northeast past Scout Carson Lake and massive Thimble Peak (elevation 9,870 feet). Along the spine of this ridge are splendid views of two drainages, Silver Lake on the left and Summit City Canyon on the right, with contrasting geology. Thimble Peak is surrounded with reddish volcanic formations, while the canyon has massive granite peaks and a plunging gorge more typical of the Sierra. The trail drops down into Sunrise Bowl at the Kirkwood Ski Resort, then follows a dirt road to Caples Lake on Highway 88, for a total distance of about 15 miles. If you don't mind the equestrian and biking traffic, which isn't too intrusive, this route makes for a great two- or three-day backpacking outing. You'll have to arrange your own shuttle, however. No permits are required.

**For trail information:** Contact the Eldorado Information Center, (916) 644-6048; Kirkwood Ski Resort, (209) 258-6000; Plasse's Resort, (209) 258-8814; or Caples Resort, (209) 258-8888.

# Tahoe Rim Trail

So many extraordinary trails exist in the Tahoe region that it would take years to explore them all. One trail that might be described as a work in progress or, rather, work almost completed, is the Tahoe Rim Trail. This is a long-running effort by a volunteer organization to build a 150-mile hiking and equestrian trail following the ridgetops of the basin. Since its inception in 1984, the Rim Trail Organization has been funded through donations and assisted by several public agencies. The trail passes through six counties in two states and incorporates a portion of the Pacific Crest Trail. Currently all but two segments of the trail are finished and open for public use; the last remaining sections are on the south and north sides of Mount Rose Highway, and between Tahoe City and the PCT. The Tahoe Rim Trail is marked with light-blue, triangular "TRT" markers, and can be accessed at six trailheads: US 50 at Spooner Summit, Highway 207 (Kingsbury Grade) at Daggett Pass, Highway 89 at Big Meadows (near Luther Pass), US 50 at Echo Summit, Tahoe City off Highway 89, and Highway 267 at Brockway Summit. The trail is moderate in difficulty with a 10-percent average grade and elevations that range from 6,300 feet to 9,400 feet. Camping is generally allowed anywhere along the trail, except along the section in Lake Tahoe-Nevada State Park on the East Shore, where it is restricted to designated campsites. Also, campfire and wilderness permits may be required in Desolation Wilderness and other Forest Service areas. They may be obtained at registration boxes at the trailheads, or from the Forest Service's Lake Tahoe Visitor Center near the Tallac Historic Site on Highway 89 north of South Lake Tahoe. The volunteer organization solicits members and has a unique, Adopt-A-Mile Program in which companies, organizations or individuals can underwrite, through a large donation, the construction of a mile of trail, for which the benefactor is given credit on a signpost.

**For trail information:** Tahoe Rim Trail Fund, 298 Kingsbury Grade, P.O. Box 4647, Stateline, NV 89449; TRT Fund Office, (702) 588-0686; or Tahoe Rim Trail Hotline, (702) 588-8799.

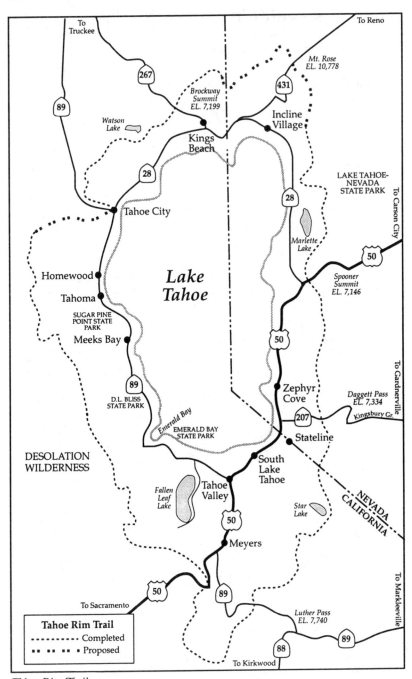

*Tahoe Rim Trail*

# BACKCOUNTRY HIKING TIPS

Travelers into the wildlands of the Tahoe Sierra should go prepared. Here are some things to keep in mind:

- Bring a compass, Forest Service map and a U.S. Geological Survey topographic map for the specific trail you're taking. *Trust no map entirely.* Contact the appropriate jurisdiction to find out the latest trail conditions, since slides, runoff, overgrowth and other natural factors can alter routes from year to year.

- Always wear sturdy hiking boots, not sneakers or sandals. Many of the trails have sharp granite scree, which can cut into thin-soled shoes.

- Your feet will appreciate you much better if you treat them well. Wear thick hiking socks and use talcum or other drying powders liberally, and bring fresh socks to change midway through an all-day hike. Carry bandages or moleskin to treat emerging blisters before they become a problem.

- Carry a day pack. My preference is for a large fanny pack, such as the type produced by Mark Pack of Oakland, with twin water bottles connected to the pack with cloth fasteners. This is more comfortable than a shoulder pack, which can dig in under your arms and impede blood circulation.

- No matter how gorgeous the weather may seem, it can change rapidly. Tahoe is known for its afternoon thundershowers any time of the summer, but particularly in June and July. This situation makes it absolutely imperative for you to bring along raingear. Failing to do so can subject you to the risk of hypothermia, a potentially life-threatening situation. Lightweight raingear, such as fold-up ponchos and two-piece suits, will do the job.

- Carry a flashlight and matches—just in case you underestimate the time it takes to finish your hike, and end up in the dark, trying to descend a rocky stairway.

- Bring extra layers of clothes. Temperatures can change radically from 6,000 feet to 9,000 feet, especially if you're climbing a peak. A sweater or sweatshirt and a windbreaker are minimal requirements.

- Don't be stingy with water. On full-day hikes, bring three water bottles (we prefer something with electrolytes such as Gatorade), or bring some water plus a water-purifying device such as a Katadyn filter. Although most hikes visit lakes or cross streams, some are on arid routes where you can't depend on finding an alternate water source.

- Be careful in fording streams. During early summer, they can be dangerously high. Even in midsummer, the morning flows may be fordable while the afternoon flows are high and treacherous. When crossing streams, you may wish to bring a pair of water slippers to protect your feet. Also, carry a hiking staff for stability.

- Do not bury or leave trash anywhere along the trail. Pack it out with you.
- In addition to a picnic lunch (one of the real treats of hiking), pack plenty of high-energy snacks such as gorp, hard candies and nuts. Take more than you think you'll need.
- Bring a wide-brimmed hat, sunglasses, sunscreen and lip balm. In summer, the sun can be ferocious, especially when reflected from hot, granite rock.
- Bring a small first-aid kit to treat cuts and scrapes. You won't need to worry about poison oak in Tahoe since it doesn't grow above 5,000 feet.
- Always fill out the wilderness permit, when required, and leave word with someone when and where you're going and when you expect to return.
- Keep your dog on a leash. You may think that it's great to led Fido run free, but he could be a nuisance to other hikers or to wildlife. Most public lands that allow dogs require them to be leashed.

*Eagle Lake, a scenic alpine lake, can be reached in a short but moderately steep hike from the Eagle Falls Trailhead.*

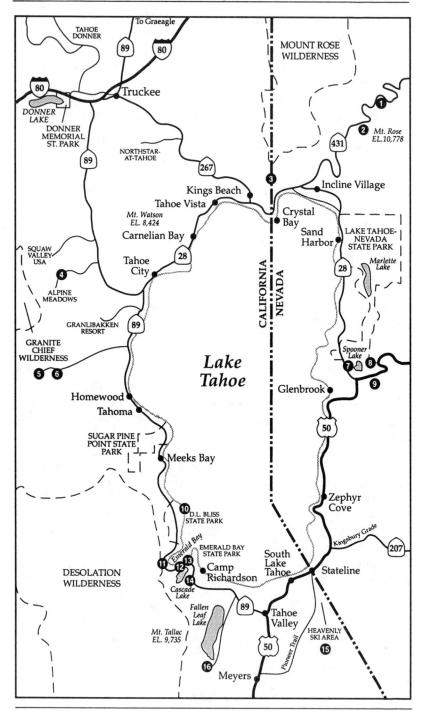

*Hiking Trails*

### Map References—Lake Tahoe Hiking Trails

◆

# North Shore

## Mount Rose Trail

*See number 1 on Lake Tahoe map, page 90*

**Difficulty:** Strenuous.
**Distance (one-way):** Six miles.
**Elevation (low/high):** 8,800 feet to 10,776 feet.
**Time (one-way):** 3.5 to 4.0 hours.
**Trailhead:** Take Mount Rose Highway (431) 7.5 miles north of Incline Village. Park at the trailhead located one mile south of the summit. Because of limited parking, the Mount Rose Campground (several hundred yards above the trailhead) provides additional space.
**Description:** In winter, alpine skiers can take chairlifts almost to the summit of Mount Rose (elevation 10,778 feet) for dramatic vistas of Reno, Washoe Valley and Lake Tahoe. In summer, it takes considerable effort to do this on foot, but it's well worth it—if you've got the stamina and lung power. From the trailhead, follow a dirt road for an easy three miles through mostly lodgepole pine forest mixed with areas of sagebrush and mule ears. In late spring and early summer, a vibrant meadow at the midpoint is awash with color from lupine, paintbrush and larkspur wildflowers. The last two miles, from the base of Mount Rose, follow steep switchbacks, sometimes on slippery rock, to the ridgeline. At the top, there's a log book where hardy souls can inscribe their names. Because of the not infrequent high winds that can rake this peak in afternoons, come with extra clothing to keep warm. By all means, bring a picnic lunch to enjoy the panorama from the highest walkable mountain in the Tahoe basin. If you're trying to decide whether to scale this peak or Mount Tallac on the west shore, consider this: The elevation gain is 1,255 feet less for Mount Rose.
**Information:** Carson Ranger District, Toiyabe National Forest, (702) 882-2766.

# Ophir Creek Trail

*See number 2 on Lake Tahoe map, page 90*

**Difficulty:** Moderate to strenuous.
**Distance (one-way):** Three miles to Upper Price Lake, six miles to Davis Creek Park.
**Elevation (high/low):** 8,600 feet to 5,300 feet.
**Time (one-way):** 1.5 to 2.0 hours for the shortest hike, 4.0 to 4.5 hours for the longest hike.
**Trailhead:** About 6.5 miles northeast of Incline Village on Mount Rose Highway (Highway 431), look for a dirt turnout on the right and a large sign marking the trailhead. (Note: You can also begin at the opposite end of the trail, at Davis Creek County Park in Washoe Valley. To reach the park, head 17 miles south of Reno on US 395 to the Franktown Road turnoff. Parking is right off US 395 on Franktown Road. Be aware that this is a tough uphill hike.)
**Description:** This trail connects the pristine Tahoe Meadows, on the southwest side of Mount Rose, to the eastern, high-desert slopes of the Sierra next to a 200-acre county park. Its chief attractions are the wild-flowers that blossom in the meadows in early- to midsummer, views of Mount Rose (elevation 10,778 feet) and a panorama of Washoe Valley and Washoe Lake. The topography changes abruptly from dense forest to rugged, open rock canyons. Along the trail are three small lakes—Upper and Lower Price and Rock—that are shallow, marshy and not really worth the effort it takes to reach them.

From the trailhead, follow the wide dirt road through moderate forest past Tahoe Meadows (you may encounter some mountain bikers). After about 1.5 miles, the trail narrows, climbs a ridge and then begins a long, steep descent through thinning forest and down an open, brushy canyon next to a huge rockfall. This side of the mountain is hot, dusty and deso-late, but the trail parallels the creek and meanders through an unmarked boulder field. Finally, it enters a canopy of forest once again, and provides distant vistas of Washoe Valley and busy US 395. A left fork drops sharply for one-quarter mile to Upper Price Lake, but this sidetrip is one you can ignore. There is no hospitable shoreline here and the bottom is muddy, with extensive algae and weed growth on the lake's surface. Both Upper and Lower Price lakes were severely damaged when part of Slide Moun-tain slid into them in 1983. If you continue on past the junction, you can catch glimpses of the lake from the main trail. Along this shaded ledge, you have the option of ending your hike and returning to Mount Rose Highway, or continuing down a steep, brushy decline to Davis Creek County Park. If you choose to do this, remember that you'll have 3,600 feet of elevation to scale on your way back.

*Information:* Carson Ranger District, Toiyabe National Forest, (702) 882-2766. Davis Creek County Park, (702) 849-0684.

## Stateline Lookout Trail

*See number 3 on Lake Tahoe map, page 90*

*Difficulty:* Easy (paved trail).
*Distance:* A half-mile loop.
*Elevation:* 7,017 feet.
*Time:* 30 to 45 minutes round-trip for the loop.
*Trailhead:* It is just off Highway 28 above the North Tahoe casinos, but there is no sign indicating a trail. Just east of the old Tahoe Biltmore Lodge and Casino, turn north on Reservoir Drive, then right on Lakeview Avenue (immediately after the fire station). Continue past residential areas until you come to an iron pipe gate; make a hard left on Forest Service Road 1601 and follow it to a fairly large parking lot. If the gate is locked, park below it and walk up the road.
*Description:* Without question, this is the most spectacular self-guided nature trail in the basin—and it is virtually unknown, even to the locals. Views of Lake Tahoe from the lookout station, built on stilts on a rocky promontory, are the North Shore equivalent of views from the Top of the Tram at Heavenly Valley in the South Shore. Unlike Heavenly, though, this place is free! The lookout, which is maintained by a citizen group, was originally constructed in 1936, but it burned down in 1979. The U.S. Forest Service rebuilt the structure, only to have vandals damage it. Now it is under the "adoption" of a volunteer group and is infrequently staffed, even in summer. From the tower, you can get sweeping panoramas of Crystal Bay and Kings Beach. The self-guided interpretive trail provides fascinating trivia about Tahoe's natural and human history. One plaque gives details of the posh Brockway Hotel and Hot Springs Resort (now gone), which was built in 1869. Another points out the site of a 4,000-foot hydraulic tramway above Crystal Bay that once carried cordwood and lumber to a water flume for transport to the Virginia & Truckee Railroad yard north of Carson City. Incline Village got its name from the tramway, and the route can still be seen from the lookout. Another section of the paved trail straddles the California/Nevada state line, with markers explaining how a survey feud in the 1870s ended with a boundary change in favor of California. With the trail located 1,000 feet above Tahoe, you can see virtually the entire lake and get the best vistas of the North Shore. This is a must for any visitor. Bring your camera!
*Information:* Lake Tahoe Basin Management Unit, (916) 573-2600.

# ★ Five Lakes Trail ★

★ *notes Author's Choice*
*See number 4 on Lake Tahoe map, page 90*

**Difficulty:** Moderately strenuous.
**Distance (one-way):** 2.5 miles.
**Elevation (low / high):** 6,040 feet to 6,920 feet.
**Time (one-way):** 1.5 to 2.0 hours.
**Trailhead:** From Truckee, travel eight miles south on Highway 89 to the Alpine Meadows Road. Turn west and drive 1.5 miles to the trailhead on the right. Parking is along the side of the road only.
**Description:** This popular, well-beaten trail gets heavy use, so much so that the Forest Service has issued severe restrictions on camping within 600 feet of the small lakes, none of which are individually numbered or named. The trail originates in a residential area and immediately starts a steep ascent along a series of forested switchbacks. Once above the trees, the trail follows the contour of a spectacular rocky canyon, and there are breathtaking views of the Alpine Meadows Ski Area and of sheer, striated granite walls. Just after the trail enters Granite Chief Wilderness, it changes to dirt and duff through a canopy of pines. At a junction, there's a quarter-mile spur to the lakes, of which only one is immediately evident. Scouting cross-country (a topographic map is helpful), you can soon reach the other lakes, which are small but attractive. Camping is prohibited near the shorelines; still, these lakes get pounded by waves of anglers, picnickers and resident dog-walkers. So impacted is the area that in 1992 the U.S. Forest Service removed 65 campsites and fire rings for revegetation. Those who want a longer hike (and are able to arrange a shuttle) can continue for another 2.5 miles to Squaw Valley USA.
**Information:** Truckee Ranger District, Tahoe National Forest, (916) 587-3558.

# ★ Barker Pass to Twin Peaks on the Pacific Crest Trail ★

*See number 5 on Lake Tahoe map, page 90*

**Difficulty:** Easy to moderate.
**Distance (one-way):** Five miles.
**Elevation (low / high):** 7,640 feet to 8,880 feet.
**Time (one-way):** 1.5 to 2.0 hours.
**Trailhead:** Drive 4.2 miles south on Highway 89 from Tahoe City to Blackwood Canyon Road. Turn right at the Kaspian Picnic Area and go 7.1 miles on paved, winding road to one-third of a mile beyond where the pavement ends and becomes dirt and gravel. The Barker Pass Trailhead is quite obvious on the right, and is usually packed with cars. There are no restrooms at this trailhead, but there are some at the Ellis Peak Trailhead

one-third of a mile back up the road.

**Description:** Although this route doesn't reach any lakes, the high elevation, easy access and lofty views of both Lake Tahoe and its major Sierra peaks make it a first-rate hike, most of which is well within the ability of families with children. The beauty of this West Shore outing is that the lion's share of the elevation gain, from Lake Tahoe to Barker Pass, is accomplished by driving. This part of the famous Pacific Crest Trail heads north from the pass, traveling along the backbone of a ridge that has wonderful vistas on both sides—one of the Tahoe basin, the other of Granite Chief Wilderness. You don't need to go the full five miles to Twin Peaks to appreciate the views; in fact, going half the distance will do. The first vista is at a ridge one mile north of Barker Peak, which has a sweeping view of Tahoe. The next one is about one mile farther, up some switchbacks to an area of crested knolls at 8,434 feet. The PCT itself does not climb to the top of Twin Peaks. The easiest access to the summit is about 0.2 miles up the trail, where it begins a gentle descent. These peaks are remnants of an ancient volcano, dated at 5 to 10 million years old. From the top, enjoy lofty views of Tahoe's dominant mountains, including Tinkers Knob, Mount Rose, Freel Peak, Mount Tallac, Dicks Peak and Pyramid Peak. This can be a hot, dusty hike, so take plenty of water.

**Information:** Truckee Ranger District, Tahoe National Forest, (916) 587-3558.

## Ellis Peak Trail

*See number 6 on Lake Tahoe map, page 90*

**Difficulty:** Moderate.

**Distance (one-way):** 2.5 miles.

**Elevation (low / high):** 7,800 feet to 8,740 feet.

**Time (one-way):** 1.75 to 2.0 hours.

**Trailhead:** At Barker Pass. Drive 4.2 miles south of Tahoe City on Highway 89 to the Kaspian Picnic Area. Turn west on Blackwood Canyon Road and go 7.1 miles until the pavement ends at the summit. The Ellis Peak Trailhead is located on the south side of the road, where it becomes dirt and gravel road. There is limited parking here and the trail gets heavy use.

**Description:** This hike combines the chance to ascend a walkable mountain, Ellis Peak, with the opportunity to enjoy a picnic at tranquil Ellis Lake. The trailhead, which begins 1,800 feet above Lake Tahoe, is easy to reach. At the outset, the trail ascends along several switchbacks in deep forest until it reaches the ridge at 8,270 feet. Follow the ridge for 1.5 miles as the trail passes through sections of open forest and meadows rich with wildflowers in spring, along with vistas of Lake Tahoe. When the trail intersects a dirt road, take the right fork for 100 yards until you reach another road branching off to the east. Follow that spur for 0.3 miles to Knee Ridge (elevation 8,520 feet); from there, it is a short distance to Ellis Peak. This lofty perch affords striking views of Tahoe to the east and Granite Chief Wilderness and Hellhole Reservoir to the west. After your climb, retrace your steps to the first intersection. To reach Ellis Lake, continue on the left fork of the road for 0.2 miles. This small lake offers a relaxing spot for lunch.

***Information:*** Truckee Ranger District, Tahoe National Forest, (916) 587-3558.

## ★ Meeks Bay Trail ★
*See Meeks Bay Trail map, below*

***Difficulty:*** Moderate.

***Distance (one-way):*** 4.5 miles to Lake Genevieve, 5.0 miles to Crag Lake, 5.7 miles to Hidden Lake, 5.9 miles to Shadow Lake, 6.3 miles to Stony Ridge and 8.0 miles to Rubicon Lake.

***Elevation (low/high):*** 6,240 feet to 8,880 feet.

***Time (one-way):*** Three to six hours, depending on the destination.

***Trailhead:*** From Tahoe City or South Lake Tahoe, take Highway 89 about 12 miles to Meeks Bay Resort. Parking is across the highway from the resort at a small dirt parking lot, and it fills rapidly on summer weekends. A wilderness permit is required and may be obtained from the U.S. Forest Service.

***Description:*** Most day hikers will choose the first lake in this lovely string of six alpine pearls, simply because of the effort and time required to reach the others. The entire route, connecting with a trail to the three Velma lakes, is a popular three- to four-day backpacking jaunt. From the trailhead, the first 1.3 miles is over a level dirt road. Then the marked trail ascends gradually (no switchbacks) through moderate

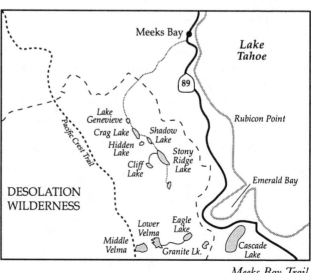

Meeks Bay Trail

forest over dirt and duff, with few vistas. It parallels Meeks Creek, passes a small spring and skirts several meadows, which are lush with wildflowers in early to midsummer. The trail becomes sandy as it climbs the eastern slopes of a canyon, and the vegetation thins a bit before you arrive at Lake Genevieve. This greenish, shallow lake, towered over by Peak 9054, is bordered by pines and has gentle, sloping contours that accommodate wading and swimming. Though quite attractive, Genevieve has its share of insects, so bring your bug repellent. The trail, which is part of the unofficial Tahoe-Yosemite Trail, continues to the left, reaching the other lakes via a series of switchbacks leading another 1,000 feet to Phipps Pass.
*Information:* Lake Tahoe Basin Management Unit, (916) 573-2600.

## Marlette Lake Trail
*See number 7 on Lake Tahoe map, page 90*

*Difficulty:* Moderate.
*Distance (one-way):* Six miles.
*Elevation (low / high):* 7,000 feet to 8,157 feet.
*Time (one-way):* Three to four hours.
*Trailhead:* Begin at Spooner Lake in the Lake Tahoe-Nevada State Park, 15 miles north of South Lake Tahoe or 12 miles south of Incline Village at the junction of Highway 28 and US 50, on the Nevada side of the lake. There is a paved parking lot, and a day-use fee is charged. (Note: This is the most popular trail in the Tahoe basin for mountain bikers, because it is the main access for the famous Flume Trail. Parking can be impossible on busy weekends.)
*Description:* Although this is a scenic outing for hikers, the trail is virtually a freeway of mountain bikes, some of which come screaming downhill from Marlette Lake. Fortunately, the trail is wide, since it is essentially a jeep path most of the way. For the first three miles, there is a gradual ascent (no switchbacks) from Spooner through North Canyon, which is a picturesque drainage with creeks, aspen groves, pines and meadows, with wildflowers in abundance during late spring and early summer. Jagged granite peaks on the east side are impressive. There is a short, steep climb to the top of Snow Pass before the trail descends to Marlette Lake. A century ago, this wooded lake, a reservoir, was used as a water source for the silver mining industry in Virginia City, located east of the ridge. Water was sent to Incline Village through a long flume, and logs were floated through a tunnel to Washoe Valley and the mines. Hiking to the north end, next to the dam, brings you to the beginning of the Flume Trail to Incline (see page 206 in chapter 8, "Bike Trails and Parks"). A short walk on this path affords a stunning view of Lake Tahoe from over 1,500 feet above its surface. Watch out for bike riders! No fishing or swimming is allowed at Marlette, and dogs are permitted only on a leash. There are

great picnic spots and sunning rocks at the south end.
***Information:*** Lake Tahoe-Nevada State Park, Nevada Parks Division,
(702) 831-0494.

## ★ Tahoe Rim Trail North ★
## (Spooner Summit)

*See number 8 on Lake Tahoe map, page 90, and Tahoe Rim Trail map, page 87*
***Difficulty:*** Moderate.
***Distance (one-way):*** Five miles to Marlette Lake, 13 miles to Tunnel
Creek.
***Elevation (low/high):*** 7,000 feet to 8,600 feet.
***Time (one-way):*** Three-plus hours.
***Trailhead:*** It's easy to miss, since it is right next to the westbound lanes
of US 50, one-half mile east of its junction with Highway 28. There is a
small dirt parking pull-off (a limited number of cars can be accommodated) and a sign designating the trailhead.
***Description:*** This is arguably the most scenic original section of the
soon-to-be-completed 150-mile hiking and equestrian trail that follows
the ridgetops of the Tahoe basin. The trail, funded by a volunteer organization, connects preexisting trails (including parts of the Pacific Crest
Trail through Desolation Wilderness) with new segments constructed
since 1984. The Spooner Lake North trail offers options of half-day, full-
day and overnight hikes, with two walk-in campgrounds around midpoint. Some of the best scenery—with bird's-eye views of Spooner Lake
and Lake Tahoe to the west and Carson City and Washoe Valley to the
east—can be enjoyed within the first 3.5 miles. There are several inspiring rocky overlooks that make for great picnic stops. Right from the trailhead, the going is mostly uphill, and ranges from exposed ridges to dense
forest. For a shorter hike, you can stop at the high points and return, or
you can continue down steep switchbacks on a fork to Marlette Lake, a
scenic swimming and sunning location, for a full day. Mountain bikes are
currently prohibited from these segments of the trail.
***Information:*** Lake Tahoe-Nevada State Park, Nevada Parks Division,
(702) 831-0494.

## Tahoe Rim Trail South
## (Spooner Summit)

*See number 9 on Lake Tahoe map, page 90, and Tahoe Rim Trail map, page 87*
***Difficulty:*** Moderate
***Distance (one-way):*** Two miles to Duane Bliss Peak, three miles to
South Camp Peak, four miles to Genoa Peak and 12 miles to Highway
207 (Kingsbury Grade).
***Elevation (low/high):*** 7,000 feet to 9,150 feet.

***Time (one-way):*** One hour for shortest route, two hours to Genoa Peak.
***Trailhead:*** On the south shoulder of US 50, one-half mile east of the junction with Highway 28, on the Nevada side. Look for the rest stop near the Nevada Department of Transportation building on Spooner Summit. There is more parking available here (as well as restrooms) than across the highway at the North Trailhead.
***Description:*** This trail winds through aspen and pine forest to a ridge-line that overlooks both Lake Tahoe and the Carson Valley. Short spur trails can take you to a rocky ledge that has a fabulous high-elevation view of Stateline and South Tahoe. By traveling cross-country, you can climb Duane Bliss Peak (elevation 8,658 feet), South Camp Peak (elevation 8,866 feet) or Genoa Peak (elevation 9,150 feet). Off-highway-vehicle roads that parallel parts of the trail are popular with mountain bikers, and can also be used for loops and access to Kingsbury Grade. If you choose to hike the entire 12 miles one-way, you'll need to do a shuttle, leaving a car at the small parking area at Kingsbury Grade. This is located at the end of Andria Drive (an extension of North Benjamin Drive), about two miles north of Highway 207.
***Information:*** Tahoe Rim Trail Fund, 298 Kingsbury Grade, P.O. Box 4647, Stateline, NV 89449; TRT Fund Office, (702) 588-0686.

# South Shore

## ★ Rubicon Trail ★

*See number 10 on Lake Tahoe map, page 90*

***Difficulty:*** Moderate.
***Distance (one-way):*** 3.1 miles to Emerald Point, 4.4 miles to Vikingsholm.
***Elevation (low / high):*** 6,230 feet to 6,580 feet.
***Time (one-way):*** 1.75 to 2.25 hours.
***Trailhead:*** At D.L. Bliss State Park on the West Shore. Take Highway 89 north 10 miles from South Lake Tahoe to the park, and drive a winding 2.5 miles on the entrance road to the shoreline beyond the campground. The trail begins at the southernmost end of the parking lot near Calawee Cove Beach. There is a fee for day-use parking. Pets are not allowed.
***Description:*** This is one of the best half-day hikes in Lake Tahoe. There is little elevation gain, the trail is well marked, and the scenery is spectacular. The path begins on a high bluff overlooking splendid rocky coves of Tahoe and follows this embankment along the rim of the lake. At Emerald Point, you can see the profusion of water traffic entering and leaving Emerald Bay—including paddlewheel excursion boats, vintage Chris Craft "woodies," jetskis, runabouts and even kayaks. From here, follow the

trail as it skirts the boat-in campground and levels off along the north shore of the bay toward Vikingsholm. This tree-shaded mansion, a replica of a Scandinavian castle, offers tours in summer, and there is a wonderful white-sand beach in front of it—a great spot for a picnic. You can return the way you came or leave a second vehicle in the parking lot above Vikingsholm, which is a steep, one-mile hike from the beach.

*Information:* D.L. Bliss State Park, California Department of Parks and Recreation, (916) 525-7277.

## ★ Eagle Falls Trail ★

*See number 11 on Lake Tahoe map, page 90*

*Difficulty:* Strenuous.

*Distance (one-way):* Five miles to Fontanillis Lake.

*Elevation (low / high):* 6,580 feet to 8,500 feet.

*Time (one-way):* 3.5 to 4.0 hours.

*Trailhead:* Take Highway 89 about eight miles north of South Lake Tahoe to the Eagle Falls Picnic Area on the left, opposite Emerald Bay. Parking in the paved area is limited to 30 vehicles and is usually full; more parking is available along the road but it, too, can be crowded. Best advice is to come early in the morning.

*Description:* One of Tahoe's signature—and most popular—hikes takes you into Desolation Wilderness and visits some of the region's most attractive alpine lakes. Prepare a picnic lunch and allow for a full-day hike, giving you enough time to enjoy each lake.

The first mile of the trail, along an uphill series of rocky stairways, seems almost like a freeway, since it's jammed with people making the short trek to Eagle Lake. There's a bridge across Eagle Creek, and when the runoff is highest it affords a good view looking down on several cataracts of Eagle Falls. Eagle Lake is a circular blue jewel, but it's constantly crowded. Keep going, up the steep trail to the left at the sign for Velma Lakes, and you'll lose the hordes. The trail is a continuous climb along an exposed granite cliff, but you can stop at many points to admire the bird's-eye view of Eagle Lake. Fortunately, the trail soon enters dense woodlands for a cool respite from the sun. After 2.5 miles of switchbacks, it reaches the crest of the hill and a fork to the left for the Bayview Trail, which leads to Granite Lake and Emerald Bay. (If you have two cars, you might consider parking one here and returning on this trail.) Keep to the right for another three-quarters of a mile and take the second fork to the left. Hike on for a half mile, enjoying lofty vistas of Middle Velma Lake to the north, until you reach another ridgeline and a junction with the Pacific Crest Trail. The sign here is somewhat confusing, but the correct route is to Dicks Lake to the right (the left fork goes to Dicks Pass). A short spur takes you to a good camping spot in trees above this nearly circular lake, and a great view of its bouldered shoreline. You can stop here to admire this pristine body of water, or continue on less than one-quarter of a mile to Fontanillis Lake, which is more spectacular.

Fontanillis is a large, elongated lake with several arms and protected granite coves. If you follow the forested trail along its east banks, you'll find a natural swimming hole and good picnic spot at the far end, in a completely sheltered arm with rock islands. This is a wonderful spot to bring an inflatable raft or float tube, and it would not be difficult to spend hours here lounging in the water or sunning on a rock. From the top of the outlet at Fontanillis, you can see Upper Velma Lake below. If you wish, follow the drainage for a shortcut side trail to this lake, over smooth rocky ledges; Upper Velma is constantly in view. (If you choose to take this route, when you reach the trail on the east shore, turn left to rejoin the path to Middle Velma Lake.) Or continue on the same trail from Fontanillis until it reaches another intersection at Middle Velma Lake. Both of these lakes have their charms. Upper Velma is a grassy, shallow lake with moderate tree cover and a flat granite plateau that forms the eastern shoreline; Middle Velma is deeper, with a pronounced, bouldered shoreline. Both lakes have excellent undesignated campsites, but Middle Velma usually has more people. To complete your long day's loop, follow the signs to the Eagle Falls or Bayview Trailhead.

***Information:*** Lake Tahoe Basin Management Unit, (916) 573-2600.

## Cascade Creek Falls Trail
*See number 12 on Lake Tahoe map, page 90*

***Difficulty:*** Easy.
***Distance (one-way):*** One mile.
***Elevation (low/high):*** 6,800 to 6,910 feet.
***Time (one-way):*** 20 to 30 minutes.
***Trailhead:*** From South Lake Tahoe, drive north on Highway 89 to the Bayview Campground, opposite Emerald Bay's Inspiration Point. There's a parking lot next to the trailhead, and wilderness permits are required.
***Description:*** This is a short but scenic hike to the top of a 200-foot waterfall, which tumbles into Cascade Lake. Take the left fork from the Bayview Trailhead, and follow a wide and well-marked path to the north ridge of Cascade Lake. The trail ascends gradually until it reaches a rocky stairway to the ledge with the falls. The best views of the falls are from this somewhat distant point. Closer to the falls themselves, the path disappears into the rocks, but it's possible to scamper through them and get near the edge of the water. Be careful! Depending on the amount of runoff, wet rocks can be slippery and the footing tricky. Get a good bearing on the route back to the trail, because it is hard to identify. From the ledge above the falls, there's a good view looking east across Cascade

Lake and, beyond, to Lake Tahoe.

*Information:* Lake Tahoe Basin Management Unit, (916) 573-2600.

## Granite Lake Trail
*See number 13 on Lake Tahoe map, page 90*

*Difficulty:* Strenuous.

*Distance (one-way):* One mile.

*Elevation (low/high):* 6,910 to 7,700 feet.

*Time (one-way):* One hour.

*Trailhead:* At Bayview, across from Inspiration Point over Emerald Bay. From South Lake Tahoe, go 7.5 miles north on Highway 89 to the Bayview Campground, which is on your left across from the Vista parking area. Drive through the campground until you see the trailhead; there is very limited parking in a paved lot here, so you may have to park at Inspiration Point across the highway. A wilderness permit is required.

*Description:* This is a short, steep and dusty hike, but Granite Lake is well worth the effort thanks to its swimming, fishing and picnicking attractions. At the trailhead, there are two forks; the other one, to the left, leads to Cascade Falls. Follow the signs on the right fork for Granite and Dicks lakes. The trail switchbacks through dense forest up the side of Maggie's Peak into Desolation Wilderness in a seemingly unrelenting ascent. About midway up, the forest cover begins to thin and there are striking views of Emerald Bay, Cascade Lake and Fallen Leaf Lake. At the top, you descend a bit off the trail to the shores of Granite Lake, a lovely spot that is ringed by granite rock and moderate fir forest. Outcroppings make for excellent swimming or casting spots, and the lake has a population of Eastern brook trout. You can turn around here for a short hike, or continue on the Bayview Trail until it intersects with the Eagle Falls Trail (see page 100) after 2.7 miles. From this junction, you can easily reach Middle and Upper Velma lakes, Dicks Lake and Fontanillis Lake. This route is a slightly longer (one-mile) alternative to the Eagle Falls Trail, but it has 330 feet less elevation gain.

*Information:* Lake Tahoe Basin Management Unit, (916) 573-2600.

## Mount Tallac Trail
*See number 14 on Lake Tahoe map, page 90*

*Difficulty:* Moderately to very strenuous.

*Distance (one-way):* 2.5 miles to Cathedral Lake, five miles to the summit of Mount Tallac.

*Elevation (low/high):* 6,480 feet to 9,735 feet.

*Time (one-way):* 1.5 to 4.0 hours, depending on the destination.

*Trailhead:* From South Lake Tahoe, drive north on Highway 89 for 3.5 miles. Watch for the Mount Tallac Trailhead sign directly across from the entrance to Baldwin Beach; turn left down the dirt road and continue to the trailhead parking. A wilderness permit is required and may be obtained from the U.S. Forest Service.

*Description:* This trail reaches two small alpine lakes—Floating Island and Cathedral—but neither is particularly attractive, and both can be swarming with mosquitoes, even in midsummer. The main reason to do this hike is to get a great view of Fallen Leaf Lake, from the backbone of a ridge on its north flank, and of Lake Tahoe, from a rocky knob that is left of the trail just before reaching Cathedral Lake. A number of hikers start up this trail with the intention of going all the way to the summit of Mount Tallac, but often find the grade a lot more than they expected. In the 1890s, Floating Island Lake had a natural, grass-covered island of twisted roots and shrubs. It was about 20 feet in diameter, sported a 12-foot-high conifer, and could support the weight of several visitors. It wasn't anchored, so enterprising anglers could paddle it around the lake. The island disappeared sometime after the turn of the century. Cathedral Lake has moderate timber on one side and a huge rockfall on the other. Considering the ravenous insects that inhabit these lakes and their lack of aesthetic beauty, neither swimming nor picnicking would be high on your list of activities here. You can turn back at Cathedral for your moderate hike, or, if you've got the stamina—and plenty of water—continue up the steep switchback of Tallac. This is where the going gets tough, big time. Those who reach the top are rewarded with an inspiring, 360-degree view of Fallen Leaf and Tahoe lakes, as well as several peaks and lakes in Desolation Wilderness. Bring a jacket, as it can be cool and windy on the summit. Congratulate yourself in accomplishing an elevation gain of almost 3,300 feet, and surviving Tahoe's toughest one-day hike. Note: There's another, somewhat easier route to Tallac via the Glen Alpine Trail (see page 104), if you take the fork to Gilmore Lake and continue on past the lake. Still, the last part is steep and rocky.

*Information:* Lake Tahoe Basin Management Unit, (916) 573-2600.

## Tahoe Vista Trail, Heavenly Ski Area
*See number 15 on Lake Tahoe map, page 90*

*Difficulty:* Moderate.

*Distance (one-way):* 1.1 mile.

*Elevation (low/high):* 8,250 feet to 9,000 feet.

*Time (one-way):* 1.5 hours (including tram rides).

*Trailhead:* At the top of the tram at Heavenly Ski Area. From US 50 at South Lake Tahoe, turn south on Ski Run Boulevard and follow the signs to the California-side parking lot. You'll need to purchase a ticket to ride the 50-passenger aerial tramway to mid-mountain. The tram fee is $10.50 per person, $6 for children 12 and under, and $8 for adults after 6 p.m.

The tram operates from 10 a.m. to 9 p.m. Monday through Saturday and 9 a.m. to 9 p.m. on Sunday. The trail begins just in front of the tram terminal and day lodge there.

**Description:** You can get a million-dollar view of Lake Tahoe and the Stateline casinos on this brief trek, without a lot of physical effort. Just below the lodge, the Tahoe Vista Trail, established in the late 1940s, hugs a ridgeline and provides terrific photo opportunities—especially around sunset. Though short, the trail is more challenging than it initially appears. There are some steep switchbacks and narrow segments that make it advisable to wear good, sturdy hiking boots (not sandals or sneakers). Half of the trail is in dense forest, with peekaboo views of the lake through majestic pines. Midway up, there's a bouldered vantage point good for more vistas. The ski area offers a self-guided trail map with information on markers, and, twice a day, provides guided hikes along the trail, usually at 11 a.m. and 1 p.m. One attraction of hiking here is being able to enjoy refreshments or a meal (lunch, dinner or Sunday brunch) afterwards.

**Information:** Heavenly Ski Area, (702) 586-7000.

## ★ Glen Alpine Trail ★

*See number 16 on Lake Tahoe map, page 90, and Glen Alpine Trail map, page 105*
**Difficulty:** Moderate to strenuous.
**Distance (one-way):** 5.8 miles.
**Elevation (low/high):** 6,560 feet to 8,120 feet.
**Time (one-way):** 3.5 to 4.0 hours.
**Trailhead:** Easily accessible from South Lake Tahoe. Travel north on Highway 89 (Emerald Bay Road) to Camp Richardson, then turn left on Fallen Leaf Road. Follow this to the western end, drive past the marina and take a narrow and bumpy asphalt road to the large, paved parking lot. A wilderness permit is required and is available at the trailhead. Restrooms are there, too.

**Description:** One of Tahoe's top hikes penetrates the heart of Desolation Valley, reaching three of the most spectacular lakes in the region. Although there are several hiking options from this trailhead, the best route takes you to Suzie and Heather lakes and, just beyond, to awesome Lake Aloha, which is a man-made labyrinth of rock pools that stretches for more than two miles in a vast rock valley. Except for the fact that the route is consistently uphill until you reach Suzie Lake, the trail is well marked and not technically difficult. It begins near a group of heavily forested summer cabins, passes Grass Lake, and begins a long series of switchbacks and rock stairways over a major ridge before dropping down to Suzie Lake. This elongated body of water with both exposed and forested shoreline, peninsulas and protected inlets, is enchanting. There are a few undesignated camping spots around the perimeter, especially on its

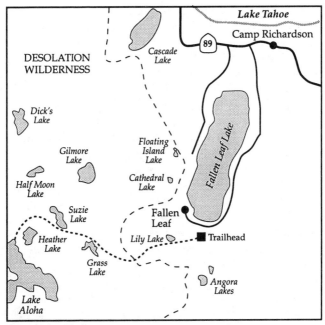

*Glen Alpine Trail*

west and north sides. Incredible as this lake is, the short, three-quarter-mile hike to Heather Lake is even more so. The trail enters the basin in a narrow cut, next to an outlet, and rises high above the north shore. The entire lake, except for one brushy area on the same side as the trail, is encased in steep granite walls, with a large rocky island. If you have Polaroid sunglasses, you can look down to the water and see large trout swimming near the surface. Be careful along this section of the trail (especially if you have children), since it drops off abruptly. The trail continues for another mile up a series of switchbacks, with stunning views of Heather, until it intersects with the Pacific Crest Trail. At this point, you can climb to one of several rocky overlooks for a view of magnificent Lake Aloha to the west and the lakes you've just passed to the east. Aloha, artificially dammed, is in the center of Desolation Wilderness. It consists of a myriad of mostly shallow granite pools, framed by Mount Price (elevation 9,975 feet), Pyramid Peak (elevation 9,983 feet) and Jack's Peak (elevation 9,856 feet). Although this is not the most spectacular vista of Lake Aloha (a better one is on the east side, off the Pacific Crest Trail from Echo Lakes), the Glen Alpine Trail is the easiest route to get there.

**Information:** Lake Tahoe Basin Management Unit, U.S. Forest Service, (916) 573-2600.

# ★ Echo Lakes Trail ★

*Difficulty:* Easy to moderately strenuous.

*Distance (one-way):* From Upper Echo Lake (via water taxi), 1.5 miles to Tamarack and 3.4 miles to Lake Aloha. From Lower Echo Lake to Upper Echo Lake, 2.5 miles.

*Elevation (low/high):* 7,420 feet to 8,430 feet.

*Time (one-way):* 1.5 hours for the short hike; 3.5 hours for the long hike.

*Trailhead:* Take US 50 from South Lake Tahoe to Echo Summit and turn onto Johnson Pass Road. Stay left through the residential area and the road will lead you to two parking lots next to Lower Echo Lake. Most likely you'll have to park in the upper lot, the larger of the two. The lower lot is adjacent to Echo Chalet, a complex that includes a store, a marina and rental cabins, and has limited parking.

*Description:* Catch a water "taxi" to the best vistas of Desolation Wilderness in what is perhaps South Tahoe's most diverse and interesting day hike. At the Echo Chalet and marina, you can pick up the lake taxi (which operates continuously between 10 a.m. and 6 p.m. in summer and costs $11 round-trip) for a delightful 15-minute cruise across Lower Echo Lake, through a snaking, narrow channel to smaller Upper Echo Lake, and to a dock that connects with a trail offering two options.

The first route is a short, relatively easy hike back to the marina on a well-maintained trail above the summer cabins that surround both lakes. It has marvelous views and makes a terrific outing for families with children, especially if you bring a picnic lunch. The second option is to follow the Pacific Crest Trail 3.4 miles to Lake Aloha, which is a considerable climb over a hot, talus-covered trail that, for nearly one-third of the route, hugs the side of a granite canyon. However, if you elect to take this trail, your efforts will be rewarded. The trail and its four spurs have access to nearly a dozen lakes, some of them reachable after a short jaunt from the main route. The first fork, at 1.5 miles, goes to Tamarack Lake, a five-minute detour. This is a lovely but windy lake with moderate forest around the shoreline and good campsites for backpackers. If you continue on the trail to Lake Aloha, pause along the way to appreciate the remarkable views of Echo and Tamarack lakes behind you. Reaching the ridgetop after a strenuous climb, the trail levels off through shaded forest, and another fork offers a sidetrip to Lake of the Woods, which is worthwhile if you have time. (You probably won't, if you want to make it to Aloha and back to Upper Echo Lake in time to catch the water taxi.)

Other spurs lead to Lucille and Margery, small lakes that you can see from the PCT. Beyond these, a somewhat confusing junction provides two routes to Lake Aloha; both, it turns out, reach the same spot at the south end of this massive lake. If you take the left fork, the water comes into view much sooner. At Aloha, you can continue on the PCT along the eastern shoreline, or take another fork to the left that follows the western shoreline. This trail goes along the top of the stone wall that forms a meandering dam, and is hard to discern in some places. If you follow it up the side of the western slopes, you can reach a rocky overlook that makes this entire effort worthwhile. Sprawling beneath you is a gigantic maze of hundreds of granite islands and ponds that make up Aloha, framed by several imposing peaks. The lake was created when it was dammed to supply water to Sacramento. Despite its artificial nature, this is a truly impressive and amazing panorama—perhaps the most spectacular in the whole of Desolation Wilderness. Bring your camera and plenty of film. If it's a warm day, pick the lake of your choice and enjoy a cool, refreshing dip, then retrace the trail back to Upper Echo Lake. At the dock, there's a telephone to call for the water taxi (carry 20 cents for this!), and be sure to get back by 6 p.m., or you'll have an additional (but relatively easy) 2.5-mile walk back to the parking lot.

*Information:* Lake Tahoe Basin Management Unit, (916) 573-2600.

## ★ Horsetail Falls Trail ★

*Difficulty:* Easy to moderate.
*Distance:* 1.5 to 2.0 miles round-trip.
*Elevation (low/high):* 6,110 feet to 6,310 feet.
*Time:* 1.5 to 2.0 hours round-trip.
*Trailhead:* At the big curve of US 50 at Twin Bridges, about 16 miles east of South Lake Tahoe. The area often is packed with cars, and you may have to park some distance up the road. A wilderness permit is required and may be obtained from the U.S. Forest Service.
*Description:* This is a great half-day hike following Pyramid Creek to Lower Horsetail Falls, so named because of its narrow column at the summit and wide plume at the bottom. The trailhead has become a popular picnic spot, with its shallow swimming holes and shaded forest. The canyon bearing the falls was carved out by glaciers, the last of which rolled through here more than 10,000 years ago. Several lakes, including Avalanche, Pitt and Ropi, feed the falls, which are at their strongest in midsummer. The trail parallels the creek much of the way, and follows granite walkways usually marked by "ducks" (rock piles). At the sign designating the boundary of Desolation Wilderness, you can enjoy good distant views of the lower and upper falls, or continue on a rougher and somewhat indistinct trail that peters out entirely once it reaches the rocky bluffs. There are some cold, refreshing ponds along the way, where you can have a picnic or take a dip. Some hikers go all the way to the top, but this is not recommended because of the poor footing, steep dropoffs and unmarked routing. You can get close to the coursing power of the lower falls, if you

want to, by inching out along the rocks. If you are bringing children, don't take them beyond the wilderness sign. As you return to the trailhead, enjoy the spectacular views of Lover's Leap, south of the highway, and other peaks of Eldorado National Forest.

*Information:* Eldorado Information Center, Eldorado National Forest, (916) 644-6048.

## Lovers Leap Trail

*Difficulty:* Moderate.
*Distance (one-way):* 2.5 miles.
*Elevation (low/high):* 5,900 feet to 6,900 feet.
*Time (one-way):* 1.5 to 2.0 hours.
*Trailhead:* Off US 50, one-quarter mile west of Strawberry (about 35 minutes west of South Lake Tahoe). Turn south at 42 Mile Picnic Site, take a right across the bridge following Packsaddle Pass Road, and go one mile to the junction with Strawberry Canyon Road. Take Strawberry for one-half mile to the trailhead.
*Description:* This trail leads through heavy forest to a dramatic high overlook of Pyramid Peak, Turtle Rock and the drainage of the South Fork of the American River. The gradual climb leads to a large, relatively flat, wide-open rock and grass summit that is about the size of a football field. You can enjoy different vistas from varying parts of the perimeter, including some of the upper slopes of the Sierra-at-Tahoe ski area to the east, Desolation Wilderness to the north, US 50 below and several attractive surrounding valleys. The sheer walls that drop toward the river are nationally popular with rock climbers. The route to the top is shared with horseback riders, joggers and mountain bikers.
*Information:* Eldorado Information Center, Eldorado National Forest, (916) 644-6048.

## Big Meadows Trail

*Difficulty:* Moderate.
*Distance (one-way):* 2.7 miles to Round Lake, 3.0 miles to Scotts Lake, 3.5 miles to Dardanelles Lake.
*Elevation (low/high):* 7,200 feet to 8,070 feet.
*Time (one-way):* Two to three hours, depending on the destination.
*Trailhead:* Off Highway 89 about five miles south of US 50, near South Lake Tahoe, in the Meiss (pronounced "mice") Country between Luther and Carson passes. Park in the Big Meadows lot on the east side of the highway. Follow the trail at the lower end of the lot about 200 yards to the highway; cross cautiously and look for the trail marker.
*Description:* This trailhead offers several good, moderate hikes to three scenic alpine lakes: Round, Dardanelles and Scotts. If you work a shuttle,

you can even do a one-way hike past Meiss Lake to Highway 88 and Carson Pass, a distance of about eight miles. Dardanelles and Round lakes can be combined easily on a single hike, while Scotts is accessible via a separate, easterly spur from Big Meadows. The trail to the first two lakes climbs steeply for one-half mile from the highway through Jeffrey pine and white fir to Big Meadows. After you cross the creek and travel across the meadow, which can be marshy, you enter a dense lodgepole forest. In another 1.5 miles, the trail drops nearly 250 feet along an aspen-covered bank to a junction. Take the left fork, which contours around a wall of fused boulders and lava mudflows. After another short climb up a small hill, the trail arrives at Round Lake, the largest lake in Meiss Country. The brownish-green lake is ideal for swimming or for fishing for cutthroat trout. To reach Dardanelles Lake on the same hike, double-back and take the left fork at the trail junction. Follow it one-quarter mile to an un-marked trail on the left that crosses the creek. The trail winds through rolling hills and past willows before crossing two more streams. A short climb up a small hill leads to the lake, which is surrounded by picturesque granite cliffs on one side and flat granite shelves on the other.

**Information:** Lake Tahoe Basin Management Unit, (916) 573-2600.

# Crystal Basin

## ★ Wrights Lake to Smith Lake Trail ★
*See Wrights Lake trails map, page 110*

**Difficulty:** Moderate to moderately strenuous.
**Distance (one-way):** 2.8 miles.
**Elevation (low/high):** 7,000 to 8,500 feet.
**Time (one-way):** 2.5 to 3.0 hours.
**Trailhead:** At Wrights Lake, a 55-minute drive west of South Lake Tahoe. Take US 50 west and turn right on Wrights Lake Road about four miles west of Strawberry. There is a sign for the turnoff, but it's easy to miss the road. It rises steeply for eight miles along switchbacks and on bumpy pavement before it reaches the Wrights Lake Campground. At the junction of three roads in the campground, take the right fork and follow it for approximately 1.5 miles past summer cabins to the Twin Lakes and the Grouse Lakes Trailhead. Parking is very limited—accommodating about 15 vehicles—so get here early. Otherwise, you'll have to park back at the campground. A wilderness permit is required at the trailhead.
**Description:** This short but vigorous outing through the "back door" of Desolation Wilderness is one of the premier hikes in the region, encom-passing four uniquely different but equally spectacular alpine lakes. Wrights Lake has something for almost everyone: one section that is deep and fishable, and another that is warm and shallow, with rock and boul-

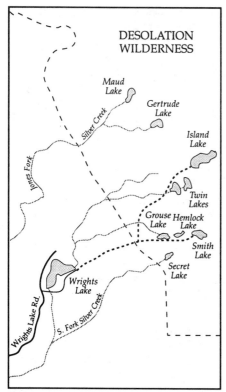

*Wrights Lake trails*

der islands. There's a pine-covered picnic area with tables and barbecues, next to the best swimming access. No outboard motors are allowed, so the lake is great for canoes, rafts and small sailing dinghies. The first of two hikes from the trailhead begins at the east end of the lake, next to an inlet. There are two forks beyond here; the left fork leads north around the lake and, not far beyond, the right fork leads to Grouse and Smith lakes (continuing straight ahead takes you to Twin Lakes). Take the right spur, and follow it across smooth but rising granite slabs, with the trail indicated by ducks (rock piles), until it climbs into red fir and lodgepole pine forest. A moderate ascent along a rocky stairway eventually reaches a creek, and the trail crisscrosses the water until it rises abruptly to a shelf. Just over the ridge is the incredibly beautiful and tranquil Grouse Lake, framed by granite walls, moderate tree cover and a small meadow. Enjoy a rest stop here before continuing a steep half mile to Hemlock Lake, with great vistas of Wrights Lake below. Hemlock, too, is magnificent; the north end has a shallow, sandy shoreline bordered with trees, while the south end has a high, sheer-walled cliff with spectacular striations. This wonderful, wind-protected lake makes for an ideal wading, swimming and floating destination. The trail continues for about one-third of a mile farther, initially on duff-covered forest trail, then up a steep, bouldered path with sections of slippery talus. There is an open promontory with lush wildflowers (including Indian paintbrush and lupine) and a lofty panorama of Crystal Basin and its reservoirs below. Beyond this point, the trail turns to granite walkways again before reaching Smith Lake. This almost perfectly round, glacial lake has deep waters and is cradled by rockfalls and towering Mount Price (elevation 9,975 feet), which separates this drainage from Lake Aloha to the east. The southwest corner of the lake has the only patch of level ground here, but there are few trees and no obvious sites for tents. Although it is marvelous to behold, the lake is quite cold, exposed to the winds, and is not hospitable for swimming. The trail ends here, so you'll need to retrace your steps (carefully!) back to Hemlock and Wrights lakes.

***Information:*** Eldorado Information Center, Eldorado National Forest, (916) 644-6048.

## Wrights Lake to Island Lake Trail
*See Wrights Lake trails map, page 110*

***Difficulty:*** Moderate.
***Distance (one-way):*** 3.1 miles.
***Elevation (low/high):*** 7,000 feet to 8,100 feet.
***Time (one-way):*** 2.5 to 3.0 hours.
***Trailhead:*** The trailhead is at the east end of the Wrights Lake Campground, eight miles north of US 50 on Wrights Lake Road, about a 55-minute drive west of South Lake Tahoe. For detailed directions, see the Wrights Lake to Smith Lake Trail on page 109. A wilderness permit is required and may be obtained from the U.S. Forest Service.
***Description:*** Of the two hikes from this trailhead into Desolation Wilderness, this is the more heavily traveled. The large lakes—Twin and Island—are popular with backpackers and anglers, and there are many small, unnamed lakes surrounding them. The thing to know about this hike is that it is mostly over crumbling rock or smooth granite, with very little tree cover. Thus the temperatures can be quite hot in summer, and extra water is advised. Families with children enjoy this hike because the outlet from Twin Lakes sends wide ribbons of water over lightly polished granite, creating natural water slides.

The trail meanders up a continuous rocky surface, paralleling a creek that cuts through a deep gorge just below Twin Lakes. All of the lakes are in a glacier-scoured canyon, amid open terrain surrounded by impressive granite walls. Flat, rocky peninsulas jut from the southern and eastern sections of Lower Twin Lake, and these make great places for sunning and picnicking. The trail to Island Lake crosses a small dam of logs and rocks at Lower Twin Lake (be careful!) and rises gradually on the north slopes, dipping down to several small ponds and scenic Boomerang Lake. At several points, the route is nearly obscured by overgrown brush and wildflowers—wear long pants or tights to avoid scratches and scruffs. Island Lake, the largest in the area, is aptly named for its handful of small rock islands. The lake's irregular perimeter is mostly elevated, with manageable, but not particularly easy, access to the water's edge. Located at the head of the canyon, the lake gets its share of wind, and the water is cold. The most impressive elements of these glacial lakes are the rock formations and peaks surrounding them. There are many photogenic

vantage points over these lakes and the Crystal Mountains. The trail ends at Island Lake; retrace your steps to the starting point.
*Information:* Eldorado Information Center, Eldorado National Forest, (916) 644-6048.

# Carson Pass/Highway 88

## Highway 88 to Meiss Lake Trail

*Difficulty:* Moderate.
*Distance (one-way):* Four miles.
*Elevation:* 8,320 feet to 8,560 feet.
*Time (one-way):* 3.0 to 3.5 hours.
*Trailhead:* Take US 50 south from South Lake Tahoe to Highway 89 and turn left. Continue to the intersection of highways 89 and 88 and turn right on Highway 88. Go one mile past the Carson Pass Sno-Park; turn left on the dirt road and park in the dirt parking area. The trailhead is located on the other side of the highway, just across from the parking area.
*Description:* With its shallow waters, Meiss is one of the warmest lakes in the Tahoe area, making it ideal for swimming. From the trailhead, follow the trail up the hillside, which is covered with mule ear and sagebrush, to a saddle. From here, enjoy views of the surrounding peaks before continuing along an old jeep route, where the trail crosses the Upper Truckee River and leads into a large meadow. Follow the path to the right 0.6 miles down the gentle slopes to Meiss Lake. Fishing here is prohibited.
*Information:* Lake Tahoe Basin Management Unit, (916) 573-2600.

## ★ Woods Lake to Round Top Loop ★

*See Woods Lake to Round Top Loop and Emigrant Trail map, page 113*
*Difficulty:* Mostly moderate, with the option of a strenuous hike to the peak.
*Distance:* Four miles round-trip.
*Elevation (low/high):* 8,570 feet to 10,380 feet at the top of Round Top Peak.
*Time:* Four to five hours round-trip.
*Trailhead:* From South Lake Tahoe, take Highway 89 south to the dead end at Highway 88, then west on Highway 88 to the Woods Lake Campground just over the crest of Carson Pass (a total distance of about 20 miles). Turn left on the two-mile paved access road to the campground, and look for the nearest available parking at the campground or on the side of the road (the 30 or so spaces at the campground often fill up before 10 a.m.!)
*Description:* One of the best hikes in the Tahoe region, this route encompasses three alpine lakes, a spectacular peak and marvelous vistas of

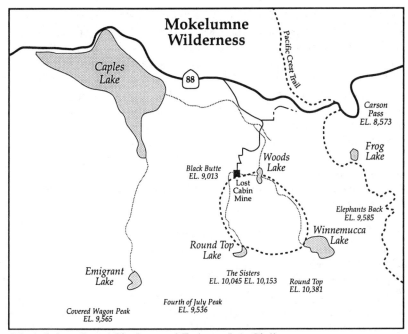

*Woods Lake to Round Top Loop and Emigrant Lake Trail*

Mokelumne Wilderness, distant Lake Tahoe, Carson Pass and Nevada's Carson Valley. The beauty of this hike is that you can make a full loop and constantly see new terrain. At the end of the hike, you can jump into tranquil, idyllic Woods Lake to cool off, or enjoy lunch on the picnic tables in the shade next to the shoreline. Look for the trailhead east of the campground (remember to fill out a wilderness permit) and begin a gradual ascent to Winnemucca Lake. The trail begins in forest but soon emerges onto rolling, hilly meadows, which are alive with wildflowers in early summer. It's an easy, 1.25-mile hike to Winnemucca, a large, rock-rimmed lake cradled in an exposed valley below a high mountain. There are a few good campsites here and sunning rocks on the lake's south side, but the area is subject to frequent winds. Continue for one mile up the well-maintained trail to Round Top Lake, enjoying gorgeous views of Winnemucca below.

At the crest of the trail, you'll have a striking vista of Round Top Lake, a shallow, almost circular body of water flanked on the south and west by the sheer, jagged cliffs of The Sisters peaks. You have a choice at this point: You can take the right fork back to Woods Lake, continue straight to Fourth of July Lake (one mile down a very steep path), or take a challenging 1.5-hour sidetrip to the summit of Round Top Peak. If you make a run at Round Top, the last third of the way is on steep, wide terrain over loose soil and unconsolidated rock, with extremely tricky footholds. Still, many people of average ability make it to the top (or the ledge just below the peak), where they are rewarded with awesome views of 50 miles or more in almost every direction. Strong, cold winds can buffet the south side of the peak, so dress accordingly. As difficult as it is scrambling to the top, it is even more difficult slip-sliding back down—in this venture, a hiking staff can come in handy. At Round Top Lake, follow the trail to Woods Lake, past the Lost Cabin Mine and down a series of moderately steep, forested switchbacks to the campground, enjoying lofty views of the lake as you descend.

*Information:* Eldorado Information Center, Eldorado National Forest, (916) 644-6048.

## Emigrant Lake Trail

*See Woods Lake to Round Top Loop and Emigrant Trail map, page 113*
*Difficulty:* Moderate.
*Distance (one-way):* Six miles.
*Elevation (low/high):* 7,758 feet to 8,600 feet.
*Time (one-way):* 3.0 to 3.5 hours.
*Trailhead:* At the west end of the dam at Caples Lake on Highway 88, approximately 22 miles southwest of South Lake Tahoe. Limited parking is available west of the dam. A wilderness permit is required and may be obtained from the U.S. Forest Service.
*Description:* This trail follows the old route of the Mormon-Emigrant Trail, which was used by pioneers in the mid-1800s, for 2.5 miles, mostly along the south side of Caples Lake and on the eastern outskirts of the Kirkwood Ski Resort. The trail then climbs to a junction, where you take the left fork, cross a stream (be careful of the water level in early summer), and continue up a series of forested switchbacks to the lake. The lake is fringed by moderate forest and is surrounded by several high peaks. It receives heavy use in the summer.
*Information:* Eldorado Information Center, Eldorado National Forest, (916) 644-6048.

## Burnside Lake Trail

*Difficulty:* Moderate to strenuous.
*Distance (one-way):* Five miles.
*Elevation (low/high):* 5,800 feet to 8,160 feet.
*Time (one-way):* 3.0 to 3.5 hours.
*Trailhead:* Located at Grover Hot Springs State Park in California, about a 50-minute drive from South Lake Tahoe. Go west on Hot Springs Road from the town of Markleeville (off highways 88 and 4). The trail-

head is in 4.5 miles on the right side of the road, before you come to Hot Springs Creek. There's also access in the camping area of the state park, although there is no parking available here.

**Description:** Because of the proximity of the campground and frequent visitors to the hot springs, this trail gets heavy use. It's a good day hike, however, and you can soak any tired muscles in the public mineral pool afterwards (temperatures hover around 102 to 104 degrees Fahrenheit; the fee is $4 for adults, $1 for children). The trail travels west along Hot Springs Valley and a small creek. Not far up the trail there is an easy, quarter-mile spur trail that leads to a pleasant 40-foot, unnamed waterfall, which is impressive during strong runoff. Beyond this junction, the well-marked trail climbs steadily to Burnside Lake, via switchbacks and straight inclines, through alternating dense forest and open, rocky terrain. In summer, this trail can get very hot, and it's wise to take twice as much water as you think you'll need. Along the way, enjoy vistas of Nevada and, occasionally, sections of the state park. The 10-acre lake is rimmed with trees and rocks, and is a popular swimming and fishing spot. Many hikers bring inflatable rafts and float tubes, as well as picnic lunches.

**Information:** Carson Ranger District, Toiyabe National Forest, (702) 882-2766. Grover Hot Springs State Park, (916) 694-2248.

# Truckee/Donner

## Summit Lake Trail

**Difficulty:** Easy.
**Distance (one-way):** Two miles.
**Elevation (low/high):** 7,200 feet to 7,400 feet.
**Time (one-way):** One hour.
**Trailhead:** From Interstate 80 at Donner Summit (west of Truckee), take the Castle Peak Area/Boreal Ridge Road exit, which is immediately west of the highway's Donner Summit Roadside Rest Area. (Unattended parking at the rest area is *not* permitted.) On the south side of the highway, look for a sign identifying the trailhead, and go east for 0.4 miles. The trailhead provides access to the Pacific Crest Trail and four other destinations, of which Summit Lake is one of the most popular.
**Description:** For the first mile, this hike follows the Pacific Crest Access Trail (Trail 15E18) east and then follows the PCT for one mile north, passing through a tunnel under Interstate 80. Shortly after the underpass, the intersection with the Summit Lake Trail (Trail 15E09) is clearly marked. The trail climbs moderately and crosses two small creeks, which are separated by a low, glaciated granite ridge. Beyond the second creek, the trail arcs through a meadow that teems with colorful wildflowers from spring through late summer. Head past the junction with the Warren

Lake Trail, keeping to the right, and continue out to the edge of an open, descending ridge. Enter a wooded area for the brief hike to the south corner of Summit Lake. Several campsites are available, and there is fishing for brook and rainbow trout.

*Information:* Truckee Ranger District, Tahoe National Forest, (916) 587-3558.

## ★ Loch Leven Lakes Trail ★

*Difficulty:* Moderately strenuous.
*Distance (one-way):* 2.2 miles to 3.5 miles.
*Elevation (low/high):* 5,680 to 6,800 feet.
*Time (one-way):* Two to three hours.
*Trailhead:* About 18 miles west of Truckee. From Interstate 80 eastbound, take the Big Bend exit; from Interstate 80 westbound, take the Rainbow Road exit. The trailhead begins one-quarter mile east of the Big Bend Visitor Center. A small parking area and restrooms are located across the road from the trailhead.
*Description:* Some wondrously beautiful small alpine lakes, with waters often warm enough for swimming, are in store for the hiker who ascends this hot, dusty trail. The trailhead itself is not well marked, but it's relatively easy to find next to the parking area. The trail works its way upward on a moderately steep grade to the southwest, climbing a rocky shelf as it rises to a vista point that overlooks busy Interstate 80. Once across the Southern Pacific Railroad tracks, it switchbacks through cool and majestic fir forest. At the summit, it opens up into granite outcroppings once again, then descends down a plateau to Lower Loch Leven. Considering the effort required to get here, it's tempting to jump into this first lake, which has accessible shoreline and smooth rock slopes for swimming and sunning. The lake is small and elongated, and you can easily swim laps across it. Those who continue on, however, will find even more picturesque scenery at Middle and High Loch Leven, both within 1.3 miles. The route climbs and descends small ridges, and offers views of valleys, high alpine meadows and glaciated mountain terrain. Good fishing and lakeside camping are available at all three lakes, though the trail is heavily used.
*Information:* Nevada City Ranger District, Tahoe National Forest, (916) 288-3231.

# Lakes Basin

## ★ Round Lake Loop Trail ★
*See Round Lake Loop Trail map, below*

**Difficulty:** Moderate.
**Distance:** 3.75 miles round-trip.
**Elevation (low/high):** 6,475 feet to 6,874 feet.
**Time:** Three to four hours round-trip.
**Trailhead:** From Truckee, drive 32 miles north on Highway 89 to Highway 49. Head six miles west on Highway 49 to the intersection with Gold Lake Road at Bassett's Station, and go right for about five miles to Gold Lake. The trailhead is at the parking lot of Gold Lake Lodge. The driving time from Truckee is around 50 minutes.
**Description:** No hike in the entire Tahoe region connects so many lakes with such varying and unique features as this one. It is the most favored day hike in the aptly named Lakes Basin, a region that is rich with volcanic rock formations, productive fishing waters, unique mountain lodges and remnants of the Gold Rush. The trail is excellent for family outings, thanks to its relatively modest elevation, minimal ups and downs, and diversity of terrain. By all means, savor this one at a leisurely pace—bring a picnic lunch, a swimsuit and a fishing rod. You can easily make it a day outing. The trail touches or overlooks nine lakes, from diminutive ponds to large impoundments. Traveling clockwise, start your hike in the direction of Round Lake, following a well-maintained trail for 1.7 miles to the lake. Stop here for a while, if you wish, but do continue on to more scenic lakes. Follow a steep, rocky trail 0.9 miles to Silver Lake, a beautiful, rock-

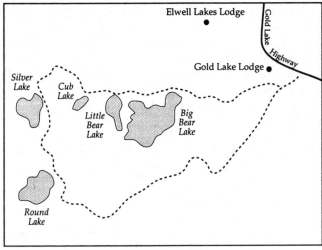

Round Lake Loop Trail

*Round Top Lake in the Mokelumne Wilderness is fringed by jagged peaks.*

rimmed body of water, which is arguably the most attractive of the group and a compelling spot for a picnic lunch. At Silver, there's a junction, and the left fork (signed for Mount Elwell) continues for about a half mile to a series of three small ponds known as Helgramite Lakes—a worthy detour. Back on the main trail, which begins a long descent, hike for about one-eighth of a mile until you reach an overlook of magnificent Long Lake, the second largest in the basin, flanked by Mount Elwell (elevation 7,812 feet). Shortly afterwards, you reach another junction; take the right fork, which passes Cub, Little Bear and Big Bear lakes (Little Bear and Big Bear offer good swimming and fishing possibilities). Beyond Big Bear, take the right fork of a third junction back to Gold Lake Lodge and the parking area. (Note: To top off a memorable day in this area, consider making dinner reservations well in advance at one of the fabled, old-fashioned lodges such as Gray Eagle, Sardine Lake or Gold Lake—see chapter 21, "Mountain Resorts and Lodges.")

*Information:* Beckwourth Ranger District, Plumas National Forest, (916) 836-2575.

## Sierra Buttes Lookout via Tamarack Lakes Trail

*Difficulty:* Strenuous.
*Distance (one-way):* 3.5 miles.
*Elevation (low/high):* 6,220 feet to 8,587 feet.
*Time (one-way):* 2.5 to 3.0 hours.
*Trailhead:* From Truckee, drive 32 miles north on Highway 89 to Highway 49. Head six miles west on Highway 49 to the intersection with Gold

Lake Road at Bassett's Station, and turn north. Continue for 1.4 miles to Salmon Creek and turn left onto the bridge. Go for about 0.3 miles and turn right onto Packer Lake Road. Proceed for 2.5 miles and turn left onto Forest Service Road 93 (Packer Saddle Road). Continue for 0.1 miles. On the left side of the road is a large sign reading "Lower and Upper Tamarack lakes and Sierra Buttes." The hike begins here; there is ample parking available.

**Description:** Of all the mountains in the Tahoe region, surely the Sierra Buttes are the most dramatic. Their jagged peaks are reminiscent of the Swiss Alps, and from almost any vantage point they command attention and awe. Thus, hiking to the fire lookout tower at the summit is virtually a pilgrimage for any self-respecting mountain trekker; many people come to this region specifically to scale the Buttes. There are easier routes to the top (one of them is from the Pacific Crest Trail higher up), but this is regarded as the most scenic, though it's no cakewalk. From the trailhead, follow the rough gravel road for one-quarter mile until it forks, then head to the right. After a half mile, you reach a sign reading "Sardine Lakes and Sand Pond via Trail." This is the Tamarack Connection Trail. Keep to the right and you will see another sign marked "Sierra Buttes L.O." in 200 yards. The twin Tamarack Lakes (elevation 6,754 feet) are on your left. Continue another half mile to a sign directing you to the left. The trail follows a ridge, above Young America Lake (elevation 7,250 feet), to the lookout. From this wildfire detection station, catch your breath and drink in the views of Mount Lassen and Mount Shasta to the north, Mount Rose to the east, and the many sparkling lakes below.

**Information:** Downieville Ranger District, Tahoe National Forest, (916) 288-3231.

# PEAK EXPERIENCES

If you've got good hiking boots and strong legs, and are in reasonably good physical condition, consider scaling one or more of Tahoe's walkable mountains. You don't need ropes or pitons to reach the summit of any of these peaks, though you may have to scramble cross-country or climb some rocks on the last portion of your hike. But once you reach the top, you'll treasure both the effort and the view. Except where noted, these are all strenuous hikes. The peaks are listed in order of descending elevation.

### ★ Mount Rose ★
*(elevation 10,778 feet; six miles one-way)*
The highest of the group, it's got views of Reno and Washoe Valley to the east and Lake Tahoe to the west. Located above Incline Village on the North Shore. (See the detailed description on page 91.)

## ★ Round Top Peak ★
*(elevation 10,380 feet; four miles one-way)*

This volcanic peak has spectacular panoramas of Carson Pass, Lake Tahoe, Carson Valley and Mokelumne Wilderness. It's tough going on loose soil and scree the last one-quarter of a mile. Bring a hiking staff and be very careful! The trail leaves from Woods Lake, east of Caples Lake. (See the detailed description on page 112.)

## ★ Mount Tallac ★
*(elevation 9,735 feet; five miles one-way)*

Splendid vistas of Emerald Bay, Cascade Lake, Fallen Leaf Lake and Desolation Wilderness are the reward for climbing Tallac. Located on the West Shore across from Baldwin Beach. (See the detailed description on page 102.)

## Little Round Top
*(elevation 9,500 feet; 2.5 miles one-way)*

From the top of Little Round Top, climbers enjoy panoramic views of Caples Lake, Carson Pass and surrounding peaks. To reach the trailhead, turn north off Highway 88 at the CalTrans Maintenance Station near Caples Lake. Continue for two miles to Schneider Cow Camp, where parking is available. Follow the four-wheel-drive road for one-half mile to the trailhead. The last part, near the junction of the Pacific Crest Trail, requires a cross-country ascent.

*Information:* Eldorado Information Center, Eldorado National Forest, (916) 644-6048.

## Ralston Peak
*(elevation 9,235 feet; four miles one-way)*

You get magnificent views of Lake Tahoe and Desolation Wilderness from this lofty perch, including Ralston and Echo lakes below and Round Top at Carson Pass to the south. The trailhead parking is across from Camp Sacramento on the north side of US 50, about six miles west of Echo Summit. The road on the east end of the parking area leads to the trailhead 200 yards away.

*Information:* Eldorado Information Center, Eldorado National Forest, (916) 644-6048.

## Genoa Peak
*(elevation 9,150 feet; four miles one-way)*

Genoa offers great views of Tahoe and the Carson Valley. Located cross-country from the Tahoe Rim Trail section between Spooner Summit on US 50 and Daggett Pass on the Kingsbury Grade on Highway 207. (See the detailed description on page 98, Tahoe Rim Trail South.)

# Mount Lola
*(elevation 9,143 feet; 4.5 miles one-way)*

This is the highest peak in Tahoe National Forest, with panoramic views of the Sierra Divide and Donner Pass. It's a strenuous climb to the top, though. To reach the trailhead, take Highway 89 north from Truckee to Forest Service Road 07 (to Jackson Meadows Reservoir). Turn west and drive 1.3 miles, then turn left on Independence Lake Road. Continue south about one-half mile to the junction with Sierra County Road S301. Turn right at the first intersection and continue west for three miles to the trailhead.

***Information:*** Sierraville Ranger District, Tahoe National Forest, (916) 994-3401.

# Tinkers Knob
*(elevation 8,950 feet; seven miles one-way)*

From Tinkers Knob, enjoy an impressive, 360-degree view of Granite Chief Wilderness, the headwaters of the North Fork of the American River and Donner Pass. To reach the Granite Chief Trailhead, go south on Highway 89 from Truckee (or north from Tahoe City), turn west on Squaw Valley Road and drive 2.2 miles to the Squaw Valley Fire Station. The trail is located on the east (right) side of the fire station and is clearly marked. It soon intersects with the Pacific Crest Trail; head north to the Tinkers Knob Saddle. It's a short climb from here to the top. This is a strenuous hike.

***Information:*** Truckee Ranger District, Tahoe National Forest, (916) 587-3558.

# Twin Peaks
*(elevation 8,800 feet; 14.5 miles one-way)*

Vistas of Lake Tahoe, Mount Rose, Tinkers Knob, Desolation and Granite Chief wilderness areas are the main attractions of this most difficult hike. The access point is Granite Chief Trailhead (see the Tinkers Knob hike above). When the trail intersects with the Pacific Crest Trail, head south to Twin Peaks.

***Information:*** Truckee Ranger District, Tahoe National Forest, (916) 587-3558.

# ★ Ellis Peak ★
*(elevation 8,640 feet; 2.5 miles one-way)*

Ellis provides impressive panoramas of Lake Tahoe to the east and Granite Chief Wilderness and Hellhole Reservoir to the west. This is the least strenuous of the peak hikes. Near Barker Pass at the end of Blackwood Canyon Road on the West Shore. (See the detailed description on page 95.)

## ★ Sierra Buttes ★
*(elevation 8,587 feet; 2.5 to 3.5 miles one-way)*

Because of its jagged profile, which is reminiscent of the European Alps, this is the most impressive-looking of all the area's mountains. This strenuous hike is 2.5 to 3.5 miles one-way, depending on the route you take. A manned fire lookout station is at the top. Near Highway 49 and the Gold Lake Road. (See the detailed description on page 118.)

## Mount Judah
*(elevation 8,243 feet; 2.5 to 6.0 miles one-way)*

Now part of the Sugar Bowl ski resort, this peak has great views of Donner Summit, Donner Lake, Truckee, Anderson and Castle peaks, as well as the more distant Sierra Buttes. The length of this strenuous hike depends on the trailhead you set off from. For the longer hike, take the Castle Peak Area/Boreal Ridge Road exit, which is immediately west of Interstate 80's Donner Summit Roadside Rest Area. (Unattended vehicles are *not* allowed in the rest area.) Follow the sign to the Pacific Crest Trail and go 0.4 miles to the PCT Trailhead. You can reduce the distance by 3.5 miles by accessing the PCT off Old Highway 40 just beyond Donner Ski Ranch, across from the Sugar Bowl ski area. Hikers must travel northeast cross-country from Roller Pass along the crest of Mount Judah to reach the highest point.

*Information:* Truckee Ranger District, Tahoe National Forest, (916) 587-3558.

## Mount Elwell
*(elevation 7,812 feet; 3.8 miles one-way)*

Located in the Lakes Basin area northwest of Truckee, this strenuous hike offers views of Long Lake, the Lakes Basin, Sierra Buttes and, to the north, distant Mount Lassen. The trailhead is on the road leading to Gray Eagle Lodge, southwest of Graeagle on the Gold Lake Road. There's lots of scree on the way up.

*Information:* Beckwourth Ranger District, Plumas National Forest, (916) 284-7126.

## Eureka Peak
*(elevation 7,447 feet; three-mile loop)*

Located in Plumas Eureka State Park, a one-hour drive northwest of Truckee, this strenuous loop trail offers a 360-degree view of the Lakes Basin and, to the north, Mount Lassen. The trail begins at the west side of Eureka Lake Dam, at the end of the county road from Graeagle to Johnsville.

*Information:* Plumas Eureka State Park, (916) 836-2380.

# Chapter 6

# Nature Trails

## ★ Author's Choice ★

### Top 10 Nature Walks

There are dozens of hiking opportunities around Lake Tahoe for backcountry purists who like to penetrate deep into the wilderness for solitude and scenery. But those who prefer brief walks, on which they can enjoy natural history, wildlife photography and beautiful vistas, will also find numerous trails around the lake and in its adjoining forests. Self-guided nature trails—some with signposts, others with maps and markers—represent wonderful learning experiences, especially for youngsters. If you'd like to identify the alpine trees and plants that grow in the Sierra, several of these walks will be informative. The meadows and marshes of public access areas can be rich with wildflowers in early summer, as well as fascinating birdlife such as ospreys, bald eagles, herons, cranes and waterfowl. To see such creatures, plan on visiting these places early in the morning or just before sunset. It's always a good idea to come with binoculars, a camera, a water bottle—and a little patience.

## Lake Tahoe Visitor Center

Several attractions and short walks are possible from the Visitor Center, the focal point of the U.S. Forest Service's Lake Tahoe Basin Management Unit:

★ *Rainbow Trail:* (★ *notes Author's Choice.*) This half-mile walk extends from Jeffrey pine forest to a mountain meadow, with a chance to see wildflowers along the way in early and midsummer. The trail goes to the Stream Profile Chamber, a wonderful underground viewing chamber on Taylor Creek that allows visitors to observe trout and other aquatic life. During fall (October), bright red kokanee salmon migrate upstream to dig their nests; these, too, can be seen through the chamber windows.

★ *Tallac Historic Site Trail:* This easy, three-quarter-mile walk is like taking a time machine back to a bygone era. From the Kiva Beach Picnic Area, walk along the historic promenade and past the remains of Lucky Baldwin's Tallac House, Tallac Casino and Tallac Hotel. Then enter the grounds of the Baldwin-McGonagle, Pope and Valhalla summer homes. Ask for the Tallac Historic Site brochure.

*Lake of the Sky Trail:* Starting just behind the Visitor Center, follow this easy, three-eighths-of-a-mile walk past the amphitheater to the shore of Lake Tahoe. Interpretive signs along the way discuss the first impressions Lake Tahoe made on notables such as author Mark Twain and naturalist John Muir.

*Smokey's Trail:* Especially educational for kids, this easy, one-eighth-of-a-mile walk ventures just outside the Visitor Center. Children who walk the trail and can remember the procedures for a safe campfire receive a reward from the Visitor Center.

*Forest Tree Trail:* This quarter-mile trail discusses Jeffrey pine, the most dominant tree in the Lake Tahoe basin. Placards trace the tree's life cycle, from germination to decomposition.

*Fallen Leaf Dam Trail:* This 2.5-mile loop begins across the highway from the Visitor Center and follows Taylor Creek to the dam at Fallen Leaf Lake. There's a two-mile extension loop to Sawmill Cove that provides more scenic vistas from the North Shore of the lake.

The Visitor Center is located four miles north of South Lake Tahoe on Highway 89. The Forest Service staffs an information desk with maps and books, and posts naturalist-led activities. Information: 870 Emerald Bay Road, South Lake Tahoe, CA 96150; Lake Tahoe Basin Management Unit, (916) 573-2600; or Lake Tahoe Visitor Center, (916) 573-2674.

## ★ Spooner Lake ★

This pleasant, 1.75-mile nature walk circles Spooner Lake, and is especially scenic in autumn when the aspen groves concentrated on the south end turn bright yellow and orange. In early summer, the adjacent meadows are a riot of wildflowers. Birdwatching can be excellent, and you might catch a glimpse of an osprey or a migrating bald eagle. Bicycles are not allowed on the trail, and no outboard motors are permitted on the lake. Swimming is not recommended because of harmless but ubiquitous leeches, and the shoreline is fairly muddy, anyway. Naturalist-rangers offer interpretive programs throughout the summer, including wildflower walks. Spooner Lake is located in Lake Tahoe-Nevada State Park on Highway 28, one-quarter mile north of the junction with US 50, near South Lake Tahoe. There is parking in a large paved lot, as well as overflow areas, which are necessary due to the large influx of mountain bikers. Day-use fees are $4 per car, $2 for a bike and $1 for hikers. Information: Lake Tahoe-Nevada State Park, (702) 831-0494.

## Sugar Pine Point State Park

There are several short to medium-length walks in this park:

★ *Dolder Trail:* For the best views of Lake Tahoe, take the trail that starts near the Ehrman Mansion to the Edwin L. Z'Berg Natural Preserve. The one-mile loop starts high, then drops down to follow the lakeshore. Along the way, it passes the world's highest (in elevation) working lighthouse, which is unnamed.

*General Creek Trail:* This 6.5-mile loop follows the General Creek drainage and enters Forest Service land. An optional side trip goes four miles from the campground to Lily Pond.

Sugar Pine Point State Park is located about 10 miles south of Tahoe City on Highway 89. It has a nature museum with several displays, maps and books next to the Ehrman Mansion. Information: Sugar Pine Point State Park, (916) 525-7982.

## D.L. Bliss and Emerald Bay State Parks

Several short nature trails exist in these two parks on the West Shore of Lake Tahoe:

★ *Balancing Rock Nature Trail:* In the northwest section of D.L. Bliss, pick up a trail guide at the park offices and follow this half-mile path along 19 numbered markers, which discuss the relationships between the soils, plants and animals found in the park. The highlight of the walk is the 130-ton granite Balancing Rock, which rests precariously on a slender stone base. Over time, the rock has been eroding away; it will eventually fall when enough material is lost to break the equilibrium between the two pedestals.

★ *Lighthouse Trail:* Another short trail at D.L. Bliss visits the site of an old lighthouse on Rubicon Point, which overlooks one of the deepest areas of the lake. From this high perch, you can see over 100 feet into the depths of Lake Tahoe.

*Vikingsholm Trail:* This is the most famous hike at Emerald Bay State Park. It follows a steep, one-mile trail from the Harvey West parking lot on Highway 89 down to Vikingsholm Castle, a Scandinavian-style estate that was constructed in 1928. Currently, park rangers conduct tours through the mansion every half hour from 10 a.m. to 4 p.m. during summer. The trail drops 500 feet in elevation, and the going is much tougher on the way back.

The parks are located about nine miles north of South Lake Tahoe on Highway 89. There's a new nature center at the entrance of D.L. Bliss State Park, with informative displays. The day-use fee for entering the parks is $5 per car. Information: D.L. Bliss and Emerald Bay State Parks, (916) 525-7277.

## Donner Memorial State Park

Two interesting, self-guided nature trails originate in this California state park, and you can combine them for a total of 2.5 miles. One begins just behind the Emigrant Trail Museum and makes a loop through the forest; it is incorporated into a Junior Ranger program for youngsters. The second self-guided trail starts next to the day-use access road and parallels Donner Lake, offering information on the geology, flora and fauna, and human history of the area. This trail meanders through forest, but there are spurs to the shoreline and beaches, and picnic sites abound. Donner Lake has a protected lagoon that is warm and excellent for swimming. Several times a week throughout the summer, rangers offer guided hikes ranging from two hours to all day. Contact the park for specific schedules and programs. The park is located at the Truckee-Donner Lake exit off Interstate 80. The day-use fee is $5 per car. Information: Donner Memorial State Park, (916) 582-7892.

## Washoe Lake State Park

This area just north of Carson City in Nevada was once the home of the Washoe Indians, semi-nomadic people who followed the animals and plants with the seasons. Near the lake they conducted rabbit drives and used willows and cattails to make baskets. This is prime birdwatching habitat. The park's wetlands and the Scripps Wildlife Management Area to the north provide refuge for many waterfowl. Ducks, coots (mudhens) and pelicans nest in the area at the south end of the lake, and the wet playa areas east of the sand dunes play host to Sandhill cranes, great blue herons and white-faced ibis. The best way to view birds is to stop at the wetlands area, about two miles off the highway, or walk along the beach on the northeast shore of the lake past the dunes. Visitors can also walk the Deadman's Creek Trail which originates in the day-use area and travels for one mile across Eastlake Boulevard 200 feet up to an overlook and gazebo. The park can be reached by taking the Lakeview exit from US 395 about one mile north of Carson City, and following East Lake Boulevard to the park entrance. The day-use fee is $3 per car from April through November 1, then it drops to $2 in winter. Information: Washoe Lake State Park, (702) 687-4319.

## Grover Hot Springs State Park

This California park, famous for its hot mineral springs, has a small, self-guided loop trail, called the Transition Trail, which comes with a brochure and 26 numbered stations that describe the area's natural history. The area covered includes glaciers, riparian vegetation, trees and the large meadow next to the springs. About 1.25 miles in length, the trail takes about an hour to walk; it begins at the Hot Springs Creek Bridge near the campground. Another trail, a half-mile walk from the campground on a dirt road, leads to an unnamed waterfalls, about 30 feet high. The park is located four miles west of Markleeville, at the end of Hot Springs Road, off Highway 4 south of its intersection with Highway 88. The day-use fee is $5 per car. Information: Grover Hot Springs State Park, (916) 694-2248.

## Angora Lakes Trail

This easy, half-mile hike, one of the best short walks in the Tahoe region, leads to two sparkling lakes framed by cliffs. The lakes are popular for swimming and fishing, and a small overnight lodge offers rowboat rentals and a snack shack. Take Highway 89 north about four miles from South Lake Tahoe to Fallen Leaf Road and turn left. Turn left again at the first paved road. Continue to Forest Service Road 12N14, a dirt and gravel road, and turn right. Continue past Angora Fire Lookout to the road's end at the parking lot. The trail has an elevation gain of just 270 feet. Information: Lake Tahoe Basin Management Unit, U.S. Forest Service, (916) 573-2600.

## Moraine Trail

This one-mile trail follows the shore of Fallen Leaf Lake on a relatively flat route through the forest. Take Highway 89 north about four miles from South Lake Tahoe to Fallen Leaf Lake Road. Continue for two-thirds of a mile to Fallen Leaf Campground. Drive through the campground and park just before campsite #75 on the right. Look for the trailhead sign near the parking area. There is no day-use fee. Information: Lake Tahoe Basin Management Unit, U.S. Forest Service, (916) 573-2600.

## ★ Page Meadows ★

Although there are no designated trails, this large meadow is considered the prime place to see wildflowers in early to mid summer. From Highway 89, two miles south of Tahoe City, turn on Pineland Drive. Turn right on Forest Service Road 15N60 or Forest Service Road 16N48 to get to the meadow. The area is popular with mountain bikers as well as hikers. Information: Lake Tahoe Basin Management Unit, U.S. Forest Service, (916) 573-2600.

## ★ Stateline Lookout Trail ★

This is one of the best high-elevation vantage points at Lake Tahoe (see page 93 in Chapter 5, "Hiking Trails"). This half-mile, paved loop trail begins at a fire lookout 1,000 feet above Crystal Bay on the North Shore, and includes detailed markers explaining the natural and human history of the area. From Highway 28, turn north on Reservoir Drive, east of the Tahoe Biltmore Lodge and Casino. Turn right on Lakeview Avenue and left on Forest Service Road 1601 (by the iron pipe gate). Park in the lot just below the lookout. Information: Lake Tahoe Basin Management Unit, U.S. Forest Service, (916) 573-2600.

## North Tahoe Regional Park

This park offers about six miles of multi-use trails, some with views of Lake Tahoe, and a large day-use area for field sports, tennis and picnicking. Trails are shared with mountain bikes, and some lead to the famous Fibreboard Freeway, a wide dirt road that follows the ridge of the North Shore. The park is located off Highway 28 at Tahoe Vista. Turn north on National Avenue and follow the signs to the parking lot. Information: North Tahoe Public Utility District, (916) 546-5043.

## Bijou Community Park

This large city park in the heart of South Lake Tahoe has several trails through meadows, with views of Freel Peak and other mountains. The park is located at 1021 Al Tahoe Boulevard, off US 50. Information: South Lake Tahoe Parks and Recreation Department, (916) 542-6055.

## ★ Tahoe Vista Trail ★

This 1.1-mile self-guided nature trail offers spectacular views from the terminal of the Heavenly Ski Area tram (see page 103 in Chapter 5, "Hiking Trails"). From the lodge, collect a brochure and follow a route that switchbacks through forest from 8,250 feet to 9,000 feet. That's a pretty decent elevation gain for a short trail, so wear hiking boots, bring water, and allow extra time. The view over Lake Tahoe and Stateline are magnificent. The tram fee is $10.50 for adults and $6 per children, but is less after 6 p.m. In fact, a wonderful time to be here is just before sunset. Information: Heavenly Ski Area, (702) 586-7000.

## Prey Meadows/Skunk Harbor

This easy, 1.5-mile walk has just 600 feet of elevation gain, and offers a pleasant stroll through a mixed conifer forest with occasional views of Lake Tahoe. You can see the remains of an old railroad grade, built in the 1870s as part of a system to supply timber to Virginia City. When you reach a fork in the road, you can take the left fork to Prey Meadows, lush with wildflowers in early summer, or the right fork to Skunk Harbor, a small picturesque cove that offers great swimming and sunbathing in the summer. Information: Lake Tahoe Basin Management Unit, U.S. Forest Service, (916) 573-2600.

## ★ Sierra Discovery Trail ★

This is one of the newest and most fascinating self-guided nature trails in the region. Created by Pacific Gas & Electric as a community service project, the one-mile trail takes you through wetlands, forest and stream-side habitats. There are interpretive signs and a waterfall along the way. The information kiosk at the parking lot describes the Drum-Spaulding hydroelectric project, which links 31 reservoirs, 12 powerhouses and 53 miles of river on the western slopes of the Sierra. A boardwalk crosses wetlands to a bridge spanning Bear River, and from there the loop trail meanders through the forest, with a scenic rest area at the midpoint. Restrooms and a nearby picnic area with tables and barbecues beside the river make for a great family outing. The trail is about 30 miles west of Truckee off Interstate 80. From the freeway, follow Highway 20 for 4.6 miles. Turn right on Bowman Lake Road, then go 0.6 miles to the parking lot. The trail is near Lake Spaulding and Fuller Lake. Information: PG&E, (916) 894-4687.

## Woodcamp Creek Interpretive Trail

Want a great, one-mile family outing? Head to the Woodcamp Creek Interpretive Trail at Jackson Meadows Reservoir, 33 miles northwest of Truckee. The trail starts at the Woodcamp Picnic Site, a day-use area next to several campgrounds on the southwest side of the lake, across the dam. A leaflet for this self-guided trail can be picked up at the trailhead. There are 26 markers that explain different types of trees, their life cycles and the local topography along the creek. Take Highway 89 about 17 miles north to Forest Service Road 19N07 (to Jackson Meadows Reservoir) and continue on this paved road for 16 miles until it reaches the campground. Information: Sierraville Ranger District, Tahoe National Forest, (916) 994-3401.

## Cottonwood Creek Botanical Trail

This half-mile nature trail helps you identify some of the common trees and plants in this mid-alpine region (about 5,400 feet). The trail originates at Cottonwood Campground, which is just off Highway 89 about 21 miles north of Truckee, and follows Cottonwood Creek, crossing it at two bridges. Get a brochure at the trailhead and proceed to 14 numbered stations to learn about white fir, black cottonwood, Jeffrey pine, Western juniper, incense cedar, bitterbrush, California wild rose and other foliage. Many people disregard a quarter-mile spur trail that branches off from the main path close to the trailhead, and this is a shame since it leads to a nice overlook of the Sierra Valley. You can do the nature trail first, then return to the overlook without retracing much ground. Information: Sierraville Ranger District, Tahoe National Forest, (916) 994-3401.

## Plumas Eureka State Park

Four trails, ranging in length from 1.3 to three miles, make this a good family destination. Here, about 60 miles northwest of Truckee, you can explore the site of the famous Jamison gold mine, recounted in the park's museum, or hike to three small lakes and a high peak.

*Madora Lake Loop:* This delightful, forested trail of 1.5 miles circles a small, lush lake surrounded by reeds and waterlillies. The trailhead is located next to a parking lot and picnic ground that is 2.5 miles east of the Museum/Park Office building via County Road A-14.

*Eureka Peak Loop:* This is a strenuous, three-mile hike if you go to the top of the mountain (see page 122 in Chapter 5, "Hiking Trails"), but you can take an easier, 2.6-mile round-trip to Eureka Lake from the ski hill parking lot.

***Little Jamison Creek Trail:*** This scenic, 1.5-mile stretch from the museum to the campground passes through a forest of white fir, Jeffrey pine and incense cedar, as well as the Jamison Mine complex.

***Grass Lake Trail:*** This trail begins at the Upper Jamison Campground, but leaves the park and enters Plumas National Forest, continuing 1.3 miles to Grass Lake. The trail continues on to more interesting and dramatic lakes, including Smith, Wades, Jamison and Rock.

Plumas Eureka State Park is located about five miles west of Graeagle on County Road A14 (to Johnsville) from its intersection with Highway 89. Information: Plumas Eureka State Park, (916) 836-2380.

## Sand Pond Interpretive Loop Trail

Near the ruggedly beautiful Sierra Buttes northwest of Truckee, this flat trail extends for three-quarters of a mile from the Sardine Lake Campground to Sand Pond, a favorite swimming hole. At the southeast end of the lake the trail splits. The right fork takes you around Sand Pond and the left fork is the Sand Pond Interpretive Loop Trail. This trail provides access to a forest/marsh transitional zone and discusses some of the natural history of the area. Among the wildlife that can be seen are, occasionally, beaver. Signs along the route explain the local ecology. To get here, take Highway 89 north from Truckee to Highway 49, then west to Gold Lake Road at Bassett's Station. Continue for about 1.4 miles, then turn left at the Salmon Creek Bridge. Proceed west toward Sardine Lake for one mile to the Sand Pond Swim Area parking lot. Information: Downieville Ranger District, Tahoe National Forest, (916) 288-3231.

## Frazier Falls Trail

This is an easy half-mile walk to a scenic fenced overlook of 100-foot Frazier Falls in the Lakes Basin area. The trailhead is located at Gold Lake Road about six miles from the Highway 89/Gold Lake Road intersection. The falls make an ideal spot for a great family picnic. Information: Beckwourth Ranger District, Plumas National Forest, (916) 836-2575.

*The shallow lagoon at the southeast corner of Donner Lake is a nice spot to wade and float.*

# Chapter 7

# Campgrounds

Every year our extended family (15 and counting) embarks on a midsummer camping expedition. With so many logistical challenges, we might as well be packing for Mount Everest. Everyone has a favorite pastime and, happily, some of them coincide with others. But the prerequisites are substantial. For example, my wife and I have a Coleman Scanoe (a combination skiff and canoe) with a small outboard motor, so we like to be near a lake for cruising and fishing. But we prefer the leeward side, so that the Sierra's almost predictable afternoon winds don't blow us off the water, or worse, swamp our little vessel. And we like being in a tent.

By contrast, my sister-in-law and her husband, after camping for years in a tent, finally succumbed to a 22-foot motor home, breaking the tradition of our clan. So now we need side-by-side campsites that are large enough to accommodate an RV and a half-dozen tents. And everyone's fussy. We have infants and mothers who want a beach or a shoreline for sunning. We have older youngsters who want a cove or shallow lagoon for swimming. Mountain bikes are high on the activity list for the older boys, so we need to be near paved or graded trails to accommodate them. You want more? The boys and fathers are fishing fanatics, so the lake had better be well-supplied with trout. My wife's favorite activity, above all others, is hiking. She wants to be near trails that lead to out-of-the-way alpine lakes, and she prefers long, strenuous forced marches of 8 to 10 miles that equal the "pump" of her high-impact aerobics classes.

Somehow, we always manage to find a place around Lake Tahoe that fills our demanding and diverse requirements. For the multi-use, multi-dimensional campers, Lake Tahoe is a paradise in the summer and early fall, and it's easy to see why sites fill up rapidly, especially in the more desirable campgrounds close to the water's edge. You can find perfect seclusion, your tent or small RV nestled deep into ponderosa pine forest. Or you can be close to the action, near town centers, with access to public transportation, and within cycling or walking distance of restaurants, night spots and other points of interest.

More than 125 public and private campgrounds exist around Lake Tahoe, Reno, Carson Valley and the surrounding areas. They are operated by the U.S. Forest Service, the California Department of Parks and Recreation, the Nevada State Department of Parks and Recreation, the Bureau of Land Management, PG&E, the U.S. Army Corps of Engineers and various city, county and regional agencies. The facilities vary in quality but, in general, the state and local agency campgrounds, and most of the private campgrounds such as KOAs, have more amenities—especially showers and flush toilets. The Forest Service sites are primitive, generally with vault toilets (the exception is in Tahoe, where all of them are flush toilets) and no showers, but they are inexpensive and tend to be in more pristine or remote locations.

Of course, if you bring a self-contained RV, you'll have all the comforts of home. Personally, I'm not keen on high-tech camping. More than once, I've set up my humble little North Face dome tent next to the Mother of All RVs, complete with portable satellite dish, color TV and gas generator. What we'd endure most of the evening was enough accessory lighting to illuminate a Broadway stage show, reruns of *Charlie's Angels* or some gawd-awful slasher video on a loud TV set, and the consistent drone of a generator to run all of this stuff. That scenario doesn't fit my definition of camping.

The key to securing a great campsite in this region is advance planning. Because the majority of public sites can be booked only through a reservation service during the high season, you may have to choose a date months in advance, and then be poised to work your phone and the redial function for an hour or longer to get through. There are a few first-come, first-served sites, and you can always take your chances. But there is such demand for these that you practically have to be standing next to someone who is vacating in the middle of the week, say on a Wednesday or Thursday, to have a shot at one. The Great Land Rush of the mid-1800s is nothing compared to the Great Camping Rush of the 1990s.

## CAMPING REGIONS AROUND TAHOE & RENO
There are six major camping regions in the vicinity:

### Lake Tahoe
The 72-mile shoreline is studded with a variety of campgrounds, most of which are on the more wooded West Shore stretching from Tahoe City to South Lake Tahoe. By far the best public campgrounds, and generally the best locations, are in the California State Parks. Emerald Bay and D.L. Bliss have wonderful shoreline access, while Sugar Pine Point is a great spot for cyclists and hikers. Donner Memorial State Park is right next to Donner Lake and close to the town of Truckee, though it gets noise from busy Interstate 80 on one side and the Southern Pacific Railroad on the other. Several federal and private campgrounds along Highway 89, from Truckee to South Lake Tahoe, are so close to the road that the constant intrusion from traffic makes them much less desirable.

For members of the RV crowd who like to be near the casinos and restaurants, the city of South Lake Tahoe has a large and well-situated campground off US 50 (Campground by the Lake, see page 149), and there's a similar but smaller campground in Tahoe City. On a section of Highway 89 from Truckee to Tahoe City, several Forest Service campgrounds parallel the road and the Truckee River. When the Truckee is flowing and fishing is good, that's a great location. But it's not quiet.

## Truckee/Donner/Interstate 80

The region stretching along Interstate 80 from Truckee to Grass Valley, all within the Tahoe National Forest, has campgrounds along the Yuba River and along a series of PG&E reservoirs, including Lake Spaulding. The best campsites are those off the main highway, particularly along the less-traveled Highway 20. A large region of hiking trails to pristine backcountry lakes in the Grouse Lake area is near here, though many of the trailheads require a four-wheel-drive or high-clearance vehicle to reach them.

## Lakes Basin

Another area not well known to non-residents is along highways 89 and 49 north of Truckee. These campgrounds are within the Tahoe and Plumas national forests. Probably the most desirable camping locations are in what is known as the Lakes Basin area, which is a network of hikable lakes stretching from Sierra City to Graeagle. Not only are the hikes spectacular here, but fishing can be great, especially in the nearby Feather River. The crown jewel and the most visible element on the landscape is the Sierra Buttes, a jagged series of peaks reminiscent of the Swiss Alps, which makes a great destination for a vigorous but not impossible hike, with rewarding vistas along the way.

## Carson Pass/Highway 88

About 40 minutes south of South Lake Tahoe, a 40-mile stretch of scenic Highway 88 affords access to wonderful campgrounds at secluded alpine lakes, with some of the best hiking, mountain biking and equestrian trails in the region. The area traverses two national forests—Eldorado in California and Toiyabe in both states. It ranges from Bear River Reservoir on the west to Indian Creek Reservoir on the east. Some tremendous small campgrounds, such as those around the Blue Lakes region operated by PG&E, can be reached on well-marked but twisty dirt roads. This area is one of the jewels of the Tahoe Sierra, and is well worth exploring.

## Crystal Basin

A labyrinth of reservoirs for boating, waterskiing and fishing, along with some pristine alpine lakes reserved for float fishing and non-motorized boats, offer the single largest camping area in this part of Northern California. And yet none of it is visible from US 50. The entire complex of lakes is accessible from only two paved roads, both of which climb a steep mountain flank and both of which are easy to miss when you're driving along the highway. Great swimming holes, fishing for trophy trout and a plethora of less well-known backcountry trails to the west side of Desolation Wilderness make this area a winner for multiple-use campers.

# Reno/Carson Valley

If you like low-alpine or high-desert camping, there is a handful of public and private campgrounds along the eastern slopes of the Sierra, all within Nevada. Some of these are in windswept, desolate places, but there is always a wetlands area, a lake, a river or some other waterway nearby. Other campgrounds hug the eastern slopes of the Sierra and Carson ranges and offer trailheads to high-elevation vistas. A lot of them, unfortunately, are next to busy highways. Some are just east of Mount Rose, the location of a recently designated national wilderness area.

*Enjoy secluded camping at Lost Lakes, in the Blue Lakes region of Carson Pass.*

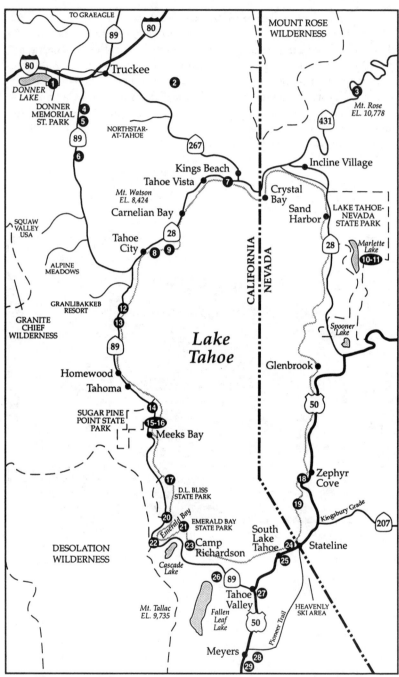

*Lake Tahoe campgrounds*

## Map References—Lake Tahoe Campgrounds

◆

# CAMPGROUNDS/RV PARKS
## Lake Tahoe

### ★ Donner Memorial State Park ★
### (California State Parks)

★ *notes Author's Choice*

*See number 1 on Lake Tahoe map, page 138*

**Amenities:** 154 sites, including 83 RV sites (28-foot maximum length), piped water, pay showers, chemical toilets, stoves, fire rings, picnic tables and swimming in the lake and a lagoon. Pets are allowed on leashes. Fee: $14. Closed in winter. Off Interstate 80 on Donner Pass Road, three miles west of Truckee.

**Comments:** This is one of the nicest and most popular public campgrounds in the Tahoe region. Nestled in pines and meandering through hills, it offers a wide range of recreational opportunities, including an excellent museum at the park entrance. There's a warm, shallow lagoon where small fry can swim, raft and canoe, as well as an extensive beach for hanging out. The lake itself accommodates fishing, windsurfing, jetskiing and waterskiing, and there's a concession that rents water craft. Rangers offer summer campfire programs at an amphitheater, along with hosted walks, and there's a self-guided nature trail. One disadvantage is noise at night from Interstate 80 and the Southern Pacific Railroad tracks, which flank the park. Also, the proximity to the highway makes it essential to take higher security measures for your belongings.

*Tip:* The best sites are in the Split Rock loop, closest to the lake and the attendant water sports concessions. Site selection is on a first-come, first-served basis, and while rangers try to accommodate specific requests, it's wise to arrive early and at least a day in advance of weekends to begin the haggling ritual.

*Information:* Donner Memorial State Park, (916) 582-7892; reservations, (800) 444-7275.

## Martis Creek (U.S. Army Corps of Engineers)
*See number 2 on Lake Tahoe map, page 138*

*Amenities:* 25 sites (all suitable for RVs), piped water, chemical toilets, barbecues, fire rings, picnic tables. Pets allowed on leash. Fee: $10. There are no reservations; all camping is on a first-come, first-served basis. Closed in winter. Off Highway 267, five miles southeast of Truckee.

*Comments:* When the lake is full, this is a beautiful campground and a great place for catch-and-release flyfishing. Most sites are under trees, and the area is close to Truckee, Northstar-at-Tahoe resort and the North Shore of the lake. Hiking and mountain biking trails are nearby. One disadvantage: The campground is next to the Truckee Airport.

*Information:* U.S. Army Corps of Engineers, (916) 639-2342.

## Mount Rose (Forest Service Concession)
*See number 3 on Lake Tahoe map, page 138*

*Amenities:* 24 sites, including nine RV/trailer sites (16-foot maximum length), piped water, flush toilets, fire rings with grills and picnic tables. Pets are allowed on a leash only. Fee: $7. Golden Age and Golden Access Passports honored. Closed in winter. Nine miles northeast of Incline Village on the south side of Highway 431, near the Mount Rose Summit.

*Comments:* This campground, the only one on Mount Rose Highway, is in Toiyabe National Forest—close to good hiking on the Mount Rose Wilderness Trail, Ophir Creek Trail and a future extension of the Tahoe Rim Trail. Also, it's a stone's throw from the popular and beautiful Tahoe Meadows, which is ablaze with wildflowers in early summer. Hikes can be made to the top of Slide Mountain for dramatic views of Reno, Tahoe and the Carson Valley, when the wind isn't blowing. The elevation is much higher than Lake Tahoe—8,900 feet—and nights can get colder. Sites 2 through 6 are on the reservation system; the rest are on a first-come, first-served basis.

*Tip:* The best sites are 13 and 14, which are at the end of a loop next to an attractive meadow.

*Information:* Carson Ranger District, Toiyabe National Forest, (702) 882-2766; reservations, (800) 280-CAMP.

# Granite Flat (U.S. Forest Service)

*See number 4 on Lake Tahoe map, page 138*

**Amenities:** 72 sites, all accommodating RVs (up to 40 feet), 17 wheelchair-accessible sites, piped water from an artesian well, vault toilets and a wheelchair-accessible river trail. Pets are allowed on a leash. Fee: $12. Closed in winter. On Highway 89, three-quarters of a mile southwest of Truckee.

**Comments:** This campground is similar to Goose Meadows Campground, with a noisy highway and lack of seclusion. But it's next to the scenic Truckee River, and close to town and golf/ski resorts such as Squaw Valley, Tahoe Donner and Northstar. Because of its centralized location, it's best for RVs.

**Information:** Truckee Ranger District, Tahoe National Forest, (916) 587-3558; reservations, (800) 280-CAMP.

# Goose Meadows (U.S. Forest Service)

*See number 5 on Lake Tahoe map, page 138*

**Amenities:** 27 sites, hand-pumped well water and older vault toilets. Pets are allowed on a leash. Fee: $8. Closed in winter. On Highway 89, five miles southwest of Truckee.

**Comments:** Situated in scattered pine alongside a busy and noisy highway, with almost no seclusion, the benefit of this place is its proximity to the Truckee River, especially when fishing is strong in the late spring and early summer.

**Information:** Truckee Ranger District, Tahoe National Forest, (916) 587-3558; reservations, (800) 280-CAMP.

# Silver Creek (U.S. Forest Service)

*See number 6 on Lake Tahoe map, page 138*

**Amenities:** 31 sites (19 of them suitable for RVs), hand-pumped well water, older vault toilets, stoves, fire rings and tables. Pets are allowed on a leash. Fee: $8. Closed in winter. On Highway 89, eight miles south of Truckee.

**Comments:** This campground has the same conditions as Granite Flat and Goose Meadow: beside a noisy highway, but also next to the scenic Truckee River.

**Information:** Truckee Ranger District, Tahoe National Forest, (916) 587-3558; reservations, (800) 280-CAMP.

# Sandy Beach Campground (Private)

*See number 7 on Lake Tahoe map, page 138*

**Amenities:** 44 sites, including 20 RV sites (35-foot maximum length), full hookups, piped water, flush toilets, showers, stoves, fire rings, tables and swimming. Pets are allowed with restrictions. Fee: $15-$20. Closed in winter. Located at 6873 North Lake Tahoe Boulevard (Highway 28), Tahoe Vista, one mile west of Kings Beach.

*Comments:* This facility is centrally located on the North Shore with access to beaches, restaurants, golf and water sports.

*Information:* Sandy Beach Campground, (916) 546-7682.

## Tahoe State Recreation Area (California State Parks)
*See number 8 on Lake Tahoe map, page 138*

*Amenities:* 31 sites, including 23 RV sites, piped water, flush toilets, showers, fire rings, picnic tables, fishing and swimming. Pets are allowed with restrictions. Fee: $14. Closed in winter. On Highway 28, one-quarter mile northeast of Tahoe City.

*Comments:* This campground has nice frontage on Lake Tahoe, but it's next to a busy highway. On the positive side, it is within walking distance of restaurants, shops and water excursions, and it's next to a paved bicycle path. This is a good venue for RVs, but not necessarily for tent campers.

*Information:* Seasonal park office, (916) 583-3074; reservations, (800) 444-7275.

## Lake Forest (Tahoe City Public Utilities District)
*See number 9 on Lake Tahoe map, page 138*

*Amenities:* 20 sites for tents and RVs (20-foot maximum length), piped water, flush toilets, freestanding barbecue pits, picnic tables, proximity to a boat ramp and swimming in the lake. Pets are allowed on a leash. Sites are on a first-come, first-served basis, with no reservations. Fee: $10, with drop box. There is a 10-day maximum stay. Closed in winter. Off Highway 28 on Lake Forest Road near the Coast Guard Station, two miles northeast of Tahoe City.

*Comments:* This campground off Highway 28 is next to the only public boat-launching ramp on the North Shore, so it's a good place to bring your boat. A public beach is within walking distance, and restaurants and shops are nearby.

*Information:* Tahoe City Public Utility District, (916) 583-5544.

## Marlette/Hobart Backcountry Area (Nevada State Parks)
*See number 10 on Lake Tahoe map, page 138*

*Amenities:* 18 hike-in (backpack) campsites just off the Tahoe Rim Trail. Pit toilets are available. The campground is close to two lakes, as well as to equestrian and mountain biking trails. There is no fee. The trailhead is at the Tahoe Rim Trail access on US 50 at Spooner Summit, east of Stateline, and the campground is about six miles farther north.

*Comments:* This is one of two hike-in sites along the eastern section of the Tahoe Rim Trail. Campers can enjoy great vistas of Lake Tahoe, Spooner Lake and Carson Valley from high points nearby.

*Information:* Nevada State Parks, (702) 831-0494.

## Marlette Peak Campground (Nevada State Parks)
*See number 11 on Lake Tahoe map, page 138*

*Amenities:* Six hike-in (backpack) campsites, picnic tables, fire rings and a pit toilet next to the Tahoe Rim Trail. About eight miles north of Spooner Summit Trailhead on US 50. There is no fee.

*Comments:* This is one of two hike-in sites along the eastern section of the Tahoe Rim Trail. Hikers can climb to the top of Marlette Peak for spectacular vistas of Tahoe and Carson Valley.

*Information:* Nevada State Parks, (702) 831-0494.

## William Kent (Forest Service Concession)
*See number 12 on Lake Tahoe map, page 138*

*Amenities:* 95 sites (40 suitable for RVs), piped water, flush toilets, barbecues, fire rings, picnic tables and swimming in the lake. Pets are allowed on a leash. Fee: $12. Closed in winter. On Highway 89, two miles south of Tahoe City.

*Comments:* Kent's proximity to the elegant Sunnyside Lodge and William Kent Beach (a Forest Service facility) are the biggest advantages. Water excursions, boating, fishing and other activities are just a stroll across the highway. And there's an inexpensive bus system (Tahoe Area Regional Transit) that stops here and can take you to points throughout the North and West shores of the lake. The campground also connects to an extensive system of paved bike trails. Sites are tucked into heavy forest, and are fairly close together; the best ones are farthest from the road. Sunnyside is a beehive of activity in summer, and there is considerable traffic congestion along the highway.

*Information:* Lake Tahoe Visitor Center, (916) 573-2674; reservations, (800) 280-CAMP.

## Kaspian (Forest Service Concession)
*See number 13 on Lake Tahoe map, page 138*

*Amenities:* 10 sites, piped water, flush toilets, stoves, fire rings, tables and swimming in the lake. Pets are allowed on a leash. Fee: $10. Closed in winter. On Highway 89, five miles south of Tahoe City.

*Comments:* This is a small campground that is close to the lake and near Homewood. It's great for water sports, but it's subject to noise from the busy highway.

*Information:* Lake Tahoe Visitor Center, (916) 573-2674; reservations, (800) 280-CAMP.

## Sugar Pine Point/General Creek (California State Parks)
*See number 14 on Lake Tahoe map, page 138*

*Amenities:* 175 sites (all suitable for RVs), piped water, flush toilets, a sanitary dump station, pay showers, barbecues, fire rings, picnic tables, swimming, hiking and cycling. Pets are allowed on a leash. Fee: $14. Open year-round. Reservations are strongly advised for May through September. One mile south of Tahoma on Highway 89.

*Comments:* This is a fairly flat campground with moderate tree cover on the west side of Highway 89, but it is well situated for many recreational activities. The best section of the park is on the east side of the highway, and contains the posh Ehrman Mansion with its manicured lawns, tall trees and scenic lake frontage; however, there are no campsites here. The long, paved West Shore Bike Path originates from this point, and at General Creek there are trailheads to several alpine lakes. For those who enjoy winter camping (without the showers), this is one of the few public campgrounds open. In summer, the campground gets heavy use, and the common facilities (including the showers) frequently seem overburdened.

*Information:* Sugar Pine Point State Park, (916) 525-7982; reservations, (800) 444-7275.

## Meeks Bay Campground (Forest Service Concession)
*See number 15 on Lake Tahoe map, page 138*

*Amenities:* 40 sites (some suitable for RVs up to 20 feet), piped water, flush toilets, stoves, fire rings, tables and swimming in the lake. Pets are allowed on a leash. Fee: $14. Closed in winter. On Highway 89, 10 miles south of Tahoe City.

*Comments:* The only things going for this rather unappealing campground are: immediate access to Lake Tahoe, and a nice, protected, white sand beach with shallow water for wading, swimming and paddling. The crescent-shaped beach is backed by pine trees, and there is a private boat-launching ramp nearby. Unfortunately, the campground is rather exposed and located much too close to the highway for any privacy or scenic beauty.

*Information:* Lake Tahoe Visitor Center, (916) 573-2674; reservations, (800) 280-CAMP.

## Meeks Bay Resort (Forest Service Special-Use Permit)
*See number 16 on Lake Tahoe map, page 138*

*Amenities:* 28 sites (10 suitable for RVs), piped water, flush toilets, showers, stoves, fire rings, tables, swimming, boating, fishing, a store and an ice cream parlor. No pets are allowed. Fee: $15-$25. Closed in winter. No reservations accepted. On Highway 89, 10 miles south of Tahoe City.

**Comments:** This historic resort is wonderful for families with children, even though the campground is unremarkable and close to the highway. RV owners will enjoy this place more than tent campers, since the resort is crowded in peak summer months. A large, white sand beach with a myriad of rentable water toys for children is the major asset of this site. There's also a general store and snack bar.

**Information:** Meeks Bay Resort, (916) 525-7242.

## ★ D.L. Bliss ★ (California State Parks)
### *See number 17 on Lake Tahoe map, page 138*

**Amenities:** 172 sites, including 21 suitable for RVs (15-foot maximum length), piped water, flush toilets, barbecues, fire rings, picnic tables, pay showers, swimming, fishing, hiking and access to Vikingsholm Castle. Pets are allowed on a leash. Fees: $14-$19. Closed in winter. Off Highway 89 south of Homewood.

**Comments:** Bliss is Tahoe's most spectacular and diverse campground, and one of the best in California. All sites are in wooded surroundings well off the highway, and many are on a hill above the lake. D.L. Bliss State Park has one of Tahoe's largest and most picturesque white sand beaches, and some ruggedly beautiful, wind-protected rocky coves, where swimming is delightful because of warmer, shallow water. The five-mile-long Emerald Bay Trail originates at the south end of the park, and provides a scenic but not too intimidating day hike along the high granite shelf of the West Shore to Emerald Bay. North of the park on Highway 89 is the lake's longest and most scenic paved bicycle trail, starting at Sugar Pine Point State Park and continuing to Tahoe City. One drawback: Sites nearest to the beach are close together and always crowded.

**Tip:** If you can assemble 10 people or several families, rent the group campsite, which is totally isolated from other sites and has an almost luxurious assortment of near-private amenities: tiled and spotlessly clean shower rooms, flush toilets and an outdoor sink. One drawback is that a dumpster nearby attracts bears. Also, the site accommodates tents or small RVs only.

**Information:** Seasonal park office, (916) 583-3074; reservations, (800) 444-7275.

## Zephyr Cove (Forest Service Special-Use Permit)
### *See number 18 on Lake Tahoe map, page 138*

**Amenities:** 170 sites (107 suitable for RVs up to 40 feet), full hookups, piped water, flush toilets, showers, stoves, fire rings, picnic tables, lake cruises, fishing, swimming, boating, restaurants, horseback riding, a recreation room and a convenience store. Pets are allowed on a leash. Fees: $15-$23. Open year-round. On US 50, four miles north of Stateline in Zephyr Cove, Nevada.

*Comments:* This is a good place for families with children, if you don't mind the lack of seclusion. Sites are closely spaced and next to a noisy highway, but most are in the trees. In summer, the campground is packed, and there's a constant influx of people for lake cruises. Major recreation amenities include the *M.S. Dixie II* paddlewheel cruiser, horseback riding at Zephyr Cove Stables, snowmobile tours in the winter, fishing charters, waterskiing and jetskiing, powerboat rentals, parasailing, beach volleyball and the *Woodwind* catamaran cruise boat. Large, attractive beach is subject to afternoon winds. Shuttles are available to Stateline casinos.

*Information:* Zephyr Cove Resort, (702) 588-6644.

### ★ Nevada Beach ★ (Forest Service Concession)
*See number 19 on Lake Tahoe map, page 138*

*Amenities:* 54 sites (30 suitable for RVs up to 24 feet), piped water, flush toilets, barbecues, fire rings, a picnic area, picnic tables, a beach, boating, swimming in the lake, fishing and volleyball. Pets are allowed on a leash. Fee: $14-$16. Closed in winter. On Elks Point Road, one mile northeast of Stateline in Nevada.

*Comments:* This is one of the two best Forest Service campgrounds at the lake (the other is William Kent; see page 143), though it sees heavy use from daytime visitors. Location is everything; it's on a wide, sandy beach (though not as scenic as the West Shore beaches), it's close to the Stateline casinos, and it's well away from the traffic of US 50. This flat site has some tree cover, though not the heavy forest typical of the West Shore. Boating at the south end (at a boat-in picnic area) and swimming opportunities abound, along with picnicking on the beach. The area, however, typically sees strong afternoon winds.

*Information:* California Lands Management (concessionaire), (916) 544-5994; reservations, (800) 280-CAMP.

### Emerald Bay Boat-In Camp (California State Parks)
*See number 20 on Lake Tahoe map, page 138*

*Amenities:* 20 sites for tents only offer piped water, chemical toilets, barbecues, fire rings, picnic tables, beaches and swimming in the lake. Fee: $9. Sites are on a first-come, first-served basis. Closed in winter. On the north shore of Emerald Bay.

*Comments:* Other than a backpack site in the high country, this is the most secluded and scenic organized camping spot at Tahoe. The lake's only boat-in campground is tucked away in protected pine forest just west of the Emerald Bay inlet, and it has a large pier and plenty of beach shoreline to accommodate everything from dinghies to opulent pleasure yachts. Views of the Sierra peaks from here are splendid, and it's an easy walk (or cruise) to Vikingsholm Castle and its scenic beach, or to the Emerald Bay Trail to D.L. Bliss State Park. The campground is popular, and the bay fills with hundreds of watercraft on a warm summer day. Evenings and mornings, however, are peaceful and devoid of traffic.

*Information:* Emerald Bay State Park, (916) 525-7277.

## Eagle Point/Emerald Bay State Park (California State Parks)

*See number 21 on Lake Tahoe map, page 138*

*Amenities:* 100 units (suitable for RVs up to 21 feet), pay showers, water, picnic tables, barbecues, flush toilets and swimming in the lake. Fee: $14. At Emerald Bay State Park about six miles north of South Lake Tahoe.

*Comments:* Situated on a high, rocky promontory on the southern flanks of Emerald Bay, this large campground, well off the highway, offers bird's-eye views of Lake Tahoe and the bay, and is one of the most popular camping spots in the region. Sites, however, are small and clustered closely together, occasionally separated by mounds of boulders, and it's a quarter-mile hike down to the beach at Emerald Bay from the nearest access point (although considering the seclusion, many campers feel the trek is worth it). The best sites are closest to the lake and have some tree cover, but they are subject to potentially strong afternoon winds.

*Information:* Emerald Bay State Park, (916) 525-7277; reservations, (800) 444-7275.

## Bayview (Forest Service Concession)

*See number 22 on Lake Tahoe map, page 138*

*Amenities:* 10 units (some suitable for large RVs), vault toilets and fire rings. Camping is free, and is available in summer only. Sites are on a first-come, first-served basis. On Highway 89 across from the Emerald Bay overlook, about seven miles north of South Lake Tahoe.

*Comments:* Although sites are undeveloped, they are fairly spacious. The campground is near a heavily traveled section of the highway, but it's a great location for hiking and fishing. The reason: One trailhead leads into Desolation Wilderness at the east end, and another goes to Cascade Lake. The latter is a short but scenic hike to Cascade Lake and Cascade Falls (about one mile away), while the former goes to Granite Lake (an excellent fishing spot) and, beyond, to the Velma lakes, which are among the more spectacular lakes in the wilderness.

*Information:* Lake Tahoe Visitor Center, (916) 573-2674.

## ★ Camp Richardson ★
## (Forest Service Special-Use Permit)
*See number 23 on Lake Tahoe map, page 138*

**Amenities:** 112 sites, group sites, showers, a boat ramp, piped water, flush toilets, barbecues, fire rings, picnic tables, swimming in the lake, horseback riding, bicycling and hiking. The campground is close to Fallen Leaf Lake, Valhalla Estates, the U.S. Forest Service Visitor's Center and Emerald Bay. No pets are allowed. Fees: $17 a night for tent campers (maximum of two tents and six people per site); up to $22 a night for RVers. Closed in winter. On Highway 89, two miles north of South Lake Tahoe.

**Comments:** Camp Richardson is popular and crowded, but it's arguably Tahoe's largest and most diverse family resort. The privately operated campground is located on flat terrain in scattered pine forest next to busy Highway 89, with little seclusion and minimal scenic appeal. But the extraordinary beaches and other recreational amenities make this a highly desirable location. Every conceivable type of water sport equipment is available for rent at the marina, including kayaking, waterskiing, jetskiing, parasailing, sailing and windsurfing. Charterboat fishing and sightseeing cruises are also possible. There's a roped-off swimming lagoon and a myriad of water toys for kids, along with four of Tahoe's most spectacular white sand beaches—Jameson, Baldwin, Kiva and Pope. A paved bike trail, an equestrian center, beach volleyball sites, and the historic estates at Tallac are next door. The Glen Alpine Trailhead into Desolation Wilderness is just up the road at Fallen Leaf Lake, and offers one of Tahoe's best day hikes. The Beacon Restaurant, on the beach, has excellent food and, with live music day and night, the best "vibes" on the lake. Camp Richardson is the closest marina to Emerald Bay; in fact, it's within easy kayaking distance.

**Information:** Richardson's Resort and Marina, (916) 541-1801 or (800) 544-1801.

### Lakeside Mobile Home and RV Park (Private)
*See number 24 on Lake Tahoe map, page 138*

**Amenities:** 43 sites (10 accommodating RVs up to 37 feet), full hookups, piped water, flush toilets, showers, cable TV, a laundry room, picnic tables, daily continental breakfast and swimming at a nearby private beach. Pets are allowed on a leash. Fee: $24.20. Open year-round. Located at 3987 Cedar Avenue, on the north side of US 50 in South Lake Tahoe (California side), three blocks from Stateline casinos and across from Crescent V Shopping Center and Raley's Supermarket.

**Comments:** This is the only RV park in the Stateline area. It is situated in a quieter motel area among mature pines two blocks off the main highway and 2.5 blocks from the lake. The park is convenient to casinos, restaurants, golf and shopping. Guests receive passes to a private beach at Lakeside Marina, with an array of water sports.

*Information:* Lakeside Mobile Home and RV Park, (916) 544-4704.

## Campground by the Lake (City of South Lake Tahoe)
*See number 25 on Lake Tahoe map, page 138*

*Amenities:* 172 sites (all suitable for RVs), piped water, showers, flush toilets, elevated barbecues, fire rings, picnic tables, a boat ramp and swimming at the lake. Pets are allowed on a leash. Fee: $16.50. Closed in winter. On US 50 in South Lake Tahoe, at South Lake Tahoe Recreation Area.

*Comments:* This is a beautifully maintained municipal campground ideally situated for RVs, although tent campers abound. It's close to the Stateline casinos, and next to bike trails, shoreline access and public bus/shuttle systems that travel throughout South Shore. Unlike the state parks, there is no extra charge for using showers. The campground is next to a large recreation complex with a heated pool, fitness center and senior center, although there are additional fees for using these facilities. Most sites are in the trees. Be forewarned: There is heavy traffic day and night on busy US 50.

*Information:* South Lake Tahoe Parks and Recreation Department, (916) 542-6096.

### Fallen Leaf (Forest Service Concession)
*See number 26 on Lake Tahoe map, page 138*

*Amenities:* 205 sites (130 suitable for RVs up to 40 feet), piped water, flush toilets, barbecues, fire rings and picnic tables. Pets are allowed on a leash. Fee: $14. Closed in winter. On Highway 89, one-quarter mile south of Camp Richardson and two miles north of South Lake Tahoe.

*Comments:* This flat campground, with moderate tree cover from scattered pines, is level and has good proximity to hiking trails. But it's a fair walk to the Tahoe shoreline, and it gets crowded, hot and dusty in midsummer. It is, however, on the road to Fallen Leaf Lake, an attractive place with fair fishing and small boating, and it is close to the trailheads for hiking and horseback riding into Desolation Wilderness. Unlike nearby Camp Richardson, most sites are well off Highway 89.

*Information:* Lake Tahoe Visitor Center, (916) 573-2674; reservations, (800) 280-CAMP.

### ★ Tahoe Valley (Private) ★
*See number 27 on Lake Tahoe map, page 138*

*Amenities:* 413 sites (301 accommodating RVs), full hookups, piped water, flush toilets, barbecues, fire rings, picnic tables, showers, a swimming pool, tennis courts, sport courts, a recreation hall, a convenience store, a visitors center, a casino and city bus service. Pets are allowed on a leash. Fee: $20-$27. Open April through October. On US 50 and C Street, at 1175 Melba Drive, South Lake Tahoe.

**Comments:** This is the most deluxe private campground in the Tahoe basin, with just about everything a camper (or even a non-camper) could want. It's a block off the main highway, on a flat location among tall pines. Sites are clean and spacious, and tent campers are as welcome as RVers. The Upper Truckee River is in back of the park, and the Factory Stores at the Y, South Shore's largest outlet center, is just next door. The park is close to two 18-hole golf courses, horseback riding and bicycle trails. It's five miles from Stateline, but it's regularly served by free casino shuttles and public buses. The campground is something of an oasis among residential and commercial development.

**Information:** Tahoe Valley, (916) 541-2222.

## Tahoe Pines (Private)
*See number 28 on Lake Tahoe map, page 138*

**Amenities:** 80 sites (50 suitable for RVs), piped water, flush toilets, showers, barbecues, a playground, fire rings, picnic tables and swimming in the lake. Pets are allowed on a leash. Fee: $19-$25. Closed in winter. At 860 US 50 in Tahoe Paradise, at the foot of Echo Summit.

**Comments:** There is nothing fancy about this place. The campground is considerably more rustic (and can be dusty from unpaved roads) than the KOA campground next door. Situated on the Upper Truckee River, it offers some swimming holes (with a private beach) when the river is flowing, and most sites are under tall pines. Noise from the busy highway can be intrusive.

**Information:** Tahoe Pines, (916) 577-1653.

## ★ KOA of South Lake Tahoe (Private) ★
*See number 29 on Lake Tahoe map, page 138*

**Amenities:** 60 sites (52 suitable for RVs up to 40 feet), full hookups, piped water, flush toilets, cable TV at some sites, picnic tables, showers, a laundry room, a recreation room, a general store, a disposal station and a swimming pool. Pets are allowed on a leash. Fees: $22-$28.50. Closed in winter. On US 50 at the bottom of Echo Pass, South Lake Tahoe.

**Comments:** This is a well-maintained campground, but it is subject to noise from busy US 50. Quieter and more secluded campsites (such as numbers 45 through 47) are off the road in the upper loop, which meanders through trees and is snuggled against a rocky hillside. The campground is located near the Upper Truckee River.

**Information:** KOA of South Lake Tahoe, (916) 577-3693.

# Truckee/Donner/
# Tahoe National Forest

### Cottonwood
### (U.S. Forest Service)

*See number 30 on Truckee/Donner map, page 152*

**Amenities:** 49 sites (28 accommodating RVs up to 35 feet), piped water, vault toilets, picnic tables and fire rings. The upper half of the campground is utilized as a group camp with a 125-person capacity. Fee: $10. Located 19.5 miles north of Truckee and 4.5 miles south of Sierraville adjacent to Highway 89, at elevation 5,800 feet.

**Comments:** Of the campgrounds along Highway 89 North, this is the nicest. It is nestled in trees next to Cottonwood Creek, it is set back from the highway somewhat, and it has an angler's trail along the creek and an overlook trail with views of the surrounding area. Sites are well dispersed, so there is no crowding. This campground is not as heavily used as it once was.

**Information:** Sierraville Ranger District, Tahoe National Forest, (916) 994-3401; reservations, (800) 280-CAMP.

### Cold Creek
### (U.S. Forest Service)

*See number 31 on Truckee/Donner map, page 152*

**Amenities:** 13 sites (some suitable for RVs up to 35 feet), piped water, vault toilets, picnic tables and fire rings. Fee: $10. On Highway 89 about 19 miles north of Truckee.

**Comments:** This campground is located next to Cold Stream, which provides some fishing for trout. It's also next to a busy highway, with little seclusion.

**Information:** Sierraville Ranger District, Tahoe National Forest, (916) 994-3401; reservations, (800) 280-CAMP.

### Bear Valley
### (U.S. Forest Service)

*See number 32 on Truckee/Donner map, page 152*

**Amenities:** 10 sites, piped water, picnic tables and fire rings. There is no fee. Six miles east of Little Truckee Summit on the Cottonwood Creek Road at elevation 6,700 feet.

**Comments:** A major forest fire burned through this area in 1994. The vault toilet and entry signs were destroyed, but these are scheduled for reconstruction. Restoration and timber harvesting projects will be ongoing throughout the area. The Bear Valley Loop Trail, an 18-mile, four-wheel-drive trail, is adjacent to the campground. The campground

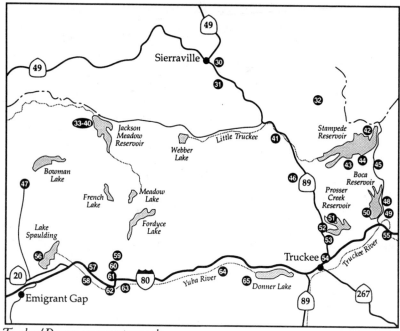

*Truckee/Donner area campgrounds*

## *Map References—Truckee/Donner area campgrounds*

and trail are still usable, but will be closed periodically during these projects.

*Information:* Sierraville Ranger District, Tahoe National Forest, (916) 994-3401.

## Jackson Meadows Reservoir Camps (U.S. Forest Service)

*See numbers 33-40 on Truckee/Donner map, page 152*

**Note:** The following Forest Service campgrounds are all in the Jackson Meadows area, which has a large, attractive lake with forested shoreline and is located 17 miles north of Truckee on Highway 89 and 16 miles west on Forest Service Road 07. Activities include boating, fishing, swimming, picnicking and hiking. There's a self-guided nature trail on the southwest side of the lake, and an RV dump station across from the information turnout. The Pacific Crest Trail runs through this area and is accessible near the East Meadow Campground. Elevation is 6,100 feet.

### Aspen Group Camp

*Amenities:* Two 25-person group camps, one 50-person group camp, picnic tables, piped water, vault toilets and central parking. Fees: $37.50 for the smaller sites, $75 for the large site. Available by reservation only. Next to the Aspen Picnic Site on the northeast shore of Jackson Meadows Reservoir.

*Comments:* Tree-shaded sites are well off the road, but near a swimming beach and a boat ramp. The adjacent parking areas are suitable for RVs, while tent camping is located within the campground. There's also a trail that leads to the lake.

*Information:* Sierraville Ranger District, Tahoe National Forest, (916) 994-3401; reservations, (800) 280-CAMP.

### East Meadow

*Amenities:* 46 sites (26 suitable for RVs), piped water, flush toilets, picnic tables and fire rings. Fee: $12. On the northeast shore of Jackson Meadows Reservoir, one mile off Forest Service Road 07 on paved access.

*Comments:* This is the most desirable campground on the east shore of the lake because of larger-than-normal sites, some lake views and flush toilets. It's located on a rise above the water. Extras include firewood for sale.

*Tip:* The best sites are 20, 23 and 24, which offer partial lake views, and sites 28 and 29, which combine to make a great two-family camping spot.

*Information:* Sierraville Ranger District, Tahoe National Forest, (916) 994-3401; reservations, (800) 280-CAMP.

## Findley

*Amenities:* 12 single-family sites, three two-family sites (some suitable for small RVs), piped water, flush toilets, picnic tables and fire rings. Fee: $11. On the west side of Jackson Meadows Reservoir, 2.5 miles across the dam on well-graded hardpack gravel road.

*Comments:* Situated on the reservoir's less-frequented west shore, this campground is worth the effort to reach it because of tree-shaded sites that are dispersed yet close to the shoreline.

*Information:* Sierraville Ranger District, Tahoe National Forest, (916) 994-3401; reservations, (800) 280-CAMP.

## Fir Top

*Amenities:* 11 single-family sites and one two-family site offer piped water, flush toilets, picnic tables and fire rings. Fee: $11. On the west side of Jackson Meadows Reservoir, across the dam.

*Comments:* See the comments for Findley Campground above— you'll find the same advantages here.

*Information:* Sierraville Ranger District, Tahoe National Forest, (916) 994-3401; reservations, (800) 280-CAMP.

## Jackson Point

*Amenities:* Boat-in only. 10 sites, vault toilets, picnic tables and fire rings. There is no water. Sites are free. On the forested shore of the reservoir one-half mile southwest of the Pass Creek boat ramp. There are no reservations; all camping is on a first-come, first-served basis.

*Comments:* Situated on a peninsula that juts out into the lake, this is a secluded and very scenic camping spot for tents. It's more exposed to afternoon winds than other campgrounds.

*Information:* Sierraville Ranger District, Tahoe National Forest, (916) 994-3401.

## Pass Creek

*Amenities:* 30 sites (15 suitable for RVs), piped water, flush toilets, picnic tables, fire rings with grills, a concrete boat launching ramp and a swimming beach at nearby Aspen Picnic Site. Fee: $12. On the northeastern shore of Jackson Meadows Reservoir.

*Comments:* This is well suited for campers with boats, due to the proximity of the boat ramp. But sites are small, located in dark, heavy forest on sloping hillsides, and are close together. There's an overflow campground just below the main campground on the road to the boat ramp, which has six sites with picnic tables and fire rings; the camping fee is $12.

*Information:* Sierraville Ranger District, Tahoe National Forest, (916) 994-3401; reservations, (800) 280-CAMP.

## Silver Tip Group

*Amenities:* Two 25-person walk-in sites (tent-camping), adjacent parking suitable for autos and RVs, picnic tables, barbecues, a campfire circle, piped water, vault toilets, central parking and access to a swimming beach at Woodcamp Picnic Site nearby. Fee: $37.50. Next to Woodcamp Campground on the southwest shore of Jackson Meadows Reservoir. Available by reservation only.

*Comments:* Of the two group camps here (the other is Aspen; see page 153), this one is better, due to its greater isolation on the scenic west shore, its spaciousness and its proximity to boat-launching, beaches, picnicking and hiking.

*Information:* Sierraville Ranger District, Tahoe National Forest, (916) 994-3401; reservations, (800) 280-CAMP.

## ★ Woodcamp ★

*Amenities:* 20 sites (10 suitable for RVs), piped water, flush toilets, picnic tables, fire rings with grills, a concrete boat launch and a swimming beach at nearby Woodcamp Picnic Site. Fee: $11. On the southwest shore of Jackson Meadows Reservoir, across the dam at the end of a well-graded gravel road.

*Comments:* This is arguably the best campground at the lake, largely because of its location to so many lakeside facilities. It is next to both the day-use site, which has the best swimming beach, and the Woodcamp Creek Interpretive Trail, a half-mile, self-guided trail with brochures available at the trailhead explaining some of the natural features of the area.

*Information:* Sierraville Ranger District, Tahoe National Forest, (916) 994-3401; reservations, (800) 280-CAMP.

## Lower Little Truckee (U.S. Forest Service)

*See number 41 on Truckee/Donner map, page 152*

*Amenities:* 15 sites (suitable for RVs up to 40 feet), piped water, vault toilets, picnic tables and fire rings. Fee: $10. Located 12 miles north of Truckee on Highway 89.

*Comments:* This campground is next to a busy highway, but it's nestled in trees adjacent to the Little Truckee River, which offers fishing and swimming opportunities. Cattle graze upstream and may pollute the river.

*Information:* Sierraville Ranger District, Tahoe National Forest, (916) 994-3401; reservations, (800) 280-CAMP.

## Davies Creek (U.S. Forest Service)
*See number 42 on Truckee/Donner map, page 152*

**Amenities:** 10 sites. There are no toilets, no campfire rings, no tables, and there is no water—in other words, it's basic dry camping. But it's free and is recommended for equestrian users. On the north shore of Stampede Reservoir. Drive to the end of Boca-Stampede Road, then head west for approximately one mile. Warning: This is a rough road and is not advised for large RVs.

**Comments:** This small campground is an open meadow between trees, but it has some shaded campsites. It's located about a half mile from the water, and there are good horseback riding opportunities north of the campground on a primitive dirt road.

**Information:** Truckee Ranger District, Tahoe National Forest, (916) 587-3558.

## Logger (U.S. Forest Service)
*See number 43 on Truckee/Donner map, page 152*

**Amenities:** 252 sites (all suitable for RVs up to 40 feet), piped water, chemical recirculating toilets, barbecues, fire rings, picnic tables, a waste dump station, and some sites and toilets with wheelchair access. Pets are allowed on a leash. Fee: $10.91, plus 10-percent local tax. Closed in winter. Exit Interstate 80 at Hirschdale, seven miles east of Truckee, and then drive eight miles north on Boca-Stampede Road.

**Comments:** Logger is nestled in a tree-shaded area on a rise over-looking Stampede Reservoir, which offers excellent fishing for kokanee salmon, as well as rainbow and brown trout. It is the most highly developed of the local Forest Service campgrounds, with paved roads and spurs. A launching ramp to Stampede is two miles west of here.

**Tip:** The best sites are at Iron Ox and Crosscut loops, which are closest to the lake. Because of the campground's size, it rarely fills up, making it an excellent choice for camping on holiday weekends.

**Information:** Truckee Ranger District, Tahoe National Forest, (916) 587-3558; reservations, (800) 280-CAMP.

## Emigrant Group Campground (U.S. Forest Service)
*See number 44 on Truckee/Donner map, page 152*

**Amenities:** Two 25-person group campsites and two 50-person campsites offer wheelchair-accessible camping as well as piped water, chemical recirculating toilets, picnic tables, fire rings, barbecues and a dump station. Fees: $35 for 25 people and $70 for 50 people, plus 10-percent local tax. The campground is tree-shaded and paved. East of Logger Campground off Boca-Stampede Road near the south shore of Stampede Reservoir, east of Truckee off Interstate 80.

*Comments:* This is one of the most popular group campgrounds in the region. It has paved roads and spurs, and is shaded with trees. Some groups return year after year, with fishing in Stampede for kokanee salmon the prime attraction. Book early, and try for a midweek date.

*Information:* Truckee Ranger District, Tahoe National Forest, (916) 587-3558; reservations, (800) 280-CAMP.

## Boyington Mill (U.S. Forest Service)
*See number 45 on Truckee/Donner map, page 152*

*Amenities:* 12 sites (all accommodating RVs), older vault toilets, barbecues, fire rings and picnic tables. There is no water. Pets are allowed on a leash. Fee: $8 per vehicle. Closed in winter. Off Interstate 80, 10 miles northeast of Truckee and two miles north of Boca Reservoir, on Boca-Stampede Road, midway between Boca and Stampede reservoirs.

*Comments:* This is an open, flat area in Little Truckee River Canyon on the Little Truckee River, with good fishing access and a somewhat cooler location than on Boca Reservoir. If the lake is down, this is a prettier place to camp.

*Information:* Truckee Ranger District, Tahoe National Forest, (916) 587-3558.

## Sagehen (U.S. Forest Service)
*See number 46 on Truckee/Donner map, page 152*

*Amenities:* 15 sites, older vault toilets, fire rings and nearby fishing. There is no water. There are no garbage containers, so pack it in and pack it out. The rough dirt access road is not recommended for large RVs. Pets are allowed on a leash. All sites are free. Closed in winter. Off Highway 89, 11 miles north of Truckee. Take the turnoff and follow signs six miles west to the campground.

*Comments:* This campground is well off the beaten path, and is popular as a wildlife-viewing area. It's located next to a large meadow, but campsites are tree-shrouded. It's close to Sagehen Creek, which harbors brook and brown trout. There's not a lot of heavy use in the summer, but fall brings hunters.

*Information:* Truckee Ranger District, Tahoe National Forest, (916) 587-3558.

## Fuller Lake (U.S. Forest Service)
*See number 47 on Truckee/Donner map, page 152*

*Amenities:* Nine tent sites, vault toilets, limited parking for trailers and cars in a paved lot, raised barbecue grills, picnic tables and fire pits. There is **no piped water** and no garbage containers. All sites are free. On Fuller Lake, four miles north of Highway 20 on Bowman Road and 3.5 miles west of the Interstate 80 intersection, about an hour's drive from

Truckee. The access road is a moderately rough dirt road one-quarter mile long and is best for trucks or four-wheel-drive vehicles. The elevation is 5,600 feet.

*Comments:* This is one of the jewels of Sierra camping, on a gorgeous, dam-filled little lake that is brimming with trout and is ideal for exploring in a canoe or rowboat. The best sites are right on the shore and are well shaded with pines. There's a day-use picnic area next to the campground. This is a tranquil, forested lake that is close to Grouse Lakes Trailhead, which is another seven miles up Bowman Road; it's also near to Lake Spaulding and the PG&E Sierra Discovery Trail, a self-guided nature area that meanders 0.8 miles through riparian wetlands next to Bear River. Note: The Forest Service may soon discontinue overnight camping here, so call ahead to check.

*Information:* Nevada City Ranger District, Tahoe National Forest, (916) 265-4538.

### Boca Rest (U.S. Forest Service)
*See number 48 on Truckee/Donner map, page 152*

*Amenities:* 29 sites (all accommodating RVs), piped water, older vault toilets, barbecues, fire rings and picnic tables. Pets are allowed on a leash. Fee: $8 per vehicle. Closed in winter. Off Interstate 80, 9.5 miles east of Truckee.

*Comments:* On the East Shore of the lake, this campground is at its best in late spring and early summer before the reservoir is drawn down; afterwards, it becomes hot and dusty.

*Information:* Truckee Ranger District, Tahoe National Forest, (916) 587-3558.

### Boca Springs (U.S. Forest Service)
*See number 49 on Truckee/Donner map, page 152*

*Amenities:* 16 sites (accommodating RVs, but there is a rough access road), a small group campground oriented to equestrian use, piped water, chemical toilets and fire rings. Fee: $8 per vehicle. In a canyon two miles east of Boca Reservoir off the Boca Springs Road, directly across from Boca Rest Campground.

*Comments:* This is an off-the-beaten-path campground with a rustic setting and some tree cover, near Boca Reservoir, a good fishing lake.

*Information:* Truckee Ranger District, Tahoe National Forest, (916) 587-3558.

### Boca (U.S. Forest Service)
*See number 50 on Truckee/Donner map, page 152*

*Amenities:* 30 primitive and dry sites (some accommodating RVs), vault toilets (one wheelchair accessible), picnic tables and fire pits. There is no water. Pets are allowed on a leash. Fee: $8 per vehicle. Closed in winter. On the west shore of Boca Reservoir off Interstate 80 at the Hirschdale exit, seven miles east of Truckee.

*Comments:* Nestled among some pines, sites are on a ridgetop overlooking the reservoir.

*Information:* Truckee Ranger District, Tahoe National Forest, (916) 587-3558.

## Lakeside (U.S. Forest Service)
*See number 51 on Truckee/Donner map, page 152*

*Amenities:* 30 undesignated and spaces for RVs, older vault toilets, some picnic tables, some barbecues and piped water (at the entrance to the campground). Pets are allowed on a leash. Fee: $8 per vehicle. Closed in winter. On the west shore of Prosser Creek Reservoir off Highway 89 on Prosser Recreation Access Road, north of Truckee.

*Comments:* This area has a few trees, but it is fairly unremarkable; it is worthwhile only when the lake is full. When Prosser Creek is drawn down, the area becomes hot, dusty and windy, and is not attractive.

*Information:* Truckee Ranger District, Tahoe National Forest, (916) 587-3558.

## Prosser (U.S. Forest Service)
*See number 52 on Truckee/Donner map, page 152*

*Amenities:* 29 sites (14 suitable for RVs), piped water, older vault toilets, barbecues, fire rings and picnic tables. Pets are allowed on a leash. Fee: $10. Closed in winter. Off Highway 89 on Prosser Recreation Access Road, two miles north of Truckee.

*Comments:* Located in a desolate area with sparse tree cover on a windy knoll overlooking the reservoir. When the lake is down, there is little to recommend this place. Geese and white pelicans are frequently seen on this side of the lake.

*Information:* Truckee Ranger District, Tahoe National Forest, (916) 587-3558.

## Prosser Group Campground (U.S. Forest Service)
*See number 53 on Truckee/Donner map, page 152*

*Amenities:* Group site accommodating a maximum of 50 people (RVs are okay), piped water, older vault toilets, large barbecue and picnic tables. Pets are allowed on a leash. Fee: $50 per night. Closed in winter. Off Highway 89 on Prosser Recreation Access Road, north of Truckee.

*Comments:* This campground has some tree cover, but its best asset is its proximity to the boat-launching ramp, which is just across the day-use parking lot.

*Information:* Truckee Ranger District, Tahoe National Forest, (916) 587-3558.

## Coachland (Private)

*See number 54 on Truckee/Donner map, page 152*

**Amenities:** 131 sites on 55 acres, full hookups, water, toilets, showers, sewage disposal, laundry, cable TV and some telephone connections. Fee: $22 a night, $133 a week, with about 25 sites reserved for short stays. At 10500 Highway 89 North at Interstate 80, Truckee.

**Comments:** This park, which is right off the freeway, is close to Prosser Creek Reservoir and Donner Lake, although there are no recreational amenities per se in the campground. Sites are nestled in the trees, but are subject to noise from both highways. This is a good spot for overnighters heading for other points in the region.

*Information:* Coachland, (916) 587-3071.

## United Trails (Private)

*See number 55 on Truckee/Donner map, page 152*

**Amenities:** 56 sites, full hookups, water, restrooms, showers, disposal, fishing, a spa, a general store and laundry. Fee: $20 (or $2 discount for Good Sam members who pay cash). On Interstate 80 at the Hirschdale exit, east of Truckee.

**Comments:** Conveniently located to Truckee and Reno, this full-service campground is near the highway and the Truckee River, and is geared to RVs.

*Information:* United Trails, (916) 587-8282.

## Lake Spaulding (PG&E)

*See number 56 on Truckee/Donner map, page 152*

**Amenities:** 25 campsites (some are walk-ins and suitable only for tents), tent spaces, five picnic areas, picnic tables, benches, fire grills, refuse containers, piped water, vault toilets, parking, fishing, swimming, a boat ramp, waterskiing and overflow camping. Fee: $10. In Tahoe National Forest about a 40-minute drive west of Truckee. Follow Interstate 80 to Highway 20; watch for the turnoff on the right.

**Comments:** This is an attractive, heavily forested campground that is near the main boat-launching ramp at this sprawling reservoir. Although sites are close together, they are well maintained, and include the luxury of brick barbecues. The campground is far enough away from the main highway to offer seclusion. One concern: Signs caution campers to "Beware of Rattlesnakes."

*Information:* PG&E Land Project, (916) 386-5164.

## Indian Springs (U.S. Forest Service)
*See number 57 on Truckee/Donner map, page 152*

*Amenities:* 35 campsites (some accommodating RVs), piped water, vault toilets, picnic tables and fire rings. Fee: $10. Sites are on a first-come, first-served basis. Take the Eagle Lakes exit off Interstate 80, about 30 minutes west of Truckee; turn north and drive one-half mile.

*Comments:* This is next to the South Fork of the Yuba River on the north side of Interstate 80, but noise from the freeway can be intrusive. Most sites are sheltered in heavy pine forest.

*Information:* Nevada City Ranger District, Tahoe National Forest, (916) 265-4538.

## Lodgepole (PG&E)
*See number 58 on Truckee/Donner map, page 152*

*Amenities:* 18 sites offer tent spaces, tables, benches, fire grills, refuse containers, water, restrooms, parking, fishing, swimming, boating, overflow camping and boat ramp nearby. Fee: $10. Located in the Tahoe National Forest. From Interstate 80, take the Yuba Gap exit to Lake Valley Reservoir.

*Information:* PG&E Land Project, (916) 386-5164.

## Lake Sterling (U.S. Forest Service)
*See number 59 on Truckee/Donner map, page 152*

*Amenities:* Six sites, vault toilets and fire rings. There is no water. Pack in and pack out—there are no garbage containers. There is no fee. Camping is on a first-come, first-served basis. Follow the directions to Woodchuck Campground, below, and proceed 3.5 miles past Woodchuck Campground to Lake Sterling. The access road to the campsites has been closed because of vehicular damage to the sites. All campers must hike in about one-quarter mile to reach the campsites. The elevation is 7,000 feet.

*Comments:* This is adjacent to Lake Sterling in a remote location, with hiking trails nearby.

*Information:* Nevada City Ranger District, Tahoe National Forest, (916) 265-4538.

## Upper Little Truckee (U.S. Forest Service)
*See number 60 on Truckee/Donner map, page 152*

*Amenities:* 26 campsites (15 suitable for RVs up to 40 feet), offer piped water, vault toilets, picnic tables and fire rings. Fee: $10. Located 12.5 miles north of Truckee on Highway 89.

*Comments:* This campground is spread out along a busy highway, but most sites are in the trees and adjoin the Little Truckee River, offering trout fishing and swimming. Cattle graze upstream and may pollute the river.

*Information:* Sierraville Ranger District, Tahoe National Forest, (916) 994-3401; reservations, (800) 280-CAMP.

## Woodchuck (U.S. Forest Service)
*See number 61 on Truckee/Donner map, page 152*

*Amenities:* Eight tent sites, some barbecues, picnic tables, vault toilets and limited parking. There is no water. Pack in and pack out—there are no garbage containers. There is no fee. Camping is on a first-come, first-served basis. Take the Cisco Grove exit off Interstate 80 and turn north. Turn left onto the frontage road after crossing over the freeway. Turn right, just before Thousand Trails, onto Rattlesnake Road. Proceed three miles to the campground.

*Comments:* This small campground is adjacent to Rattlesnake Creek at elevation 6,300 feet.

*Information:* Nevada City Ranger District, Tahoe National Forest, (916) 265-4538.

## Big Bend (U.S. Forest Service)
*See number 62 on Truckee/Donner map, page 152*

*Amenities:* 15 sites (some suitable for small RVs), picnic tables, barbecues, vault toilets, piped water, ample parking, a picnic area with two tables and one fire ring. Fee: $10. There are no reservations. From eastbound Interstate 80, take the Big Bend exit and continue east one-quarter mile to the campground. From westbound Interstate 80, take the Rainbow Road exit and continue west for 1.5 miles to the campground.

*Comments:* This campground has easy access from the freeway, but intrusive noise from traffic. There are nice wooded campsites next to the South Fork of the Yuba River behind the Big Bend Visitor Center and Museum. A real plus is its proximity to the trailhead for Loch Leven Lakes, a series of three glacial tarns that are scenic and wonderful for swimming. The campground also is near Rainbow Lodge and its excellent restaurant.

*Information:* Nevada City Ranger District, Tahoe National Forest, (916) 265-4538.

## Hampshire Rocks (U.S. Forest Service)
*See number 63 on Truckee/Donner map, page 152*

*Amenities:* 31 sites (some suitable for RVs), picnic tables, barbecues, vault toilets, piped water and limited parking. Fee: $10. Sites are on a first-come, first-served basis. Take the Rainbow Road exit off Interstate 80. The campground is off a frontage road on the south side of the freeway.

**Comments:** This is a lovely campground with heavily wooded sites, but noise from the freeway is intrusive. On the plus side, it's close to the Loch Leven Lakes Trailhead, a highly recommended route to beautiful backcountry lakes, and to Rainbow Lodge, which has an excellent restaurant if you tire of barbecued weenies. The sites are adjacent to the South Fork of the Yuba River.

**Information:** Nevada City Ranger District, Tahoe National Forest, (916) 265-4538; reservations, (800) 280-CAMP.

## Kidd Lake Campground (PG&E)
*See number 64 on Truckee/Donner map, page 152*

**Amenities:** Group sites here can accommodate up to 100 people, with tent and RV spaces, tables, benches, fire grills, refuse containers, water, restrooms, parking, fishing, swimming and boating. Fee: $15. Take the Soda Springs exit on Interstate 80. Turn right on Soda Springs Road and head 0.8 miles to Pohatsi Road, then turn west and continue to the end of the pavement. Follow signs for another 2.8 miles to the campground. The elevation is 6,750 feet.

**Comments:** This is an excellent group campground with paved roads and spurs, and enough tree cover for shade. Its viability depends on the water level at Kidd Lake, which can be drawn down substantially in mid- to late summer. There's a good hiking trail nearby. The access road can be bumpy for big rigs, and is somewhat difficult to find.

**Information:** PG&E Land Project, (916) 386-5164.

## Serene Lakes Lodge & RV Park (Private)
*See number 65 on Truckee/Donner map, page 152*

**Amenities:** 10 undeveloped campsites (three with electrical hookups), hot showers, restrooms, a restaurant, a bar, a beach, volleyball, swimming, fishing, horseshoes, hiking, biking, canoeing and sailing. Pack in and pack out—there are no garbage containers. Fee: $10. Open year-round. Reservations recommended. On the Donner Summit at 1100 Soda Springs Road. Take the Soda Springs/Norden exit from Interstate 80. Turn right on Soda Springs Road and follow it to the end of the pavement.

**Comments:** This is a rustic, weathered resort, but it has lots of charm. The mirror-smooth lakes, great for paddling and fishing (electric motors are allowed), are surrounded by pines and cabins, and there are hiking trails nearby. For kids, there's plenty to do—there's even a video arcade and game room in the lodge. The campground is well away from busy highways, although it is not exactly isolated since it is at the end of a residential area in Soda Springs. It's close to Painted Rock, Palisade Creek and Lower Lola Montez hiking trails.

**Information:** Serene Lakes Lodge & RV Park, (916) 426-9001.

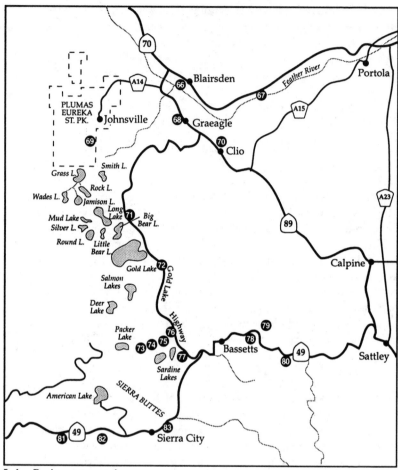

*Lakes Basin campgrounds*

## Map References—Lakes Basin campgrounds

66. Little Bear RV Park—p. 165
67. Feather River RV Park—p. 165
68. Movin' West Trailer Camp—p. 166
69. Plumas Eureka State Park—p. 166
70. Clio's River Edge Trailer Resort
    —p. 167
71. Lakes Basin—p. 167
72. Snag Lake —p. 167
73. Berger—p. 168
74. Packsaddle Camping Area—p. 168

75. Diablo Camping Area—p. 168
76. Salmon Creek—p. 169
77. Sardine—p. 169
78. Sierra—p. 170
79. Chapman Creek—p. 170
80. Yuba Pass—p. 170
81. Union Flat—p. 171
82. Loganville—p. 171
83. Wild Plum—p. 171

# Lakes Basin

## Little Bear RV Park (Private)

*See number 66 on Lakes Basin map, page 164*

*Amenities:* 95 sites, 80 with full hookups, 10 with water and electricity only, and five that are dry. No tents are allowed. Facilities include picnic tables, satellite TV, fire rings, laundry, a shower room, toilets, a club room, horseshoes, shuffleboard, ping pong, swings and a small market. Open April 1 to November 1, weather permitting. Reservations are accepted up to one year in advance. Fee: $17 to $20 a night; $126 to $133 weekly, double occupancy, with $3 for extra persons (5 and older). At 102 Little Bear Road in Blairsden.

*Comments:* This destination camping park managed by owners Don and Sue Frisk is adjacent to the Middle Fork of the Feather River, and is within a five-minute drive of the area's four golf courses. In fact, just across the street is the nine-hole Feather River Golf Course. Although quiet time begins at 10 p.m., no one mentioned that to the trains, which roar through the Feather River canyon tooting their horns at all hours of the night. Most sites are shaded, and there are two common lawn areas.

*Information:* Little Bear RV Park, (916) 836-2774.

## ★ Feather River RV Park ★ (Private)

*See number 67 on Lakes Basin map, page 164*

*Amenities:* 99 spaces, 30 with full hookups (for rigs up to 40 feet), 35 with no hookups (for tents and self-contained RVs), and 28 pull-throughs. Facilities include flush toilets, hot showers, dump station, laundry, public phones, a grocery store, ice, picnic tables, fire rings, firewood, a recreation room, a video game room, pool tables, a heated swimming pool, a "tot lot" playground and areas for horseshoes, volleyball and badminton. There are tables at each site and a common large picnic area. Fees: $15 to $18, with a maximum restriction of four adults per site. Extra adults, $3 apiece; extra children, $2 apiece. Pets are accepted with no extra charge. The season is May 1 through September 30. Advance reservations accepted and guaranteed. At 71326 Highway 70, six miles east of Blairsden.

*Comments:* This Good Sam-approved park, a former KOA with impressive recreation facilities, is the only campground in the region where tent campers can make advance reservations or be accepted (most local public campgrounds are on a first-come, first-served basis). While other Mohawk Valley private RV parks cater to retirees, this one caters to families with children. Most sites are situated in the trees. The park is not close to the Feather River, but it is within easy driving distance (10 minutes). Owners McClenn and Alta Sly are personable and accommodating.

*Information:* Feather River RV Park, (916) 836-2183.

## ★ Movin' West Trailer Camp ★ (Private)

*See number 68 on Lakes Basin map, page 164*

**Amenities:** 47 sites for RVs up to 40 feet, full hookups, showers, cable TV, picnic tables, fire pits, a bath house, a grassy picnic area, a dump station and a horseshoe area. A group area is available with a large barbecue pit. Fee: $18.81, plus tax, or $127.06 a week, double occupancy. Open May 1 through October. Reservations strongly advised. At 305 Johnsville Road in Graeagle.

**Comments:** Tucked within tall pine trees, this is the only campground located right in the center of Graeagle. It is next to the nine-hole Feather River Park Golf Course, and within a brief walk of shops and restaurants. A short drive will take you to the Lakes Basin hiking trails and the historic Plumas Eureka State Park. The park is enormously popular, and is often booked months in advance. It is owned and operated by Ron Madden.

**Information:** Movin' West Trailer Camp, (916) 836-2614.

## ★ Plumas Eureka State Park ★ (California State Parks)

*See number 69 on Lakes Basin map, page 164*

**Amenities:** 67 sites (many suitable for RVs), free hot showers, picnic tables, barbecues, food lockers, piped drinking water, restrooms, laundry tubs, hiking trails, lakes and a mining history museum. Camping is on a first-come, first-served basis. Fees: $12 to $14, depending on season; an extra vehicle is $5; dogs are $1; and there are discounts for seniors. Dogs must be on leashes only and are not permitted on hiking trails, except the U.S. Forest Service trail to Grass Lake. Located five miles west of Graeagle in Johnsville.

**Comments:** This inviting, secluded campground is well off the main highway and is nestled in a heavily wooded area. It has impressive views of high, surrounding peaks, four hiking trails to high- and low-elevation lakes and to lofty Eureka Peak, and an excellent museum on mining history at the park entrance. The park is close to the Middle Fork of the Feather River and four golf courses, as well as the spectacular Lakes Basin region. The only unfortunate aspect is that this park is the only one of the Sierra region parks that is not on the reservation system, making it difficult for campers to try "pot luck" after a long drive. Most times it's easy to get a spot in the middle of the week, however.

**Information:** Plumas Eureka State Park, (916) 836-2380.

## ★ Clio's River Edge Trailer Resort ★ (Private)

*See number 70 on Lakes Basin map, page 164*

*Amenities:* 210 sites for RVs only (40-foot maximum length), full hookups, some telephones, some picnic tables, a bathhouse with tiled hot showers, restrooms with flush toilets, cable TV, patios, fire rings, firewood and laundry. Recreation on the grounds includes badminton, horseshoes and volleyball. The season is from May 1 through October 31. Fee: $20 a night, $118.35 a week. Advance reservations accepted for the same year only. Located 3.5 miles south of Graeagle at 3754 Highway 89 in Clio.

*Comments:* This park, a favorite with retirees who stay for a month or more, is next to the Middle Fork of the Feather River, and it's the largest campground in eastern Plumas County. Only RVs are permitted; tents are forbidden. The park is close to golf courses and hiking trails. Sixty percent of the spaces are among the trees, and all sites are paved. Twenty overnight sites have picnic tables.

*Information:* Clio's River Edge Trailer Resort, P.O. Box 111, Clio, CA 96106; (916) 836-2375.

## Lakes Basin (U.S. Forest Service)

*See number 71 on Lakes Basin map, page 164*

*Amenities:* 24 sites (some suitable for RVs), picnic tables, elevated barbecues, fire pits, vault toilets, hand-pumped water and a group campground. Off Highway 89, eight miles south of Graeagle on Gold Lake Highway; the elevation is 6,400 feet.

*Comments:* This is a nice, forested venue that is located well off the highway. The trailhead for Long Lake originates here, and the campground is two miles northwest of the Gold Lake boat ramp.

*Special note:* This campground is **closed during 1995** for rehabilitation.

*Information:* Mohawk Ranger Station, Plumas National Forest, (916) 836-2575.

## Snag Lake (U.S. Forest Service)

*See number 72 on Lakes Basin map, page 164*

*Amenities:* 16 undesignated sites (some suitable for small trailers), vault toilets and fire rings. There is no water. There are no fees. Camping is on a first-come, first-served basis. Five miles north of Bassetts on Gold Lake Highway next to Snag Lake, at elevation 6,600 feet.

*Comments:* This is an attractive, small lake, but the sites, though located among pines, are right on the highway and the area is subjected to strong afternoon winds. Fishing is fair to good, and small boats, such as canoes and rowboats, can be launched from the shoreline. Boat rentals are available at Salmon Lake Lodge.

*Information:* North Yuba Ranger Station, Tahoe National Forest, (916) 288-3231.

## Berger (U.S. Forest Service)
*See number 73 on Lakes Basin map, page 164*

*Amenities:* 10 undesignated sites (some suitable for small trailers), vault toilets, primitive fire pits and some picnic tables. There is no water. There are no fees and no reservations. Two miles west of Gold Lake Highway on the Packer Lake Road, at elevation 5,900 feet.

*Comments:* Most sites are in shaded areas, and the campground has a creek flowing through it.

*Information:* North Yuba Ranger Station, Tahoe National Forest, (916) 288-3231.

## Packsaddle Camping Area (U.S. Forest Service)
*See number 74 on Lakes Basin map, page 164*

*Amenities:* 14 undeveloped sites (some suitable for RVs), new vault toilets, picnic tables, fire rings, a corral and ample parking for pack and saddle stock. There is no piped water (although it is close to a stream). Fee: $6. Camping is on a first-come, first-served basis. Located 2.5 miles west of Gold Lake Highway on Packer Lake Road, at elevation 6,000 feet.

*Comments:* This campground was designed for equestrian use, with plenty of room for horse trailers. It was recently upgraded. There's a multi-use trail to Deer Lake (about 3.5 miles from here), and the campground is close to the Tamarack Lakes Trailhead to the Sierra Buttes, as well as to Packer and Sardine lakes.

*Information:* North Yuba Ranger Station, Tahoe National Forest, (916) 288-3231.

## Diablo Camping Area (U.S. Forest Service)
*See number 75 on Lakes Basin map, page 164*

*Amenities:* Roughly 20 undesignated sites, one vault toilet, picnic tables and fire pits. There is no piped water. All sites are free. Camping is on a first-come, first-served basis. Located 1.5 miles west of Gold Lake Highway on Packer Lake Road, at elevation 5,800 feet.

*Comments:* This is a rustic but not unattractive camping area, with most sites set among the trees. It is close to Packer and Sardine lakes and popular trailheads in the shadow of the Sierra Buttes. There's a short but rough dirt entryway from the road.

*Information:* North Yuba Ranger Station, Tahoe National Forest, (916) 288-3231.

## Salmon Creek (U.S. Forest Service)
*See number 76 on Lakes Basin map, page 164*

***Amenities:*** 32 sites (seven suitable for RVs), piped water, vault toilets, picnic tables, stone fire pits and metal barbecues. There is room for RVs off the paved access road. Fee: $8. Camping is on a first-come, first-served basis. Two miles north of Bassetts on Gold Lake Highway near Salmon Creek.

***Comments:*** This is an excellent venue among scattered evergreens and aspens. The campground is on an open, elongated site next to a creek and meadow, and a short trail leads to Sand Pond and other hiking trails. There is close proximity to Sardine Lake and to high-country trailheads, including those to the Sierra Buttes.

***Tip:*** The most desirable sites are on the west side of the paved road and along the creek: numbers 16 through 29. The most secluded site is 33.

***Information:*** North Yuba Ranger Station, Tahoe National Forest, (916) 288-3231.

## ★ Sardine Lake ★ (U.S. Forest Service)
*See number 77 on Lakes Basin map, page 164*

***Amenities:*** 23 sites (18 suitable for RVs up to 30 feet), piped water, barbecues, picnic tables, fire pits, new vault toilets, wash basins, a fish-cleaning station, a swimming pond with beach, wheelchair-accessible sites and a self-guided nature trail. Camping is on a first-come, first-served basis. Fee: $8. Located 1.5 miles north of Bassetts on Gold Lake Highway, and one-half mile southwest on Sardine Lake Road. The elevation is 5,800 feet.

***Comments:*** Of the available Forest Service campgrounds near the Lakes Basin, this is the best, with close proximity to the spectacular Sardine Lakes, among the jewels of the Sierra. The sites were recently upgraded with the latest conveniences, and most sites are under pine trees. Nearby is a delightful swimming hole—Sand Pond, which is warm and shallow (about seven feet deep), but there is no lifeguard on duty. The campground is close to good hiking trails, including one to the Sierra Buttes, the most prominent peak in the region. Boat rentals and fishing are available at Sardine Lake Resort, which also has one of the area's top restaurants and the most magnificent view of any lodge in the area.

***Tip:*** Best site is 13.

***Information:*** North Yuba Ranger Station, Tahoe National Forest, (916) 288-3231.

## Sierra (U.S. Forest Service)
*See number 78 on Lakes Basin map, page 164*

*Amenities:* 15 sites (seven suitable for RVs), vault toilets, picnic tables and fire rings. There is no water. There are no fees. Camping is on a first-come, first-served basis. Seven miles northeast of Sierra City on Highway 49 on the North Fork of the Yuba River.

*Comments:* This campground is next to the river, but also next to the highway. Sites right on the river are the best ones.

*Information:* North Yuba Ranger Station, Tahoe National Forest, (916) 288-3231.

## Chapman Creek (U.S. Forest Service)
*See number 79 on Lakes Basin map, page 164*

*Amenities:* 27 sites (most suitable for RVs), metal fire rings, piped water, vault toilets, picnic tables and barbecues. Fee: $8. Camping is on a first-come, first-served basis. Located eight miles northeast of Sierra City across Highway 49 from the North Fork of the Yuba River.

*Comments:* This is perhaps the nicest campground in the Yuba Pass area. Sites are set among the trees, with a large meadow in the middle. There's a nice hiking trail along Chapman Creek, and a trail to Haskell Peak is nearby. This is not a heavily used campground, and it frequently has sites available on weekends and holidays.

*Tip:* The best sites, numbering in the 20s, are next to the meadow. They are also the quietest.

*Information:* North Yuba Ranger Station, Tahoe National Forest, (916) 288-3231.

## Yuba Pass (U.S. Forest Service)
*See number 80 on Lakes Basin map, page 164*

*Amenities:* 20 sites (nine suitable for RVs to 30 feet), piped water (purify before drinking), vault toilets, picnic tables and metal fire rings. Fee: $8. Camping is on a first-come, first-served basis. On Highway 49, 11 miles west of Sierraville at Yuba Pass Summit.

*Comments:* Sites are in an old-growth red fir stand bordering the headwaters of the North Fork of the Yuba River, next to a large meadow that attracts deer.

*Tips:* The best, most spacious sites are 3, 4, 7-9 and 18, which are next to the meadow.

*Information:* North Yuba Ranger Station, Tahoe National Forest, (916) 288-3231.

## Union Flat (U.S. Forest Service)
*See number 81 on Lakes Basin map, page 164*

*Amenities:* 13 sites (six suitable for RVs), piped water, vault toilets (one wheelchair accessible), fire rings and barbecues. Fee: $8. Camping is on a first-come, first-served basis. Six miles east of Downieville on the North Fork of the Yuba River on Highway 49, at elevation 3,400 feet.

*Comments:* Gold panning and dredging are the main attractions at this campground next to the river.

*Information:* North Yuba Ranger Station, Tahoe National Forest, (916) 288-3231.

## Loganville (U.S. Forest Service)
*See number 82 on Lakes Basin map, page 164*

*Amenities:* 18 sites (four suitable for RVs), picnic tables, fire rings and vault toilets but no water. Fee: $8. Camping is on a first-come, first-served basis. Two miles west of Sierra City on the North Fork of the Yuba River on Highway 49, at elevation 4,200 feet.

*Comments:* This is a little-used campground near Sierra County Historic Park and the Kentucky Mine Museum. Sites are among oak and young pine trees. RVs should stick to the lower loop; the upper sites are not advisable for large vehicles. Fishing is possible in the river.

*Information:* North Yuba Ranger Station, Tahoe National Forest, (916) 288-3231.

## Wild Plum (U.S. Forest Service)
*See number 83 on Lakes Basin map, page 164*

*Amenities:* 47 sites (21 suitable for RVs up to 30 feet), piped water, vault toilets, barbecues and fire rings. Fee: $8. Camping is on a first-come, first-served basis. One mile east of Sierra City on the Wild Plum Road along Haypress Creek, off Highway 49, at elevation 4,400 feet.

*Comments:* Sites here are under large mature trees next to Haypress Creek. There is good proximity to the Wild Plum Trail, the Pacific Crest Trail, the Kentucky Mine Museum and Sierra City's restaurants and shops. Swimming, fishing and gold-panning are available in the creek. This is a popular campground, with a spectacular view of the Sierra Buttes and within easy range of the Lakes Basin area.

*Tip:* The best sites in the three loops are next to the creek.

*Information:* North Yuba Ranger Station, Tahoe National Forest, (916) 288-3231.

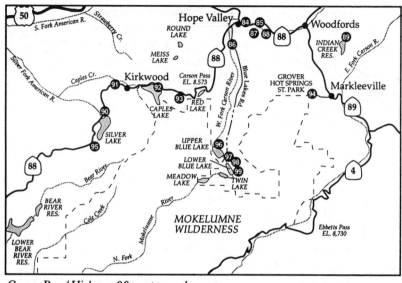

*Carson Pass / Highway 88 campgrounds*

## Map References—Carson Pass / Highway 88 campgrounds

◆

# Carson Pass/Highway 88

## Kit Carson Campground
## (Forest Service Concession)

*See number 84 on Carson Pass / Highway 88 map, above*

**Amenities:** 12 units offer vault toilets, picnic tables, water and fire pits. Fee: $7. Camping is on a first-come, first-served basis. Golden Age and Golden Access Passports honored. Closed in winter. On Highway 88 east of the Highway 89 junction.

**Comments:** This is a small, wooded campground next to a busy road, but it's close to fishing in the West Fork of the Carson River.

**Information:** Carson Ranger District, Toiyabe National Forest, (702) 882-2766.

## Snowshoe Springs (Forest Service Concession)
*See number 85 on Carson Pass/Highway 88 map, page 172*

**Amenities:** 13 units offer water, picnic tables and fire pits. Fee: $7. Camping is on a first-come, first-served basis. Golden Age and Golden Access Passports honored. On Highway 88, two miles east of the junction with Highway 89.

**Comments:** This is a small campground next to a busy highway and the West Fork of the Carson River, in a spectacular canyon setting. It's close to Sorensen's Resort, Indian Valley Reservoir, Markleeville and Grover Hot Springs State Park.

**Information:** Carson Ranger District, Toiyabe National Forest, (702) 882-2766.

## Hope Valley (Forest Service Concession)
*See number 86 on Carson Pass/Highway 88 map, page 172*

**Amenities:** 20 sites (suitable for tents and RVs), drinking water, vault toilets, picnic tables, fire pits, limited wheelchair access, and close proximity to a store and a restaurant. Fee: $7. Reservations accepted. Golden Age and Golden Access Passports honored. Open June through September. On Blue Lakes Road in Toiyabe National Forest, near the Highway 88/89 junction in Hope Valley, 14 miles south of South Lake Tahoe.

**Comments:** This is a nice, wooded campground in scenic Hope Valley, near the region's spectacular meadow and close to the West Fork of the Carson River, a good fishery in early summer. Historic Sorensen's Resort, with a restaurant and small store, is nearby, and the popular boating and fishing mecca of Blue Lakes is 11 miles south.

**Information:** Carson Ranger District, Toiyabe National Forest, (702) 882-2766; reservations, (800) 280-CAMP.

## Hope Valley RV Park (Private)
*See number 87 on Carson Pass/Highway 88 map, page 172*

**Amenities:** 13 sites for RVs, full hookups, showers, flush toilets, water and phone. Pets are permitted. Fee: $18. Reservations accepted. On Highway 88 about two miles east of the junction with Highway 89, in Hope Valley.

**Comments:** This is right on a busy highway, but it's located in a spectacular canyon next to the West Fork of the Carson River. It's a good location for hiking, fishing and visiting Grover Hot Springs State Park.

**Information:** Hope Valley RV Park, (916) 694-2292.

## Crystal Springs (Forest Service Concession)
*See number 88 on Carson Pass/Highway 88 map, page 172*

**Amenities:** 22 sites offer picnic tables, water, vault toilets and fire pits. Fee: $7. Camping is on a first-come, first-served basis. Golden Age and Golden Access Passports honored. Closed in winter. On Highway 88, four miles east of Highway 89 junction.

**Comments:** This is next to a busy highway, adjacent to the West Fork of the Carson River. Nearby is Indian Valley Reservoir, a great flyfishing lake, and Grover Hot Springs State Park, with its relaxing mineral pools.

**Information:** Carson Ranger District, Toiyabe National Forest, (702) 882-2766.

## Indian Creek Campground (Bureau of Land Management)
*See number 89 on Carson Pass/Highway 88 map, page 172*

**Amenities:** 29 units offer group sites, a dump station, showers, water, flush toilets, a boat ramp and swimming. Fee: $6-$8. Closed in winter. Camping is on a first-come, first-served basis. Four miles off Highway 4, just south of the Highway 88 turnoff at Woodfords.

**Comments:** This is a clean, pleasant campground with lots of conveniences set in moderate tree cover next to Indian Valley Reservoir. For flyfishing and float-tubing, this is an excellent trout fishery. The campground is close to historic Markleeville and Grover Hot Springs State Park.

**Information:** Carson City District, BLM, (702) 885-6000.

## ★ Silver Lake, East ★ (U.S. Forest Service) ★ Silver Lake, West ★ (PG&E)
*See number 90 on Carson Pass/Highway 88 map, page 172*

**Amenities:** The East Campground has 62 units and the West has 35 units (most suitable for RVs). They offer piped water, vault toilets, picnic tables, barbecues, fire pits, overflow vehicle parking, boat rentals and a store nearby. Fee: $9 East, $10 West. West sites are first come, first served. At Silver Lake, 32 miles southwest of South Lake Tahoe on Highway 88. In Silver Lake East, sites 3, 5, 6, 8, 9, 16, 17, 20, 29, 34, 39, 44, 45, 46, 53, 55 and 56 may be reserved. The elevation is 7,200 feet.

**Comments:** Of the two campgrounds, which are located across the highway from each other, the East side has the more spacious and centrally located sites. There's a trail from here to Kit Carson Lodge (with its store, a restaurant and boat rentals), and to the east end of Silver Lake, which has some pretty coves, beaches and a small island. Nearby options include horseback riding, hiking and fishing, though afternoon winds can be strong. Both campgrounds are well situated in thick forest. The West Campground has access to the American River. A nice nearby hiking trail goes to Shealor Lakes, a short jaunt with good swimmin' hole possibilities.

*Tip:* The best sites in the East Campground are 46, 55 and 57. The best sites in the West Campground are 75 and 76.

*Information:* For the East Campground—Amador Ranger District, Eldorado National Forest, (209) 295-4251. For the West Campground— PG&E Land Projects, (916) 386-5164; reservations, (800) 280-CAMP.

## Kirkwood Lake (U.S. Forest Service)
*See number 91 on Carson Pass/Highway 88 map, page 172*

*Amenities:* 12 sites (best for tents), piped water, vault toilets, picnic tables, barbecues, fire pit and pay telephone. Fee: $8. Camping is on a first-come, first-served basis. Located 28 miles southwest of South Lake Tahoe on Highway 88, and one-half mile west of turnoff to Kirkwood Ski Resort. Trailers are not advisable due to a narrow road access. No motor boats, no swimming or washing are allowed in the lake. The elevation is 7,600 feet.

*Comments:* This is a beautiful, small campground on an equally beautiful, small lake, one-half mile off the highway down a steep, paved road. Sites are in a "rock garden" close together among moderate pine cover. The bouldered lake offers fishing and canoeing, and many recreation amenities are nearby, including Kirkwood, riding stables, and hiking and cycling trails. This is a wonderful, idyllic retreat for tent campers.

*Information:* Amador Ranger District, Eldorado National Forest, (209) 295-4251.

## Caples Lake (U.S. Forest Service)
*See number 92 on Carson Pass/Highway 88 map, page 172*

*Amenities:* 35 units (many suitable for RVs), piped water, vault toilets, picnic tables, barbecues, fire pits and access to a boat ramp, boat rentals, mountain bike rentals, a convenience store and a restaurant. Fee: $9. Camping is on a first-come, first-served basis. Located 26 miles south of South Lake Tahoe on Highway 88. The elevation is 7,800 feet.

*Comments:* This is a great camping location on the Carson Pass for many activities, including hiking, fishing, boating and mountain biking. Sites are generally small, mostly set among the trees and nestled against a hillside. Some are beside a busy highway. Caples Lake and its namesake resort are directly across the road, offering supplies and fishing boat rentals. The lake has good fishing for trout, and spectacular vistas of magnificent Round Top (elevation 10,380 feet) and Thimble (elevation 9,827 feet) peaks. If you're tired of camp food, Caples Lake Resort has an excellent gourmet restaurant. The area is near good hiking trails to Emigrant, Round Top and Winnemucca lakes, and a mountain bike route over Schneider Cow Camp to US 50 at Echo Pass.

*Tip:* The best sites are 25 and 26, located at the end of a cul-de-sac against a granite rock wall.

*Information:* Amador Ranger District, Eldorado National Forest, (209) 295-4251.

## ★ Woods Lake ★ (U.S. Forest Service)
*See number 93 on Carson Pass/Highway 88 map, page 172*

*Amenities:* 25 sites (a few suitable for RVs, but most for tents), piped water, vault toilets, picnic tables, eight picnic sites adjacent to the lake, barbecues and fire pits. Fee: $8 ($16 for one multiple unit). Camping is on a first-come, first-served basis. Two miles south of Highway 88 near Carson Pass. No motor boats allowed. The elevation is 8,200 feet.

*Comments:* This is the highest and, some might argue, the prettiest of the Carson Pass public campgrounds. It is well off the road in a secluded, beautifully forested valley next to a picturesque jewel of a lake that offers paddling and swimming. Campsites are well dispersed, meander around hills and depressions, and are mostly in shade. Trailheads originate here to Round, Winnemucca and Fourth of July lakes, and a spectacular though strenuous hike can be made to the summit of Round Top Peak (elevation 10,380 feet). There's a large picnic area with shallow, sandy lake access for wading. The location is very popular with day users, including picnickers and hikers. The small parking lot fills quickly on weekends.

*Information:* Amador Ranger District, Eldorado National Forest, (209) 295-4251.

## ★ Grover Hot Springs State Park ★ (California State Parks)
*See number 94 on Carson Pass/Highway 88 map, page 172*

*Amenities:* 76 sites (many suitable for RVs), showers, water, flush toilets, picnic tables, barbecues, fire pits, a phone, swimming, natural hot springs, a fishing pond and self-guided nature trails. Fee: $14. Reservations accepted. Open year-round. On Hot Springs Road, six miles west of Markleeville.

*Comments:* This is one of the finest state-run campgrounds in the region, made more attractive by its proximity to the natural hot springs pools (0.3 miles away). Sites are well-dispersed, off paved access roads and mostly under pine trees, close to attractive meadows and a hiking trail to Burnside Lake. Sparkling clear night skies make for excellent stargazing. The hot springs offer 102- to 104-degree Fahrenheit soaks. Visits cost $4 for adults, $2 for children, and represent a great tonic for sore hiking muscles. There is excellent trout fishing at nearby Indian Valley Reservoir, as well as early season river rafting on the East Fork of the Carson River.

*Information:* Grover Hot Springs State Park, (916) 694-2248; reservations, (800) 444-PARK.

## Plasse's Resort (Private)

*See number 95 on Carson Pass/Highway 88 map, page 172*

*Amenities:* 60 sites, showers, piped water, flush and pit toilets, phones, an equestrian camping area, riding stables for backcountry trips, a store, a bar and a restaurant. Pets are permitted. Fees: $16 for weekends, $14 for weekdays (Sunday through Thursday). Reservations accepted. Open June to October. On Highway 88, on the west end of Silver Lake at Plasse's turnoff.

*Comments:* Dusty but scenic campsites are close to the lake and to historic Plasse's Resort, where there is a store, a restaurant, a bar and a post office. The resort has been run by the same family for 150 years. Equestrian routes from here follow the spectacular Mormon-Emigrant Trail to the back side of Kirkwood Ski Resort, with many striking vistas. A good restaurant serving dinner on the weekends and a lively bar (often full of buckaroos) make this an interesting place to camp. Most sites are in moderate tree cover and meander on rough roads over rocky terrain. Kids love this place and there are many repeat campers. It is ideal for people with horses.

*Information:* Plasse's Resort, (209) 258-8814 (seasonal).

## Blue Lake, Upper (PG&E)

*See number 96 on Carson Pass/Highway 88 map, page 172*

*Amenities:* 32 units (most suitable for RVs) in a clean campground with paved roads and spurs, piped water, vault toilets, picnic tables, barbecues, fire pits and a boat-launch area. Fee: $10, plus $3 for each additional vehicle and a small charge for pets. Camping is on a first-come, first-served basis. Located 1.3 miles past Upper Blue Lake Dam Campground. The elevation is 8,200 feet.

*Comments:* This is the nicest of the campgrounds in the Blue Lakes area, with recently upgraded facilities, though access roads are unpaved and dusty. There is moderate tree cover, and the campground is close to Lost Lakes, which are accessible via a four-wheel-drive vehicle or a short hike. Upper Blue Lake is the largest of the Blue lakes, and is a popular and crowded area.

*Tip:* The best sites are 8 and 12, which are large and well shaded.

*Information:* PG&E Land Projects, (916) 386-5164.

## Blue Lake Dam, Upper (PG&E)

*See number 97 on Carson Pass/Highway 88 map, page 172*

*Amenities:* 25 units, piped water, vault toilets, picnic tables, barbecues, fire pits, fishing and boating. Fee: $10, plus $3 for each additional vehicle and a small charge for pets. Camping is on a first-come, first-served basis. At Blue Lakes, one-quarter mile beyond Middle Creek Campground. The elevation is 8,200 feet.

*Comments:* There are nice campsites here in a moderately shaded area. The campground is near the trailhead to Grouse and Granite lakes, as well as four-wheel-drive roads to other nearby fishing lakes, including Tamarack, upper and lower Sunset, Summit, Twin and Meadow. These lakes may be drawn down substantially by late summer.

*Information:* PG&E Land Projects, (916) 386-5164.

## Middle Creek/Blue Lakes (PG&E)

*See number 98 on Carson Pass/Highway 88 map, page 172*

*Amenities:* Five units (some suitable for RVs), vault toilets, piped water, picnic tables, barbecues and fire pits. Fee: $10, plus $3 for each additional vehicle and a small charge for pets. Camping is on a first-come, first-served basis. The elevation is 8,200 feet.

*Comments:* This is a small unit sandwiched between the larger campgrounds at popular Blue Lakes, a favorite boating and fishing destination.

*Information:* PG&E Land Projects, (916) 386-5164.

## Blue Lake, Lower (PG&E)

*See number 99 on Carson Pass/Highway 88 map, page 172*

*Amenities:* 16 units (most suitable for RVs), piped water, vault toilets, picnic tables, barbecues, fire pits, fishing and boating. Fee: $10, plus $3 for each additional vehicle and a small charge for pets. Camping is on a first-come, first-served basis. Take Blue Lakes Road 6.6 miles east of Carson Pass or 2.5 miles west of Highway 89/88 junction for 12 miles. The elevation is 8,100 feet.

*Comments:* This is best for camping in early to midsummer when the Blue Lakes are at their fullest. Sites are in moderate forest cover, with most fairly close to the shoreline. There's a long and dusty dirt/gravel access road from Highway 88. Good fishing opportunities abound in this popular and crowded area.

*Information:* PG&E Land Projects, (916) 386-5164.

# Crystal Basin

## Northshore RV/Loon Lake (U.S. Forest Service)
*See number 100 on Crystal Basin map, page 180*

*Amenities:* 15 sites for self-contained vehicles, vault toilets, wheel-chair-accessible units. There is no water, no fee and reservations are not accepted. Tents are okay. On the north shore of Loon Lake, across from the main campground. The elevation is 6,500 feet.

*Comments:* This is the best free RV campground in the region, with a commanding, lofty view of Loon Lake and spectacular Rockbound Valley in Desolation Wilderness. There are paved access roads and spurs. This is an open area on a high ridge, with few trees, and is subject to afternoon winds. But it's a picturesque spot for watching sunsets and sunrises and, as might be expected, it's popular. Note: Some tent campers find undesignated sites nearby in small stands of pine.

*Information:* Camino Information Center, Eldorado National Forest, (916) 644-6048.

## Pleasant/Loon Lake (U.S. Forest Service)
*See number 101 on Crystal Basin map, page 180*

*Amenities:* 10 tent sites offer access by boat or trail only, with vault toilets, stream water (purify before drinking) and fire pits. There is no fee. On the northeast shore of Loon Lake. The distance from the boat ramp is 2.5 to three miles. The elevation is 6,500 feet.

*Comments:* This has similar attractions as Loon Lake Campground, described on page 179.

*Information:* Camino Information Center, Eldorado National Forest, (916) 644-6048.

## Loon Lake (U.S. Forest Service)
*See number 102 on Crystal Basin map, page 180*

*Amenities:* 53 designated sites (many suitable for RVs), two wheel-chair-accessible units, a large parking lot for overflow campers, piped water, picnic tables, fire rings, barbecues, vault toilets, boat ramp and 18 picnic units. Fee: $9. On the south shore of Loon Lake Reservoir, 29 miles north of US 50 via the Ice House and Loon Lake roads. The elevation is 6,500 feet, the highest among Crystal Basin campgrounds.

*Comments:* This excellent campground is flanked on the east by spectacular Rockbound Valley, a range of huge granite massifs. The sprawling reservoir has an irregular, rocky shoreline. The campground is well-positioned for long day hikes or overnight pack trips into the less-crowded portion of Desolation Wilderness, via the Loon Lake Trailhead. Tree cover is more sparse than at lower lakes, sites are rockier and closer

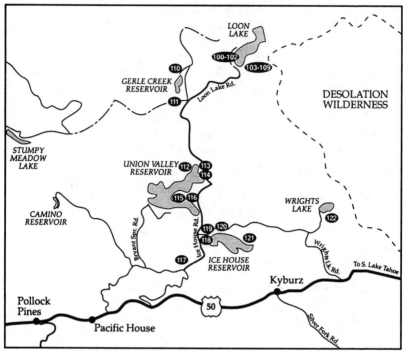

*Crystal Basin campgrounds*

## Map References—Crystal Basin campgrounds

100. Northshore RV/Loon Lake—p. 179
101. Pleasant/Loon Lake—p. 179
102. Loon Lake—p. 179
103. Loon Lake Boat Ramp—p. 181
104. Red Fir Group Camp/Loon Lake —p. 181
105. Loon Lake Group Camp #1—p. 181
106. Loon Lake Group Camp #2—p. 182
107. Loon Lake Equestrian —p. 182
108. Loon Lake Equestrian Group Camp—p. 182
109. Gerle Creek—p. 182
110. South Fork—p. 183

111. Yellowjacket—p. 183
112. Wench Creek—p. 183
113. Wench Creek Group Camp—p. 184
114. Fashoda Tent —p. 184
115. Sunset—p. 184
116. Silver Creek—p. 185
117. Robb's Valley Resort—p. 185
118. Jones Fork—p. 185
119. Northwind—p. 185
120. Ice House—p. 186
121. Strawberry Point—p. 186
122. Wrights Lake—p. 186

together, and the area is subject to strong afternoon winds. Occasionally there is good fishing for trout, but the lake is busy with waterskiers and pleasure boaters. A nice picnic area with tables overlooks the water near the boat ramp. Spectacular sunsets bathe Rockbound Valley, especially McConnell (elevation 9,099 feet) and Silver (elevation 8,930 feet) peaks. Reservations may be made for sites 1-17 from May 27 through September 11.

*Tip:* The best sites are 32 and 33, on a high embankment with gorgeous lake views.

*Information:* Camino Information Center, Eldorado National Forest, (916) 644-6048; reservations, (800) 280-CAMP.

## Loon Lake Boat Ramp (U.S. Forest Service)
*See number 103 on Crystal Basin map, page 180*

*Amenities:* 10 sites for self-contained RVs, vault toilets, wheelchair-accessible units. There is no water. No campfires are allowed. Fee: $5. At Loon Lake, next to the boat ramp.

*Comments:* This is basically an overflow camping area, and not a bad one at that. The lot is often lined with rigs shoulder to shoulder.

*Information:* Camino Information Center, Eldorado National Forest, (916) 644-6048.

## Red Fir Group Camp/Loon Lake (U.S. Forest Service)
*See number 104 on Crystal Basin map, page 180*

*Amenities:* A group site for up to 25 people and six vehicles, vault toilets, piped water, picnic tables, fire pits and barbecues. Fee: $35. Reservations are required. At Loon Lake Dam. The elevation is 6,500 feet.

*Information:* This is a better-than-average group campground with close proximity to the lake, though without the lake views enjoyed by other campsites.

*Information:* Camino Information Center, Eldorado National Forest, (916) 644-6048; reservations, (800) 280-CAMP.

## Loon Lake Group Camp #1 (U.S. Forest Service)
*See number 105 on Crystal Basin map, page 180*

*Amenities:* 10 sites for walk-in tent camping (up to 50 people), vault toilets, piped water, fire pits, barbecues and picnic tables. Fee: $50. Reservations are required. The elevation is 6,500 feet.

*Comments:* This has similar attractions as Loon Lake Campground, described above.

*Information:* Camino Information Center, Eldorado National Forest, (916) 644-6048; reservations, (800) 280-CAMP.

## Loon Lake Group Camp #2 (U.S. Forest Service)
*See number 106 on Crystal Basin map, page 180*

**Amenities:** Six sites (up to 25 people), one wheelchair-accessible site, vault toilets, piped water, picnic tables, fire pits and barbecues. Fee: $40. Reservations are required. The elevation is 6,500 feet.

**Comments:** This has similar attractions as Loon Lake Campground, described on page 179.

**Information:** Camino Information Center, Eldorado National Forest, (916) 644-6048; reservations, (800) 280-CAMP.

## Loon Lake Equestrian (U.S. Forest Service)
*See number 107 on Crystal Basin map, page 180*

**Amenities:** Nine sites, piped water, vault toilets and picnic tables. Fee: $7. Reservations may be made for sites E6-E9. The elevation is 6,500 feet.

**Comments:** This is a good staging area for independent campers bringing their horses for trips into Desolation Wilderness.

**Information:** Camino Information Center, Eldorado National Forest, (916) 644-6048; reservations, (800) 280-CAMP.

## Loon Lake Equestrian Group Camp
## (U.S. Forest Service)
*See number 108 on Crystal Basin map, page 180*

**Amenities:** Sites for up to 25 people, piped water, vault toilets and picnic tables. Fee: $35. Reservations are required. The elevation is 6,500 feet.

**Comments:** This is a large horse camping area for groups, not far from other facilities but away from the lake.

**Information:** Camino Information Center, Eldorado National Forest, (916) 644-6048; reservations, (800) 280-CAMP.

## Gerle Creek (U.S. Forest Service)
*See number 109 on Crystal Basin map, page 180*

**Amenities:** 60 sites (some suitable for RVs), piped water, vault toilets, fire pits, barbecues, tables, four picnic units, a self-guided nature trail along the creek, and a paved, wheelchair-accessible trail. Fee: $8. On Gerle Creek Reservoir, 27 miles north of US 50 via Ice House Road. No motorboats allowed. The elevation is 5,300 feet.

**Comments:** Although the campground is unspectacular, with closely spaced sites, the reservoir is a wondrous playground for swimmers, paddlers and float-tube flyfishers. It has a spectacular mountain setting, a large rocky island within swimming distance, and a self-sustaining population of brown trout. The area is popular with day users because of access to warm, shallow water. It has a fishing pier and several strategic picnic spots with rocky outcroppings that invite sunbathers. This is an excellent family venue for lazing in a raft or canoe, since the lake isn't too large. It has interesting coves and a sloping, forested shoreline. Reservations may be made for sites 1, 3-8 and 33-50 from May 27 through September 11.

*Information:* Camino Information Center, Eldorado National Forest, (916) 644-6048; reservations, (800) 280-CAMP.

### South Fork (U.S. Forest Service)
*See number 110 on Crystal Basin map, page 180*

*Amenities:* 17 sites (some suitable for RVs), vault toilets, picnic tables, barbecues, fire pits and stream water (purify before drinking). There is no fee. Located 23 miles north of US 50 via Ice House Road. Elevation: 5,200 feet.

*Comments:* Sites have some tree cover, but they are mostly dusty and dry. However, the campground is not far from the South Fork of the Rubicon River. Access is on a dirt road. There are two or three decent sites.

*Information:* Camino Information Center, Eldorado National Forest, (916) 644-6048.

### Yellowjacket (U.S. Forest Service)
*See number 111 on Crystal Basin map, page 180*

*Amenities:* 40 sites (most suitable for RVs), a boat ramp, piped water, vault and flush toilets, picnic tables, barbecues and fire pits. Fee: $8. On the north shore of Union Valley Reservoir two miles off Ice House Road and 19.5 miles north of US 50. Sites 1-19 may be reserved late May through mid-September. The elevation is 4,900 feet.

*Comments:* This is heavily wooded campground similar to Sunset. There are a few sites with glimpses of the lake.

*Tip:* The best site is 20, with a view of the lake.

*Information:* Camino Information Center, Eldorado National Forest, (916) 644-6048; reservations, (800) 280-CAMP.

### Wench Creek (U.S. Forest Service)
*See number 112 on Crystal Basin map, page 180*

*Amenities:* 100 sites (many suitable for RVs), piped water, flush and vault toilets, picnic tables, barbecues and fire pits. Fee: $8. No reservations are accepted. On the east shore of Union Valley Reservoir, about 15 miles north of US 50 via Ice House Road. The elevation is 4,900 feet.

*Comments:* This campground has sparse to moderate tree cover, with lots of forest debris. If you haven't got a reservation elsewhere in Crystal Basin during a popular weekend, this is the place to try.

*Tip:* The best sites are 70 and 71, which have lake views, and sites 79, 80 and 81.

*Information:* Camino Information Center, Eldorado National Forest, (916) 644-6048.

## Wench Creek Group Camp (U.S. Forest Service)
*See number 113 on Crystal Basin map, page 180*

*Amenities:* Two group sites suitable for RVs (up to 50 people each), piped water, flush and vault toilets, picnic tables, barbecues and fire pits. Fee: $50. May be reserved May 27 through October 1. On the east shore of Union Valley Reservoir. The elevation is 4,900 feet.

*Comments:* When the lake level is up, this is a decent location for several families or two large groups.

*Information:* Camino Information Center, Eldorado National Forest, (916) 644-6048; reservations, (800) 280-CAMP.

## Fashoda Tent (U.S. Forest Service)
*See number 114 on Crystal Basin map, page 180*

*Amenities:* 30 walk-in sites (one is wheelchair accessible), piped water, vault toilets, fire pits, a large parking area and five picnic units. Fee: $8. Camping is on a first-come, first-served basis. On the peninsula at Union Valley Reservoir, 14 miles north of US 50 via Ice House Road. The elevation is 4,900 feet.

*Comments:* Sites here are located in pine forest, with several situated right on the beach. There's a good launching point for canoes and other small boats. The area is shared with day users.

*Information:* Camino Information Center, Eldorado National Forest, (916) 644-6048.

## Sunset (U.S. Forest Service)
*See number 115 on Crystal Basin map, page 180*

*Amenities:* 131 sites (many suitable for RVs), piped water, vault toilets, picnic tables, fire pits, barbecues, picnic area, swimming beach, boat ramp and sanitary dump station. Fee: $10; $15 for double sites. On the peninsula at Union Valley Reservoir, 14 miles north of US 50 via Ice House Road. A cafe and store are within five miles. The elevation is 4,900 feet.

*Comments:* This is the largest campground in Crystal Basin, with most sites set in heavy forest and some affording lake views. Reservations can be made for May 27 through September 11 for sites 19-25, 27-31, 33-36, 52-55, 57-63, 65, 72-75, 78-80, 99-111, 122-131 and double units 26, 32, 51, 56, 76 and 77.

*Tip:* The best sites are 51 (double unit) on a wooded hill with a view of the lake, 74 for a large family, also with a view, and most of sites 81-

111. Sites 112-131 are closer together and less desirable. Sites 1-36 are spacious, but have no lake views.

*Information:* Camino Information Center, Eldorado National Forest, (916) 644-6048; reservations, (800) 280-CAMP.

## Silver Creek (U.S. Forest Service)
*See number 116 on Crystal Basin map, page 180*

*Amenities:* 11 tent sites, vault toilets, fire rings and stream water (purify before drinking). There is no fee. Next to Silver Creek, seven miles north of US 50 via Ice House Road, near Ice House Resort. The elevation is 5,200 feet.

*Comments:* There is moderate tree cover here, but the access is on a rough dirt road, and the sites are not close to water.

*Information:* Camino Information Center, Eldorado National Forest, (916) 644-6048.

## Robb's Valley Resort (Private)
*See number 117 on Crystal Basin map, page 180*

*Amenities:* 28 sites (most suitable for RVs), piped water, barbecues, fire pits, flush toilets, pay showers, a convenience store, a restaurant and a bar. Fee: $8 (1994). On Ice House Road, between Ice House and Union Valley reservoirs, 21 miles north of US 50.

*Comments:* This campground is moderately tree-shaded but dusty. It offers several "extras," including a rustic bar with bearskins on the walls. This place has no telephone number, no address and no way to make advance reservations. It's sort of a take-your-chance operation, but if the other campgrounds are full, you may find a spot here.

*Information:* There is no phone number for information.

## Jones Fork (U.S. Forest Service)
*See number 118 on Crystal Basin map, page 180*

*Amenities:* 10 sites (some suitable for RVs), vault toilets, tables and fire pits. There is no water. There are no fees. Camping is on a first-come, first-served basis. Off Ice House Road near the Jones Fork of Silver Creek near Union Valley Reservoir. The elevation is 4,900 feet.

*Comments:* You can see the lake from here, but there is no lake frontage.

*Information:* Camino Information Center, Eldorado National Forest, (916) 644-6048.

## Northwind (U.S. Forest Service)
*See number 119 on Crystal Basin map, page 180*

*Amenities:* 10 sites for self-contained vehicles, vault toilets, wheelchair access, picnic tables and barbecues. There is no water. Tents are okay. There is no fee. On the north shore of Ice House Reservoir. The elevation is 5,500 feet.

**Comments:** This is a nice, wooded area on a high point overlooking the reservoir, but there isn't much seclusion. In fact, sites are close together and crowded.

**Information:** Camino Information Center, Eldorado National Forest, (916) 644-6048.

## Ice House (U.S. Forest Service)
*See number 120 on Crystal Basin map, page 180*

**Amenities:** 83 sites (most suitable for medium to large RVs), some double units, three wheelchair-accessible units, piped water, vault toilets, picnic tables, fire rings, elevated barbecues, a picnic area, boat ramp and sanitary dump station. Fee: $10 ($15 for double units). At Ice House Reservoir, three miles from Union Valley Reservoir and 1.5 miles north of US 50 via Ice House Road. The elevation is 5,500 feet.

**Comments:** This is one of the most attractive and popular campgrounds in Crystal Basin. Sites are spacious, shaded and nestled among towering, old-growth pines. Several are close to the lake, where there's a shallow cove ideal for hand-launching small boats or for swimming. Some sites offer relative seclusion for tent campers. The campground is close to Ice House Resort, where there's gas, a large general store, a restaurant, ice and showers. Reservations may be made from May 27 through October 15 for Lower Loop sites 21-38, Upper Loop sites 50, 52, 55, 57, 61, 63, 67, 68, 70, 71, 75, 77, 78, 80-83, and double units 51, 58 and 73.

**Information:** Camino Information Center, Eldorado National Forest, (916) 644-6048; reservations, (800) 280-CAMP.

## Strawberry Point (U.S. Forest Service)
*See number 121 on Crystal Basin map, page 180*

**Amenities:** 10 sites for self-contained vehicles, vault toilets. There is no water. Tents are okay. There is no fee. On the north shore of Ice House Reservoir. The elevation is 5,200 feet.

**Comments:** This is a windy, high camping point with a narrow paved access road that is usually crowded with large RVs. Other than a view of the lake, it isn't aesthetically pleasing here. It's close to a small boat-launching area.

**Information:** Camino Information Center, Eldorado National Forest, (916) 644-6048.

## ★ Wrights Lake ★ (U.S. Forest Service)
*See number 122 on Crystal Basin map, page 180*

**Amenities:** 70 sites (20 for tents only, a half dozen for walk-ins, the rest for RVs), piped water, vault toilets, picnic tables, barbecues, fire pits,

10 picnic units, trails to Desolation Wilderness and a free horse camp nearby. Fee: $10. Reservations required from July to early September. No motor boats are allowed. Located 34 miles east of Placerville and eight miles north of US 50 at Wrights Lake Road. The elevation is 7,000 feet.

*Comments:* For those who enjoy hiking, fishing and non-motorized boating, this is the finest campground in Eldorado National Forest, and one of the finest in the Sierra. Its many features include excellent, tree-shaded sites; separate loops that give tent campers their own area, if they wish; a stunningly beautiful natural lake dotted with rocky islets; warm shallow areas for swimming; a green freshwater marsh with a creek channel that is wonderful for canoeing; an adjoining lake, Dark Lake, that is a kind of Golden Pond for float-tube flyfishers; and a half-dozen high-country trails to some of the most spectacular lakes in Desolation Wilderness, most reachable on day hikes. A large wooded picnic area has magnificent vistas of the lake and Sierra peaks. There are a number of cabins available at both Wrights and Dark lakes. This is the closest lake in Crystal Basin to Lake Tahoe, but it is the most off the beaten path. Still, the lake is extremely popular and booked well in advance.

*Tip:* The best tent sites are 17 and 18, which are more spacious than the others, and the best RV sites are 25 and 26, which are on a corner of a loop, are extra large, and are nearest to the lake. This is one of the few campgrounds for which you can reserve specific sites—a big advantage for those who know the area.

*Information:* Camino Information Center, Eldorado National Forest, (916) 644-6048; reservations, (800) 280-CAMP.

# Reno/Carson

## ★ Boomtown RV Park ★ (Private)
*See number 123 on Reno/Carson Valley map, page 188*

*Amenities:* 200 spaces, full hookups, a swimming pool, two spas, private showers, 24-hour security, cable TV, video rentals, a 24-hour mini-mart, fuel, a casino and a children's arcade. Fee: $14.50-$15.50. On Interstate 80, seven miles west of Reno at Garson exit.

*Comments:* This is a wide-open campground sequestered in rolling hills, but it's part of the mini theme park of Boomtown and it's within 10 minutes of the strip in Reno. A merry-go-round, indoor miniature golf, video thrill rides and other goodies are there to attract youngsters. The building has an Old West-style facade.

*Information:* Boomtown Hotel Casino, P.O. Box 399, Verdi, NV; (702) 345-6000 or (800) 648-3790.

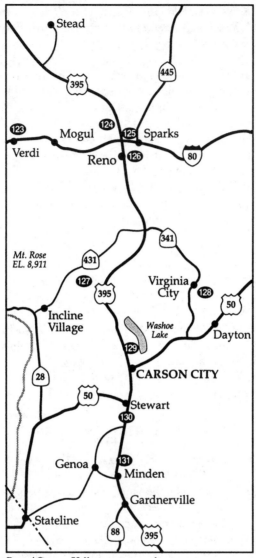

*Reno / Carson Valley campgrounds*

## Map References—Reno / Carson Valley campgrounds

123. Boomtown RV Park—p. 187
124. Shamrock RV Park—p. 189
125. River's Edge RV Park—p. 189
126. Reno Hilton RV Park—p. 189
127. Davis Creek County Park—p. 190
128. Virginia City RV Park—p. 190
129. Washoe Lake State Park—p. 190
130. Comstock Country RV Resort—p. 191
131. Carson Valley RV Resort—p. 191

## Shamrock RV Park (Private)
*See number 124 on Reno/Carson Valley map, page 188*

**Amenities:** 121 sites, full hookups, some cable TV, a heated swimming pool, laundry, showers, a store, a dump station and a shuttle to downtown Reno. No tents allowed. Fees: $20 to $22. At 260 Parr Avenue at intersection with North Virginia Street, Reno, Nevada.

**Comments:** This park is in the open desert on blacktop a bit north of the strip (2.5 miles, to be exact), and is well away from the hubbub of the central business district. The park has a large picnic area and strictly controls access (no rigs older than 1978) and noise (no loud music). This park is highly rated and very clean, and has strong repeat business. It is a Good Sam park.

**Information:** Shamrock RV Park, (702) 329-5222.

## River's Edge RV Park (Private)
*See number 125 on Reno/Carson Valley map, page 188*

**Amenities:** 164 sites, full hookups, swimming pool, laundry, showers, propane, a dump station and shuttle service to downtown Reno/Sparks casinos. Fee: $18.36. At 1405 South Rock Boulevard, Sparks, Nevada, off exit 17 from Interstate 80.

**Comments:** This park is situated next to the Truckee River, close to cycling and hiking trails, and near golf courses. It is AAA-approved and is a Good Sam park.

**Information:** River's Edge RV Park, (702) 358-8533.

## Reno Hilton RV Park (Private)
*See number 126 on Reno/Carson Valley map, page 188*

**Amenities:** 264 RV sites, full hookups, a swimming pool, spas, laundry, bathrooms, showers, shows, a store and a dump station. No tents are allowed. Fees: $10 to $25, depending on season. At 2500 East Second Street, Reno, Nevada.

**Comments:** There aren't any aesthetics here; this campground is pretty much in the open. It's adjacent to the Reno Hilton, which has restaurants, live entertainment, a kids' fun center, shopping mall, bowling center and movie theatre. Ah, but there's one big attraction: Campers can bring their pets, and there's a dog walking area for Fido to hang around while his owner is pulling on the one-armed bandits.

**Information:** Reno Hilton RV Park, (702) 789-2129 or (800) 648-5080.

## Davis Creek County Park
## (Washoe County Parks and Recreation Department)
*See number 127 on Reno/Carson Valley map, page 188*

**Amenities:** 63 tent and trailer sites, two group camping sites (maximum of 100 persons; tents only), restrooms, showers, fishing, drinking water, a picnic/barbecue area, volleyball, winter ice skating area, a three-acre pond, a dump station, hiking trails and nature displays. Open year-round. Fee: $10. No reservations except for group camps, which must be reserved in advance. Off US 395 against Slide Mountain on the eastern slope of the Sierra, south of Reno.

**Comments:** This is a large camping area with beautiful facilities, with sites under sparse pine trees in a high-desert setting. Campfires are not allowed. It is located next to the Ophir Creek Trailhead, which offers a six-mile, one-way hike to Tahoe Meadows on the Mount Rose Summit. There is easy access to and from the freeway.

**Information:** Washoe County Parks, (702) 849-0684.

## ★ Virginia City RV Park ★ (Private)
*See number 128 on Reno/Carson Valley map, page 188*

**Amenities:** 50 paved sites (all suitable for RVs), full hookups, piped water, flush toilets, showers, laundry, a market/gift shop and picnic tables. Pets are allowed on leashes only. Fee: $16.50 to $19.50, depending on season. Open year-round. In Virginia City, Nevada, three blocks north of the central business district.

**Comments:** This is the only RV park in this historic mining town. It is within walking distance of shops, museums and restaurants. It is AAA-approved and a Good Sam park.

**Information:** Virginia City RV Park, (702) 847-0999.

## Washoe Lake State Park
## (Nevada State Parks)
*See number 129 on Reno/Carson Valley map, page 188*

**Amenities:** 49 sites (all suitable for RVs), piped water, flush toilets, showers, barbecues, fire rings, picnic tables, telephones, hiking, a boat launch, group picnic grounds, a dump station, a grassy shaded picnic area and an equestrian area. Pets are allowed on leashes only. Fee: $7. Open year-round. Off US 395 north of Carson City on State Route 428.

**Comments:** The lake is full again after a long drought, and this makes Washoe a highly desirable camping area. There's a pleasant wildness about this place, with the high-desert sage, occasional elm trees and frequent animal and birdlife (including dear and coyotes). The area is a favorite for hang-gliding pilots and mountain bikers. Although most campsites are in open sage country (and quite hot in summer), the first loop has cabanas over the picnic tables—a nice touch. The day-use area has huge shade trees and a well-manicured lawn with picnic facilities. Washoe is close to the museums and restaurants of Carson City, and not far from the silver mining district of Virginia City.

*Information:* Washoe Lake State Park, (702) 687-4319.

## ★ Comstock Country RV Resort ★ (Private)

*See number 130 on Reno / Carson Valley map, page 188*

*Amenities:* 153 RV and tent sites, piped water, cable TV, flush toilets, showers, laundry, store, dump station, tennis courts, horseshoe pits, picnic tables, swimming pool, basketball court, volleyball court and spas. Pets are allowed with restrictions. Fees: $18 to $20. Open year-round. At 5400 South Carson Street (US 395), Carson City, Nevada.

*Comments:* This campground at the south end of Nevada's state capital is clean and well managed, and there's a popular restaurant (Bodine's) within a short walk. Lake Tahoe is just 20 minutes over the hill, and a unique railroad museum is a mile north.

*Information:* Comstock Country RV Resort, (702) 882-2445.

## ★ Carson Valley RV Resort ★ (Private)

*See number 131 on Reno / Carson Valley map, page 188*

*Amenities:* 70 sites, full hookups, spas, cable TV, laundry, showers, a dump station, a general store and gas and diesel fuel. It's adjacent to the Carson Valley Inn, which has two restaurants, three lounges, a casino, free nightly entertainment, a children's fun center, banquet rooms and a wedding chapel. Fee: $14.40, plus tax. At 1639 US 395 in downtown Minden, Nevada.

*Comments:* This is in an open, grassy area within short walking distance of the casino complex. The park has paved access roads and pads, as well as a lawn area for each site. One advantage is that the main hotel has a day-care center for young children, and campers have complete access to the hotel spa deck with its two hot tubs.

*Information:* Carson Valley RV Resort, (702) 782-9711 or (800) 321-6983.

*Camping and boating make perfect companions at Union Valley Reservoir at Crystal Basin Recreation Area.*

**Previous page:** *A hiker pauses at a mountain pool along Horsetail Falls, a popular attraction off Highway 50.*

**This page, top:** *Camp Richardson, near South Lake Tahoe, offers a fine beach and a variety of family recreation opportunities.*

**Left:** *Horseback riding, such as this excursion in Eldorado National Forest, provides riders with many sweeping vistas.*

**At right:** *Railroad buffs can actually drive a famous diesel locomotive at this unique outdoor museum in Portola, north of Truckee.*

**Below:** *Snowmobilers are rewarded with this lofty view of northern Lake Tahoe from 8,424-foot Mount Watson.*

**Top:** Some 150 balloons rising in unison create Reno's most colorful spectacle, the annual Hot Air Balloon Races in September.

**Left:** Sugar Bowl, one of Tahoe's oldest ski resorts, offers challenging runs and spectacular views of Donner Summit from Mount Judah.

**Opposite Page:** Dogsled rides in Hope Valley, off Highway 88 south of Lake Tahoe, are a regular attraction in winter.

**Top:** *Guided ocean kayak tours from Camp Richardson to Emerald Bay provide scenic shoreline vistas.*

**Bottom:** *The Resort at Squaw Creek offers ice skating and luxurious accommodations near the base of the Squaw Valley ski area.*

**Top:** *Edgewood Country Club, the premier golf course at Lake Tahoe, offers wooded and lakeside vistas.*

**Right:** *Mountain biking on the Flume Trail, Tahoe's most famous cycling route, provides thrills and bird's-eye views of the lake.*

**Next page:** *Float-tube flyfishing is the best way to entice spunky trout in Tahoe's high-elevation lakes.*

# Chapter 8

# Bike Trails
# & Parks

## ★ Author's Choice ★

### *Top 5 Paved Trails*

### *Top 5 Mountain Bike Trails*

On any given summer day, it seems as if half the visitors in Lake Tahoe are pedaling and puffing. With paved cycling trails bordering much of the lake, and with some of the country's most captivating mountain bike routes, Tahoe has become a cycler's paradise. Perhaps the signature trail in the basin, one that is among the world's most dramatic, is the Flume Trail, a single-track route that is notched into the side of plunging cliffs on the eastern shoreline high above the lake (see page 206). If you traveled no other path in the entire region, you would have done one of the all-time great treks in cycling.

But there is a cornucopia of delightful two-wheel outings throughout the basin and, as the region develops a collective approach to signage and trail management, Tahoe could well become the alpine cycling Mecca of the West Coast. Even now, the number and variety of trails are substantial, and they accommodate a range of abilities, from easy-going sightseers with children to hard-core pedalers with Camelback water slings. Some of the local visionaries would like to see a paved trail circling all 72 miles of the lake, and that may well happen within the next five years.

As for venturing into the backcountry, there are hundreds of miles of Forest Service roads and trails throughout the region. Unfortunately, trail markers are scarce, many maps are outdated, and it's easy to get lost. Even local riders spend a lot of time in trial-and-error scouting to sort out the maze of forks and logging roads, some of which lead to dead-ends. Realizing the potential of Tahoe for cycling, the various recreational agencies and user groups are discussing plans to inventory and mark the trail systems. Until then, mountain biking is best approached with a high degree of caution and planning. Before setting out, even on the established routes described here, check out trail conditions thoroughly with the appropriate governmental jurisdictions and experienced riders, such as employees at a local bike shop. Trail configurations can change from year to year, depending on the harshness of the winter and on logging activity, and old maps may not be reliable. Whenever you head into the high country, always leave word with someone on where you're going and when you expect to return. It's a good idea to ride with a companion.

Except for the paved trails on the perimeter of the lake, everything goes up—way up. If you haven't done much high-altitude cycling, the 6,000 to 9,000 feet where most of the trails exist can feel like climbing Mount Everest with lead boots. There are steep uphill ascents, roller coaster descents and a lot of variable terrain. While Lake Tahoe offers some truly rewarding vistas for mountain bikers, there are few easy or entry-level rides. A good way to ease into the trail system is to visit one of Tahoe's mountain biking parks, the oldest of which are at Northstar and Squaw Valley ski areas and North Tahoe Regional Park. Taking lifts makes it easier to cover the elevation, and riding downhill is not as exhausting as climbing uphill.

Whenever you cycle off-road in the basin, consider the following guidelines:

- Always wear a helmet (even on paved trails) and carry a first-aid kit. Knee pads aren't a bad idea, either. It's easy to hit a rut and take a dive.
- Carry more water than you think you'll need. With the high elevations (6,000 to 9,000 feet) and warm summer temperatures, you'll need it. Don't embark on an all-day trip without a minimum of three water bottles (preferably pint-sized) per person. As a backup, you might carry a water filter/purifier such as Katydyn, which filters *Giardia*, a microorganism that is becoming more frequent in wilderness lakes and streams.
- Carry a repair kit for patching flat tires and making other adjustments. Know how to fix gears, reinstall a chain and repair brakes.
- Carry a flashlight, extra food, matches and warm clothes. You may think that you'll be back before dark, but don't count on it. If your bike breaks down beyond your ability to repair it, or if you sustain an injury, you might need to spend a night outdoors.
- Take as many maps as you can lay your hands on, but always update your information by checking with a local bike shop, or with the appropriate offices of the U.S. Forest Service. (If the seasonal aide isn't familiar with your particular route, ask to speak with a recreation supervisor.) Carry a U.S. Geological Survey topographic map, a Forest Service map and perhaps one of the privately produced maps available locally. Don't forget your compass. Even with all of this material, there's the problem of inadequate signage, construction activities, vandalism and, sometimes, official indifference. If you come across a trail fork that should have a sign but doesn't, you can do everyone a favor by reporting it to the local Forest Service office. With so many roads and trails to maintain each year, and with diminishing staffs, each forest can use all of the help it can get.
- If you're renting a bike—and there are plenty of places to do so— check the policy of the rental agreement to make sure that it covers off-road cycling.

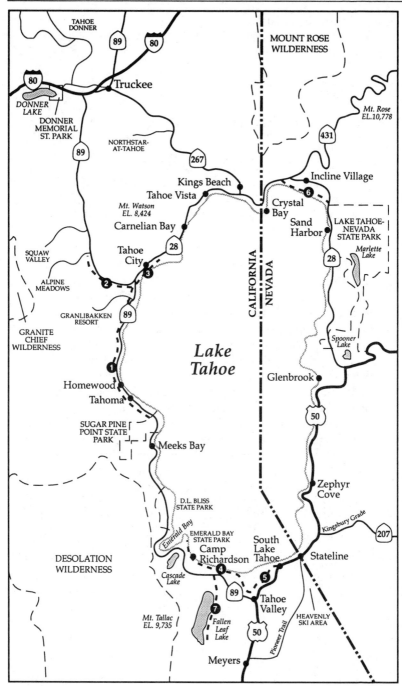

Paved roads and trails

## *Map References—Paved Roads and Trails*

◆

# PAVED BIKE TRAILS

Of Lake Tahoe's 72-mile shoreline, 20 miles have designated bike paths, which parallel the highways. Most of them are on the West and South shores, and they are in five unconnected segments. Although it's possible to ride on the road, it's not advisable to do so. There are steep hills, hairpin turns and narrow shoulders, and cyclists must share the road with retirees driving Winnebago motor homes, 18-year-olds with souped-up four-wheel-drive vehicles and raging hormones, and gamblers who have lost their last buck and imbibed too many free cocktails. Does this sound like a winning combination? Not exactly. Until more paved bike trails are constructed, the best advice is to stay off the main roads. They are too congested and too dangerous. Herewith is a rundown of the bike paths and a few side trips in Lake Tahoe and Reno:

## ★ West Shore Bike Path ★
*See number 1 on map, page 196*

***Distance:*** Nine miles, one way.
***Difficulty:*** Easy to moderate.
***Location:*** On Highway 89 at Tahoe City on the north and Sugar Pine Point State Park on the south.
***Description:*** This is the longest and most scenic paved bike trail in the basin. With only minor ups and downs, it winds along the wooded West Shore from Tahoe City to Sugar Pine Point State Park. There are stunning vistas of the lake, some good beaches and several small towns including Tahoma and Homewood. Picnic tables and rest stops are scattered along the route, so you can pack a lunch, or if you wish, eat at any of several popular restaurants along the way. This is a great family outing, with one caveat—parts of the trail consist of bike lanes along busy Highway 89, and the trail crosses the road at several points. Dismount from your bike and cross with care! Other parts of the trail pass through residential areas just west of the highway, and there are some minor uphills and downhills. While the main section of trail stretches between Tahoe City and Sugar Pine Park, there are two connecting trails that branch north and east of Tahoe City, creating interesting sidetrip options for

lengthening your casual ride to an all-day outing, if you wish.

**Trailheads and parking:** If you're staying in Tahoe City or along West Shore Boulevard (Highway 89), the path and starting point are just outside your door. Otherwise, park your vehicle at one of these places:

• *General Creek Campground, Sugar Pine Point State Park:* Located one mile south of Tahoma on Highway 89. There's a $5 day-use fee required, but there's ample parking.

• *Ehrman Mansion, Sugar Pine Point State Park:* East of Highway 89, in another section of the park, is an even better option—parking at the historic Ehrman Mansion, which has large, grassy, tree-shaded grounds with a pier and considerable shoreline access. This is an idyllic spot for a picnic or a rest after your ride. One suggestion: Get here early, because parking is limited. During summer, you can take a guided tour of the mansion, which is fully furnished and is one of Tahoe's grand old estates. By parking at Sugar Pine, you can cycle to Tahoe City, pausing, if you wish, at the beachfront marinas at Homewood, Chambers Landing and Sunnyside, all of which offer excellent and upscale lakeside restaurants. Other popular cycling stops include Black Bear Tavern, Norfolk Woods Inn (formerly Alpenhaus) and Bridgetender's Café.

• *Truckee River Recreation Trail and Public Access:* This has a large parking lot one-half mile south of Tahoe City on Highway 89, with several picnic tables and vault toilets next to the river. From here, you can go in one of three directions—south to Sugar Pine, north to River Ranch or east to Dollar Point. You can do out-and-back rides on any of these trails, or combine them. Pedal round-trip on all three trails for a total trip distance of 30 miles.

• *Kaspian Campground:* This public campground, managed by the U.S. Forest Service, is located at the intersection of Highway 89 and Blackwood Canyon Road, four miles south of Tahoe City, and includes parking, restrooms with flush toilets and special bicycle campsites. There are three options from here as well: north, south or west. You can follow the bike trail along the lake, or, if you're ambitious (and very much in shape), head up Blackwood Canyon Road. If you elect to do the latter, be prepared for a long, gradual uphill grade for four miles or so, then a steep switchback for another three miles. The views are spectacular from the summit of Barker Pass. You can stop at the Pacific Crest Trail, just beyond where the pavement ends. You'll find a trailhead that is jammed with cars and four-wheel-drive vehicles. As of 1994, there were no toilets here. If you haven't had enough exercise at this point, consider locking your bike and hiking for a bit on the trail to enjoy the vistas of the Sierra and Lake Tahoe. Or rest and then coast back down the way you came. Traffic is not heavy on this road, but it's wise to be cautious on switchbacks and curves.

## ★ Truckee River Recreation Trail ★
*See number 2 on map, page 196*

**Distance:** 4.5 miles one-way.
**Difficulty:** Easy.
**Location:** Parallels the Truckee River and Highway 89 in North Tahoe.
**Description:** This is a gentle but scenic paved trail that borders the meandering river and highway for 3.5 miles, from Tahoe City to the River Ranch Lodge at Alpine Meadows Road. A new extension, recently completed, offers an additional mile of trail to Midway Bridge. In normal to high-water years, float tubers, rafters and flyfishers can be seen along the river, and River Ranch is a great hangout for lunch or people-watching on the spacious outdoor patio that overlooks the river.
**Trailheads and parking:** The trailhead is at a large parking lot one-half mile south of Tahoe City on Highway 89. Three trails set off from here, including the West Shore Bike Path (see above).

## ★ Dollar Point Trail ★
*See number 3 on map, page 196*

**Distance:** 2.5 miles one-way.
**Difficulty:** Easy to moderate, with a half-mile climb to Dollar Hill.
**Location:** Parallels Highway 28 from Tahoe City east along the North Tahoe shoreline.
**Description:** This trail is short but it has good places to stop along the way, including Lake Tahoe-Nevada State Park, Burton Creek State Park and Lake Forest Beach and boat ramp. You can picnic along the way, on the beach, or stop at any of several restaurants. There are some nice vistas of aspens, pines and, in early summer, wildflowers. You can use this paved trail as a feeder route to the network of dirt mountain bike trails that originate at the Lakeview Cross-Country Ski Area, which is in residential area just one-half mile north of Highway 28. Look for the sign that designates the ski area.
**Trailheads and parking:** The trailhead is at Tahoe State Park, east of Tahoe City on Highway 28. Parking is at the park.

## ★ Pope-Baldwin Bike Path ★
*See number 4 on map, page 196*

**Distance:** 3.4 miles one-way.
**Difficulty:** Easy.
**Location:** On the southwest side of the lake on Highway 89, just one-half mile north of the "Y" intersection with US 50.
**Description:** This is a nearly level cycling path that covers two of South Lake Tahoe's most spectacular beaches and a complex of three famous, old estates. The path begins at Highway 89, north of the "Y" junction

with US 50, in the area where four lanes narrow to two. There are bicycle rental outfits all along this road, and even family four-wheel cycling wagons (at Camp Richardson). Picnic spots are along the way at Pope and Baldwin beaches, or at Fallen Leaf Campground. Probably the best public parking spot is at the Tallac Historic Site, a series of lakefront homes once inhabited by the rich and famous. There's a museum with free admission and, on certain days, a tour of the Pope Estate. Art and music festivals are regularly held here during the summer. Tallac is situated in pine trees, behind Baldwin Beach, and you would be hard-pressed to find a more inspirational place on the South Shore. You can picnic here, or have a great repast at The Beacon Restaurant at Camp Richardson, which has outdoor dining on a large patio on the beach and, frequently, live music (everything from jazz to rock to country and folk) that keeps the place hopping.

***Trailheads and parking:*** Parking is available at Camp Richardson and Tallac Historic Site (for directions, see page 27 in chapter 2, "Lake Tahoe Points of Interest").

## South Lake Tahoe Bike Path
*See number 5 on map, page 196*

***Distance:*** Five miles one-way.
***Difficulty:*** Easy.
***Location:*** At El Dorado Beach and Picnic Area on US 50, in the city of South Lake Tahoe.
***Description:*** This increasingly popular paved bike path connects to other bike trails and lanes throughout the city of South Lake Tahoe and into Nevada. Part of the meandering bike trail bridges Trout Creek and the Upper Truckee River, with views across Truckee Marsh to Lake Tahoe. Bike lanes along US 50 continue to the Pope-Baldwin Bike Path, but these should be used with caution due to heavy traffic.
***Trailheads and parking:*** Parking is available at the beach and picnic area.

## Incline Village/Lakeshore Drive Bike Path
*See number 6 on map, page 196*

***Distance:*** 2.5 miles one-way.
***Difficulty:*** Easy.
***Location:*** In Incline Village, North Tahoe.
***Description:*** Known locally in Incline Village as "The Joggers Trail," this wooded, paved trail starts at Gateway Park on Highway 28. Maintained by Washoe County, the trail passes close to the shore of Lake Tahoe's Crystal Bay, accesses two beaches that are reserved for Incline Village residents and guests, offers views of many million-dollar-plus homes and gated estates, and ends at the Hyatt Regency.

***Trailheads and parking:*** Parking is available at Gateway Park on Highway 28.

## Fallen Leaf Lake Paved Roads
*See number 7 on map, page 196*

***Distance:*** 3.5 miles one-way.
***Difficulty:*** Moderate.
***Location:*** In South Lake Tahoe, beginning at intersection of Lake Tahoe Boulevard and Tahoe Mountain Road, west of the "Y" intersection of US 50 and Highway 89. To follow the route in the opposite direction, park at Camp Richardson.
***Description:*** This route has some incline on residential roads to the intersection with Angora Ridge Road (a dirt and gravel road), then goes downhill until it reaches Fallen Leaf Road. You can ride north to Highway 89 and the beaches around Camp Richardson, then merge with the bike lane back to the "Y" intersection near your starting point. If you have a mountain bike, consider a sidetrip to Angora Lakes (about three miles one-way), where there's a log bike rack to lock your bike (at the parking area), a short trail to the lakes and a lodge with a snack stand and rowboat concession. This is a favorite swimming hole. Other side trips can be made down Fallen Leaf Road to Glen Alpine Falls or Fallen Leaf Lake Dam. Bicyclists may ride free of charge onto the fee beaches. Bicycles are not allowed in Desolation Wilderness, on the self-guided trails around the Forest Service visitor center, in Taylor Creek Marsh, or on dirt paths within the Tallac Historic Site. Use caution on the narrow roads and trails around Fallen Leaf Lake.

## Reno Bike Trails
Like the Lake Tahoe paths, Reno's trails also border bodies of water. Some of the city's most scenic routes are listed below.

★• *The Truckee River Trail* is Reno-Sparks' longest path at 6.5 miles. It begins at Broadhead Park, near Wells Avenue and Kuenzli Lane, and continues along the river, ending near the Vista Boulevard off-ramp on Interstate 80.

• *The Idlewild Route* also follows the Truckee River. Considerably shorter at 3.3 miles, the path begins at Riverside and First streets and continues through Idlewild Park to Caughlin Ranch.

• *Virginia Lake,* while not a bike path, affords a scenic and easy one-mile loop. Picnic tables, barbecue grills and restrooms are on site.

• *Bowers Mansion to Franktown* is a scenic, sparsely traveled country road. This four-mile stretch starts at Bowers Mansion, a turn-of-the-century home, then makes a right turn on Franktown Road. Franktown winds through farmlands, meadows, towering pines and large estates. Bowers Mansion is approximately 15 miles south of Reno.

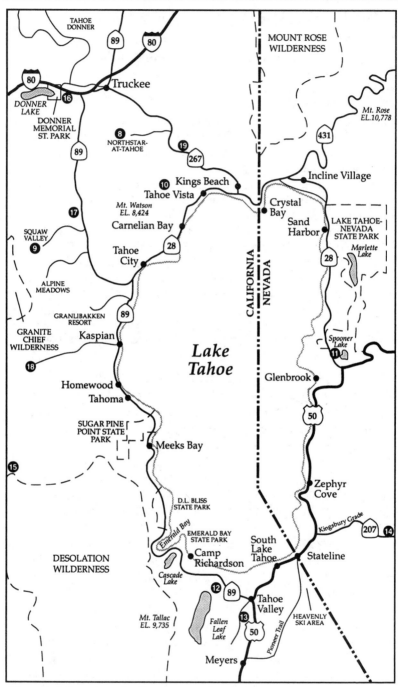

*Mountain bike parks and trails*

## Map References—Mountain Bike Parks and Trails

◆

# MOUNTAIN BIKE PARKS

Mountain bike parks offer unique cycling advantages, and Lake Tahoe has three of them: the downhill ski resorts of Northstar-at-Tahoe and Squaw Valley and North Tahoe Regional Park in Tahoe Vista. At the ski areas, the obvious attraction is being able to ride a chairlift to the top of a slope, then ride downhill—which saves on the grunting and groaning. The network of service roads and trails that crisscross most ski areas makes for an excellent trail system, and the chances of getting lost are considerably less than being on unmarked forest roads. Also, there's a bike shop around to make repairs, and snack bars or restaurants to serve munchies.

## Northstar-at-Tahoe

*See number 8 on map, page 202*

At this all-seasons resort six miles south of Truckee, two chairlifts serve an elaborate trail system, which offers everything from easy meadow jaunts to an all-day ride to a mountain lake. There are roads and single-track trails, and some are tricky to negotiate, especially with sand and unconsolidated rock. The resort has over 100 miles of trail, and one of them connects with the North Shore's most popular mountain route—the Fibreboard Freeway, which goes to Brockway Summit on the east and Tahoe City on the north. Unlike the labyrinth of trails that covers the high terrain of North Tahoe, the Northstar routes are well marked. There is no charge for using the trails—only for riding the lifts. If you're ambitious and don't mind a lot of climbing (about 1,500 feet worth), you can start cycling from Northstar Village. But if you're of average ability, do yourself a favor—take the lifts. All cyclists are required to wear safety helmets. Here are some routes available at Northstar:

★• *Watson Lake Loop*—Taken at a leisurely pace, this makes a nice half-day trip (a round-trip of 9.2 miles) for intermediate cyclists, especially if you combine a picnic lunch with a stop at Watson Lake. Take the Echo and Lookout lifts at Northstar to Route 507, at elevation 7,800 feet.

Follow that for three-tenths of a mile to Route 500, then ride on this fairly level road for 1.6 miles with a gradual climb to Route 100. It's two-tenths of a mile farther to Route 114, and then seven-tenths of a mile on that to Watson Lake. There are nice views of Lake Tahoe all along the trail. Watson Lake is set in a meadow with some sunning rocks, but because of the cold water temperature and muddy bottom, it's not a good place for swimming. The lake gets heavy use in summer from cyclists and some off-road-vehicle enthusiasts. To return to Northstar, retrace your path to Route 100, which is the Fibreboard Freeway. It's a gradual down-hill all the way for 1.75 miles to Sawmill Flat, where there's a caboose used as a warming hut for cross-country skiers during winter. From there, it's about two miles back to Northstar Village on the Big Springs Trail or Village Run.

• *Sawmill Flat Loop*—This makes a good beginner or family trip, since it is relatively short (three miles round-trip), has a view of Northstar Reservoir and surrounding mountains, and has an elevation gain of just 200 feet. From the top of the Echo Lift, take Route 501 to Route 500, and follow that until you reach the caboose. Between here and the reservoir is an open meadow with good places for a picnic. To return, follow the same route back, and at the top of Echo Lift take the Big Springs Trail back to Northstar Village, enjoying views of Martis Valley on the way down. An alternate return is the Village Run, but this is steeper and rockier.

• *Tahoe City (one-way)*—This 12-mile ride (buy a one-ride lift ticket) follows the same trail as the Watson Lake Loop (see above), but joins new Route 115 (the continuation of the Fibreboard Freeway) to Tahoe City, a distance of 7.6 miles from Mount Watson. This is a well-graded, wide but unmarked road. Park a second car at Tahoe City (one good spot is near the high school), or return the same way to the trails that lead back to Northstar Village (a long round-trip of about 25 miles). If you do this route, allow for a full day and about seven hours of riding. You can stop for lunch at one of the restaurants in Tahoe City.

**Amenities:** Two chairlifts modified to carry bicycles; the Mountain Adventure Shop in Northstar Village, which offers rentals and repairs; a mountain bike school; a day lodge with restrooms and phone; and Northstar Village restaurants.

**Fees:** Single-ride ticket—adult, $12; child, $9. Multi-ride ticket—adult, $17; child, $13. Rentals (including helmet, free souvenir water bottle and trail map): Full day—adult, $30; junior, $24; child, $15. Four hours or less—adult, $25; junior, $18; child, $10.

**Information:** Northstar-at-Tahoe, (916) 562-1010, or Mountain Adventure Shop, (916) 562-2248.

## Squaw Valley Bike Park
*See number 9 on map, page 202*

The system of roads and single-track trails that wend their way throughout Squaw Valley are better suited to strong intermediate and advanced riders. Only one lift operates for bikes—the cable car to the High Camp Bath and Tennis Club. The easiest trails are at this point, at elevation 8,200 feet. A long (and difficult) intermediate trip downhill follows the Mountain Run—a descent of 2,000 vertical feet. A gentler trail is the High Camp Loop (around the Links Chairlift), or you can do an out-and-back ride on Ridge and Newport roads, both rated as easiest. Advanced riders can try the difficult road to Shirley Lake, or a long, high route to Cornice II and Red Dog, which drops back to the base area at elevation 6,200 feet. Most of the Squaw Valley trails have two features in common: lots of bumpy granite rock and almost no tree cover. While it can get quite warm here in summer, one advantage is that you can always take a swim in the outdoor lagoon at High Camp, or enjoy the restaurant. Note: Helmets are required for all riders, and everyone using the park must purchase a trail pass at the Squaw Valley Sport Shop.
***Amenities:*** One cable car; Squaw Valley Sport Shop for rentals, clothing and accessories; and food services at the High Camp Bath and Tennis Club.
***Prices:*** Unlimited rides, $25; single ride, $17. Rentals: All-day suspension bike (including helmet), $24; half-day (four hours), $17; hourly, $6. All-day helmet rental is $5.
***Information:*** Squaw Valley USA, (800) 545-4350 or (916) 583-5585.

## North Tahoe Regional Park
*See number 10 on map, page 202*

This major recreation area, set well off of Highway 28 at Tahoe Vista (just west of the intersection with Highway 267 at Kings Beach), has both gentle and advanced terrain, and the system of trails connects with other North Tahoe mountain biking trails including the Fibreboard Freeway. The agency also has a mile-long paved trail that begins in the parking lot and goes through a wooded area of tall trees to Pinedrop Street and out to Highway 267. To access the park, go north on National Avenue from Highway 28 until it reaches the recreation complex, which includes restrooms and a parking lot (fee charged).
***Amenities:*** A mountain bike race track, picnic areas, a softball field, a playground, a parcourse, nature and hiking trails, restrooms and sled hills.
***Prices:*** $2 parking fee per car. Admission to the park is free.
***Information:*** North Tahoe Public Utility District, Recreation and Parks Department, (916) 546-5043.

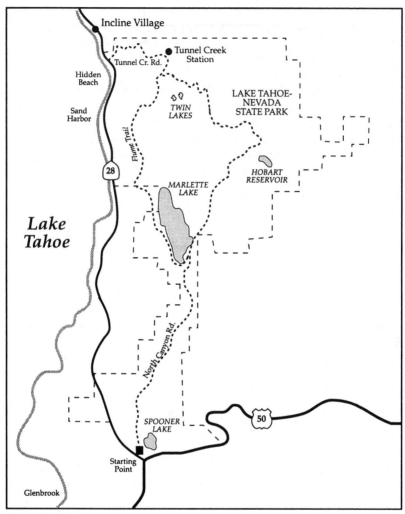

*Flume Trail*

## MOUNTAIN BIKING TRAILS
### ★ Marlette Lake/Flume Trail ★
*See number 11 on map, page 202 • Also see Flume Trail map, above*
**Distance:** Five miles to Marlette Lake and 12 miles to Incline Village
one-way.
**Difficulty:** Strenuous; not for beginners or anyone afraid of heights.
**Elevation (low/high):** 7,000 to 8,300 feet.
**Access:** Take Highway 28 to the Spooner Lake parking lot in Lake

Tahoe-Nevada State Park. A parking fee ($4 per vehicle) is charged, and there is strict enforcement on parking in designated areas. If you take a second car to arrange a shuttle, limited parking is available at Tunnel Creek Road by Ponderosa Ranch at Incline Village.

***Description:*** This is not just another mountain bike ride. It is THE ride of Lake Tahoe. If you have just one day to do an off-road cycling trip, if you are not a beginner, if you are in decent physical shape, and if you are not afraid of heights (such as a narrow trail with a sheer drop-off of 1,500 feet), this is a truly magnificent experience. The Flume Trail definitely is not a family ride and children should not be on it. It's tough even for adults, since there's a long climb uphill to Marlette Lake, and you may have to walk your bike for a good part of the distance. Also, there are some tricky spots just below the Marlette Lake Dam, where the Flume actually begins, and erosion has begun to eat away into some sections of the trail. Finally, unless you've got a lot of stamina to do the round-trip (not recommended for most riders), you'll need to park a second car at the bottom of Tunnel Ranch Road. (The state park is considering proposed shuttle concessions that will make the return to Spooner Lake much easier.)

Historically, the trail was part of an old water flume line that once carried timber from Lake Tahoe to the silver mines in Virginia City. Long abandoned, it was "rediscovered" only a few years ago by local resident Max Jones, an avid mountain biker who also operates the Spooner Cross Country Ski Area. Jones cleared debris from much of the trail and, in a few short years, it has become the single most popular mountain bike route in the basin—drawing up to 400 riders a day on weekends.

The trail begins east of the picnic area near Spooner Lake. Turn left on the dirt road that heads toward the meadow and follow a sandy road for five miles to Marlette Lake (a scenic place to stop, rest and have lunch). Turn left across the dam, where a sign announces the actual start of the Flume Trail. After negotiating a few technical spots down sandy embankments, you reach the ledge and its awesome view of Lake Tahoe. From here, the single track follows a narrow ridge at 7,700 feet—fully 1,500 feet above Lake Tahoe. You may encounter hikers and a few bass-ackward cyclists coming UP the trail (the fools!). Continue along this route until you reach Tunnel Creek Road, which in turn emerges on a street at Ponderosa Ranch. If you are super ambitious, you can make a loop by turning right and riding to the top of the ridge. You will reach Twin Lakes in one-half mile. Seven-tenths of a mile past the lake sign, turn right or continue to the next main road and turn right. Turn right again on Forest Service Road 504, climb the ridge and where the road forks, continue straight to Marlette Lake. From there, it is back to Spooner (and sliding down some sandy, squirrelly turns). The worst alternative is returning to

Spooner by riding on Highway 28, a very dangerous route considering the traffic and narrow to nonexistent shoulders.

***Information:*** Lake Tahoe-Nevada State Park—Sand Harbor, (702) 831-0494, or Spooner Lake, (702) 831-0494.

> ***Note:*** The descriptions of the following mountain bike trails are provided by the U.S. Forest Service, except where noted.
> Be aware that trail conditions can change and that signage may not be consistent. Know your abilities and do not try any of these routes unless you have experience riding off-road.
> Always contact the respective Forest Service office and local cycling shops for the latest information before setting out on the trail, and observe all sign postings that restrict access for cyclists.

## Angora Ridge
*See number 12 on map, page 202*

***Distance:*** Two miles to Angora Lookout; four miles to Angora Lakes one-way.

***Difficulty:*** Moderate.

***Elevation (low / high):*** 6,360 to 7,440 feet.

***Access:*** From South Lake Tahoe, drive two miles north of Highway 89. Turn left on Fallen Leaf Lake Road. Park past Fallen Leaf Campground on the right.

***Description:*** Enjoy a moderate ride that ends with spectacular views of Fallen Leaf Lake and Mount Tallac. Ride along Fallen Leaf Lake Road, take the first left, continue one-half mile and turn right on Angora Ridge Road (Forest Service Road 12N14). You can park or lock your bike at a trailhead to Angora Lakes and continue by foot. There's a lodge, cabins and good swimming opportunities.

***Information:*** Lake Tahoe Basin Management Unit, (916) 573-2600.

## Twin Peaks
*See number 13 on map, page 202*

***Distance (one way):*** A one- to two-mile loop.

***Difficulty:*** Moderate to strenuous.

***Elevation (low / high):*** 6,400 to 7,010 feet.

***Access:*** Off Lake Tahoe Boulevard approximately two miles from the intersection of US 50 and Highway 89. Turn left on Sawmill Road.

***Description:*** This short, steep ride to the top of a mountain peak has great views of Lake Tahoe. A shorter one-mile loop may be taken on the trail as well. It is open for public use from 9 a.m. to 7 p.m. daily. Caution: This is a very popular off-highway-vehicle area.

***Information:*** Lake Tahoe Basin Management Unit, (916) 573-2600.

# ★ Genoa Peak ★
*See number 14 on map, page 202*

**Distance:** 8 to 12 miles one-way.
**Difficulty:** Moderate.
**Elevation (low/high):** 7,720 to 8,680 feet.
**Access:** From South Lake Tahoe and US 50, take Kingsbury Grade (Highway 207) 2.5 miles and turn left on North Benjamin Road, which turns into Andrea Drive in one-half mile. Continue to the end of the pavement and park.
**Description:** Enjoy a moderate ride along a ridgeline with scenic views of the Lake Tahoe Basin to the west and Carson Valley to the east. Several spurs off the main road access peaks, with Genoa Peak the highest (elevation 9,150 feet). An excellent 10-mile loop off the main ridge is possible. Note: Mountain bikes are not allowed on the Tahoe Rim Trail, from Highway 207 to Spooner Summit and from Spooner Summit to Tunnel Creek. Take Genoa Peak Road (Forest Service Road 14N32). A longer trip is possible if you take arrange a car shuttle. Park the second vehicle off of US 50 behind the Nevada Department of Transportation Station (NDOT), one-quarter mile south of the Highway 28 and US 50 junction.
**Information:** Lake Tahoe Basin Management Unit, (916) 573-2600.

## McKinney-Rubicon Trail
*See number 15 on map, page 202*

**Distance:** 6 to 18.5 miles one-way.
**Difficulty:** Moderate to strenuous.
**Elevation (low/high):** 6,400 to 7,200 feet.
**Access:** From Highway 89 north of Tahoma, turn west onto McKinney-Rubicon Springs Road. Drive one-quarter mile and turn left on Bellevue. Continue one-quarter mile and turn right on McKinney Road. Bear left onto McKinney-Rubicon Springs Road and continue to a one-lane dirt road and park one-quarter to three-quarters of a mile along the road (there are wide turnouts). To arrange a car shuttle (see below), continue about five miles on Highway 89 to the Ellis Peak Trailhead in Blackwood Canyon.
**Description:** This is a world-class off-highway-vehicle road, which offers a variety of biking opportunities from loop rides to difficult peak climbs. This bumpy road traverses numerous areas of river rock, and is used frequently by all-terrain vehicles, motorized dirt bikes and four-wheel-drive vehicles, which can make it quite dusty. A great, but challenging loop is possible by arranging a car shuttle, parking the second car at Blackwood Canyon. From the McKinney-Rubicon Trailhead, ride 1.9 miles and head northwest on the Buck Lake Trail. Continue about 1.5

miles to the Ellis Peak Trail. Follow the Ellis Peak Trail northwest through Barker Pass to Blackwood Canyon. (Warning: Roads beyond the McKinney-Rubicon Springs Road to Barker Pass have few or no signs.)
***Information:*** Lake Tahoe Basin Management Unit, (916) 573-2600.

## Coldstream Canyon Trail
*See number 16 on map, page 202*

***Distance:*** 20 miles round-trip.
***Difficulty:*** Strenuous, on dirt road and single-track trail.
***Elevation (low / high):*** 6,000 to 8,600 feet.
***Access:*** Take Interstate 80 to the first Truckee exit, Donner Pass Road. Turn south off Donner Pass Road just east of Donner Memorial State Park onto Coldstream Road (unmarked). Follow the road for four-tenths of a mile. Park where the pavement ends.
***Description:*** One-tenth of a mile up the dirt road, take the right fork. Follow this short, steep, paved section—it very soon becomes a dirt road again. Veer right, staying on the main road that runs along the right side of two large ponds and continue the gradual climb up the valley. (Some of the valley is private property, so please stay on the road and respect the landowner's rights.) When you come to the 180-degree bend in the railroad, cross the tracks and continue on the road. Stay left at the next two forks. After crossing the creek, you will begin a short, steep climb that intersects a newly built logging road. Continue the gradual climb that follows the South Fork of Cold Creek. At the end of the logging road, a single-track trail, once an old jeep road, begins to climb the last few miles to the saddle below Tinkers Knob. Portions of the climb are steep and technical. You will cross the creek two more times; if you look carefully along the west bank of the creek, you can see the old flume used to transport logs off the mountain by the early loggers. Once at the saddle below Tinkers Knob, you will be rewarded with a breathtaking view of the Deep Creek drainage to the south. The saddle is an excellent spot to stash your bike, grab your lunch and hike the short, steep trail to the top of Tinkers Knob (elevation 8,950 feet). Descend the same way you rode up. Watch for horses on the single-track section of the ride and cars after the 180-degree bend in the railroad. (Note: The Pacific Crest Trail is located just beyond the saddle. Remember, bikes are not permitted on the PCT.)
***Information:*** Tahoe National Forest, Truckee Ranger District, (916) 587-3558.

## Pole Creek Area

*See number 17 on map, page 202*

**Distance:** 3 to 10 miles one-way.
**Difficulty:** Easy to moderate.
**Elevation (low/high):** 6,000 to 8,100 feet.
**Access:** From Truckee, take Highway 89 south for approximately seven miles. Across the street from Big Chief is a parking area where Forest Service Road 8 begins. Park here.
**Description:** There are many mountain biking options in the Pole Creek and Silver Peak area. To get to the spectacular scenery below the ridgeline and the head of the drainage, follow Forest Service Road 8, which climbs gradually. You will come to a sign for Upper Pole Creek; turn left here and continue climbing. You will experience forested areas, beautiful meadows and awesome mountain peaks. With a good topo map, you can find Silver Peak (south of the head of the Pole Creek drainage) and easily bike to the summit in an hour. As always, use caution descending the well-graded lower portion of Forest Service Road 8.
**Information:** Tahoe National Forest, Truckee Ranger District, (916) 587-3558.

## Ellis Peak and Ellis Lake

*See number 18 on map, page 202*

**Distance:** Four miles one-way.
**Difficulty:** Difficult, due to steepness over single-track trail and dirt road.
**Elevation (low/high):** 7,800 to 8,640 feet.
**Access:** From Interstate 80 in Truckee, take Highway 89 south to Tahoe City. Continue south on Highway 89 another 4.2 miles to the Kaspian Picnic Area. Drive or ride west on Blackwood Canyon Road on the seven-mile climb to Barker Pass. The Ellis Peak Trailhead is on the south side of the road, where the pavement ends on the summit.
**Description:** This motorcycle/biking/hiking trail is very steep going until you reach the ridge. The grind is worthwhile thanks to the view from the ridge. The stretch where the trail becomes rideable again is breathtaking. Follow the ridge for 1.5 miles, riding through beautiful flower-filled meadows and later through sections of open forests. The trail soon intersects Forest Service Road 14N40. To reach Ellis Lake, follow the road to the left for two miles. To reach Ellis Peak, follow the road to the right. Approximately 100 yards down the road, another marked dirt road will veer off to the east (left). Follow that road for three-tenths of a mile. Stash your bike and hike the last steps to Ellis Peak (elevation 8,640 feet). The view of Tahoe to the east, Granite Chief Wilderness and Hellhole Reservoir to the west and Desolation Wilderness to the south is breathtaking.
**Information:** Lake Tahoe Basin Management Unit, (916) 573-2600.

## ★ Brockway Summit to Martis Peak ★
*See number 19 on map, page 202*

***Distance:*** Five miles one-way.
***Difficulty:*** Moderate to strenuous.
***Elevation (low / high):*** 7,120 to 8,660 feet.
***Access:*** Drive north on Highway 267 from Kings Beach to Brockway Summit. Park one-half mile past the summit on Forest Service Road 18NO2.
***Description:*** The Martis Peak Road is a short five-mile climb, but it's steep and windy all the way. At the top, you get a nice view overlooking Lake Tahoe.
***Information:*** Lake Tahoe Basin Management Unit, (916) 573-2600.

# Meiss Country

## ★ Meiss Trail ★
*See Meiss Country map, page 213*

***Distance:*** Five miles one-way.
***Difficulty:*** Moderate to strenuous.
***Elevation (low / high):*** 7,280 to 8,400 feet.
***Access:*** Take Highway 89 five miles south from Meyers to the Big Meadows parking lot. Follow the trail at the southern end of the parking lot which leads across the highway to the trailhead.
***Description:*** Rising abruptly from Highway 89 for the first half mile, this trail levels off as it reaches Big Meadows. Trails leading to Round, Scotts and Dardanelles lakes provide access into Meiss Country with views of aspen-covered hills from lodgepole-cloaked forests. Note: This trail eventually intersects the Pacific Crest Trail, where mountain bikes are not allowed.
***Information:*** Lake Tahoe Basin Management Unit, (916) 573-2600.

## Tahoe Rim Trail
*See Meiss Country map, page 213*

***Distance:*** 18 miles one-way.
***Difficulty:*** Moderate to strenuous.
***Elevation (low / high):*** 7,280 to 9,600 feet.
***Access:*** From Meyers, drive 5.5 miles south on Highway 89 to the Big Meadows parking lot. The trail starts at the north end of the parking area.
***Description:*** Experience breathtaking scenery with exceptional views of Lake Tahoe. Take the Tahoe Rim Trail past Freel Peak, the highest peak in the basin (elevation 10,881 feet). A longer trip is possible by arranging a car shuttle and parking one car at Heavenly Ski Area's Stagecoach parking lot. The trailhead begins one-eighth of a mile up Stagecoach Run.

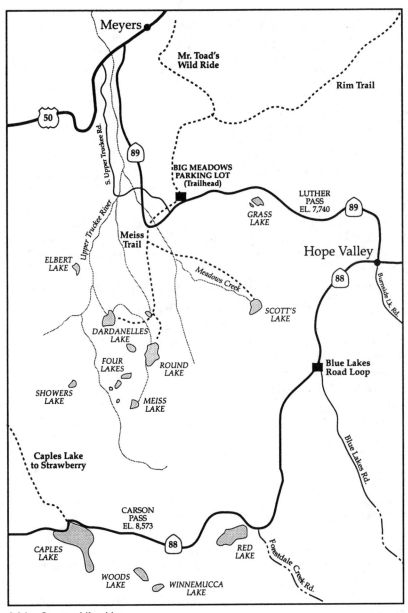

*Meiss Country bike rides*

Note: Mountain bikes are not allowed on the trail from Armstrong Pass north to Fountain Place nor from Star Lake north to High Meadows (this is private property).
*Information:* Lake Tahoe Basin Management Unit, (916) 573-2600.

## Mr. Toad's Wild Ride
*See Meiss Country map, page 213*

*Distance:* Three miles one-way.
*Difficulty:* Strenuous.
*Elevation (low / high):* 6,800 to 9,000 feet.
*Access:* Take Highway 89 five miles south from Meyers to the Big Meadows parking lot for the Tahoe Rim Trail.
*Description:* A technical ride for the experienced mountain biker, this trail drops from 9,000 feet to 6,800 feet in three miles. Take the Tahoe Rim Trail from the Big Meadows parking lot 2.5 miles to Tucker Flat. Turn left and follow the drainage of Saxon Creek. In two miles, the trail forks again. The right fork leads to Oneidas Street off of the Pioneer Trail. The left fork leads to Highway 89, south of the Highway 89/50 junction. Watch for hikers and equestrian riders on the trail and pass with caution and courtesy.
*Information:* Lake Tahoe Basin Management Unit, (916) 573-2600.

## Blue Lakes Road to Red Lake
*See Meiss Country map, page 213*

*Distance:* Four miles one-way, eight miles round-trip or a 21-mile loop.
*Difficulty:* Moderate to strenuous.
*Elevation (low / high):* 8,050 to 8,200 feet.
*Access:* From Highway 88 in Hope Valley, follow the Blue Lakes Road through Faith Valley and then into Charity Valley. There the county road turns to dirt and rises in elevation, eventually cresting at Blue Lakes. From Blue Lakes, follow Forestdale Creek Road (Forest Service Road 013) to Red Lake and Highway 88. You can go back the way you came or take Highway 88 back to Hope Valley (use caution along the highway) for a 21-mile loop back to Blue Lakes.
*Description:* This heavily traveled, off-highway-vehicle trail leads to several scenic alpine lakes and undesignated campsites. Along the way, you get spectacular high vistas of Sierra peaks. Experience steep descents and rough four-wheel-drive road for about two miles from the starting point. From there, the road levels out and is well-graded through moderate forest before reaching Red Lake. The gravel and dirt road from Hope Valley back to Blue Lakes is heavily traveled by RVs and four-wheel-drive vehicles on weekends.
*Information:* Toiyabe National Forest, Carson Ranger District, (702) 882-2766.

## Caples Lake to Strawberry
*See Meiss Country map, page 213*

*Distance:* 12 miles one-way.
*Difficulty:* Strenuous.
*Elevation (low/high):* 5,500 feet to 8,600 feet.
*Access:* From Highway 88 at Caples Lake, turn off at the Caples CalTrans Maintenance Station, and look for the jeep road to Schneider Cow Camp. This area is used for the Kirkwood Cross-Country Center in winter, and the route is skied in the famous Echo Summit to Kirkwood Race each March.
*Description:* This is a lodge-to-lodge tour, from Caples (where you can rent mountain bikes) on Highway 88 to Strawberry on US 50. It's advisable to arrange a shuttle here (allow 90 minutes for this), parking a second car at Strawberry. Considering the elevation drop of over 3,000 feet, there's a long and steep downhill from the top of a ridge beyond Schneider Cow Camp. The entire route is on a jeep trail, and since you start at 7,797 feet, you gain just 800 feet before starting your long descent. Views of Caples Lake, Thimble Peak, Round Top and Little Round Top mountains are spectacular along the four-mile stretch of road from the maintenance station to the top of the ridge. The eight-mile Strawberry Canyon Jeep Trail has some steep sections, so be careful on the descent. Take your topo map and carry lots of water; the rocky areas can get quite hot. At Strawberry Lodge, you can relax, have an ice cream cone or eat lunch at the restaurant.
*Information:* Caples Lake Resort, (209) 258-8888.

## Verdi Peak from Boca Rest Campground
*Distance:* 28 miles round-trip via Forest Service Road 72 from Boca Rest Campground.
*Difficulty:* Strenuous, mostly due to the distance.
*Elevation (low/high):* 5,600 to 8,400 feet.
*Access:* Take Interstate 80 east to the Hirschdale exit and turn left. Cross the bridge and the railroad tracks and continue to the Boca Rest Campground. Look for the Forest Service sign indicating that Verdi Peak is in 14 miles; the sign is across the street from the campground. Begin the ride here.
*Description:* Follow the Verdi Peak Road (Forest Service Road 972) for the majority of the gradual climb. At the junction of Forest Service roads 72 and 72-28, turn right onto Forest Service Road 72-28. This is the home stretch—it's approximately three more miles up to the peak and fire lookout. Descend back to the junction of forest service roads 72-28 and 72. Either turn left here and retrace your ascent back to the Boca Rest Campground or turn right on Forest Service Road 72 and descend to

Henness Pass Road. Turn left on the Henness Pass Road and descend to the junction with the paved Stampede Road, where you will turn left. The last leg of your ride is on Stampede, heading back to the campground.
*Information:* Tahoe National Forest, Truckee Ranger District, (916) 587-3558.

## Lower Lola Montez Trail

*Distance:* Three miles one-way.
*Difficulty:* Moderate, over single-track trail and dirt road.
*Elevation (low/high):* 6,640 to 7,200 feet.
*Access:* Take the Soda Springs exit off Interstate 80 on the north side of the freeway. Follow the paved road east for three-tenths of a mile to the parking area.
*Description:* Since much of the trail is over Toll Mountain Estates, a private gated community, bikers are requested to stay on the trail and observe the property rights of the landowners. From the trailhead, follow the trail north for one-quarter mile to a marked dirt road. Turn right. The road will take you to lower Castle Creek crossing. (The creekbed is lined with wire meshing—use caution in crossing to avoid flat tires.) The single-track trail begins again one-quarter mile after the creek crossing, and then climbs steeply for another one-quarter mile. Turn right where it ties in with the road again. For the next quarter mile, the road gently ascends. At the end of the road, which is also the beginning of the Motor Vehicle Restricted Area, the trail leads to an open meadow. From there, it is one-quarter mile to Lower Lola Montez Lake, a popular camping place that is wonderful for swimming. The trail is well marked throughout, and receives heavy use by hikers, especially on the weekends. Remember to be considerate and controlled during your descent.
*Information:* Tahoe National Forest, Truckee Ranger District, (916) 587-3558.

## Mills Peak Lookout Ride

*Distance:* Six miles one-way.
*Difficulty:* Moderate to strenuous, on gravel, rock, graded and dirt roads.
*Elevation (low/high):* 6,500 to 7,340 feet.
*Access:* From Highway 89 near Graeagle, take the Gold Lake Highway (County Road 519) to the junction with Mills Peak Road (County Roads 721/822). Or from Highway 49, take the Gold Lake Highway approximately eight miles north to the junction with Mills Peak Road. Park across from this intersection at the turnout.
*Description:* Travel 1.5 miles on County Road 721, then turn north on County Road 822 and continue 4.5 miles to the Mills Peak Lookout. The

lookout offers vistas of eastern Plumas County. Forest Service lookout personnel may be on duty during summer months. There is an easy 0.4-mile Red Fir Nature Trail with interpretive signs off County Road 822. (Note: Graeagle, Elwell and Gold Lake lodges are situated along the Gold Lake Highway.)

*Information:* Plumas National Forest, Beckwourth Ranger District, (916) 836-2575.

> *Note:* The following trail descriptions are provided by the Tahoe North Visitors & Convention Bureau.

## Ward Canyon to Stanford Rock to Twin Peaks

*Distance:* Nine miles one-way.

*Difficulty:* Moderate to strenuous (at times you may need to carry your bike).

*Elevation (low/high):* 5,900 to 7,199 feet.

*Access:* Take Pineland Drive off Highway 89 and follow it to Twin Peaks Road; turn left. This road turns into Ward Creek Boulevard. After one mile, there is a rock erosion system on your right, and a dirt turnout on your left, with a sign below that reads "Stanford Rock, four miles."

*Description:* Cross the creek and start the long ascent to Stanford Rock. The trail to Twin Peaks is down and to the left of Stanford Rock. Stay on the ridgeline until you get to the saddle before starting up the side of Twin Peaks. As you climb, look for the turn that drops down back into Ward Canyon (you will take this trail back down). The trails may be a little hard to spot, but there are cliffs on all sides, so it is hard to wander off! The view from Twin Peaks is spectacular. After your rest, go back to the trail you saw that takes you down and to the left. Do not start climbing up toward the rock; you should head downhill for approximately two miles of steep switchbacks to the side of Ward Creek and then back to the pavement.

*Information:* Tahoe North Visitors & Convention Bureau, (916) 583-3494.

## Brockway Summit to Glenshire

*Distance:* 10 miles one-way.

*Difficulty:* Easy to moderate on good dirt roads.

*Elevation:* 7,120 to 8,660 feet.

*Access:* Take Highway 267 from Kings Beach just past the crest of Brockway Summit to the dirt access road on the right. (Heading from Truckee, the dirt access road is just before the summit on the left.)

*Description:* Follow the main dirt road and take the third left. Soon after this left, you will start a long, eight-mile descent beside a creek, then into Klondike Meadow, continuing along West Juniper Creek. Stay straight along this road and don't turn at any intersections. When you find yourself on the pavement (Glenshire Road), make your first left. This road will bring you to downtown Truckee in approximately five miles. Commercial Row offers an abundance of restaurants, bike shops and great shopping.

***Information:*** Tahoe North Visitors & Convention Bureau, (916) 583-3494.

# Chapter 9

# Fishing Waters & Guides

## ★ Author's Choice ★

I magine a six-pound mackinaw trout peeling out line like a runaway fire truck. Or a five-pound Lahontan cutthroat trout dancing on the surface of a mirror-smooth lake. The fish that inhabit the waters of Lake Tahoe and its surrounding lakes and streams are feisty and strong, and they represent worthy adversaries for freshwater anglers. The entire region is a mighty fish trap, drawing thousands of anglers a year from every corner of the globe. Whether you tease these fish with a worm and a flasher, a damselfly nymph or a big Rapala, you'll find that the sheer variety of trout (nine species by one count) create an amazing, year-round fishery. Add to these some prized kokanee and chinook salmon, a smattering of black bass, perch and mountain whitefish, and you've got quite a stew.

After wetting a line, more than a few believers have left this region feeling that it may be the single best freshwater fishing destination in the lower 48 states. Consider a few salient points:

- Within a 75-mile radius of Lake Tahoe are more than 450 lakes, reservoirs, rivers and streams.
- Most of the popular trout species sought by anglers exist here—lake trout (mackinaw), rainbows, German brown trout, golden trout, cutthroat trout and brook trout. There are also several hybrids, as well as the feisty kokanee salmon and recent arrivals such as chinook salmon. You can find largemouth and smallmouth bass and catfish as well.
- Though hundreds of lakes exist in the high country, with many of them stocked regularly by various public agencies, fishing pressure is amazingly light. Of those who trek into Desolation Wilderness, for example, 15 to 20 percent fish, and of those only 5 to 10 percent go there strictly to fish. This means that a lot of big, smug fish are swimming around in alpine lakes with scarcely a tease from humans.
- While high-elevation fisheries elsewhere in the country shut down for winter, Tahoe and many of its neighboring waters offer year-round access. You can fish for mackinaw any time of the year in Tahoe, Fallen Leaf and Donner lakes. Most rivers and streams in Nevada, on the eastern slopes of the Sierra, are legally fishable all year. Furthermore, the high desert lakes east of Tahoe, particularly Pyramid and Topaz lakes, can offer great action in mild, shirt-sleeve temperatures, even in January.
- Wild trout, the most coveted prize of flyfishers, exist in several lakes where "zero kill" regulations are in force, thus giving casters multiple opportunities to land trophy-sized fish. Among these waters are Martis Creek Lake and Spooner Lake. There are also minimum size

requirements that encourage the development of larger fish in designated stretches of the Truckee River, the East Fork of the Carson River and the North Fork of the Yuba River. The majority of these are within an hour's drive from most points around Lake Tahoe or Reno.

• There's more than quantity and diversity in the Tahoe fisheries. If you consider big fish to be a measure of an area's worth, you'll find lunkers in Tahoe (the record mackinaw was 37.5 pounds and the record kokanee was four pounds, 13 ounces), Donner Lake (which once held a state record for brown trout), Lake Davis (large rainbows up to nine pounds), Red Lake (trophy-sized brook trout to 18 inches), and Pyramid Lake (Lahontan cutthroat trout up to 10 pounds).

Virtually every fishing technique known to humanity is employed in the quest for these fish. At Tahoe and Donner Lake, you can troll deep with long, lead-core line, or with monofilament on downriggers; you can jig with live minnows and lures, drift with minnows, or top-line with plugs. On the surrounding lakes and reservoirs, you can use the standards for trout: spinners, spoons, salmon eggs, worms and Power Bait. Flyfishers can run the gamut of patterns, from dry flies on the high alpine lakes to nymphs in the rivers. Nymphing, in fact, is a highly practiced art form in rivers such as the Truckee and the East Fork of the Carson, and in lakes such as Martis and Davis.

If you're fishing a body of water for the first time, you'll learn its idiosyncrasies much faster by hiring a guide, or by enrolling in one of the local flyfishing schools. Over 50 guides provide half-day, full-day or multi-day fishing excursions in the Tahoe/Reno area. Tahoe alone accounts for the lion's share of outfitters, with some two dozen offering boat trips. And there are a dozen flyfishing guides and instructors who can show you the techniques of casting, wading, reading the water and learning the local entomology. Guides' fees range from $60 for four to five hours, with all gear provided, to $175 per day for a backcountry trip (generally for up to two anglers).

Once you've learned successful angling methods from a professional, you'll have a much better chance of catching fish on your own. Nothing beats the benefit of years of experience, and it's an investment worth making if you plan to continue your forays for fish around Tahoe. Also, to supplement your knowledge with the latest fishing conditions, contact the tackle shops and outfitters listed below.

One point to keep in mind is that fishing regulations and license fees vary between California and Nevada. At Lake Tahoe, which is two-thirds in California and one-third in Nevada, a license from either state is sufficient to fish the entire lake, from shore or on the water. However, Nevada has certain regulations that do not apply to California; one of them is a prohibition against fishing more than one rod per person. California allows two rods to be fished at a time (for a fee of $7.90 with a stamp that goes on the fishing license and restricts fishing to lakes and reservoirs), but as soon as you cross the invisible boundary into Nevada, you can be cited. The same situation exists at Topaz Lake, which also straddles the border. Then there are the rivers, some of which involve both states. California sets specific seasons for its jurisdiction on the Truckee and East Carson rivers, but Nevada allows year-round fishing on its sections.

Be aware of license requirements. A license issued by either state is good for Tahoe and Topaz, but if you fish just one small stretch of the Truckee River that crosses the state line, you'll need licenses from both states. And there are even more vagaries. At Pyramid Lake, which is in Nevada, anglers need to purchase a permit from the Paiute Indian Reservation. This is available from fishing guides or local stores on the reservation. Check the regulations wherever you intend to fish, because seasons, limits, access and the best fishing methods are always subject to change.

## ★ FISHING LAKE TAHOE ★
★ *notes Author's Choice*

Fishing Lake Tahoe for the first time can seem like a daunting task at best. There's a lot of water in a lake that is 22 miles long, 12 miles wide and 1,645 feet deep. Without a boat, chances of success are close to zilch, and even with a boat your odds are slim unless you have the requisite electronic fish-finding gear. Statistics have shown that an unguided angler typically fishes for 10 hours before getting a mackinaw. The best strategy for new arrivals is to go out with a guide and learn the ropes. So many factors affect the success rate that someone with years of experience can shorten your learning curve tremendously. Tahoe has between 20 and 25 guides, with boats ranging from spartan to decadent, and you can always find a charter if the weather is decent.

What you discover is that while there are certain places that tend to attract fish (usually not the deepest points in the lake), nothing is predictable. A mackinaw trout, the largest species, can be one heck of a monster. The record mack, caught in 1974 by guide Robert Aronsen, weighed in at 37 pounds, six ounces, but biologists believe there are lake trout here that exceed 50 pounds. When you consider the fact that an average-sized mackinaw caught by anglers is about seven years old, it's possible that these fish might live 40 or more years. During late summer and fall, kokanee salmon can add to your creel, and rainbow are possible at any time with surface trolling. Brown trout, once a major species, have been on a severe decline as a result of an extended drought that dried up spawning streams and seriously impacted the fishery. The California

Department of Fish and Game and the Nevada Division of Wildlife annually stock more than 60,000 catchable rainbows in the lake. Mackinaw and kokanee are planted sporadically, but most are sustained by natural reproduction.

The gamefish feed on minnows, chubs and tiny freshwater shrimp, among other food sources. (Anglers have a rare chance to observe just exactly how they feed by visiting the Taylor Creek Stream Profile Center at the Lake Tahoe Visitor Center, operated by the U.S. Forest Service near Camp Richardson on the West Shore.)

Because Tahoe never freezes over, you can fish the lake all year, if you go prepared with warm clothes and a boat heater. Often the best fishing is during the winter months, when you may catch your limit of mackinaw (two) within an hour of leaving the dock. (In total, your limit cannot exceed five gamefish.)

## Methods of Catching Lake Trout

How do you catch a mackinaw? Just count the ways:

**Long Lining**—The old-timers, some of them dyed-in-the-wool traditionalists, swear by deep trolling with Rapalas or Rebels behind lead-core or metal line. When fish are 300 feet deep—not unusual for midsummer—this can mean putting out 1,200 feet of line. Cranking in that kind of yardage is tedious and tiring, and you hardly feel the fish fight, anyway. But it may be just the ticket for those who like to sit back, sip a margarita and watch the scenery go by.

**Drifting**—Although it is not consistently productive, drifting or "mooching" with live minnows and light monofilament line of six- to eight-pound test, with a medium sinker, is perhaps the most interesting and challenging way to entice the Mighty Mack. You drag the sinker along the bottom, with the minnow swimming a few feet above it. Strikes are almost imperceptible; often they consist of one or two slight twitches, so it's necessary to keep a consistent and careful eye on your rod tip. When you get a bite, your immediate impulse is to set the hook. Don't do it, or you've lost a fish. Open the bale and let the fish take

### RELEASING A MACKINAW

Fisheries biologists who have seen some of the manhandling that goes on with attempts to release mackinaw are appalled. Some anglers yank the fish into the boat, let it gasp for a minute or longer in the air, grab it by the gills, puncture its air-inflated bladder with a nail, and then dump it overboard as it bleeds. Even if the fish disappears into the depths, the chance of survival with this method is slim to none.

Because mackinaw are brought up from great depths, often over 200 feet, the bladder inflates, causing the fish to swell like a balloon. Before the fish can be returned, you must gently deflate it. Be careful not to touch the sensitive gills. A hypodermic needle (especially a large one) works fine, because it doesn't leave a permanent puncture wound. Also, advise biologists, the longer you leave a fish out of water, the less chance it will have to survive. If you intend to release the fish, especially during the summer, keep it in the net overboard while you remove the hook (preferably with a needle-nose pliers) and deflate the bladder, or place the fish in a live well or container of water while you work on it.

Decide in advance of going on a charter boat if you intend to keep your fish, and advise the skipper. There's no point in wasting fish if you don't have a place to store your catch until it is time to eat it.

out as much as 100 feet of line, for what may seem like an eternity. If a mackinaw detects any resistance while he's mouthing the bait, he'll spit it out. Once he bites, you've got a great fight on your hands. In general, drifting works best in the spring, at places such as Emerald Bay.

**Downrigging**—A good trolling compromise to the long-line system is using a downrigger. Most of the charter boat skippers are equipped with both downriggers and outriggers, so they can troll at varying depths with different lures. With a downrigger, you can use medium-weight monofilament or wire line (12-pound test or greater), a medium-weight rod, a salmon-type quick-release, and lures or live bait. When a fish strikes, you'll need to set the hook immediately; once you've got him, there's no extra weight between you and Mighty Mack. Another advantage of downriggers is that, when used with electronic fish-finders, you can adjust for depth and be on the fish with more precision. Still, it's a rather boring style of fishing; you won't have much to do until a fish hits.

**Jigging**—This is the *nouveau* style of fishing at Lake Tahoe, though it has its critics. The standard setup is a medium-weight rod with a level-wind reel, medium-weight line and a minnow on a treble hook with a four-ounce (or larger) Bomber jig. Varying the depth, you work the rod constantly with light jerks. The idea is to make a mackinaw mad enough to attack your bait. Unfortunately, he might just swipe at it with his body, and you could end up foul-hooking him in the side. If he swallows the hook, it will be tough extracting a barbed treble hook in time to release the fish without killing him. (Unless you're using a single barbless hook and you keep the fish in water when removing the hook, the chances of the fish surviving after release are slim.) Jigging has also been practiced with large chrome bars, though this is less popular. Fish are particularly susceptible to jigging during the spawning months of early fall. Some guides swear by this as the most productive method; others swear at it.

# Special Restrictions at Lake Tahoe

You can fish at Tahoe with either a valid California or Nevada fishing license. However, California rules that allow fishing with two rods (at an extra fee) to the angler are not observed in Nevada, and you are subject to a citation if you exercise this practice across the state line (wherever *that* may be!).

On the California side of the lake, fishing is prohibited in tributary streams (to protect spawning trout) and within 300 feet of the mouth of these streams from October 1 to June 30. On the Nevada side, closed areas are within a 200-yard radius of the mouths of Third, Incline and Wood creeks; within a 500-yard radius of the Sand Harbor Boat Ramp; and within the boat-launch area inside the jetty at Cave Rock Boat Ramp. Only specific minnows and suckers caught from Lake Tahoe can be used as bait.

## FISHING DESOLATION WILDERNESS

One of the best-kept secrets of Tahoe fishing is Desolation Wilderness, a vast mountain kingdom of granite lakes and free-flowing streams on the west side of Lake Tahoe. While Desolation is acknowledged as the most popular wilderness in the region, and quotas are set for overnight camping, only a small percentage of these backcountry travelers seem inclined to wet a line. Surveys have shown that just about five percent of all visitors enter Desolation with the primary purpose of fishing, though 15 to 20 percent fish the region as an incidental activity. Still, it's estimated that as many as 40,000 people enjoy fishing there.

The California Department of Fish and Game annually stocks around 100 lakes in the wilderness, using planes and daredevil pilots who swoop down into box canyons and over plunging ridgetops to spray lakes with fingerling trout. This unique aerial stocking program, which began in the 1950s, has created vibrant fisheries in what otherwise might be barren lakes. The Department of Fish and Game plants over 120,000 fingerlings each year, including golden, brown, mackinaw, rainbow, Eastern brook and, occasionally, cutthroat trout.

Now, however, the department's stocking program in Desolation, as well as in nearby Mokelumne Wilderness, is facing a serious challenge from the U.S. Forest Service. Biologists have been recording a severe and persistent decline in populations of amphibians and reptiles in lakes throughout the Sierra Nevada, and there is the perception—though unproven by scientific research—that the planted trout are threatening yellow-legged frogs with extinction. What makes the demise of the amphibians so puzzling is that there are lakes where both trout and frogs coexist in healthy numbers, lakes that have trout but no frogs, as well as lakes with frogs but no trout and lakes with neither.

To help determine the level of interest and experience of backcountry anglers, the California Department of Fish and Game is dispersing comment cards to overnight users, and is encouraging people to voice their opinions on whether the fish-planting program should be discontinued. (Comments can be sent to the California Department of Fish and Game, Region 2, Fisheries Management, 1701 Nimbus Road, Suite A, Rancho Cordova, CA 95670.)

In terms of fishing the lakes in Desolation, just after the thaw and early in the fall are the productive periods, when the fish are feeding. If you elect to fish early in the summer, be prepared for mosquitoes feeding on you, unless you smother yourself with repellent. The grassy, wooded lakes that offer such a great food source for fish tend to have large populations of insects. If this doesn't sound appealing, head for higher ground at the rockbound, granite lakes. Look for inlets that can host spawners, and lakes that have populations of forage fish such as redside shiners. These should provide good angling opportunities.

Day hikers have a disadvantage when it comes to fishing these high lakes, especially in midsummer. Unless you get started very early, the bite may well be a bust by midday. You can improve your odds, however, with a float tube or raft. When trout go deep during the heat of the day, follow them with nightcrawlers, Power Bait or salmon eggs. Use a sinker on light line, bounce or drift it on the bottom, and float the bait about four feet above it. As for flies, try black woolly worms with a flash of purple, and a local pattern called the Antron Caterpillar, used with sinking line. The value of floating cannot be overstated; if the shore is too brushy or wooded for casting, this may be your only viable option. When we go backpacking, we take a two-person raft, and we've never been skunked at any high-mountain lake.

Those who fish Desolation regularly have their favorite fishing holes. Here are the ones that seem to be on every list from those in the know:

**Gilmore Lake:** Located off the Glen Alpine Trailhead (near Fallen Leaf Lake), this lake seems to have an embarrassment of riches, including Kamloops, large browns and mackinaw. It's easy to reach on a day hike, and consequently has its share of people.

**Heather Lake:** Also accessible from Glen Alpine, this lake is spectacular, with granite walls and rock islands. It also holds some of the biggest brown trout you'll find in the backcountry. You can watch them swimming near the surface from the trail that follows a ledge high above the water on the north side. Obviously, they know what you've just realized—that you'll never reach them. These fish achieve their size and lack of interest in lures or baits from the rich food source of shiners and chub in the lake.

**Granite Lake:** From the Bayview Trailhead, this attractive lake is just a mile away, but the steep terrain you have to traverse to reach it puts off many people. Because of the short distance and hiking time, this is probably the best shot you've got for a morning or evening rise. It's a good place for brook trout, its main species.

**Cathedral Lake:** It's not particularly attractive, it has its share of bugs, and it's on the heavily traveled route to Mount Tallac. Still, this circular lake with a big rockfall is the easiest to reach for the prized golden trout. With its relatively small surface and protected location, there is rarely any wind to stir a ripple. So these fish are wary and skittish. Still, the alternative for catching a golden is to hike up some miserable, talus-covered, off-trail slope.

**Middle Velma Lake:** Although you can hike there and back within a day (a long trek), the best way to fish the spunky rainbows here, which achieve respectable sizes, is to backpack in and camp overnight. Of the lakes accessible from the Eagle Falls Trailhead, this is usually the top producer. Although hikers abound, fishing pressure is light.

## OTHER HIGH-COUNTRY LAKES

Apart from Desolation Wilderness, there are several other good fishing lakes within an hour's drive of Lake Tahoe, among them:

**Fourth of July Lake** in Mokelumne Wilderness, accessible from the Woods Lake Trailhead off Highway 88 at Carson Pass. The trail to get here is steep and has some tricky sections, but can be reached on a day hike. There are good populations of self-sustaining brook trout.

**Star Lake,** near the section of the Tahoe Rim Trail that traverses the South Tahoe peaks. It's about a six-mile hike from the Big Meadow Trailhead on Highway 89, 5.5 miles south of US 50. The lake has a burgeoning population of brook trout, and fishing for this small, spunky fish is often quite good.

**Grouse Lake area,** north of Interstate 80 and Lake Spaulding in Tahoe National Forest. Motorized vehicles are prohibited in this area, making the lakes accessible only by foot or by bicycle. Vehicles, mainly four-wheel drives, can be driven to Grouse Ridge Lookout or to Meadow Lake. Trailheads are located off Bowman Road or at Summit City on a dirt road off paved Jackson Meadows Road northeast of Truckee. Among lakes with good reports are Baltimore (large brookies up to 17 inches), Milk (brookies to 10 inches and rainbows to 13 inches), Glacier (golden trout) and Big Downey (some trophy rainbows, but bring your float tube).

**Big Bend/Kingvale area,** on trails south of Interstate 80. Good reports come from Natalie (10- to 12-inch cutthroat trout), Upper Loch Leven (lively brook trout fishery) and Salmon (a good population of brookies, with some 14 to 16 inches).

# LAKES, RESERVOIRS, RIVERS & STREAMS

The following is a list of major fishing waters close to Lake Tahoe. In most cases, the season for trout is open year-round, and the general limit is five of any species or combination, including mackinaw. But there are exceptions. One is Lake Tahoe, where the fish limit is five, but only two can be mackinaw. For Eastern brook trout, California anglers can take 15 if at least 10 are less than eight inches total length, or five if they are over eight inches. The exception to this is Red Lake, which is managed as a trophy brook fishery and has a strict limit of five total, regardless of size.

## Desolation Wilderness Area

### Echo Lakes

*See Desolation Wilderness area map, page 229*

**Location:** Just north of US 50 at Echo Summit, via Echo Lakes Road; a 20-minute drive from South Lake Tahoe.

**Elevation:** 7,414 feet.

**Fish:** Rainbow, brook and cutthroat trout, and kokanee salmon.

**Tackle and bait:** Spinners, spoons and worm-and-flasher combinations trolled from boats. The lakes are not generally considered to be productive for flyfishing.

**Limit:** Five, plus 10 brookies under eight inches.

**Season:** Year-round, but the lakes are icebound in winter.

**Fish plants:** Annually. In Lower Echo Lake, the California Department of Fish and Game plants 8,000 rainbow catchables, 11,000 rainbow fingerlings and 11,560 cutthroat fingerlings. In Upper Echo Lake, the DFG plants 10,000 rainbow fingerlings.

**Comments:** Rainbow and cutthroat trout averaging 12 inches (but occasionally reaching up to 14 inches) are the most productive in these beautiful lakes, which are framed by granite peaks and provide an entry point to Desolation Wilderness. Neither brook trout nor kokanee are planted here, so they are apparently spawning on their own. Biologists surmise that brookies are migrating from upstream lakes in Desolation, and they tend to congregate in Upper Echo Lake. Kokanee are relatively small and are caught mainly in spring. The two lakes are connected by a narrow channel, and summer homes line the shorelines. Upper Echo Lake is smaller and easier to fish from outboards or canoes. Lower Echo Lake is large, exposed and subject to powerful afternoon winds. There's a marina with a boat-launching ramp, general store and cabins at Lower Echo Lake, and a "water taxi" that runs regularly to Upper Echo Lake and the trailhead to Desolation Wilderness. No waterskiing is allowed. Parking is difficult in summer.

**Information:** Echo Chalet, (916) 659-7207.

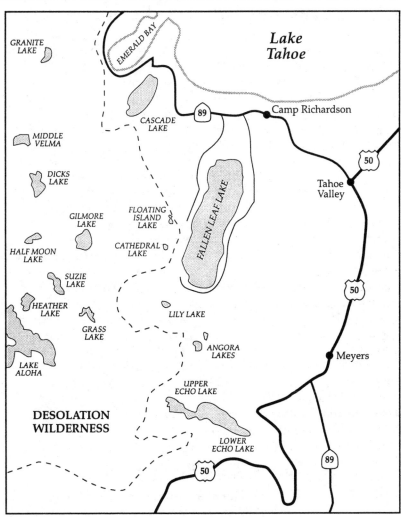

*Desolation Wilderness area lakes*

## Fallen Leaf Lake
*See Desolation Wilderness area map, above*

**Location:** Off Highway 89 on Fallen Leaf Road, near Camp Richardson, about five miles north of the "Y" at South Lake Tahoe.

**Elevation:** 6,400 feet.

**Fish:** Kokanee salmon and rainbow, brown and mackinaw trout.

**Tackle and bait:** Live minnows (but only those caught from Fallen Leaf), worms-and-flashers, spinners and Rapalas.

**Season:** Year-round, but the road is snowbound in winter.
**Limit:** Five.
**Fish plants:** Annually. The California Department of Fish and Game plants 50,000 kokanee fingerlings.
**Comments:** The amazing thing about this lake is that it is close to the Tahoe resorts but receives very little fishing pressure. Too bad, since this is a decent place to catch kokanee salmon and mackinaw. Fallen Leaf, in fact, is managed as a kokanee fishery, although it has limited numbers of rainbow and brown trout, and abundant numbers of smaller-sized mackinaw trout (one to three pounds). Early-morning trolling is the best fishing method, using Imperial Magics, Al Wilson blades and lead-core line. Begin with four or five colors early in the year, then drop to 8 to 10 colors by fall. The kokanee bite usually begins in late July and runs through September. For mackinaw, try drift-fishing with minnows. One of the problems with this large lake is the limited access for boats, consisting of a pay ramp at Fallen Leaf Marina. Most of the surrounding land (except for a U.S. Forest Service campground on the south end) is privately controlled, with several exclusive summer homes (including one featured in the movie *The Bodyguard*) and a summer retreat owned by Stanford University. Residents, many of whom have long-term leases from the Forest Service, are not keen on outside visitors, nor are they keen on allowing adequate and timely releases of lake water into Taylor Creek to ensure successful kokanee spawning for Lake Tahoe. The creek, controlled by a dam at Fallen Leaf, is the single most important spawning habitat on Tahoe for kokanee.
**Information:** The Sportsman in South Lake Tahoe, (916) 542-3474. Fallen Leaf Marina, (916) 544-0787.

# Carson Pass/Highway 88

## ★ Caples Lake ★

*See Carson Pass/Highway 88 area map, page 231*

**Location:** On Highway 88 four miles west of the Carson Pass, southwest of South Lake Tahoe.
**Elevation:** 7,800 feet.
**Fish:** Rainbow, brown, brook and mackinaw trout.
**Tackle and bait:** Rapalas, Rebels, FlatFish, Torpedoes, Triple Teasers, Canadian Wonders, feathered crappie jigs, salmon eggs, Power Bait and worms.
**Limit:** Five, plus 10 brookies under eight inches.
**Season:** Year-round, but the lake freezes over in winter.
**Fish plants:** Annually by both the California Department of Fish and Game and Alpine County—35,000 rainbow catchables, 6,000 brown

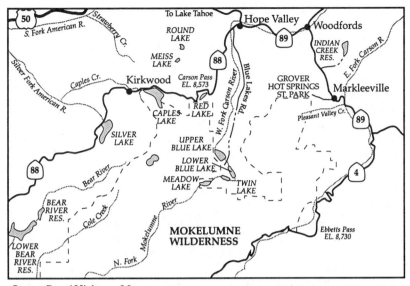

*Carson Pass / Highway 88 area waters*

trout catchables, 4,320 brook catchables, 6,000 mackinaw fingerlings and 23,000 brook trout fingerlings.

**Comments:** Here's a marvelous Mulligan stew of trout. Take your pick—just about every kind lives in this man-made lake. Shore anglers do fair, but trollers with small powerboats do better. The beauty of this 600-acre lake is that you don't have to be up at the crack of dawn to catch fish. Caples Resort guide Bruno Huff starts at around 9 a.m. and catches fish all day. Rainbows average 10 to 14 inches. Trolling just off the north, east and south shorelines with spinners and spoons is effective; worms or Power Bait with flashers also work well. If you seek the big lake trout, you'll have to go deeper with downriggers or jigs. Caples is a popular ice-fishing lake in winter, but check on ice conditions with the resort before venturing out. It's too large and too deep for flyfishing, and winds can be a problem in the afternoon. However, Caples is quite scenic, surrounded by spectacular volcanic peaks. The single resort here has boat rentals (there's a five mile-per-hour speed limit on the lake), a launching ramp and tackle, along with an excellent restaurant. A Forest Service camp-ground is across the highway, and there are some great undesignated boat-in camp spots along the eastern arm of the lake.

**Information:** Caples Lake Resort, (209) 258-8888.

## ★ Indian Creek Reservoir ★
*See Carson Pass/Highway 88 area map, page 231*

**Location:** Four miles off Highway 4/89 on Diamond Valley Road between Woodfords and Markleeville, south of the Highway 88 junction.
**Elevation:** 5,600 feet.
**Fish:** Rainbow, brook, Kamloops and Lahontan cutthroat trout.
**Tackle and bait:** Green or gold Panther Martins, pink or orange Power Bait, salmon eggs, Super Dupers and large garden worms. Flies include size-10 black woolly worms, black leeches, green matukas, silver Hiltons, Muddler Minnows and Antron Caterpillars, a local pattern. Try Adams or mosquito patterns in the evening.
**Limit:** Five, except for a bonus of 10 brookies under eight inches.
**Season:** Year-round.
**Fish plants:** Annually. The California Department of Fish and Game plants 8,100 rainbow catchables and 48,375 rainbow subcatchables. Alpine County plants varying stocks of Kamloops, rainbow, brook and Lahontan cutthroat trout.
**Comments:** This is one of the best lakes for flyfishing and float tubing for large trout. Although it used to be a catch-basin for wastewater from South Lake Tahoe, this 160-acre lake is now supplied with fresh water from the spring runoff and the West Fork of the Carson River. While the best chance of landing big fish is by belly boat, raft or canoe, shore anglers have success near the two dams. There's a small but attractive public campground with 29 sites run by the Bureau of Land Management, complete with hot showers, but camping is on a first-come, first-served basis.
**Information:** The Fish Connection, Gardnerville, (702) 782-4734. Monty Wulff's Trading Post, (916) 694-2201.

## Red Lake
*See Carson Pass/Highway 88 area map, page 231*

**Location:** On Highway 88 east of Carson Pass and west of the junction with Highway 89.
**Elevation:** 8,002 feet.
**Fish:** Brook, cutthroat and rainbow trout.
**Tackle and bait:** Power Bait, worms, Rooster Tails, Prince nymphs, woolly buggers and leeches.
**Limit:** Five, including brookies. This is a special exception to the general state limit of 10 brookies under eight inches.
**Season:** Year-round.
**Fish plants:** Annually. The California Department of Fish and Game plants 5,050 rainbow catchables, 200 Lahontan cutthroat brood stock, 8,500 brook fingerlings and 2,800 cutthroat subcatchables.
**Comments:** Want to catch trophy-sized brook trout? This is the place.

Fed by several springs and Red Lake Creek, this 85-acre lake in the shadow of Carson Pass, next to Highway 88, has become the brook trout capital of the region. The Department of Fish and Game has acquired about three-fourths of the water rights as well as surrounding lands, so the agency offers good protection for the fishery. There are no motor restrictions. Boaters will get best results working the upper end of the lake near the inlet and along the south shoreline, where there is a submerged shelf—it is the deepest place in the lake and is heavily favored by the trout. A free public launch ramp with limited parking is on the northeast end of the lake, near the dam.

*Information:* The Fish Connection, Gardnerville, (702) 782-4734. The Sportsman, South Lake Tahoe, (916) 542-3474.

## Silver Lake
*See Carson Pass/Highway 88 area map, page 231*

*Location:* On Highway 88, 40 miles southwest of South Lake Tahoe.
*Elevation:* 7,260 feet.
*Fish:* Rainbow and brown trout.
*Tackle and bait:* Worms, salmon eggs, small spinners, Power Bait, worm/flasher combinations, Panther Martins and flies such as mayflies and mosquito midges.
*Season:* Year-round, but the lake is snowbound in winter.
*Limit:* Five.
*Fish plants:* Annually. The California Department of Fish and Game plants 20,000 rainbow catchables and 5,000 brown catchables.
*Comments:* Surrounded by resorts and cabins and located next to Highway 88, Silver Lake gets heavy fishing pressure. The lake contains some big browns, going five to eight pounds, as well as lunker rainbows, going to five pounds. A few years ago, the Department of Fish and Game planted some mackinaw trout, but these apparently did not flourish. Trollers should fish 10 to 25 feet deep along the shoreline and around a large rock island. There are powerboat rentals at Kay's Silver Lake Resort, which also is the location of the launching ramp. Flyfishers will find the best action from float tubes in the fall, and earlier in the season along the Silver Fork of the American River, just across the highway. Area accommodations include Kit Carson Lodge and Kirkwood Ski Resort, and there are campgrounds operated by PG&E, the Forest Service and Plasse's Resort. Dramatic peaks frame the lake, which is rimmed by granite and forest, and on the ridge to the east runs the historic Mormon-Emigrant Trail. There are excellent restaurants at both Plasse's and Kit Carson Lodge.

*Information:* Kay's Silver Lake Resort, (209) 258-8598. Plasse's Resort, (209) 258-8814.

## ★ Blue Lakes ★

*See Carson Pass/Highway 88 area map, page 231*

**Location:** On Blue Lakes Road, 12 miles south of Highway 88, west of the junction of Highway 89. The first six miles are on paved road, but the rest is on generally adequate but occasionally bumpy dirt and gravel—okay for two-wheel drives.

**Elevation:** 8,000 feet.

**Fish:** Rainbow, brook and cutthroat trout.

**Tackle and bait:** Worms, Power Bait, Ford Fenders, Super Dupers, Kastmasters, Rooster Tails, Panther Martins and flies such as elkhair caddis, Adams, woolly worms with Flashabou, White Miller and a local pattern, the Antron Caterpillar.

**Limit:** Five trout (plus a bonus limit of 10 brookies under eight inches).

**Season:** Year-round, though snowbound in winter.

**Fish plants:** Annually. In Lower Blue Lake, 15,300 rainbow catchables and 18,000 brook trout catchables. In Upper Blue Lake, 10,000 rainbow catchables and 12,000 cutthroat fingerlings.

**Comments:** For the solo (unguided) angler, Blue Lakes provide perhaps the best chance of bagging trout in the Tahoe region, since the two lakes are heavily planted by the California Department of Fish and Game. The best methods are trolling in small boats or casting from float tubes. For shore anglers, fishing from the dams at Upper Blue Lake can be productive. Upper Blue Lake, at 344 acres, has a large population of cutthroat trout as well as rainbows, and has the most stable water level. Some beaver ponds near Lost Lakes, just above Upper Blue Lake, are full of 12- to 14-inch brook trout. The Blue Lakes region has 16 lakes, about three-fourths of them accessible by vehicle (but mainly four-wheel drive). For flyfishers, early season fishing at Wet Meadows, Granite, Tamarack and Summit lakes is worthwhile. For the evening rise, a White Miller is particularly effective. Golden trout can be caught at Raymond Lake, but the tiring, three-hour hike on slippery shale and steep switchbacks usually puts off most anglers. There are good PG&E campgrounds at both Blue Lakes.

**Information:** The Fish Connection in Gardnerville, Nevada, (702) 782-4734. The Sportsman in South Lake Tahoe, (916) 542-3474.

## ★ Carson River (East Fork, California side) ★

*See Carson Pass/Highway 88 area map, page 231*

**Location:** From Markleeville, drive nine miles north on Highway 89. Turn right onto Highway 4 and continue 2.5 miles to river access on the left side of the road.

**Fish:** Rainbow, cutthroat, brown trout and mountain whitefish.

**Tackle and bait:** Only artificial lures with barbless hooks in the wild trout section; other tackle and bait, including salmon eggs and night-crawlers, are allowed above that section. Panther Martins and Rooster Tails work well for spin casters. In warm months, nymphs such as hare's ear and woolly buggers work well for fly anglers, and in cooler months (early in the season) dry flies such as White Wulff, elkhair caddis with a yellow body, Royal Wulff and White Millers yield bites.

*Limit:* Two, with a minimum size of 14 inches in the section from Hangman's Bridge downstream to the Nevada state line (nine miles). Upstream from Hangman's Bridge, the limit is five.

*Season:* Last Saturday in April to November 15.

*Fish plants:* None in the wild trout section. The California Department of Fish and Game planted 15,000 rainbow catchables and 90 cutthroat brood stock in 1994 on the section of the river from Hangman's Bridge to Silver Creek.

*Special restrictions:* Fishing is closed year-round upstream from Carson Falls and in the tributaries here.

*Comments:* This is one of the best rivers in the region in which to catch a native trout, or perhaps a trophy brown of over five pounds. It's the only free-flowing river left on the eastern flanks of the Sierra, so without dams the native trout are able to find plenty of spawning habitat. Flyfishers will find quality but not quantity if they make short, 30-foot casts upstream. Later in the season, if the water is clear, unbroken and shallow, fish get spooky and are best approached with blind casts—definitely a challenge. In September and October, try small flies such as a Griffith Gnat or a black or gray midge, in sizes 20 to 26. For spin-casting anglers, plenty of catchable rainbows are available upstream from Hangman's Bridge, an area that is much easier to reach from Highway 4 and has lots of riffles and pockets. Two tributaries, Silver and Wolf creeks, get little pressure but can offer paydirt for those with the patience to work them. On Silver Creek, flyfishers can try a beadhead hare's ear, a black ant or a green inchworm pattern with a black head. On Wolf Creek, try any orange thorax fly fished underneath deeply cut banks. Early in the season, be careful wading during a high runoff. By mid- to late summer you should be able to wade and walk most of the East Carson on the California side.

*Information:* The Fish Connection in Gardnerville, (702) 782-4734. East Fork Resort in Markleeville, (916) 694-2229. Horse Feathers Fly Fishing School at Sorensen's Resort in Hope Valley, (916) 694-2203 or (800) 423-9949.

## ★ Carson River (West Fork) ★

*See Carson Pass/Highway 88 area map, page 231*

**Location:** Flowing from headwaters in the Blue Lakes region eastward through Hope Valley (near the Highway 88/89 junction south of South Lake Tahoe), paralleling much of Highway 88 in California.

**Fish:** Rainbow, cutthroat and brown trout.

**Tackle and bait:** For spin anglers, small (about $^1/_{16}$-ounce) Panther Martins and Rooster Tails work well. For fly anglers, try woolly buggers and White Millers, depending on the time of day.

**Limit:** Five.

**Season:** Last Saturday in April to November 15.

**Fish plants:** Annually. In 1994, the California Department of Fish and Game planted 13,800 rainbow catchables, 85 cutthroat brood stock and 17,155 brown fingerlings.

**Comments:** Though not as productive as the East Fork, the West Fork has some scenic waters in Hope Valley, and its tributaries near Blue Lakes often have brook trout as well as other species. The river downstream from Sorensen's Resort is generally accessible from Highway 88.

**Information:** Horse Feathers Fly Fishing School at Sorensen's Resort, (916) 694-2203. The Fish Connection in Gardnerville, NV, (702) 782-4734.

## ★ Pleasant Valley Creek ★

*See Carson Pass/Highway 88 area map, page 231*

**Location:** In eastern Alpine County south of South Lake Tahoe. About 1.5 miles south of Markleeville on Highway 4/89, turn west on Hot Springs Road, toward Grover Hot Springs. From there take a left onto Pleasant Valley Road. Proceed through a residential area to the top of a hill where a dirt road begins and takes you downhill to Pleasant Valley. Most of the land is private, so you should check to make sure owners allow access.

**Fish:** Rainbow, brown and cutthroat trout.

**Tackle and bait:** Only artificial flies with single barbless hooks (no live bait or lures). Try a small caddis green rock worm early in the season, a Muddler Minnow or gray grasshopper pattern. Also black ant, hare's ear, elkhair caddis and White Miller, in sizes 14 and 16.

**Limit:** Two.

**Season:** Last Saturday in April through November 15.

**Fish plants:** Annually. In 1994, the California Department of Fish and Game stocked 500 rainbow catchables and 15 brood stock cutthroat. Alpine County also planted fish.

**Comments:** This clear, spring-fed stream is a spawning area and tributary to the East Fork of the Carson River, and as such it has big brood stock, including naturally reproducing brown trout. Because of this, there's a requested catch-and-release ethic here. This is a good spot for early season fishing if the East Carson is too high.

**Information:** Horse Feathers Fly Fishing School at Sorensen's Resort, (916) 694-2203.

# Truckee Area

## Boca Reservoir

*See Truckee area map, below*

**Location:** Head east of Truckee on Interstate 80 and take the Hirschdale exit; the lake is just north of the exit.

**Elevation:** 5,700 feet.

**Fish:** Rainbow trout, brown trout and kokanee salmon.

**Tackle and bait:** Worms, eggs, Power Bait, small spinners and flies such as woolly buggers and midges.

**Limit:** Five trout.

**Season:** Year-round.

**Fish plants:** The California Department of Fish and Game plants 10,700 catchable rainbows annually, and was scheduled to plant 50,000 kokanee fingerlings for 1995.

**Comments:** This lake, covering nearly 1,000 acres, suffered heavily

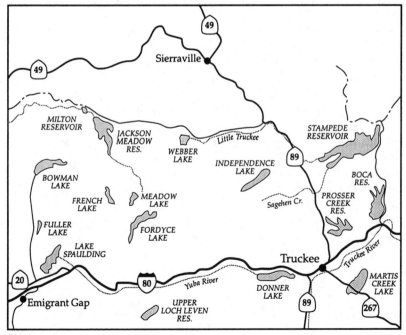

*Truckee area waters*

during the prolonged drought, when, in 1994, it dwindled to 11 percent of its normal size. Trolling in the many arms and coves is the best way to take fish here, using worm-and-flasher setups or minnow-type lures. Because of a major drawdown in recent years, call ahead to make sure boat ramps are accessible. Forest Service campgrounds are available at three locations.

*Information:* Longs Drugs, Sporting Goods Department, P.O. Box 8085, Truckee, CA 96162; (916) 587-5772.

## Donner Lake
*See Truckee area map, page 237*

*Location:* Take the Donner Pass Road exit off Interstate 80 at Truckee; follow it to the lake.

*Elevation:* 5,970 feet.

*Fish:* Mackinaw, rainbow and brown trout, and kokanee salmon.

*Tackle and bait:* Worms, salmon eggs, small spinners, Power Bait, FlatFish, Rapalas, Rebels and jigs such as minnow/Bomber combinations. (Note: Only minnows caught in Donner Lake can be used.)

*Limit:* Five.

*Fishing season:* Year-round.

*Fish plants:* Annually. The California Department of Fish and Game plants 71,800 rainbow catchables, 81,000 mackinaw fingerlings and 154,240 kokanee fingerlings.

*Comments:* Located close to the main highway, this elongated lake with over seven miles of shoreline gets plenty of fishing pressure, but for unguided anglers it's tough to fish for mackinaw and kokanee. Rainbow trout are easily caught throughout the season. As with Lake Tahoe, hiring a guide is the best approach for newcomers. Mackinaw are also among the prizes here, but anglers must fish deep for them (80 feet or more), and the best months to bag lake trout are in the spring and fall. Otherwise, early morning top-lining for rainbows and kokanee can be productive. There was once a significant population of brown trout (setting a state record a few years ago), but that fishery has declined in recent years. Rainbow trollers generally congregate at the south side of the lake, and mackinaw trollers and jiggers hover in China Cove. The beehive of waterskiers and jetskiers does not make life pleasant for boat anglers. Look out for afternoon winds in summer.

*Information:* Mountain Hardware and Sports in Truckee, (916) 587-4844.

## Fuller Lake
*See Truckee area map, page 237*

*Location:* Off Highway 20 on Bowman Lake Road, about a 50-minute drive west of Truckee, via Interstate 80.

*Elevation:* 5,600 feet.

*Fish:* Rainbow and brown trout.

*Tackle and bait:* Nightcrawlers, spinners and spoons, woolly worms and dry flies for morning and evening rises.

*Limit:* Five.

*Season:* Year-round.

*Fish plants:* Annually. The California Department of Fish and Game plants 13,800 pounds of catchable rainbows.

*Comments:* This is an attractive little reservoir, close to giant Lake Spaulding, that offers a pine-studded shoreline, scenic mountain vistas, a delightful picnic area and lots of spunky rainbow trout. Also, large brown trout persist in the lake, and many are taken early and late in the season at the inlet of Bowman Tunnel. A small outboard, rowboat, canoe or float tube is just fine for fishing Fuller, but shore anglers can have good success as well. There's a small, unimproved boat-launching area. The beauty of the lake, its easy access, and its relative lack of crowds make for an excellent family fishing spot.

*Information:* California Department of Fish and Game, 1701 Nimbus Road, Rancho Cordova, CA 95670; (916) 355-0978.

## Independence Lake
*See Truckee area map, page 237*

*Location:* Off Jackson Meadows Road from Highway 89, north of Truckee.

*Fish:* Browns, Lahontan cutthroat and brook trout, and kokanee salmon.

*Tackle and bait:* Spinners, spoons and flies. Only artificial lures with barbless hooks may be used.

*Limit:* Zero kill (catch-and-release) on all cutthroat trout; five for other species, except for an additional 10 brookies under eight inches.

*Season:* Year-round, but the lake is snowbound in winter.

*Fish plants:* None.

*Comments:* This is one of the best lakes in the region for healthy populations of naturally reproducing fish. The lake has the last remaining pool of genetically pure Lahontan cutthroat trout, which were isolated here when downstream reservoirs were built. Independence is virtually surrounded by private land, mostly controlled by Sierra Pacific Power Company, which serves northern Nevada. The only access is from one corner of the upper end, where anglers can walk in for shore fishing. Unfortunately, the lake is large and really requires the use of a boat to have much success. It is not particularly easy to fish from a float tube or a raft. Most anglers seek out the kokanee, which are not large, averaging about 10 inches. It is illegal to fish any tributaries or within 300 feet of the mouths of tributaries to Independence Lake.

*Information:* Longs Drugs, Sporting Goods Department, P.O. Box 8085, Truckee, CA 96162; (916) 587-5772.

## Jackson Meadows and Milton Reservoirs
*See Truckee area map, page 237*

*Location:* On Highway 89 and Henness Pass Road, 33 miles northwest of Truckee.
*Elevation:* 6,100 feet.
*Fish:* Rainbow and brown trout.
*Tackle and bait:* Worms, salmon eggs and small spinners for Jackson Meadows. Artificial lures with barbless hooks only for Milton.
*Limit:* Five in Jackson Meadows with no size limit; two in Milton, with a maximum size limit of 12 inches total length.
*Season:* For Jackson Meadows, year-round, but it is snowbound in winter. Milton is open the last Saturday in April through November 15.
*Fish plants:* Annually. The California Department of Fish and Game plants 26,900 rainbow catchables in Jackson Meadows, and two strains of brown trout in Milton. No regular stocking is done in Milton since the lake is managed for large trophy fish.
*Comments:* These lakes, connected by the Middle Fork of the Yuba River and located just a short distance from each other, offer great variety for both bait-and-lure anglers and flyfishers. Jackson Meadows, with a large population of redsided shiners, yields respectable rainbows for boat trollers in the 12- to 14-inch range, of which an estimated 65 percent are caught. Milton, recently recovering from a maintenance drawdown, has the capacity to kick out trophy-sized brown trout (up to 14 pounds), and until 1994 was a favorite for flyfishers. It is a diversion structure for water from Jackson Meadows, and as such has a rich food source with weeds, insects and reintroduced crayfish. The 30-acre lake, 27 feet deep, is excellent for float tubing, but it will take a couple of years for the fishery to bounce back, although anglers can now expect 8- to 12-inch fish. Wading anglers should look out for a deep hole that was used for habitat improvement in the lake bottom.
*Information:* Longs Drugs, Sporting Goods Department, P.O. Box 8085, Truckee, CA 96162; (916) 587-5772.

## ★ Martis Creek Lake ★
*See Truckee area map, page 237*

*Location:* Off Highway 267, about six miles southeast of Truckee and Kings Beach, then one-half mile on a maintained dirt road to the lake.
*Elevation:* 6,300 feet.
*Fish:* Lahontan cutthroat, Eagle Lake-strain rainbow and German brown trout.

*Tackle and bait:* Only artificial lures with barbless hooks may be used, including spinners and size 12 to 16 flies such as blood midge emergers, damselfly, caddis and callibaetis.

*Restrictions:* Boats without motors only.

*Limit:* Zero kill. All fish must be released.

*Season:* Last Saturday in April through November 15.

*Fish plants:* Annually. The California Department of Fish and Game plants 4,800 subcatchable Eagle Lake-strain rainbows.

*Comments:* This is California's first "wild trout" lake, with naturally reproducing Lahontan cutthroat trout. It is also one of the best flyfishing reservoirs in the Tahoe area for big fish, and a popular place for neophyte flycasters, because of its easy access and wide-open shoreline. Eagle Lake-strain trout have done well since they were introduced in the early 1990s. Sizes are increasing, with 20-inchers occasionally caught; these fish have large bodies and small heads. Brown trout are not faring as well; with a diminishing forage base, they may be on their way out. Also, the cutthroat trout have almost completely disappeared. This 80-acre lake, administered by the U.S. Army Corps of Engineers, is suited for float tubes, canoes and rowboats, which can be launched easily from the open shoreline. No motors are allowed on the lake. A good campground is nestled in pine trees adjacent to the lake.

*Information:* Cutters' California School of Flyfishing in Truckee, (916) 587-7005.

## Prosser Creek Reservoir
*See Truckee area map, page 237*

*Location:* Off Highway 89 about 2.5 miles north of Truckee and Interstate 80, then east on good dirt and paved roads.

*Elevation:* 5,711 feet.

*Fish:* Rainbow and brown trout.

*Tackle and bait:* Worms, salmon eggs, small spinners, Power Bait, worm/flasher combinations and flies such as nymphs, midges and black woolly buggers.

*Limit:* Five.

*Season:* Year-round.

*Fish plants:* Annually. The California Department of Fish and Game stocks 90,200 fingerling Eagle Lake-strain rainbow trout, 20,000 rainbow catchables and 10,000 rainbow fingerlings.

*Comments:* This is an open, wind-swept reservoir with 740 acres in rolling hills. Rainbows and naturally reproducing brown trout head up the main fare. Years ago, the Department of Fish and Game planted brook and cutthroat trout, but these have not become major species. Trolling is best along the shoreline close to willows and weeds, in the various arms of the lake. Boats are restricted to 10 miles per hour, so there are no waterskiers to encroach on anglers. The Forest Service maintains three campgrounds, none of which is aesthetically pleasing. There's a public boat-launching ramp. The reservoir's water level declines radically in the fall months.

*Information:* Longs Drugs, Sporting Goods Department, P.O. Box 8085, Truckee, CA 96162; (916) 587-5772.

## ★ Lake Spaulding ★
*See Truckee area map, page 237*

*Location:* 28 miles west of Truckee at the Highway 20 exit from Interstate 80 near Yuba Gap.

*Elevation:* 5,014 feet.

*Fish:* Chinook salmon, mackinaw and brown trout.

*Tackle and bait:* Rapalas, Rebels, Spaulding smelt, Bomber combinations, jigs, worm-and-flasher combinations, Apex lures, Power Bait. No live bait is allowed.

*Limit:* Five trout or salmon.

*Season:* Year-round, but the reservoir may be snowbound in winter.

*Fish plants:* The California Department of Fish and Game plants mackinaw fingerlings and brown fingerlings on a regular basis. It has recently undertaken an experimental plant of chinook salmon.

*Comments:* You thought there was no place to catch chinook salmon in the Tahoe area? Guess again. Thanks to an ambitious new program started by the California Department of Fish and Game in November, 1994, Spaulding could become the hot Sierra fishing hole for monster salmon; right now, it's the only lake in the Tahoe region stocked with the species. This historic new fishery was a cooperative effort of Kokanee Unlimited, PG&E (which owns the lake) and the Department of Fish and Game. The salmon can thrive thanks to the forage population of Japanese pond smelt and good creeks that provide spawning habitat. These days, the fish are in the 12- to 14-inch range, but in a couple of years there should be some five-pounders.

*Information:* California Department of Fish and Game, 10457 New Town Road, Nevada City, CA 95929; (916) 265-0805.

## ★ Stampede Reservoir ★
*See Truckee area map, page 237*

*Location:* Approximately eight miles north of Interstate 80 on Stampede Meadow Road at the Hirschdale exit, which is six miles east of Truckee. The lake is next to Boca Reservoir.

*Elevation:* 5,949 feet.

*Fish:* Rainbow, mackinaw, brook and brown trout, along with kokanee salmon and mountain whitefish.

***Tackle and bait:*** Worms, salmon eggs, Power Bait, small spinners, attractor blades and wedding rings with a piece of white corn, and flies such as woolly buggers, nymphs and midges.

***Limit:*** Five.

***Season:*** Year-round.

***Fish plants:*** Annually. The California Department of Fish and Game plants 126,000 kokanee fingerlings, 56,000 mackinaw fingerlings, 13,480 rainbow catchables, 24,890 brook fingerlings and 4,000 brown catchables.

***Comments:*** Of the reservoirs north of Truckee, this is by far the most popular among anglers. Despite its diverse trout population, the lake has seen its hottest action for kokanee. The productiveness of the fishery is constantly threatened by a substantial annual drawdown to supply the downstream water needs of Pyramid Lake in Nevada—primarily to support a threatened species of sucker fish called the cui-ui. In 1994, for example, Stampede was lowered to about one-third of its normal capacity. The lake, which under normal conditions encompasses 3,400 acres with 24 miles of shoreline, is operated by the U.S. Fish and Wildlife Service. For shore anglers, the best strategy is to fish the weedy flats around the inlet streams. For trollers, fish along the bottom for mackinaw and browns, and mid-depth for rainbows and kokanee. Electronic fish locators are highly advisable for finding the schools of kokanee. The best time for salmon is early in the spring when the fish are close to the surface. They go deep in summer, around 90 feet, then return to the top in fall, but by then their discoloration makes them less palatable. Fish average 12 to 14 inches. In the past, big rainbows up to seven pounds and browns up to 21 pounds have been caught, but lunkers such as these are not as common as they once were. Boaters should beware of the ferocious afternoon winds. The lake is also used by jetskiers and waterskiers. The Forest Service has good campgrounds at three locations around the lake.

***Information:*** Longs Drugs, Sporting Goods Department, P.O. Box 8085, Truckee, CA 96162; (916) 587-5772.

## Little Truckee River
*See Truckee area map, page 237*

***Location:*** There are two sections of this river. The first originates at Webber Lake and flows eastward 16 miles to Stampede Reservoir; it is accessible mainly from Highway 89 north of Truckee. The second section is sandwiched between Stampede and Boca reservoirs, north of Interstate 80 and east of Truckee.

***Fish:*** Rainbow and brown trout.

***Tackle and bait:*** For the section below Webber Lake, try lures such as Panther Martins and Rooster Tails, or flies such as caddis and woolly

buggers. In all sections of the Little Truckee, try hare's ears for nymphs or dry flies such as Parachute Adams, size 14 through 18, or Light Paradun.
**Limit:** In the section above Stampede, five.
**Season:** Last Saturday in April through November 15.
**Fish plants:** The California Department of Fish and Game plants only the section above Stampede, with 775 catchable rainbows at the campground area.
**Comments:** The upper section of the Little Truckee River, set among scenic valleys and high meadows, has a checkered pattern of ownership (Webber Lake, with the headwaters of the river, is entirely private, for example). It's important to check current maps and contact the U.S. Forest Service for the best public access points other than from the highway. This stretch of river supports both native and planted rainbow trout. The section between the two reservoirs has naturally reproducing brown trout, as well as "spill-over" rainbows from Stampede Reservoir; it has benefited from habitat improvements and regulated water flows. The best access for this area is from Boca-Stampede Road at the Hirschdale exit of Interstate 80.
**Information:** Tahoe National Forest, Truckee Ranger District, (916) 587-3558.

## Sagehen Creek
*See Truckee area map, page 237*
**Location:** This creek crosses Highway 89, about two miles north of the Hobart Mills exit north of Truckee.
**Fish:** Brown, rainbow and brook trout.
**Tackle and bait:** Artificial lures with barbless hooks from the Highway 89 bridge upstream to the gauging station at the east boundary of the Sagehen Creek Station. Use attractors and suggestive patterns such as yellow Humpies, Royal Wulffs, hare's ear and pheasant tail in sizes 14 to 18.
**Limit:** Catch-and-release only in the wild trout section.
**Season:** Last Saturday in April through November 15.
**Fish plants:** None.
**Comments:** There is relatively easy access here, and you've got a shot at catching small brown and rainbow trout in a very small meadow stream. With tight banks and trees down to the water's edge, this creek will test your casting accuracy. Successful anglers may have to crawl on their knees upstream and make precise presentations to reach these extremely spooky fish.
**Information:** Thy Rod & Staff Flyfishing, (916) 587-7333.

## ★ Truckee River (Upper Section of the Main) ★
*See Truckee area map, page 237*

**Location:** Between Truckee and Tahoe City, parallel to Highway 89.

**Fish:** Rainbow, brown trout and mountain whitefish.

**Tackle and bait:** Panther Martins, worms, salmon eggs, flies such as yellow Humpies, elkhair caddis and nymphs such as beadhead green rock worms or sparkle pupae, pheasant tail and hare's ear.

**Limit:** Five.

**Season:** Last Saturday in April through November 15.

**Special Restrictions:** No fishing from Fanny Bridge at Lake Tahoe to 1,000 feet downstream.

**Fish plants:** Annually. The California Department of Fish and Game plants 5,000 catchable rainbows.

**Comments:** The long drought drastically reduced flows along this 14-mile stretch of the Truckee, but strong runoff and spillage from Lake Tahoe could produce sufficient regulated flows to allow the California Department of Fish and Game to stock more fish here. Because of riverfront Forest Service campgrounds and easy access from busy Highway 89, this stretch of the river receives substantial fishing pressure, although anglers who fish here should be aware that much of the river frontage is private property. If you fish upstream from the Alpine Meadows Road, you'll have mostly slow water, with big pools fed by riffles where large brown trout can lurk. Then, fed by a series of seven streams, the river picks up speed, and, during normal runoff years, roars past River Ranch Lodge and can be very hazardous. Even where you feel comfortable wading, be sure to wear felt-bottomed shoes and use a wading staff to pick your way through the algae-covered rocks. In July and August, the river is heavily used for commercial rafting and tubing from Tahoe City to River Ranch, so your best strategy at that time is to fish before dusk. If dry flies aren't working on showing fish, use emerging patterns, such as soft hackles (partridge and orange, for example), or cripple patterns when trout are seemingly surface feeding. Normally, the best times to fish the Truckee are late June through early August, and again in late September through the end of the season.

**Information:** Thy Rod & Staff Flyfishing, (916) 587-7333. Mountain Hardware and Sports in Truckee, (916) 587-4844.

## Truckee River (Middle Section, California)
*See Truckee area map, page 237*

**Location:** There are several distinct sections of this river, which flows east of Truckee to the Nevada state line.

**Fish:** Rainbow and brown trout. Native wild trout exist from Trout Creek to Gray Creek in California.

*Tackle and bait:* Legal restrictions vary depending on location. From Trout Creek below Truckee to the Glenshire Bridge, only artificial lures with barbless hooks are allowed; from Glenshire Bridge to Boca Bridge, only artificial flies with barbless hooks are allowed. Beyond this bridge to the Nevada state line, any type of gear may be used.

*Limit:* Two from Boca to Gray Creek with no size restriction, and from Trout Creek to Boca Bridge the minimum size is 15 inches. From Gray Creek to the Nevada state line, the limit is five, with no size restrictions.

*Season:* Last Saturday in April through November 15.

*Fish plants:* None in the wild trout waters.

*Comments:* The Truckee River is not easy to fish at any point, but especially here. It has pocket water, riffles, pools and fast water. Footing is tricky, and accurate casting and wading are critical. The fish average 9 to 12 inches, with the occasional larger trout of 18 to 20 inches in the wild trout section of the river. Because of the somewhat confusing and varied restrictions, anglers need to pay close attention to Department of Fish and Game regulations. There is considerable fishing pressure here as the Truckee flows through shallow canyons, then enters a deep-cut gorge between Interstate 80 and the Southern Pacific railroad tracks. For fly anglers, the early season is best for presenting patterns such as stonefly initiations, beadhead hare's ear (size 14) and various sculpin imitations (sizes 2 to 6)—sculpin are the predominant forage fish here. Later in the season, from late June through early August, dry fly fishing is better at dusk, with elkhair caddis imitations, in sizes 14 to 16, and soft hackles (partridge and green, grouse and peacock) in sizes 12 to 18.

*Information:* Thy Rod & Staff Flyfishing, (916) 587-7333.

# Nevada
## ★ Pyramid Lake ★
*See Reno/Carson Valley area map, page 247*

*Location:* In Nevada, 32 miles northeast of Reno on Highway 445.

*Elevation:* 3,500 feet.

*Fish:* Lahontan cutthroat trout. An endangered, sucker-like fish called the cui-ui is protected and must be released.

*Tackle and bait:* Artificial lures only. FlatFish, Kwikfish, Krocodile spoons, Apex and Torpedoes in different colors (chartreuse, green and fluorescent orange seem to work best); and flies including size four to eight black, brown, white, olive and purple woolly worms.

*Limit:* Two per day, only one of which may be over 24 inches. The second fish may be 16 to 19 inches, or you may catch two fish that are 16 to 19 inches.

*Season:* October 1 to June 31.

**Special restrictions:**
Release all fish less than 16 inches and between 20 to 24 inches in length. All fish must be kept alive on a stringer or in a live well until you are done for the day. A Paiute Tribe permit must be purchased, at $6 for one day and $32 for the season; a state license is not required. Non-tribe members cannot use live bait.

**Fish plants:** The Pyramid Lake Paiute Tribe operates a fish hatchery and the lake is regularly stocked with Lahontan cutthroat trout.

**Comments:** Like a mirage shimmering in the high desert north of Reno, Pyramid Lake is a weirdly beautiful expanse of blue. Named after a pyramid-shaped tufa mound, this large, relatively shallow lake (300 feet deep) hosts some monster cutthroat trout. As the last vestige of prehistoric Lake Lahontan, a massive inland sea that once (a long, long, *long* time ago) covered most of Nevada and the Great Basin, the lake is owned and managed by the Pyramid Lake Paiute Indian

*Reno/Carson Valley area waters*

Tribe, and all anglers must buy a special fishing permit from the tribe (available at the marina and at stores on the reservation). The lake depends on flows from the Truckee River for its survival, and the cutthroat trout fishery has had a checkered history, a result of overfishing, cross-breeding with undesirable species, and loss of stream spawning habitat from river tributaries that were dammed up. Two hatcheries at the lake attempt to overcome those losses with the release of hundreds of thousands of cutthroat into the lake each year. Pyramid has always had a reputation for huge trout—the world record, in fact, was caught in 1925 by a Paiute Indian who landed a 41-pounder (on display at the Nevada State Museum in Carson City). Today, 5- to 10-pound fish are not uncommon. Anglers can fish the lake by motorboat or from shore, and usually the trollers have the edge. Fish can be at any part of the lake, but the regulars prefer the Artesians, the Willows and the mouth of the river. Underwater hot springs at several spots often provide good fishing grounds. Something that is unique to Pyramid is the sight of dozens of fly anglers standing on mostly submerged stepladders in the shallows near the net pens used by the hatcheries. They may cast for two to three hours before landing a fish. The best times for shore anglers are in late fall and early spring, when the water is cooler and fish are closer to the surface. Some caveats: The dry heat can cause rapid dehydration (even in winter, when temperatures can be in the 70s), and the lake is infamous for its raging afternoon winds and sudden thunderstorms, which can be very dangerous for boaters. The shoreline has sandy beaches, and there's a new marina, a launch ramp ($6 per boat) and a campground with full facilities.

*Information:* Pyramid Lake Marina, (702) 476-1156; or Pyramid Lake Tribal Council, P.O. Box 256, Nixon, NV 89424; (702) 574-1000.

## ★ Spooner Lake ★
*See Reno/Carson Valley area map, page 247*

*Location:* In Nevada at Spooner Lake, Lake Tahoe-Nevada State Park, on Highway 28 near US 50, 11 miles northeast of South Lake Tahoe.

*Elevation:* 6,981 feet.

*Fish:* Rainbow, brown, cutbow (rainbow and cutthroat cross), tiger (brown and brook trout cross) and cutthroat trout.

*Tackle and bait:* Artificial lures and single barbless hooks only—gold and silver Vibrax, Mepps spinners, Rat-L-Trap, Panther Martins, Rapalas and flies such as green, black and brown woolly buggers, Muddler Minnows and blood midges.

*Limit:* Zero kill; catch-and-release only.

*Season:* Year-round, but the lake is frozen in winter.

*Special restrictions:* No motors are allowed on the lake.

*Fish plants:* Annually. The Nevada Division of Wildlife stocks 1,000 rainbow catchables, 500 bowcutt catchables, 540 cutthroat trout catchables and 500 tiger trout catchables.

*Comments:* Nevada's only catch-and-release fishery is also the closest good stillwater flyfishing to South Lake Tahoe, just 15 minutes from the casinos at Stateline at either end of the lake. Spooner is also one of the most diverse fisheries in the region, and a patient angler might catch three or four different species in an afternoon. This is the only water in the area that contains the tiger trout, a recent cross that is planted mainly in eastern Nevada. Surrounded by aspens and pines, with a thick growth of weeds lining the shore, Spooner has a rich food source for trout, including the Lahontan tui chub, the same forage fish found in Pyramid Lake. The chub reach 6 to 12 inches in length and will readily take a fly, thus presenting something of a nuisance to anglers. Spooner is best fished from a float tube, raft or canoe, but you'll have to carry everything one-quarter mile from the parking lot of Spooner Lake. The shoreline is fairly brushy, although there are spots near the dam that accommodate shore anglers. In 1992, a random check by Division of Wildlife field workers turned up a 20-inch cutthroat and an 18-inch rainbow, the largest fish caught here to date. The best times to fish the lake are late spring and early fall. Bring your camera for proof of your catch, especially if you land a tiger trout. There's a parking fee to enter the state park.

*Information:* The Sportsman, South Lake Tahoe, (916) 542-3474. Lake Tahoe-Nevada State Park (which administers Spooner), (702) 831-0494.

## Topaz Lake
*See Reno/Carson Valley area map, page 247*

*Location:* Straddling the California/Nevada state line on US 395, 18 miles south of Gardnerville, about a one-hour drive from South Lake Tahoe.

*Elevation:* 5,000 feet.

*Fish:* Eagle Lake-strain rainbow trout, brown trout, tiger trout (hybrid of brown and brook trout), black bass and mountain whitefish.

*Tackle and bait:* Chartreuse Power Bait, nightcrawlers, black, gold or silver and gold Rapalas, Needlefish, worm-and-flasher rigs, white Rooster Tails, Panther Martins and chrome Krocodiles.

*Limits:* Five trout, 10 mountain whitefish and 15 warmwater gamefish, of which no more than five may be black bass.

*Season:* January 1 through September 30.

*Special restrictions:* The area within a 100-yard radius of Topaz Marina is closed to fishing. Also, boat anglers can fish two rods per person (for an extra license stamp fee) only in the California side of the lake. There are shore markers denoting the boundary.

*Fish plants:* Annually. The California Department of Fish and Game stocks 20,000 to 30,000 Coleman-strain rainbow catchables (around nine inches). The Nevada Division of Wildlife stocks 17,000 rainbow catchables (including Eagle Lake and bowcutt strains).

*Comments:* Big rainbows and browns make this high-desert lake, surrounded by rolling hills, sagebrush and sandy shoreline, especially popular. Lake records are set almost annually. In 1994, on opening day, an 11-pound, 11-ounce brown was caught on a rainbow-colored Rapala trolled 65 feet deep with lead-core line. Early in 1995, a 10-pound, one-

ounce rainbow was caught by an angler who was top-lining with a silver Needlefish on three-pound monofilament off the north shore. It took 90 minutes to land the fish. The average size of rainbows caught is around 1.5 pounds. Trout move all over the lake, which is 1,800 acres in size and is used for agricultural irrigation. One of the top spots is The Rock on the east side near the Douglas County Recreation Area, where shore fishing can be productive. The lake fluctuates; normally it is at 100 feet at its highest. In midsummer, when the water warms up, the trout develop small skin parasites, called anchor worms, but fisheries biologists assure anglers that these do not affect the eating quality of the fish. The Coleman strain of rainbows here is unique because they spawn in the fall rather than in the spring. Plenty of services are at the lake, including a marina with powerboat rentals, an RV park, a county campground, a restaurant and a casino. There are two boat-launching ramps, one at Topaz Marina, the other in the county park.
*Information:* Topaz Marina, (702) 266-3550.

## Carson River (East Fork, Nevada side)
*See Reno/Carson Valley area map, page 247*
*Location:* From Markleeville, drive nine miles north on Highway 89 and 18 miles north on Highway 88. Turn right onto US 395 and drive 9.5 miles through Minden and Gardnerville. Continue 2.5 miles past the last stop light (a 7-11 is at the corner). Follow the right hand turn lane into a wide dirt parking area where there is river access.
*Fish:* Rainbow, brown, brook and cutthroat trout.
*Tackle and bait:* Same as for the California side (see page 234). When the river warms up in Carson Valley, spin casters may find better luck with black and gold or black and silver Rapalas. Also, Nevada allows the use of live bait, including Tahoe suckers, mountain suckers, speckled dace, fathead minnows and mosquitofish. Buy only from dealers authorized to sell live bait in the Carson River basin.
*Limit:* Five.
*Season:* Year-round.
*Fish plants:* Annually. The Nevada Division of Wildlife planted 4,604 brown catchables in 1994.
*Comments:* This section of the river sees consistent fishing pressure, primarily from residents in the Gardnerville area. There are some steep, cut banks that are difficult to negotiate, but you'll generally get more and warmer water than the California side, and the fishery is managed for large brown trout.
*Information:* The Fish Connection in Gardnerville, (702) 782-4734.

## Truckee River (Lower Section, Nevada)

*See Reno/Carson Valley area map, page 247*

**Location:** From the Nevada state line through downtown Reno and points east.

**Fish:** Rainbow, brown and cutthroat trout.

**Tackle and bait:** There are two sections of the river, with varying regulations. The portion from the Interstate 80 bridge upstream from Crystal Peak Park to the California state line requires artificial lures with single barbless hooks. Below the bridge, there are no gear restrictions.

**Limit:** Above the Interstate 80 bridge, two trout and 10 mountain whitefish with a minimum size for trout of 14 inches. Below the Interstate 80 bridge, five trout, 10 mountain whitefish and 15 warmwater gamefish (of which not more than five may be black bass).

**Season:** Year-round.

**Fish plants:** Annually, by the Nevada Division of Wildlife. The lower section is planted with 155,000 rainbow catchables, 32,000 brown catchables and 6,000 cutthroat catchables.

**Comments:** Except for the one restricted area, it's basically open season for the section of the Truckee flowing through the casino district. If the jackpots aren't hitting in the clubs, down-and-outers can try their luck at angling. On most of the river (consult Nevada Division of Wildlife regulations for specifics), you can fish any hour of the day or night, except for within 1,000 feet downstream of Derby Dam, which is closed to fishing. Try spinners, spoons, salmon eggs, worms, flies—anything you've got. Who knows? Maybe your luck will change.

**Information:** Reno Fly Shop, (702) 825-3474.

# Crystal Basin

## Gerle Creek Reservoir

*See Crystal Basin map, page 252*

**Location:** In the Crystal Basin area at the end of Ice House Road, about 30 miles north of US 50.

**Elevation:** 5,231 feet.

**Fish:** Brown trout.

**Tackle and bait:** Spinners and spoons, such as Panther Martins, Kastmasters and Mepps; worms and Power Bait; and flies.

**Limit:** Five.

**Season:** Year-round for the reservoir; the last Saturday in April through November 15 for Gerle Creek.

**Fish plants:** None.

**Comments:** This small, rock- and pine-rimmed lake, where motorboats are prohibited, is great for anglers with rafts, canoes or float tubes. Brown

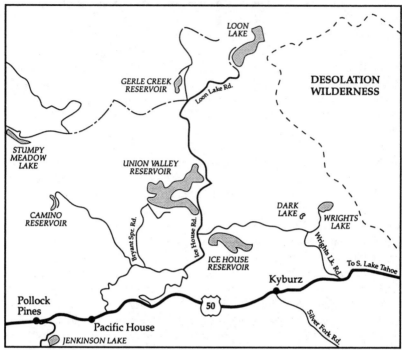

*Crystal Basin lakes*

trout naturally reproduce here, and they can get up to 18 inches. Adult browns three to five years old enter Gerle Creek in October to spawn. The lake has been made more attractive to the fish through habitat improvements from Cal Trout and REI, the major retail outdoor equipment store. Anglers can try the early morning and afternoon rises on the tree-shaded west side and on the south side near the dam. There's a rocky island that is popular with swimmers, and a cement fishing pier that is accessible to the handicapped. A Forest Service campground is next to the lake. The creek itself can be better fishing than the reservoir, with five-pounders.

**Information:** Ice House Resort, (916) 293-3321. Wild Sports in Orangevale, east of Sacramento; 9396 Greenback Lane, (916) 989-8310.

## Ice House Reservoir

*See Crystal Basin map, page 252*

**Location:** On Ice House Road, east of Placerville, 12 miles north of US 50.
**Elevation:** 5,500 feet.
**Fish:** Eagle Lake-strain rainbow, brown and brook trout.
**Tackle and bait:** Rapalas, Needlefish, Krocodiles, FlatFish, Rebels and

minnow imitations; downrigger with J-plugs; Power Bait and nightcrawlers.
**Limit:** Five.
**Season:** Year-round, but the reservoir is snowbound in winter.
**Fish plants:** Annually. The California Department of Fish and Game
plants 20,000 rainbow catchables, 4,800 brown catchables and, on occasion, Eagle Lake trout fingerlings and brook trout fingerlings.
**Comments:** Located in the Crystal Basin Recreation Area, this elongated lake of 680 acres is one of the best lakes for catching decent-sized
German brown trout, with an average size in the 12- to 14-inch range,
and the occasional monster fish. In 1993, a 10-pound brown was re-
ported. Kokanee were stocked here in the early 1980s, but they have not
become a significant fishery. Trolling with a variety of spinners and
spoons, as well as with worm-and-flasher combinations, is the best bet.
Fish near the creeks, where baitfish congregate, and along the sandy
beaches. A fine U.S. Forest Service campground with tree-shaded sites
and a public boat launching ramp are located on the west end.
**Information:** Ice House Resort, (916) 293-3321. Wild Sports in
Orangevale, east of Sacramento, 9396 Greenback Lane, (916) 989-8310.

## Jenkinson Lake
*See Crystal Basin map, page 252*
**Location:** Five miles south on Sly Park Road off US 50, a 45-minute
drive west of South Lake Tahoe.
**Elevation:** 3,478 feet.
**Fish:** Mackinaw, rainbow and brown trout, and smallmouth bass and
bluegill.
**Tackle and bait:** Blue Rapalas, chartreuse Power Bait, Needlefish,
salmon eggs, Rooster Tails (yellow and orange), and nightcrawlers with
flashers. Flies such as ant and mosquito patterns also work.
**Limit:** Five.
**Season:** Year-round.
**Fish plants:** Annually. The California Department of Fish and Game
stocks varying numbers, with many "bonus" plants depending on surplus
hatchery fish. The most recent plant was 27,000 rainbow catchables,
39,000 lake trout fingerlings and 115,000 brown trout fingerlings.
**Comments:** A mackinaw fishery that's *better* than Lake Tahoe? Hard to
believe, but many anglers swear that it's true. Heavy stocking by the
California Department of Fish and Game, a relatively low elevation,
numerous pockets and holes, and prolific Japanese pond smelt have created an incredible fishery for almost every species in the lake. In 1994, an
angler boated an 18-pound mackinaw that was 36 inches in length, and
the average mackinaw runs three to six pounds—compared to two to five
pounds in Tahoe. Brown trout are also big producers, especially in spring

and fall, with three- to six-pounders pulled in monthly, and 9- to 10-pounders on occasion. Rainbows typically run 12 to 18 inches, and most are caught on Power Bait. Motorboats are permitted on the lake, and the preferred tactic is trolling on the bottom along the shoreline with down-riggers for mackinaws and browns. The best flyfishing is in the upper arm, and the best trolling is behind the peninsula of the second dam and in the narrows near Hazel Creek Campground. Even shore anglers do well, especially from the two dams and in the upper arms, with lures such as Kastmasters. Two boat ramps are owned by the Eldorado Irrigation District (with a fee for launching), and there are 182 well-maintained public campsites along the lake.

*Information:* Sly Park Store, (916) 644-1113.

## Loon Lake
*See Crystal Basin map, page 252*

*Location:* On Ice House Road, in the Crystal Basin Recreation Area, 35 miles off US 50.

*Elevation:* 6,500 feet.

*Fish:* Rainbow and brown trout.

*Tackle and bait:* FlatFish, Rapalas, Needlefish, Kastmasters, nightcrawlers and spoons in red, chartreuse and fluorescent orange.

*Limit:* Five.

*Season:* Year-round.

*Fish plants:* Annually. The California Department of Fish and Game plants 16,000 rainbow catchables.

*Comments:* This large reservoir produces decent-sized rainbows, averaging 11 inches but occasionally reaching 16 to 18 inches, and browns averaging 14 inches but occasionally reaching 20 inches. Biologists believe there is natural brown trout reproduction from the streams. There's a large forage fish population of golden shiners, Lahontan redsides, tui chubs and California roach. The best approach is trolling next to the dams and in the upper coves. For rainbows, you seldom need a downrigger; try early morning surface trolling. For browns, try a downrigger with a Rapala or FlatFish. A public boat ramp and several Forest Service campgrounds are located on both the south and north shores. You get spectacular views of the gray, granite peaks of Rockbound Pass in Desolation Wilderness, to the east.

*Information:* Wild Sports in Orangevale, east of Sacramento, 9396 Greenback Lane, (916) 989-8310.

## Union Valley Reservoir
*See Crystal Basin map, page 252*

**Location:** In the Crystal Basin Recreation Area, 18 miles north of US 50 on Ice House Road, between South Lake Tahoe and Placerville.

**Elevation:** 4,900 feet.

**Fish:** Rainbow, mackinaw and brown trout, kokanee salmon and small-mouth bass.

**Tackle and bait:** Flashers with wedding rings, Needlefish, Rapalas and Rebels.

**Limit:** Five.

**Season:** Year-round.

**Fish plants:** Annually. The California Department of Fish and Game stocks 50,000 kokanee fingerlings, 19,400 mackinaw fingerlings and 21,000 rainbow catchables. It also sometimes stocks mackinaw catchables.

**Comments:** Dedicated local anglers who fish the Crystal Basin lakes rate this fishery the best of the bunch, primarily for rainbow trout and kokanee. The average size for kokanee runs 13 to 17 inches, and the best time to catch them is late summer or early fall near the creek inlets. Mackinaw have been caught up to 16 pounds, but are generally on the smaller side; using downriggers or deep-lining at 100 feet is necessary to bag them. The macks seem to prefer waters that are one-third to one-half the distance from the bottom. Good trolling waters are off the peninsula that has Fashoda Tent and Sunset campgrounds, or off Yellowjacket Campground on the north side. Rainbow trolling is excellent in the small forks by the power houses. You'll find public boat ramps at Yellowjacket and West Point, but Yellowjacket is the easiest to reach. Good Forest Service campgrounds are plentiful, and supplies are available at Ice House Resort nearby.

**Information:** Wild Sports in Orangevale, east of Sacramento, 9396 Greenback Lane, (916) 989-8310.

## Wrights and Dark Lakes
*See Crystal Basin map, page 252*

**Location:** Eight miles north of US 50 via Wrights Lake Road, which is about 35 miles east of South Lake Tahoe.

**Elevation:** 7,000 feet.

**Fish:** Rainbow and brown trout.

**Tackle and bait:** Power Bait, salmon eggs, small spinners and spoons, nightcrawlers and flies such as damselflies, midges, Muddler Minnows, leeches and elkhair caddis.

**Limit:** Five.

**Season:** Year-round, but the lakes are icebound in winter.

**Fish plants:** Annually. The California Department of Fish and Game

stocks 1,600 rainbow catchables and 1,600 brown catchables in Wrights, and 800 rainbow catchables and 800 brown catchables in Dark.
**Comments:** Wrights is one of the more attractive natural lakes in the Crystal Basin area, and it's a popular entry point for hiking and back-packing in Desolation Wilderness. It is heavily used by campers as well, and has a number of summer cabins around the shoreline. The fishing is spotty at best, since the water tends to be warm and is a beehive of swimmers, canoes and sailing dinghies (no motors are allowed). The best place to fish is in the upper (eastern) end, near a large creek inlet with thick growths of willows; this is also the deepest area. Much smaller Dark Lake, less than a half mile away, is a beautiful spot for float-tubing, especially during the evening rise, and it gets its share of flyfishers. Dark has rainbows and a few browns that were planted in 1992. The habitat includes lots of aquatic growth and cover at both lakes, which are rimmed with thick forest. The best times to fish are just after the thaw, in early summer and in the fall. Forest Service campsites are in high demand at Wrights, and are among the most difficult to reserve. Even if the fish aren't biting, the dramatic granite peaks are awe-inspiring. You can try fishing the Desolation Wilderness lakes on day hikes from Wrights (be sure to get a wilderness permit). It's also a short drive to the Crystal Basin reservoirs.
**Information:** Wild Sports in Orangevale, east of Sacramento, 9396 Greenback Lane, (916) 989-8310.

# Lakes Basin Area

## ★ Lake Davis ★
*See Lakes Basin area map, page 257*
**Location:** On Grizzly Peak Road or Lake Davis Road, 20 minutes north of Portola, or 45 minutes north of Truckee using the Sattley turnoff from Highway 89.
**Elevation:** 5,775 feet.
**Best catch:** Eagle Lake-strain of rainbow trout, brown trout, largemouth bass and catfish.
**Tackle and bait:** Worms, Power Bait, Rapalas, Dick Nites, crank baits, spinners, worm/flasher combos and flies such as damselfly, callibaetis and midge larva patterns.
**Limit:** Five for trout, five for bass and no limit for catfish.
**Season:** Year-round.
**Fish plants:** The California Department of Fish and Game stocks 24,000 catchable-sized Eagle Lake-strain rainbows per year.
**Comments:** As a haven for big, rainbow trout—we're talking the 10- to 12-pound variety that resemble steelhead and have pink flesh—Davis has become the undisputed champion of northern Sierra lakes. In addition to

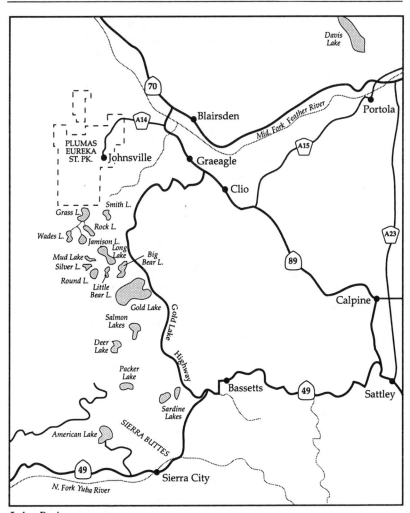

*Lakes Basin area waters*

the Eagle Lake trout, the resident German browns can reach up to eight pounds and the largemouth bass can exceed seven pounds. One of the reasons for their girth is the weed cover and the ample food supply of golden shiners. The lake, with 32 miles of shoreline on 4,000 acres, offers not only good trolling in relatively shallow water (average depth: 21 feet) for lure anglers, but is a paradise for flyfishers using waders, float tubes or prams and casting to the offshore weed beds. Fishing is best in early spring and late fall, when the bite may last all day, but becomes lethargic in high summer, when the most productive times are early morning or around sunset. Unfortunately, the future of Davis is clouded, since the

California Department of Fish and Game discovered pike there in 1994 and may have to chemically treat the lake to prevent this illegally-introduced pest from breeding. If this happens, say goodbye to the lunkers for a few years. The lake has free public boat ramps, a concession with rental boats and several U.S. Forest Service campgrounds.

*Information:* Grizzly Country Store at Lake Davis, (916) 832-0270.

# Gold Lake
*See Lakes Basin area map, page 257*

*Location:* On Gold Lake Road off Highway 89, seven miles west of the town of Graeagle, a one-hour drive north of Truckee.

*Elevation:* 6,620 feet.

*Fish:* Mackinaw, brown, rainbow and brook trout.

*Tackle and bait:* Spinners, crank baits and worms.

*Limit:* Five, any combination.

*Season:* Year-round, but the lake is snowbound in winter.

*Fish plants:* The California Department of Fish and Game stocks vary in number each year. The minimums are about 4,000 rainbow catchables, 6,000 brook trout catchables and 60,000 brown trout fingerlings.

*Comments:* This is the largest lake in the water-studded Lakes Basin northwest of Tahoe. It is best fished by trolling with Rapalas, Rebels, worm-and-flasher combinations, spinners and spoons off a shelf on the southwest end, or around a series of rock islands on the east end. There's a public boat landing just off the main road. This attractive region has several excellent lodges, most of which are booked a year in advance.

*Information:* Gold Lake Lodge, (916) 836-2350.

# Feather River (Middle Fork)
*See Lakes Basin area map, page 257*

*Location:* Fed by Frenchman and Davis lakes in Plumas County, this river parallels Highway 70 from Sloat to the junction with Highway 89 at Blairsden. From there it flows to Clio, then returns to parallel Highway 70 through Portola to Beckwourth.

*Fish:* Rainbow and brown trout.

*Tackle and bait:* Panther Martins, worms or grasshoppers, and flies such as stonefly and caddis patterns.

*Limit:* Five.

*Season:* Last Saturday in April through November 15.

*Fish plants:* Annually. The California Department of Fish and Game stocks 1,000 rainbow catchables.

*Comments:* This is a stunningly beautiful river that has easy access points at Blairsden, and as such gets a fair amount of fishing pressure at concentrated areas. Early in the season, May through mid-June, spin casters can take some decent-sized rainbows near the bridges. Flyfishers have their favorite spots, which often require hiking some distance or negotiating unmarked, four-wheel-drive roads. The La Porte Road off Highway 70 usually has the best access. Wade and cast to the downstream riffles and pocket waters; along some stretches, you'll be able to cast 45 to 50 feet. The fish in this river are robust and deep-bodied; they reach up to two pounds, in the 12- to 16-inch range, and there are naturally reproducing rainbows and a few browns. Fall is visually the most spectacular time of year for the Feather because of its bright yellow and red foliage, but trout will be skittish from the lower water. You won't get more than one cast per fish.

***Information:*** The Sportsmen's Den in Quincy, (916) 283-2733. Plumas County Visitors Bureau, (916) 283-6345 or (800) 326-2247.

## ★ Yuba River, North Fork ★

*See Lakes Basin area map, page 257*

***Location:*** In Sierra County. The river parallels Highway 49, northwest of Truckee (off Highway 89) through the towns of Sierra City and Downieville.

***Fish:*** Rainbow and brown trout.

***Tackle and bait:*** From the western boundary of Sierra City to the confluence with Ladies Canyon Creek, only artificial lures with barbless hooks may be used. Outside of this area, there are no gear restrictions. For flies, try elkhair caddis, beadhead hare's ear, blue-winged olives and stonefly nymphs.

***Limit:*** Two trout with minimum size of 10 inches in the restricted area; five in the unrestricted areas.

***Season:*** Last Saturday in April through November 15.

***Fish plants:*** Outside of the wild trout area, the California Department of Fish and Game stocked 7,890 rainbow catchables in 1994. These are stocked at bridge crossings and campground areas.

***Comments:*** You may have to rub shoulders with gold miners using dredges, but this is a scenic and generally underfished river, bordered by good Forest Service campgrounds and unique Gold Country towns. Guide Bob Cosick describes it this way: "When the insects are working and the hatch is on, you can expect 20-fish days. The majority are small native rainbows, 10 to 14 inches. There are a few browns, but they are hard to come by. The real joy of fishing here is the beauty of the canyon." Expect to do a lot of hiking to work the North Fork effectively, and don't even think of wading it until flows are below 1,000 cubic feet per second.

***Information:*** Gold Country Guide Service in Grass Valley, (916) 272-3597.

## SPECIAL FISHING FACILITIES
### Tahoe Trout Farm
The trout farm has free admission and provides use of bait and tackle at no charge. It is open to the public, with no license or boat required, no limit and payment made only for what you catch. The facility is oriented mainly to families with children. Open 10 a.m. to 7 p.m. daily (Memorial Day to Labor Day). Turn off US 50 at Terrible Herbst Gas Station.

*Information:* P.O. Box 13118, South Lake Tahoe, CA 96151; (916) 541-1491.

### Heavenly Ski Area
A high-elevation lake used for snow-making during the winter has occasionally been opened for small groups of affluent fly- and spin-casting in the summer. Trophy-sized trout are planted and guides from this South Tahoe resort can supply all the necessary gear, including float tubes and tackle. The lake is located on the Nevada side of the mountain, with lifts and day lodges nearby, but anglers are shuttled to the location in resort vehicles. The availability of the lake depends on the year-to-year summer construction program.

*Information:* P.O. Box 2180, Stateline, NV 89449; (702) 586-7000.

## CHARTER BOATS & GUIDES, LAKE TAHOE & DONNER LAKE
### North Shore/Truckee
#### Mickey's Big Mack Charters, Carnelian Bay
Mickey Daniels is considered one of the top mackinaw fishermen in Lake Tahoe, and he has two well-equipped vessels that can handle 8 to 10 people—the 32-foot *Big Mack* and the 43-foot *Big Mack II.* Both boats have V-8 inboard engines, large cabins and heaters, and plenty of deck space for roaming. Daniels is based at the Sierra Boat Company in Carnelian Bay, and sticks to the North Shore waters between Tahoe City and Stateline Point, trolling in 180 to 220 feet of water with both wire line and downriggers set up with light line and tackle. He uses custom-made rods with Penn reels for long-lining, and steelhead rods with Abu-Garcia reels for downriggers. Standard rigs include minnows with dodgers, Silver Horde lures and Lucky Louies. Fishing on the boat is by the lottery system, which means that when your number is called you work the fish; the rest of the time you can drink, sleep or sightsee. In early spring, Daniels top-lines for rainbows, which are usually incidental to the mackinaw fishing. He fishes year-round, including winter, which is the best time to

catch big fish, and he'll do both morning and afternoon runs.

**Fees:** $65 per person for five hours and, on weekdays only, $45 for three hours. Whole-boat charters go for $575 for the large vessel and $375 for the smaller one. All gear is provided, but bring snacks and liquids. MasterCard and Visa are accepted.

**Information:** Mickey's Big Mack Charters, P.O. Box 815, Tahoe City, CA 95730; (800) 877-1462 or (916) 583-4602.

## Hooker for Hire Sportfishing

Skipper Jim Brisco operates a 29-foot Phoenix diesel boat with twin turbo V-8 engines and trolls or jigs for mackinaw, rainbows and, occasionally, German brown trout. Private charters run from April through June, and can accommodate up to six anglers. Brisco uses Fenwick graphite 8.5-foot rods with Mag 10 level-wind reels, with 10-pound test line on six electric downriggers, and a variety of lures, including FlatFish, Speedy Shiner, Rebel and Rapala. Generally, he fishes the north end of the lake, from an hour before sunrise to at least six hours after, leaving from the Tahoe Boat Works. Brisco likes to troll in the 200-foot range for mackinaw, 60 feet for rainbows.

**Fees:** $400 for the boat includes gear, soft drinks and coffee.

**Information:** Hooker for Hire Sportfishing, P.O. Box 7468, Tahoe City, CA 96145; (916) 525-5654.

## Reel Magic Sportfishing

Skipper Steve Beals fishes for mackinaw trout and rainbows from April to mid-October in his 26-foot Sea Ray, which has a flying bridge, heaters, fish finders and a cabin. He prefers trolling with monofilament and lead-core line, with some downrigging and outrigging. In spring, he fishes for rainbows in 30 to 40 feet of water, and for mackinaw in 120 feet. Beals used Fenwick rods, Daiwa reels and a variety of plugs. The vessel departs twice a day from the Tahoe Boat Company, usually from 5 a.m. to 11 a.m. and from 3 p.m. until dark. The maximum number of anglers is six, but Beals prefers four.

**Fees:** $150 for one or two persons for six hours; $200 for two to four, and $240 for six. With four to six persons, Beals will fish for eight hours. All gear is provided, but clients should bring food and drink.

**Information:** Reel Magic Sportfishing, P.O. Box 10104, Truckee, CA 96162; (916) 587-6027.

## Mac-A-Tac

Skipper/owner Kevin Roach, who has 11 years of experience fishing the lake but only recently acquired this charter business, leaves out of Sunnyside Marina, on the West Shore. His 28-foot Bayliner is equipped with a Chevrolet 350 inboard engine, cabin, heaters and toilet, and can accommodate up to six anglers. Roach's preferred fishing method is trolling for mackinaw trout with downriggers 140 to 220 feet deep, and graphite rods with Penn level-wind reels and Fenwick braided 30-pound line. In spring, he fishes shallower with six-pound test line, but on downriggers with sensitive clips. Roach prefers big artificial lures such as Rapalas, but he occasionally fishes with minnows. He runs two trips a day year-round, morning and afternoon, and sticks to waters off the West and North shores of Tahoe.

*Fees:* $60 per person for 4.5 to five hours of fishing (minimum of three people), or $240 for the entire boat. All gear, along with donuts, coffee and soft drinks, are provided. Licenses are available on board.

*Information:* Mac-A-Tac, P.O. Box 433, Tahoe City, CA 96145; (916) 546-2500 or (702) 831-4449.

## Clearwater Guides

Equipped with two boats, owner-skipper Chris Turner fishes both Lake Tahoe and Donner Lake, and is the only full-time operation on Donner. At Donner, his skipper, Jay Nillian, takes up to four anglers on his 23-foot Fishrite, which has a 350 inboard engine, heater, downriggers and fish-finding electronics. Trips leave an hour before sunrise from Donner Lake Village marina, and stay out for seven hours. Sometimes he offers afternoon trips, departing at 2 p.m. and staying until dark. Nillian specializes in trophy mackinaw at Donner, trolling with FlatFish, dodgers and minnows, Rapalas, Rebels and flies from the surface to 80 feet deep. The best fishing is in spring and fall. At the North Shore of Lake Tahoe, Turner's boat is a 26-foot Farallon, with an inboard diesel engine, that can carry up to six anglers. The vessel, departing from the Tahoe City Boatworks, operates for five to six hours in the morning and four hours in the afternoon, trolling in 100 to 300 feet of water and bouncing lures off the bottom in an area between Tahoe City and Kings Beach. Mackinaw trout are the main objective, except in October and November, when Turner will top-line for rainbow trout. Turner fishes year-round on both lakes, weather permitting.

*Fees:* At Donner Lake, $70 for seven hours, or $50 for five hours in the afternoon. At Lake Tahoe, $60 for five to six hours and $50 for afternoons. Prices include all fishing tackle, coffee and donuts; all catches are cleaned and packed.

*Information:* Clearwater Guides, P.O. Box 2642, Truckee, CA 96160; (916) 587-9302 or (800) 354-0958.

# West Shore
## Kingfish Guide Service

Operating out of Homewood Marina, on the West Shore of Lake Tahoe, owners Larry and Pam Schuelke run the 43-foot *Kingfish*, the largest fishing vessel on the lake. Amenities include heaters, fish-finding electronics, radar, Fenwick rods, Penn reels, outriggers and downriggers. Pam, whose nickname is "Pamela Jean, the Fishing Machine," is one of the few female fishing captains around. Although the boat can hold up to 40 people, the Schuelkes fish a maximum of 10. Their prime method is trolling with steel line and downriggers equipped with 20-pound test monofilament, using lures such as Rapalas and Rebels. They fish year-round in waters between Emerald Bay and Stateline Point off the Cal-Neva Lodge. In winter, they jig. Fishing is mostly for mackinaw trout, with occasional runs for rainbow trout and kokanee. They also run two-hour tours of Emerald Bay in summer.

*Fees:* $65 per person, including tackle, coffee, sodas and snacks; all catches are cleaned and packed. The boat departs from 5165 West Lake Boulevard in Homewood.

*Information:* Kingfish Guide Service, P.O. Box 5955, Tahoe City, CA 96145; (916) 525-5360 or (702) 742-2472 (cellular boat phone).

# South Shore
## Prime Time Fishing Charters

Skipper John Kolesar, a South Lake Tahoe firefighter, fishes for mackinaw and kokanee on weekends out of the Tahoe Keys Marina, using a 24-foot IMP V-hull fiberglass runabout with a canvas roof. He runs primarily along the South Shore from the end of April through October. Kolesar prefers trolling, but will jig or drift according to conditions and client wishes. He supplies Abu-Garcia and Bass Pro rods with level-wind reels and 17-pound Trilene line, trolled on electric downriggers. While Kolesar will fish up to six anglers in one party, the standard party size is four. The trips depart before dawn and last five hours.

*Fees:* $70 per person (minimum two anglers), including all gear and coffee.

*Information:* Prime Time Fishing Charters, 1123 Aravaipa Street, South Lake Tahoe, CA 96150; (916) 577-7420.

## Blue Ribbon Fishing Charters
## (Formerly Dan's Sport Fishing)

Skipper John Hinson, who has been fishing the lake since 1969, is a light tackle specialist. He makes daily trips for mackinaw and kokanee from the Tahoe Keys Marina, fishing year-round, primarily along the

South Shore. Hinson uses an open Lund skiff with outboard motor, and has a trolling motor, electric downriggers and room for up to four passengers. Hinson runs full- and half-day trips, morning and afternoon.

*Fees:* $70 per person, and four anglers can go for the price of three; there is also a reduced rate for children under 12. Rods, tackle, bait and beverages are included. Your catch is cleaned, filleted and bagged.

*Information:* Blue Ribbon Fishing Charters, P.O. Box 822, South Lake Tahoe, CA 96156; (916) 541-8801.

## Don's Fishing Charters

Skipper Don Dilday runs a 30-foot Aqua Sport, with twin inboard engines and a spacious heated cabin, from Round Hill Pines, near Zephyr Cove on the East Shore of Tahoe. He fishes for both mackinaw trout and kokanee salmon—specializing in kokanee—and can take up to six anglers at a time. He trolls with downriggers and steel line, and occasionally top-lines with monofilament, or jigs with bait and lures. He's one of the few guides who also likes to drift with minnows, when that method is effective. Dilday has fished Tahoe for 18 years, and encourages catch-and-release fishing. His territory is the Nevada shoreline from Cave Rock to Skunk Harbor, and he runs twice a day, with his season lasting from April through October.

*Fees:* $60 per person, including all bait and tackle, coffee, a continental breakfast and soft drinks.

*Information:* Don's Fishing Charters, P.O. Box 10225, Zephyr Cove, NV 89448; (702) 588-4916.

## Eagle Point Sport Fishing

Located at Anchorage Marina in Camp Richardson (near South Lake Tahoe), skipper Dennis Mitchell fishes for mackinaw and kokanee, using a variety of methods that include trolling, light-tackle jigging and drifting with minnows. His 25-foot Bayliner Trophy cabin cruiser can take two to six anglers for five hours, leaving both mornings and afternoons. Mitchell will fish any part of the California side of the lake, depending on where fish are holding, but is most productive trolling afternoons off the Tahoe Keys. He's set up with two Interface fish-finders and carries custom trolling rods with level-wind Ambassador reels and Fenwick light spinning rods equipped with six-pound test monofilament for drifting. Mitchell has fished the lake for 23 years, nine of them from Camp Richardson. Apart from his fish tales, he's loaded with trivia about the film business, since he works on TV and movie productions in the winter. His season runs from April through October, and in summer he does two trips a day, one leaving before sunrise, the other at 11 a.m. Mitchell concentrates on kokanee salmon in late July and August, but will combine kokanee and mackinaw on the same trip if clients desire.

*Fees:* $70 per person (minimum of two people) for five hours, including all gear.

*Information:* Eagle Point Sport Fishing, P.O. Box 9536, South Lake Tahoe, CA 96151; (916) 577-6834.

## First Strike Sportfishing

Skipper Jeff Vogl operates two boats out of Zephyr Cove Marina—one a 25-foot Lund Sportfisher, the other a 23-foot Sunrunner. Using electronic fish-finders and lightweight tackle, Vogl specializes in jigging, using two- to four-ounce custom-made jigs, 12- to 14-pound test line, Abu-Garcia six- to seven-foot rods and Ambassador level-wind reels. Occasionally, he'll drift for mackinaw using minnows and light spinning gear. Vogl fishes the entire lake, and has been guiding for eight years. He operates year-round and, in summer, runs trips just before dawn and at 11 a.m. Charters and lake tours are welcome. Zephyr Cove is located four miles north of Stateline, Nevada.

*Fees:* $75 per person, including all bait and tackle, snacks and your catch cleaned and bagged.

*Information:* First Strike Sportfishing, P.O. Box 11268, Zephyr Cove, NV 89448; (702) 588-HOOK (4665) or (916) 577-5065.

## Hernandez Guide Service

A veteran guide on Lake Tahoe for 20 years, skipper Bruce Hernandez specializes in jigging, which he prefers over trolling because of its more interactive nature. He leaves from South Tahoe in the morning once a day on his 25-foot Tiara Pursuit cruiser, which is equipped with a Chevy 350 inboard/outboard engine, trolling motor, cabin, fish finders and variety of tackle. He uses Fenwick 6.5-foot rods with Ambassador level-wind reels, 14-pound test monofilament line, and Bomber jigs with minnows. (He won't use downriggers or long-line outriggers.) Hernandez fishes mostly the West and North shores of the lake, moving to the South Shore in October. Occasionally he drifts for rainbow and brown trout, working the shoreline and drop-offs to 70 feet. Hernandez takes up to six anglers, but prefers four, and runs March through November.

*Fees:* $65 per person, including all bait and tackle, coffee, soda or beer. Special whole-boat charter prices are available.

*Information:* Hernandez Guide Service, P.O. Box 11689, Tahoe Paradise, CA 96155; (916) 577-2246.

## George's Fishing Trips

George Dupuy, a 25-year veteran of fishing Lake Tahoe, owns a 24-foot Glastron vessel with a Chevy 283 V-8 engine, a 10-horsepower

Honda troller, a wraparound canvas cabin and a heater. He operates out of the Ski Run Marina in South Lake Tahoe (next to the *Tahoe Queen* paddlewheeler), and does deep-lining, top-lining, downrigging and drifting, with an emphasis on rainbow and brown trout. He fishes in five to 40 feet of water, using lead-core or monofilament line and lures. For mackinaw, he uses wire line or downriggers. Trips run year-round, with both morning and afternoon trips in the summer. From July through the end of September, he'll fish for kokanee salmon, if the bite is on. He accepts a maximum of six anglers.

*Fees:* $75 for five hours, with a 10-percent discount for groups of six. Dupuy can also organize large group charters (for up to 50 people) using other boats and skippers.

*Information:* George's Fishing Trips. P.O. Box 16708, South Lake Tahoe, CA 96151; (916) 544-2353.

### Rick Muller's Sport Fishing

The jig is up, or rather down, with skipper Rick Muller, who has made jigging his passion, recently producing an instructional video on jigging techniques in Tahoe. Muller, one of the self-styled "new breed" of angler and co-owner of The Sportsman outdoor equipment store in South Lake Tahoe, zips from one end of the lake to the other in his speedy 24-foot Bayliner Trophy, and boasts a 90-percent limit success rate for mackinaw trout. Moving frequently to find fish is his modus operandi. "It's nothing for me to put 60 miles a day on the boat," he says. Muller jigs with a minnow and four-ounce Bomber setup, usually in 100 to 200 feet of water. He's got the latest in electronic fish-finding gear, and has made something of an art out of locating fish. He uses 6.5-foot rods with limber tips, level-wind reels and 13- to 17-pound test monofilament line. Muller leaves seven days a week out of Tahoe Keys Marina, and can take four to six anglers.

*Fees:* $70 per person, including all bait and tackle. Special rates are available for charters.

*Information:* Rick Muller's Sport Fishing, P.O. Box 8773, South Lake Tahoe, CA 96158; (916) 544-4358.

### O'Malley's Fishing Charters

Never on Sunday, says Leonard O'Malley, who'll not fish on the Sabbath, thank you. (Somebody's got to pray for those big macks to bite!) But on the other six days of the week, he scours the lake for mackinaw, rainbow trout and kokanee, using his late-model 22-foot Radoncraft, which has a walk-around cuddy cabin, inboard/outboard engine, trolling motor and downriggers. He'll try most anything to get fish—except wire line. He trolls, jigs and drifts, but finds his best success with downriggers. O'Malley operates out of a pier near Zephyr Cove, and spends most of his time working the Nevada shoreline and the waters off South Lake Tahoe. His favorite setup is a Shakespeare 8.5-foot Ugly Stick with an Abu-Garcia 6500 level-wind reel, but he also has a few light spinning rods with eight-pound test line for drifting with minnows. O'Malley's season generally runs from March through November, and he'll take up to six anglers but prefers no more than four for his five-hour morning charters.

***Fees:*** $70 per person for five-hour morning charters and $55 per person for four-hour midday charters (from May through September), including all gear and refreshments; cleaning and bagging your catch is provided. Clients meet at Zephyr Cove and are shuttled to the boat, which is one mile away.

***Information:*** O'Malley's Fishing Charters, P.O. Box 10598, Zephyr Cove, NV 89448; (702) 588-4102.

## Don Sheetz Guide Service

Trolling and jigging are the main pursuits of veteran guide Don Sheetz, who has been fishing the lake since 1968. He runs a 21-foot Sea Ray with a Chevy 350 inboard/outboard motor, cuddy cabin, Porta-Potty, ice box, electronic fish-finder, electric downriggers and an array of fishing tackle. Sheetz leaves from the Tahoe Keys Marina and operates from April through October, taking four to six anglers. He trolls about three-quarters of the time with various lures and blades, using Walker downriggers and steel line, and jigs the rest of the time with the standard minnow-and-Bomber setup. His tackle includes light tackle rods with 16-pound line on Abu-Garcia reels. He makes one run per morning and covers waters from Edgewood Tahoe Golf Course in the south to Sugar Pine Point State Park on the West Shore, working both mackinaw and, when the bite is on, kokanee salmon.

***Fees:*** $70 per person with all gear, coffee and donuts provided. Whole-boat charters go for $260.

***Information:*** Don Sheetz Guide Service, P.O. Box 13631, South Lake Tahoe, CA 96151; (916) 541-5566.

## Tahoe Sports Fishing

With seven boats in the summer, ranging from 26 feet to 32 feet, captain Dean Lockwood runs the largest fishing charter operation at Lake Tahoe, guiding close to 1,000 trips per year. His company has been around for 40 years, the last nine of them headquartered at Ski Run Marina, near central South Lake Tahoe. Lockwood caters especially to corporate groups, families and casino guests from Stateline. His mackinaw vessels include one 34-foot Sportfisher with twin diesel engines, two 31-foot Island Hoppers, one 26-foot Offshore Fisherman, and one 26-foot

Farallon Sportfisherman. All have cabins and heaters, and can take a maximum of six anglers. Lockwood also runs a 20-footer that specializes in rainbow and brown trout; this boat has a shade top, center console and an outdrive that can be raised to maneuver in shallow waters. The boats can use all or a combination of fishing techniques for mackinaw, including slow trolling, jigging and drifting, all with live minnows. Boats also surface troll for rainbow and brown trout. The larger vessels are equipped with both downriggers and outriggers, and a selection of custom-made, 7.5-foot medium-light rods set up with salmon-sinker release systems. The queen of the fleet is the 34-foot *Dory-L,* a luxurious motor yacht with a huge cabin, flying bridge and spacious deck. Three boats fish year-round, and the others fish in summer only, with two departures in the morning and one in the afternoon. The pier is located at 900 Ski Run Boulevard in South Lake Tahoe, next to the *Tahoe Queen* paddlewheeler.

*Fees:* $75 for a five-hour morning trip; $85 for a seven-hour, all-day trip; $65 for a four-hour afternoon trip (all three-person minimum). All trips include fishing gear, tackle, bait, hot coffee, beer and soda, and cleaning and sacking your catch.

*Information:* Tahoe Sports Fishing, P.O. Box 1909, Zephyr Cove, NV 89448; (800) 696-7797 (in California) or (916) 541-5448.

## Tahoe Viking Sportfishing

Captain Ron Greer's 35-foot Viking Sportfisher is, without a doubt, the most upscale fishing vessel on Lake Tahoe. It's so posh that even if you don't get a bite, you probably won't care; just sit back, sip a brewski and watch the scenery go by. The yacht (a beamy 13.5 feet wide) has twin Caterpillar V-8 diesel engines, a Yamaha 9.9-horsepower trolling motor, a huge heated cabin and state-of-the-art fish-finding electronics. Unlike most of the Lake Tahoe mackinaw guides, Greer is not a downrigging enthusiast, nor does he drift or jig; he prefers the traditional method of slow, long-line trolling on the bottom with steel line. He stocks custom-made mackinaw rods equipped with Daiwa digital reels. He also top-lines for rainbow and brown trout with Daiwa rods and light spinning reels with six- to eight-pound monofilament line. Greer uses live minnows and a variety of lures such as Rebels and FlatFish. He operates year-round, weather permitting. In summer, the Viking departs at 6 a.m. for a five-hour trip, and occasionally does afternoon trips, fishing the waters along the West and South shores. The boat can accommodate a maximum of six anglers.

*Fees:* $85 per person, including all gear, continental breakfast, coffee, beer and soda.

*Information:* Tahoe Viking Sportfishing, P.O. Box 11885, Tahoe Paradise, CA 96155; (916) 541-1806.

# GUIDES FOR PYRAMID, CAPLES, DAVIS & OTHER LAKES

## Pyramid-Tahoe Fishing Charters

Guide Lex Moser has what most other guides envy with a passion. He fishes Pyramid Lake on the Paiute Indian Reservation in winter and early spring (and is the only non-Native American guide with those fishing rights), and switches to Lake Tahoe in late spring and summer. The prize at Pyramid is the frisky Lahontan cutthroat trout, and the lower elevation (3,800 feet, compared to 6,225 feet at Tahoe) means much warmer temperatures in the winter (even approaching T-shirt days). Moser has a 24-foot Wellcraft Airslot with a walk-around cuddy cabin that can seat four, a 260 Volvo inboard/outboard engine, a trolling prop, a heater, four downriggers, two outriggers and an electronic fish-finder. He can accommodate both lure anglers and flyfishers. Among the 17 rods stocked on the boat are Loomis trolling rods and Shimano jigging rods. He has a speed and temperature transducer, which he can put on a downrigger and locate the dozen or so underwater geothermal springs that sometimes attract fish. The trout and baitfish, called tui chubs, prefer water around 55 degrees Fahrenheit. Moser normally divides his fishing day between trolling and jigging, to provide variety. He uses light, six-foot rods and six-pound test line for jigging. Moser fishes two shifts—7 a.m. to 11:45 a.m., and 12:15 p.m. to 5 p.m., with his season on Pyramid lasting from October 1 through the end of May. For flyfishers, he pulls out the riggers and casts or wades to the shoreline. From June 1 to the end of September, he fishes Lake Tahoe, offering early- and mid-morning charters, lasting about 4.5 hours each, from the North Tahoe Marina, next to Sunsets on the Lake restaurant. The first departure is usually for mackinaw and rainbow trout, the second for rainbow and kokanee salmon.

**Fees:** For Pyramid Lake and Tahoe, $60 per person for a half day (minimum two anglers); and $90 for a full day of eight hours (minimum three anglers), including all gear and coffee. For Pyramid Lake only, clients can buy the required $6 reservation permit on the boat (no other state fishing license is needed to fish Pyramid).

**Information:** Pyramid-Tahoe Fishing Charters, 14752 Rim Rock Road, Reno, NV 89511; (702) 852-FISH (3474).

## Dave Curran

Guide Dave Curran fishes 15 lakes in the region, using a variety of motorized watercraft and specializing in trolling. The lakes covered include Davis, Frenchman, Caples, Silver, Blue, Donner, Tahoe, Topaz and, farther north, Almanor and Eagle, where he stations one boat per lake and hires other guides to run them. He has six boats ranging from 28-foot

Boston Whalers to 14-foot aluminum runabouts. Two Horizon fiberglass 18-footers have forward seats, depth finders and radar, and are Coast Guard-certified. He uses light rods with Penn level-wind reels, or sometimes ultra spinning gear in midsummer, depending on conditions. Curran, who has been guiding in the area for 30 years, cleans fish and, for an extra charge, will smoke your catch and send it to you later. He can take up to four people per trip.

*Fees:* $100 per day, per person, including all rods and tackle. You must bring your own food or drink.

*Information:* Dave Curran, 1041 Arrowhead, Gardnerville, NV 89410; (702) 265-2365.

### Bruce "Bruno" Huff

The King of Caples is one of the premier trout-fishing guides in the area, a personable man with a knack for fishing and a zest for cooking. He's the year-round chef at Caples Lake Resort, which has achieved a reputation for its fine gourmet dining, but between his stints in the kitchen he's fishing six days a week. His energy and sense of humor are reasons enough to book him as a guide, but his fishing prowess is almost legendary. In 1994, he and his clients boated 1,107 trout, and released 80 percent of them (at the request of his customers). Huff's main waters are Caples and the other lakes along Highway 88, including Silver, Bear River, Red and Blue. But he also fishes Topaz Lake and the East and West forks of the Carson River. In winter, conditions permitting, he'll ice-fish in Caples for rainbow and mackinaw trout, using the standard Swedish pimple along with feathered, crappie-style jigs. The rest of the time he trolls with lures such as FlatFish, Rapalas, Triple Teasers, Canadian Wonders, Torpedoes and a variety of spoons. On the rivers, he fishes with a combination of flies and tackle. Huff uses Fenwick and Charlie Thomas rods and Shakespeare and Abu-Garcia level-wind reels. His boat is a 17-foot Boston Whaler equipped with a 50-horsepower Mercury outboard and a 15-horsepower Johnson troller.

*Fees:* $60 per person, with a maximum of two people, for four hours. All gear is provided. Bring your own snacks and beverages.

*Information:* Bruce "Bruno" Huff, P.O. Box 263, Markleeville, CA 96120; (916) 694-2145.

### Anastasia Fishing Guide Service

Mickey Anastasia is one of a handful of tackle guides on Lake Davis, which is considered among the hottest big trout lakes in the Sierra. He fishes April to October, using a 16-foot Bay Runner with open V-hull aluminum frame and a 45-horsepower Honda outboard. Anastasia, who has been guiding on the lake since 1991, trolls 12-pound lead-core or monofilament line with worms and flashers, at depths of around 15 feet (the lake is relatively shallow, averaging 20 to 22 feet deep). Fish respond all day in the early and late parts of the season, and in the early mornings only during midsummer. He uses seven-foot Abu-Garcia graphite rods and Penn 109 level-wind reels. Anastasia fishes from first light until 1 p.m. or until limits are reached for clients, whichever comes first.

*Fees:* $55 per person (three-angler maximum), includes a daily license and all fishing gear.

*Information:* Anastasia Fishing Guide Service, 3011 Grizzly Road, Portola, CA 96122; (916) 832-5181.

## FLYFISHING GUIDES & SCHOOLS

### California School of Flyfishing, Truckee

Ralph and Lisa Cutter, husband-and-wife instructors and guides, have achieved a great reputation for their flyfishing school, the only one in the North Lake Tahoe/Truckee area, which they've operated since 1981. Lisa, one of a handful of certified female flyfishing guides, punches out 100-foot casts with great dexterity. The Cutters' classes run from May through mid-November, with both stillwater and fast-water experience, at venues that usually include the Truckee River and Martis Creek Lake. Introductory two-day courses with one to three anglers include textbook, all gear and deli lunch each day, and range from $425 for one to $725 for three. Classroom sessions are done at the Cutters' home in Truckee. Another two-day course for intermediates, called "The Complete Flyfisher," fishes both freestone and stillwater; it runs $425 per person, including deli lunch, and anglers are urged to bring their own gear. A one-day course on advanced fishing techniques is $225. Ralph, a firefighter in Incline Village, does most of the teaching, assisted by other instructors, and Lisa does most of the guiding. The Cutters use a variety of rods, including Loomis, Fenwick, Sage and Scott.

*Fees:* Class prices are listed above. For outings, prices are $200 for one person and $250 for two people for a full day (9 a.m. until 4 p.m.), or $125 and $150, respectively, for a half day (9 a.m. until 12:30 p.m. or 5:30 p.m. until dark).

*Information:* California School of Flyfishing, P.O. Box 8212, Truckee, CA 96162; (916) 587-7005 or (800) 58-TROUT.

### Horse Feathers Fly Fishing School, Hope Valley

Instructor Judy Warren has owned this school for 26 years, and has based it out of scenic Sorensen's Resort in Alpine County for the past 10 years. Her specialty is teaching novice anglers, particularly women and children, in a congenial, non-intimidating environment. Using the streams

## FISHING LICENSES

Always obtain copies of the latest fishing regulations and amendments from sporting goods and fishing tackle dealers.

### California

Licenses are required for anyone 16 and older. A one-year, resident license is $24.95; a non-resident license is $67.45. A one-day license for either residents or non-residents costs $8.95. Anglers who fish Lake Tahoe or Topaz Lake can use either a California or Nevada license from boat or shore.

*Note:* A new regulation requires all anglers to display their licenses by wearing them while fishing.

### Nevada

Licenses are required for anyone 12 and older. A one-year resident license is $15.50 for persons 16 through 64, and $5.50 for persons 12 through 15 years of age. Non-resident licenses are $45.50 for persons 16 and older and $8.50 for persons 12 through 15 years of age. A three-day fishing permit is $17.50 and a 10-day fishing

of Hope Valley, she provides quality, custom-made equipment, including J. Kennedy Fisher rods, to all clients and teaches them the basics, such as casting, reading water, knot-tying, streamside entomology and selecting flies. She is active in California Trout and is author of *Angling Alpine*, a field guide to the rivers, streams and 60 lakes of the county. Warren is also associated with Wolf Pack Station and Antelope Pack Station, which offer guided trips into Carson-Iceberg Wilderness on horseback.

*Fees:* Her "Introduction to Fly Fishing" class is $45 for the first hour and $15 per hour thereafter; fly-tying classes are $60 for five to six hours, including all equipment, or $66 including lunch at Sorensen's. She does limited guiding at $60 for the first hour and $20 an hour thereafter, but prefers to refer clients to Jim Crouse of Alpine Fly Fishing (see page 273 in this chapter).

*Information:* Horse Feathers Fly Fishing School, P.O. Box 397, Markleeville, CA 96120; (916) 694-2399.

## Reno Fly Shop

One of a handful of flyfishing shops in northern Nevada, this place has three full-time guides—Dave Stanley, Dave Bryeans and Jeff Cavender—who book exclusively through the shop. They fish the Truckee River in both California and Nevada, the Little Truckee River, and Martis, Davis, Frenchman and Milton lakes. If you like variety, you can book a half-and-half combo—morning on Martis and evening on the Little Truckee. The Nevada portion of the Truckee is legally fishable year-round (and is generally below the snowline in winter). Lakes can be fished with prams or float tubes. The shop also conducts regular fly-tying clinics, two-day dry-land casting seminars in Reno, clinics on nymphing and dry fly fishing, women-only sessions and, once a year, clinics for youngsters age 10 and older. The store is Orvis-endorsed. A full selection of local fly patterns is available at the shop, where clients meet. All fishing is strictly catch-and-release. The season runs from late March through summer. Hours are 10 a.m. to 6 p.m. weekdays and 10 a.m. to 5 p.m. Saturday and Sunday.

*Fees:* Guided trips are $200 for a full day with lunch for one or two anglers, $150 for a half day, and $90 for an evening rise (about three hours). Clients are encouraged to bring their own gear. The two-day casting clinics are $95 with all gear supplied; for dates and times, as well as information on specialty clinics, contact manager Bud Johnson.

*Information:* Reno Fly Shop, 294 East Moana Lane, Reno, NV 89502; (702) 825-FISH (3474) or (702) 827-0600.

## Alpine Fly Fishing

A veteran of 25 years, Jim Crouse provides lessons and guided trips in the prime waters of Alpine County south of Tahoe, including the East and West forks of the Carson River, Pleasant Valley Creek and Silver Creek (both tributaries of the Carson River's East Fork), and, occasionally, Indian Creek Reservoir. He fishes for native rainbows in the upper reaches of the East Fork of the Carson River, as well as the catch-and-release section on the lower river from Hangman's Bridge to the Nevada border. His territory ranges from Hope Valley to Markleeville, between highways 88 and 4. Crouse uses caddis and mayfly patterns when hatches are on, but most of the time fishing is subsurface with flies such as woolly buggers. "I try to get away with the biggest and strongest patterns that I can, and go small only when I have to," he says. He has some specialty flies that he ties and provides to his clients. Crouse also fishes Lost Lake, Granite Lake, Tamarack Lake and other waters in the Blue Lakes region. Crouse will plan morning or evening trips, or a combination; he prefers weekday trips.

*Fees:* $95 for a half day (five hours) for one angler and $125 for two anglers, including transportation, a rod-and-reel kit (J. Kennedy Fisher gear), flies and beverages. All-day trips are $190 for two persons, including lunch. Private fly-tying lessons are $30 for two hours and $15 for each additional hour.

permit is $30.50. All anglers who take or possess trout must also buy a Nevada Trout Stamp, which is $5 additional.

*Note:* Free fishing day is the second Saturday in June of each year, when anyone may fish without a license. Anglers who fish Lake Tahoe or Topaz Lake can use either a Nevada or California license from boat or shore. Anglers who fish the Truckee and East Carson rivers on both sides of the state line must have licenses from both states.

*Note:* A Nevada fishing license is *not* required for fishing Pyramid Lake, which is on the Paiute Indian Reservation. For information on Pyramid Lake, see page 246 in this chapter.

*Information:* Alpine Fly Fishing, P.O. Box 10465, South Lake Tahoe, CA 96158; (916) 542-0759.

## Thy Rod & Staff

Veteran guide Frank Pisciotta, who has fished California waters for more than 35 years, guides on the trophy trout waters of the Truckee River from Trout Creek, east of town, downstream to Floriston; Martis Creek Lake; Milton Reservoir below Jackson Meadows Reservoir; and the North Fork of the Yuba River. He is Lake Tahoe's only Orvis-endorsed guide. Pisciotta requires catch-and-release fishing and the use of barbless hooks, regardless of the regulations. All skill levels are welcome, and he will guide/instruct to the specific desires of the client. He can supply Orvis rods and reels, leaders, tippets and flies for no extra charge. Trips are wading and float-tubing, with float tubes provided if needed. Additionally, Pisciotta offers five two-day basic skills clinics, including ones specializing in float-tubing and fishing small creeks.

*Fees:* Full-day excursions (8 to 10 hours) are $185 for one angler and $235 for two anglers, and includes 8 to 10 hours of fishing, a light lunch and beverages. Half-day sessions are $125 for one person and $160 for two persons, beverages provided. Two-day skills clinics are $200 per person. All instruction is "on stream."

*Information:* Thy Rod & Staff, P.O. Box 10038, Truckee, CA 96162; (916) 587-7333.

## Johnson Tackle & Guide Service

How about mountain biking and flyfishing? Guide Randy Johnson offers this option in the Bowman Lake region of Tahoe National Forest, which is northwest of Truckee above Lake Spaulding. He cycles to a half-dozen backcountry lakes on Forest Service roads, usually on rides of about 90 minutes. And he's a veritable supply house of gear—with carbon-frame bikes, float tubes, J. Kennedy Fisher rods and his own fly designs. The only thing he won't provide are waders. Johnson's other prime spots are the Truckee River, from the catch-and-release section beginning at Trout Creek to the Nevada state line; Lake Davis in Plumas National Forest north of Truckee; Martis Lake; and the Truckee trio of Boca, Stampede and Prosser Creek reservoirs. For the larger lakes, he fishes from a driftboat or a pram, and suggests that clients have basic flycasting skills, although he customizes all trips to a client's ability. However, he will take novices—including youngsters 12 and older—on the Truckee River for personalized instruction on casting, reading the water, and stream entomology. On the river, he uses mostly subsurface nymphs such as free-floating caddis larva. At Lake Davis, Johnson fishes the offshore weed beds for the big Eagle Lake-strain trout (averaging 16 to 22 inches), using damselfly and blood midge larva patterns. All fishing is catch-and-release. The season is from April through October.

**Fees:** Full-day for one person is $150, and $180 for two anglers. He'll supply any gear except waders, and provides sodas and snacks.

**Information:** Johnson Tackle & Guide Service, P.O. Box 26, Tahoma, CA 96142; (916) 525-6575.

## Joe Heuseveldt

A school teacher by trade, Heuseveldt is a personable and articulate flyfishing instructor who specializes in fishing the Truckee River and the wild trout waters of Martis Lake. He'll take clients of any ability level, from beginners to experts, and offers clinics for up to five people on the Truckee, where he discusses wading skills, reading the water, entomology and casting. Heuseveldt's technique is to fish the river with short, rifle-shot casts of 10 feet upstream from a nine-foot rod, with no line mending. "We emphasize pinpoint accuracy, drag-free drifts and strategic wading," he says. His favorite patterns on the Truckee are yellow and royal Humpies. Clients should bring their own fishing gear, neoprene chest-waders and a wading staff. Heuseveldt will supply his special flies. He generally fishes the summer months from mid-June through Labor Day.

**Fees:** $200 a day for one person, plus $50 for each additional person.

**Information:** Joe Heuseveldt, P.O. Box 8220, Truckee, CA 96162; (916) 587-3035.

## A River Runs To It

Lake Tahoe residents and flyfishers Travis and Cheryl Adlington offer clinics and lessons on stillwater fishing, mainly during weekends and Tuesdays from May through October. Travis, an optometrist, specializes in teaching beginning to advanced techniques on local lakes, using Spooner, Martis and Davis lakes as outdoor classrooms. Sessions cover lake fishing via float tubes, prams and wading, and discuss the advantages of nymphing. Generally clients meet at Incline Village, often at the Village Green next to the Hyatt Regency, for casting instruction. The couple accept both beginning and advanced flyfishers, and also do individual casting instruction and small-group fly-tying clinics. New casters can try their skills at nearby Spooner Lake, a catch-and-release trout fishery that has ideal casting areas. The all-day clinic is a long one—lasting 14 hours (from 8 a.m. until 10 p.m.)—but is geared for people who can't spare two full days to learn all the necessary flyfishing basics. The Adlingtons supply lunch and there is a break for dinner (on your own bill). Groups of four to eight anglers are accepted.

**Fees:** $200 per day for one person and $150 for each additional person, including all gear and materials, a personalized textbook and lunch.

*Information:* A River Runs To It, P.O. Box 7133, Incline Village, NV 89452; (702) 831-8819.

## Gold Country Guide Service

Bob Cosick specializes in catch-and-release freestone and stillwater angling, with his main territory the main stem and North Fork of the Yuba River. In winter (January through March), during the stonefly hatch, and through the end of April, during the mayfly hatch, he uses a Klackacraft (a McKenzie-style driftboat) on the lower river. During summer, when flows are below 1,000 cubic feet per second and the caddis hatches are on, he fishes the river and the North Fork by foot. Occasionally, he fishes Martis Creek Lake in Truckee. Cosick has been fishing these waters since 1980. He prefers clients with basic flyfishing skills, including the ability to cast 25 to 30 feet consistently. Customers should bring their own rods and gear. He recommends rods of eight or nine feet in length, in the four to six weight categories, with 10-foot leaders in sizes 4x through 6x, with tippet material 5x, 6x and 7x.

*Fees:* Full-day trip—$180 for one angler, $230 for two. Half-day trip—$100 for one, $160 for two. Float trip—$250 for a full day and $150 for a half day (two-angler maximum). Lunch and beverages are provided on full-day trips.

*Information:* Gold Country Guide Service, P.O. Box 1966, Grass Valley, CA 95945; (916) 272-FLYS (3597). Nevada City Anglers Fly Shop, (916) 478-9301.

## Sierra Flyfishing Guide Service

With 30 years of flyfishing experience, 12 of them in the Truckee area, Art Lew is a dedicated instructor, fly-tyer and amateur entomologist. Living on the Truckee River, he fishes the catch-and-release trophy trout section with dry flies from Trout Creek to Union Bridge. He also fishes Martis Creek Lake for Eagle Lake-strain trout, as well as Milton Reservoir and the lower reaches of the Yuba River. The majority of his clients are repeat customers. Lew supplies Fisher rods and Orvis reels, as well as his own unique fly patterns. His blood midge emerger has become local legend as the "wonder fly" of Martis Reservoir. Lew emphasizes all aspects of flyfishing, including the approach and entomology, and does not fish while he's guiding.

*Fees:* $175 for a full day, $125 for a half day, including gear, lunch and beverages.

*Information:* Sierra Flyfishing Guide Service, P.O. Box 1704, Truckee, CA 96061; (916) 587-5011.

## Adams Tube Trips

Bellyboat fishing in the Lakes Basin is the specialty of part-time guide Rob Adams, who is based in Graeagle. Adams does one-day and multi-day trips among the more than 50 alpine lakes that are located within a 15-mile radius. Adams has been fishing the area for 20 years and guiding since 1992. His main destinations are Wades, Long, Spencer, Rock, Gold and Sardine lakes. He also guides on Lake Davis for big Eagle Lake rainbows, fishing the offshore weed beds with float tubes. On the one-day, high-country hikes, he leaves just before sunrise to catch the morning bite, using patterns that might include mayflies, woolly buggers, leeches, damselflies, ants and Adams, depending on time of year. Multi-day trips are by advance arrangement. The season runs June to October, depending on spring thaw. Lake Davis trips are in spring and fall, and run from before sunrise to about 1:30 p.m. Adams encourages catch-and-release fishing. Trips are customized to clients' desires and abilities.

*Fees:* $150 for one person and $200 for two, including float tube, rod, reel and waders. Multi-day trips average $125 per person per day. Clients bring snacks, lunch and beverages.

*Information:* Adams Tube Trips, P.O. Box 2003, Graeagle, CA 96103; (916) 836-4410.

## True North Guide Service, Lake Davis

Shane Sisler offers guided trips on weekends only from March through November out of the Grizzly Country Store at Davis. He takes a maximum of two anglers in his 16-foot Starcraft, which has a Mercury 45-horsepower motor, live wells, fish-finder and two casting platforms. Sisler fishes mostly nymphs, the tried-and-true pattern for this lake, but occasionally fishes dry flies if there's a hatch. The top patterns are damselfly, callibaetis and blood midge. The prize trout is the cutbow, a hybrid of cutthroat and rainbow, which averages three to four pounds and fights like a river steelhead. Most fish are caught in relatively shallow waters (five to six feet), and sometimes less. Clients cast into coves, shallows and weed beds, and may wade along the shoreline. Catch-and-release fishing is encouraged, but not required. Sisler usually departs around 8 a.m. for half-day or full-day trips. Sage rods with Orvis reels are supplied, but clients must buy leaders and flies, which can be purchased at the store. Owner Dave Takahashi, himself a flyfisher, offers his own "dirty dozen" package of local flies.

*Fees:* $250 for two anglers for a full day, or $125 for a half day. Bring lunch and beverages, as well as waders.

*Information:* True North Guide Service, 7552 Lake Davis Road, Portola, CA 96122; (916) 832-0270.

# TACKLE SUPPLIERS
## Lake Tahoe

**The Sportsman:** Rentals, sales, equipment and accessories for backpacking, camping, fishing (licenses available) and alpine skiing. Co-owners Jack Martin, Rick Muller and Stan Pomin are veteran guides, and are widely regarded as among the most knowledgeable anglers in the basin. 2556 Lake Tahoe Boulevard, South Lake Tahoe, CA 96150; (916) 542-3474.

**Hooks & Books:** This is a mail-order service providing over 500 flyfishing books and videos. Also, hard-to-get Tiemco and Daiichi hooks and flytying tools. Contact Thy Rod & Staff, P.O. Box 10038, Truckee, CA 96162; (916) 587-7333, or e-mail, 73442.374@compuserve.com.

**Tahoe Bike and Ski:** Fishing tackle and licenses. 8608 North Lake Boulevard, Kings Beach, CA 96143; (916) 546-7437.

**Swigard's True Value Hardware:** A full line of fishing supplies. 200 North Lake Boulevard, Tahoe City, CA 96145; (916) 583-3738.

**Bud's Sporting Goods and Fountain:** Fishing and camping equipment, sportswear, fishing licenses and maps. 10043 Donner Pass Road, Truckee, CA 96161; (916) 587-3177.

**Mountain Hardware and Sports:** Fishing licenses, tackle, boat and RV supplies, camping supplies, rafts and alpine ski accessories. Open 7 a.m. to 7 p.m. Monday through Saturday, 8 a.m. to 6 p.m. Sundays and summer. VISA, American Express and MasterCard are accepted. 11320 Donner Pass Road, Truckee, CA 96161; (916) 587-4844.

**The Sports Exchange:** Rentals, sales, equipment and sportswear for mountain biking, boating (canoes, kayaks, fishing boats), camping, climbing (new/used gear and climbing gyms), fishing (equipment and licenses), parachutes, skis (alpine and Nordic), snowboards, saucers, tennis and windsurfing. 10095 West River, Truckee, CA 96161; (916) 582-4510.

**Tourist Liquor and Sporting Goods Store:** Flyfishing specialists, with fishing bait and equipment. 10092 Donner Pass Road, Truckee, CA 96161; (916) 587-3081.

**Zephyr Cove Marina:** Boat (speed, fishing, waterskiing) and jetski rentals. Four miles north of the South Shore casinos on U.S. Forest Service lands in Zephyr Cove, NV. P.O. Box 830, Zephyr Cove, NV 89448; (702) 588-3833.

**Homewood Hardware:** Full line of fishing supplies. 5405 West Lake Boulevard, Homewood, CA 96141; (916) 525-6367.

**Outdoor and Flyfishing Store:** Flyfishing equipment and licenses. 3433 Lake Tahoe Boulevard, South Lake Tahoe, CA 96150; (916) 541-8208.

**Payless Drug Stores:** Biking, fishing, camping, tennis, saucers, equipment, and sportswear. 1020 Al Tahoe Boulevard, South Lake Tahoe, CA 96150; (916) 541-2434.

**A-Action High Sierra Fishing Charters:** Fishing charters and equipment. P.O. Box 17663, South Lake Tahoe, CA 96151; (916) 541-3254.

**Woodfords Station:** Fishing and camping gear, fishing licenses, market (ice, cafe, food to go, beer, wine), and tourist information. Open daily, 7 a.m. to 6 p.m. 290 Pony Express Road, Woodfords, CA 96120; (916) 694-2930.

## Plumas County

**Grizzly Country Store:** Tackle and information on fishing conditions at Lake Davis. Contact Dave Takahashi, 7552 Lake Davis Road, Portola, CA 96122; (916) 832-0270.

**Blairsden Mercantile and Hardware:** Tackle and fishing information for the Feather River and Lakes Basin areas. 282 Bonta, Blairsden, CA 96103: (916) 836-2589.

**Gold Rush Sports:** Tackle and fishing information for the Lake Davis and Feather River areas. 280 East Sierra Avenue, Portola, CA 96122; (916) 832-5724.

**Sportsmen's Den:** Tackle and fishing information for local waters in Plumas County. 1580 East Main, Quincy, CA 95971; (916) 283-2733.

## Reno/Sparks/Carson Valley

**Reno Fly Shop:** A full-service fly shop (fly-tying, rod building, equipment), stream-fishing lessons, Nevada/California licensed guide service (full and half day), cold weather clothing and accessories, and specialized equipment for Pyramid Lake fishing. Independence Square, 294 East Moana Lane, Reno, NV 89502; (702) 825-FISH (3474).

**The Fish Connection:** A full-service flyfishing and tackle shop, with hand-tied and custom-made flies, custom rods and a complete line of materials and accessories. They also offer guide services and flyfishing and fly-tying lessons. Owners Mike and Sue Solgat do one-on-one casting lessons on the East Fork of the Carson River by arrangement. They are a full source for regular fishing information in Alpine County (California) and western Nevada waters. Open 9 a.m. to 6 p.m. weekdays, 8 a.m. to 5 p.m. Saturday. 1384 US 395, Gardnerville, NV 89410; (702) 782-4734.

**The Gilly Fishing Store:** Fishing tackle (full line fly, bass, trout), rod building, reel repair, a complete line of classes and licenses. 1111 North Rock Boulevard, Sparks, NV 89431; (702) 358-6113.

**Johnson's Sporting World:** Fishing tackle and licenses. 435 Kietzke Lane, Reno, NV 89502; (702) 323-6109.

**Mark-Fore & Strike Sporting Goods:** Fishing (tackle, bait, fly-fishing), camping/outing (tents, stoves, sleeping bags), boating (mercury outboards), waterskiing and backpacking equipment. Open 8 a.m. to 6 p.m. Monday through Thursday and Saturday; 8 a.m. to 7 p.m. Friday. 490 Kietzke Lane, Reno, NV 89502; (702) 322-9559.

**Rick's Discount Fishing:** Fishing tackle, custom spoons, spinners, lake trolls and mail orders. 2166 Victorian Avenue (B Street), Sparks, NV 89431; (702) 356-6614.

## IMPORTANT RESOURCES & CONTACTS

**California Department of Fish and Game (Headquarters):** 3211 S Street, Sacramento, CA 95816; (916) 227-2244.

**California Department of Fish and Game (Region 2 Office):** 1701 Nimbus Road, Rancho Cordova, CA 95670; (916) 355-0978.

**Nevada Division of Wildlife:** P.O. Box 10678, Reno, NV 89520; (702) 688-1500.

**Alpine Chamber of Commerce:** Call for the latest in fishing and tips or pick up a complete fishing packet. P.O. Box 265, Markleeville, CA 96120; (916) 694-2475.

**Plumas County Visitors Bureau:** Knowledgeable about the Feather River, Lake Davis and Lakes Basin areas. 91 Church Street, Quincy, CA 95971; (800) 326-2247 or (916) 283-6345.

# Chapter 10

# Golf Courses

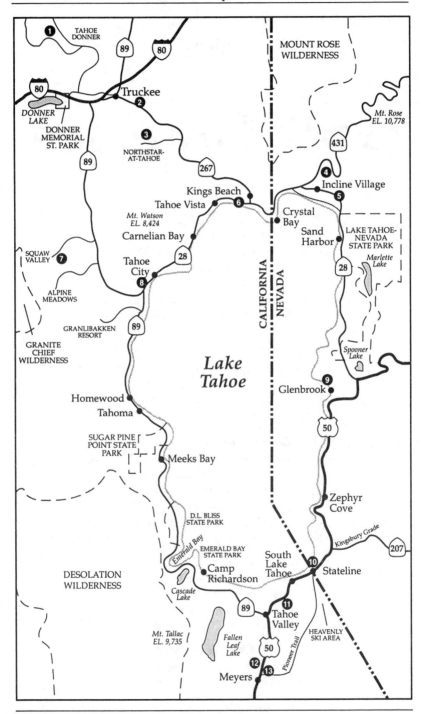

## *Map References—Lake Tahoe area golf courses*

◆

Golf is not just a casual diversion in the Tahoe-Reno area; it is a passion. Some of the top courses in the country, and some of the oldest in California and Nevada, are located within a 50-mile radius of Lake Tahoe. The region has no less than two dozen 18-hole courses, with all but two of them open for public play, and another half dozen nine-hole courses. Beyond these, at least three more 18-hole courses are on the drawing boards.

What makes a golf vacation here so attractive is the diversity of terrain. You can play a hilly, forested course at Lake Tahoe one day, and a links-style, high-desert course the next day. Expect to encounter plenty of wildlife, including deer, marmots, coyotes and waterfowl on the fairways and in the out-of-bounds areas, some of which are sensitive and protected wetlands. The top designers in the sport—Arnold Palmer, Robert Trent Jones Sr. and Jr., Peter Jacobsen and Robert Muir Graves, among others—have left their trademarks at these courses, so there is plenty of challenge for any player. Proximity is another advantage; from Reno or Tahoe, you can drive to most of these places within an hour.

As might be expected, it's tough to get tee times at the premier mountain courses because their season is short and demand is high. These include Edgewood in South Lake Tahoe, Incline Championship, Tahoe Donner, Plumas Pines, Graeagle Meadows and The Resort at Squaw Creek. You can extend the season to year-round by playing the Reno and Carson Valley courses, which are closed only by occasional snowfall. If you're having trouble getting tee times, consider these excellent but less well-known courses: Genoa Lakes, Dayton Valley, Lake Tahoe, Northstar, Incline Executive, Washoe and Wildcreek. By all means, try to play at Lakeridge in Reno, this city's most spectacular course.

For high-handicap players, there's mild terrain at Rosewood Lakes, Sierra Sage, Carson Valley, Eagle Valley and Graeagle Meadows. And the best-kept golf secrets in the entire region are Tahoe's secluded nine-holers, especially Glenbrook and Old Brockway, which have frequent elevation changes and can test all of your skills.

Keep in mind a few things when playing these courses. In summer, afternoon thundershowers are not uncommon in both the mountain and high-desert areas. When lightning is flashing close by, the last thing you want in your hands is a big, fat 9-iron. The better part of valor is to retreat to the clubhouse and wait until the storm blows over (which it often does within an hour), or just quit for the day. Another frequent environmental factor is afternoon wind—especially at the Reno and Carson Valley courses, where most players prefer morning tee times. Finally, with so many of these courses bordering nature preserves, respect the signs asking you to stay out of the wetlands. Such habitats are crucial to the local wildlife, which, after all, contribute to the enjoyment of playing golf here.

# Truckee/Donner

## ★ Tahoe Donner Golf Course ★

★ *notes Author's Choice*

*See number 1 on Lake Tahoe area map, page 282*

**Stats:** Designed by Bill Williams; 18 holes, 6,917 yards and 72 par.

**Description:** Located above Truckee on a plateau that encompasses a vast residential/resort development, this picturesque and meticulously groomed course is difficult to play, and equally difficult for securing tee times, since residents get most of the prime spots during the short season. This course has six par 5s and eight par 4s, but even big boomers will have to use finesse to avoid landing in creeks or in the heavily forested out-of-bounds areas. Although the scorecard rates the second hole as the number-one handicap, the course strategy booklet (available for a few extra dollars at the pro shop) gives that distinction to the first, a 450-yard, par 5 "warm-up" that sets the tone for the rest of your round. The hole is long and straightaway, and the narrow corridor offers little forgiveness for a hook or slice. Your drive is apt to land on an uphill slope, and you'll need a 3-iron or 7-wood for a long second shot to a two-level green that will challenge your putting skills. The 18th (421 yards, par 4) is one of the most spectacular finishing holes in the Sierra. It requires a strong downhill drive of 210 to 230 yards, then a carefully negotiated long second shot that must sail over a watery labyrinth of streams and ponds to reach a large green. On the second, third and fourth holes, you have to dodge some large trees in the fairway, which can block even solidly hit balls.

**Amenities:** Driving range, putting green, cart rentals, pro shop, restaurant, snack bar and bar.

**Fees:** Including mandatory cart, $85 ($60 preseason rate before June); special rates available after 3:30 p.m., when carts are optional. No nine-hole rates available. Club rentals: $20.

*Hours:* 7 a.m. to dusk (mid-May through mid-October).

*Pro:* Bruce Towle.

*Information:* Off Old Highway 40 in Tahoe Donner; 12850 North-woods Boulevard, Truckee, CA 96161; (916) 587-9440.

## Ponderosa Golf Course
*See number 2 on Lake Tahoe area map, page 282*

*Stats:* Nine holes, 3,018 yards and 36 par.

*Description:* One mile south of Truckee, this nine-hole course is well-maintained and mostly level, with few surprises. Wide fairways are forgiving, there are no fairway water hazards, and the course is easily walkable. There are two par 5s, four par 4s and two par 3s. The toughest hole is the 507-yard ninth, a par 5 that has a dogleg on the right, Highway 267 on the left and a well-bunkered green. The greatest elevation change is the third (145 yards, par 3), which requires a steep uphill tee shot across a road to the green. Homes and pine trees parallel the first four holes.

*Amenities:* Putting green, power and pull cart rentals, club rentals, pro shop, lessons, club repair and snack bar.

*Fees:* $35 ($20 after 3:30 p.m.). Cart rentals: $20 for 18 holes, $12 for nine holes.

*Hours:* 7 a.m. to 7 p.m. (May through October).

*Manager:* Al Bailey.

*Information:* At Highway 267 and Reynolds Way, Truckee, CA; 10040 Reynolds Way, Truckee, CA 96160; (916) 587-3501.

## ★ Northstar-at-Tahoe Golf Course ★
*See number 3 on Lake Tahoe area map, page 282*

*Stats:* Designed by Robert Muir Graves; 18 holes, 6,897 yards and 72 par.

*Description:* Here's a course with a Jekyll and Hyde personality: the front nine has friendly, wide-open fairways overlooking Martis Valley, while the back nine has a devilish layout that requires players to slash through an obstacle course of dense forest, barrancas and water hazards. Drivers in front, irons in back, lots of balls in your bag—and you have the basic strategy. But the 14th (489 yards, par 5) sneaks up on you like Jack the Ripper. Consider a 5-iron off the tee, and gauge your second shot carefully (maybe another 5-iron)—there's a small uphill rise that slopes off toward a blind green. Lurking here is a barranca, and it's better to lay up in front of it than to risk a lost ball. Scout the distance before your second stroke, and use a wedge for your third shot to the small green, taking care to avoid a deep bunker on the left. The 17th (359 yards, par 4) and the 18th (552 yards, par 5) will also give you fits; they require threading the needle between stands of pine and aspen, and the 17th veers left across a creek. Water comes into play on 14 holes, so plan on dunking a few if you're a high handicapper.

*Amenities:* Driving range, putting green, cart rentals, club rentals, pro shop, restaurant, snack bar and bar.

*Fees:* $65 (18 holes, cart and bucket of range balls). Club rentals: $25 for 18 holes, $15 for nine holes. Carts are mandatory until noon.

*Hours:* 7:30 a.m. to dark (May through October).

*Pro:* Jim Anderson.

*Information:* Located at Northstar-at-Tahoe, off Highway 267 on Basque Drive, six miles from Truckee; Basque Drive (off Northstar Drive), P.O. Box 129, Truckee, CA 96160; (916) 562-2490.

# North Shore

### ★ Incline Executive Course ★

*See number 4 on Lake Tahoe area map, page 282*

*Stats:* Designed by Robert Trent Jones, Jr.; 18 holes, 3,513 yards and 58 par.

*Description:* Carved into a lushly forested hillside above Incline Village's prestigious Championship Course, this track is not only spectacularly scenic, but is also a sterling challenge for your short game. Forget about woods; there are 14 par 3s, no par 5s and the longest hole (18th) is 399 yards. You'll get plenty of practice with your short irons and wedges, and plenty of exercise, too, since the course seesaws up and down the mountain. Perhaps the most interesting hole is the 122-yard 15th, a par 3 that has a high, elevated tee requiring an 8- or 9-iron to carry a stream to a lower green bordered by three bunkers. Short gets you in the stream and long gets you in the woods. The 17th (125 yards, par 3) is almost the reverse; you tee off to an elevated green. Narrow fairways, dense out-of-bounds and water hazards on the majority of the holes necessitate more than a few extra balls in your bag. This course has been rated as one of the top five executive courses in the U.S. It is also one of the easier courses in Tahoe for securing a tee time.

*Amenities:* Putting green, cart rentals, pro shop, snack bar and bar.

*Fees:* Including mandatory carts, $50 for nonresidents ($25 after 4 p.m.), $25 for residents ($12.50 after 4 p.m.). Off-season rates (before June 17 and after September 17): $40 for nonresidents ($20 after 4 p.m.) and $20 for residents ($10 after 4 p.m.). Club rentals: $25.

*Hours:* 6:30 a.m. to 7 p.m. (mid-May to early October).

*Pro:* Randy Cooper.

*Information:* On Golfer's Pass Road off Mount Rose Highway (Highway 431); 690 Wilson Way, Incline Village, NV 89451; (702) 832-1150.

## ★ Incline Championship Course ★
*See number 5 on Lake Tahoe area map, page 282*

**Stats:** Designed by Robert Trent Jones, Sr.; 18 holes, 6,915 yards and 72 par.

**Description:** This premier course combines the scenic beauty of green hills, aspen and pine forest, and lofty panoramas of Lake Tahoe. Set in the uncrowded "banana belt" of the lake's most upscale community (and surrounded by million-dollar-plus estates), the Championship Course is extremely popular. A diverse layout with frequent elevation changes offers four par 5s, 10 par 4s and four par 3s. Creeks and ponds provide water hazards, some of them blind, on eight holes of the front nine and four holes of the back nine. The number-one handicap hole is the par 5 fourth, a double dogleg left that is 619 yards and bordered by out-of-bounds along the length of the hole. But for a lot of players the 18th (411 yards, par 4) is more difficult. The tee shot must carry two creeks and be straight down a tight fairway lined with houses. There's a dogleg left, and if you don't get an accurate drive to a narrow landing you'll have a tough second shot. In any case, you'll have to cope with a well-bunkered and elevated green that slopes away from you. The signature hole is the 16th (406 yards, par 4), with its dramatic view over Lake Tahoe and snow-capped Sierra peaks.

**Amenities:** Driving range, putting green, cart rentals, pro shop, restaurant, snack bar and bar.

**Fees:** Including mandatory carts, $100 for nonresidents ($50 after 4 p.m.), $35 for Incline Village residents/guests ($17.50 after 4 p.m.). Off-season rates (before June 17 and after September 17): $80 for nonresidents ($40 after 4 p.m.) and $25 for residents ($12.50 after 4 p.m.). Club rentals: $25.

**Hours:** 6 a.m. to 7 p.m. (early May through mid-October).

**Pro:** Brian Alders.

**Director of golf:** John Hughes.

**Information:** 955 Fairway Boulevard, Incline Village, NV 89451; (702) 832-1144.

## ★ Old Brockway Golf Course ★
*See number 6 on Lake Tahoe area map, page 282*

**Stats:** Designed by John Dunn; nine holes, 3,400 yards and 36 par.

**Description:** It would be a mistake to dismiss this as a lightweight nine-holer, but that's what many passersby think when they see the flat, rather nondescript first and second holes from Highway 267 or North Lake Boulevard. Ah, but there's pure gold in the rest of the course, and plenty of challenge with narrow fairways, varying terrain elevations and woodlands. Not only that, but Old Brockway has a colorful history; it was the site of the first Bing Crosby Open, in 1934, long before it became a PGA-sanctioned event. The course was built in 1924, and has retained its original form. From its inception, it was intended as an amenity to the Brockway Hotel, a luxurious resort that was destroyed by fire. Hollywood's famous Rat Pack—Dean Martin, Frank Sinatra et al—used to play here regularly, and holes one, two, three, eight and nine are together known as "The Loop" or "Whiskey Run," commemorating Martin's drinking habits on the course. There's a story that another famous golfer, Bob Hope, while teeing off on the second hole, inadvertently hit a deer, causing the ball to ricochet to about 10 feet from the pin—reportedly his best shot in Tahoe. Although most of the course is invisible from the highway, it has an interesting layout, with five par 4s, two par 3s and two par 5s. Because several holes parallel homes or highway, slices and hooks will get you into fast trouble. The number-one handicap hole is the seventh, a long (553-yard) par 5 that slopes uphill and has a wide ditch fronting an elevated and bunkered green. On the short, 195-yard third hole, you tee off on top of a high rock garden through a narrow slot between homes and forest, to a lower green.

**Amenities:** Driving range, putting green, cart rentals, pro shop and restaurant.

**Fees:** $45 for 18 holes, $25 for nine holes. Cart rentals: $25 for 18 holes, $16 for nine holes. Club rentals: $15.

**Hours:** 6:30 a.m. to dark (April to November).

**Pro:** Garrett Good.

**Owner:** Lane Lewis.

**Information:** At the junction of highways 28 and 267; 7900 North Lake Boulevard, Kings Beach, CA 96143; (916) 546-9909.

## ★ The Resort at Squaw Creek ★
*See number 7 on Lake Tahoe area map, page 282*

**Stats:** Designed by Robert Trent Jones, Jr.; 18 holes, 6,931 yards and 71 par.

**Description:** "The course that Titlist built" is the way that locals describe this mean-spirited, links-style track, which has a penchant for swallowing balls. Most of the back nine resembles a waterfowl sanctuary, with elevated wooden cart paths crisscrossing the wetlands. A wayward ball off the tee will sink in the ooze like a rock in quicksand, and about the eighth time this happens you'll be ready to break your driver in half. The front nine presents some tight, narrow fairways notched into the hillside and sandwiched between rows of mature pines. You may wonder how on earth anyone managed to build a golf course here. Actually, the course was designed on about two-thirds of the normal land area. The number-one handicap is the eighth, a par 4, 338-yard hole that requires an iron off the tee and pinpoint accuracy on the second shot to reach a speck of a green, or it's lost in the marsh. By the time you get to the last holes, it's

likely that the wind will be kicking up through the meadow, and you'll be too distraught to appreciate the sweeping vistas of Squaw Valley's imposing peaks. The 429-yard 17th (a par 4) often throws a fierce headwind your way, and makes it tough to use a driver without risking the wrath of the Marsh Monster. Your second stroke must carry a creek to a diminutive green surrounded by bunkers. Arguably this course, built in 1992, is the most difficult in the Sierra. It will test the resolve of seasoned players.
*Amenities:* Driving range, putting green, cart rentals, pro shop, restaurant, snack bar, bar and accommodations.
*Fees:* Including mandatory carts, $100 weekdays, $110 weekends. Club rentals: $25.
*Hours:* 8 a.m. to dark (June to October).
*Director of golf:* Bob Hickman.
*Information:* 400 Squaw Creek Road, Olympic Valley, CA; (916) 583-6300.

## Tahoe City Golf Course
*See number 8 on Lake Tahoe area map, page 282*
*Stats:* Designed by May Webb Dunn; nine holes, 2,570 yards and 33 par.
*Description:* Located in the heart of Tahoe City, this nine-hole course is the oldest at Lake Tahoe (circa 1917), beating Brockway by seven years. Like Brockway and Glenbrook, it was a staple of Sinatra, Hope and Crosby. Except for holes four and five, the course is basically flat and wide open, but has some scenic views of the lake, which is directly across the street. There are four par 4s, four par 3s and one par 5. The 419-yard third, a par 4, has an out-of-bounds that consists of retail businesses on the left and a well-bunkered green. However, the fifth (294 yards, par 4) is the trickiest, with a slight dogleg right, water hazard on the right, and a sunken green with a narrow slot through tall pines.
*Amenities:* Driving range, putting green and pro shop.
*Fees:* $35 for 18 holes, $25 for nine holes ($16 after 4:30 p.m.). Cart rentals: $22 for 18 holes, $15 for nine.
*Hours:* Dawn to dusk (April through November).
*Pro:* Don Hay.
*Information:* In downtown Tahoe City; 251 North Lake Boulevard, Tahoe City, CA 96145; (916) 583-1516.

## ★ Glenbrook Golf Course ★
*See number 9 on Lake Tahoe area map, page 282*
*Stats:* Nine holes, 2,715 yards and 35 par.
*Description:* If you didn't have precise directions, you'd never find this secluded, forested beauty, which is set in a private, gated residential community of upscale homes but is open for public play. Glenbrook, located on the southeast corner of the lake below US 50, is one of three historic

nine-holers (the others are Old Brockway and Tahoe City) that drew the Hollywood glitterati in the 1940s and 1950s. Ben Hogan, Bing Crosby, Frank Sinatra and other heavyweights have played here over the years, and, not surprisingly, *Golf Digest* ranked this as one of the top six nine-hole resort courses in the world. Its well-groomed fairways, mature evergreens and frequent views of Lake Tahoe make this a place that rivals many 18-hole courses. This is not a short-iron course, either; there are two par 5s, three par 4s and three par 3s from the men's tees. The hole that gives players the most difficulty is the third, a short (216-yard) par 3 that requires a precise shot to a well-bunkered green with a left-to-right dropoff. Most players are forced to lay up in front of the green, not exactly friendly territory, and overhitting can put your ball down an embankment against a fence. The second hole is a long, downward-facing dogleg left, with a lake to the left of the green. Because of its seclusion, Glenbrook is relatively uncrowded, but it is certainly a worthy venue for visiting golfers.

**Amenities:** Driving range, putting green, cart rentals, pro shop, restaurant, snack bar and bar.

**Fees:** 18 holes for $45 ($20 after 4 p.m.); nine holes for $28. Optional cart rental: $20. Club rental: $20.

**Hours:** 7:30 a.m. to 6 p.m. (April through October).

**Pro:** Lane Christiansen.

**Information:** North of Cave Rock; Pray Meadow Road; 2070 Pray Meadow Road, Glenbrook, NV 89413; (702) 749-5201.

# South Shore

## ★ Edgewood Tahoe Golf Course ★

*See number 10 on Lake Tahoe area map, page 282*

**Stats:** Designed by George Fazio; 18 holes, 7,491 yards and 72 par.

**Description:** This is the Grand Dame of Sierra courses, with lakeside frontage and an elegant, palatial clubhouse that contains a gourmet restaurant and enough banquet rooms to host a myriad of social functions, weddings and conferences. Edgewood is the site of the annual Isuzu Celebrity Championship, a major televised event held each July. But perhaps its greatest distinction is having the only two holes—the signature 17th (207 yards, an easy par 3) and the finishing 18th (574 yards, par 5)—that are right on the shore of Tahoe. It's easy to be swept up by the scenic lake vistas and the carefully manicured fairways and greens, but you'd better pay attention if you're going to avoid bogeys. Try for a fade off the tee on the tough, 462-yard ninth, a par 4 with a narrow fairway, a dogleg right, out-of-bounds to the left and trees to the right. The 10th (431 yards, par 4) has a lake that eats into most of the fairway and guards the green along with four bunkers. On the 15th (372 yards, par 4), an uphill tee shot that slopes to a hidden fairway requires a look-see through a periscope, but is less difficult than it seems. And on the 16th, an island of a green is surrounded by bunkers, virtually assuring you of practice with your sand wedge. On most of the holes, the greens are designed to make Silly Putty out of frustrated putters. Note: Edgewood is the most popular course on the lake, and the most difficult for getting tee times.

*Amenities:* Driving range, putting green, cart rentals, pro shop, restaurant, banquet rooms, snack bars and bar.

*Fees:* Including carts, $125. Club rentals: $20.

*Hours:* 7 a.m. to 3 p.m. (May through October).

*Pro:* Lou Eiguren.

*Information:* Located behind Horizon Casino; Lake Parkway (P.O. Box 5400), 180 Lake Parkway, Stateline, NV 89449; (702) 588-2787 or (702) 588-3566.

## Bijou Golf Course
*See number 11 on Lake Tahoe area map, page 282*

*Stats:* Nine holes, 2,028 yards and 32 par.

*Description:* Built in 1920, this scenic nine-holer, which is located in Bijou Meadows just off US 50 near the center of South Lake Tahoe, is a respectable track for players of all abilities. Operated by the city, the course takes no advance reservations, but is one of the easiest to get on in the Tahoe Basin. There are five par 4s and four par 3s, and Bijou Creek provides water hazards on five holes until midsummer. Pine trees line many of the holes, and there are vistas of Freel Peak and Heavenly Ski Area. The number-one handicap hole is the 370-yard sixth, a par 4, which has a demanding first shot that must carry a creekbed and meadow. The ideal landing is 220 yards off the tee, providing the best approach to a very small green. The eighth (215 yards, par 3), plays straightaway to an equally diminutive green that is surrounded on three sides by the creekbed and a trap on the left; overhit, and you're in the ditch. In general, greens are small and have lots of tricky undulations. The course has seen a major restoration program during recent years, and there are plans to relocate and redesign it.

*Amenities:* Driving range, putting green, cart rentals, pro shop and snack bar.

*Fees:* $10 for nine holes ($6 after 4 p.m.). Handcart rentals: $2. Club rentals: $5.

*Hours:* 7:30 a.m. to 6:30 p.m. (April through October).

*Manager:* Don Radford.

*Information:* Located at 3464 Fairway (at Johnson Boulevard) in South Lake Tahoe. For information, write 1180 Rufus Allen Boulevard, South Lake Tahoe, CA 96150; (916) 542-6097.

## ★ Lake Tahoe Golf Course ★
*See number 12 on Lake Tahoe area map, page 282*

**Stats:** 18 holes, 6,707 yards and 71 par.

**Description:** Owned by the California Department of Parks and Recreation, this course is one of Tahoe's sleepers. It is frequently easier to get tee times here than on the lake's premier tracks, and it has a modern and spacious new clubhouse. But the course is not exactly a breeze; there are potential water hazards on 16 holes, including sections of the Upper Truckee River, although there are enough straightaway fairways to make up for double bogeys. The number-one handicap hole is the 13th, a sticky, 447-yard par 4 that requires a long and straight drive into the wind to a narrow landing that has a hidden pond on the right and bunkers on the left. Your second shot requires a fairway wood or long iron to a small green with bunkers in front, though most players will settle for laying up short of the green and hoping for a precise chip shot and putt. Of the other holes, the ninth (589 yards, par 5) has three different water hazards—a lake, a creek and a pond—and the 10th (427 yards, par 4) demands an accurate drive that must carry two water hazards and avoid wooded out-of-bounds to the right, with a second shot to a narrow green that slopes from back to front. This course has great diversity, including scenic riparian habitat with pines and aspens, and a huge rocky bluff behind the 10th that is unique in the region.

**Amenities:** Driving range, putting green, cart rentals, pro shop, snack bar and bar.

**Fees:** Including mandatory cart, $45 for 18 holes, weekends and holidays. Early-bird and twilight rates available. Cart rentals: $12. Club rentals: $20.

**Hours:** 6 a.m. to 8 p.m. (April through October).

**Pro:** Bob Billings.

**Manager:** Dave Rowe.

**Information:** Off US 50 between the South Lake Tahoe Airport and Meyers; 2500 US 50, South Lake Tahoe, CA 96150; (916) 577-0788.

## Tahoe Paradise Golf Course
*See number 13 on Lake Tahoe area map, page 282*

**Stats:** 18 holes, 4,070 yards and 66 par.

**Description:** "Like playing golf in your hallway" is the way one starter describes this tight course of narrow fairways through pine thickets, although what's visible from US 50 looks anything but difficult. There are 12 par 4s and six par 3s, and two of the holes have water hazards. The top handicap hole is the ninth (377 yards, par 4), which requires a tee shot through a gap no wider than 50 yards, down to a large landing area and green that is bunkered on the right. The fifth (295 yards, par 4) is also downhill, with a dogleg right that offers a skimpy landing area and a green that slopes from back to front. As a rule, hitting behind most of the holes means "bye bye ball." The signature hole is the 14th (110 yards, par 3), which has a pond in front and a view of Mount Tallac and the surrounding peaks. In general, the course has modest facilities and fair maintenance, but with its short yardage, it seems like an executive course.

*Amenities:* Driving range, putting green, cart rentals, pro shop, snack bar and bar.

*Fees:* $29 for 18 holes; seniors (65 and over) and juniors (16 and under), $25; twilight rates, $18. Optional cart rentals: $20. Club rentals: $7.50.

*Hours:* 7 a.m. to 7 p.m. (April through November).

*Pro:* Dave Gilpin.

*Manager:* David Beeman.

*Information:* 3021 US 50 (near Meyers); South Lake Tahoe, CA 96150; (916) 577-2121.

# Reno

### ★ Sierra Sage Golf Course ★

*See number 14 on Reno/Carson area map, page 294*

*Stats:* 18 holes, 6,623 yards and 71 par.

*Description:* This links-style, high-desert course near Stead Air Field, with gently rolling hills and wide-open fairways, is a modest track that won't get any design awards but will provide high-handicap golfers with an outing that is gentle on the psyche. Fairways are mostly flat and wide, and water hazards on six of the holes won't phase experienced players. There are three par 5s, 11 par 4s and four par 3s. The toughest hole is the fifth (475 yards, par 4), which tees off over a deep depression and has an uphill lie to a blind, well-bunkered green on a dogleg left. Out-of-bounds is mostly sagebrush, and the surrounding vistas can best be described as arid and desolate. Stead is a workingman's town with various industrial parks, and is the site of the annual Reno Air Show.

*Amenities:* Driving range, putting green, cart rentals, club rentals, restaurant and bar.

*Fees:* Weekdays (April through October), $20 for nonresidents, $15 for Washoe County residents; weekends, $23 for nonresidents, $17 for residents; nine-hole green fees, $11; winter rates, $14. Senior rates available. Club rentals: $12. Cart rentals: $19.

*Hours:* Daylight to dusk year-round.

*Director of golf:* Mike Mitchell.

*Information:* North of Reno off US 395; 6355 Silver Lake Boulevard, Reno, NV 89506; (702) 972-1564.

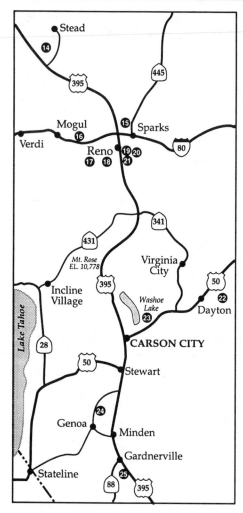

### Reno / Carson area golf courses

## ★ Wildcreek Golf Course ★

*See number 15 on Reno/Carson area map, left*

**Stats:** Two courses designed by Benz and Phelps. The Championship Course is 18 holes, 6,932 yards and 72 par; The Executive Course is nine holes, 2,840 yards and 27 par.

**Description:** Spread out over a wide area in a scenic valley north of town, Wildcreek has both a championship and a nine-hole executive course. The main course has a half-dozen holes located on hillside terraces, giving players some tricky sidehill lies and a fair amount of pitch. Ten holes have either lakes or lateral water hazards, and there are lots of bunkers and out-of-bounds areas with sagebrush, thus providing plenty of diversity. The course has four par 5s, 10 par 4s and four par 3s. The number-one handicap hole is the fifth (389 yards, par 4), which has an elongated lake on the left that half-circles the small green, and a river and bunkers to the right. The biggest trouble is off the tee, because of a narrow fairway and a tight, intimidating approach to the green. Use a 5-wood or mid- to long-iron off the tee, and a 7- to 9-iron for your second shot. The signature hole, which, at 609 yards, is also the longest, is the par 5 18th. Here you'll have to tee off into a landing area on a plateau that is difficult to see from the tee box. Your second shot will have to play down between two lakes to a fairway that is 50 yards wide, and from there you need a precise shot uphill to a green surrounded by traps. The executive course, with four lakes, is a fair test of your short game; the longest is the sixth (220 yards, par 3), which features several water hazards. Wildcreek is one of two courses owned by the Reno-Sparks Convention & Visitors Authority; the other is Northgate (see next listing).

**Amenities:** Driving range, putting greens, chipping greens, club rentals, cart rentals, pro shop, snack bar and bar.

**Fees:** Including mandatory cart, $44 for the Championship Course, $10 for the Executive Course ($2 each additional nine). Club rentals: $20 (Championship), $6 (Executive).

**Hours:** 6:30 a.m. to 7 p.m. The Championship Course is open February through December. The Executive Course is open all year.

**Pro:** Fred Elliott.

**Director of golf:** Ron Wrest.

**Information:** Off McCarran Boulevard; 3500 Sullivan Lane, Sparks, NV 89431; (702) 673-3100.

## Northgate Golf Club
*See number 16 on Reno/Carson area map, page 294*

**Stats:** Designed by Benz and Polette; 18 holes, 6,966 yards and 72 par.

**Description:** There's a lot of no-man's land between the tees and fairways on this hilly, high-desert course northwest of downtown Reno. It's full of sagebrush, rocks, ravines and sand. If you're not off the tee here, you'll spend a lot of time chasing balls in rabbit warrens. Because of the clay soil, exposed ridges, prevailing afternoon winds and hot sun, the fairways can become bulletproof in midsummer. As one of two courses operated by the Reno-Sparks Convention & Visitors Authority (the other is Wildcreek—see preceding listing), Northgate gets a lot of use. It has four par 5s, 10 par 4s and four par 3s, and there are four tee boxes on each hole. Plenty of average players will feel like beaten alley cats after spending a few hours searching for balls in the bramble. The top handicap hole is the fifth (410 yards, par 4), a hard dogleg right with a difficult landing area full of grass bunkers, and a two-tiered green that challenges your putting skill. Miss the green here and you'll be up and down like a yo-yo. But for a lot of players the greatest frustrations are in the back nine. Among the dillies are the 371-yard, par 4 15th (an uphill tee shot to a blind dogleg right guarded by grass and sand bunkers); the 436-yard, par 4 14th (a drive over sage and dirt to a narrow landing, nasty out-of-bounds on the right and grass bunkers bordering the fairway); and the

407-yard, par 4 17th (a tee shot over desert and sand bunkers to the left of the landing). Some nice touches at this course include ball-cleaners on each cart and ice water at the drinking stations.

**Amenities:** Driving range, putting green, chipping green, cart rentals, club rentals, pro shop, snack bar and bar.

**Fees:** Including cart, $42 for nonresidents, $29 for Washoe County residents; nine holes (available after 2 p.m.), $25. Club rentals: $20.

**Hours:** 6:30 a.m. to 7:30 p.m. (February through December).

**Pro:** Don Boyle.

**Director of golf:** Ron Wrest.

**Information:** West of downtown Reno and north of Interstate 80; 1111 Clubhouse Drive, Reno, NV 89523; (702) 747-7577.

## ★ Lakeridge Golf Course ★

*See number 17 on Reno/Carson area map, page 294*

**Stats:** Designed by Robert Trent Jones, Sr.; 18 holes, 6,717 yards and 72 par.

**Description:** Players flock to this challenging course in the southwest foothills of the city for one simple reason: the signature 15th hole. You can see pictures of it everywhere—an island green just off the shore of a large, mirror-smooth lake—but the impact doesn't sink in until you're on the highest tee box on a hillside 130 feet above the water with the whole of Reno stretching out in the distance. When the wind is raging, which it does with great regularity, you've got to make careful adjustments to get a par 3 on this 239-yard ego-killer. Frustrated players frequently can be seen spraying Mulligans into the drink. But the 15th is not the highest handicap hole; that distinction belongs to the fourth (599 yards, par 5). This is a dogleg right that demands a tight, well-placed tee shot to a narrow landing at the bend, and a couple of strong fairway shots with a wood or long iron to reach a well-bunkered green. Lakeridge is unquestionably Reno's premier course, though the fairways tend to harden and dry by mid- to late summer. The layout undulates through the hills, especially on the back nine, and water comes into play on 12 holes. With rocky outcroppings and abrupt elevation changes, there is a Badlands feel to the place. Local wildlife is everywhere, and includes geese as well as large, lumbering marmots called rock chucks.

**Amenities:** Driving range, putting green, cart rentals, club rentals, restaurant, snack bar and bar.

**Fees:** Including mandatory carts, $60 (Friday through Sunday). Twilight rates are available after 3 p.m. Club rentals: $25. Walkers permitted after 5:30 p.m.

**Hours:** 6 a.m. to 7 p.m. (March through December).

**Pro:** Paul Lane.

**Information:** 1200 Razorback Road, Reno, NV 89509; (702) 825-2200.

## ★ Washoe Golf Course ★

*See number 18 on Reno/Carson area map, page 294*

**Stats:** 18 holes, 6,995 yards and 72 par.

**Description:** Built in 1934 and operated by Washoe County, this is the oldest course in Reno and a favorite of local players. The front nine is relatively flat, while the back nine, much less forgiving, meanders up the hillside. Tall trees parallel the fairways throughout the course, and there are water hazards on five holes. There are three par 5s, 12 par 4s and three par 3s. Most difficult is the 12th (475 yards, par 4), which has a dogleg left, an obstructed view from the fairway and a small green, bunkered on the left, that falls away left to right. Use a driver or long iron off the tee and a fairway wood or long iron for the second shot. Even if you reach the green without mishap, you could lose strokes on putting. The ninth (426 yards, par 4) will give you something to think about as well. It's a straightaway shot into the wind uphill, to a small green with traps on both sides. Washoe is the site of the annual Reno Open, and past luminaries such as Ben Hogan have played here.

**Amenities:** Driving range, putting green, cart rentals and restaurant.

**Fees:** Weekdays (April through October), $20 for nonresidents, $15 for residents; weekends, $23 for nonresidents, $17 for residents. Twilight rates ($11) available after 4 p.m.; senior rates available; winter rates, $14. Cart rentals: $19. Club rentals: $15.

**Hours:** 7 a.m. to dark year-round.

**Pro:** Barney Bell.

**Information:** 2601 South Arlington, Reno, NV 89509; (702) 828-6640.

## Hilton Bay Aquarange

*See number 19 on Reno/Carson area map, page 294*

**Description:** If you're staying at the Reno Hilton (or even if you're not), what the heck—you might as well get some practice on the hotel's four floating greens, located in an artificial lake outside. Each green has cups with sensors, and there are different promotional giveaways for hitting cups at various ranges. A hole-in-one could get you an all-expense-paid vacation.

**Amenities:** Gift shop.

**Fees:** $6 for a large bucket of balls, $3 for three rental clubs.

**Hours:** 8 a.m. to midnight weekends, 9 a.m. to 10 p.m. weekdays (November to April); 7 a.m. to 2 a.m. (May to October).

**Information:** Reno Hilton, 2500 East Second Street, Reno, NV 89595; (702) 789-2122.

## ★ Rosewood Lakes Golf Course ★

*See number 20 on Reno/Carson area map, page 294*

**Stats:** Designed by Brad Benz; 18 holes, 6,693 yards and 72 par.

**Description:** Situated near the eastern foothills of Reno, this city-owned course is challenging but not too intimidating, and is especially popular with women. It is aptly named, since lateral water hazards come into play on all 18 holes. The layout, with four tee boxes, stretches through a labyrinth of wetlands, with cattails and marsh grass dominating the out-of-bounds ground cover. On the fifth and eighth holes, both par 3s, it's necessary to make accurate shots over the wetlands (167 and 160 yards, respectively) from tee boxes on a berm. The seventh (540 yards, par 5) is the number-one handicap hole, and requires a straight-away tee shot that stays left of berms on the right. But the 17th (401 yards, par 4) has danger written all over it; it's a dogleg right with lakes on the left and right, and a difficult approach with a river to the left of an elevated green. The 15th (547 yards, par 5) is interrupted by a lake in its midsection, requiring a drive that lays up in front of it, and an accurate approach to a well-bunkered green. Except for the last four holes, the fairways are generously wide, and high handicappers get plenty of chances for par. Waterfowl and their natural predator, the coyote, are plentiful on the course, and don't be surprised if Wile E. comes thrashing out of the reeds to present you with an unmarked hazard. The course won the Environmental Steward Award from the Golf Course Superintendent Association of America in 1992 and 1994.

**Amenities:** Driving range, putting green, cart rentals, restaurant and snack bar.

**Fees:** $24 for nonresidents, $18.50 for Washoe County residents. Twilight fees, $15 for nonresidents, $11.50 for Washoe County residents. Senior rates available. Cart rentals: $18 for 18 holes, $11 for nine holes. Club rentals: $15 for 18 holes, $7.50 for nine holes.

**Hours:** 7 a.m. to 7 p.m. (until 8 p.m. in summer); open year-round.

**Pro:** Mike Mazzaferri.

**Information:** East of Reno-Tahoe International Airport; 6800 Pembroke Drive, Reno, NV 89502; (702) 857-2892.

## Brookside Golf Course

*See number 21 on Reno/Carson area map, page 294*

**Stats:** Nine holes, 2,882 yards and 35 par.

**Description:** This used to be an 18-hole course, but it's been eaten away by the Reno-Tahoe International Airport, which owns the land, and now just nine flat, mostly straightaway holes remain. But there is some respectable distance, with two par 5s, four par 4s and three par 3s. The number-one handicap is the third (385 yards, par 4), which requires a strong drive and an approach shot to a green that is bunkered on the right and left. However, most players consider the first (540 yards, par 5) to be the most difficult, mainly because of a ditch on the left. There are lakes on three holes, and two of those sandwich a narrow fairway off the tee on the ninth (150 yards, par 3). Brookside, built in 1956, is operated by the city of Reno.

*Amenities:* Putting green, cart rentals, club rentals, snack bar and bar.
*Fees:* $10 adults, $6 seniors (62 and over), $3 juniors (17 and under). Carts (optional): $16. Club rentals: $15.
*Hours:* Daylight to dusk year-round.
*Manager:* Jerry Brown.
*Information:* Near Reno-Tahoe International Airport; 700 South Rock Boulevard, Reno, NV 89502; (702) 856-6009.

# Carson Valley

## ★ Dayton Valley Country Club ★
*See number 22 on Reno/Carson area map, page 294*

*Stats:* Designed by Arnold Palmer; 18 holes, 7,161 yards and 72 par.
*Description:* As one of the newest courses in the region, this is also one of the finest, most beautifully sculpted and manicured tracks anywhere. Located 11 miles east of Carson City, in the middle of the high desert (but in what is really an emerging planned residential community), Dayton Valley is a delight to play, as long as you adhere to one cardinal rule—get an early morning tee time. By afternoon, the winds can whip through this wide-open course with ferocity. Despite the lack of trees, however, the course has fascinating, technical terrain, with velvety, almost surrealistic fairways, creative use of hillocks, water hazards on 12 holes and a maze of bunkering. There are four par 5s, 10 par 4s and four par 3s. The most difficult is the 450-yard ninth, a par 4, which requires you to negotiate three water hazards, find a narrow landing off the tee without hitting into water on the left, and negotiate an approach with water on both sides and in front of the small, elongated green. Anything other than an accurate shot lands you in water or bunkers. The 17th (478 yards, par 4) is a minefield of large bunkers, with a fairway that zigzags between them to a postage-stamp green. There is nothing predictable or mundane about Dayton Valley; it is one of the jewels of golf.
*Amenities:* Driving range, sand traps, putting green, cart rentals, club rentals, clubhouse, restaurant, snack bar and bar.
*Fees:* Including carts, $35 weekends, $25 weekdays (November through March); $40 weekends, $25 weekdays (April); $70 weekends, $53 weekdays (May through October). Club rentals: $25.

**Hours:** Dawn to dusk year-round.
**Pro:** Jim Kepler.
**Director of golf:** Tom Duncan.
**Information:** Located east of Carson City; 51 Palmer Drive, Dayton, NV 89403; (702) 246-7888 (PUTT).

## ★ Eagle Valley East and West ★

*See number 23 on Reno/Carson area map, page 294*

**Stats:** West Course: Designed by Homer Flynt; 18 holes, 6,851 yards and 72 par. East Course: 18 holes, 6,658 yards and 72 par.

**Description:** Of the two 18-hole courses here, the East Course is flat, easy and predictable—a great track for neophytes and casual players. The West Course, however, will eat you alive. It is hilly, narrow and full of water traps and barrancas. Typical of high-desert, links-style courses, it has plenty of sagebrush, sand, jackrabbits and afternoon winds. There is a kinship, of sorts, with Northgate in Reno (see page 295), because the design and terrain are very similar, which is to say, not easy on high handicappers. And there is a bit of distraction from the trap range that thunders incessantly next to holes five and six. There are four par 5s, 10 par 4s and four par 3s. The number-one handicap is the third (567 yards, par 5), on which you must carry a water hazard off the tee and hit to a sharp dogleg left on the approach to the green. Getting the "You've gotta be kidding" award, however, is the 15th (559 yards, par 5), which has a high ridge at mid-landing (blocking any chance of seeing the green) and a barranca below that; sidecut fairways and a sharp dogleg right complete the nightmare. The sage, rocks and dry grass in out-of-bounds will steal your ball, if the rabbits don't.

**Amenities:** Lighted driving range, putting green, restaurant, snack bar, bar and free supervised children's playroom.

**Fees:** For the East Course, $21 ($10 after 4 p.m.); for the West Course, including mandatory cart rental, $37.50 (6:30 a.m. to 1 p.m.), $26.50 (1 p.m. to 4 p.m.), $18 (4 p.m. to 6 p.m.). Club rentals: $15.

**Hours:** 6:30 a.m. to 6 p.m. year-round.
**Pro:** Gary Bushman.
**Information:** North off US 50 east of Carson City; 3999 Centennial Park Drive, Carson City, NV 89706; (702) 887-2380.

## ★ The Golf Club at Genoa Lakes ★

*See number 24 on Reno/Carson area map, page 294*

**Stats:** Designed by Peter Jacobsen; 18 holes, 7,263 yards and 72 par.

**Description:** Snuggling against the eastern Sierra in Nevada's oldest town, this spectacular course, opened in 1993, has a backdrop of mountain vistas that extend southward for miles, a vast wetlands that attracts geese, ducks and shorebirds, and a sprinkling of stately cottonwoods. The long, links-style course is situated in a new, gated residential community that borders the Carson River, and is a 30-minute drive from South Lake Tahoe. *Golf Digest* recently rated it fourth in the nation among new public courses. Thirteen holes have water hazards, and the bunkers have a unique design in which the grass tapers sharply over the edges to a flat sand base. The course has four par 5s, 10 par 4s and four par 3s. There's a strategy in playing this course: Try for a morning tee time to avoid afternoon winds; play from the forward tee boxes (there are four for each hole) if you're an average player; and be off the tee to avoid trouble, which lurks everywhere. If you play from the gold tees, you'll be hitting over water on 12 holes. The number-one handicap hole is the 474-yard seventh, a par 4 that plays uphill and into a strong prevailing wind, with a tough approach shot to a green that slopes from front to back. The signature hole is the 13th, a par 5 that is Nevada's longest at 652 yards, and requires concentration to keep from losing balls on the right out-of-bounds. The 18th (449 yards, par 4) has a hard dogleg left and requires carrying a large lake, which continues as a left-side hazard all the way to the green.

*Amenities:* Driving range, chipping green, putting green, cart rentals, pro shop, restaurant and snack bar.

*Fees:* Including non-mandatory carts and range balls, $60 weekdays, $75 weekends (May through mid-October); $40 weekdays, $55 weekends (mid-October through April). Club rentals: $20. Lessons available.

*Hours:* 6 a.m. to 6 p.m.

*Director of Golf:* Randy Fox.

*Information:* Off US 395 on Jacks Valley Road; 1 Genoa Lakes Drive, P.O. Box 350, Genoa, NV 89411; (702) 782-4653 or (702) 588-4653.

## ★ Carson Valley Golf Course ★

*See number 25 on Reno/Carson area map, page 294*

*Stats:* Designed by Red Swift; 18 holes, 7,263 yards and 71 par.

*Description:* Here's a course that meanders over a wide area, just as the East Fork of the Carson River and its minor tributaries meander through most of the holes. Located off US 395, in the southern outskirts of Gardnerville, this course has four par 5s, nine par 4s and five par 3s. Although mostly on level ground, the presence of the river creates an ongoing water hazard, and there are stately cottonwood trees that frame tight fairways. The top handicap hole is the 460-yard sixth, a par 5 that features, you guessed it, the river; too long of a drive could land in the drink, and even laying up is not much help—the second shot could also end up in water, since the river extends diagonally up to the green and flanks it on the right. Safe haven is only on the narrow approach to the left. The 16th (355 yards, par 4) has a similar configuration, with the river a left-side hazard that leaves only a spit of land for the green. The 11th (260 yards, par 4), seems beguilingly easy: a wide fairway with an easy dogleg left. The problem is that the green is perched on a plateau, which in turn is snuggled against a bluff, and only an accurate wedge shot will keep it from bouncing against the "wall" or rolling off the edge. The 14th (324 yards, par 4) could use a ball with eyes, capable of navigating a phalanx of cottonwoods. In general, this course has a rustic, wilderness feeling to it, with cart paths crossing wooden bridges and following dirt river embankments. An enticement for playing here is that one of the town's better Basque restaurants is right next door.

**Amenities:** Driving range, putting green, cart rentals, club rentals, pro shop, full bar, on-course beverage cart and Basque restaurant next door (Carson Valley Country Club).

**Fees:** $20 for 18 holes, $13 for nine holes ($10 twilight rate). Cart rentals (optional): $20. Club rentals: $15.

**Hours:** 7 a.m. to 6 p.m. year-round.

**Pro:** Chris Goeschel.

**Owners:** Don and Lynn Brooks.

**Information:** Off US 395 south of Gardnerville; 1027 Riverview Drive, Gardnerville, NV 89410; (702) 265-3181.

*The 15th hole at Lakeridge Golf Course in Reno is surrounded by a lake that swallows golf balls—maybe yours.*

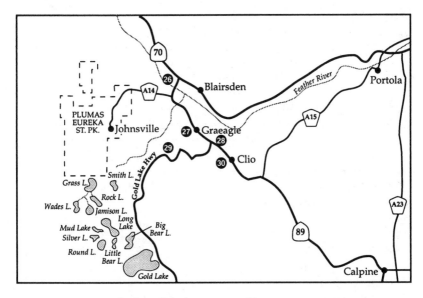

### *Lakes Basin area golf courses*

◆

# Lakes Basin

## Feather River Golf Course

*See number 26 on Lakes Basin area map, above*

**Stats:** Nine holes, 2,744 yards and 34 par.

**Description:** Built in 1915, this is the most challenging of the two nine-holers in Graeagle, and offers a good warm-up for playing nearby Plumas Pines. There are tight, tree-lined fairways on level terrain, and the course has seven par 4s and two par 3s. The second hole (411 yards, par 4) is the number-one handicap. The course is owned by the Feather River Inn, which offers accommodations and other recreation amenities.

**Amenities:** Equipment rentals and sales, pro shop, snack bar, bar, conference facility, accommodations and Sunday brunch.

**Fees:** $16 for 18 holes, $12 for nine holes on weekdays; $19 for 18 holes, $15 for nine holes on weekends and holidays ($15, seniors). Hand cart rentals: $3. Club rentals: $7.

**Hours:** 7 a.m. to dusk (April to November).

*Pro:* Hal Jamey.
*Information:* At the junction of highways 70 and 89; 65899 Highway 70, P.O. Box 67, Blairsden, CA 96103; (916) 836-2722.

## Feather River Park Resort
*See number 27 on Lakes Basin area map, page 303*
*Stats:* Nine holes, 2,582 yards and 35 par.
*Description:* This nine-holer is part of a large but low-key resort complex that has rustic cabins and various recreational amenities near the central business district of Graeagle. The flat, open course is pleasantly framed by scattered pine trees, and even the two par 5s, at 433 yards and 439 yards, can be reached in two shots. There is nothing intimidating here, the pace of play is unhurried, and the course is popular with retirees and youngsters.
*Amenities:* Pro shop, bar, accommodations and Sunday brunch.
*Fees:* $13 weekdays, $15 weekends. Cart rentals: $15 for 18 holes, $10 for nine holes. Club rentals: $7.50.
*Hours:* 8 a.m. to dusk (April to October).
*Pro:* Mike Boyd.
*Information:* Along the Middle Fork of Feather River on highways 70 and 89; P.O. Box 37, Blairsden, CA 96103; (916) 836-2328.

## ★ Graeagle Meadows Golf Course ★
*See number 28 on Lakes Basin area map, page 303*
*Stats:* Designed by Ellis Van Gorder; 18 holes, 6,688 yards and 72 par.
*Description:* This is a mostly flat but scenic course in the golfing Mecca of Graeagle, a one-hour drive north of Truckee. It's not as technical as its neighbor, Plumas Pines, and not nearly as difficult either (there are just two tee boxes per hole). But some elevated tees, water hazards and strategically located pine trees can make life interesting for players. The layout has the standard four par 5s, 10 par 4s and four par 3s, but every hole has a name, and the number-one handicap hole—"Eagle's Roost" (413 yards, par 4)—has a sharp dogleg right and a bunkered green. But some might argue that "Feather's Edge," the seventh (543 yards, par 5), is the trickiest because it tees off across the Middle Fork of the Feather River, although it's pretty much a straightaway shot to the green from there. The 16th (161 yards, par 3) has a giant pine blocking the middle of the green, which definitely puts some stress on your tee shot. The course is well maintained, and is in vogue with retirees, who give it a relaxed, unhurried pace.
*Amenities:* Driving range, pro shop, restaurant, snack bar and bar.
*Fees:* $33 ($18 twilight rate). Cart rentals (optional): $24 for 18 holes, $16 for nine holes. Club rentals: $15.
*Hours:* Dawn to dusk.

*Pro:* Bob Klein, Jr.
*Information:* 18 Highway 89, Graeagle, CA 96103; (916) 836-2323.

## ★ Plumas Pines Country Club ★
*See number 29 on Lakes Basin area map, page 303*

*Stats:* Designed by Homer Flynt; 18 holes, 6,504 yards and 72 par.
*Description:* Beautifully designed, exquisitely manicured and spectacularly scenic, this course, set in a lush valley framed by rugged Sierra peaks, is a memorable experience for any player. It demands a high level of skill with its tight, pine-framed fairways and frequent water hazards. There are blind doglegs, heavily bunkered greens and houses paralleling many of the holes, putting a premium on accuracy. Expect to lose more than your normal quota of balls. The course has four par 5s, 10 par 4s and four par 3s, with three tee boxes per hole. Duck ponds, lakes or streams come into play on 11 holes, and you'll have to carry the water on seven of them, either with tee or fairway shots. The number-one handicap hole, and the signature of the course, is the ninth (395 yards, par 4); this has a dramatic view across a small lake toward the clubhouse, which sits on a high hill overlooking the course. Your tee shot on "Hot Dog Hill" must carry the lake and stay left of a deep rough that is in a direct line to the green. Dense foliage on the left is played as a lateral hazard, and there's a slight dogleg right to an elevated green, with a sharp falloff behind the hole. Other difficult holes include the second (419 yards, par 4), which is a dogleg left with a narrow neck fairway and a lateral water hazard left; the fourth (484 yards, par 5), which has a slot of a fairway, a completely guarded green on a dogleg right, the Feather River on the left and homes on the right, and is called "Double Trouble"; and the 18th (539 yards, par 5), which has a double dogleg and out-of-bounds on the left, a lateral hazard on the right and an uphill approach to a two-tiered green. The course brochure says that some of these holes are known to make grown men cry, so keep your towel handy. The best advice is to play Plumas Pines with someone who's already been through a nervous breakdown.
*Amenities:* Driving range, pro shop, restaurant, snack bar, bar and accommodations.
*Fees:* Including carts, 18 holes and range balls before play: $60 ($30 twilight rate). Off-season fees (April to May and September to November): $50 ($30 twilight rate). Golf and dinner specials available. Club rentals: $5.
*Hours:* Dawn to dusk (May to October).
*Pro:* Tim Fernau.
*General Manager:* Michael T. Kahler.
*Information:* 402 Poplar Valley Road, P.O. Box 746, Blairsden, CA 96103; (916) 836-1420.

# Whitehawk Ranch Golf Course
*See number 30 on Lakes Basin area map, page 303*

**Stats:** Designed by Dick Bailey; 18 holes, 6,920 yards and 71 par.

**Description:** Nestled in the pristine Mohawk Valley 45 minutes north of Truckee, this brand new course (open for limited play in late summer 1995) promises to become one of the Sierra's unique and scenic tracks, and is certainly in a league with Edgewood at Lake Tahoe. As part of an upscale planned community with an elevation of 4,500 feet, Whitehawk is a study in environmental awareness and aesthetic design. There are five tee boxes for each hole, allowing plenty of options for players of varying abilities. Yardage ranges from 4,645 to 6,920, with a par of 71 for both ends. The course, with three par 5s, 11 par 4s and four par 3s, encompasses forest and open meadow, with homes bordering holes four through seven. Sulphur Creek meanders through several holes, and there are lakes on others. On the demanding 14th (435 yards, par 4), your second shot (try a 6-iron) is along a tight fairway with a lake and an obtrusive tree on the right, and a tricky back pin placement on a green that has an elevated rear deck. On the equally challenging 16th (455 yards, par 4), you'll play into the wind, cross Sulphur Creek with your tee shot, aim for a target bunker at 300 yards (staying clear of trees on the left side), and then play to a heavily bunkered hole that doglegs to the left. Among four signature holes, the fourth is the first that plays into the trees, and the 16th has a grand view of the upper Mohawk Valley and its lush pasture lands.

**Amenities:** Driving range and clubhouse.

**Hours:** Estimated limited opening in late summer 1995.

**Fees:** 1995 play for homeowners only; opening to the public in spring 1996. Green fees are yet to be determined.

**Information:** Five miles south of Graeagle at 1137 Highway 89 in Clio, CA; P.O. Box 800, Blairsden, CA; (916) 836-2021 or (800) 453-1645.

# Chapter 11

# Horseback Riding Excursions

## ★ Author's Choice ★

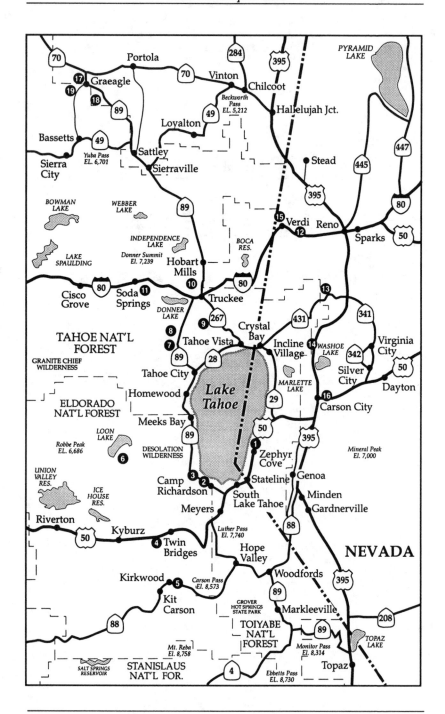

## Map References—Horseback Riding Excursions

◆

Much of Lake Tahoe's history was written by pioneers who braved the Sierra Nevada on horseback, and it seems only fitting that visitors should explore the backcountry the same way. The slap of leather and the clip-clop of hooves have a timeless appeal. Fortunately, many of the trails leading into the wilderness areas around Tahoe accommodate horses as well as hikers. The chief advantage of an equestrian trip is the ability to cover a lot of ground in a short span of time. And with style. Sit back in your saddle, cinch up your Stetson, yell "Heeaahhhh" and enjoy the scenery.

Hiring a wrangler is the best introduction to the region, though there are ample opportunities to put together your own trips if you own a horse. Guided rides lasting from an hour to several days are available through nearly two dozen corrals and pack stations scattered around Tahoe, Reno and Carson Valley. The diversity of terrain that exists for hikers is there for riders as well. You can take a leisurely jaunt along the Truckee River, a day-long excursion into a wilderness area such as Desolation or Mokelumne, or a week-long pack trip that really gives you a chance to clear the cobwebs from your mind. If you've had previous riding experience and you're particularly adventurous, you might even consider joining a cattle drive in the Black Rock Desert, a vast region of high-rock canyons and valleys north of Reno.

Horseback riding has long been a tradition in the Sierra Nevada, and it is considered a family activity. But, like any outdoor activity, there are always risks, and riders should be aware of them. Because there's a chance of falling off your horse, outfitters are emphatic about having you sign a waiver releasing them of liability. For the most part, the companies listed here have years of experience, but, like any business, they vary in quality. They may range from a makeshift corral that offers summer-only operations to a year-round facility that includes boarding stables and riding arenas. While it's difficult to evaluate the quality of an outfitter, you can usually check some of the most obvious signs: cleanliness of corral or stables; general health and disposition of the animals; and attitude of employees toward their guests. Be leery of any operation that allows or encourages unguided rides. If you ever have doubts about an outfitter, contact the county animal control office or the nearest U.S. Forest Service ranger station, whichever has regulatory authority. You won't find many shoddy operations—most of them disappeared during the great insurance crisis of the early 1980s. But you will find varying philosophies of operation. My biggest complaint is that wranglers don't interact enough with riders, or don't share the history and lore of the area. Horse-packing is a profession that certainly is not immune to burn out, especially when wranglers are doing four or five rides a day.

Of course, the most important relationship is the one between you and your horse. In years of backcountry riding, I've come to accept the fact that all horses are not created equal. They have idiosyncrasies, and they're not reluctant to test a rider. You can expect some kind of quirk from your assigned steed, whether it's squeezing your leg against a tree trunk, traveling under low-hanging branches, or stopping frequently to nibble on foliage. Right off the bat, you need to establish who's in control by showing firmness and resolve.

While horseback riding is considered a family activity, I wouldn't advise taking youngsters under 10 on long rides, unless they are already comfortable with horses. As with many outdoor pursuits, there's always an element of risk. Backcountry trips that offer incredible vistas frequently require negotiating steep, narrow and rocky trails. The most sure-footed animal, one with experience in the mountains, is the one you want to be on, not some flatland filly that's just been added to the pack string. An educated horse inspires confidence, but it's still a good idea for the rider to help out on tough terrain. Move in sync with your horse, leaning forward on the uphill sections and backward on the downhill sections. When encountering other recreationists, such as cyclists, off-roaders or hikers, pull off the trail, stop and let the traffic go by. Horses can be spooked by different things, from motorized dirt bikes to parasailers, and taking an unexpected spill could ruin your whole day.

Deciding where to go is more than just selecting an outfitter. With a short, one- or two-hour ride, you can get a spectacular view of Lake Tahoe from one of its surrounding peaks. But the most memorable trips are the overnighters. To see jagged granite massifs and pristine alpine lakes, sign up for a pack horse trip in one of these destinations: Desolation Wilderness, Mokelumne Wilderness, Lakes Basin or the new Mount Rose Wilderness. And for a truly unique, high-desert trip—a place with natural hot springs and ochre-colored canyons—try the Black Rock Desert.

# South Shore

## ★ Zephyr Cove Resort Stables ★

★ *notes Author's Choice*
*See number 1 on map, page 308*

Just four miles northeast of the Stateline casinos on the Nevada side, this operation, which dates back to the 1930s, offers lofty views of Zephyr Cove and its resident paddlewheeler, the *M.S. Dixie II*. You and your horse will do a lot of climbing along heavily forested trail, ranging from 1,000 feet to 2,500 feet above Tahoe, depending on whether you take a one- or two-hour ride. From the highest point, you can see a big chunk of the lake, including Emerald Bay and most of South Shore. You might also pass by McFall Creek and some other scenic points in Toiyabe National Forest. Dwight and Louise McGill, who have owned the business for eight years, like to keep groups small, between four and six riders per wrangler. They have a string of 55 horses, and they can run departures every five minutes, so no one has to wait very long. Another unique feature is the addition of a lunch ride, as well as breakfast and dinner rides. All meals are served buffet-style in a picnic area about a 10-minute ride from the stables, and for dinner, a more leisurely affair, there are other activities such as horseshoe pitching, volleyball and even Western line-dancing lessons. Breakfast includes scrambled eggs, fried potatoes, ham, English muffins and fresh fruit salad. Lunch consists of hamburgers, hot dogs or barbecued chicken breasts with baked beans and potato salad. Dinner is a hearty meal with steak and chicken, corn on the cob, tossed salad, baked beans and a fresh-baked dessert, such as apple pie or cake. Meal rides are extremely popular, so book them well in advance. Another nice feature: You can get here on the free Zephyr Cove shuttle bus from many points in South Lake Tahoe. Parking at the stables is limited, on a dirt hill, but there is additional parking (for a fee) at the Zephyr Cove Resort lot across US 50.

***Types of trips:*** One-hour, two-hour, breakfast, lunch and dinner rides. No overnight or backcountry trips. All trail rides are guided. Reservations are required. Minimum age: 7. Maximum weight: 225 pounds.

***Fees, hours:*** One hour, $18; two hours, $35; breakfast, $30; lunch, $38; dinner, $35. Open 9 a.m. to 5 p.m. in summer and 10 a.m. to 4 p.m. in spring and fall. Operates May through November. Located four miles north of the Stateline casinos on US 50 at Zephyr Cove Resort.

***Information:*** Zephyr Cove Resort Stables, P.O. Box 1672, Zephyr Cove, NV 89448; (702) 588-5664.

## RIDE 'EM OPTIONS

As riding has increased in popularity in the Tahoe/Reno area, so has the list of options. Equestrian outfitters typically provide quite a variety of experiences, among them:

• **The Two-Hour Ride:** This is a "sampler" that is based on the comfort level of the average non-rider. Typically you will ride to a predetermined vista point and then follow a loop trail back to the corral. This is a popular ride among families with young children, since they won't get fatigued or bored in this short period of time.

• **Ride-A-Meal:** Several corrals offer two-hour breakfast rides, with the emphasis on the meal more than riding, as well as late afternoon or early evening dinner rides, which can last about three hours. Breakfast usually includes hot cakes, bacon and eggs, and dinner is typically barbecued steak. These rides are extremely popular and usually require several days' advance booking.

## ★ Camp Richardson Corral and Pack Station ★

*See number 2 on map, page 308*

This is one of Tahoe's historic corrals, and it has been run by the same family since 1934. Current operators Rob and Jill Ross enjoy a good reputation, and their corral is well situated for explorations of the lush, wooded West Shore attractions, such as Desolation Wilderness, Fallen Leaf Lake and a couple of hillside overlooks of Lake Tahoe. It's about a 15-minute drive from Stateline, or a few minutes north of the "Y" intersection on Highway 89. If you're staying in town, you can take the Tahoe Trolley or the beach shuttle to get here. For guests of Camp Richardson Resort, one of the lake's premier family lodges, the stables are just a short walk away. The one- and two-hour rides travel through meadows or pine forest, and offer vistas of Lake Tahoe or Fallen Leaf Lake. The corral usually has a couple of dozen horses available, and the animals are well cared for. The facility itself is spacious, with several buildings and a large parking lot, along with an outdoor picnic area. But there isn't much personalized interaction with guests, and sometimes the wranglers seem just plain bored.

***Types of trips:*** One-hour, two-hour and half-day guided trail rides over the Aspen, Meadow and Fallen Leaf Lake trails. (Half-day rides include Floating Island Lake, a heavily wooded backcountry lake that is undistinguished, except as a breeding ground for mosquitoes.) Breakfast rides, evening steak rides (through wooded trails across Taylor Creek), hay rides and boarding are available. Winter sleigh rides are available December to March.

***Fees, hours:*** One hour, $18; two hours, $34; half day, $60; breakfast rides, $27.50; steak rides, $32.50; wagon rides, $10. Spot packs (per animal cost), overnight pack trips to a high-country lake to fish or relax ($300), and extended pack trips into the Desolation Wilderness ($150 per day) also are available. Minimum age: 6. Open May to September (weekdays, noon to 4 p.m.; weekends, 10 a.m. to 4 p.m.). Reservations necessary. Located on Emerald

Bay Road at Fallen Leaf Road.

*Information:* Camp Richardson Corral and Pack Station, P.O. Box 8335, South Lake Tahoe, CA 96158; (916) 541-3113.

## ★ Cascade Stables ★
*See number 3 on map, page 308*

Not only is this one of the oldest and best-run stables in the region, but it is also located on the most attractive piece of real estate of any equestrian center in the basin. Well off Highway 89 on the West Shore, just before you ascend to Emerald Bay, Cascade has lakeside frontage that is to die for, with an excellent picnic spot on a sandy beach. Owner Harold "Shrimp" Ebright is the latest member of the Ebright clan to manage the business, which has been going since 1935. He accommodates guests for one- and two-hour rides, mostly on private trails, up to an around Cascade Lake and Cascade Falls, as well as to a meadow next to the shoreline of Lake Tahoe. His backcountry "spot trips"—packing you and your gear into a predetermined site for several days—are among his most popular offerings. The corral is on the doorstep of Desolation Wilderness, and the recommended trip, leisurely enough for most riders, covers Dicks, Fontanillis and the three Velma lakes, with camping at Dicks or Middle Velma. Surrounded by jagged peaks and granite canyons, these are among Desolation's most spectacular lakes. But you'll encounter plenty of hikers, anglers and backpackers on the trail. As another option, Ebright will trailer horses to the popular Meeks Bay Trail that covers Genevieve, Crag and Stony Ridge lakes. Breakfast, on a private beach next to Lake Tahoe, usually includes ham and eggs and fried potatoes and onions. Dinner includes steak, fried potatoes and onions, salad, corn on the cob, garlic bread and dessert of watermelon or pie.

*Types of trips:* Hourly guided rides, breakfast rides, dinner rides and pack charters. Reservations are required for breakfast and dinner rides. Boarding is available.

*Fees, hours:* One hour, $18; two hours, $32;

**• Half-Day Ride:** On a four-hour ride, you can enjoy venturing far afield into the countryside and enjoy a sandwich or picnic, or maybe try a bit of fishing at one of the Sierra's high-alpine lakes.

**• All-Day Ride:** Eight hours in the saddle is not for those with sore backs, sore butts or sore knees, unless you stop every two hours for long breaks. This is recommended for experienced riders who are mileage junkies or are half bow-legged already.

**• Overnight Pack Trip:** This is a great way to enjoy a camp out with extra time to fish, hike or just sing songs around a fire. Usually the outfitter includes everything except tent and sleeping bag, and prepares all of your meals. For the deluxe tours, expect basic, hearty food such as steak, beans and baked potatoes—or, if you're lucky, a fresh-caught trout.

**• Spot Pack:** If you like going deep into the wilderness for solitude but don't feel like hauling everything on your back, this is the best alternative. The wrangler takes your group and gear to the place of your choice, drops you off and then returns with the horses on a predetermined date to pack you out. This works best when you can set up a "base camp" that allows for other activities such as hiking or fishing.

**• No-Frills Wrangler-Guided Trip:** This has the benefit of an experienced guide who tends to the route and the livestock, but the lower cost of doing everything else on your own. You choose the number of days you wish to go, and even the route. Also, you bring your food and gear and handle all of the camp chores, so if you burn the beans, it's *your* fault.

**• Extended All-Expense-Paid Trip:** Now this is a real expedition. Plan an itinerary or make one up as you go. This allows a leisurely horseback riding experience, with the opportunity to take side trips, break camp each day for new exploration, or stay at one place for a while. The packer brings every-

breakfast ride, $32; dinner ride, $35; $65 a day for a horse, $50 for a half day; $125 for a packer and a horse. Pack trip costs do not include food. Stables are closed in winter. Located off Highway 89 near Cascade Lake and Emerald Bay in South Lake Tahoe.

***Information:*** Cascade Stables, 2199 Cascade Road, South Lake Tahoe, CA 96150; (916) 541-2055.

## ★ Strawberry Canyon Stables ★
*See number 4 on map, page 308*

Located on US 50 next to Strawberry Lodge (a 25-minute drive west of South Lake Tahoe), this modest operation of 24 horses offers riders a glimpse of what owner Lynn Chilgren calls the "Little Yosemite" of Eldorado National Forest, a place surrounded by impressive granite formations. There are views of the American River Canyon; a lofty vista from the top of Lover's Leap, where riders can see Horsetail Falls, Pyramid Peak and Hogsback Peak; and a small but picturesque backcountry lake named Cody. Any of these points can be reached within a three- or four-hour ride. For overnight trips, you can follow the Pacific Crest Trail south to a variety of lakes. All rides are guided, and the outfitter has accepted children as young as 3, but recommends that parents try a one-hour ride before attempting anything longer. Highly recommended are the premier rides to Lover's Leap and Cody Lake. But there are spectacular views of granite canyons even on the one-hour ride. Lynn and his wife Monica put a special emphasis on personalized service and reasonable prices, and there is strong repeat business. The stables—nothing fancy—are located in a meadow next to the South Fork of the American River, and future plans include the creation of an 18-unit RV campground.

***Types of trips:*** One-hour, two-hour, three-hour, half-day, full-day and multiple-day trips in the mountains on 200 square miles of forest land. Hay rides, sleigh rides (in winter) and trips to Lover's Leap and Cody Lake are available. All trips require reservations.

***Fees, hours:*** One hour, $15; each additional

hour, $10; Lover's Leap Trip, $35; Cody Lake Trip, $50; hay rides, $6; sleigh rides, $5. Children 3 and under ride double with a parent. Open year-round (weather permitting), 8 a.m. to 6 p.m. daily (summer) and 10 a.m. to 5 p.m. on weekends. Located in Strawberry, CA, between Kyburz and South Lake Tahoe at 17480 US 50.

thing (except your personal gear) and prepares all meals. For larger groups, a cook often accompanies the party.

**Information:** Strawberry Canyon Stables, P.O. Box 8, Kyburz, CA 95729; (916) 659-7728.

# Kirkwood/Highway 88

## ★ Kirkwood Stables & Lazy K Pack Station ★

*See number 5 on map, page 308*

Carson Pass is one of the undiscovered gems of Lake Tahoe, even though it was clearly "discovered" nearly 150 years ago by Kit Carson and became a major route for settlers migrating across the Sierra. Kirkwood is a bustling ski resort in winter, but in summer it becomes a quiet, peaceful gateway to Mokelumne Wilderness and a great escape from the crowds at Tahoe. The stables are operated by Jim Hagan, who has painstakingly built a network of trails that parallel a series of dramatic bluffs and pinnacles surrounding the resort. Hagan has a string of 30 horses with stables in two locations, one next to the Kirkwood Inn on Highway 88, and the other at Plasse's Resort on Silver Lake, seven miles west. From Kirkwood, short rides can be made along the Red Cliffs Trail to Thunder Saddle Bowl in the ski area; from Plasse's, one-day rides explore Beebe, Pardoe and Cole Creek lakes. But the premier excursion, over one of the most scenic equestrian routes in Northern California, is an overnight ride from Silver Lake to Kirkwood. Much of the 18-mile journey is along the old Mormon-Emigrant Trail, now a Jeep road, and it offers vistas from a ridgeline that overlooks two drainages. On the north side is Thimble Peak (elevation 9,827 feet), a reddish volcanic formation that flanks the Kirkwood ski area on the west and resembles the Utah Badlands. On the south side is Summit City Canyon, a deep drainage with sheer

*Horseback riding along the historic Mormon-Emigrant Trail offers a slice of history and spectacular panoramas.*

granite walls. From the trail, mostly above treeline, you can see both areas simultaneously—an incredible experience. There are also high views of Silver and Scout Carson lakes. Hagan's horses are dependable, sure-footed animals, and that's a good thing, too, because there are steep descents on rough terrain, especially dropping into Sunrise Bowl behind Thimble Peak.

**Types of trips:** Guided rides (from one hour to all day) on private and Eldorado National Forest lands; pack trips to the Mokelumne Wilderness and Carson Pass (fishing and swimming available); spot trips to the place of your choice; wagon rides in a Western-style wagon; and horse-drawn sleigh rides in the winter. Campground sites are available at Caples and Silver lakes (PG&E and U.S. Forest Service), and at Plasse's Resort (private tent or RV sites with campsites that can accommodate horses). Reservations are recommended.

**Fees, hours:** One hour, $20; each additional hour, $10; full day, $70. Meals are provided on overnight rides. The stable has locations at Kirkwood Ski Resort and Silver Lake Plasse's Resort off Highway 88. Open 9 a.m. to 5 p.m. daily from June to October.

**Information:** Kirkwood Stables and Lazy K Pack Station, P.O. Box 89, Kirkwood, CA 95646; (209) 258-7433 (Kirkwood) and (209) 258-7434 (Silver Lake).

# Crystal Basin/US 50

## ★ Crystal Basin Pack Station ★

*See number 6 on map, page 308*

Crystal Basin, on the west slope of the Tahoe Sierra, has fewer hikers and backpackers than the east slope, in many ways making it a more desirable entry point to Desolation Wilderness. It is brimming with natural alpine lakes as well as reservoirs. This outfitter, the only one in the region, is on the doorstep of Rockbound Valley, an area replete with pristine lakes and jagged grey peaks. Since the valley is too vast to be reached in day hikes, horseback riding affords an excellent means of exploring some of the Sierra's best out-of-the-way wilderness areas. Packer Barry Gorman, with 30 years of experience, operates from the Van Vleck Ranch, which he owns, and breeds all of his horses to provide well-tempered and trustworthy mounts. The ranch, with a pack string of about 30 horses and mules, is 22 miles off US 50 and six miles off Ice House Road on a chip-sealed road. Day rides go to Shadow Lake, Lake #3 and Bassi Ranch. Longer, overnight trips enter the Rubicon drainage and cover Schmidell Lake, 4 Q Lakes, Red Peak and Rubicon Lake, which has excellent trout fishing and an island campground that is accessible by horseback. Allow three days minimum to explore Rockbound Valley, more if you can spare the time. Gorman specializes in family groups and will take up to 10 people at a time. On full-service trips, all meals are provided.

*Types of trips:* Wilderness trail rides, trout fishing, spot trips and overnight pack trips. Pasture boarding and endurance horse training and conditioning available. Family and group camping is permitted in High Mountain Meadow (catering available). A two-bedroom bunkhouse is available by the weekend or week.

*Fees, hours:* One hour, $20; half day, $45; full day, $80; overnight, $100; weekend, $225. Pack stock horses and mules are also available for $75 per day. Van Vleck Ranch is a 50-minute drive east of Placerville in the Crystal Basin Recreation Area (Eldorado National Forest). Riding instruction and summer youth riding camps are also offered at Gorman's Placerville ranch.

*Information:* Crystal Basin Pack Station, 6115 Windle Straw, Placerville, CA 95667; (916) 626-5349 or (916) 622-4626 (home).

# North Shore

## Alpine Meadows Stables
### *See number 7 on map, page 308*

A half-day ride to Page Meadows, one of the best places to view mountain wildflowers in June and July, is a major attraction at this easy-to-reach corral, which is just off Highway 89 between Truckee and Tahoe City, not far from the popular River Ranch Lodge. Shorter rides of one and two hours follow forested trails to a rock formation called the Munchkins or to various overlooks of Alpine Meadows, including the ski area of the same name. If you're intent on having a view of Lake Tahoe, however, then the half-day ride is the ticket, as long as you're prepared for an uphill climb to the ridgetop. At the edge of Page Meadows, which is also popular with mountain bikers, you'll have time to eat a picnic lunch or stretch your legs. The corral, which is nothing fancy, is run by Larry Courtney and his wife, Teri, who own a string of 18 to 20 horses. The operation has been in the family since 1967.

***Types of trips:*** One-hour, two-hour and half-day rides. All tours are guided. Pack charters available.

***Fees, hours:*** One hour, $15; two hours, $30; half day, $50. Open 9 a.m. to 6 p.m. seven days a week, from May 15 to November 1. Located three-quarters of a mile off Highway 89 on Alpine Meadows Road between Tahoe City and Truckee.

***Information:*** Alpine Meadows Stables, 2600 Alpine Meadows Road, Tahoe City, CA 96145; (916) 583-3905.

## Squaw Valley Stables
### *See number 8 on map, page 308*

When the new golf course was built on the meadows at Squaw Valley and the ski area was expanded in 1992, this horseback trip lost some of its allure. But you'll still get picturesque views of Lake Tahoe, the valley and several high peaks, depending on the duration of your ride. Probably the best ride for scenery is the half-day trip to High Camp, a large restaurant and recreation complex (with swimming pools, ice skating and bungee jumping) that is midway up the mountain. Riders climb some 2,000 feet along the Mountain Run Trail, and there are views of the ski lifts, gondola and tram, which together form one of Tahoe's largest ski resorts and the site of the 1960 Winter Olympics. At High Camp, there is an hour for lunch (bring your own or dine at the restaurant), and time to enjoy the lofty vistas. The shorter, three-hour rides ascend about 700 feet to Juniper Ridge, with views of the valley, Lake Tahoe and the posh Resort at Squaw Creek. Shorter rides go part way up the hill. All rides are on private land, and all are guided. The stables have been operated by Eric and Maita

Pavel since 1981, but historically date back to the 1930s, when a train that used to go from Truckee to Tahoe City would drop off recreationists at Squaw Valley. The Pavels have a string of about 30 horses, mostly quarter horses, plus several Shetland ponies.

*Types of trips:* One-hour, two-hour, three-hour and half-day rides. No overnight trips. Pony rides, private rides, lessons and boarding are also available. All tours are guided, and leave about every 20 minutes. Minimum age is seven and maximum number of riders per tour is seven.

*Fees, hours:* One hour, $17; two hours, $34; three hours, $48; half day, $64; pony rides, $6 per half hour. Open daily 8:30 to 4:30 p.m. from the week before Memorial Day to Labor Day. Closed in winter. Reservations are required. Located at the Squaw Valley exit off Highway 89, between Tahoe City and Truckee.

*Information:* Squaw Valley Stables, 1525 Squaw Valley Road, Squaw Valley, CA 96146; (916) 583-7433.

## ★ Northstar Stables ★
*See number 9 on map, page 308*

Northstar-at-Tahoe is the area's first true four-seasons resort, and it has a cornucopia of recreational amenities ranging from an excellent ski hill to an 18-hole golf course. One unique feature of the stables, here since 1975, is that it offers rides during the winter, over snow-covered trails. In summer, there is access to a network of trails north of Mount Watson (elevation 8,424 feet) and some sweeping if distant views of Lake Tahoe east of Mount Pluto (elevation 8,617 feet). The most popular outings are the 45-minute rides in Martis Valley, with the best view from Porcupine Hill. Half-day rides follow wooded trails east of the downhill ski area, to a lookout that embraces the valley and Donner Pass, or to points near Brockway Summit, which affords a commanding vista of Lake Tahoe. Full-day rides, for experienced riders only, reach the crest of the ridgeline, encompassing the Tahoe Rim Trail and points such as Watson Lake. Other destinations include Gray Lake in the new Mount Rose Wilderness, east of Highway 267 off the Brockway Summit, and Red Rock Desert, 20 miles north of Reno on the west side of Pyramid Lake. Breakfast rides offer eggs, sausage and pancakes; dinner rides offer steak, chicken or sea bass, with corn on the cob, beans, salad, French bread and dessert. Meals are served after the ride in a picnic area behind the stables. This well-established facility, operated by Teri Cartelleri, has a string of about 34 horses.

*Types of trips:* In summer, trail rides 45 minutes on the hour, half-day, breakfast and dinner rides. In winter, trail rides and sleigh rides only. All tours are guided. Longer rides, pony rides, lessons and boarding are available.

***Fees, hours:*** Trail rides, $15; breakfast trips, $20; dinner trips, $25; half-day trips, $50; overnight trips, $85. Winter sleigh rides: adults, $12; children between 5 and 12, $8; kids 4 and under ride free when accompanied by an adult; private sleigh rides for two, $40. Pony rides for children under 7 are available ($5 for 15 minutes). Meal and overnight trips require a minimum of six people. Open year-round: 8 a.m. to 6 p.m. in summer; 10 a.m. to 4 p.m. in the off-season. Reservations are recommended. Located six miles north of Lake Tahoe at the Northstar Drive exit off Highway 267.

***Information:*** Northstar Stables, 910 Northstar Drive, P.O. Box 129, Truckee, CA, 96161; (916) 562-1230.

## ★ Tahoe Donner Equestrian Center ★
*See number 10 on map, page 308*

Although Tahoe Donner doesn't have the grandeur of Desolation Wilderness, it does have ridgeline vistas and a mini-forest of quaking aspens, which are vivid in the fall months. This sprawling bedroom community is set on a plateau above the town of Truckee, and the shorter rides overlook much of the residential development and traverse the small alpine ski area. Probably the most scenic view is of the lush, green Euer Valley to the north. Longer rides offer views of Donner Pass and Summit Lake. Particularly impressive about this facility are the clean corrals, well-mannered horses, personable and outgoing employees, and unique five-day summer riding camps for youngsters. With practice arenas for English and Western riding, this is the most elaborate equestrian center close to Tahoe and a place that is popular with families.

***Types of trips:*** One-hour, two-hour, half-day, full-day, barbecue and full moon (Saturday nights only) trail rides on 63 kilometers backing Tahoe National Forest. All tours are guided. Private rides, pony rides, lessons, horsemanship camps (English and Western, beginning through advanced), and boarding available.

***Fees, hours:*** One hour, $18; two hours, $34; half day, $54; full day, $108; barbecue, $40; full moon tour, $25; half-hour pony rides, $6; riding lessons, $35; and five-day horsemanship camp, $250. Closed in winter (end of September). Reservations are recommended. Head three miles north of Truckee on Highway 89 and turn left on Alder Creek Road to the center.

***Information:*** Tahoe Donner Equestrian Center, 15275 Alder Creek Road, Truckee, CA; (916) 587-9470.

## Summit Corral
*See number 11 on map, page 308*

This is small string of 10 horses operated by Sandy Harmon out of Donner Ski Ranch, near the Donner Summit south of Interstate 80. Most rides are one or two hours in duration, and go to areas such as Lytton Lake, a small impoundment in a lush, green valley.

**Types of trips:** One- and two-hour rides. Reservations are suggested.

**Fees, hours:** Open daily 9:30 a.m. to 5 p.m. (last ride at 4 p.m.) July and August. Closed in winter. Located at Donner Ski Ranch, 3.5 miles off Interstate 80 at the Soda Springs/Norden exit.

**Information:** Summit Corral, 19320 Donner Pass Road, P.O. Box 95, Norden, CA 95724; (916) 426-3622.

# Reno/Carson Valley

## Truckee River Stables, Reindeer Station & Old Washoe Stables

*See numbers 12, 13 and 14 on map, page 308*

While these places are widely scattered along the eastern slopes of the Sierra, all of the riding facilities are run by the same operator, Michael Stockwell, all are within a few minutes' drive of the casinos in downtown Reno, and all can be connected in interesting ways. In fact, riders can do a two-night trip that reaches all three properties, starting in either direction. Stockwell has a string of 70 horses that are apportioned among the three stables. Riders can do rides of almost any duration, from an hour to several days. At Truckee River Stables, the most popular ride parallels the river near the hamlet of Mogul, off Interstate 80, and extends partly up the open, rocky flanks of the Sierra. At Reindeer Station, a quirky place that is part restaurant, part tavern, part antique store and part junkyard, riders go deep into the forest of the Mount Rose Wilderness and along pristine Galena Creek. The property is on the eastern side of the Mount Rose Highway, well before the ski resort of the same name. And Old Washoe Stables, formerly Winters Ranch, offers foothill terrain and meadows some 15 miles south of Reno. Riding to these three destinations takes three days and two nights, with a total of 12 hours in the saddle. Or you can start at one ranch and ride to the next closest one. The largest operation is Truckee River Stables at Mogul, where there are also boarding stables, riding arenas and Western and English lessons, along with picnic areas for meal rides.

**Truckee River Stables:** Hourly guided trail rides along the river. Horse or wagon rides, $18 per hour; lessons, $40 per hour. Overnight rates by negotiation. Customized catered dinner rides with live entertainment, such as band music and actors dressed up as gunfighters. Roping arena for weekly competitions. Open daily year-round, 8 a.m. to 7 p.m. Located at exit 7 off Interstate 80, in Mogul, NV; (702) 345-7433.

**Old Washoe Stables:** Hourly guided mountain trail rides winding through meadows and over creeks. Tethered horse rides for kids under 8

## BACK-COUNTRY RIDING TIPS

• Discuss your riding ability with the wrangler before the trip, so that you can be matched with a compatible horse. If you want a gentle plod-der, make your wishes known. Refuse to ride any horse named "Thunderbolt."

• Make sure that wranglers adjust the stirrups properly for your legs. Long or short stirrups can cause problems, such as cramping or knee stress.

• Don't wear shorts, no matter how warm it is. Denims or slacks are best. And always wear a hat for shade from the intense, high-elevation sun.

• Take plenty of water. Wranglers seem to be able to live on a thimbleful for days, but the altitude and dry air will make you thirsty. Don't depend on anyone else to carry your water.

• It is common for saddle cinches to loosen as the horse exercises, so don't hesitate to ask for a recheck if you find that your saddle is rolling sideways.

available. $18 per hour. Open in spring and summer, 8 a.m. to 7 p.m. daily. Closed in winter. 1201 US 395 North, Washoe Valley, NV; (702) 849-1200.

***Reindeer Station:*** One-hour, two-hour rides and longer trips by arrangement in the Mount Rose Wilderness. $18 per hour. Located on Mount Rose Highway; (702) 849-9902.

## Crystal Peak Equestrian Center
*See number 15 on map, page 308*

Newly acquired by Glenn and Linda Holloway, longtime local residents, this former dairy ranch is a complete equestrian center that offers a full plate of activities, from trail rides to wagon rides, from English and Western lessons to equestrian summer camps for kids. There's a nice picnic area nestled in a grove of quaking aspens adjacent to the Truckee River, and the 317-acre complex includes barns, corrals, pastures and riding arenas. The rental string includes 15 to 20 horses. The center operates seven days a week, year-round, and if there's enough snow on the ground, they'll run sleigh rides. Trails, generally on private land, range over rolling, open foothills north of the ranch, with gradual climbs above the little community of Verdi. Hour-long rides meander along the Truckee River. Crystal Peak is located just off Interstate 80 east of Boomtown, the casino/theme park that is a major road stop, and is a 15-minute drive from downtown Reno.

***Types of trips:*** One-hour to all-day trail rides, haywagon rides and, in winter, sleigh rides. Roping, barrel racing, team penning and corporate picnics also are offered. The center can also accommodate private family or business parties, barbecues and picnics.

***Fees:*** Half hour, $15; one hour, $20; two hours, $35; half day, $70; full day (six to eight hours), $120. Wagon or sleigh rides are $10 per person. Lessons are $15 for a half hour, $30 for an hour or, with three or more students, $12.50 per person for a half hour and $25.50 per person for an hour. Five-day summer camps for kids are $200. Open seven days a week, from sunup to sundown, year-round. Reservations required. To reach the ranch, heading west from Reno, take exit 5 from Interstate 80, and go 1.3 miles to 1850 Old Highway 40 West.

***Information:*** Crystal Peak Equestrian Center, P.O. Box 327, Verdi, NV 89439; (702) 345-7600.

## ★ Tin Cup Adventures ★
*See number 16 on map, page 308*

You know it's going to be a different kind of ride when co-owner Mike Tristram (that's a she) explains that she and Dennis (that's a he), call their trips "adventures," not rides, that their idea of backcountry cooking is a stir-fry in a Chinese wok, and that intelligent campfire discussions should focus on truly practical things—such as how to talk to a coyote. This husband-and-wife team, who admit that they are refugees from the newspaper business (ah, that explains everything!), have been running trips for four years in the area recently designated as Mount Rose Wilderness. This is a region that is replete with stunning meadows and mountain wildflowers, aspen thickets and picturesque views of Mount Rose (elevation 10,778 feet), along with other peaks of Toiyabe National Forest. The wilderness extends from the Lake Tahoe side of the crest, along Mount Rose Highway, to the Carson Valley side. It is not exactly brimming with lakes, but there are creeks, springs and ponds that enhance the lushness of the area, particularly in early summer. Using both mules and horses, the Tristrams take groups of up to eight people on one-day rides (four to six hours) to Thomas Creek, where a buffet lunch is served beside the creek or in Timothy Meadows near Painted Rock. Another ride, for experienced riders, goes to Gray Lake and a high point overlooking Lake Tahoe. Campouts in the wilderness include everything except sleeping bags. For a unique experience, the Tristrams take up to 30 riders (most of whom supply their own horses) on a moonlight ride across a dry lake bed in the Black Rock Desert northeast of Reno. This is once a year in mid-August, and it is one of the more popular rides.

***Types of trips:*** Customized outings include

• Ask about any idiosyncrasies of your horse. Is he a tail biter? A frequent muncher? Is there a pecking order for the pack string? Find out about these things in advance.

• Bring full rain-gear, even if the sky is blue and you're going out for only four hours. Thunderstorms can roll in very quickly, and it's not pleasant to be drenched from head to foot in a sudden downpour.

• If you have a still or video camera, consider using a large fanny pack, with plastic bags to insulate your gear in case of rain. A fanny pack, I've found, works better than a knapsack, especially when jostling up and down in a trot.

• If you are allergic to dust, take some sinus medicine and bring a bandanna to wear around your nose and mouth. Some sections of trails can be quite dusty, especially with a number of horses.

• Although wranglers have the ability to ride for hours at a time without stopping, they tend to forget that non-riders need a break once in a while. Don't be bashful about asking to stop if you are getting sore.

• Ride single-file, especially when traveling through meadows and crossing streams, and don't allow your horse to shortcut a switchback. Minimize impact on the backcountry by sticking to established trails.

extended camping adventures (overnight trips of any duration), hiking adventures, drop camps (you run your own camp), and hiking drop camps. The Black Rock Moonlight Ride is a special mid-August overnight trip scheduled once each year to the Black Rock Desert (100 miles northeast of Reno). The destination is the Black Rock Hot Spring on the Lassen-Applegate Trail (reservations required by August 1).

*Fees, hours:* Wilderness camp trips (three days/two nights), $318; one-day adventures to Thomas Creek, $57; one-day to Gray Lake, $62. Wild horse camp trips: one day, $57; three days, $318. Customized adventures: hiking, $153; drop camps, $127 to $207; hiking drop camps, $60 to $130; extended camp trips, $106. Reservations are required on one-day adventures (minimum of three days notice) and overnight trips (minimum of 10 days notice). Open year-round (weather permitting), except overnight trips, which are open mid-May to November.

*Information:* Tin Cup Adventures, 220 Wayne Road, Carson City, NV 89704; (702) 849-0570.

# Lakes Basin/Graeagle Area

## Graeagle Stables

*See number 17 on map, page 308*

Outfitter Paul Bianco, a wrangler by way of Stanford and Silicon Valley, has run this small operation of a dozen horses for 10 years. It's situated right in the middle of downtown Graeagle, so it's easy to find. While a cursory look might lead someone to conclude that there is little proximity to the backcountry here, *au contraire:* A trail that begins right behind the stables parallels Smith Creek and leads to the northern edge of Lakes Basin. On half-day trips, there's a nice loop that reaches Smith Lake—a great spot for swimming with its shallow, sloping shoreline—then returns along Gray Eagle Creek. Overnight rides can add Wades, Jamison and Grass lakes. Once a summer, or more often if there's a demand, Bianco runs a four-day, fully catered trip from Graeagle to Sierra City, a spectacular ride along the

Pacific Crest Trail that takes in the "Little Switzerland" of the basin, including views of the rock-rimmed Sardine Lakes and the ruggedly beautiful Sierra Buttes, the most imposing mountain formation in the region. Camp is usually made at Wades and Tamarack lakes, and Bianco serves eclectic meals of wild game that might include venison, bear, goose or buffalo. In Sierra City, guests end their trip with a night at the Sierra Buttes Inn, and the horses are trailered back.

*Types of trips:* One-hour, half-day and all-day rides are the mainstay here, with two- to four-day overnight pack trips arranged with advance notice.

*Fees, hours:* One hour, $18; two hours, $35; other rates depend on time. The Graeagle to Sierra City trip starts at $595 per person and includes everything except sleeping bags and personal gear. Open May through September, 9 a.m. to 5 p.m. Closed in winter. Located in Graeagle on Highway 89.

*Information:* Graeagle Stables, P.O. Box 20072, Graeagle, CA 96103; (916) 836-0430.

## The Equestrian Center at Whitehawk Ranch
*See number 18 on map, page 308*

Whitehawk Ranch is a brand-new, all-seasons resort and residential community, with an 18-hole golf course and a fistful of plans for overnight lodging and other amenities. Built by Hugh A. White, an electronics entrepreneur turned rancher, the property encompasses 956 acres of lush pasture and rolling hills in Mohawk Valley, bordered on three sides by national forest. The equestrian center predated the homesites by five years, and originally was supposed to be a private Arabian stud farm. Now, however, this very aristrocratic-looking complex of boarding stables, riding arenas and gazebos is open to the public for short horseback and wagon rides. The center's forte, pioneered by general manager Buzz McCann, is hosting groups of 12 to 200 people for dinner rides and picnics. A secluded picnic site at the edge of a 60-acre meadow accommodates up to 12 people and is a 20-minute wagon ride from the center. The meal is served in style, with elegant glassware and tablecloths; the entree is usually steak or chicken, with corn on the cob, green salad, macaroni salad, French bread, wine or beer, dessert and coffee. Larger parties, up to 40, can be accommodated in a spacious gazebo at the equestrian center. Hay wagon rides, horseshoes, volleyball, a bonfire, entertainment and other activities are provided in deluxe group packages. The arena is constantly busy with monthly team-roping and hunter/jumper competitions, a summer youth equestrian camp and other events.

*Types of trips:* Hourly guided trail rides, dinner rides, wagon rides (10 people maximum), and romantic surrey rides for two. Overnight campouts, private parties (5 to 200 people), and sleigh rides (complete with blankets, coffee and hot chocolate; 10 people maximum) are available.

*Fees, hours:* One-hour trail ride, $16; lunch trail ride, $25; dinner wagon ride, $36.50 ($20, children 5 to 12, and $5, kids 4 and under); romantic surrey for two, $18 per couple, $90 with dinner. Wagon/sleigh rides: adults, $9; children 12 and under, $6; flat rate per hour, $65. Reservations are required. Open May to September, 9 a.m. to 5 p.m. Located six miles southeast of Graeagle on Highway 89.

*Information:* The Equestrian Center at Whitehawk Ranch, P.O. Box 800, Blairsden, CA 96103; (916) 836-0866.

## ★ Gold Lake Pack Station and Stables ★
*See number 19 on map, page 308*

You can see a half-dozen lakes in a day, or a dozen lakes in two days in this scenic but relatively undiscovered trove of lakes an hour's drive north of Truckee. Outfitter Russell Reid, a horseman for 20 years who teaches equestrian courses at Feather River College, is the largest outfitter in the region. Located at Gold Lake, his stables have immediate access to this distinctive mountain playground, which straddles the Tahoe and Plumas national forests. The most popular short ride is the 2.5-hour jaunt on the Round Lake Trail, which affords views of Big Bear, Little Bear, Silver and Long lakes. Half-day trips stop for lunch at Round Lake (bring your own or arrange with the packer). Overnight rides usually add Gold, Wades, Grass and Jamison lakes to those listed above. The best campsite is at Wades Lake, a nearly circular alpine gem flanked at one end by a sheer-walled cliff. Three- and four-day deluxe trips, custom-tailored to the pace and preferences of clients, with all meals provided, also are popular. Reid runs 25 to 30 head of horses, and has a few old-fashioned line tents at his corral that are available to guests for camping the night before their trip. Recent additions include rides in a replica of the famous Conestoga "Prairie Schooner" covered wagon, pulled by a team of Belgian horses.

*Types of trips:* Hourly, half-day, and full-day guided trail rides, pack trips (overnight, wrangler-guided and spot trips), wagon rides and cookouts. Lessons, horsemanship classes, kiddie rides and boarding available.

*Fees, hours:* One hour, $19.75; 2.5 hours, $38; half-day rides, $54; dinner rides, $35 ($20 for kids); breakfast rides, $28 ($20 for kids). Special overnight and guided trips are available. Minimum age: 5. Open May through October daily, 9 a.m. to dusk. Closed in winter. Located eight miles south of Graeagle on Gold Lakes Road, off Highway 89, in the Lakes Basin Recreation Area.

*Information:* Gold Lake Pack Station and Stables, 1540 Chandler Road, Quincy, CA 95971; (916) 836-0940 (summer) or (916) 283-2014 (off-season).

# Chapter 12

# Rafting, Ballooning
# & Other
# Summer
# Activities

If you ever tire of Tahoe's conventional outdoor activities, you won't lack for something unusual to do. Everything is possible, and everything is available. Paddle sports, from kayaking to river rafting, are high on the list of alternative summer excursions, simply because they are readily accessible and offer magnificent scenery. Several companies provide half-day or full-day outings in sturdy touring kayaks along the North Shore and West Shore of the lake, and others provide thrills rafting on California's best whitewater rivers. But the thrill of exploring this region isn't limited to the water; many aerial aficionados can find lofty experiences in hot air balloons, gliders and sightseeing planes. Of course, if you aren't nervous about high places, you might consider signing up for a rock climbing course, because peak-bagging is the rage these days. If you're looking for more down-to-earth pursuits, well, there's always a spirited game of tennis. Just bring the high-elevation balls, or you'll be doing more chasing than volleying.

## KAYAKING & RAFTING EXCURSIONS

Getting up close and personal with Lake Tahoe means getting down to the water—way down. During calm mornings, you can take guided kayak tours, usually in large ocean kayaks, around the perimeter of the lake. This is a great way to see the shoreline, its magnificent homes and its multitude of parks and beaches. Generally, you can bring your lunch or snacks and stop at a scenic spot to enjoy the beauty of the lake. Two-hole kayaks are often available for couples. Tours with lessons depart from several locations, from Camp Richardson to the North Shore. Those who have established reasonable proficiency can rent watercraft on their own, but beware of afternoon winds. Nothing is tougher than paddling against waves and gales. Here are the outfitters who offer paddling craft:

### Kayak Tahoe

Steve, Mike and Susan Lannoy have been running this unique paddling operation since 1989 from the Anchorage Marina at Camp Richardson on the South Shore. The gentle, protected waters in front of the beach are excellent for novices to practice kayak maneuvers, and the touring kayaks are beamy and stable. The top tour is to Emerald Bay, and paddlers can leave from Baldwin Beach or the Anchorage Marina, stopping at the Emerald Bay Boat-In Campground for lunch or hiking. Because of the possibility of strong afternoon winds, the Baldwin put-in is a bit easier for the return trip. This excursion takes about four hours. A two-day, one-night camping trip to the same place affords more time to explore the beach, hike the trails and enjoy the sunset and sunrise at Emerald Bay. Participants must bring their own camping gear and prepare their own meals; the guides will assist in packing the kayaks, which have ample room for tents, sleeping bags and food. Proficient paddlers may rent boats on their own for camping. The company offers a variety of lessons, sunset and moonlight tours, and river kayaking on the Upper Truckee River.

*Fees, hours:* $25 to $45 for daily tours; $30 to $90 for ocean or river kayak lessons; $30 to $125 for campouts and seminars. Rental costs are $12 per hour for touring kayaks and $35 per day for river kayaks. Open 9:30 a.m. to 5:30 p.m. May 27 through October 2. Reservations are recommended.

*Information:* Richardson's Resort, P.O. Box 11129, Tahoe Paradise, CA 96155; (916) 544-2011.

## Tahoe Paddle and Oar

Operating from Kings Beach on the North Shore, owner Phil Segal runs a sizeable enterprise with more than 100 touring kayaks and canoes for rent, and he can handle large groups of up to 40 people. Using Aquaterra, Northwest and Eddyline sea kayaks, paddlers can take guided tours along spectacular rocky coves and beaches. The put-in is at the North Tahoe Beach Center, and the route proceeds around Brockway Point to Crystal Bay and through the "boulder fields" to Buck's Beach—a pristine "locals" hangout with white sand and rocky peninsula. The tours last 2.5 hours and go five miles.

*Fees, hours:* $50 per person, minimum of two people and maximum of 30; $35 per person for kayak lessons, with a minimum of four people. Rentals are $10 to $20 per hour, with a minimum of two hours. At $10 per person more, paddlers can have an outdoor barbecue lunch and all-day access to the hot tub and pool operated by the North Tahoe Public Utility District. Open daily, 10 a.m. to 5 p.m.

*Information:* North Tahoe Beach Center, 7860 North Lake Boulevard (Highway 29), Kings Beach, CA 96143; (916) 581-3029.

## Tahoe Whitewater Tours

Mike Miltner, an experienced paddling guide for nearly 25 years, offers probably the single best kayak route along the West Shore of the lake. Participants put in from the beach at beautiful D.L. Bliss State Park, then paddle two miles south past Rubicon Point and three miles inside of Emerald Bay. Tours include van shuttles to Bliss Park from Tahoe City or South Lake Tahoe, a lunch stop at the boat-in campground or Fannette Island, fully catered meals (featuring goodies such as smoked salmon and gouda cheese sandwiches), and a visit to Vikingsholm Castle. Both single and double kayaks with closed cockpits are available on the full-day trip. No previous experience is necessary, and guides provide an orientation on equipment and paddling techniques. A minimum of four paddlers is required. The company also offers whitewater rafting on the East Fork of the Carson River, the South Fork of the American River and the Truckee River. Two-day packages offer kayaking on Tahoe one day and rafting the second day.

***Fees, hours:*** From $40 to $75 per day, with lunches provided. Reservations are required.

***Information:*** P.O. Box 7461, Tahoe City, CA 96145; (916) 581-2441 or (800) 581-2441.

## PADDLE CRAFT RENTALS
### Tahoe Water Adventures (North Shore)

Canoes and other watercraft are available here, along with a snack stand and full bar. Canoe rates: Full hour, $12; two hours, $20; all day, $50. Open daily from dawn to dusk. 120 Grove Street, P.O. Box 6341, Tahoe City, CA 96145; (916) 583-3225.

### Paradise Watercraft Rentals (South Shore)

Located at Camp Richardson, this outfit rents paddleboats (canoes, kayaks and Zodiaks), as well as water toys and other vessels. Reservations are accepted. 1900 Jameson Beach Road, South Lake Tahoe, CA 96150; (916) 541-7272.

### Reno Mountain Sports

Canoe and kayak rentals, sales and accessories. 155 East Moana Lane, Reno, NV 89509; (702) 825-2855.

## WHITEWATER RAFTING

Splash! In your face! Nothing like cold mountain water to take the edge off a hot summer day. Happily, visitors to Lake Tahoe can partake of Northern California's favorite ritual for cooling off: smashing through frothy rapids while screaming in devilish glee. Some of California's best whitewater river trips are easily accessible from Tahoe, and a few guide services offer hotel pick-up, shuttle to the river and return on the same day. The rafting season usually begins in April, with the first run-off from melting snow, but most participants prefer to wait until warmer days in mid- to late summer. No matter what time of the season you go, wearing a full wetsuit is a good idea, and generally the guides will provide them. They'll also tell you what to do if the boat flips over (a rare but possible occurrence), if it gets wrapped on a rock, or if another boat starts a water fight with bailing buckets. River rats frequently have their choice of experiences—paddleboats that require five or six folks to stroke in unison, or oar boats that invite passengers to sit back and relax while the guide does all of the work. One of the delights of a full-day trip is enjoying a catered lunch on the banks of the river, and most rafting companies excel in their gourmet repasts. Here are the main rivers within reach of Lake Tahoe:

**East Fork, Carson River:** This is a mellow to moderate rafting experience under normal run-off, with most rapids rated Class II or III. But the season is short—usually mid-April to late June—because there are no dams to control the flows. The most popular run is 19.5 miles long; it begins three miles south of Markleeville on Highway 89 at Hangman's Bridge (where vigilantes lynched an alleged murderer in 1874) and ends in Nevada five miles south of Gardnerville. While some tours can do the river in a day, most involve two days with an overnight campout on public lands. There are many notable features to recommend a trip on the East Fork, among them the transition from alpine terrain with pine trees (at 5,500 feet) to high-desert bluffs with chaparral. The scenery is spectacular and constantly changing, and the river is a good introduction to white-water. Sidewinder Rapid, rated Class III, is probably the most difficult rapid. A highlight of the trip is a stop at East Carson Hot Springs, about halfway down the run, where you can soak in a natural pool that averages 104 degrees Fahrenheit. Just before the take-out above Ruhenstroth Dam (which has a dangerous, 30-foot waterfall), you'll float through a spectacu-lar gorge that is lined by formations called "The Crags."

**South Fork, American River:** One of the nation's most popular whitewater rivers, it is about an 80-minute drive from Lake Tahoe. With its headwaters in Desolation Wilderness, the South Fork offers a rich gold mining history, waters that range from placid to pulverizing, and a pan-oramic canyon that is filled with rollicking "haystacks." The full run of 20.5 miles is normally done in two days, but outfitters also cover two stretches in single-day trips. The first, from Chili Bar to Lotus, is about 11 miles long and contains two Class III+ rapids: Meatgrinder, a long rock garden with a submerged boulder at the end, and Troublemaker, a maze of boulders and strong rapids. The second stretch, from Lotus to Salmon Falls Bridge at Folsom Lake, is nine miles long and includes hair-raisers such as Satan's Cesspool, a Class III+ rapid that has two precipitous drops, as well as a large rock where a peanut gallery of spectators usually gathers to watch the action. There are several advantages in running the American River: a low elevation (less than 1,000 feet at the highest put-in), consistently hot temperatures in summer, and good, developed camp-grounds along the route. Some outfitters have permanent midpoint sta-tions with hot showers, picnic grounds and bathrooms, along with shaded campsites. One drawback is that weekends can see 2,000 or more river rats in one day, with a succession of buses disgorging mobs of people. At Coloma, rafters pass one of California's most famous historic sites—the place where James Marshall discovered gold at John Sutter's mill in 1848, triggering the '49er Gold Rush. Those who have time after their river excursion might wish to explore the vintage towns of Placerville or Auburn, where historic districts with boutiques and antiques beckon shoppers.

**Truckee River:** From Tahoe City to River Ranch, the Truckee River is a tranquil, easygoing waterway that can be floated in inner tubes and rubber rafts, when Lake Tahoe is spilling enough water at Fanny Bridge to create sufficient flows. If you want this kind of experience, you can rent a raft in Tahoe City and do your own thing. But if you're looking for whitewater, consider a stretch that runs from a put-in east of Truckee to the Interstate 80 bridge at Floriston. The rapids are Class II and III, with a continuous stretch of rock gardens through a deep canyon. It's a moderate run for commercial guides, but it can be tricky for novices on their own. Only a few companies run this river, and in recent years a drought has made rafting generally unfeasible.

**Middle Fork, American River:** It's grueling, it's exciting and it's a hell of a long day (10 hours) on a river, but for advanced rafting aficionados it's one of the best "secrets" of the Sierra. With its headwaters rising from the Sierra west of Squaw Valley, the Middle Fork drew dozens of mining towns along its banks in the middle and late 1800s. Even today, the river gives up respectable amounts of gold and is actively dredged. River rats like the Middle Fork because it has scenic canyons and much more of a wilderness feeling than the other area rivers. There are powerful Class IV and V rapids along the 25-mile run, as well as a mandatory portage at Ruck-a-Chucky Falls. Those who sign up for this trip should be in good physical condition, because paddlers will have to negotiate tortuous sections, such as the infamous Tunnel Chute rapid, a man-made diversion slot blasted out of the rock by gold miners. Boats go through one by one, or sometimes not at all, depending on the hydraulics. The put-in is located about 23 miles east of Auburn, and the take-out is near the confluence of the Middle Fork and North forks of the American, though some companies do shorter runs. The Middle Fork with its flows controlled by dams, is runnable from May to September, and its elevation of 1,100 feet assures warm to hot temperatures during most summer days.

# RIVER RAFTING OUTFITTERS

(Note: Commercial guides for the East Fork Carson River are approved for permits on an annual basis by the Carson Ranger District of the U.S. Forest Service, in cooperation with the Bureau of Land Management. As this book went to press, the 1995 participants were not yet approved. For a list of permitted outfitters, contact the Carson Ranger District at 1536 South Carson Street, Carson City, NV 89701; (702) 882-2766.)

## Activities Unlimited

Tahoe resident Rick Wright offers rafters a complete package, since he owns both a touring bus company and a river rafting operation. Departing from any accommodation at South Lake Tahoe, Wright offers one-day guided trips on the South Fork of the American River. His big stretch mini-buses are positively luxurious, so the 80-minute ride is hardly inconvenient. The trip includes lunch, bus transportation and video taping. Open April to October. Cost: $65 to $70. Children ages 8 to 15 receive a $10 discount. Kids must be at least 8 years old. P.O. Box 798, Zephyr Cove, NV 89448; (702) 588-4722.

## Adventure Connection

Veteran river guide Nate Rangel offers one- and two-day trips on both the South and Middle forks of the American River. Open April to September. Cost: One day, $90 to $99 (lunch included); two days, $195 to $220 (five meals and camping included). Children ages 7 to 15 receive a $10 discount. Children must be at least 7 years old. Staff-supervised children's adventures (family camps providing nature hikes and games, with parental participation welcome) are available. Transportation is offered from the Lake Tahoe area. Rangel will fax maps to hotels the day before a trip. P.O. Box 475, Coloma, CA 95613; (916) 626-7385 or (800) 556-6060.

## All-Outdoors Adventure Trips

South Fork American River guided half-day, one-day and two-day trips. Open April to October. Cost: Half day, $74 to $79 (no lunch); full day, $98 to $129 (lunch included); two days, $214 to $234 (four meals and camping with your own gear) No shuttle service is available. 2151 San Miguel Drive, Walnut Creek, CA 94596; (510) 932-8993 or (800) 24-RAFTS.

## Beyond Limits Adventures, Inc.

South Fork American River guided rafting trips. Half-day, one-day and two-day trips are available. Equipment, shuttle and meals are provided on all one- and two-day trips. Open daily from April through October. Reservations are required for all trips (last-minute trips possible if space permits). P.O. Box 215, Riverbank, CA 95367; (800) 234-RAFT or (209) 869-6060.

## CBOC Whitewater Rafting Adventures

South Fork American River guided rafting trips. Half-day, full-day and two-day trips are available. Open April to September. Cost: Half day, $58 to $82 (lunch included); full day, $105 to $115 (lunch included); two days, $210 to $240 (meals and camping included); Family Affair, $25 to $50 (children 5 years and older and parents). Shuttle service is provided for groups in the Tahoe area. P.O. Box 554, Coloma, CA 95613; (800) 356-2262.

## Earthtrek Expeditions

South Fork American River guided rafting trips. Half-day, full-day and two-day trips are available. Open April to October. Cost: Half day, $69 to $84 (lunch included); full day, $89 to $104 (lunch included); two days, $189 to $219 (meals and camping included). Bus transportation to the Lake Tahoe area is provided for groups only. P.O. Box 1010, Lotus, CA 95651; (800) 229-8735.

## OARS

South Fork and Middle Fork American River guided half-day white-water trips. Equipment, life jackets, guides and transportation are included. Cost: Selected midweek days, $49; other midweek days, $59; Saturday and Sunday, $69. Any size group acceptable. Children must be at least 7 years old. Reservations are required with a minimum 24-hour notice. P.O. Box 67, Angels Camp, CA 95222; (800) 346-6277.

## Tahoe Whitewater Tours

Choose from three different guided day rafting trips (South Fork of American River, East Fork of Carson River or Truckee River). Emerald Bay Guided Sea Kayak Tours are offered from D.L. Bliss State Park (shuttle van and lunch included). Combine rafting and kayaking into a two-day trip. Cost: $40 to $75 per day. Reservations are required. P.O. Box 7461, Tahoe City, CA 96145; (916) 581-2441 or (800) 581-2441.

## Tributary Whitewater Tours

Seven-mile Truckee River half-day trips (Class II to III+). Cost: Week-days, $55; weekends, $65. Open June to September. 20480 Woodbury Drive, Grass Valley, CA 95949; (916) 346-6812.

## Whitewater Connection

South Fork American River guided half-day, full-day and two-day rafting trips. Open April to September. Cost: Half-day, $69 to $84 (lunch not included); full day, $89 to $99 (lunch included); two days, $189 to $219 (camping, three meals; camping equipment available for rent). A midweek shuttle service is available to groups in the Lake Tahoe area. Next-day reservations are available. 7170 Highway 49 (P.O. Box 270), Coloma, CA 95613; (800) 336-7238.

## Whitewater Excitement

South Fork American River guided half-day, full-day and two-day rafting trips. Open April to September. Cost: Half day, $59 (Sunday to Friday only; no lunch included); full day $75 to $110 (lunch included); two days, $185 to $220 (five meals and one to two nights camping; no camping equipment rentals available). No shuttle service is available to the Tahoe area. P.O. Box 5992, Auburn, CA 95204; (800) 750-2386.

## Whitewater Paddle Raft Adventures

Half-day, one-day and two-day rafting trips, from novice to advanced level. Choose from trips down the American River's South Fork (Class III), Middle Fork (Class IV) or North Fork (Class V). The minimum age is 6 years old. Open April to September. Cost: $59 and up; youth (ages 6 to 15) discounts available on some trips; the 13th person is free with 12 paid participants. A round-trip Lake Tahoe shuttle is available. Advance reservations are necessary. American Water Expeditions, Highway 49, Coloma, CA; (800) 825-3205.

## Whitewater Voyages

Half-day, full-day and two-day guided rafting trips on the South Fork American River. The minimum age is 7 years old. Open April to October. Cost: Half day, $60 to $75 (no lunch); full day, $90 to $99 (lunch included); two days, $184 to $214 (four meals, one to two nights camping; tent and wetsuit rentals available; additional breakfast, $10). Children 16 and under receive a 10-percent discount. No transportation is available. P.O. Box 20400, El Sobrante, CA 94820; (800) 488-7238.

# AERIAL SPORTS

Nothing makes you appreciate the tranquil beauty of Lake Tahoe and its rugged peaks as much as a bird's-eye view from a higher vantage point—namely, a hot air balloon, a glider, a parasail or an airplane. Soaring is a popular sport on the east slopes of the Sierra, where the Minden Airport caters to gatherings of gliders each spring and summer. Unique climatic conditions here create waves, which are narrow bands of moving air, as well as thermals, circular vortexes of hot air rising from the high desert. Glider pilots often can sample both conditions in a matter of days, and wave-riders have been known to follow currents for 100 miles or more. From both Minden and Truckee, you can hire pilots to give you a taste of soaring over the ridges and mountains of the Sierra—certainly an unforgettable experience.

Also unforgettable is hot air ballooning, which is celebrated with the annual Reno Hot Air Balloon Races in September. But most times of the year, including winter, if the weather is calm and the skies are clear, you can drift lazily above the Carson and Washoe valleys, or even above Lake Tahoe itself.

Chartering a helicopter or an airplane can get you over the Sierra's backcountry lakes, and the view of Desolation Wilderness, in particular, is mesmerizing. The high alpine jewels are easily visible, and the highlight is giant Lake Aloha, a granite basin of rocky ponds that stretches for miles between dramatic rocky peaks. This is a tour to be done early in the morning, however, before the winds kick up and create more turbulence than you can stomach. Also, consider a gentle flight over the Lake Tahoe shoreline, where you can view palatial waterfront mansions and the aquamarine colors of the lake. Of course, if your budget doesn't include any of these options, you can always take a quick ride on a parasail towed by a boat on the lake. Or you can go find a jumping off place at the top of Squaw Valley—on a bungee cord.

## HOT AIR BALLOON RIDES
### Alpine Adventures Aloft
Daily champagne excursions over Carson Valley are offered year-round, weather permitting. A full brunch follows each flight. Cost: $145. P.O. Box 1649, Minden, NV 89423; (702) 782-7239 or (800) 322-9997.

### Balloons Over Lake Tahoe
Choose one of four hour-long flights over Lake Tahoe or Carson Valley (weather permitting). Champagne follows. Free shuttle service is provided anywhere in the South Lake Tahoe area. Cost: $175 per person. Flights depart 6 a.m. to 10 a.m. daily in the summer (by reservation only). Reservations are required; no credit cards are accepted. P.O. Box 10037, South Lake Tahoe, CA 96158; (916) 542-5944.

### Lake Tahoe Balloons
Choose flights from Lake Tahoe and Truckee or Carson Valley (1.0- to 1.5-hour flights and shorter trips are available). Champagne brunch is served after the flight at Caesar's Cafe Roma. Cost: $165 per person for the 1.0- to 1.5-hour flight. Flights are scheduled year-round, weather permitting. Reservations are recommended 24 to 72 hours in advance. P.O. Box 19215, South Lake Tahoe, CA; (916) 544-1221.

### Instigator (Nevada's Hottest Airline)
Flights range over the Reno area. Cost: $125 per person per hour; $80 per half hour. The price includes champagne, a balloon, a photo of the flight and a commemorative pin. Discounts are available for children. Open daily, year-round. Reno, NV; (702) 323-1443.

## Mountain High Balloons

Mountain High offers champagne flights over Truckee and Tahoe City. Cost: $135 per hour; $85 per half hour. Children under 12 fly free when accompanied by an adult. Flights are available in Reno for the Hot Air Balloon Races. Open year-round. Reservations are recommended. Truckee, CA; (916) 587-6922 or (800) 231-6922.

## Sierra Cloud Dancer Balloon Company

One-hour champagne excursions are offered anywhere within 150 miles of Reno with advance arrangements and reservations. Cost: $125 per person per hour; $80 per half hour. Reno, NV; (702) 747-0107 or (800) 747-0107.

# GLIDER RIDES
## High Country Soaring

Scenic, narrated, one-passenger rides are offered over Carson Valley and Lake Tahoe. Acrobatic riding is available upon request. Cost: $70 for a 45-minute trip; $40 for a short ride over Carson Valley (a trip geared for children). There are no child rates. Open 9 a.m. to sunset, year-round. No credit cards are accepted. Douglas County Airport, Minden, NV; (702) 782-4944.

## Soar Minden

One- or two-passenger glider rides over Lake Tahoe and Carson Valley. Cost: One person, $55 to $75; two persons, $90 to $130; acrobatic rides, $125. Gift certificates are available. Open year-round. Douglas County Airport, P.O. Box 1764, Minden, NV; (702) 782-7627 or (800) 345-7627.

## Soar Truckee

Glider rides are offered over the Truckee area. 40100 Truckee Airport Boulevard, Truckee, CA; (916) 587-6702.

# AIRPLANE RIDES
## Alpine Lake Aviation

Aerial tours of Lake Tahoe and Carson Valley are offered on a seven-passenger, twin-engine Cessna. Lake Tahoe (45 minutes): Adults, $99, and children (under 12) half price. Lake Tahoe and Yosemite (90 minutes): $149 (minimum four passengers by reservation only). Children must be accompanied by an adult. Group rates are available. Free shuttle service is provided. Open year-round, seven days a week, 8 a.m. to 5 p.m. (weather permitting). Charter and wedding flights are available. Tours cancelled within 24 hours will be charged a 35-percent cancellation fee. All no-shows are charged a 75-percent fee. Mailing address: P.O. Box 5249, Stateline, NV 89449. At South Lake Tahoe Airport, South Lake Tahoe, CA; (702) LT-VISIT.

### Biplane Odyssey

One-passenger rides are offered over the Reno and Lake Tahoe area, with flying lessons along the way. Acrobatic flights are available in the Great Lakes biplane. Morning departures. Cost: $45 to $125. They are located at Reno-Stead Airport, 4895 Texas Avenue, in Reno, NV. Mailing address: 4776 Scenic Hill Circle, Reno, NV 89503; (702) 747-1907.

### Cal-Vada Aircraft

Seaplane tours are available over several areas. Tahoe City area, $45; Emerald Bay, $54; Castle Peak ride, $60; Incline area, $60; Desolation Wilderness, $64; around Lake Tahoe, $81. All prices are per person (two-person minimum). Charters to Reno, South Shore and San Francisco, and fishing and picnic trips are also available. Open year-round. Reservations are recommended. P.O. Box 265, Homewood, CA 96141; (916) 525-7143.

### Nevada-Cal Aero

Scenic flights and flying lessons are offered over the Reno-Tahoe area. Cost: $80 for one or two passengers. Flight instruction and gift certificates are available. Open seven days a week. Reno Jet Center, P.O. Box 21552, Reno, NV 89515; (702) 856-4963.

### Tahoe Aero

Biplane tours for one or two passengers are offered in an authentic Navy N3N-3 or WACO YMF-5. The flight includes a souvenir photo. Helmet, goggles, a scarf and a leather jacket are supplied. Acrobatic rides and gift certificates are available. Reservations are required. They are located at the Truckee-Tahoe Airport, Hanger F20, 10356 Truckee Airport Road, in Truckee, CA. Mailing address: P.O. Box 1725, Crystal Bay, NV 89402; (702) 831-2555.

## PARASAILING

### Hyatt Regency, Incline Village

20-minute parasailing excursions. Cost: $48. Open to the public seven days a week (Memorial Day to Labor Day). 111 Country Club Drive, Incline Village, NV 89450; Hyatt Regency Activity Desk, (702) 832-1234; or Mountain Lake Adventures, (702) 831-4FUN.

## Laker Tahoe Parasailing

Dry take-offs and landings from a custom-designed parasail boat. Private lake tours are available. Tahoe Boat Company Marina, 700 North Lake Boulevard, Tahoe City, CA 96145; (916) 583-SAIL.

## Ski Run Marina

Parasailing excursions. Cost: $40 after 10 a.m. Early-bird specials are available. Ski Run Marina, 900 Ski Run Boulevard, South Lake Tahoe, CA 96151; (916) 544-0200.

## South Shore Parasailing

Departs from Camp Richardson and Ski Run Marina. Camp Richardson, 1900 Jameson Beach Road, Camp Richardson, CA 96150; (916) 541-PARA; or Ski Run Marina, 900 Ski Run Boulevard, South Lake Tahoe, CA 96151; (916) 544-0200.

## West Lake Parasailing

Ten-minute, all-dry parasailing runs. Cost: 350-foot line, $40; 500-foot line, $60. Group rates are available, but there are no children's rates; street clothes okay. Open daily 7 a.m. to 4 p.m. (late May to early September). Sunnyside Marina, 1840 West Lake Boulevard, Tahoe City, CA 96145; (916) 583-6103.

# HANG GLIDER LESSONS
## Adventure Sports

Hang gliding instruction, tandem flights and paragliding instruction. Cost: Gliding course, $450; tandem flights, $100. 3650 Research Way #22, Carson City, NV 89706; (702) 883-7070.

# SKYDIVING
## Instead Sky Sports

Five-hour, one-day parachute lessons. Ground training, all equipment and the jump is included. Cost: $150. Open 8 a.m. to 5 p.m. daily. Reno-Stead Airport, Reno, NV; (702) 972-6493.

# BUNGEE JUMPING
## Bungee Squaw Valley

Bungee jumping from a 75-foot structure with a giant safety air bag. Cost: First jump, $39.95; each additional jump on the same day, $10. You must weigh between 80 and 250 pounds; minimum age of 10. Open daily, 7:30 a.m. to 4:30 p.m. Videos and gift certificates available. Other amenities include skiing (in season), swimming pool, spa, locker rooms, mountain biking, ice skating rink, tennis courts, fitness room, bar and restaurant. Located at the top of the cable car at Squaw Valley USA. Highway 89, High Camp Bath and Tennis Club, Olympic Valley, CA; (916) 583-4000 or (916) 583-6985.

# OUTDOOR & INDOOR CLIMBING

Lake Tahoe and its environs offer a multitude of climbing opportunities, from spectacular peaks to indoor walls. If you are new to climbing or new to the area, be sure to check with local climbers before heading to a site. If you are looking to take climbing lessons, consider one of the sources below.

## Alpine Skills International

Courses at this Donner Summit center are taught using a variety of skills and techniques to create a well-rounded rock climber. Courses include: Introduction to Rock Climbing, $138 (two days, June through September); The Next Move, $148 (two days, June through September); Learning to Lead, $158 (two days, June through September). Weekend rock-climbing courses include Saturday night dinner. Bunk and breakfast are available for $22 per night plus tax. Seminars include: Rock Anchoring Clinic, $55 (half day, June through August); Climber's Self-Rescue, $85 (one day, June through August); Rockskills Seminar, $385 (five days, June through August), $498 (including four nights lodging, four breakfasts and four dinners); Alpenskills Climbing Seminar, $498 (five-day introductory seminar to mountaineering skills, June through August). Reservations are required. Donner Summit, P.O. Box 8, Norden, CA 95724; (916) 426-9108.

## Headwall Climbing Wall

This is a 30-foot-high indoor climbing wall at Squaw Valley USA. Harness and ropes are required and supplied. Fees: Adults, $7 per hour; children (12 and under), $10 per hour; climbing shoes, $4. Open daily year-round, noon to 8 p.m. Located in the Cable Car building (no cable car ride needed) at the base of Squaw Valley USA; Squaw Valley, CA; (916) 583-7673 or (916) 583-6985.

## High Adventure at Northstar

At Northstar-at-Tahoe, you'll find this 24-foot-high outdoor climbing wall. Cost: Climbing wall, $10 per hour; all-day pass, $20. Adventure Challenge Course (games and exercises with ropes, cables and tall fir trees offered Thursday through Sunday from 11 a.m. to 4:30 p.m.), children (ages 10 to 17), $30; adults, $40. Orienteering Course (hiking exploration, Wednesday through Sunday): Introductory, $15 (including lesson, map, compass and vest rental); intermediate, $18 (including lift ride, map and compass rental). Shoe rentals are available. Climbing wall hours: Daily, 9 a.m. to 7 p.m. Mountain Adventure Shop in Northstar Village: Open 9 a.m. to 12:30 p.m. Wednesday through Sunday. Northstar-at-Tahoe (off Highway 267), P.O. Box 129, Truckee, CA 96160; (916) 562-2285.

## The Sports Exchange

Two indoor climbing rooms offer top roping and bouldering. Cost: All-day pass, $8 (adults and children); climbing shoe rentals, $3. Family rates and monthly passes are available. Children under 10 must be accompanied by an adult. Other services include a retail consignment shop and cafe. Open daily, 10 a.m. to 9 p.m. 10095 West River, Truckee, CA 96161; (916) 582-4510.

## Tahoe Mountaineering

This outfit provides instruction and guide services for private, individualized wilderness experiences. Choose from rock climbing, camping and peak-bagging. Beginning rock climbing lessons are offered at Gad Gym in South Lake Tahoe; outdoor lessons are offered at the Pie Shop, 90-Foot Wall and Castle Rock. Multi-pitch guiding includes intermediate climbing at Lover's Leap. Wilderness peak-bagging and camping include one- to three-day walking and camping expeditions in Tahoe at Jobes Peak and Phipps Peak (you must be at least 13 years old). Fees: $12 per hour (minimum four hours); $120 per day (overnight trip expenses include gasoline, food and personal gear). Jim Campbell, P.O. Box 729720, South Lake Tahoe, CA 96157; Tahoe Mountaineering, (916) 544-5199, or Gad Gym, (916) 544-7314.

**Note:** Unsupervised rock climbing areas from beginner to advanced levels abound in the Lake Tahoe region. Some of the popular sites include Big Chief (between Tahoe City and Truckee), Cave Rock (advanced climbing at Zephyr Cove, Nevada), Donner Summit area (over 400 different routes off Old Highway 40 west of Truckee), Eagle Creek Canyon (beginner climbing on a 75-foot wall near Emerald Bay), Lover's Leap (off US 50 near Strawberry), and Twin Crags (beginner climbing area on Highway 89 north of Tahoe City). For further information regarding trail locations, maps and supplies, contact The Sierra Mountaineer at (702) 856-4824 in Reno or (916) 587-2825 in Truckee.

# SCUBA DIVING

The incredible clarity of the water at Lake Tahoe makes it especially attractive for diving. Underwater visibility approaches the kind of "vis" that warm-water divers experience in the tropics, and it's possible to see unique underwater rock formations, fish and, occasionally, the wreckage of an old boat. However, divers should be aware that the risks of high-elevation diving exceed those of sea level. Special diving depth tables are needed to determine safe, no-decompression times, and in general the times are considerably less than in the ocean. Because of the cold temperatures of the lake, full wetsuits are required all summer, and dry suits are required in winter. If you intend to dive in Tahoe, go with an experienced local diving guide and watch out for the frequent boat traffic on the surface.

## DIVE SHOPS & TOURS
### Diving Edge
Scuba instruction (PADI certified), dive travel, sales, rentals and air fills. Cost: $99 per person. 176 Shady Lane #B, Stateline, NV; (702) 588-5262.

### Sierra Diving Center
Scuba instruction and equipment. Open 9 a.m. to 5 p.m. on weekdays; 9 a.m. to 9 p.m. on Wednesdays; 10 a.m. to 5 p.m. on Saturdays. 104 Grove Street #E, Reno, NV; (702) 825-2147.

### Strictly Scuba
Dive travel, sales, service, rentals and lessons. 131 West 10th, Carson City, NV; (702) 884-3483.

### Tropical Penguins Scuba and Water Sports
Private and group instructions, adventure trips, equipment rentals, sales and service. Old Town Mall Annex, 180 West Peckham #1160, Reno, NV; (702) 828-3483.

## OFF-HIGHWAY VEHICLES
If you've got a few spare tires, a replacement front end, an axle or two and maybe super-duper shocks, you might be ready for what Tahoe can dish out to man and machine. The national forests and other public lands around the basin are laced with four-wheel-drive and dirt bike roads, often shared with mountain bikers and hikers. Literally hundreds of miles can be explored with four-wheel-drives, and the rewards can include isolated fishing lakes and campsites. If you don't want to batter your own vehicle, however, you can always sign up for a tour. People with bad backs need not apply.

## OHV Tours
### High Mountain Outback Adventures
This comapny offers guided tours on all-terrain vehicles from Homewood Ski Area over the Rubicon Trail. Half-day tour, $79 (morning or afternoon ride, guide, helmet and goggles, free snack); full-day rough

ride, $129 (same package, rugged terrain); three-day and two-night adventure, $595 (same package plus two breakfasts, three lunches, two dinners, tent, sleeping bag, cooler, covering the entire Rubicon Trail in both directions). Children ages 3 and older may drive electric miniature Jeeps (supervised). A personalized video is available. You must be a licensed driver to operate machines. All drivers must wear issued helmets. The minimum age is 14 for the half-day tour and 18 for the full-day and three-day tours. High Mountain Outback Adventures, 2286 Utah, South Lake Tahoe, CA 96150; (916) 541-5875 or (916) 546-0132. Reservations required.

## Seventh Cavalry Patrol

Guided four-wheel-drive tours into the scenic backcountry of the Pine Nut Mountains and historical areas surrounding Virginia City. Introductory tour, $59; half-day, $99; full day, $189. Tours include food, beverages and a free shuttle. Nighttime tours are available. Open seven days a week, 8 a.m. to 12 noon; 1 p.m. to 4:30 p.m; 8 p.m. until conditions warrant (night patrol). Reservations are recommended. Virginia City, NV, (702) 882-1840.

# OHV Trails

## National Forests

The national forests around Lake Tahoe and the Bureau of Land Management areas east and south of Carson City offer a multitude of off-roading possibilities. One of the most famous Jeep and dune buggy trails in America—the Rubicon Trail—extends from Georgetown in the Gold Country foothills west of Tahoe to the very shores of the lake, a distance of 22 miles. The narrow passages, rocky climbs and occasional mud holes make this route very difficult. For a detailed description of off-roading trails in national forests, contact the following:

• **Lake Tahoe Basin Management Unit,** 870 Emerald Bay Road, South Lake Tahoe, CA 96150; (916) 573-2600.

• **Truckee Ranger District, Tahoe National Forest,** P.O. Box 399, Truckee, CA 95734; (916) 587-3558.

• **Sierraville Ranger District, Tahoe National Forest,** P.O. Box 95, Highway 89, Sierraville, CA 96126; (916) 994-3401.

## Bureau of Land Management Areas

Off-roading trails on BLM-managed lands are mostly in Nevada and include the following developed areas:

**Sand Mountain:** Sand dunes of a vast, 4,795-acre recreation area are located 25 miles east of Fallon (which is east of Carson City). Speed is limited to 15 miles per hour around the camp area and 25 miles per hour on all access roads. All off-highway vehicles must use a fluorescent orange whip flag eight feet above ground level. Bureau of Land Management, Carson City District, 1535 Hot Springs Road #300, Carson City, NV 89706-0638; (702) 885-6000.

**Sand Springs:** Located 25 miles east of Fallon, NV, this half-mile, self-guiding interpretive loop trail winds through the fenced, 40-acre Sand Springs Desert Study Area. Learn about the plants and animals of the Great Basin. You'll also see a historic 1860 Pony Express Station, which was buried under sand until archaeologists discovered and excavated it in the 1970s. Bureau of Land Management, Carson City District, 1535 Hot Springs Road #300, Carson City, NV 89706-0638; (702) 885-6000.

# TENNIS

Tennis, anyone? If you've got the lungs for an energetic game at 6,300 feet, go for it. You'll find tennis just about everywhere—at resorts, hotels, public recreation areas and schools. Be sure to use the hard, high-elevation balls if you don't want your game to wind up in the stratosphere.

# North Shore

**Granlibakken Racquet Club:** Six public courts, professional staff, tennis camps and clinics. Cost: $20 per hour. Every summer the Nike Lake Tahoe Tennis Camp is held for youngsters from 9 to 18 years old (see page 452 in Chapter 17, "Kid Stuff," for fee and program information). Highway 89, west of Tahoe City, CA; (916) 583-4242.

**Incline Village Tennis Complex:** Seven courts (two lighted), a pro shop and lessons. Cost: $6 to $9. Reservations are necessary. On Southwood Boulevard off Highway 28, Incline Village, NV; (702) 832-1235.

**Lakeside Tennis Club:** Nine courts, a pro shop and lessons. Cost: $16 per hour. Open 9 a.m. to 6 p.m. on weekdays; 9 a.m. to 5 p.m. on weekends (high summer hours extended). On Highway 28, 955 Tahoe Boulevard, Incline Village, NV; (702) 832-4860.

**North Tahoe Regional Park:** Five lighted tennis courts. First come, first served. Fee: resident, $3; nonresident, $5. Group reservations can be made for $6 per hour per court (minimum three courts for three hours). Donner Road and National Avenue off Highway 28, Tahoe Vista, CA; (916) 546-7248.

**Northstar-at-Tahoe:** Ten courts. Free, but for the exclusive use of guests and residents. Lessons are offered and open to the public. Two- and five-day tennis camps, taught by Northstar's USTA pro and staff, are available for adults and juniors. On Highway 267 between Truckee and Kings Beach; (916) 562-1010.

# Squaw Valley

**High Camp Bath and Tennis Club:** Two tennis courts. Squaw Valley USA, (916) 583-6985 or (800) 545-4350.

# West Shore

**Sugar Pine Point State Park:** One court. First come, first served. Park entry, $2; no playing fee. Off Highway 89 between Tahoma and Meeks Bay, CA; (916) 525-7982.

# Chapter 13

# Beaches, Spas & Picnic Areas

## ★ Author's Choice ★

### Top 10 Public Beaches

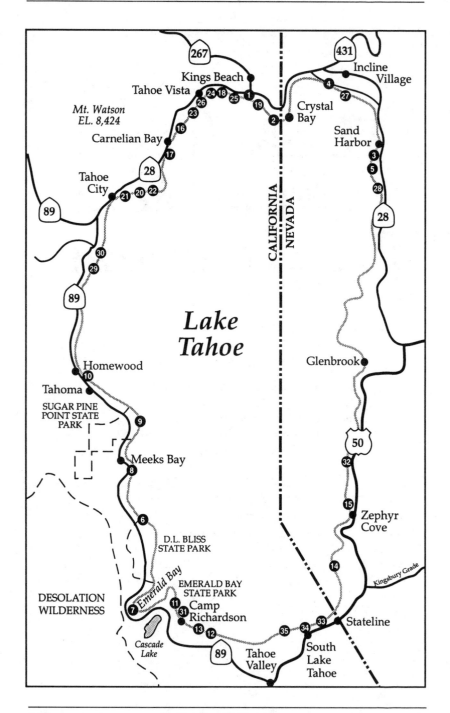

## Map References—Beaches

◆

Even if Lake Tahoe didn't bask in the splendor of snow-capped Sierra peaks or boast the greatest concentration of ski resorts in North America, it would still be famous for its beaches. No other alpine lake in the country is blessed with the kind of white sand beaches that rim much of Tahoe's 72-mile shoreline. Some of these beaches extend for miles, and offer a dazzling combination of aquamarine waters, bays, coves, rocky points and forest.

Each major city and community around the lake has its own beaches. There are also numerous private beaches at resorts and townhouse developments. Although the lake is cold all year in its deeper areas, the shallows can be brisk but comfortable, especially on warm days. What is particularly captivating is the clarity of the water everywhere. Mirroring the sand and rocks below, the lake shifts its colors, from a bright turquoise close to the surface to a rich, deep blue as the shelf gradually disappears into the depths. The hues are striking from the high vantage points along the West and East shores, and the effect reminds more than one visitor of a tropical island paradise.

Over 30 developed public beaches offer a multitude of recreational opportunities, from simple sunbathing to kayaking, jetskiing and parasailing. Each beach has its own personality and attracts its own following. There are beaches suited to families with small children, who can play on pedal boats, dinghies and other water toys while their parents enjoy a much-deserved rest. Some beaches primarily draw teenagers, who thrive on loud music, volleyball and mutual admiration. And there are beaches that have become popular with the clothing-optional set.

Some of the best beaches offer an insight to Lake Tahoe's heady social history, with magnificent mansions nestled in the trees just above the white sand. Emerald Bay, Baldwin Beach and Sugar Pine Point State Park all have venerable estates that are open to the public, as well as fine swimming beaches. Also, there's a bit of culture at Sand Harbor, on the East Shore, where an annual summer Shakespeare Festival holds forth. Nothing goes better than the Bard and the beach. To beach or not to beach? That is the question. Or is it?

# BEST BEACHES
## North Shore
### Kings Beach State Recreation Area
*See number 1 on map, page 348*

Usually crowded and very visible from Highway 28, this wide, sandy beach is a hangout for the younger set, primarily because it has so many water sports and water toy concessions (including jetskis and kayaks), and because there's a huge area for impromptu beach volleyball games and the attendant preening. This relatively flat beach extends for nearly 3,000 feet alongside the community of Kings Beach, affording access to shops and restaurants. While the beach is free, parking is $4. Come here for swimming, sunbathing, jetskiing and volleyball. Amenities include a seven-acre day-use park, a playground, a boat launch, restrooms and a picnic/barbecue area. Paddle/rowboat rentals are available. Power boats are prohibited. On North Lake Boulevard, west of Deer Street, in Kings Beach, California; North Tahoe Parks and Recreation Department, (916) 546-7248.

### ★ Buck's Beach (Speedboat Beach) ★
*★ notes Author's Choice*
*See number 2 on map, page 348*

This is one of the locals' hideaways, and it's easy to see why. The beach is hidden behind a few blocks of houses just west of the Cal-Neva Lodge at Crystal Bay Point. It is a relatively small but scenic area, with a protected sandy beach, a bouldered promontory jutting into the water, and a series of rock islets. The beach is a favorite with kayakers and canoeists, many of whom land here from nearby Kings Beach. Parking is very limited—on the street only—and the access is between private homes along a narrow path and stairway that lead to the shoreline. No fee. Located at the end of Speedboat Road at Crystal Bay, Nevada; North Tahoe Parks and Recreation Department, (916) 546-7248.

# East Shore

## ★ Sand Harbor, Lake Tahoe-Nevada State Park ★
*See number 3 on map, page 348*

With its wonderfully transparent waters, unique smooth rock formations and protected coves, this is arguably Tahoe's finest and most visually
spectacular white sand beach. Like something out of the South Pacific,
the offshore colors are striking, varying from turquoise to indigo with the
depth of the water. The beach is a mile long, bordering the south and west
sides of Sand Point, a small, slightly elevated peninsula off Highway 28.
The combination of granite boulders and Jeffrey pines adds to its distinctive appearance, and there are shallow coves for swimming as well as for
launching boats. Of course, the views of snow-capped peaks across the
lake add to the ambience. Beachgoers will enjoy swimming, picnicking,
volleyball or just hanging out on the sand. Other assets include the annual
Shakespeare at Sand Harbor Festival, a series of plays performed by
visiting theater companies in an outdoor, sandy amphitheater. Performances are held several evenings each week (for more information, see
page 502 in Chapter 19, "Annual Events"). There's a large parking lot off
the highway. Amenities include restrooms, covered picnic facilities, paved
walkways allowing handicap access, barbecue grills, a boat launch, lifeguards, nature trails and a visitor's center. There is a nominal admission
fee. Located on Highway 89 four miles south of Incline Village, Nevada;
Lake Tahoe-Nevada State Park, (702) 831-0494.

## Burnt Cedar Beach
*See number 4 on map, page 348*

This beautifully maintained beach and adjacent grassy picnic grounds
are available only to residents and guests staying at condominiums and
homes in Incline Village. The quality and cleanliness of the facilities,
including the Olympic-size swimming pool, are compelling reasons for
vacationing at Incline. If you rent a condo, be sure to ask for beach passes
from the owner. Amenities include restrooms, picnic facilities, fire pits, a
barbecue grill, playgrounds, a pool and a large lawn. Lakeshore Drive,
Incline Village, Nevada; Incline Village General Improvement District
(IVGID), (702) 832-1310.

## ★ Chimney Beach ★
*See number 5 on map, page 348*

Sandwiched among the scenic smooth rock gardens of the East Shore,
this small sand beach south of Sand Harbor is largely undeveloped, and is
a favorite among locals. Getting to the beach, and its great views of snow-
capped peaks across the lake, requires a one-quarter-mile walk from

Highway 28. Limited parking is available in U.S. Forest Service lots, and users are advised not to park on the road. Amenities include restrooms, fire pits and barbecue grills. Dogs are permitted. On Highway 28 south of Sand Harbor; U.S. Forest Service, (702) 355-5302 or (702) 882-2766.

# West Shore

## ★ Lester Beach, D.L. Bliss State Park ★
*See number 6 on map, page 348*

Blissful? You bet. Located in a 1,237-acre state park, this spectacular, 3.5-mile-long beach on the West Shore has just about everything—wide and flat sandy areas, rocky points, secluded coves and an elevated, forested shoreline where one of Tahoe's most scenic hiking trails originates. There are shallows warm enough for swimming, and plenty of areas for picnicking and water sports, including kayaking. Motor and sail yachts frequently anchor in a small cove here, and tall pine trees line the hill above the beach. The area is adjacent to a large campground, but the beach is nearly two miles off of Highway 89. The five-mile Emerald Bay Trail begins at the south end of Lester Beach, and a trail to Rubicon Point starts at the north end. The views from here, especially in the late afternoon, are truly inspiring. Amenities include restrooms, picnic facilities, fire pits, barbecue grills, hiking trails and camping facilities. Open May through October, weather permitting. The day-use fee is $5 per vehicle. Located 11 miles south of Homewood on Highway 89 in Tahoma, California; California Department of Parks and Recreation, (916) 525-7277.

## ★ Emerald Bay Beach ★
*See number 7 on map, page 348*

Would you walk a mile for a spectacular beach? This one will test your stamina, especially going back uphill, which is an elevation gain of 500 feet. But it is so romantic and idyllic, it's worth the sweat. The beach fronts the famous Vikingsholm Castle, a replica of a Scandinavian castle, which is open for tours in summer. Beachgoers are surrounded on three sides by steep-walled mountains, and little Fannette Island, the only island in the lake, is a short distance offshore. The beach is popular with motorboaters and users of other water craft, and the bay itself—the most photographed place in Tahoe—is a constant beehive of activity. When the water is calm, particularly in the morning, this is a wonderful spot to bob lazily on a rubber dinghy. Amenities include restrooms, picnic facilities, a one-mile hiking trail and a pier. Open from mid-June through Labor Day. Vikingsholm Castle tours are scheduled 10 a.m. to 4 p.m. daily every half hour. Fees: Adults, $2; children (12 and under) and seniors (65 and over), $1. At the base of Emerald Bay State Park; on Highway 89, eight miles north of South Lake Tahoe, California; California Department of Parks and Recreation, (916) 525-7277.

## Meeks Bay Beach
*See number 8 on map, page 348*

There are two beaches here, one managed by the U.S. Forest Service, another by Meeks Bay Resort. Ensconced in a scenic, wind-protected cove on the West Shore south of Sugar Pine Point State Park, the public beach is small but visually appealing. Parking is in a pine-shaded lot, and the small, level, white sand beach is just a few steps away. This is an excellent location to launch a kayak or rubber dinghy to paddle along the shoreline. The resort beach next door has a myriad of water toys for rent, and is especially popular among families with young children. Both beaches are close to Highway 89, so expect some noise from the traffic. Amenities include restrooms, picnic facilities, fire pits, barbecue grills and a small boat launch (at the resort). Admission is $5; parking is $3. Ten miles south of Tahoe City, California; Meeks Bay Resort, (916) 525-7242; or U.S. Forest Service, (916) 573-2674.

## Sugar Pine Point State Park
*See number 9 on map, page 348*

The largest of Lake Tahoe's California parks is 2,000 acres in size and divided into two sections by Highway 89. The smaller east side has the stately Ehrman Mansion and a huge grassy area, shaded by pine trees, that slopes gently down to the shoreline. This is one of the finest picnic areas on the lake, and it's less well-known because it is set off from the road. There's a pier and mostly rocky shoreline, but a small beach is available for swimming and sunning. The park is laced with cycling trails and connects with the West Shore Bicycle Path. Amenities include restrooms, showers, picnic facilities, fire pits, barbecue grills and a free pier. Hiking, mountain biking, tennis and swimming are nearby. There is a $5 admission fee for autos. On Highway 89, 10 miles south of Tahoe City, California; California Department of Parks and Recreation, (916) 525-7982.

## Chambers Beach
*See number 10 on map, page 348*

Located at Chambers Landing on the West Shore, this is a small and not particularly inspiring public beach that is situated next to one of the more exclusive townhouse enclaves on the lake, which has a private dock and the famous Chambers Landing Restaurant. This is a peculiar arrangement, with a private beach reserved for owners and their guests right next to the public beach. Parking is available in the lot only for owners and those dining at the restaurant; everyone else must pay or park along Highway 89 and walk in. Amenities include a picnic area and restrooms. Highway 89, near McKinney-Rubicon Springs Road, Tahoma, California; Tahoe City Public Utility District, (916) 583-3796.

# South Shore

## ★ Baldwin Beach ★
*See number 11 on map, page 348*

This white sand beach is backed by the meandering Tallac Historic Site, a series of shaded lakefront mansions tucked into stands of stately pine. Tallac frequently hosts fairs, art shows and music festivals, a plus for beachgoers. Sloping trails and stairways lead from Tallac to this relatively narrow but very scenic beach. There's a public parking area, but you'll have to walk a bit to reach the beach. Amenities include restrooms, picnic facilities, fire pits and barbecue grills. Swimming is available. There is an admission fee. No dogs are allowed. Nearby is the Lake Tahoe Visitor Center, offering several nature walks and the Stream Profile Chamber. Highway 89, four miles north of the "Y," South Lake Tahoe, California; U.S. Forest Service, (916) 573-2674.

## ★ Pope Beach ★
*See number 12 on map, page 348*

This wide, sandy beach offers inspiring views of South Lake Tahoe, the Tahoe Keys and Heavenly Ski Area. It is a lazy, languid kind of place with plenty of room to accommodate large crowds (which it draws). The Upper Truckee River empties into the lake near this beach. There's a parking lot, but it fills up fast on weekends. Amenities include restrooms, picnic facilities, fire pits and barbecue grills. Swimming is available. There is an admission fee. No dogs are allowed. Highway 89, two miles north of the "Y," South Lake Tahoe, California; U.S. Forest Service, (916) 573-2674.

## Jameson Beach
*See number 13 on map, page 348*

Located next to Anchorage Marina at Richardson's Resort, this privately managed beach on Forest Service land is Action City. It has a swimming area in the lake, a cornucopia of watercraft, a water trampoline, parasailing rides, a waterski school, cruise boats and kayak tours. Live music, from jazz to rock, gushes forth from the patio of the Beacon Restaurant, a popular beachfront bistro, offering hip vibrations while you tan. There are places for beach volleyball, and a short walk will take you to the Tallac Historic Site or Baldwin Beach, a public facility, next door. The view from Jameson Beach to the north includes striking West Shore peaks and the vibrant blue of the lake. Bike rentals and a paved bike trail are at the entrance of the resort, and a lot of cyclists bike to the beach (certainly the easiest access). Parking in a small lot next to the beach is extremely limited, and most motorists must park along Jameson Beach Road. Amenities include picnic tables, a beach volleyball net, barbecue grills, a marina complex with watercraft rentals, a swimming lagoon and parking (there is a day-use fee). Located 2.5 miles north of the "Y" in South Lake Tahoe, California; Richardson's Resort, (916) 541-1801.

### ★ Nevada Beach ★
*See number 14 on map, page 348*

This is the closest quality beach to Stateline, and it is just far enough off the beaten path to offer relief from the traffic along US 50. Located at the end of Elk Point Road on the east side of Tahoe, the beach is adjacent to a large and popular campground. It has a series of rolling dunes, formed by the strong afternoon winds that blow on this side of the lake. The best time to come here is morning to early afternoon. Amenities include restrooms, picnic facilities, fire pits, barbecue grills and a boat-in area (at south end). No dogs are permitted. Off US 50 on Elk Point Road near Round Hill, Nevada; U.S. Forest Service, (916) 573-2674.

### ★ Zephyr Cove Beach ★
*See number 15 on map, page 348*

Nestled in beautiful Zephyr Cove, so named because of the strong afternoon "zephyr" winds noted by early pioneers, this scenic, mile-long beach offers a myriad of water sports. It is also the site of a pier that is home for the *M.S. Dixie II* paddlewheel cruiseboat and the *Woodwind* sailing trimaran. A campground and a resort with cabins are adjacent to the beach, and two restaurants are on-site. If you're too lazy to get up and fetch a margarita and nachos, relax—a cocktail waitress from the Sunset Bar and Grill will be along shortly to take your order. Recreationists will find plenty of room for volleyball as well as other beach sports such as parasailing, pedal boats, ski boats, jetskis and fishing charters. Amenities include restrooms, picnic facilities, fire pits, barbecue grills, boat rentals, food and cruises. The parking day-use fee is $4. US 50 at Zephyr Cove, Nevada; U.S. Forest Service, (702) 588-6644.

# Donner Lake

## Donner Memorial State Park

The "other" big lake near Tahoe has its share of beach hangouts. The southeast corner of the park, close to the campground, has a series of narrow but delightful sunning beaches and a shallow lagoon where the water gets pleasantly warm during summer days. This lagoon is a great place to bring a canoe or inflatable raft, and probably the warmest natural swimming area for kids in the region. Waterskiers, windsurfers and jetskiers all share the beaches, and there's a concession stand with additional water toys. The picnicking/day-use area is just west of the campground, under the shade of pine trees. Amenities include hiking trails, picnic areas and a museum (open all year). Boating, fishing and waterskiing are options. Off Interstate 80, Donner Pass Road, Truckee, California; California Department of Parks and Recreation, (916) 582-7892.

## ★ West End Beach ★

This is a large, family-oriented beach on the west end of Donner Lake, and it gets its share of users since it's fairly visible from Interstate 80 above. There are scenic views of the surrounding peaks, and the beach is an active place for sailboaters and windsurfers, who enjoy the strong afternoon winds that kick up on the lake. There's a large, grassy area and a boat ramp close by. Amenities include restrooms, picnic facilities, fire pits, barbecue grills, concession stands, horseshoes, playgrounds and a swimming area. Boating, waterskiing, volleyball, basketball and tennis are options. Admission is $5 for adults. End of Donner Pass Road, Truckee, California. Truckee Donner Parks and Recreation District, (916) 582-7720.

# MORE BEACHES
## North Shore

**Carnelian Bay Beach:** *(See number 16 on map, page 348).* A large stony beach area, which was recently acquired for public use. Picnic tables and fire pits. Off Highway 28, between the Sierra Boat Company and Gar Woods Grill, Carnelian Bay, California; North Tahoe Parks and Recreation Department, (916) 546-7248.

**Patton Beach:** *(See number 17 on map, page 348.)* Picnic facilities, fire pits, barbecue grills and a 150-foot rocky beach. At Onyx Street and Highway 28, Carnelian Bay, California; North Tahoe Public Utility District, (916) 546-7248.

**North Tahoe Beach Center:** *(See number 18 on map, page 348.)* A large clubhouse with a sauna, a 26-foot hot tub and exercise facilities, plus restrooms, picnic facilities, fire pits and barbecue grills. Spa admission: Adults, $7. At the intersection of Highway 28 and Highway 267, Kings Beach, California; North Tahoe Public Utility District, (916) 546-7248.

**Coon Street Picnic Area:** *(See number 19 on map, page 348.)* Restrooms, picnic facilities, fire pits, barbecue grills, playgrounds and a long, wide beach. Parking fee: $4. At Coon Street and Brockway Vista Avenue, Kings Beach, California; North Tahoe Public Utility District, (916) 546-7248.

**Tahoe State Recreation Area:** *(See number 20 on map, page 348.)*
Restrooms, picnic facilities, fire pits, barbecue grills, 39 campsites, showers, a playground and a small beach (open dawn to dusk). Just east of
Tahoe City on Highway 28, past the Lighthouse Shopping Center on the
right; Tahoe State Recreation Area, (916) 583-3074.

**Commons Beach:** *(See number 21 on map, page 348.)* Restrooms,
picnic facilities, fire pits, barbecue grills, a sandy beach, large grassy area,
playground and a small parking lot. Off Highway 28 on Commons Beach
Road, next to the fire station in Tahoe City, California; Tahoe City Public
Utility District, (916) 583-5544.

**Skylandia Park and Beach**: *(See number 22 on map, page 348.)* A
picnic/barbecue area, restrooms, swimming, a pier and bicycling/hiking
trails. Lake Forest Road and Highway 28, Tahoe City, California; (916)
583-3796.

**Agatam Beach:** *(See number 23 on map, page 348.)* Restrooms, picnic
tables, fire pits, barbecue grills and a 300-foot beach with a lawn area. At
Highway 28 and Agatam Street, Tahoe Vista, California; North Tahoe
Public Utility District, (916) 546-7248.

**Moondunes Beach**: *(See number 24 on map, page 348.)* Restrooms, fire
pits, barbecue grills and 600-foot sunbathing and a swimming beach. At
Highway 28 and National Avenue near Pino Grande, Tahoe Vista, California; North Tahoe Public Utility District, (916) 546-7248.

**Secline Beach**: *(See number 25 on map, page 348.)* Picnic facilities and a
300-foot beach. Off Highway 267 at the end of Secline Street, Kings
Beach, California; North Tahoe Public Utility District, (916) 546-7248.

**Tahoe Vista Recreation Area:** *(See number 26 on map, page 348.)*
Picnic/barbecue area, restrooms, swimming, a turf area and a boat ramp.
National Avenue at North Lake Boulevard, Tahoe Vista, California; (916)
546-7248.

# East Shore

**Incline Beach:** *(See number 27 on map, page 348.)* Located across from
the Hyatt Regency in Incline Village, this beach is smaller than Burnt
Cedar (see page 351) and is also off-limits to non-residents. Restrooms,
picnic facilities, fire pits, barbecue grills, playgrounds, a boat launch and a
grassy area. Lakeshore Drive, Incline Village, Nevada; Incline Village
General Improvement District, (702) 832-1310.

**Secret Harbor/Paradise Cove:** *(See number 28 on map, page 348.)*
An undeveloped beach area, occasionally frequented by nudists. Restrooms and parking. Dogs permitted. South of Sand Harbor off Highway
28, Nevada; U.S. Forest Service, (916) 573-2674.

# West Shore

**Kaspian Picnic Area:** *(See number 29 on map, page 348.)* Cobble and coarse stone beach with restrooms, lakeside picnic tables, fire pits, barbecue grills, campsites (across the highway), shore fishing and access to Blackwood Canyon (with hiking, mountain biking, four-wheeling and rollerblading opportunities). Highway 89, south of Sunnyside Lodge, Tahoe City, California; U.S. Forest Service, (916) 583-3642 or (916) 573-2674.

**William Kent Campground:** *(See number 30 on map, page 348.)* Camping sites, restrooms, picnic tables, fire pits, barbecue grills and a rocky beach with room for sunbathing. Highway 89, south of Tahoe City, California; U.S. Forest Service, (916) 583-5544 or (916) 573-2674.

# South Shore

**Kiva Beach:** *(See number 31 on map, page 348.)* Restrooms, picnic facilities, barbecue grills and swimming. Leashed dogs permitted. Highway 89, 2.5 miles north of the "Y," South Lake Tahoe, California; U.S. Forest Service, (916) 573-2674.

**Cave Rock:** *(See number 32 on map, page 348.)* Picnic/barbecue area, fishing, swimming, waterskiing, restrooms and a boat ramp. US 50, seven miles north of Stateline, Nevada; Lake Tahoe-Nevada State Park, (702) 831-0494.

**Connolly Beach:** *(See number 33 on map, page 348.)* Restrooms, picnic facilities and a boat launch available at a nearby resort (Timber Cove Lodge). No lifeguards on duty. At US 50 across from Johnson Boulevard, behind Timber Cove Lodge, South Lake Tahoe, California; South Lake Tahoe Parks and Recreation Department, (916) 542-6055.

**El Dorado Beach:** *(See number 34 on map, page 348.)* Restrooms, picnic facilities, fire pits, barbecue grills and a boat launch available (subject to lake level). No lifeguard on duty. Between Rufus Allen Boulevard and Lakeview, South Lake Tahoe, California; South Lake Tahoe Parks and Recreation Department, (916) 542-6055.

**Regan Beach:** *(See number 35 on map, page 348.)* Restrooms, picnic facilities, playgrounds, volleyball, swimming, a grassy field and food stands. No alcohol, dogs or fires permitted. West of US 50, Lakeview and Sacramento streets, South Lake Tahoe, California; South Lake Tahoe Parks and Recreation Department, (916) 542-6055.

# HOT SPRINGS

**Grover Hot Springs State Park:** This unique California state park offers both hot and cold outdoor mineral pools, with little sulphur content. Summer hours are 9 a.m. to 9 p.m. daily, and winter hours are 2 p.m. to 9 p.m. on weekdays and 9 a.m. to 9 p.m. on weekends. Fees: $4 for adults 18 and over; $2 for youths. Swimsuits are required, and there are cramped changing rooms and showers available. The park, in an idyllic valley surrounded by mountains, is located four miles west of Highway 89 on Hot Springs Road just outside of Markleeville. It is about a 45-minute drive from South Lake Tahoe. Grover Hot Springs State Park, (916) 694-2248 (park office).

**Walley's 1862 Hot Springs Resort:** This clean and modern outdoor hot springs resort was originally built by David and Harriet Walley more than a century ago. It had a luxury hotel with gourmet dining, and it was adjacent to the Pony Express Route and the Mormon-Emigrant Trail. The upscale visitors over the years have included President Ulysses S. Grant, author Mark Twain, and actors Clark Gable and Ida Lupino. Located near Genoa, 12 miles from South Lake Tahoe via the Kingsbury Grade, the resort has several outdoor pools at varying temperatures, as well as one large pool for swimming. It has large changing rooms, a full health club and massage services, along with modern showers and a small shop. Open seven days a week from 9 a.m. to 10 p.m., and fees are $12 per person for all-day use. At 2001 Foothill Road in Genoa, Nevada. Walley's 1862 Hot Springs Resort, (702) 883-6556 or (702) 782-8155.

**Carson Hot Springs Resort:** This private hot springs spa, located in a considerably less scenic venue than the other spas, offers private indoor baths, an outdoor pool and patio, and an adjoining bar. Open 8 a.m. to 11 p.m. daily, except Christmas. The cost for the outdoor pools is $10 for adults and youth (over 12) and $8 for seniors over 55 and children 12 and under. Private, indoor hot tubs with the same mineral water cost $12 for adults and $9 for seniors, with a time limit of two hours. At 500 Hot Springs Road, Carson City, NV; Carson Hot Springs Resort, (702) 882-9863 or (702) 884-0666.

# SPAS

**Euro Spa:** This is Cal-Neva Lodge's in-house spa, and it features massage therapy, body and skin care treatments, scalp massage, manicures, pedicures, a fitness facility, lockers, Jacuzzi, steam/sauna and a relaxation lounge. Robes, slippers, towels and hair dryers are provided. Open 9 a.m. to 9 p.m. daily; advance appointments required. Cost: $30 to $55 for massage therapy, $35 to $40 for body and skin care treatments.

Cal-Neva Lodge, 2 Stateline Road, P.O. Box 368, Crystal Bay, NV; (702) 832-4000 or (800) CAL-NEVA.

**Cho-Cho:** The health spa at Caesar's Tahoe on the South Shore offers something called "European thalassotherapy," which involves body polishing and scrubbing, a seaweed bath, a massage and a thermal wrap. The seaweed bath contains a formula of 90-percent microburst seaweed at a temperature of 96 to 100 degrees Fahrenheit. Open 9 a.m. to 7 p.m. daily. Cost: $175 for the complete body treatment, which takes two hours; $125 for the mini-body/facial, which takes one hour; and $95 for the soak and scrub. Appointments are recommended. At Caesar's Tahoe, Stateline, NV; (702) 588-4243.

**North Tahoe Beach Center:** This large facility has a hot spa, a dry heat sauna, a fitness and weight room facility, lockers, showers, ping pong, a volleyball net, a beach, disposable bathing suits, boat rentals, windsurfing rentals, picnic areas, video games, a fireplace lounge and a big-screen TV. Open 10 a.m. to 10 p.m. daily, except 7 a.m. to 10 p.m. on Monday, Wednesday and Friday. Cost: $7 for adults and $3.50 for children under 12. On Highway 28 near Highway 267 at 7860 North Lake Boulevard, Kings Beach, CA; (916) 546-2566.

**Massage Therapy:** Swedish, Shiatsu, reflexology, sports massage, stress relief, Reiki, lymphatic drainage, aromatherapy and creative visualization are among the treatments here. Open 9 a.m. to 9 p.m. daily, with appointments recommended. Cost: $40 for a half hour, $50 for an hour, and $70 for 90 minutes. At Nephele's Center, 1169 Ski Run Boulevard, South Lake Tahoe, CA; (916) 541-4269 or (916) 542-4374.

# PICNIC AREAS

Lake Tahoe and the surrounding areas, from the high mountain region to the Carson Valley, beckon to those with a picnic basket, a bottle of Chardonnay, a crab salad and maybe a loaf of sourdough bread, the glue that holds San Francisco's gourmet reputation together. Although picnics can be enjoyed for their own intrinsic pleasure, they seem to go better with some activity such as bicycling, fishing, hiking or boating. The following dedicated picnic areas can be combined with outdoor sports, nature or history walks. This list is not exhaustive and, in fact, is more of a supplement to the campgrounds profiled in Chapter 7, beginning on page 133. Virtually every campground has some area for independent picnicking, but not all picnic areas offer camping. One thing to keep in mind is to avoid leaving scraps for the local wildlife. In fact, when picnicking in high-elevation forest, make a point of keeping your food locked tightly in your car (inside of coolers and other containers) before and after your meal.

Here are my favorite spots to picnic in the Tahoe area:

**Woods Lake:** This is one of the most attractive picnic areas in the high country, some 35 miles southwest of South Lake Tahoe, just west of Carson Pass. Located west of Carson Pass next to a small, wooded alpine lake and excellent hiking trails into Mokelumne Wilderness. Picnic tables, water and barbecues are near the water's edge, but parking is limited and fills fast on weekends. (For more information, see page 176 in Chapter 7, "Campgrounds.") Highway 88, California, in Eldorado National Forest; (209) 295-4251.

**Spooner Lake:** This is a popular starting point for the Flume Trail mountain bike ride, as well as a diverse recreational fishery. You'll enjoy excellent fall colors with the aspens. Picnic tables, restrooms, barbecue grills, hiking and cycling trails. Located at intersection of highways 28 and 50 on the Spooner Summit, Nevada; Lake Tahoe-Nevada State Park, (702) 831-0494.

**Ferguson Point:** This scenic, high-country picnic area is located on the east shore of Silver Lake near the Kit Carson Lodge. Amenities include 10 picnic sites, tables, benches, refuse containers, restrooms, and a nearby boat ramp. Fishing, swimming and waterskiing are available. In the PG&E Recreation Area in Eldorado National Forest. West of Carson Pass on Highway 88, California; U.S. Forest Service, (916) 386-5164 or (916) 644-6048.

**Grover Hot Springs State Park:** Delightful hot mineral pools make this a worthy spot for picnicking. A nice, wooded campground is nearby. Amenities include natural hot springs, a swimming pool, a fishing stream, self-guided nature trails, 76 camping sites, water, showers, restrooms and picnic facilities. Open year-round. Hot Springs Road, three miles west of Highway 89, Markleeville, California; Grover Hot Springs State Park, (916) 694-2248.

**Washoe Lake State Park:** Enjoy swimming, birdwatching, fishing, windsurfing, romping in sand dunes, horseback riding on equestrian trails and...picnicking, of course. Amenities include restrooms, a dump station, a birdwatching area and a boat ramp. Off US 395, between Lakeshore and East Lake boulevards, north of Carson City, Nevada; Washoe Lake State Park, (702) 849-1825.

**Bowers Mansion Regional Park:** Outside historic Bowers Mansion (tours are available), visitors will find a picnic/barbecue area, a playground, a swimming pool, restrooms, volleyball and horseshoes. Tours of the mansion are offered daily. Open 11 a.m. to 4:30 p.m. Fees: Adults, $3; children (12 and under) and seniors (65 and over), $2. At 4004 US 395 North (next to Davis Creek County Park), north of Carson City, NV; (702) 849-1825 or (702) 849-0201.

**Davis Creek County Park:** Picnic/barbecue area, camping, fishing, nature exhibits, restrooms, volleyball and hiking trails. Off US 395 at 25 Davis Creek Road, north of Carson City, Nevada; (702) 849-0684.

**Donner Memorial State Park:** The pine-shaded picnicking/day-use area is just west of the campground. Amenities include hiking trails, picnic areas and a museum (open all year). Boating, fishing and waterskiing are options. Off Interstate 80, Donner Pass Road, Truckee, California; California Department of Parks and Recreation, Donner Memorial State Park, (916) 582-7892.

**Bijou Community Park:** This large city park in the heart of South Lake Tahoe, south of US 50, offers many recreation facilities: Picnic/barbecue areas, basketball, horseshoe, jogging trails, grassy fields, a playground, restrooms, volleyball, a concession stand, a gazebo, a nine-hole golf course and a skateboard area. Al Tahoe Boulevard near Johnson Street, South Lake Tahoe, California; (916) 542-6056.

**Martis Creek Lake Recreation Area:** There is a nice, tree-shaded picnic area next to a campground and favorite catch-and-release flyfishing waters, close to Truckee. Amenities include picnic/camping facilities and 3,000 acres of wildlife refuge. Power boats are prohibited. Highway 267, three miles north of Northstar Drive, North Truckee, California; (916) 639-2342.

# Chapter 14

# Alpine Ski Resorts

## ★ Author's Choice ★

### Top 5 Resorts for Beginners
Tahoe Donner—p. 372
Diamond Peak Ski Resort—p. 382
Sierra-at-Tahoe—p. 389
Northstar-at-Tahoe—p. 379
Boreal Ski Resort—p. 374

### Top 5 Resorts for Intermediates
Sierra-at-Tahoe—p. 389
Alpine Meadows Ski Area—p. 368
Northstar-at-Tahoe—p. 379
Heavenly Ski Area—p. 387
Kirkwood—p. 390

### Top 5 Resorts for Experts
Squaw Valley USA—p. 370
Kirkwood—p. 390
Sugar Bowl—p. 377
Mount Rose—p. 381
Alpine Meadows Ski Area—p. 368

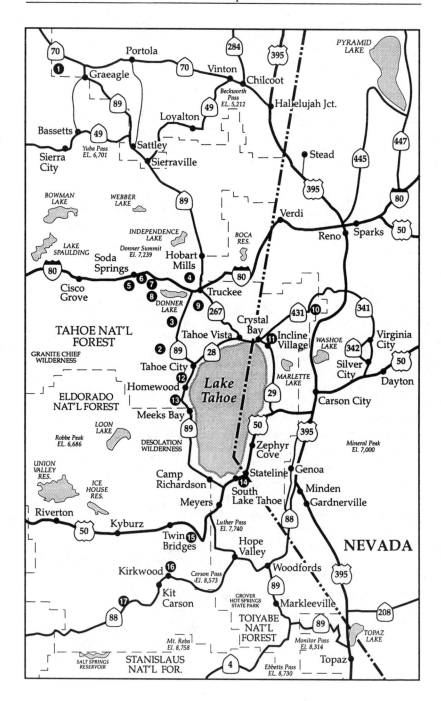

## Map References—Alpine Ski Resorts

◆

No mountain region in North America can offer the profusion of ski resorts and lifts that encircle Lake Tahoe, and nowhere in the world will skiers find as much variety within an hour's drive of wherever they're staying. When you add up the chairlifts, gondolas and trams—more than 135 at last count—it's hard to find a comparable destination. No fewer than 17 resorts, some of them of international caliber, grace the snowy peaks of this region. And when it comes to après-ski life, Tahoe is all aces, thanks to the proximity of major casinos and their year-round roster of big-name acts and Broadway-style entertainment. Tahoe wins the aesthetics award as well, with a huge lake that never freezes in winter and million-dollar views from every corner of the basin. Not surprisingly, Lake Tahoe has become popular with skiers from Europe and Japan, as well as from all over the United States.

Tahoe historically gets more snow than the Rocky Mountains. Typically, Sierra snow has a higher moisture content than that of the Rockies, and more of it falls at one time than almost anywhere else in the interior of the U.S. (the only exceptions are Snowbird and Alta in Utah). Two- to four-foot dumps are not uncommon, and these create an excellent base for skiing. But the white stuff does not fall uniformly around the basin. Ski areas closest to the water, such as Heavenly and Diamond Peak, tend to experience warmer climates, which can affect the storm track. But both resorts have more than compensated for these conditions by installing extensive snowmaking systems. Few will argue that the true snowbelt is Donner Summit, often described as the snowiest place in America (with an average of 500-plus inches a year). Storms rake the peaks of the Summit with a fury, and areas such as Sugar Bowl, Donner Ski Ranch and Boreal reap the benefits.

Weather-predicting is no easy task in the Sierra, and it's possible to have a blizzard sitting on Donner Summit while the South Shore is clear and dry. The lake and its environs are a collection of micro-climates, so there's always varying snow depths and conditions. During storms, strong winds can shut down the highest peaks and ridges, or clouds can create dense whiteouts. Happily, there's always a port in the storm—lower-elevation resorts tucked in the forest that offer protected skiing.

First-time visitors to Lake Tahoe find it difficult to grasp the distances around the basin. From one end of the lake to the other, it's 22 miles—easily a 45- to 60-minute drive. There is good public transportation within South Tahoe and most of the North Shore, but not much linking them. On weekends, the narrow two-lane roads and resort parking lots can be jammed, and it's best to take buses and shuttles where they are available. Skiers staying at the South Tahoe hotels and motels have the best network of transportation—a luxury coach that runs between Stateline and Reno-Tahoe International Airport 14 times a day, and frequent free or low-cost shuttles to Heavenly, Sierra-at-Tahoe and Kirkwood. There's also a daily shuttle to Squaw Valley (reservations required), and a ferry service on the Tahoe Queen to the West Shore, where skiers can select Homewood, Alpine Meadows or Squaw Valley. On the North Shore, the Tahoe Area Regional Transit system (TART) and ski area buses serve most of the region, with pick-up points at numerous locations. From Reno, daily buses serve major North Shore resorts, and the savings in staying in a less pricy room may justify that expense.

For the greatest mobility, you may want to get a rental car. Having your own wheels also helps when dining out, shopping or sightseeing, especially on the North Shore. But be aware that driving can be hazardous on icy roads, and chains or four-wheel-drive vehicles may be required during snowstorms. Sometime, perhaps in the not-so-distant future, Tahoe will have a regional transportation system that will help eliminate the traffic jams, pollution and hassle of winter driving.

There are three tiers of ski resorts in the region: the big names (Squaw Valley, Heavenly, Alpine and Kirkwood); the big areas with less fame but no less enjoyable terrain (Sierra-at-Tahoe, Northstar, Sugar Bowl, Diamond Peak, Mount Rose and Homewood); and the self-proclaimed "family" resorts with less daunting slopes (Boreal, Donner Ski Ranch, Tahoe Donner and Carson). For beginners and lower intermediates, the smaller resorts provide unintimidating environments as well as individualized attention. For intermediates, some of the best slopes and base amenities are at the middle group of ski areas. The beauty of spending a ski week in Tahoe is the opportunity to sample several resorts, and various packages, such as one offered by the Tahoe North Visitors & Convention Bureau, include a discounted interchangeable lift ticket that is valid at multiple locations.

Variety is really the hallmark of Lake Tahoe skiing. There is every type of terrain imaginable—from open bowls to intimate forests. Because of slope configurations and the complexity of Sierra mountains, runs tend to be narrower than in the Rockies, and there are more traverses and access trails. But grooming is practiced with near-fanaticism, and ski areas know how to make the most of their snow cover and conditions. The couloirs, gulleys and chutes are welcomed by snowboarders, who have more natural halfpipes in Tahoe than anyplace else in the country.

One of the great pleasures of skiing at Lake Tahoe is that when the lifts close, the action doesn't stop. Fine restaurants, nightclubs, casino showrooms and 24-hour gaming can entertain even the most hopeless insomniac. And if you just want to relax, there's always a spa or a hot springs close by.

*Note: All prices listed are based on the 1994-95 ski season, and are subject to change.*

## Plumas Eureka Ski Bowl
*See number 1 on map, page 364*

**Location:** One hour north of Truckee, on Johnsville Road five miles west of Graeagle (off Highway 89 North), at Plumas Eureka State Park.

**Information:** Plumas Eureka State Park, 310 Johnsonville Road, Blairsden, CA 96103; (916) 836-2380.

**Lifts:** Two pomas, one tow.

**Vertical descent:** 650 feet.

**Terrain:** 20 runs (longest, one mile) in open bowls and forested slopes. Base elevation: 5,500 feet; summit: 6,150 feet. Open weekends and holidays only.

**Lift ticket prices:** Adults, $17 or $13 for a half day; children (12 and under), $13 or $10 half day.

**Off-site lift ticket sales:** None.

**Description:** Historic ski site dates back to 1860, and is the oldest recorded sport skiing and racing area in the western hemisphere. In the old days, gold miners at Johnsville created a ski lift out of the mining ore buckets moving up the hill, and skied down on free-heel longboards. Today the hill is operated by the non-profit Plumas Ski Club under lease from Plumas Eureka State Park, and has two poma surface lifts serving the lower flanks of Eureka Peak. There's also a rustic warming hut with restrooms, food service and storage lockers. While the majority of skiers are local, alpine-style downhillers, telemarking also is popular. Snowboarders can access the mountain but cannot use the lifts.

**Strategy for skiing the mountain:** Beginners stick to the left side of the mountain, off Rainbow Poma, and intermediates use the right side, off Squaw Poma.

**Best beginner run:** Lower Rainbow Ridge.

**Best intermediate run:** Upper/Lower Squaw Ridge.

**Best expert run:** Cornices.

**Restaurants/bars:** Café food service in warming hut.

**Equipment rental:** None.
**Instruction:** None.
**Transportation:** None.
**Day care:** None.
**Snowboarding:** Yes (but use of lifts not permitted).
**Special programs / camps:** None.
**Major event of the season:** None.
**Other services:** Warming hut: fireplace, storage locker (free with own lock), restrooms.

## ★ Alpine Meadows Ski Area ★

*See number 2 on map, page 364*

**Location:** Off Highway 89 south of Truckee.
**Information:** 2600 Alpine Meadows Road, P.O. Box 5279, Tahoe City, CA 96145; (916) 583-4232 or (800) 441-4423. Snowphone: (916) 581-8374.
**Lifts:** Two high-speed quads, two triples, seven doubles, one surface.
**Vertical descent:** 1,800 feet.
**Terrain:** 2,000 acres, 100-plus runs (longest, 2.5 miles). Beginner, 25 percent; intermediate, 40 percent; advanced, 35 percent. Base elevation: 6,835 feet; summit, 8,637 feet. Snowmaking.
**Lift ticket prices:** Adults, $43; children (7-12), $18; children (under 6), $6; seniors (65-69), $29. Seniors 70 and over ski free. A New Alpine 10-Pak (purchase before mid-December) is $288 for 10 days. Family multi-day, group pass and interchangeable lift ticket packages are available.
**Off-site lift ticket sales:** At Cal-Neva Lodge, Granlibakken and Hyatt Regency. Call the Alpine Meadows Information Desk, (800) 441-4423, for details.
**Description:** This is one of Tahoe's titans. Big bowls, powder chutes, open meadows and scenic forest create a sizeable and marvelously diverse playground for all abilities. Alpine's reputation for having the longest season in the region, typically running until Memorial Day, is based on the huge catch-basin known as Alpine Bowl, which seems to stockpile snow in copious amounts when storms roll across Ward Peak (elevation 8,637 feet). Sherwood, the back bowl, is the most distant section of the resort; it offers sunny, east-facing slopes with open powder fields for inter-mediates and experts. From the top of the Summit Quad, skiers have a 360-degree panorama of the lake, the surrounding peaks and Ward Valley, an area slated for future development. Alpine's philosophy is traditional, and the resort resists anything trendy, including snowboarding, which is prohibited. Purists—the older crowd and the classic, proficient skiers—are the main clientele. The place has a European quality to it, with its steep slopes and aging double chairlifts. It's worth noting that winds atop Ward

Peak can be fierce during inclement weather.

***Strategy for skiing the mountain:*** If there's fresh powder, head for Sherwood Bowl first thing; by midday, the snow will be heavy and warm. Follow the sun to Alpine Bowl, well before the early afternoon winds kick up. Scott Peak (elevation 8,289 feet) is a nice, protected slope for afternoon skiing, and there's a good view of the lake from the top. The greatest congestion is around the base of the Alpine Bowl and Roundhouse chairs.

***Best beginner run:*** Weasel to Meadow.

***Best intermediate runs:*** Sherwood Rim in Sherwood Bowl and Rock Garden off Summit Chair.

***Best expert runs:*** Scott Chute, Waterfall in Wolverine Bowl.

***Restaurants / bars:*** Cafeteria (burgers, salads, ethnic foods), Mexican Cantina (full service), Kealy's Alpine Bar, Treats (espresso, desserts), Chalet (mid-mountain chalet serving soups, sandwiches, desserts) and Compactor Bar (drinks, cocktails, big-screen TV).

***Equipment rental:*** Standard, high-performance/demo and telemark packages (skis, boots, poles) available.

***Instruction:*** Group lessons: Adults, $30 half day, $40 full day. Private lessons: Adults, $55 per hour.

***Transportation:*** Free ski-area shuttle service is available around Tahoe Basin (Incline Village and Sunnyside to Alpine Meadows). Call (916) 583-4232 for shuttle schedule. Daily connections with Tahoe Area Regional Transit (TART) buses; call (916) 581-8225 for schedule. For information on the Tahoe Queen Ski Shuttle (breakfast buffet and après-ski party included), call (916) 541-3364 or (800) 238-2463.

***Day care:*** None.

***Snowboarding:*** Prohibited entirely.

***Special programs / camps:*** Children's Snow School (ages 4-6), $39 (full-day package with lesson, rental, lift ticket and lunch). Kid's Ski Camp (ages 6-12), $48 full day, $38 half day (lunch optional). First-Time Beginner Ski Package, $48 (lesson, rental, lift ticket). Learn-to-Ski Package, $90 (includes two days' lift tickets, rentals, six hours of group lessons). Tahoe Handicapped Ski School. NASTAR Racing for all levels (December through April).

***Major events of the season:*** NFL Ski Challenge with National Handicapped Sports (February) and Family Ski Challenge (March).

***Other services:*** Breeze Ski and Sports Shop, Alpine Repair Shop, lockers (50 cents), basket check room ($1) and overnight RV parking.

# ★ Squaw Valley USA ★
★ notes *Author's Choice*
See number 3 on map, page 364

**Location:** Off Highway 89, six miles north of Tahoe City and 12 miles south of Truckee off Interstate 80 at the Truckee exit.

**Information:** P.O. Box 2007, Olympic Valley, CA 96146; (916) 583-6985. Snowphone: (916) 583-6955.

**Lifts:** 150-passenger aerial cable car, six-passenger super gondola, four express quads, eight triples, 15 doubles, four surface lifts.

**Vertical descent:** 2,850 feet.

**Terrain:** 8,300 acres, six peaks (longest run, three miles). Base elevation: 6,200 feet; summit: 9,050 feet. Beginner, 25 percent; intermediate, 45 percent; advanced, 30 percent. Limited snowmaking.

**Lift ticket prices:** Adults, $43 ($29 half day); children (under 12) and seniors (65 and over), $5.

**Off-site lift ticket sales:** None.

**Description:** Spread out over six peaks, this former Winter Olympics site is one of the world's top ski areas, with a reputation that is based on its hairball runs and its profusion of Olympic-caliber skiers. This is the most insistently European-style layout in Tahoe, with the majority of runs above treeline in vast, naked bowls. There is a plethora of nooks and crannies to challenge skiers with nerves (and legs) of steel: cornices, steep faces, endless mogul fields and couloirs. Peaks rise abruptly from the valley floor, and an ascent in the tram over the sheer wall and jagged rocks of Broken Arrow (elevation 8,020 feet) is a thrill unto itself. The resort is divided into three sections: the lower mountain (elevation 6,200 feet); the upper mountain (mid elevation of 8,200 feet); and Snow King, on the east side next to The Resort at Squaw Creek. The most challenging runs are chairlifts that originate at the lower mountain and reach points such as KT-22 (elevation 8,200 feet), so named because an average skier needs 22 kick-turns to get down. The best beginner and lower-intermediate skiing is on the upper mountain, though runs are short there by Tahoe's standards. Because of its dearth of trees and its high exposure, this area is subject to powerful winds and whiteouts during inclement weather, making it easy to become disoriented. The most protected skiing is off Snow King (elevation 7,550 feet), which is largely in the trees and has longer intermediate runs. In general, there are frequent terrain changes—bumps, undulations, drops and gullies—throughout the ski area. Intermediate skiers may find that a lot of runs are either too boring or too difficult. Squaw Valley has reasonably priced restaurants and creative food throughout its lift system, and a delightful sit-down restaurant at scenic (and windy) High Camp, which is also the location of an ice-skating rink and bungee jumping concession.

***Strategy for skiing the mountain:*** On weekends, the crush to get to the top is daunting, with the heaviest crowds and longest wait at the cable car. It's moderately faster to take the gondola, and a lot faster to take the Squaw One Express, a quad chair. Better yet, make your warm-up runs off Red Dog and Squaw Creek chairs, then work your way over to the upper mountain. If you come early and reach the top without a long wait, head immediately for the Shirley Lake and Solitude lifts, which have the most protected snow. By late morning, Siberia Bowl and Emigrant soften and offer good skiing. On weekends the worst congestion is at Gold Coast and Shirley Lake. At the end of the day, downloading on the gondola or cable car may be preferable to skiing the Mountain Run, which is something of a zoo. For advanced and expert skiers, some of the resort's hidden treasures are off these chairs: Olympic Lady, Silverado and Granite Chief.

***Best beginner runs:*** Riviera, East Broadway (at elevation 8,200 feet).

***Best intermediate runs:*** Shirley Lake, Emigrant, Red Dog.

***Best expert runs:*** Headwall, Cornice II, West Face of KT-22.

***Restaurants/bars:*** High Camp Bath and Tennis Club; Alexander's Restaurant, Poolside Bar and Grill, Terrace Bar and Grill, Oyster Bar.

***Equipment rental:*** Standard and high-performance/demo packages (skis, boots, poles), and snowboards available.

***Instruction:*** Group lessons, $26. Private lessons, $60 per hour ($20 each additional person). Snowboard lesson, $26.

***Transportation:*** A free ski-area shuttle service is available for skiers daily from The Resort at Squaw Creek; call (916) 426-3651 or (916) 583-6985 for information. Sierra Nevada Gray Line operates daily ski shuttle service (December through April) from downtown Reno casino hotels; call (702) 331-1147 or (800) 222-6009. For information on the Tahoe Queen Ski Shuttle (breakfast buffet and après-ski party included), call (916) 541-3364 or (800) 238-2463.

***Day care:*** Yes.

***Snowboarding:*** Yes.

***Special programs/camps:*** Children's World (ages 12 and under): $60 (lift, lesson, lunch; rentals $12 extra). Day care (ages 3-12): $60 (supervised play, lunch, snacks, rentals, lift ticket; ski lesson $7 extra). First-time snowboard or ski package: $49 (rentals, lift ticket, lesson).

***Major events of the season:*** Christmas Torchlight Parade, New Year's Eve Party (live band).

***Other services:*** High Camp Bath and Tennis Club: Olympic-size ice skating rink, heated swimming lagoon (summer only), spa, tennis courts, bungee jumping, climbing wall, volleyball/basketball courts, retail shops, halfpipe snowboard park, lockers ($1) and overnight ski check ($5).

# ★ Tahoe Donner ★
*See number 4 on map, page 364*

**Location:** Four miles off Donner Pass Road and two miles west of Truckee in Tahoe Donner residential community. Follow signs off Interstate 80 from the first exit in Truckee, Donner Pass Road.

**Information:** 11509 Northwoods Boulevard, Truckee, CA 96161; (916) 587-9444. Snowphone: (916) 587-9494.

**Lifts:** Two doubles, one surface lift.

**Vertical descent:** 600 feet.

**Terrain:** 120 acres, 11 runs (longest, one mile). Base elevation: 6,750 feet; summit: 7,350 feet. Beginner, 50 percent; intermediate, 50 percent.

**Lift ticket prices:** Adults, $26; children (7-12) and seniors (60-69), $12. Seniors 70 and over and children 4 to 6 ski free when accompanied by an adult.

**Off-site lift ticket sales:** Mountain Hardware. Bass TM Tickets, (800) 225-2277.

**Description:** This is a small resort with one large, open ski bowl and two chairlifts, located in the Tahoe Donner residential resort community above Truckee. Since it is primarily a learn-to-ski area, there isn't much for strong intermediates or advanced skiers. The terrain has scant tree cover and not much variation. Still, beginners will find lots of economical lift and lesson deals.

*Tahoe Donner ski area offers wide-open slopes ideal for beginners.*

**Strategy for skiing the mountain:** This is a good, uncrowded area for families with small children. The layout is obvious and easy.

**Best beginner run:** Mile Trail.

**Best intermediate run:** Race Course.

**Best expert run:** Skip's Plunge (the only expert run).

**Restaurants/bars:** Café, restaurant at clubhouse.

**Equipment rental:** Standard packages (skis, boots, poles) available.

**Instruction:** Group (90-minute lesson): Adults and children 7 and older, $22. Private lessons (one hour), $45 ($20 each additional person).

**Transportation:** The Tahoe Donner Shuttle runs daily; call (916) 562-6257 for schedule information.

**Day care:** None.

**Snowboarding:** Yes.

**Special programs/camps:** First-time lesson package: $34 (limited surface lift tickets, 90-minute lesson, rentals). Beginner ski package: Adults, $49; children 7-12, $39 (lift ticket, 90-minute lesson, rentals).

**Major events of the season:** Coca Cola Race (January), Children's Pog Championship Tournament (February).

**Other services:** Retail ski shop, short lockers (50 cents) and tall lockers ($5).

## Soda Springs
*See number 5 on map, page 364*

**Location:** One mile off Interstate 80 on Highway 40 at the Soda Springs/Norden exit, 13 miles west of Truckee.

**Information:** P.O. Box 39, Truckee, CA 96160; (916) 426-3666. Snowphone: (916) 426-3669.

**Lifts:** One triple midway stop, one double.

**Vertical descent:** 652 feet.

**Terrain:** 200 acres, 16 runs (longest, one mile). Base elevation: 6,700 feet; summit: 7,352 feet. Beginner, 30 percent; intermediate, 50 percent; advanced, 20 percent.

**Lift ticket prices:** Adults, $20; children (7-12) and seniors (60-69), $5. Children 4 and under and seniors 70 and over ski free.

**Off-site lift ticket sales:** None.

**Description:** One of the first ski areas in the Tahoe region, now owned by neighboring Boreal resort and operated on weekends and holidays only. A quick exit from Interstate 80 on Donner Summit, the area offers a good venue for beginners, or for intermediates looking to get in a half day of skiing. The vertical is almost the same as at Boreal. All intermediate to advanced runs are off the Crystal triple chair, and all beginner runs are off the Lion's Head double.

**Strategy for skiing the mountain:** You don't need one—this is the best place for uncrowded skiing on busy or holiday weekends.

**Best beginner run:** Sunshine.
**Best intermediate run:** Meadow.
**Best expert run:** Mad Dog.
**Restaurants / bars:** Cafeteria (breakfast, lunch, dinner).
**Equipment rental:** Standard and high-performance / demo packages (skis, boots, poles), and snowboards available.
**Instruction:** Group 90-minute lessons: Adults and children (7-12), $22. Private lessons: $45 per hour (one to two people).
**Transportation:** None.
**Day care:** None.
**Snowboarding:** Yes.
**Special programs / camps:** First-time lesson package: Adults, $34; children (7-12), $31 (rentals, lift ticket, lesson). Beginner snowboard lesson package: Adults and children (7-12), $41 (rentals, lift ticket, lesson). Soda Springs tickets may be used for Boreal night skiing.
**Major events of the season:** Christmas Day Celebration, New Year's Eve Torchlight Parade.
**Other services:** Lockers ($1), ski check ($1) and retail ski shop.

## ★ Boreal Ski Resort ★
*See number 6 on map, page 364*

**Location:** Off Interstate 80 at Donner Summit, at Castle Peak exit, 10 miles west of Truckee.
**Information:** P.O. Box 39, Truckee, CA 96160; (916) 426-3666.
**Lifts:** Two quads (one high-speed detachable), two triples, five doubles.
**Vertical descent:** 600 feet.
**Terrain:** 380 acres, 41 runs (longest, one mile). Beginner, 30 percent; intermediate, 55 percent; advanced, 15 percent. Base elevation: 7,200 feet; summit: 7,800 feet. Snowmaking on 100 acres.
**Lift ticket prices:** Mondays, weekends and holidays: Adults, $33; children (12 and under) and seniors (60-69), $10; seniors 70 and over ski free. Tuesday through Thursday: Adults, $21; children and seniors, $5.
**Off-site lift ticket sales:** None.
**Description:** There isn't much elevation here; what you see from the freeway is mainly what you get: short, fall-line runs from the ridge. Boreal's assets consist of quick access from the highway, a snowmaking system that usually enables it to claim the earliest opening date (around mid-October), high elevation, consistent snowfall and popularity with snowboarders and beginning skiers. The resort is spread out lengthwise, with most of the tree-lined runs at opposite ends. Several short but steep runs are in the drainage between Accelerator and Mineshaft chairlifts. The large day lodge is well positioned for non-skiing parents to watch the progress of their children on easy slopes off the Gunnar's and Claim

Jumper lifts. Jibassic Snowboard Park, with jumps and obstacles, is off the Mineshaft Chairlift, and the resort, an early proponent of the sport, offers a myriad of boarding programs. When you're not busy skiing, check out the ski museum next to the parking lot; it contains fascinating memorabilia and photography of skiing's long history in Lake Tahoe. By the way, the food here is good and reasonably priced, and includes conveniences such as a salad bar.

***Strategy for skiing the mountain:*** If you're not on a learning curve, stay away from the slopes fronting the day lodge, which are filled with novice skiers and snowboarders. Less crowded skiing is at opposite ends of the area, and on the back side. Take the Accelerator Quad lift to the top and work your way to one of these areas. You'll find few skiers on the Cedar Ridge and Lost Dutchman triples. If snowpack is ample (or if conditions are a little icy), try the Quicksilver Quad on the back side.

***Best beginner run:*** Sunset Boulevard, which is also the longest run at Boreal (one mile) and its most scenic, winding down from the top of the ridge.

***Best intermediate run:*** Central Pacific.

***Best expert run:*** Waterfall on the front side.

***Restaurants / bars:*** Cafeteria (breakfast, lunch, dinner), bar, espresso bar.

***Equipment rental:*** Standard and high-performance / demo packages (skis, boots, poles), and snowboards available.

***Instruction***: Group lessons (90 minutes): Adults and children, $20. Private lessons: $45 per hour (one to two people).

***Transportation:*** None.

***Day care:*** None.

***Snowboarding:*** Yes. Unlimited, with snowboard park.

***Special programs / camps:*** Animal Crackers Kids (ages 4-8), $49 (full-day rental, ticket, lesson, lunch). Easy Learn-to-Ski Package: Adults, $40; children (8-12), $33 (beginner two-hour lesson, rental, ticket). Skill Improvement Package: Adults, $57; children (ages 8-12), $35 (lesson, rental, ticket). Snowboard Lesson Package: Adults, $50; children (8-12), $43 (lesson, rental, ticket).

***Major events of the season:*** New Year's Eve Extravaganza; snowboarding competitions (February).

***Other services:*** Two snowboard parks (one for daytime and one for nighttime) with halfpipes, Boreal Inn Hotel, lockers ($1), ski check ($1) and retail ski shop.

# Donner Ski Ranch
*See number 7 on map, page 364*

**Location:** On the Donner Summit, Soda Springs/Norden exit off Interstate 80, 10 miles west of Truckee.

**Information:** P.O. Box 66, Norden, CA 95724; (916) 426-3635.

**Lifts:** One triple, five doubles.

**Vertical descent:** 750 feet.

**Terrain:** 400 acres, 45 runs (longest, 1.2 miles). Base elevation: 7,031 feet; summit: 7,781 feet. Beginner, 25 percent; intermediate, 50 percent; advanced, 25 percent. Snowmaking.

**Lift ticket prices:** Weekends and holidays: Adults, $20; children/seniors, $10. Midweek, non-holiday: Adults, $10; children/seniors, $5.

**Off-site lift ticket sales:** Promotions available through various ski and snowboard retail stores in Northern California.

**Description:** The cheapest adult lift ticket in Tahoe combined with the usually dependable natural snowfall on Donner Summit make this one of the great ski values of the region. In exchange for such a deal, skiers must forego the usual frills, including a fancy day lodge and high-speed lifts. The lodge is almost ramshackle in appearance, and the interior might charitably be described as rustic. Lifts are aging and slow, and there are no quads. Parking is limited, and nothing about the food could be described as gourmet. Still, there are 400 acres worth of terrain out there, once you get beyond the limitations of the front side—the only part that's visible from the entrance. An inspiring view of Donner Lake to the east is off the top of Chair 1, but the majority of cruisin' stuff is on the back side, a tranquil valley full of lovely, gladed ski runs. There are no flats to pole over, and while most of the runs are around one-half mile in length, lift lines are short and there is amazing variety. The ski area allows snowboarding without restriction.

**Strategy for skiing the mountain:** Don't let the steep face under Chair 1 scare you; warm up on the South Trail, then take the scenic North Trail for the eagle's view of Donner Lake from Signal Peak (elevation 7,851 feet), then work your way to the back side, skiing chairs 3, 2 and 5, in that order. If morning conditions are icy, head immediately to Chair 5, which is south-facing and softens first. Most intermediates prefer Chair 3 with its sense of seclusion and its idyllic, forested environment.

**Best beginner run:** BJ's Road.

**Best intermediate run:** Lyla's.

**Best expert run:** The Face.

**Restaurants/bars:** Old Highway 40 Restaurant/Bar, cafeteria (breakfast, lunch, dinner, snacks), Tinker Station, Ranch Bar.

**Equipment rental:** Standard and high-performance/demo packages (skis, boots, poles), and snowboards available.

*Instruction:* Group lessons (90 minutes): Adults and children, $12. Private lessons: $40.
*Transportation:* None.
*Day care:* None.
*Snowboarding:* Yes. Unlimited on the mountain.
*Special programs / camps:* Children's ski school (12 and under), $25 (rental, lift ticket, lesson). Snowboarding lessons (rentals, lift ticket, lesson): Adults, $45; children, $40. Night skiing (4 p.m. to 7 p.m.) Wednesday through Sunday, $5.
*Major events of the season:* Rage'n at the Ranch U.S. Amateur Snowboard Association (USASA)-sanctioned snowboard series (December through February), and Anniversary Week (late January), with adult and child lift tickets at $6 and rentals at $10.
*Other services:* Ski shop (accessories, souvenirs, ski and snowboard maintenance/repairs), lockers (50 cents), condos and a snowboard park.

## ★ Sugar Bowl ★
*See number 8 on map, page 364*

*Location:* On old Highway 40 off Interstate 80 at the Soda Springs/ Norden exit, 15 miles west of Truckee.
*Information:* P.O. Box 5, Norden, CA 95724; (916) 426-3836 or (916) 426-3651. Snowphone: (916) 426-3847.
*Lifts:* One gondola, three quads, five doubles.
*Vertical descent:* 1,500 feet.
*Terrain:* 1,110 acres, 58 runs (longest, three miles). Base elevation: 6,883 feet; summit: 8,383 feet. Beginner, 15 percent; intermediate, 40 percent; advanced, 45 percent. Limited snowmaking.
*Lift ticket prices:* Adults, $37; children (5-12), $10; seniors, $17 (midweek, non-holiday, 60 and over). Children 4 and under ski free. Half-day rates available.
*Off-site lift ticket sales:* Albertsons markets (coupon vouchers).
*Description:* Built in 1939, this resort has retained its Old World charm for more than a half-century, and it is now on an expansion kick that saw a new mountain, Judah, opened in the winter of 1994-95. The place has an aristocratic, Tyrolean ambience, and, in fact, the inspiration for its design, along with the first ski school director (the noted Hanness Schroll), was Austrian. Sugar Bowl was once the playground of the rich and famous, among them Walt Disney, who was an early investor, actor Errol Flynn and many of the social and business elites of San Francisco (who still own it). The Sugar Bowl Lodge, in a rambling, wood-frame building, offers 40 rooms (almost always booked throughout the season) and one of the best gourmet restaurants in the region. Access to the base area used to be exclusively by the Magic Carpet gondola from the parking lot, but now

with a second base area at Mount Judah, skiers can drive directly to the slopes. Sugar Bowl has a reputation as the snowiest ski resort in Tahoe—smack in the middle of the Donner Summit—allowing for early and late season skiing on natural snow. The ski area has three mountain faces, dominated by Mount Lincoln (elevation 8,383 feet) and Mount Disney (elevation 7,953 feet). Most of the runs from these peaks are advanced to expert, and there are some narrow chutes and gullies that create natural halfpipes for snowboarders, who are much in evidence. Most of the intermediate runs are on the west side of Disney, the east side of Lincoln and the new Mount Judah. As Judah expands, it will almost certainly become popular with cruising skiers because of its tree-lined runs and scenic vistas of Donner Pass and Castle Peak.

***Strategy for skiing the mountain:*** If possible, take shuttles from Donner Lake or Soda Springs. Parking is limited at the Magic Carpet base, but more readily available at the new Mount Judah base. Warm up on Christmas Tree Ridge (where most of the beginner and lower intermediate runs are located), then tackle Disney, Lincoln and Judah. Crow's Nest off Mount Disney has some of the least crowded intermediate runs, with best snow conditions before midday. Lincoln and Judah have good north-facing runs that hold powder well into the afternoon. If you want to avoid lines at the gondola by day's end, either leave early or park at Judah.

***Best beginner runs:*** Jerome's Hill, Sleigh Ride.

***Best intermediate runs:*** Mogul Ridge, MacTavish.

***Best expert runs:*** Bacon's Gully and Silver Belt.

***Restaurants/bars:*** Cafeteria, hotel dining room, two bars.

***Equipment rental:*** Standard and high-performance/demo packages (skis, boots, poles), and snowboards available.

***Instruction:*** Group lessons: $25 (two hours) or $45 (all day); private lessons: $45 per hour ($20 each additional person).

***Transportation:*** A free ski shuttle along Donner Summit is available, on weekends and holidays only. Call (916) 426-3651.

***Day care:*** Yes.

***Snowboarding:*** Yes.

***Special programs/camps:*** ABC Beginner Ski or Snowboard Program: Adults, $45; children 6-12, $35 (two-hour lesson, rentals, lift ticket). Powder Kids (ages 6-12): $52 (lift ticket, rentals, lesson, lunch). Sugar Bears (ages 3-6): $48 (lift ticket, rentals, lesson, lunch).

***Major events of the season:*** New Year's Eve DJ Dance Party and Fireworks, Sierra League Race (January).

***Other services:*** Retail ski shop and lockers.

# ★ Northstar-at-Tahoe ★

*See number 9 on map, page 364*

**Location:** Off Highway 267, six miles south of Truckee.

**Information:** P.O. Box 2449, Truckee, CA 96160; (916) 562-1010. Snowphone: (916) 562-1330. Reservations: (800) GO-NORTH.

**Lifts:** Six-passenger high-speed gondola, three express quads, two triples, three doubles, two surface lifts.

**Vertical descent:** 2,280 feet.

**Terrain:** 2,000 acres, 61 runs (longest, 2.9 miles). Base elevation: 6,330 feet; summit: 8,610 feet. Beginner, 25 percent: intermediate, 50 percent; advanced, 25 percent. Snowmaking coverage on 50 percent of runs (200 acres).

**Lift ticket prices:** Adults, $42; children (5-12), $18; seniors (60-69), $21; seniors (70 and over), $5. Children under 5 ski free. Half-day, multi-day rates available.

**Off-site lift ticket sales:** None.

**Description:** A complete year-round resort, Northstar is one of Tahoe's most popular intermediate mountains, with meticulously groomed runs in an intimate, secluded forest environment. Its well-designed layout has ego-building lower intermediate and beginner runs on the front side, and advanced intermediate and expert runs on the back side. This is the only ski area in Tahoe with a "village," and one of the few ski-in, ski-out over-night lodging complexes. Most skiing begins one-third of the way up the mountain, at a day lodge that is reached by a gondola or chairlift. Begin-ner runs are concentrated on the lower mountain, with a long, flat road back to the village. The majority of expert runs off the front face of Mount Pluto (8,610 feet) are short and steep, while those on the back are longer and more varied. Cruising terrain is the mainstay on the front side, with scenic runs off West Ridge providing views of Martis Valley and Truckee. The back side consists of long, fall-line runs on advanced inter-mediate terrain (even though the trails are marked black diamonds), and tree skiing in fresh powder. Because of its wind-protected location and dense forest, Northstar is one of the best foul-weather ski venues in North Tahoe. The main day lodge offers typical skier's fare, but the Mountaintop Summit Deck and Grill provides gourmet Mexican cuisine (including the finest salsa in Tahoe). But this is not the place to be during inclement weather, since there is no indoor seating. You'll find good restaurants for lunch and dinner in the village (try Timbercreek). Among Northstar's attributes are one of the country's best instructional programs for youngsters. For techno-weenies, the ski area pioneered Club Vertical, an electronic lift pass that calculates vertical feet skied.

**Strategy for skiing the mountain:** With long lines forming at the gondola and access chair at the village, weekend skiers should go early or late. Intermediates should stay clear of the congested mid-mountain area around Main Street, filled with beginners and converging skiers. The best skiing is on the back side early in the morning, before the crowds arrive. Trails on the east side, including Logger's Loop, Sunshine and Sidewinder, seem to get the least use most times of the day. Because of Northstar's popularity, the parking lots can fill quickly and lift sales are halted when the mountain reaches capacity on weekends and holidays. If you're not staying there, go early and have breakfast.

**Best beginner run:** Village Run.

**Best intermediate runs:** Isolated and uncrowded Logger's Loop on the front side, West Ridge/Iron Horse (advanced intermediate) on the back side.

**Best expert run:** Burn Out on the back side.

**Restaurants/bars:** In the village: Timbercreek Restaurant (steaks, poultry, seafood), Pedro's Pizza, Village Food Company (gourmet deli items, espresso), Alpine Bar and Lounge. On the mountain: Big Springs Day Lodge (breakfast, lunch, barbecue), Lookout Sub Shop (deli sandwiches, wine, beer), Nordic Cafe (sandwiches, wine, beer), Summit Deck and Grill (mountaintop restaurant with outdoor seating). Below the mountain: Basque Club Restaurant (traditional Basque dinner).

**Equipment rental:** Standard and high-performance/demo packages (skis, boots, poles), and snowboards available.

**Instruction:** Skill Improvement—1.75-hour group lessons: Adults and children (5-12), $25. Private lessons: Adults and children, $50 per hour ($20 each additional person).

**Transportation:** Free daily ski-area shuttle service is available (December through March) between Tahoe Vista, Kings Beach, Incline Village, Truckee and Northstar. Call (916) 587-0257 for the Northstar schedule. Northstar's ski shuttle connects to TART public buses for skiers from West Shore and Tahoe City.

**Day care:** Yes, at Minors' Camp.

**Snowboarding:** Yes (no snowboard park).

**Special programs/camps:** Minors' Camp (ages 2-6): $40 (supervised play, lunch); $51 (90-minute lesson, rentals, lift ticket, lunch); $58 (2.5-hour lesson, rentals, lift ticket, lunch). Ski Cubs Package (ages 3-6): $49 (90-minute lesson, rental, lift ticket, lunch). Super Cubs Package (ages 5-6): $58 (90-minute lesson, rental, lift ticket, lunch). Star Kids Program (ages 5-12), $55 (four-hour lesson, lift ticket, lunch, souvenir water bottle, pin, balloon); $65 (all of above, plus rentals). New beginners lesson package: $42 (1.75-hour lesson, lift ticket, rentals). Advanced beginner lesson package: $57 (1.75-hour lesson, lift ticket, rentals). Dynastar Center: $10 (demo unlimited Dynastar skis for four hours). Three-day ski clinic: $185. Club Vertical Electronic Ticketing: Adults, $69; children/seniors, $49 (allowing skiers to charge ticket and food purchases, access separate lift lines, get discounts, and access a message center for lost/found people; interchangeable with Sierra-at-Tahoe lift ticket).

***Major events of the season:*** Snowfest Winter Carnival (March) and Special Olympics (March).

***Other services:*** Village Mall: general store, ski rental shop, repair shop, souvenir/gift/video store, gas station, recreation center (outdoor spas, saunas, exercise/arcade room); overnight ski storage; ski and basket check; mountain photos; sleigh rides; transport gondola. Snowmobiles available for guided tours: $69 for one rider, $89 for two.

## ★ Mount Rose ★

*See number 10 on map, page 364*

***Location:*** On Mount Rose Highway (Route 431) 12 miles from Incline Village and 22 miles from Reno.

***Information:*** 22222 Mount Rose Highway, Reno, NV 89511; (702) 849-0704. Snowphone: (702) 849-0706; outside Nevada, (800) SKI-ROSE.

***Lifts:*** Three triples, two quads, one double.

***Vertical descent:*** 1,440 feet.

***Terrain:*** 900 acres, 41 runs, longest run 2.5 miles. Base elevation: 8,260 feet; summit: 9,700 feet. Beginner, 30 percent; intermediate, 35 percent; advanced, 35 percent.

***Lift ticket prices:*** Adults, $34; children (6-12), $14; seniors, $17. Children 5 and under ski free. Daily specials.

***Off-site lift ticket sales:*** None.

***Description:*** Bring your ski legs for this mountain, which rises to the west of Reno and is the third highest in the Tahoe region (next to Heavenly and Kirkwood). This is not a cruisers' paradise, though intermediates will find enough to keep them occupied. What defines this area are its challenging advanced runs, which require you to keep sharp edges. The resort actually comprises what used to be two separate areas (Mount Rose and Slide Mountain) on opposing flanks of the peak. From the summit you can ski either side, and there are services such as ticket sales, parking, cafeteria and restrooms on both sides. But the ski school, rental and retail departments and most of the food services are on the Mount Rose side. Terrain varies from steep, tree-lined runs at Rose to the wide-open Sunrise Bowl at Slide. There's good beginner terrain from the two lower chairlifts at Rose, but none at Slide. On powder days, this area excels, and its high elevation holds snow late into spring. (Note: Trail ratings are a notch higher than most other ski areas, so that runs marked intermediate at Slide are really advanced.) Strong winds, a not unusual occurrence, can harden slopes quickly. From the summit, there are sweeping views of

Reno, Washoe Valley and Lake Tahoe. The Mount Rose day lodge, remodeled several times in recent years, serves quality meals (Mexican food is a specialty) and has one of the most efficient ski/boot rental operations in Tahoe. Management seems responsive to customers, and there is strong repeat business from Reno residents. On stormy days, the steep and winding access road can be hazardous and may be closed.

***Strategy for skiing the mountain:*** With its northeastern exposure, the Slide side has the sunniest disposition in the morning, but it's hardly the easiest place for a warm-up run. Still, early in the day is best for skiing Slide; then work your way back to Rose. If the wind picks up, the runs off the Lakeview Chair will be more protected than those from the top of the Northwest Passage Chair.

***Best beginner run:*** Galena on the Rose side.

***Best intermediate run:*** Bruce's on the Slide side.

***Best expert run:*** Northwest Passage on the Rose side.

***Restaurants/bars:*** Cafeteria (breakfast, lunch deli/food court), tavern (full bar).

***Equipment rental:*** Standard and high-performance packages (skis, boots, poles), and snowboards available.

***Instruction:*** Two-hour group lessons: Adults and children (6-12), $22. Private lessons: $45 per hour ($20 for each additional person).

***Transportation:*** Sierra Nevada Gray Line operates one daily ski shuttle package service for $29 (half-day lift ticket, round-trip from downtown Reno, John Ascuaga's Nugget, Sands Regency Hotel Casino, Reno Hilton and Clarion Hotel Casino, December through April). Call (702) 331-1147 or (800) 222-6009.

***Day care:*** None.

***Snowboarding:*** Yes, on the Slide side.

***Special programs/camps:*** First-time skier package: Adults, $45; children (12 and under), $28 (rental, beginner lift ticket, lesson). Rosebuds Ski School (ages 3-5), $25 (lift ticket, supervised play, rentals $5 extra).

***Major event of the season:*** None.

***Other services:*** Snowboard terrain (Zephyr Park), sports shop, repair shop, lockers (50 cents), and outdoor barbecue deck.

## ★ Diamond Peak Ski Resort ★
*See number 11 on map, page 364*

***Location:*** Incline Village, two miles above Highway 28 on the Nevada side of the lake.

***Information:*** 1210 Ski Way, Incline Village, NV 89451; (702) 832-1177. Snowphone: (702) 831-3211; reservations: (800) GO-TAHOE.

***Lifts:*** One quad, six doubles.

***Vertical descent:*** 1,840 feet.

**Terrain:** 655 acres, 35 trails (longest, 2.5 miles). Base elevation: 6,700 feet; summit: 8,540 feet. Beginner, 18 percent; intermediate, 49 percent; advanced, 33 percent. Snowmaking: 75-percent coverage, including 20 acres of advanced terrain in Solitude Canyon.

**Lift ticket prices:** Adults, $35; children/seniors, $14. Children ages 5 and under and seniors 70 and over ski free.

**Off-site lift ticket sales:** Hyatt Regency activities desk (guests only).

**Description:** Magnificent, close-up views of Lake Tahoe from the scenic east shore, coupled with long intermediate romps from Crystal Ridge and the summit of Diamond Peak (elevation 8,540 feet), provide the chief attractions for this resort. Its base facilities are modest (greatly over-crowded on weekends) and natural snowfall is less dependable here be-cause of a "banana belt" effect next to the lake. But the resort can cover most of its holdings with snowmaking, and a recent expansion of the Snowflake mid-mountain lodge has doubled the seating capacity there, providing more deck space for a spectacular panorama of Lake Tahoe. The lower mountain, which is the original ski area, contains the majority of lifts and has mostly short, north-facing runs. But two-thirds of the terrain is on the upper mountain, reached by just one chairlift, the Crystal Quad. This area is a totally different environment, with lengthy interme-diate trails, expert powder chutes off the ridge, and acres of tree skiing in Solitude Canyon and Golden Eagle Bowl for powder fanatics. West-facing exposure, winds on the exposed ridges and less snowmaking here often shorten the season for this part of the mountain, but when the snow is right, Diamond Peak is one of the great secrets of Tahoe skiing. The area is no slouch with statistics—it has the fourth longest vertical at Lake Tahoe. Other pluses include a friendly attitude, better-than-average food service and one of the region's best and most affordable programs for children.

**Strategy for skiing the mountain:** Warm up on Red Fox or Coyote on the lower mountain, then get to the top of Crystal Quad. Intermediate and advanced skiers can ski the upper mountain most of the day. Make a point to have lunch at Snowflake Lodge for the view of the lake. If winds pick up in mid-afternoon, finish your day on the lower, more protected slopes.

**Best beginner run:** Lodgepole.

**Best intermediate run:** Crystal Ridge—also the longest and most scenic.

**Best expert run:** Lightning.

**Restaurants/bars:** Base Lodge, Snowflake Lodge (expanded deck with barbecue atop Lakeview Lift).

**Equipment rental:** Standard and upgraded (not high-performance) packages (skis, boots, poles), and snowboards available.

**Instruction:** Two-hour lesson: Adults and children, $20.

***Transportation:*** Free daily ski-area shuttle service is available through-out Incline Village and Crystal Bay. Call (702) 832-1177. The Reno Shuttle is available.
***Day care:*** Ages 3-6, $20 for two hours or $35 for four hours.
***Snowboarding:*** Yes.
***Special programs / camps:*** Children's ski school (ages 4-6), $57 all day (four hours of instruction and supervision; rental gear $10 extra); Family Package starting at $38 for one adult and one child (6-12); First-Time Skier Package, $29. Handicapped lift ticket rates: Adults, $20 ($14 weekdays); children, $9 ($6 weekdays) with free rental of standard equip-ment only.
***Major events of the season:*** Northern Lights Celebration (December), Nevada Special Olympics (March).
***Other services:*** Snowboard park, lockers (50 cents to $1), ski check (no basket check) and Village Ski Loft retail store.

## Granlibakken Ski Resort
*See number 12 on map, page 364*

***Location:*** 625 Granlibakken Road off Highway 89, one-half mile south of Tahoe City.
***Information:*** P.O. Box 6329, Tahoe City, CA 96145; (916) 583-6203. Snowphone: (916) 583-9896.
***Lifts:*** One poma.
***Vertical descent:*** 300 feet.
***Terrain:*** Open slope with two runs. Base elevation: 6,330 feet, Summit: 6,610 feet. Beginner, 50 percent; intermediate, 50 percent.
***Lift ticket prices:*** Adults, $15; children (12 and under), $8.
***Off-site lift sales:*** None.
***Description:*** This is the oldest ski area in the Lake Tahoe basin, with one small, open hill and two runs geared mainly to beginners. A cozy, rustic day lodge offers meals, lessons and rentals. The name Granlibakken is Norwegian for "the hill sheltered by fir trees." Built in 1927 by the Southern Pacific Railroad and the Tahoe Tavern Resort, the area was used historically as a site for Olympic ski jumpers. For three decades, Olympic tryouts were held here, along with the Junior National Jumping Championships, and the hill was maintained by the Lake Tahoe Ski Club until the late 1950s. Famous jumpers who competed here included Roy Mikkelsen (1932 and 1936 Olympics) and Wayne Poulsen, founder of Squaw Valley USA and 1938 California state champion for jumping, downhill and slalom. The ski area has been owned by Bill and Norma Parson since 1978. While it is not really much of a ski hill, the Parsons keep it open primarily for sentimental reasons. The surrounding Granli-bakken Resort is a full-service conference center with excellent condo-

minium accommodations, meeting rooms and restaurant. There's a popular snowplay area next to the ski hill. Granlibakken is the closest skiing to Tahoe City.

**Restaurants/bars:** Snack bar in warming hut.

**Equipment rental:** Standard packages (skis, boots, poles) available.

**Instruction:** Group lessons: Adults and children (12 and under), $15; private lessons, $25 per hour.

**Transportation:** A shuttle is available from Reno-Tahoe International Airport, if flying in ($35 for one person, $20 per person if more than one skier in cab).

**Day care:** None.

**Snowboarding:** None.

**Special programs/camps:** Beginner lesson package: Adults and children, $30 (one-hour lesson, rentals, lift ticket). Lodge/Lift Package, $59 (lodging: double occupancy with two skiers in room, lift ticket, breakfast).

**Major event of the season:** Torchlight Parade on Christmas Eve.

**Other services:** Snow play area open daily ($4), saucer rentals ($3) and Ski Hut Retail Shop.

## Ski Homewood
*See number 13 on map, page 364*

**Location:** On Highway 89 in Homewood, six miles south of Tahoe City.

**Information:** 5145 West Lake Boulevard, P.O. Box 165, Homewood, CA 96141; (916) 525-2992. Snowphone: (916) 525-2900. Lodging: (800) TAHOE-4-U.

**Lifts:** One quad, two triples, two doubles, five surface lifts.

**Vertical descent:** 1,650 feet.

**Terrain:** 1,260 acres, 57 runs (longest, two miles). Base elevation: 6,230 feet; summit: 7,880 feet. Beginner, 15 percent; intermediate, 50 percent; advanced, 35 percent. Snowmaking on 15 acres.

**Lift ticket prices:** Adults, $32; youths (9-13), $11; seniors, $12. Children 8 and under ski free with an adult. Midweek rates available.

**Off-site lift ticket sales:** Bass TM Ticket Sales; (800) 225-2277.

**Description:** The best "hidden" family resort in Lake Tahoe. From Highway 89 on the West Shore, you can see only a fraction of what is a spacious, medium-sized resort with extraordinary close-up views of the lake. Don't be put off by the steep face at the base of the mountain. There are two separate base areas (the second was once a separately owned ski area sharing the same ridge). Between the two mountain faces are 33 intermediate runs and 20 expert runs, providing all the variety any skier could want. Skiing on the north side is mostly in trees, but the south side offers one large bowl (Quail Face) that is for experts only. A decent beginner's area, with five lifts, is at the base of the north side, with longer runs on the south side. Homewood installed one of the nation's first quad chairs, though it is not high-speed. Its protected location makes for a great bad-weather skiing venue, but low elevation and proximity to the lake can cause rapid thaws on the bottom runs, especially in spring. The area specializes in low-cost children's programs and midweek two-for-one adult lift deals. It also has one of Tahoe's more active snowboard programs, including lessons for older adults. A unique feature of the resort is its accessibility by ferryboat; the *Tahoe Queen* runs a daily breakfast trip (skiers and weather permitting) from the end of Ski Run Boulevard in South Lake Tahoe across the lake to Homewood Marina, where skiers merely walk off the boat and across the road to the lifts. The return voyage is accompanied by live music and dancing.

***Strategy for skiing the mountain:*** Park in the less crowded South Lot, or take the Tahoe Area Regional Transit (TART) bus from various North Shore pick-up points. The best sun exposure and warm-up runs are off the Quail double chair. Then work your way up the Ellis triple chair and over the ridge to the intermediate's paradise off The Quad. Avoid snaking Lombard Street, aptly named, at the end of the day.

***Best beginner runs:*** Rainbow Ridge, Homeward Bound (connecting trails) on the ridge and south side, together offering one run that is two miles long.

***Best intermediate runs:*** High Grade, Smooth Cruise on the south side.

***Best expert runs:*** Dutch Treat on the south side, Glory Hole on the north side.

***Restaurants/bars:*** Hofbrau, Hava Java, South Side Lounge, Warming Hut Snack Bar.

***Equipment rental:*** Standard and high-performance/demo packages (skis, boots, poles), and snowboards available.

***Instruction:*** Group two-hour lesson: Adults and children (6 and older), $25. Private lesson: $45 per hour ($15 each additional person).

***Transportation:*** Free ski shuttle service is available between North and South Lodge and downtown Homewood; call (916) 525-2992 for schedule information. North and West Shore access is provided by Tahoe Area Regional Transit (TART) with connections to Reno-Tahoe International Airport. Use TART and receive full bus fare refund towards lift ticket; call (916) 581-6365 for information. For information on the Tahoe Queen Ski Shuttle (breakfast buffet and après-ski party included), call (916) 541-3364 or (800) 238-2463.

***Day care:*** Yes.

***Snowboarding:*** Yes.

***Special programs/camps:*** Adult beginner ski package: $39 (four-hour lesson, lift ticket, rentals). Children's beginner ski package (ages

6-13): $29 (four-hour lesson, lift ticket, rentals). Child care (ages 2-5): $45 (full-day supervised play, lunch, snacks). Super Sliders Program: Adults, $175; children (5-18), $135 (eight-week series of ski instruction).

***Major events of the season:*** Ho Ho Homewood Toy Drive (December), Telemark Race (February).

***Other services:*** Repair/sports shops and new snowboard terrain park lockers (50 cents).

## ★ Heavenly Ski Area ★
*See number 14 on map, page 364*

***Location:*** At the end of Ski Run Boulevard, off Highway 50, South Lake Tahoe.

***Information:*** P.O. Box 2180, Stateline, NV 89449; (702) 586-7000. Reservations: (800) 2-HEAVEN. Snowphone: (916) 541-7544.

***Lifts:*** One aerial tram, three express quads, eight triples, seven doubles, five surface lifts.

***Vertical descent:*** 3,500 feet.

***Terrain:*** 4,800 skiable acres, 79 runs (longest, 5.5 miles). Base elevation: 6,540 feet (California side), 7,200 feet (Nevada side); summit: 10,040 feet. Beginner, 20 percent; intermediate, 45 percent; advanced, 35 percent. Snowmaking on 66 percent of cleared trails.

***Lift ticket prices:*** Adults, $42; youths (13-15), $30; children (6-12), $18. Children 5 and under ski free. Half-day, multi-day and group rates available.

***Off-site lift ticket sales:*** Safeway (outside Tahoe Basin) and local stores.

***Description:*** The only Western ski area that straddles two states (California and Nevada), Heavenly also has the highest top elevation (10,040 feet) in the region. While it is a vast ski complex with bowls, glades and ridgetops, it is known primarily as an intermediate skier's mountain. One of the largest snowmaking systems in North America guarantees good coverage in lean snow years. The lower California side below Gunbarrel features an intimidating face of moguls and steep terrain, with most cruising stuff higher on the mountain. The best powder, longest intermediate runs and best protection from winds are on the Nevada side. The highest and most impressive view of Lake Tahoe in the basin is from the Top of the Tram day lodge, which has a sit-down restaurant, bar and large deck and is the terminus of a 50-passenger tram. Three modern lodges on the Nevada side offer superior facilities and fair food compared to the California base lodge, which is aging and cramped. Most of the advanced and expert runs are concentrated on the upper portion of the Nevada side, in Milky Way Bowl and Mott's and Killebrew canyons. There are some narrow, congested trails and convergence points that increase the risk of skier collisions—especially on Ridge Run. Heavenly has very little beginner terrain for the size of the mountain, but it is well utilized by the ski school here, which is under the progressive leadership of Stu Campbell, instructional editor for *Ski Magazine*. A snowboard park was introduced for the 1994-95 season. Heavenly's free bus shuttle system to and from area lodging is the most extensive in Tahoe.

***Strategy for skiing the mountain:*** To newcomers, this is the most confusing ski resort in Tahoe, largely because of its size and maze of connecting trails. My first bit of advice is to take the free ski bus from your hotel or motel, and avoid the parking crunch. If you're an intermediate skier, forget about skiing the lower California side; your options to return at the end of the day are a snaking beginner's trail that isn't worth the effort, downloading on the tram (too long of a wait) or downloading on the Gunbarrel Chair, which is the best alternative (with a million-dollar view of Tahoe and Stateline to boot). Reaching the top of the California side is pokey; allow an hour on weekends to ride the three necessary chairlifts. For quicker access, take the less frequent shuttle from South Shore to one of the Nevada bases (Stagecoach or Boulder) and ride just two lifts to the summit. If you enter Nevada from the California side, heed the warnings to begin your journey back well before the lifts close. In general, skiing is less crowded and snow quality is better on the Nevada side.

***Best beginner run:*** Mombo Meadows on the California side.

***Best intermediate run:*** Olympic Downhill on the Nevada side.

***Best expert runs:*** Milky Way Bowl on the Nevada side, Gunbarrel on the California side.

***Restaurants/bars:*** Peak Cafe at the Top of Tram (breakfast, lunch, dinner), Sky Meadows Deck and East Peak Lodge (two outdoor barbecues), Mountain Peak (full-service bar), Slice of Heaven (Italian, pizza), Black Diamond Cantina (Mexican) at Boulder Lodge and four bars.

***Equipment rental:*** Standard and high-performance/demo packages (skis, boots, poles), and snowboards available.

***Instruction:*** Two-hour group lessons: Adults (13 and over), $28. Private lessons: $50 per hour (additional person, $25 per hour).

***Transportation:*** Free shuttle service is available from Heavenly bus stops located near most lodging properties, leaving every 20 to 30 minutes (8 a.m. to 5:30 p.m. daily).

***Day care:*** None.

***Snowboarding:*** Yes, including a new snowboard park.

***Special programs/camps:*** Children Ski Explorers (ages 4-12), $58 (full day including lesson, lunch, rental, lift ticket). First-Timers Package, $43 (ticket, rental, three-hour lesson).

***Major events of the season:*** Winter Carnival (January), Mogul Competition (January).

***Other services:*** Sports shop, lockers (75 cents), free ski checks (at base and top of tram), basket check ($1) and snowboard park.

# ★ Sierra-at-Tahoe ★

*See number 15 on map, page 364*

**Location:** Off Highway 50 at Echo Summit, on Sierra-at-Tahoe Road, 12 miles west of South Lake Tahoe.

**Information:** 1111 Sierra-at-Tahoe Road, Twin Bridges, CA 95735; (916) 659-7453. Snowphone: (916) 659-7475.

**Lifts:** Three high-speed quads, one triple, five doubles, one surface lift.

**Vertical descent:** 2,212 feet.

**Terrain:** 2,000 acres, 44 runs (longest, 3.5 miles). Base elevation: 6,640 feet; summit: 8,852 feet. Beginner, 25 percent; intermediate, 50 percent; advanced, 25 percent.

**Lift ticket prices:** Adults, $37, $25 half day; youths (13-19), $27, $20 half day; seniors (60-69) and children (6-12), $17, $13 half day. Seniors 70 and over and children 5 and under ski free.

**Off-site lift ticket sales:** Lodge/lift packages available at Best Western, Horizon and Lakeland Village in South Lake Tahoe.

**Description:** This is Tahoe's most underrated resort, often overlooked by out-of-towners because of its low profile and modest distance (25 minutes) from South Lake Tahoe. This is an amazingly well-designed mountain, with exceptional terrain for all ability levels. It features north-facing, fall-line runs, an intimate, forested setting and an enlightened management that listens to consumers. Sierra-at-Tahoe has the region's most extensive beginner terrain, with a top-to-bottom run (Sugar n' Spice) that allows new skiers maximum access to the mountain. Intermediates have one section of the ski area to themselves, with a series of wide, undulating runs through sylvan forest from the Puma and Slingshot quad chairs. The highest peak is Huckleberry Mountain (elevation 8,852 feet), where challenging, advanced runs cascade down the front, and intermediate and beginner runs fan out from the back. On the summit, there's a world-class vista of Lake Tahoe from a large day lodge that houses the Grand View Grill and Lake View Deck. The back side has a unique and challenging snowboard park and, in fact, the resort is considered one of the top snowboard destinations in America. Recently acquired by the company that owns Northstar (near Truckee), new improvements in food services and instruction, combined with a joint lift ticket and the electronic Club Vertical program, make this resort an outstanding experience for any type of skier. Beginners are well pampered here, and they have more terrain to ski than at any other Tahoe resort. The resort's only drawback is a cramped base lodge with a rabbit-warren of corridors.

**Strategy for skiing the mountain:** By all means, take the free shuttle buses from South Lake Tahoe. Begin your day on the back side, the sunniest area in the morning. Then ski down the ridgeline to the Nob Hill lift, and from there over to the runs off Puma, where the afternoon sun creates a particularly spectacular view of Desolation Wilderness to the north.

**Best beginner run:** Sugar n' Spice.

**Best intermediate run:** Powder Horn.

**Best expert run:** Castle.

**Restaurants/bars:** Cheeseburgers in Paradise, Sierra Pub, Grand View Grill and Lake View Deck at Summit (barbecue), Slingshot Snacks.

**Equipment rental:** Standard and high-performance/demo packages (skis, boots, poles), and snowboards available.

**Instruction:** Group lessons (Breakthrough Clinic): $25. Private lessons, $45 per hour ($25 for each additional person).

**Transportation:** A free ski shuttle bus stops at 30 different locations at South Shore. Call (916) 541-7548 for schedule information.

**Day care:** Yes.

**Snowboarding:** Yes. Unlimited access, plus a snowboard park.

**Special programs/camps:** Introduction to skiing or snowboarding: $37 (rentals, lesson, lift ticket). Two-day introduction to skiing package: $67 (rentals, lessons, lift tickets). Wild Mountain Children's Center introduction to skiing (ages 4-12): $50 full day, $35 half day (lesson, lunch, rentals, lift ticket). Dyno-Tykes Day Care (ages 2-5), $45 (supervised play, lunch, snacks). Interchangeable lift tickets available (good for Heavenly, Kirkwood, Northstar-at-Tahoe, Alpine Meadows and Squaw Valley).

**Major events of the season:** U.S. Amateur Snowboard Event (January), Coca Cola Cup Challenge (February).

**Other services:** Ski repair, sports shop, snowboard park/terrain garden, lockers (75 cents) and ski basket check ($2).

## ★ Kirkwood ★

*See number 16 on map, page 364*

**Location:** Off Highway 88 at Carson Pass, 30 miles southwest of South Lake Tahoe.

**Information:** P.O. Box 1, Kirkwood, CA 95646; (209) 258-6000. Reservations: (800) 967-7500. Snowphone: (209) 258-3000.

**Lifts:** Six triples, four doubles, one surface lift.

**Vertical descent:** 2,000 feet.

**Terrain:** 2,000 acres, 65 runs (longest, 2.5 miles). Base elevation: 7,800 feet; summit: 9,800 feet. Beginner, 15 percent; intermediate, 50 percent; advanced, 35 percent.

**Lift ticket prices:** Adults, $40; youths and students (13-24), $30; children (6-12), $5. Children 5 and under ski free. Half-day and multi-day rates available.

**Off-site lift ticket sales:** Bass TM Ticket Sales; (800) 225-2277.

**Description:** With its awesome, serrated peaks, this might be the most visually impressive resort in the Tahoe region. One look from Kirkwood

Meadows and there's no doubt about it: This is a skier's mountain. Much like Squaw Valley, the resort is in a box canyon, but its topography—ridgelines capped with pinnacles and bizarre fingers of rock—is vastly different. Recently acquired by Telluride of Colorado, Kirkwood will be appreciated most by strong intermediate to super-expert skiers. From Thimble Peak (elevation 9,876 feet), there are no less than 11 double-black-diamond runs, and they represent a world of hurt for lesser skiers. In fact, there's a skull-and-crossbones sign at the base of the Wagon Wheel Chair to underscore the point. Kirkwood's got every kind of terrain a ski area could want—bowls, cornices, saddles, chutes, glades and, fortunately, a few flats for beginners. The resort, with its high base elevation (7,800 feet) is a favorite with early- and late-season skiers. Pluses include a variety of lodging (all in condos), good food services and high-quality, user-friendly ski instruction. Negatives include its distance from South Lake Tahoe, occasional tricky driving over high passes, and the lack of shopping or other après-ski activities for overnight guests.

***Strategy for skiing the mountain:*** Make sure your ski legs are warmed up before tackling anything serious on this mountain. Be aware that the trail ratings are deceptive; some intermediate-signed runs would be diamond runs at other resorts, and some diamond-signed runs are readily negotiable by strong intermediates. Ski the Sunrise Bowl first thing in the morning, then Juniper and Flying Carpet off the Caples Crest Chair, then work your way over to the Cornice lift, where most intermediates find Sentinel Bowl the easiest way down. Modest cruising runs are off the Solitude and Hole 'n Wall chairs.

***Best beginner runs:*** Snowkirk, Graduation.

***Best intermediate runs:*** Devil's Draw, Sunrise Bowl.

***Best expert runs:*** Eagle Bowl, Thunder Saddle (double diamond), Olympic.

***Restaurants / bars:*** Red Cliffs Lodge (cafeteria, Mexican food), Timber Creek Lodge and Snoshoe Thompson's (cafeteria, pizza), Cornice Cafe (gourmet), Kirkwood Inn (home-style dining), five bars.

***Equipment rental:*** Standard and high-performance/demo packages (skis, boots, poles), and snowboards available.

***Instruction:*** Group lessons (90 minutes): Adults and children (ages 4-12), $12. Private lessons: Adults and children (ages 4-12), $55 per hour ($20 for each additional person).

***Transportation:*** A shuttle from South Shore lodging properties is available seven days a week ($2 round-trip fare).

***Day care:*** Ages 3-6, $5 per hour (two-hour minimum) or $35 full day, 8 a.m. to 5 p.m.

***Snowboarding:*** Yes.

***Special programs / camps:*** Pro Turn ski clinics ($12 for 90 minutes);

free Avid Skier cards (ski four days and get fifth day free); adult first-time ski package, $30 (90-minute lesson, rental, lift ticket); snowboard lesson package, $50 (rentals, lift ticket, two-hour lesson); children's ski package (ages 4-12), $50 (lift ticket, rentals, all-day lesson, lunch).
***Major event of the season:*** New Year's Eve Torchlight Parade.
***Other services:*** Alpine Village (two specialty ski shops, general store, post office and six condo complexes), lockers (75 cents), ski basket check ($2), daily sleigh rides (adults, $10; children 12 and under, $5).

## Carson Ski Resort/Iron Mountain
*See number 17 on map, page 364*

***Location:*** Off Highway 88, 42 miles east of Jackson.
***Information:*** 99981 Mormon-Emigrant Trail, Pioneer, CA 95666; (209) 258-8700 or (702) 782-4745.
***Lifts:*** Three doubles, two triples.
***Vertical descent:*** 1,300 feet.
***Terrain:*** 1,200 acres, 45 runs (including 10 new trails); longest, 3.5 miles. Base elevation: 6,500 feet; summit: 7,800 feet. Beginner, 20 percent; intermediate, 50 percent; advanced, 30 percent.
***Lift ticket prices:*** Weekends and holidays: Adults, $27.50; youths (13-18) and seniors (65 and over), $18; children (6-12), $10; children 5 and under ski free. Weekdays: Adults, $18; youths/seniors, $12; children, $10. Half-day weekends: Adults, $15; youths/seniors, $12; children, $8. Half-day weekdays: Adults, $12; youths/seniors, $7.50; children, $6. Family Day Passes (two adults and two youths or two children): $65 weekends, $50 weekdays.
***Off-site lift ticket sales:*** None.
***Description:*** The Tahoe region's only "upside down" ski area is under new ownership after being closed for the 1993-94 season. The summit is actually the parking area and day lodge, where you ski down, so there's no waiting to start your first run of the day. Although the ski area is basically invisible from Highway 88 (and you can easily miss the small entrance road), it contains respectable terrain across two bowls, with skiing above and below treeline and with long intermediate runs (up to 3.5 miles in length). The wind-protected, north-facing area is a natural catch-basin for snow, which is usually ample in the Carson range. Emphasis is on afford-able family skiing and snowboarding (there are two halfpipes), and close proximity to Sacramento Valley and San Francisco, with fewer snow miles and no passes to drive. This area is the farthest (42 miles) from Lake Tahoe. The season is long, and can run to late spring.
***Strategy for skiing the mountain:*** No lines, no waiting.
***Best beginner run:*** Marmot.
***Best intermediate run:*** Northwest (3.5 miles).

**Best expert run:** Cinnamon Grade.

**Restaurants/bars:** Day lodge with restaurant.

**Equipment rental:** Standard packages (skis, boots, poles) and snowboards available.

**Instruction:** Group lessons (90 minutes): Adults, $16; Private lessons: Adults, $20.

**Transportation:** None.

**Day care:** None.

**Snowboarding:** Yes. Unrestricted.

**Special programs/camps:** Beginner ski or snowboard school: Adults, $39 (lesson, lift ticket, rental); children (6-12), $39 (full-day lesson, lift ticket, rentals, supervised care, lunch).

**Major event of the season:** None.

**Other services:** Dorm and motel units (ski-in/ski-out) across from day lodge, retail shops and ski check ($1).

> **NOTE:** As of the 1994-95 season, Carson Ski Resort was closed. At press time, its future operation was uncertain.

*Snowboard parks, such as this one at Sierra-at-Tahoe ski area, offer jumps and bumps for "shredders."*

# INSTANT SKI & WEATHER INFORMATION
## Ski Reports

The following services provide recorded telephone reports on Lake Tahoe ski conditions:

California State Automobile Association Ski Report Hotline: (415) 864-6440.

The *San Francisco Chronicle's* City Line has specific ski reports, updated daily by Tahoe ski areas and the National Weather Service. Call (415) 512-5000 and enter one of the following numbers:

Alpine Meadows, 6411
Boreal/Soda Springs, 6413
Carson Ski Resort, 6418
Diamond Peak, 6426
Donner Ski Ranch, 6415
Heavenly, 6416
Kirkwood, 6419
Mount Rose, 6421
Northstar-at-Tahoe, 6423
Sierra-at-Tahoe, 6424
Sierra Summit, 6425
Squaw Valley, 6427
Sugar Bowl, 6429
Tahoe Donner, 6429

## Weather Reports

For weather reports updated daily by the National Weather Service, call the *San Francisco Chronicle's* City Line at (415) 512-5000. Enter 3140 for weather conditions in the Sierra.

## Road Conditions

Call (800) 427-7623 or (916) 445-1534 for updated highway conditions in California, and (702) 793-1313 for conditions in Nevada.

## Chapter 15

# Cross-Country Ski Areas & Trails

### ★ Author's Choice ★

#### Top 5 Resorts for Beginners

#### Top 5 Resorts for Intermediates

#### Top 5 Resorts for Experts

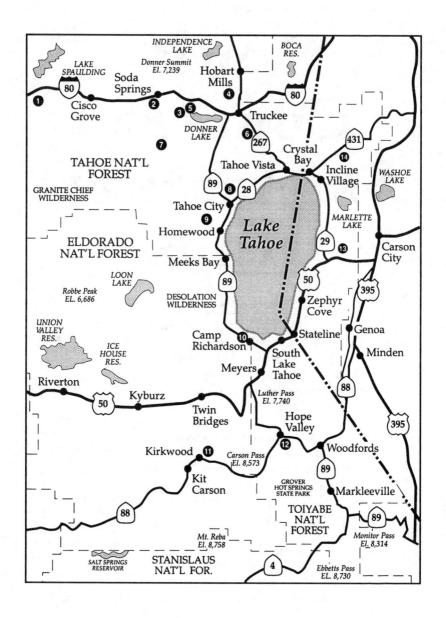

## *Map References—Cross-Country Ski Resorts*

◆

Just as Lake Tahoe boasts the greatest concentration of downhill ski lifts in North America, so, too, does it offer the cross-country skier a bounty of riches. The region is justly famous as the home of Royal Gorge, the largest Nordic resort on the continent. But a dozen other privately operated cross-country areas, combined with numerous routes on public lands, create an unparalleled opportunity for skinny skiers to find their favorite vistas of the Sierra.

Around the perimeter of Tahoe itself are no less than five organized cross-country areas, all of them with spectacular panoramas of the lake from varying elevations. It isn't necessary to be a strong skier or to negotiate arduous trails, either, to be rewarded with such vistas. Beginners can get lofty views from an easy trail at the Diamond Peak Cross-Country Center on the North Shore, or ski right on the beach itself at Camp Richardson on the South Shore. Cheap skiing (free or for minimal charges of $3 to $5) is almost everywhere you turn—at a number of trails operated by public agencies, such as the U.S. Forest Service and the California and Nevada state parks systems. One compromise in using these trails, however, is to forego the comforts of grooming and machine-set track (with a few notable exceptions). Most of the public trails are on the West Shore of the lake, extending from Tahoe City in the north to South Lake Tahoe, and are easy to reach from Highway 89. But don't overlook the locally operated community trail systems, especially ones maintained by the North Tahoe Public Utility District and the city of South Lake Tahoe.

There's plenty of excellent skiing outside of the basin, as well. Notable venues include Kirkwood to the south, Crystal Basin and Donner Summit to the west, and the Plumas and Lakes Basin areas to the north. Also, between Truckee and the North Shore of the lake are several "hidden" trail systems, less well-known routes to destinations such as Martis Peak or along the backbone of mountains framing the North Shore.

Every area has its own unique charm. You can stride or skate in open meadows, explore secluded valleys that seem miles from nowhere but are quite close to civilization, climb to scenic overlooks of frosted peaks and plunging canyons, or follow meandering mountain streams through aspen and pine forest to frozen alpine lakes. Enjoying an outdoor picnic lunch on a huge granite outcropping, with a million-dollar view before you and a warm midday sun above, is one of the great pleasures of backcountry skiing. The more adventurous can even sign up for full moon tours or overnight snow-camping.

Considering the prodigious amounts of snow that can blanket the Sierra, there are several caveats to be aware of. One is that after a storm the usually high moisture content of the snow can create avalanche hazards on many steep slopes. If you're venturing into the high country on trails that are not patrolled, or are cutting your own tracks, contact the local office of the U.S. Forest Service for the latest information on avalanche conditions. Outside of the developed areas, it's not wise to travel alone. Even when skiing with a friend, tell someone where you're going and when you expect to return. More than one skier has been caught in a sudden change of weather and become lost or disoriented. Carry a fannypack or knapsack with extra food and liquids, and have sufficient layers of clothing to survive lower temperatures.

Another consideration when taking Forest Service trails is that they are minimally signed, or sometimes lack signs altogether. If you are not familiar with orienteering—using a compass and USGS topo maps—then don't venture out on unmarked routes. Wherever you go, be especially careful in crossing streams or skiing on ice-covered lakes; if you are uncertain about your footing, use an alternate route. Remember that snow conditions are constantly changing. Consider also your altitude, your physical conditioning and the dangers of hypothermia.

One final note: Many cross-country areas recently have begun offering snowshoe rentals, so even non-skiers now have the chance to explore the backcountry. Snowshoes are noted in the listing when they are available. (For more on snowshoeing in the Tahoe region, see page 446 in Chapter 16, "Snowmobiling, Sleigh Rides & Other Winter Activities.")

*Note: All prices are based on the 1994-95 season, and may be subject to change.*

# CROSS-COUNTRY SKI RESORTS
## ★ Eagle Mountain Nordic ★
★ *notes Author's Choice*
*See number 1 on map, page 396*

*Location:* One mile off Interstate 80 about 30 minutes west of Truckee. Take the Yuba Gap exit and head south. The base elevation, at 5,800 feet, is the lowest of any Nordic area in the Tahoe region.

*Kilometers of track:* 75K of groomed track.

*Types of trails:* 25 ski trails and skating lanes (25 percent beginner, 45 percent intermediate and 30 percent advanced).

*Trail pass fee:* Adults, $15 (all day) and $12 (after 1 p.m.); children (7 to 12) and seniors (65 and over), $10. Children 6 and under ski free. Open 9 a.m. to 5 p.m. (trails close at 4:30 p.m.). Closed Christmas Day.

*Description:* Step into the stunningly beautiful log day lodge and you immediately feel the warmth that owner Gene West has imparted to this Nordic area. The lodge, surrounded by a huge wooden deck, is attractively furnished with Native American handicrafts and a large wood-burning stove, and it overlooks a meadow of aspens and the start of an extensive trail system. West, a Hollywood model and actor, has made special efforts to create a family environment here. The gentle base trails, including Meadowlark, a 1.8-kilometer loop, have a great comfort level for youngsters, and even non-skiing adults can join them on snowshoes. For intermediate and advanced skiers, an extensive system that partially follows the Mormon-Emigrant Trail affords sweeping views of Yuba Gap, especially from the top of Eagle Mountain (elevation 6,140 feet), which is 340 feet above the lodge. A more ambitious trek, with steady elevation gain, climbs to Cisco Butte, a rocky promontory with a telephone tower and 360-degree views of the surrounding mountains, including Castle Peak, Devil's Peak, Red Mountain, Donner Pass and even the distant Sacramento Valley. Trails skirt close to two frozen lakes, Kelly and Snowflower.

*Warming huts, day lodge:* Two warming huts, one day lodge.

*Services:* Cafe in the day lodge, rentals and lessons.

*Rental packages:* Striding, telemark and skating skis, boot and poles, and snowshoes available.

*Instruction:* Groups, $18 per person; private, $25, $15 for each additional person. Minimum age: 7 years old.

*Major events of the year:* 5-10K Snowshoe Race (January) and Full Moon Ski Tour every month (with dinner, live entertainment and bonfire), $20; annual National Off-Road Bicycle Association (NORBA) Winter Nationals (mountain bikes on snow).

*Special programs:* Packages of lessons, ski rentals and trail passes for adults, $35; discounted group and school rates available. Snowshoe tours weekly.

**Information:** Eagle Mountain Nordic, 15250 Ventura Boulevard, Suite 710, Sherman Oaks, CA 91403; (800) 391-2254 or (916) 389-2254.

## ★ Royal Gorge Cross Country Ski Resort ★
See number 2 on map, page 396

**Location:** Take the Soda Springs/Norden exit off Interstate 80 on Donner Summit. The Van Norden Trailhead is one mile east on Old Highway 40, and the Summit Station is another three-quarters of a mile beyond. Follow well-marked signs.

**Kilometers of track:** 328K of groomed, set track on 9,172 acres.

**Types of trails:** Striding, skating and telemark skiing on 88 trails (16 advanced, 44 intermediate and 28 beginner), with elevations ranging from 5,800 feet to 7,538 feet. There are four surface lifts for telemark and downhill skiing on cross-country micro-skis.

**Trail pass fee:** Adults, $19.50 on weekends, $16.50 on weekdays; children (ages 7 to 14), $8.50; children under 7 ski free.

**Description:** Perched on snowy Donner Summit, this is North America's largest cross-country ski area, and it has just about everything you could want: an immaculate trail system that is revitalized daily with a fleet of snow-grooming machines; an extensive network of warming huts; a backcountry overnight wilderness lodge, unique among U.S. Nordic ski areas, which serves gourmet meals; four surface lifts that form something of a mini downhill ski area served by a large day lodge with a restaurant and sundeck; and rental equipment that is always on the cutting edge of technology. John Slouber, the owner of Royal Gorge, has created not only the ultimate cross-country resort, but one of the great winter resorts of the world. A former downhill racer who was educated in France, Slouber is one of the sport's most persistent innovators, and his standards for client service are the highest in the industry. Apart from the physical layout of the resort, what stands out is the quality of the staff, consisting of amiable and helpful young people from Australia, New Zealand, South Africa and Europe, who give Royal Gorge a true international flavor.

Guests who stay a week in the Wilderness Lodge are treated to sumptuous French-style buffets for breakfast and lunch, and a full-course dinner with table service and wine. The lodge, an old hunting retreat built in the late 1800s, is not exactly a luxury hotel; there are private bedrooms with bunks, but toilets are shared and all shower facilities are located outside in a separate building. If you can deal with these minor inconveniences, you'll enjoy the meals and the posh, knotty-pine sitting room with its big, overstuffed couches, wood-burning heaters and vast library of books and games. (Guests who want more deluxe accommodations can stay at Rainbow Lodge, also owned by Royal Gorge, which is described on page 539 in Chapter 21, "Bed & Breakfasts & Other Unique Inns.")

Royal Gorge has eight track systems, and it would take more than a week for most skiers to explore them all. The best beginner terrain is at Lake Van Norden, a wide-open area with a shallow, frozen lake and no substantial elevation changes. Additional low-impact terrain weaves through dense forest from Summit Station (the main day lodge and parking area) to the Wilderness Lodge, but there are few vistas from these trails, and some of them parallel a not-very-scenic powerline. To see the spectacular sights, you've got to be a strong intermediate skier—or better—and spend most of a day on the trails. A moderately strenuous but recommended intermediate route of 16 kilometers round-trip is to the base of Devil's Peak (elevation 7,704 feet), a jagged, dramatic uplift whose walls rise abruptly from an open meadow. There's a warming hut here from which you can admire the view. More difficult, with steeper ups and downs, is the track to Point Mariah in the Palisade Peak System. Those who make it (an all-day trip of 22 kilometers round-trip from Summit Station) get a bird's-eye view of the awesome Royal Gorge, which plunges 4,417 feet down sheer granite cliffs to the South Fork of the American River. Over on the Ice Lakes Track System, the adrenaline rush is along a new expert trail called Razorback, which follows a narrow ridgeline that overlooks Serene Lakes on the north and a steep drop-off to the south. Several trails connect with the Sugar Bowl ski area at one end of the system, and with Rainbow Lodge (12 kilometers from the Wilderness Lodge) at the other end, making it possible to do an inn-to-inn ski tour of several days.

***Facilities:*** Two overnight lodges, one day lodge, four trailside cafes and 10 warming huts.

***Services:*** Snowmaking, private or group lessons, tours, video clinics, telemark or skating clinics, rentals, sleigh rides, children's snow school and skiable disability program.

***Rental packages:*** Micro-skis with boots and bindings, skating skis with bindings, high-performance and demos skis, and snowshoes available.

***Instruction:*** Learn-to-ski packages for adults, $39 (including rentals, group lesson and trail pass). Pee-Wee Snow School (ages 4 to 8), $42 all day (including rentals, trail pass, supervision, lesson and lunch).

***Transportation:*** A free shuttle bus runs daily between Rainbow and Summit Station for Rainbow guests and skiers on the Interconnect Trail. Limousine service is available from and to Reno-Tahoe International Airport.

***Major events of the year:*** Flying Kilometer Race (December) and Emigrant Trail Tour (February).

***Special programs:*** Participant in the Tahoe North Visitors & Conven-

tion Bureau's Cross-Country Interchangeable Trail Pass.
*Information:* Royal Gorge Cross Country Ski Resort, 9411 Hillside
Drive, P.O. Box 1100, Soda Springs, CA 95728; (916) 426-3871.

## Clair Tappaan Lodge
*See number 3 on map, page 396*

*Location:* On Old Highway 40 off the Soda Springs/Norden exit of
Interstate 80.
*Kilometers of track:* 10K of machine-groomed trails (60 percent
beginner, 40 percent intermediate).
*Types of trails:* Striding trails, telemark area and one skating lane,
through mixed forest, meadows and ridges.
*Trail pass fee:* Adults, $5; children (12 and under), $2.50.
*Description:* This modest track system winds through the Donner Pass
area behind the Sierra Club lodge, and nudges close to the adjacent
Donner Ski Ranch alpine ski area. The terrain is mostly scattered forest
and open meadow. The snowy summit has some of the most dependable
snow cover in the Sierra, and is especially ideal for spring.
*Warming huts, day lodge:* One overnight lodge.
*Services:* The lodge is owned by the Sierra Club, but is open to non-
members as well as members.
*Rental packages:* Striding, telemark and skating skis, bindings and
boots, and snowshoes available.
*Instruction:* Offered daily except Friday. Group lessons, $14 for two
hours; private, $25 per hour.
*Transportation:* A free shuttle runs to the Royal Gorge and Norden
area, via Sugar Bowl ski area buses.
*Special programs:* Discounts for midweek groups.
*Information:* Clair Tappaan Lodge, P.O. Box 36, Norden, CA 95724;
(916) 426-3632.

## ★ Tahoe Donner Cross-Country ★
*See number 4 on map, page 396*

*Location:* Five minutes north of Truckee. Take the Donner Memorial
State Park exit from Interstate 80. Drive one-half mile east on Donner
Pass Road to the bottom of Northwoods Boulevard. Turn left onto
Northwoods and follow the signs to the cross-country center, about three
miles from the turnoff.
*Kilometers of track:* 70K of machine-groomed track.
*Types of trails:* Skating lanes with 33 trails (30 percent beginner, 40
percent intermediate and 30 percent advanced).
*Trail pass fee:* Adults, $14; teens (ages 13 to 17) and seniors (60 to 69),
$12; children (ages 7 to 12), $9.

**Description:** Despite the fact that this sizeable ski area originates in a populated residential community above Truckee, the trail system allows for a blissful escape from civilization—especially in the isolated and remarkably beautiful Euer Valley, located three kilometers north of the lodge. Although this pristine valley is just 100 feet below the plateau that supports the cross-country center, it might as well be another world. In summer the Circle E Ranch, owned by descendants of a pioneer family, uses the lush meadow for grazing cattle, but in winter it becomes a wonderful tour route for beginning- and intermediate-level skiers. Trails parallel the South Fork of Prosser Creek and pass some rustic line cabins and barns. The entire valley is surrounded by several major peaks, including Castle (elevation 9,103 feet), Red Mountain (elevation 7,900 feet) and Prosser Hill (elevation 7,171 feet). A good, easy tour route is Last Round-up, a 4.9-kilometer loop from the lodge. Once in the valley, you can stay there all day, since a large warming hut, the Euer Valley Cookhouse, provides full food and beverage service on weekends and complimentary, self-service hot tea and spring water during weekdays. But if you can tear yourself away from here, another, larger system of trails called Home Range meanders through aspen groves and scattered pine, and offers a large meadow for beginners in front of the lodge. For the best views, intermediates and experts can climb for six kilometers along Hawk's Peak to the top of Sunrise Bowl, which sits on Donner Ridge at 7,800 feet (a 1,100-foot elevation gain from the base area). Here you'll find another warming hut, with southwest-facing vistas of Donner Summit and Castle Peak. The entire ski area is groomed and managed well, with special features like the excellent homemade goodies at the Donner Party Cafe, a fully-stocked equipment rental department and a myriad of programs for kids. The Tiny Tracks Snow School is something of a signature for the Nordic center, which has an Old West Kiddie Corral and weekend instruction for youngsters ages five to nine in all aspects of ski technique.

**Warming huts, day lodge:** Two trail warming huts, one cookhouse/ warming hut and one day lodge.

**Services:** Half-day and multi-day trail passes, twilight, night skiing, lessons, rental equipment and the Tiny Tracks Snow School.

**Rental packages:** Striding and skating skis, demos and snowshoes available.

**Instruction:** Group learn-to-ski, $34 (including trail pass, lesson and rental); and Tiny Tracks Ski School for children (ages 5 to 9), $25 (including trail fee, lesson and rental).

**Major events of the year:** Tahoe Donner President's Cup (February) and Tour D'Euer (March).

**Special programs:** Participant in Tahoe North Visitors & Convention Bureau's Cross-Country Interchangeable Trail Pass.

*Information:* Tahoe Donner Cross-Country, 15275 Alder Creek Road, P.O. Box 758, Truckee, CA 96160; (916) 587-9484.

## Alpine Skills International
*See number 5 on map, page 396*

*Location:* Off Old Highway 40, at the Soda Springs/Norden exit of Interstate 80, on the top of Donner Summit.
*Kilometers of track:* None.
*Types of trails:* Backcountry mountaineering routes only.
*Trail pass fee:* None.
*Description:* This is basically a ski mountaineering program, with no organized trail system. Tours are made daily on Donner Summit and near the Sugar Bowl ski area. There are great views of Donner Lake from many routes. The program's overnight lodge is set near trail systems at Royal Gorge, Clair Tappaan and Donner Summit.
*Warming huts, day lodge:* One day lodge, no huts.
*Services:* Tours, telemark lessons (on Forest Service lands, by special arrangement with Tahoe National Forest) and overnight accommodations.
*Rental packages:* Backcountry rentals (skis, boots and poles), telemark skis and snowshoes available.
*Instruction:* Telemark and backcountry group lessons, $45.
*Special programs:* Weekend packages with lodging, lessons and meals for $198 (telemark) and $188 (backcountry).
*Information:* Alpine Skills International, P.O. Box 8, Norden, CA 95724; (916) 426-9108.

## ★ Northstar-at-Tahoe Cross-Country Center ★
*See number 6 on map, page 396*

*Location:* Eight miles south of Truckee at the Northstar-at-Tahoe resort, on Northstar Drive, off Highway 267.
*Kilometers of track:* 65K of groomed track.
*Types of trails:* Skating lanes with 38 trails (30 percent beginner, 40 percent intermediate and 30 percent advanced). Lift access is only via the Big Springs Express Gondola and Echo Triple Chair.
*Trail pass fee:* Adults, $15; children, $8.
*Description:* The cross-country area here is integrated with the downhill ski area, and a lot of Nordic skiers feel that the parking, lift access and crowds are too much of a hassle to deal with. That's a shame, since the trail system escapes the alpinists and affords tranquility and wonderful views of Lake Tahoe and Martis Valley. There's also a unique warming hut—an old railroad caboose at Sawmill Flat. The area is divided into three trail systems, all of them beginning at the cross-country day lodge within walking distance of the mid-mountain alpine lodge. You'll have to

board the Big Springs Express Gondola or the Echo Triple Chair from Northstar Village to reach this point. From there, you can explore the Big Springs network, mostly beginner and intermediate trails, with great views of Martis Valley. An easy to intermediate outing connects the Holiday and Picnic trails, about a 4.3-kilometer loop that circles through forest but has several open vista points, some of them with picnic tables. You can make a longer tour (9.6 kilometers round-trip) by taking the Schaffer's Camp Trail to the second trail system, which is an out-and-back route with a warming hut at the end. On the east side of the resort, Sawmill Flat has the greatest variety of trails, as well as the best view of Lake Tahoe, along the Tahoe beginner trail. From the Nordic lodge, this vantage point is about four kilometers, and a lot of skiers choose this for their lunch stop. A good halfway rest point is the caboose, a novel but effective warming hut located in an open meadow. Although it's necessary to wade through the parking and lift system with alpine skiers, all three of the trail systems are well away from the lifts and there is no feeling of commingling on the hill. Also, Northstar's variety of on-the-hill lodging (condos and a motel) make access to the trails a matter of walking out your door in the morning.

***Warming huts, day lodge:*** Two warming huts, one day lodge.

***Services:*** Rentals, lessons and tours.

***Rental packages:*** Striding, skating and telemark skis, boots and bindings, and snowshoes available.

***Instruction:*** Group lesson, $20; private lessons, $35 per hour, $20 for each additional person. Children's lessons: Minors' Camp (ages 2 through 6), $51 with lesson and rentals; Star Kids (ages 5 to 12), $65.

***Transportation:*** Free shuttles run from Truckee and all points within Northstar.

***Major events of the year:*** Telebration and Annual Telemark Race (January) and Guided Backcountry Tour (April).

***Special programs:*** Participant in Tahoe North Visitors & Convention Bureau's Cross-Country Interchangeable Trail Pass.

***Information:*** Northstar-at-Tahoe Cross-Country Center, P.O. Box 2499, Truckee, CA 96160; (916) 562-2475 or (800) 533-6787 for reservations.

## ★ The Resort at Squaw Creek ★ Cross-Country Ski Center

*See number 7 on map, page 396*

***Location:*** At The Resort at Squaw Creek, in Squaw Valley. From Truckee, drive 10 miles south on Highway 89 and turn right into the main Squaw Valley parking lot. Continue one-third of a mile; the Squaw Valley Cross-Country Center is on the left.

***Kilometers of track:*** 20K of groomed track.

***Types of trails:*** Striding and skating lanes with 11 trails (60 percent beginner, 25 percent intermediate and 15 percent advanced).

***Trail pass fee:*** Adults, $12; children and seniors, $10.

***Description:*** If you're looking for a trail system that is easy on the body, look no further. You won't find much difficult terrain here. Most of the trails, named after Olympic venues such as Cortina and Grenoble, are on the golf course and the adjacent meadow fronting the palatial Resort at Squaw Creek. There are three intermediate trails with modest ups and downs, and two advanced trails that extend up the hill behind the hotel. This is a good area for novice and senior skiers, and the vista of Squaw Valley and its massive peaks provides pleasant surroundings.

***Facilities:*** No warming huts; all facilities at the hotel ski shop.

***Services:*** Twilight skiing, private or group lessons, rentals and retail store.

***Rental packages:*** Standard, upgraded recreation and high-performance demo skis, boots and poles available.

***Instruction:*** Group striding, $30; package, $35 (including complete rental, lesson, trail pass). Private lessons, including skating and telemarking, $35.

***Special programs:*** Participant in the Tahoe North Visitors & Convention Bureau's Cross-Country Interchangeable Trail Pass.

***Information:*** The Resort at Squaw Creek Cross-Country Ski Center, 400 Squaw Creek Road, P.O. Box 3333, Olympic Valley, CA 96146; (916) 583-6300.

## ★ Lakeview Cross-Country Ski Area ★
*See number 8 on map, page 396*

***Location:*** The route to get here passes through a residential area above Highway 28, two miles east of Tahoe City. Look for a small sign on the highway, or for the Shell Station at Dollar Hill. If you're headed east, turn left at Fabian Way, then right on Village Drive. Go around the corner, turn left at Country Club Drive, and the ski area day lodge is on the left.

***Kilometers of track:*** 65K of machine-set track.

***Types of trails:*** 17 trails (30 percent beginner, 40 percent intermediate and 30 percent advanced).

***Trail pass fee:*** Adults, $13; children, $5.

***Description:*** This is the closest major cross-country center to Tahoe City, and it is surprisingly large and scenic considering its out-of-sight venue. The trail network, with both skating and striding lanes, has been here for 18 years, and is well known to the mountain bike set. Most of the trails meander below Mount Watson (elevation 8,424 feet), one of the highest points on the North Shore. They range from aspen- and pine-fringed avenues to meadows and high ridges, and some of the property includes Burton Creek State Park, a protected wildlife sanctuary. The most scenic trail is Eagleview, rated intermediate, which has a moderate uphill grade to a short but sweeping view of Lake Tahoe; the lookout point is about four kilometers from the lodge. On the west side of the ski area, Red Tail, another intermediate loop, is a mostly open hill with striking vistas of Mount Watson. For experts, the Great Ski Race Trail, used for an annual race between Truckee and Tahoe City, will test your stamina. Area operator Mike Wolterbeek, a longtime member of the Tahoe Nordic Search and Rescue Team, has completely refurbished the rental shop and snack bar. Track is machine-set by snow groomers on a daily basis.

*Warming huts, day lodge:* One warming hut, one day lodge/cafe.

*Services:* Moonlight tours.

*Rental packages:* Striding and skating skis, boots and bindings available.

*Instruction:* Striding and skating group lessons, $15; private, $25.

*Major event of the year:* The Great Ski Race (March) from Truckee to Tahoe City.

*Special programs:* Participant in Tahoe North Visitors & Convention Bureau's Cross-Country Interchangeable Trail Pass.

*Information:* Lakeview Cross-Country Ski Area, P.O. Box 1926, Tahoe City, CA 96145; (916) 583-9353.

## Granlibakken Resort
*See number 9 on map, page 396*

*Location:* At the end of Granlibakken Road off Highway 89, one-half mile south of Tahoe City.

*Kilometers of track:* 7.5K, primarily on one trail.

*Types of trails:* No set track, but the first 1.5 miles are packed with a snow groomer, with the remaining 1.5 miles to Page Meadows ski-set (25 percent beginner, 75 percent intermediate). There is one poma chairlift.

*Trail pass fee:* None.

*Description:* This is one of Tahoe's great, off-the-beaten-path cross-country ski treks. Granlibakken is a secluded, all-seasons resort of clustered condominiums that has one of Tahoe's original downhill ski areas. From the top of the poma lift you can follow a fire road uphill for one mile to Lookout Point, with its view of Lake Tahoe, and for another two miles to Page Meadows, for a round-trip of six miles. Or you can take a longer route from the ski hut at the downhill area along a path that reaches the fire road farther east, via a short but substantial uphill climb. None of these trails is maintained, and there are no signs at all in Page Meadows.

*Facilities:* One warming hut at the ski hill.

*Services:* None.

*Rental packages:* Striding and skating skis, boots and bindings available.

*Instruction:* None.
*Special programs:* None.
*Information:* Granlibakken Resort, P.O. Box 6329, Tahoe City, CA 96145; (916) 583-9896.

## Camp Richardson Cross-Country Ski Center
*See number 10 on map, page 396*

*Location:* At Richardson's Resort on Emerald Bay Road (Highway 89), two miles north of the "Y" intersection of Highway 89 and US 50.
*Kilometers of track:* 18K of groomed track; other routes tracked out by skiers.
*Types of trails:* Striding area next to the West Shore of Lake Tahoe or through the woods to Fallen Leaf Lake Road and Taylor Creek.
*Trail pass fee:* None.
*Description:* This is a small operation, but it offers the only organized cross-country skiing that is actually on the shores of Lake Tahoe; in fact, you can ski on a snow-covered beach next to the Beacon Restaurant and Camp Richardson cabins, although trails are not set or marked. The main system is behind the shop (across the road from the resort), and extends to Fallen Leaf Lake Road, which is unplowed in winter and offers additional ski routes. You can also ski up to Taylor Creek and take the marked Forest Service trails from there to the east shore of Fallen Leaf Lake. As a new operation, the emphasis of the center is on beginners and families, and the trail system is expected to expand in the coming years.
*Facilities:* Rental shop across the road from the Camp Richardson main lodge, which stays open all year.
*Services:* Overnight lodging, rentals and meals at the Beacon Restaurant, on the beach, which serves lunch and dinner.
*Rental packages:* Skis, boots, bindings and poles available.
*Instruction:* Lessons by advance arrangement near the shop; cost is $10 for the first half hour with two people, $5 for each additional half hour.
*Special programs:* Friday night ski tour along the beach with bonfire and entertainment, weather permitting; call for details.
*Information:* Camp Richardson Cross-Country Ski Center, Highway 89, P.O. Box 9028, South Lake Tahoe, CA 96158; (916) 541-1801.

## ★ Kirkwood Cross-Country Center ★
*See number 11 on map, page 396*

*Location:* On Highway 88 at Kirkwood Meadows, next to Kirkwood Inn.
*Kilometers of track:* 80K of machine-groomed track.
*Types of trails:* Skating lane with three interconnected trail systems (20 percent beginner, 60 percent intermediate and 20 percent advanced).
*Trail pass fee:* Adults, $13; children, $7; seniors, $9.

**Description:** This is one of the largest and best-maintained cross-country resorts in the region, with unique topography that includes lava rock buttes, sloping tiers of granite boulders, and picturesque views of Caples Lake and Little Round Top Mountain. Kirkwood is a must for any visiting Nordic skier. There are three separate trail systems, each with its own attractions, but all of them, except for three trails, are negotiable by intermediates. Most of the gentle beginners' trails are in Kirkwood Meadows, from the base of the downhill ski area to Highway 88, a distance of five kilometers. This is open, flat terrain bordered by condominiums and houses. Across the road, next to the large cross-country center, a vast, unseen intermediates' Mecca drops down into a valley and extends through the woods, crossing Caples Creek several times. This area includes a Kiddies' Kilometer, festooned with wooden wildlife figures. It also includes the scenic High Trail, which rises back to the ridgeline for a view of the lower drainage. The system here offers loop trails ranging from 1K to 5K, some interesting rock formations, and two of the three expert trails (Agony and Ecstasy), which ascend steep slopes to connect with the upper trail system. That system, called Schneider, can be reached more easily by driving two miles east on Highway 88 and turning north on Schneider Cow Camp Road to a parking lot. From here, there's another large beginner network, on the lower trails, and a labyrinth of intermediate trails that eventually lead to Coyote Pass, the route used for the annual Echo Summit to Kirkwood Cross-Country Race. The most scenic trails are Lower and Upper Outpost, flanked on one side by bizarre lava buttes and on the other by a stunning panorama of Caples Lake and peaks of the Mokelumne Wilderness. Because the intermediate trails are generally above the treeline, or are sparsely vegetated, there are almost uninterrupted views. Kirkwood provides meticulously groomed and machine-set trails, as well as an excellent staff of instructors managed by Debbie Waldear, a former Olympic contender who exemplifies the best in the sport. Not surprisingly, the area is a favorite of Tahoe residents.

**Warming huts, day lodge:** Three warming huts, two lodges.

**Services:** Restaurant/bar, lessons, rentals and tours.

**Rental packages:** Striding, skating and telemark gear, and snowshoes available.

**Instruction:** Group lesson (striding, skating or telemark), $15, $30 for lesson, rentals and trail pass. Private lesson, $25 per hour, $15 for each additional person.

**Major events of the year:** Rossignol/Kirkwood 20K Race (January), Echo Summit to Kirkwood Cross-Country Race (March) and Telemark Clinic (March).

**Special programs:** Two-day, one-night backcountry ski/camping tours with community tent, including one dinner and one breakfast, for $105.

**Information:** Kirkwood Cross-Country Center, Highway 88, P.O. Box 1, Kirkwood, CA 95646; (209) 258-7248 and (800) 967-7500 for reservations.

## Hope Valley Cross-Country Ski Center
*See number 12 on map, page 396*

**Location:** At Sorensen's Resort, located on Highway 88 just west of the intersection with Highway 89.

**Kilometers of track:** 60 kilometers of marked trails (10 kilometers groomed).

**Types of trails:** Striding and telemark.

**Trail pass fee:** None.

**Description:** Hope Valley, in Toiyabe National Forest, is an idyllic place with beautiful frozen lakes and distant vistas of Carson Pass and its prodigious peaks. Operator Steve Lannoy runs a small cross-country program out of historic Sorensen's Resort, where one of the trails (Indian Head) originates. Most skiers, however, will need to drive to one of seven other trailheads. The closest is the Burnside Lake Trail, where a large flat serves as the teaching area and the starting point for a 14-mile round-trip to the lake, which is at the end of a wide Forest Service road. But a less ambitious loop of five or six miles, mostly on machine-set track, can be made on the Sawmill Trail, which branches off from Burnside. Stronger skiers who continue on will get dramatic views from Sweet Vista, which overlooks Stevens Peak (elevation 10,061 feet) and Red Lake Peak (elevation 10,061 feet) to the west, as well as the drainage for the West Fork of the Carson River. Other good trails are north on Highway 89, not far from its intersection with Highway 88. There's a good beginner trek on the south side of Grass Lake, with flat but scenic terrain through ponderosa and Jeffrey pine. The best views of Hope Valley are from the Willow Creek Trail, a five-mile, out-and-back, intermediate track that branches eastward from Highway 89, and from the Snowshoe Thompson Trail, a meandering six-mile trail from Luther Pass to the highway intersection. The modest Nordic center at Sorensen's has a full-service rental and instruction program. Most of the trails do not have machine-set track, so skiers will have to cut their own after new snow. There are no skating lanes on trails. Trail systems on Forest Service lands are open to other winter uses, including snowmobiling.

**Warming huts, day lodge:** One day lodge, no warming huts.

**Services:** Overnight lodging, sauna, cafe, rentals, lessons and tours.

**Rental packages:** Striding, Europa telemark skis, demos and snowshoes available.

**Instruction:** Group striding lessons (1.5-hour session), $26 (including equipment); private lessons, $25, $20 for each additional person (including both striding and telemark techniques).

***Major event of the year:*** Indian Head Challenge Tour (February).
***Special programs:*** Guided wildlife and moonlight tours and back-country skills seminars.
***Information:*** Sorensen's Resort, 14255 Highway 88, Hope Valley, CA 96120; (916) 694-2203.

## ★ Spooner Lake ★
*See number 13 on map, page 396*

***Location:*** The closest major cross-country area to South Lake Tahoe, 12 miles from the Stateline casinos on the Nevada side of the lake. It is located just north of the junction of US 50 and Highway 28, at the parking lot for Lake Tahoe-Nevada State Park. Incline Village is 12 miles north.
***Kilometers of track:*** 91K of machine-groomed track.
***Types of trails:*** 21 trails (30 percent beginner, 40 percent intermediate, 30 percent advanced).
***Trail pass fee:*** Weekends: Adults, $10; children (7 and over), $8. Weekdays: Adults, $5; children, $3. Seniors (over 70) and children (6 and under) ski free.
***Description:*** Relatively undiscovered, Spooner Lake is one of the gems of Lake Tahoe, even though passersby can see little more than a modest trail system that encircles a frozen, snow-covered lake. Ah, but what you see is only a fraction of what there is. For intermediate to expert skiers, this is one of the most spectacular trail systems anywhere. The route to the high-country trails around Snow Pass climbs gradually along a drainage fringed with aspen and pine forest, leading to three challenging routes: Marlette Lake, 9.7 kilometers from the lodge; the Carson Range Trail, a 20-kilometer loop from Marlette Lake with plenty of steep climbs; and the Bear Mountain Loop, 13.2 kilometers from the lodge. All three are expert routes, and they reward you with some of the best vistas of Tahoe, especially Bear Mountain, where a high trail comes close to the lake. The trail to Snow Pass is the same one used by mountain bikers in the summer to reach the famous Flume Trail, which begins just northwest of Marlette Lake. In winter, the Flume Trail is closed, even to skiers. As it happens, Max Jones, the man who made the Flume Trail famous, operates the cross-country area, most of which is in Lake Tahoe-Nevada State Park. Although strong Nordic skiers thrive on the higher trails, the flat loop around Spooner Lake is a very scenic 4.5-kilometer tour. Most of the trails throughout the 8,000 acres of terrain are buffed daily with a large snow-grooming machine.
***Warming huts, day lodge:*** One warming hut, one day lodge.
***Services:*** Full moon guided ski tours, snack service, lessons and rentals.
***Rental packages:*** Skis, boots and bindings, and snowshoes available. Kids 6 and under get free rentals.

**Instruction:** Adults, $14; students, $12; children, $10. Ski skating lessons: Adults, $16; students, $14.

**Special programs:** Participant in Tahoe North Visitors & Convention Bureau's Cross-Country Interchangeable Trail Pass.

**Information:** Spooner Lake, P.O. Box 11, Glenbrook, NV 89413; (702) 887-8844 or (702) 749-5349.

## ★ Diamond Peak Cross-Country ★
*See number 14 on map, page 396*

**Location:** Five miles up Mount Rose Highway (Highway 431) from Highway 28 in Incline Village. The area, situated on the right side of the road, is easy to miss, since the trailhead and mobile home used for the day lodge are set off the highway. Parking is at a wide, roadside turnout west of the entrance, and there is a bit of a walk uphill to reach the center.

**Kilometers of track:** 35K of machine-groomed track.

**Types of trails:** 12 trails with skating lanes (20 percent beginner, 50 percent intermediate and 30 percent advanced).

**Trail pass fee:** Adults, $13; children (6 to 12) and seniors (60 to 69), $8. Children 5 and under and seniors 70 and over ski free.

**Description:** One of the most scenic trail networks in Tahoe, this area offers lofty views of the lake from its beginner and intermediate trails. In fact, nowhere around Tahoe can neophyte Nordic skiers reach such a spectacular vantage point. Take your camera and head out on the Vista View Trail, where you can make an easy trek to Knock Your Socks Off Rock, 1.5 kilometers from the trailhead. This is a granite promontory that provides a breathtaking panorama of Tahoe, and it has picnic tables for those who wish to spend some time here. The lake views continue a bit farther, along an intermediate loop called Rim O'Lake, and together the two trails offer a great 5K outing. Another good perspective, with a view of the associated downhill ski area, is from Diamond Peak, just off the Hawk's View Intermediate Trail. For expert skiers, there are steep ascents and descents off the Great Flume and Folsom Camp trails, which overlooks the site of a historic logging operation. Diamond Peak Cross-Country has a variety of terrain, ranging from heavy forest to open ridgelines and plateaus. It is also beautifully groomed, and there are skating as well as striding lanes. Even in lean winters, the snowpack usually is excellent because Diamond Peak has the highest elevation of any cross-country resort in the basin (8,500 feet to 9,200 feet). The area is operated by the Incline Village General Improvement District, which also runs the downhill ski resort.

**Warming huts, day lodge:** One warming hut at the cross-country center.

**Services:** Lessons, rentals, food and beverages.

*Rental packages:* Standard and demo skis, boots and bindings for touring and skating.

*Instruction:* Group striding, $22 (including lesson and trail pass); private (striding and skating), $27.

*Transportation:* A free shuttle service runs throughout Incline Village and Crystal Bay, but only on weekends and holidays to the cross-country area, and with only two departures per day.

*Major events of the year:* Host of 10K and 20K Nordic races (March) and the Folsom Camp Snowshoe Race (March).

*Special programs:* Participant in Tahoe North Visitors & Convention Bureau's Cross-Country Interchangeable Trail Pass.

*Information:* Diamond Peak Cross-Country, 1210 Ski Way, Incline Village, NV 89451; (702) 832-1177.

# OTHER TRAILS & PUBLIC CROSS-COUNTRY SKIING AREAS

The following trail descriptions are provided by several public agencies, including the U.S. Forest Service, California Department of Parks and Recreation, City of South Lake Tahoe and North Tahoe Public Utility District.

## Truckee/Donner

### Big Bend

*Level, terrain:* Beginner to intermediate. The slope is moderately steep; there are granite boulders and rock outcrops from the trailhead to the South Fork of the Yuba River.

*Mileage, elevation:* No set trails. 5,700 feet to 7,000 feet.

*Description:* Big Bend is a dispersed recreation area with no marked trails, which is open to all users. While the region is open to motorized vehicles such as snowmobiles, it is mainly used for skiing, snowshoeing and snow play. Elevation changes approximately 1,000 feet from canyon floor to ridgetop. The south slope of the canyon changes from granite to forested slope and back to granite at the top to the ridge. Users should consult Forest Service maps for road and trail locations and private land designation.

*Trailhead:* Parking is available at the Loch Leven Lakes Trailhead parking area. From Reno, take Interstate 80 about 45 miles west to the Big Bend exit. Turn left onto Hampshire Rocks Road and follow it one-quarter mile to the parking lot. Restrooms are available.

*Topographic maps:* Cisco Grove, Soda Springs.

*Information:* U.S. Forest Service, Tahoe National Forest, Truckee Ranger District, (916) 587-3558.

## Cabin Creek Trail

*Level, terrain:* Intermediate to advanced; gently rolling slopes.
*Mileage, elevation:* Nine-mile loop. 6,000 feet.
*Description:* A marked route follows along old logging roads and the Cabin Creek Road. It's a nice area for downhill practice while cross-country skiing. The trail is becoming popular among skiers; it also receives moderate snowmobile use.
*Trailhead:* From Interstate 80, take Highway 89 south three miles. Turn right onto Cabin Creek Road. The unmarked trailhead is one mile from Highway 89. There is limited parking in the road cut, when plowed.
*Topographic map:* Truckee.
*Information:* U.S. Forest Service, Tahoe National Forest, Truckee Ranger District, (916) 587-3558. Backcountry and avalanche information, (916) 587-2158.

## Donner Memorial State Park

*Level:* Beginner; gentle terrain.
*Mileage, elevation:* 2.5-mile loop; 6,000 feet.
*Description:* A flat, marked loop trail follows a campground access road around the southeast shoreline of Donner Lake, to Split Rock, and returns through the forest. The trail has groomed, machine-set track, but no skating lanes. It sees heavy weekend and moderate weekday use.
*Trailhead:* Southeast of the Donner Lake exit off Interstate 80. Parking is available at the Donner Memorial State Park Museum. A $3 Sno-Park permit is required and may be purchased at the park museum from 10 a.m. to 4 p.m. daily.
*Topographic map:* Truckee.
*Information:* California Department of Parks and Recreation, Donner Memorial State Park, (916) 582-7892.

## Peter Grubb Hut/Castle Peak/ Donner Summit

*Level, terrain:* Intermediate to advanced. There is a moderate upslope toward the hut and a difficult downhill over Castle Pass.
*Mileage, elevation:* Three miles one-way. 7,200 feet at trailhead; 7,800 feet at hut; 9,100 feet at Castle Peak.
*Description:* A marked Nordic ski trail begins at the Castle Peak/Boreal Interchange at Donner Summit and follows the summer road approximately one-quarter mile to an intersection. From this intersection, Nordic skiers can take the trail to the north, which continues up Castle Valley and over Castle Pass. From there, an unmarked trail continues on to the Peter Grubb Hut. For experienced skiers, more difficult routes continue on to Castle and Basin peaks. Make reservations to stay at the Peter Grubb Hut

through the Sierra Club at the Clair Tappaan Lodge at Norden; phone
(916) 426-3632 for details. This is a very popular skiing area. Snowmobiles are prohibited in Castle and Round valleys.
*Trailhead:* Along the north side of Interstate 80 at the Castle Peak
interchange. Sno-Park parking is available along the Boreal frontage road
south of the freeway. A $3 permit is required.
*Topographic maps:* Norden, Soda Springs.
*Information:* U.S. Forest Service, Tahoe National Forest, Truckee
Ranger District, (916) 587-3558. Backcountry and avalanche information,
(916) 587-2158.

## Pole Creek Trail System

*Level, terrain:* Beginner to very advanced.
*Mileage, elevation:* 11 miles one-way; 6,200 to 8,400.
*Description:* These unmarked trails follow Forest Service roads along
the Pole Creek and Silver Creek drainages. The area is a popular cross-
country skiing destination. Some loops offer downhill practice areas. It is
closed to snowmobiling.
*Trailhead:* Six miles south of Truckee on Highway 89. Some free parking is available on the west side of the road.
*Information:* U.S. Forest Service, Tahoe National Forest, Truckee
Ranger District, (916) 587-3558. Backcountry and avalanche information,
(916) 587-2158.

## Sagehen Summit

*Level, terrain:* Intermediate to advanced; there is a gradual incline.
*Mileage, elevation:* Five mile loop; 6,400 feet.
*Description:* This unmarked route follows a road up a creek bottom.
Lateral roads offer many side trips for the adventurous. Sagehen Campground (2.5 miles west of Highway 89) makes a good winter camp. Cross-
country skiing is popular in the area. The area is also used by snowmobilers; the route crosses a groomed snowmobile trail one-quarter mile
in from Highway 89.
*Trailhead:* At Sagehen Summit on the west side of Highway 89, eight
miles north of Truckee. There is limited parking for four to six vehicles
when the road is plowed.
*Topographic maps:* Hobart Mills, Independence Lake.
*Information:* U.S. Forest Service, Tahoe National Forest, Truckee
Ranger District; (916) 587-3558. Backcountry and avalanche information,
(916) 587-2158.

## Wheeler Loop

*Level, terrain:* Beginner; relatively flat area with open timber and marsh.
*Mileage, elevation:* Five-mile loop from Highway 89; 6,400 feet.

**Description:** This marked route follows a county road around the north side to Kyburz Flat. The open, flat area offers plenty of skiable terrain, and receives moderate use. The access from Highway 89 is County Road 450.

**Trailhead:** Drive 17 miles north of Truckee on Highway 89 to the marked trailhead. If you reach Jackson Meadow Road, you've gone one mile too far. Parking is difficult if the road shoulder has not been plowed. (Note: Cross-country skiing south of Kyburz Road from February 1 to July 15 is discouraged, because of waterfowl nesting in Kyburz Marsh.)

**Topographic maps:** Sardine Peak, Sierraville.

**Information:** U.S. Forest Service, Tahoe National Forest, Truckee Ranger District; (916) 587-3558.

# North Shore

## Martis Lookout Trail

**Level, terrain:** Advanced; a moderate climb to Martis Peak.

**Mileage, elevation:** Eight-mile loop. 7,200 feet at trailhead; 8,650 feet at Martis Peak.

**Description:** The unmarked route follows Martis Lookout Road to Martis Peak, with views of Lake Tahoe, the Sierra crest and Mount Rose. This is a very popular area, which can be a problem as there is only limited parking.

**Trailhead:** One-quarter mile north of Brockway Summit. A limited area adjacent to the highway is plowed for parking.

**Topographic map:** Martis Peak.

**Information:** U.S. Forest Service, Tahoe National Forest, Truckee Ranger District, (916) 587-3558.

## North Tahoe Regional Park

**Level, terrain:** Beginner to advanced.

**Mileage, elevation:** 17 miles of wide, multi-use trails. 6,000 feet to 6,600 feet.

**Description:** This 132-acre regional park, located above Tahoe Vista off Highway 28, is one of the bargains of cross-country skiing, if you don't mind the occasional rough edges and intermittent grooming. Although it is used mostly by skiers, it is shared with snowmobilers, since the trail is supported by the California Off-Highway-Vehicle Program (green sticker) fund. Parking is available for over 100 vehicles in a large lot and along the access road, and there are restrooms at the trailhead. An "iron ranger" self-pay system requires $3 for an all-day pass and $2 for a half day. Beginner trails afford some of the best views of Lake Tahoe, along the Lake View Trail. Intermediate routes go through dense forest and can actually be followed to Old Brockway at Kings Beach, next to the junction of highways 267 and 28. Advanced trails follow a high ridgeline with more views of the lake. Most are designed to be loop routes. The trails are patrolled on a part-time basis, and may have bare spots on lower elevations. A snowmobile concession operates from the park, and popular snowmobiling routes use the Fibreboard Freeway, which is accessed nearby from Brockway Summit on Highway 267.

*Trailhead:* From Truckee, take Highway 267 south to Kings Beach at Lake Tahoe. Turn west on Highway 28, right on National Avenue and follow signs for one mile to the park.

*Information:* North Tahoe Parks and Recreation, (916) 546-7248.

# East Shore

## Tahoe Meadows

*Level, terrain:* Beginner; gentle.

*Mileage, elevation:* No set trails; 7,000 feet.

*Description:* This is not only a great place to try moonlight skiing, but this fairly flat meadow also offers a great place to exercise. Snowmobiles are allowed.

*Trailhead:* From Incline Village, take Highway 28 to Mount Rose Highway (Highway 431). Just before the summit, where the road levels out, look for a large meadow to the right. Park in the turnout by the meadow.

*Information:* U.S. Forest Service, Toiyabe National Forest, Carson Ranger District, (702) 882-2766.

# West Shore

## Angora Road

*Level, terrain:* Advanced.

*Mileage, elevation:* Two miles to Angora Lookout, four miles to Angora Lakes. 7,200 feet to 7,470 feet.

*Description:* This trail provides some of the best available views of Lake Tahoe and Fallen Leaf Lake, but it's a steep grade at several points. Some snowmobiles are usually present. There's a lodge with cabins at the lakes, but they are open only during summer. Granite shorelines surround the lakes, which are frozen in winter.

*Trailhead:* Take Lake Tahoe Boulevard 2.5 miles south of the "Y" in South Lake Tahoe. Turn right on Tahoe Mountain Road and climb to the ridgetop. Turn right at the "T" intersection on Glenmore Way. Take an immediate left on Dundee Circle and another left on the next street. Park along the road. Ski or walk down the road and turn left on Forest

Service Road 12NI4. This road leads to Angora Lookout and up to Angora Lakes.

*Information:* U.S. Forest Service, Lake Tahoe Basin Management, (916) 573-2600.

## Blackwood Canyon Road

*Level, terrain:* Intermediate to advanced.

*Mileage, elevation:* 2.5 miles to the meadow, seven miles to Barker Pass. 6,200 feet to 7,680 feet.

*Description:* This unmarked road winds through Blackwood Canyon. Follow the road to an obvious junction and stay to the right. This path will lead you to a beautiful meadow where snowmobiles are not allowed. For a longer, more strenuous outing, continue upward to Barker Pass, where it meets the Pacific Crest Trail. There are some steep uphill climbs to get here, but at the top are views of the canyon and Lake Tahoe. Snowmobiles are allowed on this part of the trail.

*Trailhead:* Take Highway 89 three miles south of Tahoe City to Blackwood Canyon Road, across from the Kaspian Picnic Area. Continue to the Blackwood Canyon Sno-Park (a $3 permit is required) next to the highway.

*Information:* U.S. Forest Service, Lake Tahoe Basin Management Unit, (916) 573-2600.

## McKinney-Rubicon Springs Road

*Level, terrain:* Intermediate.

*Mileage, elevation:* Two miles to McKinney Lake, three miles to Lily Lake. 6,400 feet to 7,120 feet.

*Description:* Following the tree-lined road along McKinney Creek, this trail has a 700-foot elevation gain and is unmarked. The moderate path leads through forest to two lakes. Snowmobiles are allowed on some parts of the trail.

*Trailhead:* From Highway 89, south of Homewood, turn west onto McKinney-Rubicon Springs Road and drive one-quarter mile. Take the first left on Bellevue and drive one-quarter mile. Take the second right on McKinney Road (follow the signs to Miller Lake) and drive another quarter mile. Bear left on McKinney-Rubicon Springs Road. Go straight at the stop sign and park where the snowplowing ends. Parking is limited.

*Information:* U.S. Forest Service, Lake Tahoe Basin Management Unit, (916) 573-2600.

## Meeks Creek

*Level, terrain:* Beginner to intermediate.

*Mileage, elevation:* 3.5-mile loop. 6,200 feet.

*Description:* Follow an old logging road along Meeks Creek for 1.75

miles. You can ski the full loop by crossing the creek and following the road back to Highway 89. For some more exercise, try skiing the meadow. Use caution crossing snow bridges, as they may be weak. Snowmobiles are not allowed.

*Trailhead:* Drive 12 miles south on Highway 89 from Tahoe City. South of Homewood, parking is located along the highway one-quarter mile south of the Meeks Bay fire station or one-half mile north of Meeks Bay Campground.

*Information:* U.S. Forest Service, Lake Tahoe Basin Management Unit, (916) 573-2600.

## Page Meadows

*Level, terrain:* Beginner to low intermediate.

*Mileage, elevation:* No set trails. 6,400 feet.

*Description:* Page Meadows is mostly flat, surrounded by a scenic forest. The tricky part is to avoid getting lost since there are no signs or set track.

*Trailhead:* From Highway 89, two miles south of Tahoe City, turn right on Fountain Avenue, left on Tahoe Park Heights Drive, right on Big Pine Drive and left on Silvertip. Park along the street where the snowplowing ends. Parking is extremely limited. Ski down the road to the meadow. Snowmobiles are not allowed.

*Information:* U.S. Forest Service, Lake Tahoe Basin Management Unit, (916) 573-2600.

## Sugar Pine Point State Park

*Level, terrain:* Beginner to intermediate.

*Mileage, elevation:* Four marked trails totaling 8.3 miles. 6,400 feet.

*Description:* This expansive California state park, open all year (including the campground), stretches across both sides of Highway 89 and offers two distinct environments: one along General Creek in the forest near the campground, the other along the shoreline of Lake Tahoe on the grounds of Ehrman Mansion. The shortest route is the 1.1-mile Orange Trail and the longest is the 3.3-mile Red Trail. The easier routes are on the east side of the park. Park rangers groom all four trails, but on an irregular basis. There's a $5 day-use fee for each vehicle. Camping, with toilets but no showers, is available at $12 per day. No snowmobiles are allowed.

*Trailhead:* The park is located one mile south of Tahoma on Highway 89.

*Information:* California Department of Parks and Recreation, Sugar Pine Point State Park, (916) 525-7982.

## Tallac Historic Site Trail

*Level, terrain:* Beginner.

*Mileage, elevation:* Two-mile loop; 6,200 feet.

*Description:* This is a flat, marked trail that winds through historic estates just above the shore of Lake Tahoe. See great views of Mount Tallac. Rental equipment is available from Camp Richardson, next door.

*Trailhead:* Parking is located three miles north of South Lake Tahoe on Emerald Bay Road (Highway 89). A $3 Sno-Park permit is required for parking. This route can connect to the Taylor Creek Trail across the highway. Snowmobiles are not allowed.

*Information:* U.S. Forest Service, Lake Tahoe Basin Management Unit, (916) 573-2600.

## Taylor Creek

*Level, terrain:* Beginner to intermediate.

*Mileage, elevation:* Fallen Leaf Dam Trail, 2.5-mile loop; Fallen Leaf Campground, 2.5-mile loop; Sawmill Trail, two-mile loop. You can combine the dam and sawmill trails for a 4.5-mile loop. 6,200 feet.

*Description:* These flat ski trails are suitable for all skill levels of cross-country skiers. The loop trail traverses open meadows and aspen groves. At the dam and Sawmill Cove, there are views of Fallen Leaf Lake. The developed trails cover a large area. Although they are heavily used, they are not congested.

*Trailhead:* Take Highway 89 north from South Lake Tahoe approximately 3.5 miles to the Taylor Creek Sno-Park. A $3 Sno-Park permit is required. Snowmobiles are not allowed.

*Information:* U.S. Forest Service, Lake Tahoe Basin Management Unit, (916) 573-2600.

# South Shore

## Bijou Community Park

*Level, terrain:* Beginner to low intermediate.

*Mileage, elevation:* Four miles of machine-set track; 6,000 feet.

*Description:* This is the only cross-country ski area that is located in the center of South Lake Tahoe, and it is operated by the city's Parks and Recreation Department. The groomed trail system meanders through 154 acres of mostly flat meadow, with some hilly wooded areas. There is a skating lane as well as a striding track. A plowed parking lot and restrooms are available. There is no fee for the trails.

*Trailhead:* At the Bijou Community Park recreation complex, which is at the corner of Al Tahoe Boulevard and Johnson Street (off US 50 on Al Tahoe) in South Lake Tahoe.

*Information:* City of South Lake Tahoe, Parks and Recreation Department, Bijou Community Park, (916) 542-6055.

# Carson Pass/Highway 88

## Grass Lake

*Level, terrain:* Beginner.
*Mileage, elevation:* Three miles to Hope Valley; 7,000 feet.
*Description:* You can ski over a frozen bog surrounded by aspen groves. Unmarked paths lead to Hope Valley. Grass Lake is also popular for moonlight skiing.
*Trailhead:* Take Highway 89 south from South Lake Tahoe to Luther Pass and park in one of the plowed turnouts. Snowmobiles are not allowed.
*Information:* U.S. Forest Service, Lake Tahoe Basin Management Unit, (916) 573-2600.

## Hope Valley

*Level, terrain:* Beginner to intermediate.
*Mileage, elevation:* An open meadow area—no set trails. 7,000 feet.
*Description:* This large, flat meadow is surrounded by aspen and pine. Use caution crossing streams, as ice or snow bridges are usually weak.
*Trailhead:* Take Highway 89 south from South Lake Tahoe to Highway 88. Limited parking is available along the road near the Burnside Lake turnoff. Cross the road and ski the meadow northwest of the road. Snowmobiles are not allowed on land managed by the California Department of Fish and Game, but are allowed on Forest Service lands. Cross-country rental equipment and instruction are available at Sorensen's Resort, just east of the intersection.
*Information:* California Department of Fish and Game, (916) 355-0978. U.S. Forest Service, Lake Tahoe Basin Management Unit, (916) 573-2600.

## Winnemucca Lake Loop

*Level, terrain:* Intermediate to advanced.
*Mileage, elevation:* Six-mile loop. 7,900 to 8,650 feet.
*Description:* This trail climbs from Carson Pass to Winnemucca Lake, then descends to Woods Lake east of Caples Lake. From there, it follows the road from Woods Lake to the old highway, which it follows in a gentle grade back up to Carson Pass. This route provides a beautiful tour through the high Sierra. It is not recommended for beginners because of its length and steepness, but has several bowls that offer a great opportunity to try out your telemark turns. The trail is marked with X-C symbols, blue diamonds and pink flagging. Be aware of possible avalanche danger

along this trail near Round Top Peak.
***Trailhead:*** At Carson Pass on Highway 88, just west of Hope Valley and the Highway 88/89 junction.
***Information:*** U.S. Forest Service, Eldorado National Forest, Amador Ranger District, (209) 295-4251.

# Crystal Basin/US 50
## Trout Creek/Fountain Place
***Level, terrain:*** Advanced.
***Mileage, elevation:*** Six miles one-way. 6,400 feet to 7,720 feet.
***Description:*** This unmarked trail leads through a meadow and down an unplowed road. Snowmobiles are allowed. Ski two miles along Fountain Place Road to Trout Creek. Advanced skiers may continue on to Fountain Place, approximately four miles.
***Trailhead:*** From Meyers on US 50, turn right on the Pioneer Trail. Continue three-quarters of a mile to Oneidas Street and turn right. Park on Oneidas where the snow plowing stops.
***Information:*** U.S. Forest Service, Lake Tahoe Basin Management Unit, (916) 573-2600.

## Echo Lakes
***Level, terrain:*** Intermediate to advanced.
***Mileage, elevation:*** 2.5 miles to the northwest corner of Upper Echo; five miles to Lake Margery, and six miles to Lake Aloha. 7,420 feet to 7,470 feet (Echo Lakes only).
***Description:*** An unmarked, almost flat trail parallels the lakes before climbing in elevation to Desolation Wilderness. If you are planning a trip into the backcountry, be sure to check the avalanche danger and obtain a wilderness permit. Day-use permits are available at the trailhead; overnight users must register at the U.S. Forest Service office in South Lake Tahoe or at the Eldorado Information Center in Camino on US 50. Pick up the "Echo Lakes Cross-Country Skiing" brochure from the Forest Service office for additional information. Snowmobiles are not allowed.
***Trailhead:*** Take US 50 to Echo Summit and turn north onto Echo Lakes Road. Park in the Echo Lakes Sno-Park ($3 permit required). Overnight parking is allowed for Desolation Wilderness campers. Parking is not allowed on the north side of the road.
***Information:*** U.S. Forest Service, Lake Tahoe Basin Management Unit, (916) 573-2600.

## Loon Lake Winter Recreation Area

*Level, terrain:* Beginner to advanced.

*Mileage, elevation:* 9.75 miles of ungroomed, marked and unmarked trails. 6,378 feet to 6,700 feet.

*Description:* This relatively undiscovered trail system sets off from elegant Loon Lake Chalet, a spacious warming hut. Facilities here include a dining area, a small kitchen with a stove and hot water, a propane barbecue, outside restrooms and a loft for overnight use (reserve in advance). A staff ranger is always on duty for search-and-rescue missions. Seven defined trails, ranging from one to four kilometers, offer a variety of touring experiences in the Crystal Basin area, with views of steep, granite peaks in Desolation Wilderness to the east. Only one of the trails—South Shore—is unmarked; this extends from the Loon Lake Campground along the shoreline. A more challenging route for intermediate to advanced skiers connects the North Star Trail (2.5 miles) to the Telemark Loop (1.5 miles) on the north shore of the lake. Trailheads are signed with trail name, mileage, kilometers and difficulty. Trails are not groomed and track setting occurs only on an intermittent basis.

*Trailhead:* From South Lake Tahoe, travel west on US 50 to Riverton (where the highway goes from two to four lanes). Turn right on Ice House Road and continue 30 miles to the lake. Call ahead for road conditions. Limited parking is available at the chalet.

*Information:* U.S. Forest Service, Eldorado National Forest, (916) 644-6048.

# Lakes Basin

## Plumas Eureka State Park

*Level, terrain:* Beginner to intermediate.

*Mileage, elevation:* Three trails totaling 5.8 miles. 5,150 feet.

*Description:* This California state park, located in the heart of Gold Country, offers three ungroomed trails. Longest is the Jamison Canyon Loop Trail, a marked, three-mile beginner route that starts at the state park museum, winds through the campground, crosses two creeks and returns to the main road. It also accesses more advanced skiing in the canyon and Grass Lake basin. The loop ends at County Road A14, and you'll need to make a short walk along the road in order to return to the museum and the parking lot. One section of the trail (along the access road to the campground) has potential avalanche danger. Another trail, around Madora Lake, also begins at County Road A14, and provides an unmaintained trailhead with skiing along an ungroomed loop trail of 1.5 miles. The third trail, an ungroomed, intermediate route of 1.3 miles, begins at the parking lot of Plumas Eureka Ski Bowl and goes to Eureka

Lake. Advanced skiers can continue to the historic Eureka Peak. When the ski area is open, cross-country skiers can purchase a single-ride ticket to the top of the hill ending near the lake.

**Trailhead:** From Graeagle on Highway 89, turn left on County Road A14 and go five miles to the state park museum and park office.

**Information:** California Department of Parks and Recreation, Plumas Eureka State Park, (916) 836-2380.

## Gold Lake Road

**Level, terrain:** Beginner to intermediate; easy, gradual slope.

**Mileage, elevation:** 17 miles one-way. 5,400 feet at the Highway 49 and Gold Lake Road junction, increasing to 6,400 feet at Gold Lake.

**Description:** The Gold Lake Road is groomed for snowmobile and skiing use through the Off-Highway-Vehicle Program (please use caution when a snow groomer is on trail). Since this route is also a county highway, the slope in any direction is gradual and travel is easy for a beginner. The route follows Gold Lake Road from its junction with Highway 49 to Graeagle. The snow-covered roadway offers excellent cross-country opportunities for beginning and intermediate enthusiasts. This route provides great views of the Sierra Buttes and the surrounding area. Limited parking is available across from Bassett's Station. The route receives heavy use by snowmobilers and cross-country skiers. The Little Truckee Summit-Yuba Pass Trail can be accessed by following (for approximately 12 miles) the marked snowmobile trail which intersects this trail.

**Trailhead:** At the junction of Highway 49 and Gold Lake Road. Limited parking is available at the trailhead parking lot.

**Topographic maps:** Haypress Valley, Gold Lake and Clio.

**Information:** U.S. Forest Service, Tahoe National Forest, Sierraville Ranger District, (916) 994-3401. Downieville Ranger District, (916) 288-3231.

## Upper Sardine Lake

**Level, terrain:** Beginner to intermediate; fairly gradual, but beginners may have trouble with the last one-half mile.

**Mileage, elevation:** 3.5 miles one-way; seven miles round-trip. 5,400 feet at junction of Gold Lake Road and Highway 49; 6,000 feet at Upper Sardine Lake.

**Description:** This route is not marked, but follows Gold Lake Road approximately 1.5 miles, then turns left onto Sardine Lake Road. The route continues for one mile to Lower Sardine Lake, then branches to the right and continues around the shore of Lower Sardine Lake for one mile to Upper Sardine Lake. It's very scenic and offers the visitor one of the best winter views of both Sardine Lakes and the Sierra Buttes. The route

receives moderate use by cross-country skiers and snowmobile enthusiasts.
*Trailhead:* At the junction of Highway 49 and Gold Lake Road (near
Bassett's Station). Limited parking is available.
*Topographic maps:* Sierra City and Haypress Valley.
*Information:* U.S. Forest Service, Tahoe National Forest, Sierraville
Ranger District, (916) 994-3401.

## Packer Lake Trail

*Level, terrain:* Beginner to intermediate; a very gradual slope, but the
long round-trip distance may deter beginners.
*Mileage, elevation:* 5.5 miles one-way; 11 miles round-trip. 5,400 feet
at the junction at Gold Lake Road and Highway 49; 6,400 feet at Packer
Lake.
*Description:* This route is not marked. It follows the Gold Lake Road
for about 1.5 miles, then turns left, following the Upper Sardine Lake
route. The route branches to the north onto Packer Lake Road and con-
tinues for four miles to Packer Lake. Along the way, you get great views of
the Sierra Buttes and Packer Lake. It receives moderate use from cross-
country skiers and snowmobilers.
*Trailhead:* At the junction of Highway 49 and Gold Lake Road (near
Bassett's Station). Limited parking is available.
*Topographic maps:* Haypress Valley, Gold Lake and Sierra City.
*Information:* U.S. Forest Service, Tahoe National Forest, Sierraville
Ranger Station, (916) 994-3401.

## Henness Pass Road

*Level, terrain:* Beginner to advanced; an easy, gradual slope, but the
trail is ungroomed.
*Mileage, elevation:* Unmarked trails in a remote, 20-mile area. 4,900
feet.
*Description:* Henness Pass Road heads about 20 miles one-way to
Jackson Meadows, where it ties into the Yuba Pass Trail. Skiers wind
through plantations on this unmarked, ungroomed trail. The ridgetop
location offers expansive views. The road receives light to moderate use.
*Trailhead:* From Truckee, drive 17 miles north on Highway 89. Head
eight miles west on Henness Pass Road to the Yuba Pass junction. Take a
right on Ridge Road from Highway 49. Drive 18 miles to the Pliocene
Ridge Guard Station, where plowing stops, at the junction of Henness
Pass and Pliocene Ridge roads. Parking is limited but adequate.
*Topographic maps:* Allegheny and Downieville.
*Information:* U.S. Forest Service, Tahoe National Forest, Downieville
Ranger District, (916) 288-3231.

## Yuba Pass Sno-Park

***Level, terrain:*** Beginner to advanced.
***Mileage, elevation:*** 100 miles of skiing opportunities. 6,700 feet.
***Description:*** Trails are groomed both north and south of the Sno-Park through the California Off-Highway-Vehicle Program. The area is very popular with snowmobilers and skiers. Wheeled vehicles are prohibited on groomed routes. You'll find an excellent, 4.5-mile (one-way) Nordic trail heading to Bear Trap Meadows; the trailhead is north of the Sno-Park, marked "Snowmobile and Nordic Ski Trailhead." Snowmobiles share the route for one mile, then cross-country skiers have it to themselves.
***Trailhead:*** From Truckee, drive 25 miles on Interstate 80 to the Sierraville/Quincy exit of Highway 89. Follow Highway 89 toward Sierraville, then turn left on Highway 49. Drive 18 miles on Highway 49 to Bassett's Station. The Sno-Park is six miles east of Bassett's Station on Highway 49. Sno-Park permits are $3 and may be obtained at Bassett's Station.
***Topographic maps:*** Sattley, Webber Peak and Haypress Valley.
***Information:*** U.S. Forest Service, Tahoe National Forest, Sierraville Ranger Station, (916) 994-3401.

## Lunch Creek/Yuba Pass Ski Trail

***Level, terrain:*** Intermediate.
***Mileage, elevation:*** Nine-mile loop. 5,000 feet to 6,700 feet at Yuba Pass.
***Description:*** This marked ski trail leads north and west from Yuba Pass through Bear Trap Meadows and along Lunch Creek Road. There are several hills adjacent to Lunch Creek Road that lend themselves to telemark practice. Approximately one mile of the trail overlaps a snowmobile trail. By parking one car at Lunch Creek and one at Yuba Pass, skiers can make an excellent loop. The trail receives light to moderate use by skiers, and moderate use by snowmobilers in the immediate vicinity of Yuba Pass.
***Trailhead:*** Access to the trail is at Yuba Pass and Lunch Creek Road, approximately one mile west of Yuba Pass. Limited parking is available at Lunch Creek. Yuba Pass is a Sno-Park area and a $3 permit is required. Permits can be obtained at the Sierraville Service and Country Store, one-quarter mile south of the Highway 89/49 junction in Sierraville; (916) 994-3387.
***Topographic maps:*** Haypress Valley, Clio, Calpine and Sattley.
***Information:*** U.S. Forest Service, Tahoe National Forest, Sierraville Ranger District, (916) 994-3401.

# Chapter 16

# Snowmobiling, Sleigh Rides & Other Winter Activities

W hat if you don't ski? Or what if your muscles burned out skiing KT-22 at Squaw Valley USA? There's more than one way to play in the snow at Lake Tahoe. Whether you're taking a break during a ski vacation or looking for activities to entertain young children, the lake affords a wealth of winter recreational alternatives. Snowmobiling tends to be the number-one option, and guided tours use hundreds of miles of scenic trails, encompassing several national forests and most sides of Tahoe. Then there are sleigh rides, some of which can include dinner, and dog sled tours, which are great for kids and couples. Recently, snowshoeing has become popular at several state parks and at most of the cross-country ski areas, and it's possible to take short, easy hikes through frosted meadows and forest or even along snow-covered beaches. For hearty adventurers, there's winter camping, ice climbing and backcountry skiing. And for those who just want an hour or two of gliding along the ice, Tahoe's outdoor ice-skating rinks may fill the bill.

## DOG SLED RIDES
### Husky Express

Dotty Dennis is an institution at Lake Tahoe. This diminutive lady with a big voice is a veteran 20-year "musher" who runs the area's only commercial dog sled tours. It's always enjoyable—some would even say romantic—to scoot along on the snow, bundled up in blankets in the sled, behind Dotty's powerful team of huskies. Her trail system is in Hope Valley, one-half hour south of South Lake Tahoe off Highway 88. She schedules trips by advance reservation (weather and snow permitting), and offers special children's rides during an annual series of dog sled races held at Hope Valley. Her sled holds 375 pounds (two adults and one or two small children). Dotty and her partner, David Beck, also offer guided backcountry skiing, hut skiing and wilderness sled dog/ski expeditions, as well as avalanche, survival and musher courses.

*Fees, hours:* Adults, $50, children, $20, for a one-hour ride ($90 minimum per sled); $175 for a two-hour picnic ride. Moonlight and event rides available. Cross-country ski lessons available for $30 (lesson, skis, boots, poles; two-student minimum). Reservations are required. Checks and cash accepted only; no credit cards.

*Contact:* Husky Express and Sierra Ski Touring, P.O. Box 176, Gardnerville, NV 89410; (702) 782-3047 or (800) 833-MUSH.

# SLEIGH RIDES
## Borges Sleigh Rides

Dashing through the snow, in the proverbial one-horse open sleigh, the Borges family spins tales of Tahoe while passengers enjoy a pleasant ride through aspens and meadows at a site that is just across the street from Caesar's Tahoe. The family has operated the sleigh rides, and more recently carriage rides, at Stateline for over 20 years. Visitors can ride in one of five handmade sleighs, which seat from two to 20 passengers and are pulled by 2,000-pound blond Belgian or rare American-Russian Bashkir Curlies. The 35-minute ride features running commentary from the driver, who might regale passengers with songs, poems and history. Everyone is snuggled up in warm blankets.

***Fees, hours:*** Adults, $10; children (12 and under), $5. Rides are offered daily in winter from 10 a.m. to 4 p.m. (weather and snow conditions permitting). Carriage rides are available in summer at three locations: Horizon, Caesar's and Embassy Suites. In summer, rides begin daily at 12 p.m. Sleigh and carriage rides can be hired for weddings. Borges is located on private land adjacent to Caesar's Tahoe, on US 50 at Stateline, Nevada.

***Contact:*** Borges Sleigh Rides, P.O. Box 7496, South Lake Tahoe, CA 95731; (916) 541-2953.

*Sleigh rides, such as this one with the famous Borges family at Stateline, are popular winter excursions at Tahoe.*

## Kirkwood Ski Resort

The Meadows are the soul of Kirkwood, a four-seasons resort west of Carson Pass on Highway 88. And taking a horse-drawn sleigh ride across the Meadows is one way to appreciate the rugged beauty of the high peaks that comprise the box canyon surrounding the resort. Kirkwood Stables operates the rides, as well as summer trips.

***Fees, hours:*** Adults, $10; children (12 and under), $5. Sleigh rides start daily at 2:30 p.m. The resort is located on Highway 88, 30 miles southwest of South Lake Tahoe.

***Contact:*** Kirkwood Ski Resort, P.O. Box 1, Kirkwood, CA 95646; (209) 258-7433.

## Camp Richardson Corral

Located on the West Shore, just a four-mile drive on Highway 89 north of the "Y" intersection in South Lake Tahoe, Camp Richardson Corral offers sleigh rides lasting about 45 minutes, when snow conditions permit. The sleigh holds 12 to 14 people, and rides meander through the forest or along the shoreline of the lake. Dinner rides, with a minimum of six to eight people, enjoy an hour in the sleigh, then return to the corral for a full-course steak dinner.

***Fees, hours:*** Adults and children, $10; children 3 and under are free. Dinner rides are $30 for adults and $15 for youngsters 4 to 8. Rides begin at 11 a.m. and depart every hour on the hour. Dinner rides depart at 5:30 p.m. Reservations are required.

***Contact:*** Camp Richardson Corral, P.O. Box 8335, South Lake Tahoe, CA 96158; (916) 541-3113.

## Northstar-at-Tahoe

Combining a sleigh ride with a full-course Basque dinner is a unique feature of Northstar Stables, which is located at the golf course of this four-seasons resort located between Truckee and Kings Beach on Highway 267. Sleigh rides begin at the Basque Club Restaurant and go through Martis Valley for approximately 30 minutes.

***Fees, hours:*** Adults, $12; children 5 to 12, $8. Youngsters 4 and under are free. Rides are offered 3 p.m. to 7 p.m. on weekdays and noon to 8 p.m. on weekends. Horseback trail rides are open throughout the year, snow conditions and weather permitting. Reservations are recommended.

***Contact:*** Northstar-at-Tahoe, P.O. Box 129, Truckee, CA 96160; (916) 562-1230.

## Truckee Carriage and Coach Company

Sleigh rides lasting about 25 minutes are offered daily between The Resort at Squaw Creek and Squaw Valley USA. The 100-year-old carriage, which seats up to four adults, is pulled by a pair of blond Belgian draft horses.

**Fees, hours:** Adults and children, $20 per person (two-mile tour); $50 per person (six-mile tour); children 6 to 12 are half price, and under six are free when accompanied by an adult. Rides depart from The Resort at Squaw Creek from noon to 6 p.m. Thursday through Monday.

**Contact:** Truckee Carriage and Coach Company, P.O. Box 11212, Truckee, CA 96162; (916) 587-3867 or (916) 591-3867.

# ICE SKATING
## Olympic Ice Pavilion

This Olympic-sized ice-skating rink located at High Camp Bath and Tennis Club at the top of Squaw Valley's tram has a grand view of the ski area and its spectacular, rocky peaks. Since it can get pretty windy here, it's best to phone ahead and check conditions before visiting. There are wind enclosures to protect the rink, and on a sunny day this is a magnificent experience (though you might get a bit winded from the 8,200-foot altitude). Other amenities at the club include restaurants and bars, retail shops, a heated swimming lagoon, a spa and bungee jumping.

**Fees, hours:** Adults, $17; children 12 and under, $10 (including cable car ride, rentals and two hours skating). A Cheap Skate Discount Package runs Sunday through Thursday from 4 p.m. to 9 p.m. and costs $9 for adults and $6 for children. Lessons (all levels) cost: group, $6 (children only, Wednesday and Sunday from 5 p.m.); private (by appointment only), $18 for 20 minutes, $25 for a half hour and $40 for an hour. The pavilion is open daily year-round, 11 a.m. to 9 p.m. Squaw Valley Ski Resort is located off Highway 89, 12 miles south of Truckee, at 1960 Squaw Valley Road.

**Contact:** Squaw Valley USA, 1960 Squaw Valley Road, Squaw Valley, CA 96146; (916) 581-7246.

## The Resort at Squaw Creek

Squaw Valley has a corner on ice-skating arenas, and this magnificent resort, the largest in the valley, has a spacious outdoor rink that is open to the public. Skaters can enjoy fine views of the adjacent meadows, Squaw Valley Ski Resort and the surrounding mountains. Sessions are two hours each and run continuously, with a half-hour break, from 9 a.m. to 5 p.m.

**Fees, hours:** Adults, $10; children 6 to 13, $7; children 5 and under, $3. Cost includes skating and rentals. Lessons (all levels): $40 for a one-hour private session, $25 for a half-hour private session; $10 for each additional person. No group lessons are available.

**Contact:** The Resort at Squaw Creek, 400 Squaw Creek Road, Squaw Valley, CA 96146; (916) 581-6624 or (916) 583-6300.

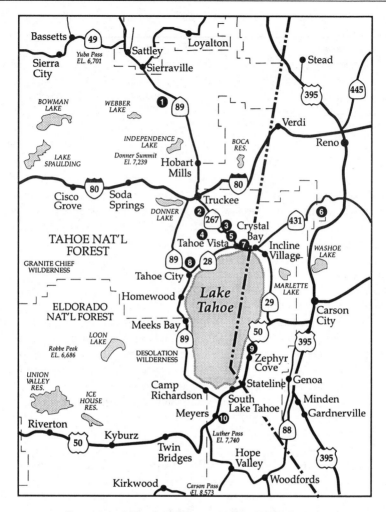

## *Snowmobile Outfitters in the Tahoe Area*

1. Eagle Ridge Snowmobile Outfitters—p. 434
2. Northstar-At-Tahoe—p. 434
3. Snowmobiling Unlimited, Inc.—p. 435
4. High Country Snowmobiling—p. 436
5. High Sierra Snowmobiling—p. 436
6. Reindeer Lodge—p. 437
7. Mountain Lake Adventures—p. 437
8. TC SNO MO'S—p. 438
9. Zephyr Cove Snowmobile Center—p. 439
10. Lake Tahoe Winter Sports Center—p. 439

# SNOWMOBILING

Sure it's noisy. But snowmobiling is one heck of an adrenaline rush. It's also the fastest way to see some of Lake Tahoe's spectacular backcountry vistas, including dramatic views of the lake itself. There isn't much of a learning curve needed to run a snowmobile, and guides provide advance instruction before every tour. About all that you need to know is how to start the engine (with a pull-cord, just like cranking up your lawnmower), how to go (depress the thumb throttle), and how to stop (apply the hand-grip brakes, just like in a bicycle). Then there is strategic "leaning": If one side of the snowmobile starts to sink into soft snow, you and your passenger lean to the other side. Leaning also helps when rounding corners. That's about all there is to it. One thing to know about snowmobile trails is that they can be full of washboard ruts if they're heavily used or if there is not enough snow to groom them every day. That means that your body will absorb a fair amount of pounding—not terrific if you have a back problem. It's also a good idea not to drink a lot of coffee beforehand, or you'll need to make unscheduled stops, which is difficult if you're in a large group.

When you sign up for a snowmobile trip, it isn't necessary to bring anything with you. Some riders wear their own ski clothing, but because of occasional oil spots (or pine tar from trees), you're better off renting a one-piece snowmobile suit, which is a lot warmer, anyway, even if it makes you look puffed out like an astronaut on a moon walk. Helmets are mandatory, and you can also rent boots and gloves. If you want to bring a camera, snacks or drinks, bundle them up in a fanny pack or knapsack, and use the rear rack on your snowmobile.

One of the decisions you'll need to make is whether to ride single or tandem. Children (who must be age 6 or older) are always assigned to ride with a parent, but two adults will find that sharing a snowmobile is rather uncomfortable—for the second rider. It's more enjoyable if everyone has their own machine, even though it costs more. Teens must be at least 16 years old and have a driver's license before they are allowed to operate solo.

Although snowmobiles are powerful vehicles that can rip through the woods, the guided tours are not races. A lead guide sets the pace, and with larger groups, usually 12 people or more, a chase guide follows in the last machine. Often groups will be divided, with parents and kids in a slow group, and single-rider machines in a faster group. The tours normally last about two hours, and the guide will make frequent stops to explain points of interest, have refreshments and check on everyone in the group.

Almost every snowmobile outfitter in the Tahoe Basin has a specific territory, and the scenery varies depending on whom you go with. Trips can range from short excursions with panoramic vistas of Lake Tahoe to extended all-day trips into the mountainous backcountry north and south of the lake. You can arrange for a picnic lunch, if you wish, and some companies offer overnight rides with stays in local lodges. If the size of the group matters to you (or if you want a more personalized experience), you may wish to schedule a separate ride for your family, book on a weekday rather than a weekend, or go with a smaller outfitter. The large companies can be hectic on busy weekends, when the staff often seems overwhelmed with business and short on patience.

## Eagle Ridge Snowmobile Outfitters
*See number 1 on map, page 432*

Owners Brad and Sue Ehrhorn offer a variety of tours on nearly 200 miles of groomed trails that traverse 650 square miles in Tahoe National Forest. From the trailhead at Little Truckee Summit, 14 miles north of Truckee on Highway 89, groups head out on two- and three-hour trips to places such as Webber Lake, Hobart Mills, Treasure Mountain and Jones Valley. This is the only outfitter that offers all-day tours to the spectacular Sierra Buttes and Lakes Basin, usually with a barbecue along the trail or lunch at historic Bassett's Station on Highway 49. The Gold Lake Road is frozen over in winter, and makes an excellent, scenic snowmobile route past the jagged and awesome buttes, one of the undiscovered treasures of Tahoe. On the longer rides, snowmobilers may travel cross-country most of the time, breaking fresh powder in meadows and glades. The company offers moonlight rides and two- and three-day overnight tours. The equipment consists of 12 Polaris machines.

***Fees, hours:*** Rates include helmets, boots, and clothing—Hobart Mills or Webber Lake (two hours): $80 single, $100 double; Treasure Mountain and Jones Valley or a moonlight ride (three hours): $100 single, $125 double; Bassett's Station (full day): $170 single, $195 double; the overnighter (two full days, including meals, accommodations, snowmobile and one night ride): $350 single only; and the three-day trip (same as the overnighter package with one extra day and additional areas covered): $495 single only. There is a minimum of four people per tour. Hot beverages and snacks are served on every ride. Videotaping is available. MasterCard, Visa and American Express are accepted.

***Contact:*** Eagle Ridge Snowmobile Outfitters, P.O. Box 4581, Incline Village, NV 89450; (916) 546-8667 or (702) 831-7600.

## Northstar-at-Tahoe
*See number 2 on map, page 432*

Snowmobile tours are a recent introduction at this large ski area between Kings Beach and Truckee. Two-hour tours begin near Northstar Village, follow groomed trails on the perimeter of the downhill ski area, and enter the trail system of the cross-country center up to Sawtooth Ridge, which overlooks Martis Valley and the town of Truckee. Two-hour moonlight tours also are available to the famous lookout of Mount Watson, with an elevation gain of about 2,000 feet. The resort offers nine new snowmobiles with heated handlebars, and two tour guides; there is no minimum group size for departure. Day tours leave at 10:30 a.m. and 1:30 p.m. December through March. Make reservations through the Northstar Activities Center.

***Fees, hours:*** Two-hour tours: $69 single, $89 double (includes guided tour, snowmobile rental and helmet). Rental clothing (adult and child) costs $12 for the complete package (jacket, bib, gloves and boots). Separate rental of insulated jacket, bib, gloves or boots is $4 each. Tours operate daily from 8 a.m. to 5 p.m., Saturdays from 7:30 a.m. to 5:30 p.m. There is a 300-pound weight limit per machine; machine operators must be at least 15 years old (parental consent is needed for children under 18). MasterCard, Visa, American Express and Discover cards are accepted. Reservations are recommended.

***Contact:*** Northstar-at-Tahoe, P.O. Box 129, Truckee, CA 96160; (916) 562-1010.

## Snowmobiling Unlimited, Inc.
*See number 3 on map, page 432*

With 14 years under their belts, Bob and Cindy Wolff operate the oldest snowmobile operation in Lake Tahoe, and their motto is "doing whatever it takes to please the customer." That may explain their high rate of repeat business. Their territory covers 75 square miles of national forest land in North Lake Tahoe, on the trail system that surrounds Mount Watson. Guided tours begin on the Brockway Summit three miles north of Kings Beach on Highway 267, and are available in shorter increments, such as one to one-and-a-half hours (more suitable for families with young children), as well as the standard two-hour outing. The crowning view, available from the longer rides, is from Mount Watson, which overlooks Lake Tahoe. The Wolffs will organize custom rides for almost any occasion—birthdays, weddings, anniversaries—and they can offer trail riding or off-trail riding. All trips must be reserved in advance, and there are no specific times for daily departures; these are at the convenience of the customer. The weight limit is 300 pounds per machine. Drivers must be at least 16 years old, and youngsters must be able to hang on for at least an hour (preferably age 4 and up). The equipment consists of about 20 machines.

***Fees, hours:*** One-hour tour (approximately 14 miles): $40 single, $60 double; one-and-a-half-hour tour (approximately 16 to 19 miles): $60 single, $90 double; two-hour tour (approximately 22 to 24 miles): $75 single, $110 double. All gear—suits, helmets, gloves and boots—is provided. They are open daily, 7 a.m. to 7 p.m., December through April, weather permitting.

**Contact:** Snowmobiling Unlimited, Inc., P.O. Box 1591, Tahoe City, CA 96145; (916) 583-7192 or (916) 583-5858.

## High Country Snowmobiling
*See number 4 on map, page 432*

Joe and Angelique Boyd have been the exclusive snowmobile concessionaires at North Tahoe Regional Park since 1989. They offer two unique features: the largest double oval snowmobile track on the lake, and a short, 45-minute tour on 11 miles of groomed trail that includes a high vista of Lake Tahoe. The park is at the top of National Avenue in Tahoe Vista, just off Highway 28 on the North Shore (west of the junction with Highway 267). Because the trail system is shared with other users (notably cross-country skiers), daytime rides are conducted only during weekdays. On weekends, all wilderness trail rides are at night. Rides are available on the oval day or night, every day. The equipment consists of 20 Polaris and Skidoo snowmobiles.

**Fees, hours:** Use of the track is $30 per machine (per half hour) for day rental and $50 for night rental. Trail tours are $50 per machine (45 minutes for a day ride, midweek only) and $65 (45-minute moonlight ride, midweek and weekends). There's a two-machine minimum, and single riders are required except when a child accompanies an adult. Helmets are provided. The track is open seven days a week, 10 a.m. to 5 p.m. All trail tours, night or day, are by reservation only. MasterCard and Visa are accepted.

**Contact:** High Country Snowmobiling, P.O. Box 1025, Carnelian Bay, CA 96140; (916) 546-0132 or (916) 546-2629 (evenings).

## High Sierra Snowmobiling
*See number 5 on map, page 432*

This is a large oval track on Old Brockway Golf Course, at the intersection of highways 267 and 28 on the North Shore. It is geared primarily to families with kids who want to take a spin on a snowmobile. The equipment consists of 16 Skidoos.

**Fees, hours:** Adults and youths 16 and over, $30 per machine (per half hour). You must have a valid driver's license to operate a machine. All children must be accompanied by a parent. Open daily, 9 a.m. to 5:30 p.m. MasterCard and Visa are accepted.

**Contact:** Brockway Golf Course, 7900 North Lake Boulevard, Kings Beach, CA 96143; (916) 546-9909.

## Reindeer Lodge
*See number 6 on map, page 432*

This is a unique, maybe even quirky place, filled with antiques, resident ghosts and miscellaneous "stuff" on the Mount Rose Highway (Highway 431), between Reno and Incline Village in Nevada. There's a restaurant and bar inside, where you can spend a fair amount of time pondering who collected so much "stuff." For snowmobiling, everything is do-it-yourself. There's a 2.5-acre site located adjacent to the lodge, and it offers a practice course that includes open areas, trees, curves and moguls. Or you can rent a snowmobile at an off-site venue nine miles up the road on a 1,000-acre open meadow near Mount Rose. Transport and pick-up is $10 per machine, with a minimum of two machines, or you can haul them up yourself. There are no guides at either location. Equipment consists of about two dozen snowmobiles.

*Fees, hours:* On-site—$12.50 single cylinder, $15 twin cylinder for 15 minutes; $20/$30 for 30 minutes; $30/$45 for an hour; $50/$80 for two hours; and $90/$140 for four hours. Off-site—$40 single cylinder, $55 twin cylinders for one hour; $65/$95 (two hours); $110/$170 (four hours); $190/$280 (eight hours); and $240/$340 (24 hours). Trailer rental rates range from $15 for a two-place trailer with hitch for two hours to $50 for a four-place trailer with hitch for 24 hours. Clothing rental is available—gloves, $2; boots, $2; suits, $6; or the total outfit, $7. Helmets are available at no charge. Amenities include food service (breakfast, lunch, dinner, barbecues, banquets), hot drinks, cocktails, arcades, billiards, slots and an antique museum. The lodge is open daily year-round, 8 a.m. to 7 p.m. Discover cards are accepted.

*Contact:* Reindeer Lodge, 9000 Mount Rose Highway, Reno, NV 89511; (702) 849-9902 or (702) 849-1960.

## Mountain Lake Adventures
*See number 7 on map, page 432*

This is one of several companies that offer trips to Mount Watson, the highest point on the North Shore of Lake Tahoe. A commanding vista of the lake from this lofty perch, as well as views of several ski resorts, are the main attractions of the two-hour, 26-mile tours. Clients meet at The Sports Station at Kings Beach, get outfitted and then drive three miles up Highway 267 to a parking area just short of the Brockway Summit. The route follows a series of machine-groomed trails along a ridgeline behind Northstar-at-Tahoe ski resort, then climbs to a rocky vantage point high above the lake. The equipment consists of 30 Polaris snowmobiles. Each rental includes full suits, boots, gloves and helmets; to reflect this, fees are higher than those of other companies.

*Fees, hours:* Grand Adventure (two hours): $75 single, $110 double;

Moonlight (three hours): $110 single, $150 double; Private Party and Powder (single riders only): $100 for two hours, $150 for three hours, $175 for four hours and $260 for six hours (lunch included in the six-hour trip). Open daily, 8 a.m. to 5 p.m., November through April. Group discounts are available (10 percent off) with a minimum of six machines. Tours depart at 11:30 a.m. and 2 p.m. Machine operators must be at least 16 years old with a driver's license, and children must be at least 4 years old and accompanied by parent (double-rider price). MasterCard and Visa are accepted. Reservations recommended. The Sports Station is located at 8299 North Lake Boulevard in Kings Beach, California.

**Contact:** Mountain Lake Adventures, P.O. Box 9653, South Lake Tahoe, CA 96158; (916) 583-9131 or (702) 831-4202.

## TC SNO MO'S
*See number 8 on map, page 432*

Located at the Tahoe City Golf Course, this small, personable operation provides both an oval track and regular backcountry tours. The 90-minute, 22-mile guided outings reach Mount Watson for a million-dollar view of Lake Tahoe from 2,000 feet above the shore. The trail begins at the historic, nine-hole golf course, then zigzags up the hillside through aspen and pine forest to the top of a cinder cone. From here, there is a commanding view of distant Martis Valley, Donner Pass and Castle Peak to the north. Then the trail follows a forest road along a ridgeline, with spectacular views en route to a rocky knob at Mount Watson. The panorama of the lake from here is positively inspiring; it is arguably the best overlook of Tahoe, and it allows you to see virtually the entire lake from north to south. Late afternoon is a particularly enchanting time, because of the muted sunlight that casts a warm glow on the basin. Groups are small, with one guide for every five people; the guides themselves are both knowledgeable and amiable. The equipment consists of 20 Polaris snowmobiles, divided between the oval track and the tours. Trips depart at 10 a.m., noon and 2 p.m. daily. The adjoining track on the golf course consists of 10 acres of groomed area.

**Fees, hours:** All rentals includes a free, mandatory helmet. Wilderness tours (1.5 hours): $65 single, $85 double. Track: $30 per machine per half hour (single or double riders). Drivers must be at least 16 years of age; youngsters accompanying parents must be at least 4 years of age. Amenities include a restaurant and bar. The tours and track are open daily, 9 a.m. to 5 p.m. It is located off Highway 28 at the Tahoe City "Y" behind Lucky's and the Bank of America. MasterCard and Visa are accepted. Reservations are recommended.

**Contact:** TC SNO MO'S, P.O. Box 1198, Tahoe City, CA 96145; (916) 583-1516 or (916) 581-3906.

## Zephyr Cove Snowmobile Center
*See number 9 on map, page 432*

This is the largest snowmobile tour service on the West Coast. Zephyr Cove runs 100 Yamaha and Skidoo snowmobiles, and has an extensive shuttle bus system that picks up riders at the Stateline hotels. All outfitting is done at Zephyr Cove Resort, four miles from South Lake Tahoe. From there, guests are taken to the trailhead at Spooner Summit on US 50, northeast of Stateline in Nevada. Weekends can be incredibly busy, so if you're looking for a more personal experience, schedule a tour on a weekday. With so many machines on the trail system at one time, it's frequently necessary to detour on spurs to allow other groups to pass. The route is quite scenic; it includes a high ledge at 9,000 feet with a bird's-eye view of Lake Tahoe and the Stateline casinos, and an overlook of Carson Valley and points east in Nevada. Bring your camera. Trails meander through pine and aspen forest, and the return route to the staging area can be rather steep (depending on snow cover). There's a spot where the group stops for hot chocolate, about midway through the tour. Equipment includes 30 single-rider and 50 double-rider machines. Three two-hour tours are offered daily, and a three-hour "Top of the Top" tour provides single riding over the best available terrain.

*Fees, hours:* Two-hour tours—$69 single, $99 double (combined weight limit of 400 pounds). Clothing rentals are available: parkas, gloves, bibs and boots, $3 per item; $8 for the complete package. Helmets are free and mandatory for all trips. Moonlight and private tours are available. Families, groups and first-time riders are welcome. Zephyr operates daily from 8 a.m. to 10 p.m. Machine operators must be at least 15 years old and have written parental consent; all riders are required to sign a risk acknowledgment, and leave a damage deposit on a credit card. Children as young as 5 can ride along. The season runs from November through April. MasterCard, Visa, American Express, Discover and some ATM cards are accepted. Reservations are required.

*Contact:* Zephyr Cove Snowmobile Center, 760 US 50, P.O. Drawer 830, Zephyr Cove, NV 89448; (702) 882-0788 or (702) 588-3833.

## Lake Tahoe Winter Sports Center
*See number 10 on map, page 432*

This is one of the larger operations at Lake Tahoe, running 50 to 60 Arctic Cats out of a staging area in Hope Valley on Blue Lakes Road, just south of Highway 88. One advantage is that it owns a fleet of buses to pick up guests at their hotels in South Lake Tahoe. They are taken to the rental center on US 50, outfitted with rental gear and helmets, and then shuttled to the trailhead, about a 30-minute drive. The trail explores the scenic Carson Pass area, with vistas of high, snow-capped peaks from an elevation that reaches 9,000 feet. You drive through meadows, on snow-covered roads, through forest and along ridgelines in Toiyabe National Forest, for a 25-mile round-trip. Tours leave every two hours, starting at 10 a.m., and half- and full-day tours with lunch can be arranged. The Winter Sports Center also operates an oval track nearby.

*Fees, hours:* Two-hour trips: $59 single, $89 double for the 10 a.m. tour; $69 single, $99 double at other departures (includes helmet, machine and shuttle). Single riders are recommended. There is a maximum of seven snowmobiles per guide. You must arrive 45 minutes before bus departure. Each machine has a 350-pound weight limit. First passengers must be at least 16 years old; children and second passengers must be able to hold on for two hours. Snowmobiling on the center's oval track costs $25 for a single rider and $40 for doubles (per half hour). Rental clothing is available: snowsuits, $5; boots, goggles, gloves, $3 each; complete package, $14. The center is also a full snowmobile dealership (sales and service). Open seven days a week, November through May. MasterCard, Visa and American Express are accepted. Reservations are recommended.

*Contact:* Lake Tahoe Winter Sports Center, P.O. Box 11436, Tahoe Paradise, CA 96155; (916) 577-2940.

## SNOWMOBILE TRAILS IN NATIONAL FORESTS

Snowmobiling is open on most national forest lands within the Tahoe Basin, provided there are at least six inches or more of snow on the ground. Wilderness, roadless areas and developed ski areas are closed to all motorized vehicles. If you are venturing into these areas on your own, go prepared with food, water and survival equipment. Always carry maps and contact the local office of the U.S. Forest Service for the latest trail conditions. Be aware that fresh storms can create avalanche hazards, and the roar of a snowmobile can set off slides. Be sure to obtain a Sno-Park permit for parking in designated California Sno-Park areas.

## North Shore
### Brockway Summit

Thirteen miles of groomed trails lead to Mount Watson, Watson Lake and Stumpy Meadows. Along the three- to four-hour ride, you get great views of Lake Tahoe and Martis Meadows. From Kings Beach on Highway 28, take Highway 267 four miles to Brockway Summit. Park along the highway (parking is limited). Several commercial outfitters also operate in this area.

*Contact:* Lake Tahoe Basin Management Unit, 870 Emerald Bay Road #1, South Lake Tahoe, CA 96150; (916) 573-2600. (Winter hours: Monday through Friday, 8 a.m. to 4:30 p.m.)

## Tahoe Meadows

Beautiful ungroomed trails on this meadow in the shadow of Mount Rose in Nevada provide great views of Lake Tahoe. This area is shared with cross-country skiers. From Incline Village, take Highway 28 to Mount Rose Highway (Highway 431). Just before the summit where the road levels out, look for a large meadow to the right. Park in the turnout by the meadow (parking is limited).

***Contact:*** Lake Tahoe Basin Management Unit, 870 Emerald Bay Road #1, South Lake Tahoe, CA 96150; (916) 573-2600. (Winter hours: Monday through Friday, 8 a.m. to 4:30 p.m.)

## Little Truckee Summit/Yuba Pass

Located in Tahoe National Forest, just north of Truckee off Highway 89, this trail network is the largest in the region for snowmobilers. It extends west of the highway near Prosser Creek Reservoir past privately owned Webber Lake and Jackson Meadows Reservoir to Bassett's Station. From there, it continues along Gold Lake Road to Gold Lake. The routes are used by a commercial snowmobiling outfitter, although they are open to the general public. A detailed map can be obtained from the U.S. Forest Service.

***Contact:*** Truckee Ranger District, P.O. Box 399, Highway 89, Truckee, CA 95734; (916) 587-3558.

# East Shore
## Spooner Summit

Groomed trails, enough for two to three good hours of riding, lead to panoramic views of Lake Tahoe. Take US 50 to Spooner Summit. Park in the large turnout in front of the Spooner Rest Stop. These trails are used by commercial outfitters, but are open to the general public.

***Contact:*** Lake Tahoe Basin Management Unit, 870 Emerald Bay Road #1, South Lake Tahoe, CA 96150; (916) 573-2600. (Winter hours: Monday through Friday, 8 a.m. to 4:30 p.m.)

# West Shore
## Blackwood Canyon Sno-Park

This Sno-Park provides views of Barker Pass, Ellis Peak and Bear Lake, with unmarked, ungroomed trails featuring big bowls, meadows and forests winding through Blackwood Canyon. This is a good day trip; most of the route follows a paved road that is snowbound in winter. Avalanche danger exists after storms. This is a popular cross-country ski area as well, so watch for pedestrians. Take Highway 89 three miles south of Tahoe City to Blackwood Canyon Road, across from the Kaspian Picnic Area. Continue to Blackwood Canyon Sno-Park. A Sno-Park permit is required ($3 day use).

**Contact:** Lake Tahoe Basin Management Unit, 870 Emerald Bay Road #1, South Lake Tahoe, CA 96150; (916) 573-2600. (Winter hours: Monday through Friday, 8 a.m. to 4:30 p.m.)

# South Shore
## Hell Hole

Good for a two- to three-hour trip, this forested, ungroomed ride provides limited views of Lake Tahoe from the top. Some avalanche potential exists in the Hell Hole area after a storm. From US 50 in Meyers, take Pioneer Trail 1.5 miles to Oneidas Street and turn right. Park where the snowplowing ends. Follow Fountain Place Road three miles to Hell Hole Road and turn right.

**Contact:** Lake Tahoe Basin Management Unit, 870 Emerald Bay Road #1, South Lake Tahoe, CA 96150; (916) 573-2600. (Winter hours: Monday through Friday, 8 a.m. to 4:30 p.m.)

## Hope Valley/Blue Lakes

Although used for commercial snowmobiling, the unattached snowmobiler can ride a network of groomed and ungroomed trails in Toiyabe National Forest from Highway 88 (near the Forest Service's Hope Valley Campground) southward to just west of Ebbets Pass on Highway 4. Obtain a detailed trail map from the Forest Service.

**Contact:** Carson Ranger District, 1536 South Carston Street, Carson City, NV 89701; (702) 882-2766.

# Lakes Basin
## Lake Davis

Snowmobilers will find an ungroomed trail around the lake, starting from a staging area at the lake's southeastern end (Lake Davis Road and Grizzly Road). Access to Lake Davis via Grizzly Road is usually kept plowed and well-maintained. An additional three-mile loop trail to the Smith Peak Lookout is located on the west side of Lake Davis. Services are available nearby. From Truckee, drive north on Highway 89 to the Sattley turnoff. Heading toward Sattley, drive to Highway 70. Turn left, heading toward Portola, and drive 1.25 miles to the Lake Davis turnoff. Turn right on Grizzly Road and drive five miles to Lake Davis.

**Contact:** Plumas County Visitors Bureau, 91 Church Street, P.O. Box 4120, Quincy, CA 95971; (800) 326-2247 or (916) 283-6345.

## Lakes Basin Recreation Area

Gold Lake Highway winds through the Lakes Basin (connecting highways 89 and 49) and is snowbound in winter. The road is groomed and marked for snowmobilers and cross-country skiers. There are numerous ungroomed trails branching off the main route, including a route to the Mills Peak Lookout. A staging area at the highway's northern end moves with the snowline, ranging from Mohawk Chapman Road to Gray Eagle Lodge Road. A second staging area with restrooms is located at Bassetts, at the southern end of Highway 89 at the Highway 49 intersection.

*Contact:* Plumas County Visitors Bureau, 91 Church Street, P.O. Box 4120, Quincy, CA 95971; (800) 326-2247 or (916) 283-6345.

# SNOW-PLAY AREAS
## (SLEDDING & TUBING)

It doesn't take much to create a spot for sliding down the snow; usually a modest hill will do. There are plenty of ad hoc snow-play hills throughout Tahoe, and anyone with a saucer, a tube or a cardboard box can get in on the action. It should be pointed out that while this kind of snow-sliding can be fun and exhilarating for youngsters, it frequently leads to injuries of limbs, back, hip and head. Aging adults should not try any of these shenanigans, and kids ought to wear helmets, at the very least, for protection, since rocks and trees are not very soft landing zones. Here are some of the more well-known spots:

### Bassett's Station

Parking is available, but often crowded. A popular gathering spot is Bassett's Station at the intersection of Gold Lake Road and Highway 49, northwest of Truckee. There is a $3 day-use parking fee.

*Contact:* Tahoe National Forest, (916) 265-4531.

### Blackwood Canyon Sno-Park

This snow-play area is located on the west side of Highway 89, three miles south of Tahoe City. There is avalanche danger—avoid steeper terrain along the north side of Blackwood Canyon. Parking is available, but often crowded. A good spot to try is at the intersection of Jackson Meadow Road and Highway 89. There is a $3 day-use fee.

*Contact:* Tahoe National Forest, (916) 265-4531.

### Boreal Ski Resort

In addition to its ski slopes, Boreal features a snow-play area. Only plastic disks may be used; the $5 entry fee includes disk rental. It's located off Interstate 80 at Donner Pass. Parking is available in front of the Boreal Lodge, but it's often crowded.

*Contact:* Boreal Ski Resort, (916) 426-3666.

## SNO-PARK AREAS & PERMITS

Snow-cleared parking lots are located on main highways (marked by distinctive brown highway signs) in the central Sierra Nevada snow country of California. The season is November 1 to May 30 each winter (weather permitting).

Vehicles must have a Sno-Park permit displayed on the dashboard. The parking fee is $3 per day (good at any Sno-Park on the date issued) and $20 for a season permit (good at any Sno-Park during the entire winter season). Cars parked without a valid permit displayed are subject to a $75 citation.

Permits are sold at a variety of sporting goods stores throughout central California, businesses located near the Sno-Parks, and all Northern California State Automobile Association offices (for members only).

For mail orders, send a check made out to the California Department of Parks and Recreation for $20 (season permit) or $3 for each day

## Cisco Grove

Here you'll find a snow-play area, a sled slope, hot food, groceries, local information and a snowmobile and cross country area. There is no overnight parking. The day-use parking fee is $3. (A Sno-Park permit is available at campground.) Cisco Grove is located off Highway 80. Take the Cisco Grove exit; the snow-play area is off the north side of the freeway at the entrance to Thousand Trails Campground.

***Contact:*** Thousand Trails Campground, (916) 426-3362.

## Donner Memorial State Park

There is a snow-play area, but no sled slope. The day-use parking fee is $3. (A Sno-Park permit is available at the park.) No snowmobiles or overnight parking are allowed. The snow-play area is next to the Emigrant Trail Museum. From Highway 80, take the Donner Lake exit. The park is on Donner Pass Road.

***Contact:*** Emigrant Trail Museum, (916) 587-3841.

## Echo Summit

This is a popular snow-play area, with an extensive sledding hill and some cross-country skiing. No snowmobiles are allowed. The day-use parking fee is $3. (A Sno-Park permit is available at the lodge.) The area is on the south side of US 50 at Echo Summit.

***Contact:*** California Conservation Corps, (916) 659-0642.

## Granlibakken Ski Resort

South of Tahoe City, this resort features a snow-play area on a 40-foot hill. It's saucers only and open daily, 9 a.m. to 4 p.m. Day use is $4; saucer rentals are $3. Amenities include a warming hut and refreshment stand. The resort is located off Highway 89 at the end of Granlibakken Road.

***Contact:*** Granlibakken Ski Resort, (916) 583-6203.

## Hansen's Toboggan & Saucer Hill

This tube and saucer hill features banked turns and packed runs. All equipment is furnished (and what's more, no outside equipment is allowed). Rates are $9 per person for three hours and $5 for one hour. Group rates are available. It's located at Hansen's Resort, near Heavenly Ski Area, at 1360 Ski Run Boulevard in South Lake Tahoe.

*Contact:* Hansen's Resort, (916) 544-3361.

## North Tahoe Regional Park

This snowhill welcomes toboggans, saucers and inner tubes. Best of all, there is no charge for use of the play area. Equipment rentals are available, at $3 for a disk or tube. It's located on the North Shore at the top of National Avenue off Highway 28 at Tahoe Vista.

*Contact:* North Tahoe Regional Park, (916) 546-5043 or (916) 546-7248.

## Mount Rose

Bring your own equipment or rent at Reindeer Lodge (see below). This is an undeveloped area eight miles up from Reno on the Mount Rose Highway (Highway 431). There is no contact phone number.

## Reindeer Lodge

There is no snow-play area on the premises, but saucer rentals are available (take them anywhere): saucers, $3; small raft, $6; medium raft, $8; large raft, $10. Other amenities include food service (breakfast, lunch, dinner, barbecues), hot drinks, arcades, billiards and an antique museum. On-site and off-site snowmobile rentals are also possible (see page 437 in this chapter). The lodge is open daily year-round, 8 a.m. to 7 p.m. Discover cards are accepted.

*Contact:* Reindeer Lodge, (702) 849-9902 or (702) 849-1960.

## Taylor Creek

Here you'll find a snow-play area, a small sledding hill and cross-country skiing access to Fallen Leaf Lake. The day-use parking fee is $3. No snowmobiles are allowed. The area is on the west side of Highway 89 near Camp Richardson, one mile west of Echo Summit.

*Contact:* South Tahoe Shell, (916) 541-2720.

permit (specify dates to be used) to: Permit Sales, Sno-Park Program, P.O. Box 942896, Sacramento, CA 94296-0001. Allow two weeks for processing. Call (916) 653-8569 for a site map of all Sno-Park locations.

## Yuba Pass

You'll find a snow-play area, cross-country skiing (north of Highway 49) and groomed snowmobile trails. Parking is available, but often crowded. There is a $3 day-use parking fee. On the south side of Highway 49 at Yuba Pass.

***Contact*** Tahoe National Forest, (916) 265-4531.

## Yuba Gap

It's got a snow-play area, sled slopes, cross-country skiing and hot food. No snowmobiles, buses or overnight parking are allowed. The day-use parking fee is $3. From Highway 80, take the Yuba Gap exit. Turn right on Frontage Road and follow signs for one-half mile to the snow-play area at Naco West Snowflower Campground.

***Contact:*** Snowflower Country Store, (916) 389-8241.

# SNOWSHOEING

It takes little skill to immediately enjoy over-the-snow hiking on today's modern snowshoes. Apart from the old-fashioned wooden snowshoes, several companies have introduced lightweight aluminum alloy models that are sleek and easy to use. Many of these are available for rent at winter sports stores and at cross-country ski centers around Lake Tahoe. In fact, most Nordic resorts offer snowshoeing on designated trails (seechapter 15, "Cross-Country Ski Areas & Trails" beginning on page 395 for details). Also, snowshoe tours are frequently offered by rangers in the state parks and national forests. In California, Donner Memorial State Park near Truckee and Sugar Pine Point State Park on the West Shore, and in Nevada, Lake Tahoe-Nevada State Park on the East Shore, occasionally offer guided snowshoe nature walks during the winter.

## Boca-Stampede Reservoir

This is a level snow play area for beginners. There is a $3 day-use parking fee. Drive five miles east of Truckee on Interstate 80 and take the Hirschdale Road exit. Head north about one-half mile toward the reservoir.

***Contact:*** The Sierra Mountaineer in Truckee, (916) 587-2025, or in Reno, (702) 856-4824.

## Carson Pass Area

Trails fan out on mild to rugged terrain in the Hope Valley area, along scenic creeks and around frozen lakes. There is a $3 day-use parking fee (Sno-Park Pass). Take Highway 89 south of South Lake Tahoe to Highway 88; watch for turnouts around the junction.

***Contact:*** The Sierra Mountaineer in Truckee, (916) 587-2025, or in Reno, (702) 856-4824.

## Donner Memorial State Park

The park offers flat terrain for beginners. There are no snowshoe rentals available. Take the Donner Pass Road exit from Interstate 80 in Truckee, then head south to the park entrance.

***Contact:*** Emigrant Trail Museum, (916) 582-7892.

## Mount Rose/Tahoe Meadows

This is a great beginner's location, with a flat area off the highway (near a hut provided by the Tahoe Rim Trail Association) which fans out into the meadows. It's one-half mile west of the summit from Reno to Incline Village off Highway 431.

***Contact:*** The Sierra Mountaineer in Truckee, (916) 587-2025, or in Reno, (702) 856-4824.

## Peter Grubb Hut

Here's another spot with level terrain. There is a $3 day-use parking fee (Sno-Park permit). It's along the Pacific Crest Trail off Interstate 80 at the Boreal exit (approximately one-half mile from Boreal Ski Resort), on the Donner Summit.

***Contact:*** The Sierra Mountaineer in Truckee, (916) 587-2025, or in Reno, (702) 856-4824.

# BACKCOUNTRY SKIING

Backcountry skiing is also known as telemark, free-heel, pinning, touring and *rondonée* (using skis with three-pin toe bindings). Because of the possibility of avalanches, skiers should always carry survival equipment, food, liquids and detailed maps, and inform friends or relatives of intended routes and dates of return. Tahoe is full of stories of backcountry skiers caught in sudden and intense blizzards. If you've got the yen for this kind of adventure, consider contacting one of the professional guide organizations below, rather than striking out on your own.

## Alpine Skills International (ASI)

ASI has special-use permits with Tahoe National Forest throughout the ski season. The school provides tours and instruction, from novice through advanced cross-country and telemark skills to backcountry camping. The ASI lodge, located on Old Highway 40 on the top of Donner Summit, also has comfortable and reasonably priced overnight accommodations. Tours include the Introduction to Ski Camping at $168, a weekend ski tour for advanced beginners or intermediate Nordic skiers, which is offered several times from January through March. There's also the High Tour Seminar at $262, which includes a traverse from Sugar Bowl to Squaw Valley, a three-day seminar, one night of lodging, a breakfast and two dinners. This requires strong intermediate skiing skills, and is offered several times from February through April. Reservations are required. MasterCard, Visa and Discover are accepted.

**Contact:** Alpine Skills International, P.O. Box 8, Norden, CA 95724; (916) 426-9108.

### Sierra Ski Touring

Veteran backcountry ski guide and author David Beck provides individualized instruction for backcountry skiers, at $245 per day. Cross-country ski lessons are $30 (including lesson, skis, boots and poles, with a two-student minimum). Other services offered include hut skiing, wilderness dog sled/ski expeditions (ride on a sled pulled by a team of huskies), and avalanche, survival and musher courses. Beck is a partner with Husky Express (see the listing on page 428 of this chapter). Two-day tours (including lodging and food) are $195 for the Avalanche weekend, $145 for the Telemark weekend, and $225 for the Musher midweek expedition. All camping is in the backcountry—there is no lodge or ski hut. Meet at Carson Pass for skiing. Reservations are required. No credit cards are accepted; cash and checks only.

**Contact:** Sierra Ski Touring, P.O. Box 176, Gardnerville, NV 89410; (702) 782-3047 or (800) 833-MUSH.

# ICE CLIMBING &
# WINTER MOUNTAINEERING
## Alpine Skills International (ASI)

Seminars at this Donner Summit lodge focus on the skills most important for adapting to this special environment. The Introduction to High Altitude Mountaineering (offered from June through July) is $196 and covers fundamental skills and mountaineering safety; it requires very good physical conditioning. The Altitude Alpine Style Glacial Ice Seminar is a five-day program for $495; six sessions are offered from June through July. The Introduction to Snow Climbing is $152; it is a two-day seminar at Donner Pass in May and Tioga Pass (Yosemite) in June. The Intermediate Snow and Ice Climbing Seminar is $172 and consists of a two-day seminar, requiring an introductory or equivalent course and good conditioning as prerequisites; it is offered from August through September. Reservations are required. MasterCard, Visa and Discover are accepted.

**Contact:** Alpine Skills International, P.O. Box 8, Norden, CA 95724; (916) 426-9108.

# SNOW & WINTER CAMPING

It may sound like a cold, uncomfortable activity, but snow camping has its aficionados. Cross-country ski centers, especially Kirkwood, offer overnight snow camping trips on an occasional basis, usually in early spring when the threat of winter storms has abated. If you've a mind to try snow camping on your own, consider the various Forest Service campgrounds that can provide uncrowded venues. These are not open with full services during the winter, but some of the areas can still be used. Here are two popular locations:

## Highway 49 North of Truckee

Chapman Creek, Sierra and Yuba Pass campgrounds, operated by Tahoe National Forest, are good locations for snow camping. Parking is limited at both Chapman and Sierra. Yuba Pass is quite popular as a day-use area and parking is available. In the Lakes Basin area off the Gold Lake Highway (which is closed because of snow in winter), you can ski-hike with a backpack to Sardine Lake, Salmon Lake, Berger Creek and Snag Lake campgrounds. Visitors must pack out their trash, and provide their own toilet paper and drinking water. No fees are charged. Please be sure to leave a clean camp.

***Contact:*** Tahoe National Forest, 631 Coyote Street, P.O. Box 6003, Nevada City, CA 95959-6003; (916) 265-4531.

## Highway 89/Little Truckee Summit

From the parking lot here, overnight camping is permitted between November and April for five days or less. This is also a popular parking area for cross-country skiers and snowmobilers. Prosser Campground is open in winter, but it requires a 1.5-mile ski or hike to the campground. Visitors must pack out their trash and provide their own toilet paper and drinking water. No fees are charged. Please be sure to leave a clean camp.

***Contact:*** Tahoe National Forest, 631 Coyote Street, P.O. Box 6003, Nevada City, CA 95959-6003; (916) 265-4531.

# OTHER INFORMATION SOURCES
## Alpenglow Lake Tahoe

Knowledgeable personnel can point out various backcountry locations around the area. This is a retail store selling backcountry equipment, clothing, books and maps. It's located at 415 North Lake Boulevard in Tahoe City, CA; (916) 583-6917.

## The Sierra Mountaineer

This retail store sells backcountry equipment, clothing, books and maps. Staff members can describe various backcountry locations around the area. There are two locations: one in Truckee at Bridge and Jibboom streets (on Commercial Row), (916) 587-2025; and another in Reno, at 155 North Edison Way, (702) 856-4824.

# Chapter 17

# Kid Stuff

Whardd W hen is it time to cut the kids loose? Here are some hints:
(A) When they've blasted holes through the roof of your motor
home with a slingshot.
(B) When your dog starts running *away* from them.
(C) When they've redecorated your rustic cabin with Sega and Nintendo
games.
(D) When you or they need some personal "space."

Let's face it, children prefer to be with other children, and adults are
pretty low on the food chain. While you and your spouse are fawning over
some remarkable wildlife sighting—a bald eagle, perhaps—your child
may be preoccupied with zapping a pesky sibling with laser tag.

In the Lake Tahoe and Reno areas, there's a lot of kid stuff. It ranges
from excellent summer and day camps (tennis, anyone?), to those electronic junior slot machines known as video arcades. Happily, a lot of
things for small fries don't have to cost much. For example, you can tour a
trout hatchery for free. If your goal is to enhance your child's education,
by all means visit one or more of the excellent museums in Lake Tahoe,
Reno, Virginia City and Carson City (and covered in other chapters in
this book). In particular, the railroad museums (there are three in the
region) are usually a hit. So is the Ponderosa Ranch, with its Western
town, petting animals and movie sets. Also, consider the nature centers
and self-guided walks at state parks and U.S. Forest Service visitor centers
(see chapter 6, "Nature Trails," beginning on page 123).

When all else fails, or if the Great Outdoors is pelting you with liquid
sunshine or copious white flakes, there are certainly the indoor theme
parks, and Reno has a corner on the market for those. The new Silver
Legacy hotel, Reno's answer to Las Vegas, is guaranteed to keep everyone
wide-eyed. And Boomtown, with its indoor mini-golf and motion theater,
is a youngster's paradise. One thing to keep in mind is that if you feel like
climbing the walls, or if you've reached the end of your rope, both you
and your offspring can reconnect at a climbing wall or a ropes course, of
which there are several in the Tahoe basin.

## SUMMER & DAY CAMPS
### Nike Lake Tahoe Tennis Camp, Granlibakken Resort

If you want your physically talented son or daughter to swat balls like
Chris Evert or Andre Agassi, here's the place to start. This is an annual
seven-day, six-night tennis camp for young people from ages 9 to 18. It
includes meals, housing, 30 hours of instruction, video analysis and personal skills evaluation. Special off-court activities include swimming,
beach games, river rafting, ice skating at Squaw Valley, volleyball, bingo,
ice cream/movie/pizza nights, miniature golf, arcade, casino night, Fri-

day graduation and dance. The camp runs from June to August. Fees: resident, $645; extended days, $545 (8:30 a.m. to 9 p.m.) and $495 (8:30 a.m. to 4:30 p.m.). Multiple-week camps are available. Deposit policy: $200 per week. If you cancel 14 days or longer from the start date, you receive a refund minus $50; less than that and you get full credit towards the next camp session or refund of payments less $200 per week. For information, write to 919 Sir Francis Drake Boulevard, Kentfield, CA 94904, or phone (800) NIKE-CAMPS. The camp is held at Granlibakken Resort, 625 Granlibakken Road, Tahoe City, CA 96145.

## Nike Junior Golf Camp, Northstar

Offered from June through August, this is a six-day, five-night golf camp for boys and girls, ages 10 to 18, at this large, four-seasons resort six miles south of Truckee. The camp includes meals, housing, golf instruction (beginner through advanced) and greens fees. Fees: $795. Northstar-at-Tahoe, Highway 267 and Northstar Drive. For information, write to 919 Sir Francis Drake Boulevard, Kentfield, CA 94904, or phone (415) 459-0459 or (800) 645-3226.

## Tahoe Donner Equestrian Center, Tahoe Donner

This is Tahoe's most complete equestrian center, and it is set up with permanent riding arenas and instructors. It's located in the Tahoe Donner residential resort community above Truckee, and the instructors are first-rate. Five-day horsemanship camps, offered from June through August, teach basic through advanced levels of Western and English riding styles. Fees start at $250. Book early, because the courses fill rapidly. Reservations are required. Closed during winter (beginning at the end of September). 151509 Northwoods Boulevard, Truckee, CA 96161; (916) 587-9470.

## Walton's Grizzly Lodge

This is a unique facility located at the headwaters of the Feather River near Portola in Plumas County, about a 45-minute drive north of Truckee or an hour north of Reno. It's at a 5,000-foot elevation (above the smog and poison oak), and has been a family-operated summer camp for boys and girls, ages 7 to 14, for many years. The campground is nestled among 50 acres of ponderosa pine and features a private lake. Dormitories accommodate children by age group and contain indoor showers and restrooms. Activities include campouts, hiking, creek swimming, fishing, horseback riding, archery, volleyball, softball, soccer, ping pong, trampoline, rollerblading, wrestling, gymnastics, tennis, golf and challenge courses. Other activities are campfire entertainment, theme dances, games, computers and arts and crafts. Cost—one week, $650; two weeks,

$1,300; three weeks, $1,900; four weeks, $2,400. The camp meets flights at the Reno-Tahoe International Airport from around the world. Open from June through August. Free video by request. P.O. Box 519, Portola, CA 96122; (916) 832-4834.

## Little People's Adventures, Truckee

This is an outdoor recreation day camp for children ages 5 to 12. Planned adventures are offered in bowling, rock climbing, hiking, horseback riding, ice skating, swimming, rollerblading, biking, bouldering, miniature golfing, water sports and other games and activities. Camp counselors are certified for first aid and CPR. Fees: $30 per day, including activities, transportation, snack, instruction and supervision. Discount packages include Ultra Fun Pass (10 adventures for the price of nine); Traveler's Ticket (six adventures for the price of five); and Family Pack Discount ($5 off each additional child). Children must bring lunch, water, equipment (discounts available at local shops) and proof of medical coverage. Reservations must be made at least 12 hours prior to planned activity. Space is limited to 15 children per day. Reservations are accepted. Camp hours are 9 a.m. to 3:30 p.m. June to September, and weekends only from September to October. P.O. Box 2914, Olympic Valley, CA 96146; (916) 581-4LPA.

## Mountain Buddy's Club, The Resort at Squaw Creek

This lavish resort at Squaw Valley has earned high marks for its supervised children's and teen's programs, which are available to guests throughout the year. There's an organized selection of activities including arts and crafts, games, sports, cooking and science. Separate programs are scheduled for teens and kids 3 to 13 (children must be toilet-trained). Babysitting is available for children under three years old. Located at the Resort Activity Center on the second floor. Fees: $45 all day (9 a.m. to 5 p.m., lunch included) or $20 half day ($5 additional for lunch). You receive a 10-percent discount for each additional child. A one-time membership fee of $10 includes a T-shirt and quarterly newsletter. Reservations must be made 24 hours in advance and a cancellation notice of four hours is required. The Resort at Squaw Creek, 400 Squaw Creek Road, Squaw Valley, CA 96146; (916) 581-6624.

## Camp Hyatt, Hyatt Regency, Incline Village

Taking care of families with children is a specialty at this hotel, and there are always supervised programs available in both summer and winter. For hotel guests, Camp Hyatt has activities such as chaperoned hiking, beach play, crafts, skiing or snow play for youngsters ages 3 to 12, giving Mom and Dad a chance to whoop it up on their own. Inquire about specific programs and times. There's also a video arcade that's open

24 hours daily. P.O. Box 3239, Incline Village, NV 89450-3239; (702) 832-1234 or (800) 553-3288.

## Granlibakken Resort and Conference Center, North Tahoe

This all-seasons resort offers a variety of programs and sports camps for kids, as well as corporate team-building sessions for adults. A new addition is an impressive ropes course that has a series of both low- and high-element challenges using poles, cables and native pine trees. Activities are designed to increase personal self-confidence and mutual respect within a group, as well as improve communication, problem solving and productivity. Certified trainers guide you and your team through the course, providing a safe and secure environment. The full-day session runs from 9 a.m. to noon and 1 p.m. to 5 p.m. The half-day session is 9 a.m. to 1 p.m. or 1 p.m. to 5 p.m. Prices vary depending on group size and program. Discount rates are available for large groups and non-profit organizations. Sierra Challenge at Granlibakken Resort, Granlibakken Road, Tahoe City, CA 95730; (702) 829-7673 or (800) 552-4494.

## Camp Homewood, Lake Tahoe

This West Shore ski area offers several summer activities, including hiking, mountain biking, canoeing, kayaking, swimming, nature hikes, sports, games and archery. Four-day sessions are held for boys and girls ages 7 to 14. Open in July and August. Fees: $275 per session (families with two or more children can deduct $25 per child). A non-refundable deposit of $50 is required with the application. Located at Homewood Ski Area, P.O. Box 5262, Tahoe City, CA 96145; (916) 581-4319.

## Galena Creek Park Campfire Programs, Reno

This Washoe County park on Mount Rose Highway offers a Friday night campfire hour with storytelling and singing. Bring a lawn chair, a blanket and marshmallows. It's free and runs from 8:30 p.m. to 9:30 p.m. on Fridays, from July to September. Take the north entrance to Galena Creek Park, 18350 Mount Rose Highway, Reno, NV 89511; (702) 849-2511.

## Karate Kids, Stateline

At this day camp for boys and girls ages 6 to 13, kids learn street smarts, play fun games, and enjoy daily outside seasonal activities. Children must bring proper clothing and a towel for water activities. Fees: $45 per day, including activities, lunch and snacks; $40 for each additional family member; $30 per evening session Friday to Sunday. The day session runs from 8:30 a.m. to 3:45 p.m., and evening session runs from 6 p.m. to 10 p.m. Open year-round. P.O. Box 2238, Stateline, NV 89449; (702) 588-0752.

# CLIMBING & ROPES COURSES

## Headwall Climbing Wall, Squaw Valley

Located in the tram building of the Squaw Valley ski resort, this unique wall features a 30-foot-high indoor course, with both easy and difficult routes. It's a challenging workout (at 6,200 feet!) for both kids and adults. Harness and ropes are required and supplied. Fees: adults, $7 per hour; children (12 and under), $10 per hour. Climbing shoes are $4. Open daily year-round, from noon to 8 p.m. Located at the Cable Car Building of Squaw Valley USA; 1960 Squaw Valley Road, Squaw Valley, CA 96146; (916) 583-7673.

## Adventure Park, Northstar-at-Tahoe

Active kids who have limitless energy will find plenty of things to challenge them at this ropes course and 24-foot outdoor climbing wall. Operated in the summer at this all-seasons resort south of Truckee, programs include Adventure Challenge Ropes, Junior Ropes, a climbing wall and orienteering courses. Adventure Challenge Ropes courses include games and exercises with ropes, cables and tall fir trees. Orienteering courses emphasize hiking exploration techniques, including map and compass reading. The fee for children (ages 10 to 17) is $30 and for adults it's $40. The course is open from noon to 5 p.m. Thursday through Sunday. The fee for the Junior Ropes course for children 4 to 9 is $10, and it is open daily from 9 a.m. to 5 p.m. The climbing wall course costs $10 per hour or $20 for a day pass (with harness and staff supervision); shoe rentals are available. The wall is open daily 9 a.m. to 7 p.m. The orienteering course is $15 to $18 for adults and $10 to $13 for children, with youngsters 7 and under admitted free when accompanied by an adult. Open from June to September. Reservations are recommended. For information, write to 1030 Merced Street, Berkeley, CA 94707; phone (916) 562-2285 or (510) 525-9391 (Adventure Associates). Participants meet at the Mountain Adventure Shop in Northstar Village, Truckee, CA.

## The Sports Exchange, Truckee

This used sports equipment store features two indoor climbing rooms designed for top roping and bouldering. A day pass costs $8; climbing shoes rent for $3. Family rates and month passes are available. Children under 10 must be accompanied by an adult. The store also has a new cafe and sells used equipment on consignment. Open daily from 10 a.m. to 9 p.m. 10095 West River, Truckee, CA 96161; (916) 582-4510.

## Tahoe Mountaineering, South Lake Tahoe

Private, individualized wilderness experience, guide service and lessons are available for rock climbing, camping and peak bagging. Wilderness

Peak Bagging and Camping (ages 13 and older) features one- to three-day walking and camping expeditions in Tahoe (Jobes Peak and Phipps Peak). Fees: $12 per hour (four-hour minimum); $120 per day (overnight trip expenses include gasoline, food and personal gear). Write to Jim Campbell, P.O. Box 729720, South Lake Tahoe, CA 96157. Phone Tahoe Mountaineering, (916) 544-5199, or Gad Gym, (916) 544-7314.

# FISHING PONDS
## Trout Farm, South Lake Tahoe

If the fish aren't cooperating in Tahoe's many lakes and streams, you might try this place. It offers free admission and use of bait and tackle. Public fishing requires no license, boat or limit. You pay only for what you catch. Open 10 a.m. to 7 p.m., from Memorial Day to Labor Day. VISA and MasterCard are accepted. Turn off US 50 at Terrible Herbst Gas Station, 1023 Blue Lake Avenue, South Lake Tahoe, CA 96151; (916) 541-1491.

## Saw Mill Pond, South Lake Tahoe

This is an attractive little fishing area just west of the "Y" intersection of US 50 and Highway 89. Free fishing for children 13 and under. You must supply your own bait and equipment. The California Department of Fish and Game stocks the pond with trout in the spring. Open from April to November, weather permitting. Past the "Y" at the corner of Lake Tahoe Boulevard and Saw Mill Road. Lake Tahoe Basin Management Unit, 870 Emerald Bay Road, Suite 1, South Lake Tahoe, CA 96150; (916) 573-2600.

# NATURE CENTERS
## Animal Ark, Reno

This non-profit nature center and wildlife sanctuary features educational information about predators of North America. Many wildlife species are located at the center. Fees: Adults, $4; children (3-12) and seniors (65 and older), $3; free to children 2 and under. Open Saturday and Sunday, 10 a.m. to 5 p.m. Closed in winter, from October to April. Take US 395 to Red Rock. Travel north for 11 miles, then turn right on Deerlodge. 1265 Deerlodge, Reno, NV 89506; (702) 969-3111.

## Lahontan National Fish Hatchery

Five miles south of Gardnerville, Nevada, this hatchery features cutthroat and rainbow trout. It offers free, self-guided tours, interpretive exhibits and brochures. Special guided tours can be arranged. Open daily from 8 a.m. to 3 p.m. during summer. 710 US 395, Gardnerville, NV 89410; (702) 265-2425.

## Lake Tahoe Visitor Center, South Lake Tahoe

The visitor center provides free maps, brochures, wilderness permits, interpretive programs and six self-guided nature trails. A Stream Profile Chamber is located along the interpretive Rainbow Trail; you can watch cutthroat and rainbow trout, kokanee salmon and other aquatic life through the windows of this underground viewing chamber. Campfire programs are available in August. Open daily through October, from 8 a.m. to 5:30 p.m. Interpretive programs are scheduled between 10 a.m. and 8 p.m. (June through Labor Day). On Highway 89, four miles south of the "Y" intersection of US 50 and Highway 89. Lake Tahoe Basin Management Unit, 870 Emerald Bay Road, Suite 1, South Lake Tahoe, CA 96150; (916) 573-2600.

# THEME PARKS & AMUSEMENT CENTERS

## Ponderosa Ranch, Lake Tahoe

Your kids probably never heard of television's most popular Western series, "Bonanza," but they'll love the assortment of Western-style happenings at this outdoor theme park on a hillside above Incline Village. The Cartwright Ranch House here is the actual set used in the series (as well as several recent "Bonanza" TV movie spin-offs). Tours of the park, an entire Western theme town and a vast open-air museum of vintage cars and wagons will appeal just as much to adults. Amenities include video arcades, indoor and outdoor shooting galleries, the Mystery Mine, retail shops, a saloon, walking tours and gunfight shows. Pony rides and a petting zoo are free with admission. Haywagon breakfast rides (wagons pulled by tractors) depart daily from 8 a.m. to 9:30 a.m. in summer, and offer flapjacks and other vittles on a hill overlooking the lake. Or the wee ones can have a Hossburger for lunch. An authentic 1870s church is available for weddings. Open daily from 9:30 a.m. to 5 p.m. (late April through October, weather permitting). 100 Ponderosa Road, Incline Village, NV 89451; (702) 831-0691.

## Silver Legacy, Reno

This brand-new, 37-story casino/hotel/theme park in downtown Reno, a joint project of Circus Circus Enterprises and Eldorado Hotel Casino, covers two city blocks and has a climate-controlled family entertainment center. As this edition went to press, Silver Legacy was planning a late summer, 1995 opening. The park's theme is the Old West mining era of the mid- to late 1800s, and the centerpiece is a huge dome with a 120-foot-high automated mining machine that is built of steel and glass with brass accents. 407 North Virginia Street, P.O. Box 3920, Reno, NV 89505; (702) 329-4777.

*The Old West façade beckons visitors to Boomtown, a combination casino, hotel and indoor theme park east of Reno.*

## Boomtown, Reno

Commanding a prominent location on a hill next to Interstate 80 west of Reno, this casino/funhouse hybrid is a great spot to turn the kids loose. While the place is mostly wall-to-wall slot machines and gaming, the Family Fun Center is an indoor wing devoted to over 100 arcade and video games. There's an antique carousel, a themed 18-hole miniature golf course and a Dynamic Motion Theater, where the seats move to the action. The theater, with four or five different features, is fairly intense and realistic, even for adults, and the mine shaft theme, in particular, will scare the daylights out of you. The Tumbleweed Pizza Cafe, a party room and a prize redemption center are adjacent to the action. There's a hotel, RV park, gas station and restaurants at Boomtown, as well. Fees: miniature golf, $3.50; motion theatre, $3.50; carousel, 75 cents. An all-day pass provides access to all activities and includes $2 in game tokens. Open daily year-round from 10 a.m. to 10 p.m. Interstate 80, P.O. Box 399, Verdi, NV 89439; (702) 345-6000 or (800) 648-3790.

## Wild Island, Sparks

When the mercury starts soaring in the high desert of Reno, as it inevitably does in midsummer, this is the place to cool off. The 11-acre park just east of John Ascuaga's Nugget off Interstate 80 has a series of water rides that include speed slides, a wave pool and a lazy river. If that's not enough adventure, there are two 18-hole miniature golf courses that use theatrical settings and coordinating soundtracks, and include scenes such as a European street, a 41-foot castle and an old grist mill. A futuristic game arcade, called Tut's Tomb, and a go-cart raceway that has electric mini cars, sprint cars and adult-sized Indy cars, also are at the park. Golf costs $3.95 for 18 holes and $5.95 for 36 holes. Indy cars (42-inch minimum driving height) are $3.50; Sprint cars (42-inch maximum height) are $2.50. Water slides are $10.95 for kids under four feet; $15.95 for kids over four feet. Winter hours: 1 p.m. to 9 p.m. weekdays, 10 a.m. to 9 p.m. weekends. Summer hours: 10 a.m. to 11 p.m. Sunday through Thursday; 10 a.m. to midnight Friday and Saturday. Water slide park hours: 11 a.m. to 7 p.m. weekends (beginning one week before Memorial Day), and 11 a.m. to 7 p.m. daily in July and August. 250 Wild Island Court, Sparks, NV 89434; (702) 331-WILD or (702) 359-2927.

## Circus Circus Hotel Casino, Reno

It's the Big Top under the Big Roof, with jugglers, trapeze artists, wirewalkers and other daredevils who are there to take your mind off your losing streak, or to keep the kids occupied while you roll the dice. The Midway features carnival games, a redemption center, a video arcade, a shooting gallery and free circus acts every half hour. Restaurants and restrooms are located above the Midway. Open 10 a.m. to midnight on weekdays; 10 a.m. to 1 a.m. on weekends. Circus acts are performed daily from 11 a.m. to midnight. 500 North Sierra, Reno, NV 89503; (702) 329-0711.

## Performing Elephants at the Nugget, Sparks

Bertha and Angel perform as the opening act at the celebrity showroom every day except Tuesday. Visitors may see the elephants in their home at Elephant Palace, which is adjacent to the Nugget building. Open daily from 10 a.m. to 2 p.m. in the summer (outside), 12 p.m. to 1 p.m. in the winter (inside the barn), weather permitting. Admission for adults and children 6 and older is $12.50 Sunday through Friday and $15 on Saturday. The Elephant Palace visit is free. At John Ascuaga's Nugget, off Interstate 80 east of Reno (Nugget Avenue exit). 1100 Nugget Avenue, Sparks, NV 89431; (702) 356-3300 or (800) 648-1177.

## Idlewild Playland, Reno

This 49-acre park features amusement rides (a train, electric cars, a carousel, planes, a rollercoaster and a tilt-a-whirl). Animal rides are also available. Other amenities include picnic and party areas, a swimming pool, volleyball courts and baseball fields. Rides cost 65 cents each; an $11 family pack containing 20 tickets is available. Open daily from 11 a.m. to 6 p.m. Closed during winter until February (weather permitting). 1900 Idlewild Drive, Reno, NV 89509; (702) 329-6008.

## Harrah's Casino Hotel, Lake Tahoe

The new, 12,000-square-foot Family Fun Center on US 50 features a Play Pal Jungle Gym, a redemption center, virtual reality laser tag and video games. No child-supervised care is available. Open 9 a.m. to midnight on weekdays, 9 a.m. to 1 a.m. on weekends. P.O. Box 8, Stateline, NV 89449; (702) 588-6611 or (800) HARRAHS.

## Tahoe Amusement Park

This outdoor facility on US 50 features a mini-Ferris wheel, a large slide and a merry-go-round. Other amenities include a video arcade, miniature golf, electric cars and carnival-style games. Closed during winter. 2401 Lake Tahoe Boulevard, South Lake Tahoe, CA 96105; (916) 541-1300.

## Reno Hilton Fun Quest Center

An indoor arcade in this large casino hotel features video arcade games, Q-Zar laser tag, bumper cars and a Kid Quest jungle gym. Fees: Q-Zar, $6 per person; bumper cars, $2; Kid Quest (children ages 3 to 8), $5. Open daily year-round from 10 a.m. to midnight. In the Reno Hilton, at the corner of Mill and Glendale. 2500 East Second Street, Reno, NV 89595; (702) 789-2FUN.

# SLOT CAR RACING & GO-CARTS

**Celebrity Golf and Entertainment, Carson City:** Go-carts are available from noon to 7 p.m. Monday through Friday, 10 a.m. to 7 p.m. Saturday, 10 a.m. to 5:30 p.m. Sunday. Fees are $3.50 for five minutes. Birthday party facilities and group rates are available. 4729 South Carson Street, Carson City, NV; (702) 883-7335.

**Flag to Flag Slot Cars, Reno:** An indoor racetrack for slot cars, accessories, sales, rentals and races. Track rates start at $2; car and control, $5 for 15 minutes. Open from 2 p.m. to 10 p.m. Wednesday through Friday, noon to 10 p.m. Saturday, and noon to 8 p.m. Sunday (weather permitting). 295 Gentry Way #7, Reno, NV; (702) 825-4199.

# MAGIC SHOWS

**Magic Shop, Reno:** Free magic shows are presented every hour on the hour from 11 a.m. to 5 p.m. Brief instruction is given free with every purchase. Private lessons are by appointment only. Free magic classes are offered every other Thursday from 6 p.m. to 7 p.m. Open 10 a.m. to 6 p.m. Monday through Saturday, 11 a.m. to 5 p.m. Sunday. 1 North Virginia Street, Reno, NV; (702) 786-6544.

# MINIATURE GOLF

**Fantasy Kingdom Miniature Golf, South Lake Tahoe:** Outdoor 23-hole course with castles, dragons, sharks and whales. Open daily during summer. 4046 US 50, South Lake Tahoe, CA; (916) 544-1491.

**Magic Carpet Golf, North Tahoe:** Miniature golf course. Closed during winter. 5167 North Lake Boulevard, Carnelian Bay, CA; (916) 546-4279.

**Magic Carpet Golf, South Lake Tahoe:** 19-hole and 28-hole golf courses. Fees: 18 holes are $4 per day, $4.50 per night; 28 holes are $5.50 per day, $6 per night. 2455 Lake Tahoe Boulevard, South Lake Tahoe, CA; (916) 541-3787.

**Graeagle Miniature Golf and Driving Range:** Located 50 minutes north of Truckee on Highway 89. Closed during winter. Highway 89, Graeagle, CA; (916) 836-2107.

**Celebrity Golf and Entertainment, Carson City:** Outdoor miniature golf course. Open from noon to 7 p.m. Monday through Friday, 10 a.m. to 7 p.m. Saturday, and 10 a.m. to 5:30 p.m. Sunday. Fees are $3.50 for children and adults, $2.50 for seniors. Birthday parties and group rates are available. 4729 South Carson Street, Carson City, NV; (702) 883-7335.

**Magic Carpet Golf, Reno:** Outdoor miniature golf courses (two 19-hole courses and one 28-hole course). Party packages are available. The cost is $4 for 19 holes. Open daily from 11 a.m. to 6 p.m., weather permitting. 6925 South Virginia Street, Reno, NV; (702) 329-6008.

# ROLLER SKATING

**Kings Skate Country, Sparks:** Roller skating rink, snack bar, rentals and sales. Skating fees: weekend mornings, $3; weekdays, $3.50; weekend evenings, $4. Skate rentals: $1.50. Open Monday 6:30 p.m. to 9 p.m., Tuesday 7:30 p.m. to 10 p.m., closed Wednesday and Thursday for private parties, Friday noon to 2 p.m. (only children 10 and under with parent) and 6 p.m. to midnight, Saturday 10:30 a.m. to 1 p.m. (children's session) and 3 p.m. to midnight, Sunday 10:30 a.m. to 1 p.m. (children's session) and 4 p.m. to midnight. Open year-round. 1855 East Lincoln Way, Sparks, NV; (702) 359-5572.

**Kings Skate Country, Reno:** Roller skating rink, snack bar, rentals and sales. Skating rentals: weekend mornings, $3; weekdays, $3.50; weekend evenings, $4. Skate rentals: $1.50. Hours: closed Monday and Tuesday for private parties; Wednesday, 5 p.m. to 9 p.m.; Thursday, 7:30 p.m. to 10 p.m.; Friday, noon to 2 p.m. (only children 10 and under with parent) and 6 p.m. to midnight; Saturday, 10:30 a.m. to 1 p.m. (children's session) and 3 p.m. to midnight; Sunday, 10:30 a.m. to 1 p.m. (children's session) and 4 p.m. to 7 p.m. Open year-round. 515 East Seventh, Reno, NV; (702) 323-5464 or (916) 329-3472.

# BATTING CAGES

**Celebrity Golf and Entertainment, Carson City:** Seven outdoor batting cages. Open noon to 7 p.m. Monday through Friday, 10 a.m. to 7 p.m. Saturday, and 10 a.m. to 5:30 p.m. Sunday. Fees: $1 for 20 balls. Birthday party facilities and group rates are available. 4729 South Carson Street, Carson City, NV; (702) 883-7335.

**Grand Slam USA, Sparks:** Indoor batting cages for soft and hard ball hitting. Batting and pitching lessons are available. Fees: $1.25 for 20 pitches; $25 per hour. Open 9 a.m. to 8 p.m. Monday, Tuesday and Friday; 9 a.m. to 6 p.m. Wednesday, Thursday and Saturday; 9 a.m. to 4 p.m. Sunday. 1855 East Lincoln Way #F, Sparks, NV; (702) 358-4487.

# ZOOS

**Sierra Safari Zoo, Reno:** Families can get close to over 200 animals and 40 species. Hands-on experience is emphasized with a one-acre petting area (people can feed deer, exotic sheep and goats) and nursery pen (pet bottle-fed babies). Fees: adults, $5; seniors, $4; children (ages 2 to 12), $3; kids under 2 are free. Group rates are available. Open from 10 a.m. to 5 p.m. daily (closed during winter until April 1). Take US 395 to the Red Rock exit in Stead; 10200 North Virginia Street, Reno, NV; (702) 677-1101.

*A Western theme celebrates the famous Cartwright family of television's "Bonanza" at the Ponderosa Ranch.*

# Chapter 18

# Wedding Sites & Services

## ★ Author's Choice ★

### *Top 10 Places to Get Married*

Emerald Bay/Vikingsholm Castle
*(see page 20 in "Lake Tahoe Points of Interest")*

Top of the Tram, Heavenly Ski Area—p. 476

Sand Harbor
*(see page 24 in "Lake Tahoe Points of Interest")*

On Lake Tahoe, Via Cruiseboat—p. 478

Cal-Neva Lodge—p. 469

Harrah's Tahoe Wedding Chapel—p. 471

Ehrman Mansion/Sugar Pine Point State Park
*(see page 25 in "Lake Tahoe Points of Interest")*

Genoa Community Church—p. 487

Ponderosa Ranch Chapel—p. 481

Silver Lake Chapel—p. 487

Something about Lake Tahoe tugs at the heart. Nature's handiwork of glacier-carved mountains, pristine bays and sandy beaches has created a place for hopeless romantics. Tahoe works its magic in many ways: the grandeur of Emerald Bay, the paddlewheel excursion boats plying the waters, the stunning sunsets from the top of Heavenly's tram, the miles of white sand beaches and rocky shoreline, the twinkle of lights in the evening around the lake. There are towering hotels that overlook more riches than any slot machine could deliver, European restaurants where you can dine on soft-shell crab as water laps at the piers, and cozy little inns with big fireplaces that invite togetherness. Could a more ideal spot be found for two people to join in matrimony?

Unique in the world among alpine lakes, Tahoe has become a popular destination for couples to say their vows—as well as enjoy a romantic honeymoon. You can take your pick of just about any venue imaginable for a wedding: a historic church, a famous lakeside estate, a rocky overlook at Emerald Bay, an excursion boat, a ski resort, a hotel, a beautiful beach, or any one of over two dozen wedding chapels that have sprung up in recent years. You can have an elaborate affair for a large group, with dancing and entertainment, or a simple ceremony in a small chapel.

Nevada has always had a reputation as an easy place to get a marriage license and a cheap, quick ceremony. South Lake Tahoe, in particular, has catered to this business, and production-line weddings are nothing unusual in the summer. Recent changes that facilitate the issuance of licenses in California have generated even more business. Everybody, it seems, has a chapel, even if it's a converted motel room or a former knickknack shop in a casino. The chapels range from inauspicious places, with enough highway noise to drown out the pastor, to elaborate venues with artificial lighting and video camera systems. Because of fierce competition among wedding providers, the cost of a basic, no-frills ceremony can be dirt cheap (as little as $150). Of course, you can also go soup-to-nuts and hold an elegant, luxurious event that everyone in your party will enjoy.

In recent years, as the wedding industry has grown, so, too, have the demands from consumers. There is now a more upscale, sophisticated environment for those who want it. Wedding planners can customize a ceremony to very exacting (and sometimes quirky) specifications. Outdoor weddings have become nearly as popular as indoor weddings, and there are dozens of lakefront sites with gazebos, lawns or decks to accommodate vows with a view.

The only restrictions in planning your special day are your imagination and budget. Using Tahoe and its landscape as an outdoor chapel, you can devise a beautiful ceremony that doesn't have to be expensive. Over the years, Yvonne Watcher, wedding director and ordained minister for the Fantasy Inn, one of Tahoe's premier wedding services and hotels, has performed a number of unique weddings. Among them:

- Hiking to the top of Mount Tallac, an exhausting climb with an elevation gain of 3,255 feet (to the summit at 9,735 feet). The bride and groom wore hiking boots with their wedding attire, and by the time they reached the top, after six hours on foot, it was amazing that they had any stamina left to say their vows. Afterwards, the couple ate chocolate eclairs and drank champagne.
- Sailing above Tahoe in a hot air balloon. One couple not only recited their vows 4,000 feet in the air, but wrote a poem after their lofty experience and included it in cards sent out afterwards to friends and family.
- A beach ceremony at Sand Harbor, on the Nevada side of the lake, in which the bride made her entrance by walking barefoot through the water across a shallow cove. She and her fiancé were married at the end of a carpeted aisle, and following the ceremony, their families and guests blew bubbles above the newlyweds.
- A winter wedding in which the couple took the Heavenly resort ski tram to its mid-mountain terminal, said their vows from the deck of the lodge, and then skied off into the horizon.

Consider a wedding I helped organize in June, 1994, for Japanese television and film actress Yumi Morio and her fiancé, Naoki Kawai. Working with Fantasy Weddings and a Japanese-speaking colleague, Jana Walker, we developed an elaborate spectacle that was filmed by a Tokyo television station and covered by a bevy of reporters and magazine editors. The couple chose Lake Tahoe as their wedding spot because Kawai-san had proposed there during a ski trip. They had given us just one specification: They wanted an outdoor wedding on the shore of Emerald Bay.

The wedding day, as luck would have it, dawned with perfect, warm weather (after several days of wind, rain and even snow flurries). The couple was taken from the Horizon Casino Resort by a white stretch limousine to the dock at Zephyr Cove. There, joined by nearly 100 relatives, friends and media, the party boarded three luxury yachts for a 45-minute journey across the lake to Emerald Bay.

The boats motored through the narrow inlet and across the mirror-smooth bay, facing an awesome backdrop of snow-crested peaks, white beach and Vikingsholm Castle. After the guests disembarked onto the beach, the ceremony began at a site facing the bay, beneath a white arch fronted by flowers. Before and after the vows, a singing duo with guitar and flute played "Love Song from The Godfather," a nod to the filming of *The Godfather, Part II* at the nearby Fleur du Lac estate. Small boats bobbed gently in the bay next to Fannette Island, the lake's only true island, home

## HOW TO OBTAIN A MARRIAGE LICENSE

**CALIFORNIA Confidential Marriage License:** No blood test or waiting period. Applicants must sign a form stating they are living together as husband and wife. Must be at least 18 years old and bring picture identification. It is required that you purchase the license (approximately $45) in the county where the ceremony will be performed.

Licenses may be obtained from the following: California wedding chapels; El Dorado County Recorder, Clerk Office, in South Lake Tahoe at (916) 573-3408; Placer County Clerk-Recorder in Auburn at (916) 889-7983; or Placer County Sheriff's Department at (916) 581-6305.

**Regular License:** Blood tests are no longer required. The couple must be at least 18 years old, possess picture identification, and have a witness. Obtain a license from your home town county courthouse or the El Dorado County Recorder, Clerk

to a small, stone teahouse on its rocky summit.

Afterwards, the party reboarded the yachts and returned to South Lake Tahoe for a reception at Edgewood Country Club, the famous golf resort that borders the lake and has an elegant clubhouse with banquet rooms and beamed cathedral ceilings. Kawai-san and his bride arrived at the reception in a horse-drawn, white carriage. After the emotion-filled day, there wasn't a dry eye in the house.

Other celebrities have said "I do" at the lake in years past, although with less fanfare. Actor Tom Selleck, for example, married his lady love on a quiet and secluded sand beach on the Nevada side. And comedian-actor Robin Williams also chose Tahoe for his wedding.

The opportunities for a memorable wedding (and a fun-filled honeymoon) beckon from every corner of this alpine paradise. No doubt about it, Tahoe is for lovers.

## WEDDING CHAPELS & SITES

There are as many wedding possibilities as there are attractions in Lake Tahoe. Outdoor weddings next to the shoreline or on a mountain overlooking the lake are among the more popular ceremonies. You can tie the knot in a state park, in a national forest or in one of Tahoe's several historic estates. When considering any of these options, it's best to work through a local wedding coordinator who knows how to deal with the paperwork, especially if you want a ceremony on public lands. Usually, most chapels and some churches will perform off-site ceremonies. The following list includes the major hotels, resorts, churches, theme parks and chapels that regularly perform weddings. But the possibilities extend far beyond this group. For other ideas, consult the chapters on accommodations, resorts, beaches, major points of interest, restaurants and nightclubs.

The prices listed for the wedding chapels, venues and services below, while valid as this book went to press, are always subject to change. Advertised or unadvertised specials may be offered, especially during slow periods. In general, minister fees range from $35 to $150, photography from $30 to $625, video photography from $65 to $150, flowers from $50 to $1,250, catering from $10 to $125 per guest, cakes from $25 to $275, and live music from $75 to $425. Prices are usually open to negotiation for large and elaborate weddings.

# HOTELS
# North Shore

## ★ Cal-Neva Lodge ★

*★ notes Author's Choice*

Perched on a rocky knoll overlooking Crystal Bay, Cal-Neva Lodge has the most picturesque setting of any major hotel on the lake. Exquisite lake views from the balconies and patio terraces of the hotel provide several idyllic backdrops for a wedding ceremony. Cal-Neva supplies convenient catering services, a relaxation spa and all the elements to ensure a cozy honeymoon. If you're looking to have a grand reception, there's the historic Indian Room with its wood-beamed ceilings and rustic memorabilia. One of the popular settings for vows is a gazebo on a large elevated patio, but there are also two indoor chapels to choose from. This hotel has lots of history, some of it spicy, including rumored dalliances between Marilyn Monroe and John F. Kennedy. The property was once owned by Frank Sinatra. Because the hotel straddles the state line, you can have your choice of a wedding in either California or Nevada.

**Amenities:** Three chapels with lake views and ministers are available. They include a gazebo overlooking the lake, with a seating capacity of 400; the Lady of the Lake Chapel, with its church-like setting and a capacity of 120; and the Lakeview Chapel, with a seating capacity of 50. The hotel has a full-service wedding department, including florist, wedding boutique and beauty salon. Several honeymoon packages are available.

**Information:** Cal-Neva Lodge, 2 Stateline Road, P.O. Box 368, Crystal Bay, NV 89402; (702) 832-4000 or (800) 225-6382.

Office, (916) 573-3408. License fees vary by county (approximately $50) and can be used anywhere in California.

**NEVADA**

No blood test or waiting period required. The couple must be at least 18 years old and bring picture identification. Those 16 to 18 years of age can be married with parents or legal guardians either present or by notarized written consent.

Licenses ($42 fee, cash only) can be obtained by the following: Douglas County Clerk in Minden at (702) 782-9015; Carson City Clerk at (702) 887-2084; Douglas County Administration Building in Stateline at (702) 588-7100; or Washoe County Justice Court in Incline Village at (702) 832-4166.

## The Resort at Squaw Creek

Rising out of the forest next to the foothills of Squaw Valley USA ski area, this luxurious hotel offers a lot of atmosphere for weddings—spacious outdoor patios and decks, a top-ranked golf course, award-winning restaurants and banquet rooms with majestic views of the valley and towering peaks. The resort's beamed ceilings and massive windows impart grandeur and sophistication. The superb catering and service, offered at a multitude of indoor and outdoor wedding sites, work to create a memorable setting for any ceremony. If money is no object, and you want to impress your guests with gourmet food and sparkling mountain vistas, this is a place to do it.

***Amenities:*** The resort has a variety of wedding locations, some as bucolic as a wooden bridge over a stream. Receptions include catered two- or three-course meals, wedding cakes, linen, tables, chairs, and a dance floor, bandstand and DJ (lunch menus are $36 to $50 per person, dinner menus $52 to $125 per person; customized menus available). A wedding planner arranges ministers, florists, photographers, menus and entertainment, and you can even order ice sculptures. Wedding packages for any time of the year offer ceremonies on-site with a complimentary wedding night suite.

***Information:*** The Resort at Squaw Creek, 400 Squaw Creek Road, P.O. Box 3333, Olympic Valley, CA 96146; (916) 583-6300 or (800) 327-3353.

## Hyatt Regency, Lake Tahoe

Nestled among the tall trees at Incline Village, the Hyatt Regency has its own private beach with grand views of Lake Tahoe. The brand new Lakeside Lodge, which is across the street from the main building, is the best location to tie the knot because it's right on the beach and it has wonderful vistas. But the hotel also makes use of its banquet rooms, ballroom and large tents that can be set up on the lawn. The Hyatt is close to great restaurants, golf and other points of interest on the North Shore, and the interior has recently had a major facelift that makes it one of the more attractive casino resort properties on the lake.

***Amenities:*** Wedding, reception and honeymoon packages are available. Locations consist of the Lakeside Lodge, with three sections each seating 100 to 120 people; the Donner Room, which seats 10 to 40; the Pool Deck, which seats 25 to 75; the Water Gardens, which seats 200; the Regency Ballroom, which seats up to 900 in sections of 50 guests; and the outside lawn, which offers special tents and can seat up to 400. Rental fees range from $250 to $1,500. The hotel can provide tables and linen, silver plates and crystal glassware, fine China, professional personnel, a dance floor, a bandstand and a wedding coordinator. Breakfast, lunch, dinner menus, and wine and bar service are also available. Couples must hire their own music, pastor, photographers and florists (a recommendation list is provided).

*Information:* Hyatt Regency, P.O. Box 3239, Incline Village, NV 89450; (702) 832-1234, ext. 4460.

# South Shore

## Caesar's Tahoe Wedding Chapel

Do you like special effects? If you're a fan of Hollywood movie magic, this may be the place for your nuptials. Clearly the most "high tech" of the wedding chapels at Tahoe, this one has a novel feature—an "environmental" ceiling. By pushing a few buttons, the wizards behind the scenes can produce any mood or time of the day—from dawn to moonlight, or even a combination, if you prefer. The setting is quite ethereal, from the grand white player piano to the marble altar. Video cameras film everything, and the resulting tape has fade-ins, fade-outs and a moody soundtrack. The chapel is on the ground floor of the hotel and its location is a little strange; it's next to the hotel's indoor swimming pool. Fortunately the grand foyer is air-conditioned, and there are bridal finishing rooms for final touches.

*Amenities:* A chapel, minister, candles, grand piano music, videography, still photography and flowers are available. Couples must obtain their own marriage license from Douglas County. The hotel is available for receptions and accommodations. Chapel fees range from $65 to $180 and up, and a non-refundable deposit of $100 is required to reserve a date. The minimum chapel time is 30 minutes.

*Information:* The Wedding Chapel at Caesar's Tahoe, 55 US 50, P.O. Box 6930, Stateline, NV 89449; (800) 833-4422 or (702) 588-4422.

## ★ Harrah's Tahoe Wedding Chapel ★

Opened in the spring of 1995, the newest casino chapel is the highest at the lake—on the 16th floor of the hotel next to The Summit restaurant. It has a commanding view of South Shore, the lake and the surrounding peaks. The interior has a contemporary, European feel to it, not church-like, and the audience faces the windows to enjoy the panorama. Gold leaf is set into a pale concave ceiling, and the overall effect is one of sophistication.

*Amenities:* The chapel is 1,000 square feet, and has two spacious mountain-view bridal suites with restrooms, generous seating and state-of-the-art video and sound system. Other services include an on-site wedding coordinator, packages with accommodations, receptions, catering, flowers, cakes, photography, a bridal boutique and a hair and nail salon.

The chapel is owned and operated by the hotel.

*Information:* Harrah's Casino Hotel, US 50, P.O. Box 8, Lake Tahoe, NV 89449; (702) 588-6611, ext. 2293.

## Harvey's Wedding Chapel

This is an attractive chapel with a not-so-attractive view of the rear parking lot from the 18-foot-high windows. The interior is nicely appointed, with a marble altar, a mirrored and concave ceiling and comfortable upholstered chairs. The chapel is on the third level next to the convention center. As a hotel, Harvey's has many excellent features, including spacious and modern rooms with dramatic lake views, good service and some of the best restaurants in Tahoe.

*Amenities:* The hotel can provide a pastor, chocolates, champagne, a cake, a reception, photography, video and music. Flowers and off-site weddings also are available. Packages that include the service and accommodations begin at $375. Reservations require a $50 non-refundable deposit.

*Information:* Harvey's Wedding Chapel, US 50, P.O. Box 128, Stateline, NV 89449; (702) 588-2411, ext. 2125, or (800) HARVEYS.

## Embassy Suites Wedding Services

South Lake Tahoe's newest hotel, located on the California side of Stateline, offers two attractive indoor chapels next to a sweeping, elegant lobby with towering skylights, a mining-era sluice box with gushing water, lush vegetation and a vast indoor courtyard that is ideal for receptions. Oversized suites with separate bedrooms and living rooms, free morning breakfast and afternoon Happy Hour, an indoor pool, a restaurant and a nightclub are all features to attract a wedding party. And the casinos are just outside the door. The wedding services are operated independently of the hotel.

*Amenities:* The large chapel seats 100, and a garden atrium chapel seats over 250. Services available include the ceremony, pastor, flowers, video, still photography, a wedding cake, a marriage license and catering. There's a non-refundable deposit of $50 to reserve a date.

*Information:* Embassy Suites Wedding Services, 4130 Lake Tahoe Boulevard, Suite 224, South Lake Tahoe, CA 96150; (916) 544-2300 or (800) 722-6660.

## Fantasy Inn

This is the lake's most unusual small hotel, designed with European-Tahoe architecture and with elaborate theme rooms geared specifically to couples. These include Romeo and Juliet, Graceland, Rainforest and Roman suites. A small but elegant, tastefully decorated chapel with video cameras adjoins the inn lobby, and there's a lawn for outdoor ceremonies and small receptions. The on-site coordinator can arrange weddings here and in other locations around the lake. The theme suites, always popular, make great honeymoon retreats with their oversized tubs for two, oversized beds and ceiling-mounted televisions. Everything is deluxe and intimate, with no crowds or clanging slot machines.

*Amenities:* Among the services available are indoor and outdoor weddings, a candlelight ceremony, video, flowers, a marriage license and certificate, music and romantic gifts. Packages include the full service, a honeymoon suite, toasting glasses with champagne, and breakfast in bed.

*Information:* Fantasy Inn, 3696 Lake Tahoe Boulevard, South Lake Tahoe, CA 96150; (916) 541-6666, (800) 624-3837 or (800) 367-7736.

### Horizon Casino Resort

The motto for The Chapel at Lake Tahoe Horizon is "Weddings with a View," but you won't get a view of anything except the walls of what used to be a store in the ground floor arcade. Many of the guest rooms, however, have great views of the lake, because the hotel is situated on the shoreline side of the highway. The hotel has recently undergone an extensive remodeling, but the chapel is basically a square room with simple appointments. However, for both a view and a memorable ceremony, you can always ask for the Elvis Presley Suite, where the King himself used to stay during his performances at what once was called the Sahara Tahoe. The large suite, which has a kitchen, a living room, a dining room, an exercise room and a separate bedroom, also makes a perfect honeymoon retreat, and it has a sweeping high vista of the lake. The chapel seats 50, but ceremonies also can be arranged on the courtyard or by the lake, as well as on skis or from a horse-drawn sleigh or carriage.

*Amenities:* The hotel can provide a pastor, music (vocalist, pianist or pre-recorded), video, photography, champagne, flowers and candles. Full wedding packages start at $230. There's a $50 non-refundable deposit required to reserve a date.

*Information:* Horizon Casino Resort, US 50, P.O. Box 6539, Stateline, NV 89449; (702) 588-6637 or (800) 850-3434.

# LODGES & RESORTS
## North Shore
### Christy Inn

Once the home of Wayne and Sandy Poulsen, founders of the Squaw Valley USA ski area, this rustic property includes a rambling guest house and a gourmet restaurant, called Graham's. Weddings can be performed in the restaurant or outside on the summer garden area and deck, with the reception inside. There's a deposit of half the estimated food cost to reserve a date.

*Amenities:* The indoor seating capacity is 80, and the outdoor capacity is 200. Rooms run $85 to $180 per night, and catering menus range from $25 to $35 per person, with drinks, tax and gratuity extra.

*Information:* Christy Inn, P.O. Box 2008, Olympic Valley, CA 96146; (916) 583-3451 or (916) 583-0454.

### Northstar-at-Tahoe

This forested, four-seasons resort a few miles north of Lake Tahoe has skiing in the winter, and golf, tennis and cycling trails in summer. Wedding and reception sites can be arranged at any of several indoor and outdoor locations, from the clubhouse to the ski hill.

*Amenities:* On-site wedding and lodging facilities are available. The Romance at Tahoe Ski Package (starting at $345) offers two nights lodging, two-day lift tickets, a sleigh ride, dinner, champagne and a chocolate basket in the room, and access to Northstar's Recreation Center.

*Information:* Northstar-at-Tahoe, P.O. Box 2499, Truckee, CA 96160; (916) 562-1010 or (800) 466-6784.

### Diamond Peak Ski Resort

This medium-sized ski resort on the East Shore of the lake offers dramatic vistas, along with indoor and outdoor wedding venues. Small weddings can be accommodated during the winter, but most are held in summer, either at the main lodge or at the mountaintop Snowflake Lodge, which has a new deck and offers a spectacular, close-up vista of Lake Tahoe. It can accommodate over 100 people. There's only one problem: You need a four-wheel-drive vehicle to get there. By the summer of 1996, however, a new quad lift will offer easier transportation.

*Amenities:* The regular day lodge is available throughout the summer, but the Snowflake Lodge requires advance arrangements and access by all-terrain vehicles. Rates vary depending on time of year and location of residence (locals get a better deal). Deposits are required, and there is a prime time and regular season use, with additional charges for other facilities and cleaning. The wedding party must provide all catering, pastor, photographer, flowers and music. The ski area will provide set-up and tear down of tables and chairs.

*Information:* Diamond Peak Ski Resort, Group Sales Office, 1210 Ski Way, Incline Village, NV 89451; (702) 832-1132.

### Squaw Valley USA Ski Area

Now a four-seasons resort, this ski area operates the High Camp Bath and Tennis Club, a complex of restaurants and recreation facilities at elevation 8,200 feet. Weddings can be held any time of the year, winter or summer, on a spacious patio or deck above sheer granite cliffs and the distant valley 2,000 feet below. The wedding party and guests arrive on the Squaw Valley tram, which terminates at High Camp.

*Amenities:* Five indoor seating areas are available, along with outdoor venues for the ceremony. The independent concession that runs High Camp can provide all catering, beverages, and set-up and tear down, as well as provide recommendations for the pastor, cake, flowers and entertainment. Prices are variable, depending on the size and wishes of the wedding party.

*Information:* High Camp Food and Beverage, P.O. Box 2288, Olympic Valley, CA 96146; (916) 583-2555.

## Sugar Bowl

When the lifts close down in summer, the historic, European-style lodge remains open for special functions and meetings, including weddings. This classic, Bavarian building has one of the best outdoor decks in the Sierra, as well as a grand dining room and lots of stone and wood accents. There's also a 40-room hotel (with a deluxe suite for honeymooners) that can accommodate the wedding party and guests. Access is by gondola or road. There are great photo opportunities nearby at the famous Rainbow Bridge on the Donner Summit overlooking Donner Lake.

*Amenities:* Sites include the lodge lounge, an outside lawn next to a creek, a large deck overlooking the mountains, and the dining room. The resort can provide a fully catered buffet or sit-down meal in the restaurant or on the lodge deck, with a capacity of up to 500 people. The staff can perform other planning tasks as well, including selection of a minister, a photographer, flowers and entertainment. The lodge is available from June through October, any day of the week. Prices for rental of the facility start at $450.

*Information:* Sugar Bowl, Old Highway 40, P.O. Box 5, Norden, CA 95724; (916) 426-3836, ext. 540.

## Rainbow Lodge

This 1920s bed and breakfast has a country feel, with stone, wood and warm interior colors. There's a large dining room, a lobby with a fireplace, and a full bar, along with attractive spots for a ceremony beside the Yuba River.

*Amenities:* The inn is available for weddings in summer only, from June to September. An outdoor garden with a gazebo is located behind the lodge and seats 150 people. The indoor wedding seats 45 people. A buffet catered by the lodge can be stationed in the dining room, on an outdoor deck and on a lawn. A $450 rental fee includes linen, glassware, set-up and cleaning. The bride and groom must arrange all other services, such as the marriage license, a minister, cake, flowers, photography and music, and a referral list is provided for those services. Lodging accommodations are also available for the wedding party.

**Information:** Rainbow Lodge, P.O. Box 1100, Soda Springs, CA 95728; (916) 426-3871.

# South Shore

### ★ Heavenly Ski Area ★

The main attraction here is the Top of the Tram, which is 2,000 feet above the lake level and has a huge deck providing South Tahoe's most dramatic view of the basin and Stateline casinos. Weddings can be arranged, winter or summer, at six different mountain locations, with full catering and banquet facilities available. There's a restaurant, a full bar and seating for up to 150 people indoors or 250 outdoors.

**Amenities:** Heavenly offers catering services and the tram ride; all other arrangements, including those for a pastor, a photographer, flowers, cake, music, a limousine, formal wear and accommodations, must be made by the couple, and a referral list is provided. Prices for meals range from $11 to $20 per person, and group tram rides of 25 or more cost $8 for adults, $6 for children 4 through 12, and are free for children 3 and under.

**Information:** Heavenly Ski Area, P.O. Box 2180, Stateline, NV, 89449; (916) 542-5153 or (702) 586-7000, ext. 6228.

### Timber Cove Lodge Weddings

This is a large but moderately priced lodge located on the shoreline of Lake Tahoe, with its own chapel, grassy knolls, a boathouse, a banquet room and a beach with a pier. Weddings can be arranged at any of these sites.

**Amenities:** Packages can include a marriage license, photography, video, flowers, champagne, toasting glasses and a wedding cake. Services arranged at no fee include music, limousine, hair styling and makeup, reception and accommodations. A $50 non-refundable deposit is required.

**Information:** Timber Cove, 3411 Lake Tahoe Boulevard, P.O. Box 128, South Lake Tahoe, CA 96150; (916) 541-6722, (916) 541-8494 or (800) 44-TO-WED.

### Strawberry Lodge

Nestled among the Sierra pines along the banks of the American River stands this historic, rustic lodge where weddings have been performed since 1858. The lodge has marvelous common facilities, including a big lobby with stone fireplace, a gazebo outside, a large recreation room, and beautiful guest rooms with antique furnishings.

*Amenities:* Wedding parties have use of the grounds and main ballroom, a full bar, a restaurant with extensive wine list, a fixed-price buffet menu for 35 or more persons, a rehearsal dinner in the lodge's celebrated wine cellar, and 40 hotel rooms ($45 to $100). A minister, honeymoon suite and river house are also available. The bride and groom must arrange decorating, musical entertainment, photography and the wedding cake. A non-refundable, one-third deposit is required to reserve the lodge.

*Information:* Strawberry Lodge, 17510 US 50, Kyburz, CA 95720; (916) 659-7200.

## Carson Pass/Highway 88

### Sorensen's Resort

This rustic and historic resort is set in beautiful Hope Valley, about a 20-minute drive south of Lake Tahoe. If you're looking for a simple, casual ceremony in a woodsy setting, with a cozy log cabin for your wedding night, this is an ideal Tahoe retreat. Weddings can be held near a pond, on a deck or in the authentic Norway House, and there's a small but excellent cafe for receptions. Accommodations are quite diverse in the various cabins and structures on the property.

*Amenities:* Indoor and outdoor sites, catering, flowers, champagne, reception and log cabin accommodations are available. Fees, based on the number of guests over and above any lodging and food costs range from $250 for 25 people to $1,000 for 100 people. Wedding/honeymoon packages begin at $125 per person, double occupancy. There's a non-refundable consultation fee of $250 charged to all wedding parties due at the time of booking. Fifty percent of food, lodging and facility fees are required within seven days of booking.

*Information:* Sorensen's Resort, 1255 Highway 88, Hope Valley, CA 96120; (916) 694-2203 or (800) 423-9949.

### Kirkwood

This four-seasons resort in the uncrowded Carson Pass area of Highway 88 offers both winter and summer venues, from the mountain to the meadows.

*Amenities:* The resort can supply catering, indoor and outdoor facilities, accommodations in condominiums, restaurants and a horse-drawn sleigh or wagon. All other services must be supplied by the wedding couple.

*Information:* Kirkwood Ski Resort, P.O. Box 1, Kirkwood, CA 95646; (916) 258-6000.

# Reno/Carson Valley

## Mackay Mansion

This is a popular and noteworthy estate in the one-time silver mining boomtown of Virginia City. It is a lovely, authentic Victorian mansion with a grand parlor, an outdoor garden for ceremonies of any size and a full wedding planning service. It is the most idyllic place in an otherwise desolate high-desert area, but the town and its historic buildings are fascinating, and the mansion, once owned by a silver baron, is elaborate and impressive. The bride can even arrive in a horse-drawn buggy.

***Amenities:*** The mansion offers an indoor wedding facility seating 30, a one-acre outdoor garden seating 500, a band pavilion, a dance floor, flowers, video and still photography, round-trip transportation from Reno (up to eight people), and carriage rides around Virginia City. A referral list is available for caterers, wedding cakes, entertainment and Victorian-era vintage clothing. Services are performed by a retired minister or a Justice of the Peace. The wedding couple must obtain a marriage license.

***Information:*** Mackay Mansion, 291 South D Street, Virginia City, NV 89440; (702) 847-0173.

# CRUISE BOATS

## ★ Lake Tahoe Cruises ★

The *Tahoe Queen* is a Mississippi River-style paddlewheel cruiser that has several decks and private areas for weddings. The boat operates all year from Ski Run Marina in South Lake Tahoe, has a glass bottom, and seats 500 passengers. It also has a full kitchen and huge dining facility, an area for private parties, and a regular dance band that plays during dinner cruises. When weather permits, weddings are conducted in the open on the third level observation deck, with park benches used for theater-style seating. Otherwise, vows are exchanged in the second deck oak room near the stern, overlooking the paddlewheels. The captain of the vessel can perform the ceremony, but only for those with a California wedding license. A singer can be provided to furnish an appropriate love song. Full dinner service is available (at one of two seatings), and the band usually cranks up for dancing and entertainment in the second deck cocktail lounge.

***Amenities:*** Wedding parties may choose a daytime cruise to Emerald Bay, which lasts just over two hours, or a dinner cruise with live music, which lasts 3.5 hours. Services include a wedding coordinator (at extra charge), a singer, a band or a DJ during the day, champagne, a wedding cake, photography, video and flowers. A deposit of $500 is due at the time of booking (refundable 30 days in advance), with the balance due two weeks before the date. Fees for boarding are $14 per person for daytime cruises and $18 for dinner cruises (the meal is extra). The same company also operates the *Miss Tahoe,* a private charter boat used for parties that seats 150 passengers. Rates for the charter range from $1,500 for two hours to $2,000 for four hours, plus the cost of meals and drinks.

**Information:** *Tahoe Queen,* US 50 at Ski Run Marina. P.O. Box 14292, South Lake Tahoe, CA 96151; (916) 541-3364 or (800) 23-TAHOE.

## M.S. Dixie II

This is Lake Tahoe's newest and largest cruise boat, and it sails daily out of Zephyr Cove on the Nevada side of the lake. Weddings can be conducted with a pastor of the couple's choice on the top observation deck prior to departure. Ceremonies may be held during any one of three cruise itineraries: the sunset dinner-dance (Sunday through Friday), the champagne brunch or the historic Glenbrook breakfast. The ship's captain does not perform ceremonies.

**Amenities:** The *Dixie* can supply food and beverages, including champagne, along with a keyboardist or acoustic guitar player for the ceremony. The wedding party is obliged to arrange everything else, including the cake, flowers and photography. There are no facilities to accommodate gifts. Rates range from $18 per person for adults on the daytime cruises to $34 for the dinner-dance cruises, and there is a fee of $50 for parties of four or more.

**Information:** Zephyr Cove Resort, P.O. Box 1667, Zephyr Cove, NV 89448; (702) 588-3508.

### Tahoe Para-Dice

Sailing out of Camp Richardson on the West Shore of Lake Tahoe, this vessel is a modern, luxurious 70-foot motor yacht with a flying bridge, a hot tub on the upper deck, a barbecue, a large cabin for seating and a hosted bar. It can accommodate up to 49 passengers, and its home port of Richardson's Resort is the closest launching site to Emerald Bay. The lounge can be customized with tables, chairs, tablecloths, silverware and china, and the charter company can arrange all or part of your wedding. For a small- to moderate-sized wedding party, this boat is ideal because it can be fully chartered, offering a private, exclusive wedding.

**Amenities:** The upper deck, normally set up with tables and chairs, is used for both the ceremony and dancing, while the lower salon is available for the reception. This deck has tables, chairs and a custom couch, along with large picture windows and a full bar. Live entertainment is available. Cost for charters ranges from $700 for an hour to $1,500 for three hours. Catering is extra, and can include brunch or buffet dinner.

An advance deposit of $500 is required to reserve a date, and 50 percent of the contract balance is due three weeks prior to the cruise date.

**Information:** *Tahoe Para-Dice*, P.O. Box 11436, Tahoe Paradise, CA 96155; (916) 541-7499.

## Woodwind

There's just enough room in the cockpit of this spectacular trimaran to hold a memorable ceremony. Just ask country singer Reba McIntire, who chartered the boat for her wedding a few years ago. A popular tradition on Lake Tahoe since 1975, the *Woodwind* operates up to seven cruises a day out of Zephyr Cove Marina from April 1 through October 31. Complete weddings can be performed on this very stable boat, which is 41 feet long and 24 feet wide and has a glass-bottom viewing area. The ceremony normally takes 90 minutes and is conducted under full sail.

**Amenities:** The *Woodwind* can provide the minister, photographer, videographer, flowers, champagne and informal catering with trays of hors d'oeuvres from Zephyr Cove Resort. Weddings must be booked months in advance, and couples must supply their own wedding license (from Nevada or California). Either formal or casual attire is suitable, and standing or sitting is available on the deck as well as in the cockpit. The cost ranges from $350 for a weekday to $600 for a weekend.

**Information:** Woodwind Sailing Cruises, P.O. Box 1375, Zephyr Cove, NV 89448; (702) 588-3000.

## The Party Boat

This 52-foot luxury yacht, which operates on a charter basis out of Tahoe Keys Marina, can handle a wedding party of up to 49 people. The boat features a spacious indoor cabin, an upper deck, a flying bridge, conference cabins and two bathrooms.

**Amenities:** Chairs are available, but the wedding party must provide all other services, including a pastor, food, drinks, photography and flowers. The vessel can do scenic cruises to Emerald Bay and other points on Lake Tahoe by request. The cost is $450 per hour, with a three-hour minimum. There's a refundable security deposit of $250, and a 15-percent gratuity for the captain and crew. The boat is available year-round, weather permitting.

**Information:** Tahoe Keys Marina, 2435 Venice Drive East, Suite 100, South Lake Tahoe, CA 96150; (916) 541-2155.

## Tahoe Gal

North Shore's newest cruiseboat, a small paddlewheel excursion vessel launched in the summer of 1994, offers a spacious top deck and an enclosed cabin that can handle up to 150 passengers. There's also the private Commodore Salon, which is available during regular cruises only and can seat up to 25 people. The boat normally sails along the West Shore of the lake, and on some departures visits Emerald Bay. The *Tahoe Gal* operates daily during the summer and is available for charters any time of the year.

*Amenities:* The vessel has a full bar, a galley for lunch and dinner, and catering facilities. The ship's captain can perform the wedding ceremony, and staff members can assist with other arrangements including flowers, photography, video, a limousine and lodging. Local pick-up can be provided for charters.

*Information:* *Tahoe Gal*, 850 North Lake Boulevard, P.O. Box 7317, Tahoe City, CA 96145; (916) 583-0141.

# RESTAURANTS, MEETING HALLS & THEME PARKS

## ★ Ponderosa Ranch ★

Among its various wedding venues, this Western theme park at Incline Village has an authentic 1870 country church that seats 125 people and is available from May through October. The ranch includes sets used for the filming of television's most popular western, *Bonanza*, during the 1960s and early 1970s, and a made-for-TV movie sequel in 1993. There's a large saloon/dance hall with complete catering available, an outdoor picnic area with rustic tables and a hilltop barbecue area. Also, a photographer on site can provide old-fashioned tintype pictures. The wedding service is performed by the Church of the Ponderosa minister.

*Amenities:* Ponderosa provides a variety of services, including flowers, champagne, a horse and buggy, photography, an antique limousine, a cake, catering and reception areas. Wedding packages begin at $150, and a license must be obtained by the couple. Tablecloths, napkins and plates are not supplied for outdoor receptions. Advance reservations are required.

*Information:* Ponderosa Ranch, 100 Ponderosa Ranch Road, Incline Village, NV 89451; (702) 831-0691.

## Gar Woods Grill and Pier

With its shoreline location and long guest pier, this North Shore restaurant is a popular site for weddings, especially if the couple wants to roar off into the sunset by boat. Ceremonies can be held on the beach, the pier, the deck or inside the restaurant.

*Amenities:* The restaurant is available for catered receptions, either during regular meal times or at other times. The cost to reserve the restaurant for private parties over 150 is $1,000. Meals range from $19 to $30 per person, and there's a $300 charge for the ceremony. A 20-percent gratuity and tax are added, and a deposit of 25 percent is required to reserve a date (nonrefundable 60 days prior to event).

*Information:* Gar Woods Grill and Pier, 5000 North Lake Boulevard, P.O. Box 1133, Carnelian Bay, CA 96140; (916) 546-3366, (702) 833-1234 or (800) BY-TAHOE.

## North Tahoe Conference Center

This private beachfront setting at Kings Beach on the North Shore has a lakefront room and a deck that can accommodate up to 500 people.

*Amenities:* On-the-spot marriage license, a minister, catering, beverage service and photography are available. Special Sweetheart Deal packages range from $150 to $1,500.

*Information:* North Tahoe Conference Center, P.O. Box 69, Kings Beach, CA 96143; (916) 546-7249.

# PRIVATE CHAPELS AT LAKE TAHOE
## North Shore

### A Chapel by the River

Adjacent to the Truckee River, this rustic Tahoe-style chapel features open beam ceilings, track lighting, fresh greenery and a cream-colored interior. The building was recently renovated.

*Amenities:* The riverside wedding chapel seats two to 36 people, and off-site group seating is available for up to 400 people. California confidential licenses are issued with no blood tests or waiting. The minister is always on site. Professional consultation and planning services include arranging for the minister, the ceremony, the marriage license, music, flowers, catering, photography, video, a limousine and lodging. The chapel can plan events around the lake (including wedding ceremonies on the snow or on the lake). The chapel fee is $100, which includes recorded music, dressing rooms for the bride and groom, and coordinator services. The reception room and deck are $100 per hour. There is an $80 nonrefundable deposit to reserve a date, with a one-week advance reservation recommended.

*Information:* A Chapel by the River, 115 West Lake Boulevard, P.O. Box 90, Tahoe City, CA 96145; (916) 581-2757 or (800) 581-2758.

### Dream Maker Wedding Chapel

This chapel specializes in lakeside and panoramic lakeview, mountaintop weddings. One of the more famous (and quiet) ceremonies was the wedding of actor Tom Selleck. The chapel is open daily, except Thanksgiving and Christmas Day.

*Amenities:* The main chapel seats 42 and is located at 907 Tahoe

Boulevard. The smaller chapel is located next to the Marriage License Bureau at the Center Point Building, 865 Tahoe Boulevard, Suite 104. Facilities include the chapel, a bridal dressing room, a minister, a hostess, a witness and recorded music for one hour. The main chapel costs $135, while the smaller chapel is $110, which includes a 25-minute ceremony but has no bridal dressing room. Out-of-chapel wedding packages include indoor or outdoor ceremonies with panoramic views. Advance payment in full is required to reserve a date. Other services include a DJ, photography, video, a cake, catering, flowers, wedding accessories, romantic gifts, formal wear, gowns, accessories, a limousine and accommodations.

*Information:* Dream Maker Wedding Chapel, 907 Tahoe Boulevard, P.O. Box 6395, Incline Village, NV 89450; (702) 831-6419 or (800) 252-3732.

### A Light in the Forest Wedding Chapel
A two-sided view of the lake is captured through this chapel's picture windows. Simple ivy, wood interior, turquoise window seats and gray chairs decorate the intimate setting.

*Amenities:* Choose from an indoor lakeview chapel that seats 50, an outdoor lakeview veranda, or alternative indoor and outdoor sites. The chapel rental is $50, with a $25 additional fee for rearranging seating or cleaning. The minister is available for off-site wedding ceremonies. An optional meeting or counseling prior to the ceremony is complimentary. A red rose ceremony or evening trinity candlelight service are available upon request.

*Information:* A Light in the Forest Wedding Chapel, 590 North Lake Boulevard, P.O. Box 7584, Tahoe City, CA 96145; (916) 581-5117.

# South Shore
### A Country Chapel
This 1930s ranch house has been converted to a romantic country chapel.

*Amenities:* A reception area seats up to 400 people. A California non-blood test marriage license is offered with the notary fee waived. In addition to ceremonies performed here, the coordinators have organized ceremonies at Heavenly's Top of the Tram, Tallac Vista and Valhalla Estates, in a hot air balloon, in a horse-drawn sleigh, on skis and snowmobiles, and on a 52-foot yacht. Coordination services include photography, video, a cake, flowers, live musical performers, catering, decorator, a limousine and a minister. A $50 non-refundable deposit is required for reservations. No refunds are given for cancellations of less than 21 days.

*Information:* A Country Chapel, 1154 Emerald Bay Road, South Lake Tahoe, CA 96150; (916) 544-4896 or (800) 896-4656.

# A Lakefront Wedding Chapel

Panoramic lake and mountain views are featured from this lakefront chapel on the beach. Chapel decor includes wooden chairs with mauve cushions, soft floral wallpaper, and mirrors capturing the spectacular lake views.

*Amenities:* The indoor chapel seats 50; the outside terrace seats 100 and rents separately from $79 to $150. Wedding packages (except midweek specials) range from $298 to $798 and include a marriage license and certificate, a notary fee and reception coordination. Some packages include photography, video, live music, a limousine, a sleigh ride and ski lift tickets. A non-refundable $100 deposit is required to reserve the wedding date and time.

*Information:* A Lakefront Wedding Chapel, 3351 Lake Tahoe Boulevard, Suite 14, South Lake Tahoe, CA 96150; (916) 544-6119 or (800) 656-LOVE.

# A Touch of Love Wedding Chapel

The chapel's garden features a gazebo.

*Amenities:* The chapel seats 20 people and the garden seats 50. A California license with no blood test may be issued. Other services include fresh or silk flowers, rings, video, photography and various locations of your choice for weddings and receptions. VISA and MasterCard accepted.

*Information:* A Touch of Love Wedding Chapel, US 50, 986 Edgewood Circle, South Lake Tahoe, CA 96150; (916) 544-1904 or (916) 541-4748.

# Beverly Lodge and Wedding Chapel

This Victorian-style chapel seats 20.

*Amenities:* Chapel rental and license are $100, and a license is issued with no blood test or waiting. Full-service weddings, receptions and lodging are available.

*Information:* Beverly Lodge and Wedding Chapel, 3480 Lake Tahoe Boulevard, South Lake Tahoe, CA 96150; (916) 544-4410 or (800) 865-4411.

# Chapel of the Bells

This chapel has a convenient location near major hotels and attractions at South Lake Tahoe.

*Amenities:* The chapel seats 25. An outdoor gazebo and garden seats 40 and stands 100. The inside chapel fee is $116, the outside gazebo chapel fee is $136, and off-premise services are $149. Fees include the license and clerical fee. Other services include photography, video, flowers, a cake, reception, accessories and accommodations.

*Information:* Chapel of the Bells, 2700 US 50, P.O. Box 18410, South Lake Tahoe, CA 96151; (916) 544-1112 or (800) 247-4333.

## Chapel of the Pines

This chapel offers a variety of indoor and outdoor venues throughout Tahoe and the Carson Valley.

*Amenities:* Indoor venues include the *M.S. Dixie II*, Genoa Church ($200 rental fee), a lakefront wedding chapel ($75 to $100 rental fee), and a hotel or private home where you are staying (no charge). Outdoor venues range in price from $15 to $600, and include Logan Shoals Vista Point, Spooner Lake Meadow, a beach site, a 90-minute cruise on a 42-foot trimaran, on horseback, Eagle Falls at Emerald Bay, on a ski slope, tram and sleigh. Other services include photography, video, flowers, live music, catering, a cake, personal services, formal wear and lodging. A deposit, half of the total wedding cost, is required to set the date; 48-hour cancellation notice is required.

*Information:* Chapel of the Pines, P.O. Box 1519, Stateline, NV 89448; (702) 588-2821 or (800) 426-2858.

## Cloud 9 Chapel

The formal church-like setting with pews seats 60 people, and the informal chapel with a pink floral interior seats 30.

*Amenities:* Both chapel fees are $50. California and Nevada marriage licenses may be issued on the premises with no blood tests or waiting. Other services include photography, flowers, off-site wedding locations, wedding consultations, receptions and honeymoon suites.

*Information:* Cloud 9 Chapel, 2659 US 50, P.O. Box 13884, South Lake Tahoe, CA 96151; (916) 544-1411 or (800) 545-0611.

## Edelweiss Chapel

This dollhouse-like chapel features pews, an altar, stained-glassed windows and silk flower arrangements. A flower shop is housed within the chapel.

*Amenities:* The $95 wedding package includes the license, chapel rental, minister services and the ceremony. There are no other donations or hidden charges. Other services include flowers, garters, rings, photography and videos.

*Information:* Swiss Chalet Village, 2540 Lake Tahoe Boulevard, P.O. Box 14182, South Lake Tahoe, CA 96151; (916) 541-4301.

## Lake Tahoe Wedding Services

This Victorian chapel features brass chandeliers and mauve accents with an outdoor garden area and gazebo setting.

*Amenities:* The chapel seats 40 people, the garden area seats 60, and the gazebo seats 25. The chapel rental fee is $68. Other services include full California and Nevada wedding arrangements, off-site wedding locations (Emerald Bay, lakeside and yacht), wedding consultation, reception facilities, and tuxedo and gown rentals. A free wedding packet is available upon request.

*Information:* Lake Tahoe Wedding Services, US 50, 3135 Lake Tahoe Boulevard, South Lake Tahoe, CA 96150; (916) 541-1566, (800) 824-6393 or (800) 874-0808.

### Love's Lake Tahoe Wedding Chapel

This is one of South Shore's oldest chapels, set on a hill above a busy intersection. (It is on US 50 at the bottom of Kingsbury Grade.)

*Amenities:* The garden setting in the upstairs informal chapel seats 16, while the downstairs formal chapel seats 50. Chapel rental fees range from $35 to $139. Lakeside and off-site wedding services can be performed in California and Nevada. Other services include photography, flowers, reception facilities, formal attire, a gift shop, limousines, video and accommodation arrangements. The couple must supply a marriage license. A $50 deposit is required to reserve the date and time. Cancellations must be made at least three days in advance.

*Information:* Love's Lake Tahoe Wedding Chapel, P.O. Box 2308, Stateline, NV 89449; (702) 588-6112, (702) 588-2044 or (800) MARRY-US.

### Mountain Lake Weddings

This business offers a variety of locations around Lake Tahoe, in addition to its own chapel.

*Amenities:* Chalet-style chapel seats up to 45 with a reception area that seats 400. Some off-site locations include Heavenly's Top of the Tram, Tallac Vista, Valhalla Estates, in a hot air balloon, on a horse-drawn sleigh, on skis and snowmobiles and on a 52-foot yacht. Coordination services include photography, video, a reception, a wedding cake, flowers, live musical performers, catering, a decorator, a limousine and a minister. A $50 non-refundable deposit is required for reservation. No refunds are given for cancellations less than 21 days notice. American Express, VISA and MasterCard are accepted.

*Information:* Mountain Lake Weddings, P.O. Box 14399, South Lake Tahoe, CA 96151; (916) 544-4896; (800) 896-4656).

### Wedding Paradise

This small wedding chapel is located near a golf course on the outskirts of South Lake Tahoe.

*Amenities:* The chapel seats 20 and the outdoor gazebo seats 75. Chapel rental fees range from $116 to $149 and include license and clerical fee. Other services include custom photos, videos, fresh or silk flowers, wedding cake, reception, accessories and accommodations.

*Information:* 1000 US 50, Meyers, CA. Mailing address: P.O. Box 18410, South Lake Tahoe, CA 96151; (916) 577-1051 or (800) 237-9316.

# UNIQUE CHURCHES

**St. John's in the Wilderness Episcopal Church:** Without a doubt, this is Lake Tahoe's single most inspiring church for a wedding. An old stone building right on the East Shore of the lake, the church has an incredible view through a window behind the pulpit that frames the basin and snow-covered mountains. For non-congregational weddings, either the bride or the groom must be Episcopalian, and even then there is considerable negotiating and advance preparation (at least one year for reserving a date). The church seats 240 people. Marriage classes are free with any local Episcopal priest. Fees are $150 for the priest and $100 for the building. Catering on site is available. Contact St. John's Episcopal Church, 1776 US 50, P.O. Box 236, Glenbrook, NV 89413; (916) 542-1127 or (702) 882-8460.

★ **Silver Lake Chapel:** This small church, situated near the shore of Silver Lake in the Carson Pass area, has a large picture window that faces the water and Thunder Mountain, a unique hollowed-out tree pulpit, and antique benches seating approximately 100 people. There's no electricity in the chapel, although a generator is available. The chapel, built by local volunteers, requires that the wedding ceremony be performed by licensed clergy. No beverages of any kind may be served in the chapel, no nails or tacks may be used to hang decorations, no furniture may be moved, no receptions are permitted in or around the chapel, and dripless candles must be used. The church is open from July 4 through Labor Day. A donation of $75 should be received no later than two weeks prior to wedding. The chapel is located on Highway 88, at the south end of Silver Lake at Plasse's Resort, southwest of South Lake Tahoe. Contact Norma Cuneo for information and reservations at 245 Boarman Street, Jackson, CA 95642; (209) 223-0464.

★ **Genoa Community Church:** Built in 1859, this is one of Nevada's oldest churches in the state's oldest town, and is among the most delightful wedding sites in the region. Just 30 minutes from South Lake Tahoe, the church is an old-fashioned white clapboard building with a steeple and a bell, and it's located in a quiet, tree-shaded area with ministerial views of grazing cattle, mountains and a small historic community. The church seats 75 people (wooden pews seat 50 and chairs 25), is available for outside ministers, and has a fully operating antique organ. Two-hour rentals for weddings are available seven days a week, at $150 per wedding. There's an elegant bed and breakfast inn next door, with a bridal suite. The town does not arrange for the services of a minister, photographer, florist or caterer, but will provide names of local sources. Reservations are required. The church is operated by the Town of Genoa, P.O. Box 14, Genoa, NV 89411. (702) 782-8696; (702) 782-2518.

# MORE CHURCHES
## North Shore

**Assumption Catholic Church:** Catholic or interfaith marriages are performed. Requirements: four months' advance notice for preparation and marriage counseling with a priest. Fee: $150 church donation, minister donation welcome. Reservations are required. 10116 E Street, Truckee, CA 96161; (916) 587-3595.

**Church of Christ Truckee:** Bible Church of Christ. Seats 250 people. Fees: church donation, minister $150 (counseling, rehearsal and wedding ceremony). Minister requires the bride and groom to have six to eight hours of counseling if he performs the ceremony. Reservations are required. P.O. Box 8519, Truckee, CA 96160; (916) 587-4551.

**First Baptist Church of Truckee:** Seating capacity is 90. The minister will marry anyone anywhere in California. Fees: building, $100 ($25 additional for kitchen use); minister, $150 (includes rehearsal, $25 additional for off-site weddings farther than 20 miles away). Reservations are required. 11605 Deerfield Road, Truckee, CA 96161; (916) 582-4045.

**Four Square Gospel Church of Incline Village:** This is a plain, simple structure without a kitchen or reception area. Seating capacity is 100. Fees: church, $50; minister, $100. Reservations are required. 918 Northwood Boulevard, Incline Village, NV 89451; (702) 831-5030.

**Incline Village Community Presbyterian Church:** Four sessions are arranged with the minister (wedding preparation, premarital session and ceremonial session) three months in advance. The couple must obtain a Nevada marriage license. The sanctuary seats 160 to 180 people, and an outdoor chapel that is open in July and August only seats 150. Fees: building, $100 for 1-75 guests, $200 over 75. Restrictions: No alcohol or smoking is allowed in church. Reservations are required. 736 McCoury Boulevard, Incline Village, NV 89451; (702) 831-0784.

**Lakeside Christian Essene Church:** This is a non-denominational church performing traditional and contemporary wedding services. Fees: Donations are welcome for the church and minister's use. Reservations are required. 907 Tahoe Boulevard, Incline Village, NV 89451; (702) 831-6419.

**Our Lady of the Lake Catholic Church:** Catholic or interfaith marriages are performed. Requirements: four months' advance notice for

preparation and marriage counseling with priest. Fee: $150 church dona-
tion, with a priest donation welcome. Reservations are required. 8363
Steelhead Avenue, Kings Beach, CA 96143; (916) 546-2291.

**St. Patrick's Episcopal Church:** This is a large, formal church
with a chapel. Requirements: Couples must give three months' advance
notice, undergo premarital counseling, and be members of the Episcopalian faith. Fee: Donations are welcome for the building and the minister's
use. Reservations are required. 341 Village Boulevard, Incline Village, NV
89451; (702) 831-1418.

**Seventh Day Adventist Church:** The building has a stained glass
window of three angels and seats 125 people. Fees: building, $200; minis-
ter, by donation. The minister can perform off-site weddings in California
and Nevada. Church restrictions: There is no Saturday wedding service
(except Saturday evening). Minister's requirements: Bride and groom
must both be Seventh Day Adventists and attend one week to one month
of marital counseling. However, couples may bring in a minister who
marries any Christian denomination. Reservations are required. 11662
Brockway Road, Truckee, CA 96161; (916) 587-5067.

**Tahoe Family Charismatic Worship Center:** No restrictions are
set by this church. Fee: donation welcome to the church and minister for
weddings performed. Reservations are required. 296 Deer Road, Kings
Beach, CA 96161; (916) 546-0705.

**Tahoe Incline Christian Fellowship:** This is a non-denominational church, with a maximum indoor seating of 30. Clergy will perform
outdoor and off-site weddings (including Aspen Grove, Hyatt Water
Garden and Sand Harbor Beach). No premarital counseling is required
but is provided if requested. Fees: Donations to the church and minister
are welcome. Reservations are required. 811 Tahoe Boulevard, Incline
Village, NV 89451; (702) 831-1277.

## South Shore

**Calvary Chapel:** This non-denominational church seats 100 people.
Requirements: minimum of three sessions with minister. Fee: donations
welcome for use of church and minister. Reservations are required. 2100
Eloise Avenue, South Lake Tahoe, CA 96150; (916) 544-7320.

**Church of Jesus Christ of Latter-Day Saints:** Seating capacity
is 500. Requirements: Both bride and groom must be active Mormons
and receive written permission from their bishop; all arrangements to be
made through the couple's church; and marriages are performed only in
California. Fee: donations accepted by church and minister. Reservations
are required. 3460 Spruce Avenue, South Lake Tahoe, CA 96150; (916)
544-6369.

**First Baptist Church of South Lake Tahoe:** The interior consists of knotty-pine walls, a 15-foot-high ceiling, stained glass entryway and chairs seating up to 150 people. No marriage counseling is required. Fees: church, $100; minister, by donation. Janitorial service and live music are available. Reservations are required. 1053 Wildwood Avenue, South Lake Tahoe, CA 96150; (916) 544-2743.

**Hope Lutheran Church:** The sanctuary seats 125 people. The minister requires an informal meeting prior to the ceremony with two or three marital counseling sessions, and the church will marry anyone in the Christian faith. Fees: church, $50; minister, $50 minimum; organist, $50 minimum. Open all year. Reservations are required. 930 Julie Lane, South Lake Tahoe, CA 96150; (916) 541-1975.

**Lake Tahoe Community Presbyterian Church:** Seating capacity is 150. No marital counseling is required. Fees: church use, $100; minister, $75; deacon, $75; organist, $75. No smoking or drinking are allowed in church, and no birdseed, rice or confetti may be thrown on church property. A $50 deposit is required to reserve the date on the church calendar. 2733 Lake Tahoe Boulevard, South Lake Tahoe, CA 96150; (916) 544-3757.

**St. Theresa's Catholic Church:** This church seats 600 people. Requirements: Paperwork must be filed at this church with four months' advance notice, and couples must have contact with the priest. One party must be Catholic, and neither can be divorced. A six-week marriage preparation program may be taken at your own church. Fee: $500 building rental. Reservations are required. 1041 Lyons Avenue, South Lake Tahoe, CA 96150; (916) 544-3533; (916) 541-9022.

**Seventh Day Adventist Church:** Seats 60 people. No marital counseling required for those outside the church. The minister will marry anyone in the Christian faith. Fees: church, $75; minister, $25 minimum. Restrictions: There are no Saturday morning services and only sacred music is allowed in the church. Reservations are required. 3609 Vanda Lee Avenue, South Lake Tahoe, CA 96150; (916) 544-3525.

**Temple Bat Yam Jewish Congregation of South Lake Tahoe:** Seats 80 people (120 full capacity if extra chairs are rented). Building has a kitchen and large parking lot. Fees: donation to temple and rabbi for Jewish wedding services provided. Marriages can be performed by a rabbi or by a student rabbi with a Justice of the Peace. Meeting with the rabbi is required. 3260 Pioneer Trail, South Lake Tahoe, CA 96150; (702) 588-4503.

# Reno

**Lakeside Community Church:** This church offers a non-denominational indoor or outdoor setting, as well as wedding consulting services. Reservations are required. 4685 Lakeside Drive, Reno, NV 89509; (702) 826-0566.

**Temple Emanu El:** Conservative Jewish synagogue. The rabbi will only perform Jewish weddings (no interfaith marriages). The sanctuary seats 250 people ($250 to non-members) and includes the use of a *chupah*. 1031 Manzanita Way, Reno, NV 89509; (702) 825-5600.

*Outdoor weddings, such as this one on a deck at Cal-Neva Lodge, offer lofty views of Lake Tahoe.*

# Chapter 19

# Annual
# Events

H istory, geography and just plain cabin fever contribute to the diversity of special events that are held throughout Lake Tahoe, Reno and Carson Valley each year.

The basin specializes in participant and outdoor sports, such as mountain bike tours, vintage boat shows, ski competitions, sled dog races and winter carnivals. Reno has a flare for highly visual and dramatic crowd-pleasers such as the Great Balloon Race, the National Championship Air Races and a celebration of the 1950s hot-rod lifestyle called Hot August Nights, which is the city's biggest blowout. And Carson Valley, with its tradition of silver mining, railroading and lumbering, offers events centered around historic places and people—among them the famous author and newspaperman Mark Twain. Virginia City, where the Comstock Lode silver mine propelled a desolate high-desert valley into a cradle of riches, does almost anything to get attention. Its signature event is the International Camel Races, which are always held in September. Recently, it has added a unique event called the Outhouse Races.

Visitors planning a trip to any of these communities during major events should book accommodations early. Hot August Nights, which draws over 3,000 cars of the 1950s and 1960s, sells out virtually every room in Reno eight months in advance. Lodging, however, can often be found in neighboring Lake Tahoe and Carson City. Apart from these marquee events, there are less flamboyant but equally charming local festivals that exemplify the lifestyle and culture of the area. Lake Tahoe has a burgeoning arts community that continues to offer quality events such as jazz, bluegrass and classical music concerts, art displays, and food and wine tastings. Native Americans, especially the Washoe and Paiute tribes, have powwows in Carson City and Lake Tahoe where visitors can explore their traditions and handicrafts. The annual Arts and Crafts Fair and Pow Wow at the Stewart Indian Museum in Carson City each June is one of the biggest gatherings.

The following listings are of annual events. It is important to check with the organizers to verify dates and locations, since changes are not only possible, but frequent.

## JANUARY

★ **Celebrity Sports Invitational:** Want to see a falling star? Then check out this early January event at Squaw Valley, where some of Tinseltown's finest demonstrate how to misbehave in the snow. There are unusual ski races, a concert by a big-name group and a fundraising auction for charity. Information: The Resort at Squaw Creek, (916) 583-6300, ext. 6203.

★ **Historic Skiing Revival Series:** Residents of Plumas County dress in historic costumes to commemorate one of the oldest American sites for skiing, dating back to the 1860s. Anyone over the age of 18 can try to ski on 12- to 14-foot-long skis. There is a series of three races beginning in late January and continuing through March at Plumas Eureka Ski Bowl in the historic town of Johnsville, CA. Information: Plumas County Visitors Bureau, (800) 326-2247 or (916) 283-6345.

★ **South Lake Tahoe Annual Winter Celebration:** Sure, things are slow this time of year after the holidays, so South Lake Tahoe has a few ideas to keep the party going. This month-long series of events in January includes fireworks, torchlight parades, a beer festival, talent shows, music concerts, an ice-sculpting contest, downhill professional and amateur ski races, snowboard competitions and the televised Celebrity Ski Classic at Heavenly Ski Resort. Most of the major events are on weekends. Information: Lake Tahoe Visitors Authority, (916) 544-5050; Tahoe Douglas Chamber of Commerce, (702) 588-4591.

## FEBRUARY

**Emigrant Trail Tour:** This cross-country ski tour retraces the path of pioneers at Royal Gorge Cross Country Ski Resort on the Donner Summit, at Soda Springs, CA. Information: Royal Gorge Cross Country Ski Resort, (916) 426-3661.

**International Police Winter Games**: Heavenly Ski Area, South Lake Tahoe, CA. Information: (702) 586-7000.

★ **Sierra Sweepstakes Sled Dog Races:** Snow permitting, this weekend series of sled dog races at the Truckee-Tahoe Airport offers a chance to view a variety of teams and events in an open field. The "drivers" work hard, but the Siberian huskies usually steal the show. Spectators can number in the thousands. Information: Truckee-Donner Chamber of Commerce, (916) 587-2757.

## MARCH

★ **Annual Great Ski Race:** This challenging 30-kilometer cross-country race, held in early March, runs from Lakeview Cross-Country Ski Area to the Cottonwood Restaurant in The Hilltop Lodge at Truckee and raises funds for the Tahoe Nordic Search and Rescue Team. It is considered the largest cross-country ski event in the West, with more than 800 participants. Information: (916) 583-9353 (Lakeview).

**Cross Country Ski and Food Festival:** Held at Northstar-at-Tahoe, Truckee, CA. Information: Northstar-at-Tahoe, (916) 562-1010.

★ **Echo Summit to Kirkwood Cross-Country Race:** For Nordic skiers in good shape, this challenging 18-kilometer, mid-March event spans two drainages and a mountain pass, from Echo Summit on US 50 to the Kirkwood Cross-Country Center on Highway 88. Information: Kirkwood, (209) 258-7248.

**Gold Mountain Pioneer Ski Celebration:** Held in Johnsville, CA. Information: Plumas County Chamber of Commerce, (916) 283-6345 or (800) 326-2247.

**Mother Earth Annual Pow Wow:** Competitive dancing, arts and crafts from several area Native American tribes are displayed at the Stewart Indian Museum grounds in Carson City, NV. Information: Stewart Indian Museum, (702) 882-1808.

★ **Snowfest Winter Carnival:** In early March, North Lake Tahoe and Truckee pull out all the stops for a 10-day extravaganza of winter events that includes a parade, ice carving, ski and snowboard races, live comedy and music, the legendary Polar Bear Swim, a torchlight ski parade and fireworks, a dress-up-your dog contest, a children's costume contest, a crafts fair, food events and many humorous spectator activities. The entire North Shore, including over a dozen alpine and cross-country ski areas and several communities, participate in more than 125 events. Information: Snowfest, P.O. Box 7590, Tahoe City, CA 96145; (916) 583-7625.

## APRIL

★ **Auburn Foothills Century VII Bicycle Race:** This historic Gold Rush town in the western foothills of the Sierra Nevada is a beehive of cycling. Route options include eight miles, 16 miles, 50 kilometers, 100 kilometers and 100 miles. Information: Auburn Bicycle Club, 9490 Crater Hill Boulevard, Auburn, CA 95603; (916) 885-3861 or (916) 624-2453.

**Easter Egg Hunts:** Bijou Community Park (South Lake Tahoe, CA), (916) 541-4611; Kings Beach State Recreation Area (Kings Beach, CA), (916) 546-7248; and Truckee River Regional Park (Truckee, CA), (916) 587-3587.

**Feather River Dixieland Jazz Concert:** A series of musical events running April through June in Graeagle, CA. Information: Plumas County Visitors Bureau, (800) 326-2247 or (916) 283-6345.

**Fête du Printemps:** Cross-country ski tour followed by a picnic. Information: Royal Gorge Cross Country Ski Resort, Soda Springs, CA; (916) 426-3871.

**Mountain Man Spring Rendezvous:** He-man stuff such as shotgun shoots, candle shoots, a survival walk and cannon shoots draw major crowds to an encampment southwest of Carson City along Canyon Road. It is usually held in late April. Information: Eagle Valley Muzzleloaders, (702) 887-1221.

# MAY

**Cinco de Mayo Chili Cook-off and Parade:** Virginia City, Nevada. Information: Virginia City Chamber of Commerce, (702) 847-0311.

★ **Comstock Historic Preservation Weekend:** This event in the former silver-mining boomtown of Virginia City, Nevada, includes a Victorian house and garden tour and a Mark Twain walking tour of historic sites. Twain was a reporter for the *Territorial Enterprise* during the heyday of the Comstock Lode. Events include a costume ball, history lectures, plays, entertainment, a parade and tours of vintage homes. Information: Virginia City Chamber of Commerce, (702) 847-0311.

★ **Fiesta Nevada:** Latin and mariachi bands, acrobats, folk dancers and food line the streets of Victorian Square for this two-day event celebrating Cinco de Mayo in Sparks, Nevada. Entertainment spans the Hispanic cultures of Mexico, Guatemala, Brazil and Peru on the first weekend after May 5. Over 50,000 people attend this annual gathering. Information: Sparks Redevelopment Agency, (702) 353-2291.

**High Desert Mountain Bike Race:** Held on May 20, out of Virginia City. Information: Virginia City Chamber of Commerce, (702) 847-0311.

**Motocross/Grand Prix:** Dirt bike races are held in the desert at the edge of Virginia City, Nevada, on a closed seven-mile track. Information: Virginia City Chamber of Commerce, (702) 847-0311.

★ **Sportsfest:** Various cycling events are held during the last weekend in May (Memorial Day) at Incline Village, Nevada, including mountain bike races, family fun races and a guided tour of the famous Flume Trail from Spooner Lake to Incline Village. Information: Incline Village/ Crystal Bay Visitors & Convention Bureau, (702) 832-1606.

# JUNE

★ **America's Most Beautiful Bike Ride:** Here's the only chance of the year for cyclists to circle the 72-mile perimeter of Lake Tahoe on road bikes under controlled circumstances. The route follows US 50 and highways 89 and 28, and the event draws hundreds of participants. It's usually held in early June. Information: Curtis Fong, event promoter, (702) 588-9658.

★ **Arts and Crafts Fair Pow Wow:** This is a major three-day gathering of over 35 tribes with dancing and other Native American cultural events. Food, a parade and arts and crafts exhibits fill the grounds of the Stewart Indian Museum, located on 5366 Snyder Avenue just east of downtown Carson City, Nevada. Information: Stewart Indian Museum, (702) 882-1808.

**Beer Fest:** Northern California microbreweries provide unique beers for tasting at the lodge at Northstar-at-Tahoe. Information: Northstar-at-Tahoe, (916) 562-1010.

**Celebrate the River:** A festival of food, music, arts and crafts, and shopping lines the Raymond I. Smith Truckee River Walk in downtown Reno. Information: Reno Redevelopment Agency, (702) 334-2077; or Reno-Sparks Convention & Visitors Authority, (800) 367-7366.

**Founder's Day:** This quirky two-day celebration in Virginia City, Nevada, commemorates the founding of the Comstock Lode silver boom in 1859, and is usually held during the first week in June. Events involve townspeople in period dress, with local characters. Information: Virginia City Chamber of Commerce, (702) 847-0311.

**Kit Carson Rendezvous and Wagon Train:** This is a re-creation of a mountain encampment, complete with a Native American village and a Civil War camp. You'll find live country music, arts and crafts, and food booths at Mills Park, Carson City, Nevada. Usually held on the second weekend in June. Information: Event promoter, (702) 884-3633.

★ **Lake Tahoe Wagon Train Rendezvous:** Dressed in period costumes, hundreds of people ride horses, authentic covered wagons and buggies along the original route of the Pony Express, retracing the trail from Zephyr Cove, Nevada to Old Hangtown (Placerville) in California. The mile-long train becomes a major parade as it rolls through South Lake Tahoe, usually during the second week of June. There are two days of events including gunfights, Civil War reenactments, fiddlers, clogging demonstrations, square dancing and barbecues at Round Hill Center in Nevada and the Campground by the Lake in South Lake Tahoe. Information: Highway 50 Association, (702) 883-4551.

**Living History Day:** Volunteers dress up in period clothing of this vintage mining town and operate several facilities at Plumas Eureka State Park in Johnsville, eastern Plumas County, including the blacksmith shop. Information: Plumas Eureka State Park, (916) 836-2380.

★ **Reno Rodeo:** This is one of the West's largest rodeos, and it draws thousands of spectators to the Reno Livestock Events Center in Reno, Nevada. There's also a parade through downtown Reno with a celebrity Grand Marshal, as well as country music concerts. Held in mid-June. Information: Reno Rodeo Association, (702) 329-3877; Reno-Sparks Convention & Visitors Authority, (800) 367-7366.

**Special Kit Carson Trail Spring Walk:** Participants can take a one-mile walk back in time to visit some of Carson City's vintage homes, with guides and hosts/hostesses dressing in period clothing and giving narrated tours. The one-day event is usually held in mid-June and starts at the Nevada State Legislative Plaza. Information: Carson City Convention & Visitors Bureau, (702) 687-7410.

**Valhalla Renaissance Festival:** This two-day event includes knights in combat, archery contests, jugglers, period crafts, plays, harpists, jugglers and mandolin players. It is held at Richardson's Resort, South Lake Tahoe, CA. Information: Richardson's Resort, (916) 541-1801.

★ **Valhalla Summer Arts and Music Festival:** A summer-long series of concerts featuring major jazz, bluegrass, New Age, folk, Latin and classical artists begins in late June and lasts through early October at the Tallac Historic Site, which is located 3.5 miles north of South Lake Tahoe on Highway 89. The weeknight and weekend concerts, along with arts and crafts festivals, are sponsored by the non-profit Tahoe Tallac Association, which raises funds for the restoration of the historic estates. Concerts are held in the Valhalla Grand Hall. For a program, contact the Tahoe Tallac Association at P.O. Box 19273, South Lake Tahoe, CA 96151; (916) 541-4975 (summer) or (916) 542-4166 (winter).

**Western States 100-Mile Run:** Ultra distance runners trek through snow, ice and broiling granite canyons in this test of high-elevation endurance from Squaw Valley to Foresthill in Auburn. Information: Squaw Valley USA, (916) 583-6985.

## JULY

**Arts and Crafts Fair:** Held in downtown Graeagle. Information: Plumas County Visitors Bureau, (800) 326-2247 or (916) 283-6345.

**Brewfest:** A variety of micro-brewed beer, music, dancing and food are served up at Harvey's Resort Casino at Stateline, Nevada. Information: Harvey's, (702) 588-2411.

**Cannibal Cruise and Car Show:** This is a car show, dance and rally at Truckee Regional Park in Truckee. Information: Truckee-Donner Chamber of Commerce, (916) 587-2757.

**Death Ride:** This difficult road bike ride starts at Markleeville in Alpine County. Information: Alpine County Events, (916) 694-2571.

**Firemen's Muster:** The "muster" consists of a parade, a competition with antique fire-fighting equipment (some from as early as the 1840s), breakfasts, barbecues, dancing and live music. The event rotates annually between Virginia City and Carson City, and is usually held in mid-July. Information: Carson City Convention & Visitors Bureau, (702) 687-7410.

★ **Fourth of July Celebration, South Shore:** Of the various fireworks displays in and around Lake Tahoe, this is the most extravagant. Pyrotechnics burst with dazzling colors over the water in front of the Stateline casinos, and the summer's largest audience gathers for the show. The best vantage point is a coveted berth on one of the various cruise boats such as the *M.S. Dixie II* or the *Tahoe Queen*, which view the fireworks from the lake. Information: Lake Tahoe Visitors Authority, (916) 544-5050.

## Other Fourth of July Celebrations:

- Donner Lake, Truckee. Information: Truckee-Donner Chamber of Commerce, (916) 587-2757.
- Kings Beach State Recreation Area, Kings Beach. Information: North Tahoe Public Utility District, (916) 546-7248.
- Mills Park, Carson City, Nevada. Information: Carson City Convention & Visitors Bureau, (702) 687-7410.
- Mohawk Valley Independence Celebration. At Graeagle in eastern Plumas County. Information: Plumas County Visitors Bureau, (800) 326-2247 or (916) 283-6345.
- The Resort at Squaw Creek in Squaw Valley. Information: (916) 583-6300.
- Tahoe City. Information: North Tahoe Chamber of Commerce, (916) 581-6900.
- Virginia City, Nevada. Information: Virginia City Chamber of Commerce, (702) 847-0311.

★ **Isuzu Celebrity Golf Championship:** This six-day event, usually beginning the day after July 4th, attracts top entertainment and sports stars such as Dan Marino, John Elway, Steve Young, Michael Jordan, Smokey Robinson, Randy Quaid and some 70 others for the three-day stroke-play competition. Players with accredited U.S. Golf Association handicaps of 10 or less can compete in the tournament, which is televised live on national networks. The public can buy gallery tickets for all days of the event at the gate. It's held at Edgewood Tahoe Golf Course, rated one of America's top courses. Information: Lake Tahoe Visitors Authority, (916) 544-5050.

★ **Lake Tahoe Summer Music Festival:** This series of outdoor concerts, among the most ambitious at Lake Tahoe, runs from July through August at various sites on the North Shore, including Topol Pavilion at Homewood, Granlibakken Resort, Squaw Valley, Sand Harbor and Tahoe Donner. A variety of music spans the gamut of classical, folk, operatic, Broadway and jazz. For a program write to the Music Festival at P.O. Box 62, Tahoe City, CA 96145, or call (916) 583-3101.

**Native American Fine Arts Festival:** Held at the Tallac Historic Site near South Lake Tahoe. Information: Tallac Historic Site, (916) 541-5227.

**Sports Cars & All That Jazz:** Hundreds of sports cars, from modern Italian custom cars to hot rods, share the limelight with name jazz artists at various locations around Reno, including casino showrooms. Information: DRA Special Events (promoter), (800) 535-3045.

★ **Tahoe Fat Tire Festival:** This is a nine-day series of mountain biking races, polo, observed trials, guided tours for various ability levels, rallies, parties and other activities around Lake Tahoe, usually starting at

Tahoe Vista Recreation Area. Held late July through early August. Information: Cyclepaths Bike Store, (916) 581-1171.

★ **Truckee-Tahoe Air Show:** Over 100 airplanes, including bi-planes, aerobatic planes, racing planes, sailplanes and other aircraft fill the skies over Truckee for this three-day show, usually held the third weekend of June. Other events include wing-walkers, fireworks, hot air balloon rally, barbecue, rides and dancing. It's held at the end of July at the Truckee-Tahoe Airport, 10356 Truckee Airport Road, Truckee, CA. Information: Truckee Airport District, (916) 587-4119.

**The Way It Was Rodeo:** This old-fashioned rodeo event in Virginia City, Nevada, features riding, roping and dogging contests. It's usually held the second weekend of July. Information: Virginia City Chamber of Commerce, (702) 847-0311.

## AUGUST

**Arts and Crafts Fair:** Kings Beach State Recreation Area, Highway 28 in downtown Kings Beach. Information: Kings Beach Library, (916) 546-2021.

**Blackwood Backwood Mountain Bike Challenge:** Mountain bikers climb up a steep West Shore canyon. Information: Venturing Out Promotions, (916) 583-3753.

**Carson City Invitational Hand-Car Races:** This two-day event pits teams against each other on railroad hand-cars, using dual tracks at the Nevada State Railroad Museum in Carson City, on the last weekend in August. Information: Nevada State Railroad Museum, (702) 687-6953.

**Civil War Encampment and Reenactment:** This lavish event is put on by a group called Nevada Civil War Volunteers, at the Mackay Mansion and Virginia & Truckee Railroad in Virginia City, Nevada. Activities include an authentic Civil War camp, mock battles and a train stick-up. Usually held the third weekend of August. Information: Virginia City Chamber of Commerce, (702) 847-0311.

★ **Concours d'Elegance Wooden Boat Show:** This is the largest and longest running show of antique and classic wooden boats in the country. Over 125 vessels, including many old "woodies" dating back to the early 1900s, are on display, usually at the Sierra Boat Company in Carnelian Bay on the North Shore of Lake Tahoe. The event is generally held the second weekend in August as part of Tahoe Wooden Boat Week. Proceeds benefit a future Tahoe Heritage Marine Museum. Information: Tahoe Yacht Club, (916) 525-5225.

**Graeagle Fall Festival Art Show:** This outdoor arts and crafts festival is held at the Community Square in Graeagle in eastern Plumas County. Information: Collette Promotions, (702) 322-4544.

★ **Great Gatsby Festival:** The Tallac Historic Site, a complex of vintage mansions on the southwest shore of Lake Tahoe, comes alive with the sights and sounds of the early 1900s, with an antique boat show, antique automobiles, barbecue, living history celebration, Dixieland music, games, crafts and food. Information: Tallac Historic Site, (916) 541-5227.

★ **Hot August Nights:** This is one of the largest events in the region, a big four-day blowout of car mania that celebrates the hot rods, music and lifestyle of the 1950s and 1960s. Nightly cruising on Virginia Street (The Strip) in downtown Reno is combined with free live music, name bands (such as The Beach Boys and Smokey Robinson) in concerts, a car auction, a massive automotive flea market, show 'n' shine car shows in parking lots everywhere, and rallies. Reno hotels sell out a year in advance, so plan ahead. Several events are also held at Lake Tahoe. It happens the first week of August. Information: Hot August Nights, (702) 829-1955; or Reno-Sparks Convention & Visitors Authority, (800) FOR-RENO.

**Nevada State Fair:** Held at the Reno Livestock Events Center in Reno, Nevada, this includes livestock exhibits and events, entertainment, rides and midway games. Information: Nevada State Fair, (702) 688-5767.

**Outhouse Races:** Otherwise known as "Power to the Potties." Teams put wheels on outhouses and make a run through downtown Virginia City on C Street. Other activities include the Toilet Paper Plunge and the Corncob Toss. Held in late August. Information: Virginia City Chamber of Commerce, (702) 847-0311.

**Portola Railroad Days:** Festivities center around the Portola Railroad Museum, a large open-air museum with still-operating diesel engines in downtown Portola. Information: Portola Railroad Museum, (916) 832-5348.

**Rod Hall 300:** This off-road vehicle race with dune buggies, four-wheel drives and motorized dirt bikes runs for 300 miles in the desert, beginning at Fernley, 30 miles east of Reno. Open to spectators and entrants in late August. Information: Rod Hall International, (702) 331-4800.

★ **Shakespeare at Sand Harbor Festival:** Otherwise known as the Bard on the Beach, this series of Shakespearean plays by noted troupes is performed in a natural amphitheater with a stage and props at Sand Harbor, Lake Tahoe-Nevada State Beach. You can bring your own short beach chair or rent one, and food and drink are available during the evening performances. Several plays are held on dates in August through early September. Information: Incline Village/Crystal Bay Visitors & Convention Bureau, (702) 832-1606.

**Tevis Cup 100-Mile Equestrian Ride:** This famous horseback endurance ride travels the same route as the foot race in June, from

Squaw Valley to Foresthill in Auburn. Information: Squaw Valley USA, (916) 583-6985.

★ **Truckee Championship Rodeo:** Two days of bucking broncos, bull riding, steer wrestling, calf riding and other events are held at McIver Arena, on Highway 267 in Truckee. The weekend rodeo, usually in mid-August, is preceded by a week of activities that includes a fashion show, hay rides, a tack auction, a beard and mustache contest, Western karaoke and celebrity team penning. Information: Truckee-Donner Chamber of Commerce, (916) 587-8808; or Truckee-Donner Horsemen's Association, (916) 587-0780.

# SEPTEMBER

**Annual Donner Party Hike:** This hike seeks to retrace, albeit with a less drastic outcome, the ill-fated route of the Donner Party of the 1840s, half of whom perished during an early winter. Information: Donner Memorial State Park, (916) 587-8808.

**Antique Fair:** More than 50 sellers of antiques display their wares on Labor Day weekend at Graeagle, eastern Plumas County. Information: Plumas County Chamber of Commerce, (916) 832-5444.

**Carson City Run:** Motorcycles rev up in Carson City for a series of competitions, games, shows, food, equipment exhibits and live entertainment in Mills Park. Held on the second weekend in September. Information: Performance Productions, Inc. (promoter), (415) 756-8704.

**Ferrari Club of America Hill Climb:** This event in Virginia City, Nevada, includes a parade and car show, along with timed races up the 7.4-mile truck route from Silver City to Virginia City. Ferraris and Shelby Cobras participate, and there is a viewing stand for spectators. Held the last weekend of September or the first weekend of October. Information: Virginia City Chamber of Commerce, (702) 847-0311.

★ **The Great Reno Balloon Race:** This is one of the most colorful spectacles of the year in Reno, and it is totally free to the public. The nation's top 140 balloonists make a mass ascent in balloons of weird shapes and sizes from Rancho San Rafael Park. There is a Dawn Patrol for super-early risers, and the rest of the balloons take off at first light. Food booths and displays are on the field north of town. Held the second weekend of September. Information: Event promoter, (702) 829-2810.

★ **National Championship Air Races:** Hundreds of planes soar into the high-desert skies in the world's longest-running air race, which includes pylon racing, aerobatics, skywriting, skydiving and other events during the third week of September at Reno-Stead Airport. Information: Reno-Sparks Convention & Visitors Authority, (800) 367-7366; or Reno Air Races, (702) 972-6663.

**Nevada State Railroad Museum Steam Up:** Steam engines are cranked up for rides and other festivities over Labor Day weekend at the Nevada State Railroad Museum in Carson City, Nevada. Information: Nevada State Railroad Museum, (702) 687-6953.

**One Hundred Mile Endurance Race:** This equestrian endurance ride is held over two days, and includes two laps out and back from the desert, beginning at Virginia City, Nevada. Information: Virginia City Chamber of Commerce, (702) 847-0311.

**Splendor of the Sierra Fine Arts Show:** Exhibit of local crafts people at Northstar Village near Truckee. Information: Northstar-at-Tahoe, (916) 562-1010.

★ **Virginia City International Camel Races:** People with nothing else to do race camels around an arena. Some of them also race water buffalo and ostriches. There are (other) humorous events, a parade and general quirkiness in Virginia City, Nevada, on the second weekend in September. Information: Virginia City Chamber of Commerce, (702) 847-0311.

★ **World's Championship Chili Cook-off and Americana Food Festival:** This major event fills downtown Reno with more than 100 chili chefs cooking their award-winning recipes for chili aficionados. Music, food, entertainment, arts and crafts spice up the activities. Usually held in late September. Information: Reno-Sparks Convention & Visitors Authority, (800) 367-7366.

## OCTOBER

★ **Autumn Food and Wine Jubilee:** Here's a great way to sample the award-winning recipes of North Shore restaurants, along with accompanying wines. More than 50 of Tahoe's finest restaurants and West Coast wineries offer bites and sips at The Resort at Squaw Creek in Squaw Valley. Information: North Tahoe Chamber of Commerce, (916) 581-6900.

**Italian Festival:** A Columbus Day parade, Italian food booths, entertainment, grape stomping and a spaghetti tournament are the highlights of this event in early October at the Eldorado Hotel Casino in downtown Reno, Nevada. Information: Eldorado Hotel Casino, (702) 786-5700 or (800) 777-5325.

**Kit Carson Trail Ghost Walk:** Apparitions of the past come back to haunt the old homes of Carson City in this tour. Volunteers dress up in ghostly apparel to regale visitors with their tales, usually in late October. The tour meets at the Legislative Plaza. Information: Carson City Convention & Visitors Bureau, (702) 687-7410.

★ **Kokanee Salmon Festival:** This event in early October is held in conjunction with the annual spawning run of landlocked salmon up

Taylor Creek in South Lake Tahoe. Two days of family activities include a Kokanee Kookoff, educational programs, art displays, nature walks, a children's fishing booth, and tours of the Lake Tahoe Visitor Center's Stream Profile Chamber, an underground viewing area with windows below the water level. Information: U.S. Forest Service, Lake Tahoe Basin Management Unit, (916) 573-2600.

★ **Native American Snow Dance Festival:** Begun as an attempt to end a recent drought in the mountains around Lake Tahoe, this event (wildly successful for the winter of 1994-95) is now an annual affair. It includes dancing demonstrations, arts, crafts and food of Native American tribes indigenous to the area. Held on the first weekend of October, the event attracts more than 5,000 spectators. Located next to the Hyatt Regency in Incline Village, Nevada. Information: Incline Village/Crystal Bay Visitors & Convention Bureau, (800) 468-2463 or (702) 832-1606.

★ **Nevada Day Celebration:** Yes, Nevada joined the Union as a state on Halloween, so this event competes with ghosts and goblins every October 31st in Carson City, Nevada. It includes a parade, live music, a rock-drilling contest, a music and art show, a beard contest and a ball at the Governor's Mansion. Wear your finest 1864 period clothing. All of downtown Carson City is closed off to traffic to accommodate booths and merriment. Information: Nevada Day Committee, (702) 882-2600.

**Octoberfest:** Located at Alpine Meadows Ski Area, this late October celebration includes music, food and drink. Information: North Tahoe Chamber of Commerce, (916) 581-6900 .

**Professional Team Penning Association, National Finals:** This is held at the Carson City Fairgrounds, also known as Fuji Park, and involves professional team ropers displaying their prowess. Information: Event coordinator, (702) 882-4458.

# NOVEMBER

★ **Celtic New Year:** Celtic village settings, dancing, food, live entertainment and a bagpipe band parade highlight this event at various locations in Reno, including Rancho San Rafael Park, Virginia Street downtown and other venues. Information: DRA Special Events, (800) 535-3045.

**Christmas on the Comstock:** Held the day after Thanksgiving, this event features fireworks, a candlelight parade and a Christmas tree lighting ceremony at the end of town. Information: Virginia City Chamber of Commerce, (702) 847-0311.

**Christmas on the River:** Caroling, hot cider, storytelling, tree lighting, food and entertainment hold forth along the Raymond I. Smith Truckee River Walk in downtown Reno the day after Thanksgiving. Information: Event promoter, (702) 334-2414.

# DECEMBER

★ **Alpenlight Festival:** Festive holiday events throughout the North Shore of Lake Tahoe include evening parties, ice sculptures, sleigh rides, window decorating contests and other holiday pursuits in venues such as Alpine Meadows, The Resort at Squaw Creek and downtown Tahoe City. Information: North Tahoe Chamber of Commerce, (916) 581-6900.

**Christmas Eve Torchlight Parade:** Held at Squaw Valley USA. Information: (916) 583-6985.

**Cross Country Guided Tour:** This includes a caroling party and candy cane children's race at Northstar-at-Tahoe resort near Truckee. Information: Northstar-at-Tahoe, (916) 562-1010.

★ **First Night, Lake Tahoe:** This is a family-oriented, alcohol-free New Year's Eve celebration (December 31st) with art, food and parties held at various locations around South Lake Tahoe (which is not known as a teetotallers town). Information: Tahoe Prevention Network, (916) 541-8935.

**Fischer-Tahoe Nordic Ten:** This is a 10K cross-country ski race at Lakeview Cross-Country Ski Area in Tahoe City. Information: (916) 583-9353.

**New Year's Eve Celebration:** Music, entertainment and fireworks are held at Northstar Village near Truckee. Information: Northstar-at-Tahoe, (916) 562-1010.

**Night Race:** This is a 5K cross-country race at Tahoe Donner Cross-Country ski area. Information: (916) 587-9444.

★ **Northern Lights Celebration:** This week of festivities includes free skiing at Diamond Peak Ski Resort in Incline Village, Nevada, evening parties and special discounts at local businesses to jump-start the ski season around Lake Tahoe. Information: Incline Village/Crystal Bay Visitors & Convention Bureau, (800) 468-2463.

★ **Silver and Snowflake Festival of Lights:** Usually held during the first weekend of December in Carson City, Nevada, this event includes a ceremonial lighting of the big tree in front of the state capitol (the oldest tree in the town), caroling, live music, sleigh rides and other merriment. Information: Carson City Convention & Visitors Bureau, (702) 885-0411.

# Chapter 20

# Mountain Resorts & Lodges

## ★ Author's Choice ★

If you're looking for a rustic mountain cabin with a wood-burning stove and a front porch from which to watch the sunset—and no television and telephones in sight or sound—you'll find it in the Lake Tahoe region. If your style runs more to the contemporary, with a modern suite overlooking an 18-hole golf course or a vibrant ski area, you'll find that here, too. If you're seeking atmosphere, such as a great lake for fishing or boating that is practically at your front door, several resorts will fill that bill.

Although at first glance Lake Tahoe looks like little more than a few high-rise casino hotels and a multitude of lakefront motels, there is more here than meets the eye. Some of the best resorts are not even on the lake; they are tucked away in mountain valleys and at the ends of narrow, dirt roads. On Lake Tahoe itself, there are two trends: The first combines modern conveniences with a woodsy but gentrified environment, while the other celebrates rustic simplicity and an emphasis on old-fashioned family togetherness. Each approach has its following. Sunnyside, a new lodge on the West Shore of the lake, is an example of the former. Richardson's Resort, on the South Shore, is an example of the latter. Of course, the large four-seasons resorts—Squaw Creek, Northstar and Kirkwood—all have excellent ski slopes and a range of recreation. Most resort accommodations, with the exception of Squaw Creek, are condominiums.

One way to choose a resort is to determine which activities appeal to you the most. If golf is your passion, you probably won't be happy in an isolated mountain cabin. If hiking, fishing and mountain biking are your main pursuits, you may want to be away from the crowds and the main roads. Check the brochures and descriptions carefully; a lot of places that call themselves resorts may be just motels with a fancy name and very few on-site amenities. While the definition of a resort may be somewhat nebulous, those listed here include lakefront and riverfront lodges or major properties with a multitude of activities such as on-site golf, skiing, fishing or cycling.

There are four major resort regions in the area: Lake Tahoe, with its proximity to boating, cycling trails and beaches; Carson Pass, with its emphasis on history, nature and hiking; the Lakes Basin area, with its unique string of 1920s-style small lodges and magnificent hiking trails; and the Feather River Country, with its golf courses, historical towns and scenic river frontage. Moreover, Lake Tahoe encompasses several subregions, including Donner Lake, Echo Lakes, Fallen Leaf Lake and Angora Lakes. Although not as crowded as Tahoe during the summer, all of these places do brisk business, and accommodations can be difficult to secure during peak seasons.

Some truly unique lodges exist in the Carson Pass and Lakes Basin areas, both within an hour's drive of Tahoe. Along Highway 88, south of

Lake Tahoe, some of the lodges have their roots in the pioneering days of the mid-1800s, when Kit Carson forged a route, later known as the Mormon-Emigrant Trail, that brought thousands of settlers across the Sierra to California. Small trading posts that sprang up to serve these westward immigrants later became resorts. In the Lakes Basin country north of Tahoe, the miners, loggers and railroad workers who established camps in the area opened the door for the resorts that materialized in the early 1900s.

It can be difficult to book rooms and cabins in Tahoe's outlying areas. A short summer season and limited accommodations put these places in high demand; typically, they have long waiting lists, often a year or two in advance. The seven rustic lodges along the Gold Lake Highway from Bassett's Station to Graeagle, for instance, have less than 80 cabins among them. Most of these lodges are leased from the U.S. Forest Service and are restricted in their ability to expand or improve their properties. So demand always outstrips supply. Some families have been coming to these places for decades, and repeat business runs 80 percent or higher. The best chance of getting a spot is to book in the early or late season (May through June and September through October), or engage in the lottery system for new arrivals. These months can be delightful, or they can be rainy, snowy and cold; you can never predict weather patterns in the Sierra. Another thing to know about these lodges is that they are mostly family-run businesses, often handed down through the generations. Thus, attitudes toward guests can range from folksy to frosty, and you should not expect the kind of management efficiencies you'd get at a major resort. You may encounter the occasional cantankerous soul who ought to find some other line of work; however, most of the owners are laid back and accommodating. They are running these lodges because of tradition, obligation or just because they like living in the mountains.

# North Shore
## ★ The Resort at Squaw Creek ★
### ★ notes Author's Choice

Tahoe's newest and most elegant resort, situated at the site of the 1960 Winter Olympics, has propelled Squaw Valley into a year-round destination. Already known for its challenging ski slopes, the valley now has an equally gnarly golf course, an 18-holer that spreads out from the lower slopes of the mountain to a marshy meadow. The course was named one of the "Top Five Resort Courses" in the U.S. by *Golf Digest* magazine. The Resort at Squaw Creek covers 626 acres, and is chockablock with other sports amenities: tennis courts, an executive fitness center, a cross-country ski center and an aquatic center with three swimming pools (including a

120-foot water slide). In winter, guests need only step outside their rooms to immediately board a chairlift that accesses the mountain's more protected intermediate runs. Also, Squaw Creek is near a riding stable, several good hiking trails and a mountain bike park on the ski hill.

The resort complex is divided into two main buildings—one housing the lobby, meeting rooms and restaurants, the other housing the 405 rooms and suites. Suites are roomy and lavishly appointed, and most of them have striking views of the forest or the valley. One inconvenience is that the two buildings are not interconnected, so guests must walk outside (sometimes in a blizzard) to get from their rooms to the lobby or the restaurants. The exterior layout is one of the resort's more attractive features; it has meandering rock and stone terraces for outside dining, sunning and sitting, and a commanding, 250-foot cascading waterfall. Employees are courteous and energetic, though they clearly expect to be tipped often and well. Five restaurants serve everything from sandwiches to gourmet meals, and tend to be in the higher price range for Tahoe. Although the resort caters to the executive conference trade, it has excellent supervised recreation programs for youngsters and teens, perhaps the best in Tahoe for upscale families. With all of its accolades, the resort picked up a Gold Key Award in 1994, one of the hotel industry's highest honors.

***Rooms:*** 405 guest rooms and suites, two-speaker phone, television, some kitchens, Continental breakfast and some fireplaces.

***Resort amenities:*** Five restaurants and lounges (Glissandi, Cascades, Ristorante Montagna, Bullwhacker's Pub and Sweet Potato Deli), retail shops (clothing, ski rentals, accessories), an art gallery, laundry facilities, three heated pools, a water slide, four spas, a salon, a complete fitness center, an eight-court Peter Burwash International Tennis Center ($12 per hour, $5 rental), a mountain biking park, an 18-hole Robert Trent Jones, Jr. golf course (see page 288 in chapter 10, "Golf Courses," for fees), ice skating rink, ski-in/ski-out service via a triple chairlift to Squaw Valley USA (see page 370 in chapter 14, "Alpine Ski Resorts," for details), convention facilities (33,000 square feet), Mountain Buddies for kids ages 3 to 13, and special teen programs. Nearby activities include snowmobiling, horseback riding, flyfishing and rafting. Host of the Celebrity Sports Invitational (January).

***Rates:*** $148 to $270.

***Information:*** 400 Squaw Creek Road, P.O. Box 3333, Olympic Valley, CA 96146; (916) 583-6300 or (800) 327-3353.

## ★ Northstar-at-Tahoe ★

As a moderately priced family destination, this giant four-seasons resort has it all: a challenging 18-hole golf course, one of the best intermediate ski areas in the state, the basin's most developed mountain biking park, a small "village" with three good restaurants, horseback riding stables, a cross-country ski center and a wealth of other recreation options. The resort and its residential community encompass 2,560 forested acres, with many distinctive homes, especially near the golf course. The recommended Northstar experience is staying in a condominium, each of which is decorated according to the preference of its owner. The ones closest to the ski hill offer ski-in, ski-out access. A motel-style lodge in the village has the convenience of underground parking and proximity to the lifts, but the units are modest in size and decor.

As Northstar nears its 25th anniversary, the resort has been systematically refurbishing and upgrading its facilities. Also, more attention is being given to summer programs, including new mountain bike routes, a new ropes course and an outdoor climbing wall. Northstar has its own internal shuttle system for guests, and is six miles from either Truckee or Lake Tahoe's North Shore. Its location on an access road off Highway 267 gives Northstar a great off-the-beaten-track feeling and mountain ambience. Just smell the pine needles!

***Rooms:*** 252 units, ranging from hotel-style rooms in the Village Lodge (51 rooms and village lofts with kitchens and living rooms) to four-bedroom condos and houses (some daily rentals, others weekend rentals) with phone, cable television, fireplace, linens and some maid service.

***Resort amenities:*** A ski hill, an 18-hole golf course, a summer golf camp, hard-surface tennis courts and tennis lessons (summer only), a mountain bike park, a cross-country ski center, snowmobile tours, horseback riding stables, a sauna, a Jacuzzi, a pool (summer only), a recreation room, retail stores, four restaurants (Timbercreek, Village Food Company, Pedro's and Golf Club House), sports equipment rentals and some covered parking. Shuttles run between Northstar and Truckee hourly in summer, daily in winter (twice daily on winter weekends). The resort will pick up guests with advance notice at Truckee-Tahoe Airport, Amtrak or Greyhound stations. Aero Trans, a private limo service, operates from Reno-Tahoe International Airport.

***Rates:*** Winter is $129 to $641; summer is $99 to $425. A deposit is required. MasterCard, Visa, American Express and Discover cards are accepted.

***Information:*** Northstar Drive and Highway 267 (P.O. Box 2499), Truckee, CA 96160; (916) 562-1113 or (800) GO-NORTH.

## Granlibakken Resort

Tucked away in a forested valley two miles south of Tahoe City, this tranquil resort has developed a reputation as a wonderfully secluded conference center and family sports retreat. But Granlibakken has an honored place in the history of American skiing, because the small but steep slope that it adjoins hosted the ski jumping tryouts for the 1932 Winter Olympics. Athletes who came here and went on to compete in the Games at Lake Placid, New York, were the elite skiers of their day, long before downhill and slalom events took over the limelight. The site, built by a resort called Tahoe Tavern (which later burned down), was the first developed skiing at the lake. The area wasn't called Granlibakken until 15 years later, however, when a Norwegian jumper named Kjell Rustad leased the land from the U.S. Forest Service and installed a 450-foot rope tow. The name means "a hillside sheltered by fir trees," and refers to a place in Norway where Rustad skied as a youngster. Today, the ski hill and rope tow are still operating, but the alpine jump is just a memory.

Current owners Bill and Norma Parson have developed a sizable conference center that can host up to 450 people. Surrounding it are 76 condominium units and a new $3 million Executive Lodge, which opened in March, 1995. The expansion includes additional condominiums, with spacious first-floor living rooms, and second-floor entertainment and family rooms with fireplaces. The new facilities feature a gourmet kitchen, and can accommodate groups of up to 72 people, while larger groups of up to 300 can use the preexisting conference center.

The main building has banquet and meeting rooms, dining rooms and a large outdoor terrace that hosts performing arts events in summer. Condos are well appointed, comfortable and woodsy, and are shaded by forest. Summer recreation includes the annual Nike Tennis Camp for youngsters, a new and impressive ropes course for team-building, and a trailhead for mountain biking and hiking into spectacular Page Meadows, one of Tahoe's best wildflower areas. Just down the road are three ski areas—Alpine Meadows, Squaw Valley and Ski Homewood. Perhaps Granlibakken's most enduring asset is that it is close to the action at Tahoe City and the lake, yet physically removed from the traffic and noise of Highway 89.

*Rooms:* 120 condominium units with phones, televisions, some kitchens, some fireplaces, a full buffet breakfast and some laundry facilities.

*Resort amenities:* A spa, a sauna, a pool (summer only), a ski hill, cross-country trails, a snow-play area and facilities for conferences, weddings and banquets.

*Rates:* $85 to $95 per unit for a one- to two-bedroom lodge room, and $195 to $350 for one- to four-bedroom condos.

*Information:* 625 Granlibakken Road, P.O. Box 6329, Tahoe City, CA 96145; (916) 583-4242 or (800) 543-3221.

# Truckee/Donner Pass

## Donner Lake Village Resort

Often overshadowed by Tahoe, Donner Lake is a delightful, self-contained community with homes, lodges, beaches and virtually every type of water sport, yet it is just a couple of miles from historic Truckee's fine restaurants and eclectic boutiques. This lakefront resort is the largest at Donner, and it has a full marina where guests can berth their boats (at no extra charge) or rent one on site, lounge on the private beach, and cook steaks on one of several shoreline barbecues. Accommodations vary in type and quality, from modern, nondescript motel-style lodgettes and studios to rustically furnished two-story townhouses. Lakeside one-bedroom suites have the best views of Donner. There is complimentary tea and coffee in the morning, but no restaurant. A small conference room can accommodate up to 20 people. The lake itself offers fishing for trout (including mackinaw), waterskiing, jetskiing, sailing and swimming, and there's a museum and substantial beach at Donner Memorial State Park on the southeast side. In winter, the resort is minutes away from the Donner Summit ski areas of Sugar Bowl, Boreal and Donner Ski Ranch, as well as Squaw Valley, Alpine Meadows and Northstar.

*Rooms:* 66 modern lodgettes, studios and one- and two-bedroom condominiums with direct-dial phones, color TVs, some kitchens, some fireplaces with wood-burning stoves, wheelchair access, non-smoking rooms, daily maid service, and rollaways and cribs on request.

*Resort amenities:* Complimentary coffee and tea, laundry facilities, guest saunas, a private beach, a private marina and a conference room.

*Policies:* No pets are allowed; bicycles and skateboards are not allowed in the courtyard or surrounding walkways; one night's deposit is required to reserve accommodations.

*Rates:* $60 to $205.

*Information:* 15695 Donner Pass Road, Suite 101, Truckee, CA 96161; (916) 587-6081 or (800) 621-6664.

## Serene Lakes Lodge & RV Park

Guests have plenty of serenity at this rustic, family-run lodge located in Soda Springs on Donner Summit, next to two small alpine lakes. Reportedly, famed author Mark Twain happened upon the lakes during his travels, and named them after his daughters, Serene and Dulzura. There is nothing fancy about the lodge, which has a weathered, wooden exterior. It was originally built as an ice house in the early 1900s, when workers used to cut large blocks from the lakes and ship them by rail for refrigeration use by cities. Today, the lodge is open year-round, though it can be quite snowbound in winter. Guests stay in 16 small, private rooms and share common bathrooms and showers. There's a spacious dining room and bar with a massive stone fireplace, a game arcade for kids, and a large outdoor patio that overlooks the lakes. No motors are allowed on the lakes, which are easily navigated in canoes, rowboats or sailing dinghies. Adjoining the lodge are picnic grounds, a sandy beach, a volleyball net, horseshoe pits, a swimming area, an RV campground, and hiking and biking trails. The lodge is located at the end of a residential street, but is well removed from Interstate 80. Several ski areas, including Sugar Bowl and Royal Gorge Cross Country Ski Resort, are just down the road.

**Rooms:** 16 private rooms (one or two queen-size beds per room); common restrooms and showers.

**Resort amenities:** A lodge restaurant (serving breakfast, lunch and dinner), a cocktail bar, meeting and banquet facilities (catering for private parties, social events, company picnics and business groups), an RV and tent campground with showers and restrooms, propane for sale, a large outdoor patio, a picnic area, a sandy beach, a volleyball net, horseshoe pits, snow-play areas and a free shuttle to local ski areas. Fishing, swimming, canoeing and sailing are available on the lake; ice skating is possible in winter. Three National Forest hiking trails are located nearby (Painted Rock, Palisade Creek and Lower Lola Montez trails). The resort hosts the Half Marathon and 10K Wilderness Run in October. Open year-round for lodging and dining.

**Rates:** $30 to $70 per night. Reservations are recommended.

**Information:** 1100 Soda Springs Road, P.O. Box 811, Soda Springs, CA 95728; (916) 426-9001.

# West Shore

## Sunnyside Lodge

This luxurious, small lodge, which resembles an elegant bed and breakfast, reflects the Tahoe style of wood and rock, but in a contemporary setting. Built just a few years ago and blessed with one of the best locations on the lake, this consistently popular lodge has two styles of accommodations: lakefront suites and smaller rooms without views. The suites are by far the more impressive units (worth the extra $30 to $35); they are elegantly decorated in rich burgundy and dark green, and all have balconies right on the lake. The sunrises and sunsets are magnificent—this is truly a place for romance to blossom. Regular rooms are smaller and face parking lots.

Still, Sunnyside manages to be sold out most weekends of the year. One reason might be its sumptuous cuisine. In the morning, a continental breakfast, which comes with the price of the room, is served upstairs in the library, and includes fresh orange juice, cereal, banana nut bread and fresh fruit. Lunch (in summer only) and dinner are served downstairs in the restaurant, and include a selection of pastas and fresh seafood. There's a cozy lobby with beamed ceilings and a big stone fireplace, fine for an après-ski toddy. In summer, a sweeping outdoor deck with tables and chairs is a popular hangout; this fronts Sunnyside's own marina, where rental boats, jetskis, fishing charters and sightseeing cruisers are available. Located two miles south of Tahoe City on Highway 89, Sunnyside is on the West Shore cycling path, and bike rentals are within walking distance. During winter, ski-area shuttles stop here, and in summer the Tahoe City Trolley services the area. Traffic along Highway 89 can be severely congested on busy summer weekends, and there's a constant bustle of people in and out of the U.S. Forest Service campground across the road. A word of advice in booking Sunnyside: Do it months in advance.

*Rooms:* 23 rooms and suites with private decks, some lakefronts, some lakeviews, some fireplaces, some wet bars, continental breakfast and complimentary afternoon tea.

*Resort amenities:* Chris Craft restaurant (indoor dining and summer deck), concierge, meeting facilities (catering large parties, weddings, banquets and conferences), ski locker rooms, bike racks, a full-service marina, ski and sailboat rentals and a skier shuttle service.

*Policies:* No pets allowed. Discounts available to guests for major ski resorts, ski rentals, sleigh rides and snowmobiling. Open year-round.

*Rates:* $75 to $170, with the less expensive rates in spring, fall and winter. Midweek lodging discount packages available. Visa and MasterCard accepted.

*Information:* 1850 West Lake Boulevard, P.O. Box 5969, Tahoe City, CA 96145; (916) 583-7200 or (800) 822-2SKI (California only).

## Meeks Bay Resort

With an attractive beach, a protected cove and reasonably priced boat launching, this is a great spot on Lake Tahoe for a summer family vacation. Located 10 miles south of Tahoe City on Highway 89, the site was once used by the Washoe Indians as a camp for fishing and foraging. In the 1920s, the resort was established by Oswald Kehlet, who built a large home bordered by the lake on three sides. The residence was later owned by William Hewlett, co-founder of the Hewlett-Packard Corporation, and then by San Francisco billionaire Gordon Getty, who used it as a summer home. Today, the Kehlet Mansion is a popular rental for groups (it has seven bedrooms, three baths and an observation deck over the water). But there are 20 additional units at the resort, including one- and two-story cabins and condominiums, most of which have lake views. Kids love the beach, where they can find a roped-off swimming lagoon and a variety of water toys for rent. The resort also operates a campground right next to busy Highway 89. A general store and snack stand serve the beach crowd.

Meeks Bay is close to major hiking and cycling trails, and to the boating Mecca of Emerald Bay. A trailhead for several alpine lakes in Desolation Wilderness is just across the street.

***Rooms:*** 21 one- and two-story cabins, lakefront condominiums and the Kehlet Mansion. Larger condos have big living rooms and fireplaces, separate bedroom, full kitchens and bathrooms with tubs/showers. Two-story cabins have open beams with upstairs sleeping loft and downstairs bedroom, and all cabins have kitchens. Other features include some fireplaces, eating utensils, rollaways, cribs and special linen services.

***Amenities:*** Campfires allowed (no permits required), showers, laundry facilities, non-power boat rentals, marina slips and launching facilities.

***Policies:*** No pets allowed. There is a 14-day stay limit. Cleaning and security fees range from $100 to $500. Open June to September.

***Rates:*** From $550 to $2,750 a week.

***Information:*** 7901 Highway 89 in Meeks Bay, CA; P.O. Box 411, Tahoma, CA 96142; (916) 525-7242.

# South Shore
## ★ The Ridge Resort ★

This is Tahoe's classiest condo-hotel, a luxurious resort of private suites. Located on a Nevada peak six miles above Stateline, the Ridge is frequently used as a hideaway for celebrities performing at the casinos. Here, they can breathe the crisp mountain air, stay clear of the crowds and indulge in their favorite pastimes. One of those is skiing; in fact, there's a private, 10-passenger gondola that runs guests between the resort and the Nevada side of Heavenly Ski Area. Other amenities include an indoor/outdoor swimming pool, indoor and outdoor tennis, a state-of-the-art fitness center, sauna and spa, and indoor racquetball courts. Each suite can sleep up to six people and is luxuriously appointed with a fireplace, a wet bar, a kitchen and a living room entertainment center. Balconies have gas barbecues, as well as spectacular views of Carson Valley, Heavenly Ski Area or South Shore. The Ridge Club offers a restaurant and cocktail lounge with piano bar, and the meals are usually exceptional. Underground parking and hourly shuttles to the Stateline casinos complete the picture. Is this a great place for a honeymoon, or what?

***Rooms:*** 254 suites, one- and two-bedroom units with phones, televisions, VCRs, some stereos, fireplaces, kitchens, a complimentary bottle of champagne and fresh-baked banana nut bread in the room upon arrival.

***Resort amenities:*** A restaurant, a concierge, maid service, gift and grocery stores, a cocktail lounge, a children's playground and arcade, tennis and racquetball courts, a sauna, a heated indoor/outdoor pool, a health spa, conference rooms (10 to 75 people, equipment and catering), a shuttle to casinos and a private lift to Heavenly Ski Area.

**Policies:** Advance deposit of one night's stay within 10 days of booking date (four or more nights require two nights' deposit). Deposits are fully refunded if cancelled more than 48 hours in advance (holidays require 15-day notice).

**Rates:** $105 to $340 per night, or $625 to $2,025 per week.

**Information:** 400 Ridge Club Drive, P.O. Box 5790, Stateline, NV 89449; (702) 588-3553.

## ★ Richardson's Resort ★

If a resort can be measured by its energy output, this place would score number one in wattage. As a hangout for the younger crowd, this is *the* spot in South Shore. One reason may be the constant beat of live music from the outdoor deck of The Beacon restaurant, which is right on the beach. Another reason may be the ebb and flow of watercraft, which range from kayaks to waterski boats, from parasailing runabouts to sightseeing cruisers. The pier at Anchorage Marina is constantly busy, and seems to be a magnet for the sunworshippers who line the sparkling, white sand beaches north and south of here. Location is everything, and Richardson's, a vintage family-oriented resort that has been around since the 1920s, has the enviable position of being at the center of Tahoe's recreational universe. Its leeward site offers protection from winds, and it has the closest full-service marina to Emerald Bay. The resort is also on a popular paved bike trail, is within a short stroll of the famous Tallac Historic Site and its resident artists' colony, has a riding stable across the street, and is within four miles of the major hiking routes into Desolation Wilderness, including trailheads at Glen Alpine, Bayview and Eagle Falls. Shopping, golf and casinos are minutes away, and guests can hop on the inexpensive South Tahoe Trolley to reach most points of interest. Accommodations at Richardson's include small rooms in a large, rustic lodge with bed and bath; a motel-type complex next to the beach with spacious rooms and bath; a lakeside condominium; nearly 40 cabins; and campgrounds for tents and RVs. The cabins, named after vintage automobiles, have the requisite knotty-pine ceilings and most amenities except TVs and telephones. They are tucked into pleasant pine forest well off the main highway, but close to the beach. Richardson's, a private concession on U.S. Forest Service land, is open year-round. In winter, there's a small cross-country ski center with trails along the beach and through the woods. In summer, the Tallac estates next door hold major music, art and other events.

**Rooms:** Lakefront cabins and condos, rustic ski cabins, hotel and inn rooms, and tent and RV campsites. Crib rentals ($5) and rollaways ($10) available.

***Resort amenities:*** The Beacon Restaurant (lunch, dinner, Sunday brunch; private party and banquet facilities; outdoor dining and entertainment in summer), an ice cream parlor, a deli, a meeting/reception facility, an adult and children's playground, a country store, a gas station, a casino shuttle bus, hiking and biking trails, bike rental shops and tours, a tennis court, volleyball courts, cross-country skiing, charter and boat rentals, a launch ramp and a sandy beach. Horseback riding is available through a nearby stable.

***Policies:*** No pets are allowed. A 50-percent, nonrefundable deposit ($100) must be received within two weeks after reservations are booked; no refund for early departure.

***Rates:*** Lakefront cabins and condos, from $495 to $1,260 per week; lodge and beach inn rooms, from $59 to $89 per night; campsites from $17 to $22 per night.

***Information:*** P.O. Box 9028, South Lake Tahoe, CA 96158; (916) 541-1801 or (800) 544-1801.

## ★ Zephyr Cove Resort ★

Mark Twain wrote about the "Washoe Zephyrs"—the western winds—that kick up many afternoons on the east side of the lake, especially in spring and fall. But this cove a few miles north of Stateline does have its tranquil moments, when it is arguably the most picturesque cove on the lake, its beauty second only to Emerald Bay. The rustic resort of cabins and campsites here is the East Shore counterpart of Richardson's Resort. Zephyr is the home of two of Tahoe's most famous cruiseboats, the *M.S. Dixie II* and the *Woodwind* sailing yacht. It also has a lively beach scene, with waterskiing, parasailing, fishing, jetskiing and volleyball. There's a big, rambling lodge next to US 50 that houses a restaurant, a grocery store and guest rooms. The rustic cabins are located between the lodge and the beach, and a campground for tents and RVs is across the highway. As might be expected, crowds are a fact of life here in summer. There's a constant stream of traffic on the road, as well as buses arriving with hundreds of passengers for the *Dixie* cruises. Other attractions include a horseback riding stables across the street, and snowmobile tours of Spooner Summit in the winter. Public transportation is available between Zephyr and the casinos, and the resort is near trailheads for the Tahoe Rim Trail, the famous Flume Trail for mountain bikes, and one of the area's best catch-and-release fishing lakes at Spooner Lake, Lake Tahoe-Nevada State Park (see page 248).

***Rooms:*** 33 units. Lodge rooms sleep two to six; cabins, some housekeeping units, sleep two to eight, and have twins, doubles, sleeper sofas, television, some kitchens, some fireplaces and limited linen and towel service.

*Resort amenities:* A restaurant, a beachside bar and grill, a campground, an RV park with a dump station and showers, tent sites, coin-operated laundry, a general store, a gift shop, a video arcade, one mile of sandy beach, a marina, boat charters (*M.S. Dixie II*, *Woodwind* and fishing), boat rentals, parasailing rides, horse stables and a snowmobile center.

*Policies:* Pets are allowed in the RV park, campground and cabins ($2 per day or $7 per week charge); 72-hour cancellation notice is required for refund (cabins only). There is a 14-day stay limit.

*Rates:* $45 to $75 for lodge rooms, $55 to $185 for cabins, $15 for tent sites ($95 per week), and $23 for RV sites ($145 per week.) Visa, MasterCard, American Express and Discover cards accepted.

*Information:* 760 US 50, P.O. Box 830, Zephyr Cove, NV 89448; (702) 588-6644.

## Angora Lakes Resort

Here's one of those off-the-beaten-path resorts that never advertises. Although it's a bit difficult to find (just above Fallen Leaf Lake on a dirt road), the resort is a little piece of paradise that constantly has a waiting list. The lakes are twin alpine jewels that are popular with local cyclists, hikers and swimmers, and there is considerable day use, especially at Upper Angora Lake, where the resort operates a beach, rowboat rental concession and snack stand (famous for its homemade lemonade!). To get here, take Highway 89 north from the South Shore, turn left on Fallen Leaf Lake Road, then take the first left up the hill and watch for a poorly marked dirt road on the summit (Forest Service Road 1214). Follow this along the ridge to the unused Angora Fire Lookout, and park in the lot (there's room for about 100 cars, but it fills fast on weekends). From here, you'll need to walk one-half mile on a hiking trail to Upper Angora Lake (Lower Angora Lake has several privately leased cabins). The upper lake is located in a granite-rimmed bowl flanked by Echo and Angora peaks, and is named after a herd of Angora goats that were pastured here by homesteader Nathan Gilmore in the 1870s.

The resort was opened in 1921 by the Holdinger family, and today it is still operated by their descendants, Jim and Gloria Holdinger. They offer eight rustic cabins, each with electricity, hot showers and chemical toilets. Every cabin has a different layout, ranging from studios to two-bedroom configurations. The lake, about one-third of a mile across, provides swimming from a beach of decomposed granite—okay for bare feet. A snack shed, with tables and chairs on a porch, sells cold drinks, sandwiches, ice cream and candy. The resort is in such demand for overnight stays that the Holdingers say they are "backlogged" with demand. The best advice is to book a year or two in advance.

*Rooms:* Eight cabins, each accommodating four to six people. These are housekeeping units and guests must bring their own linen and towels; there is no maid service or washing machine available. No meals are included with overnight stays. The season is from mid-June to mid-September.

***Resort amenities:*** A swimming beach, 10 rowboats for rent, hiking and cycling trails nearby, and a snack stand that operates daily. Arriving guests and their luggage will be picked up by a truck using a private road parallel to the trail. Guests will need to park their vehicles in the main lot next to the fire lookout.

***Rates:*** $650 to $750, minimum one-week rental.

***Information:*** Angora Lakes Resort, Angora Ridge Road, South Lake Tahoe; (916) 541-2092 in summer or (916) 577-3593 in winter.

## Echo Chalet

Echo Lake is close to South Lake Tahoe but, like Angora Lakes, it's off the beaten path. Everyone who comes to the region should make an effort to visit this place. Nestled between high granite peaks, it is a truly magnificent body of water with a wealth of natural and recreational attractions. Take US 50 west of South Lake Tahoe, then look for Echo Lake Road (a poorly marked right turn from the highway just west of Echo Summit), and drive through a residential area for two miles before reaching the lodge and marina. One of the important trailheads into Desolation Wilderness begins at Upper Echo Lake, on the Pacific Crest Trail, and hikers can access it via a boat taxi from Lower Echo Lake. Even if you don't trek into the backcountry, there's a marvelous three-mile, mostly level trail that follows the east rim of the lakes. Several attractive summer homes and cabins are sprinkled around the shoreline. Lower Echo Lake is a happening place; it has a launch ramp, a dock, sightseeing and rental boats, a store, a post office and several housekeeping cabins. The cabins are weathered and basic, and are located on a shaded hillside overlooking the chalet. Some have kitchenettes, small living rooms and equally small bedrooms. Furniture and appliances are old, and the interiors could use some sprucing up. The best accommodations at the lake are the few—and highly prized—summer homes that occasionally are available for rent, mostly by word of mouth.

***Rooms:*** Eight housekeeping cabins with beds, kitchenettes, living rooms and balconies. There are no telephones or televisions in the cabins.

***Resort amenities:*** A chalet store with groceries, fishing tackle, boat equipment and fountain service (ice cream!); a picnic area with barbecues; a service station with gasoline, stove and lantern fuel, kerosene, propane, boat and motor sales and service; sightseeing trips around both Echo Lakes ($8 adults, $5 children) and daily summer taxi service to the Desolation Trailhead ($6.50 one-way or $11 round-trip for adults, $4 and

$7 for children, and $2 and $3 for dogs); fishing boat rentals from $15 an hour and up; a boat-launch ramp ($6 to $10); and overnight slips ($15 per night).

**Rates:** Cabins are from $66 per day and from $396 per week, double occupancy.

**Information:** Echo Chalet, 9900 Echo Lakes Road, Echo Lake, CA 95721; (916) 659-7207.

## Carson Pass/Highway 88

### ★ Sorensen's Resort ★

It is only 20 minutes from South Lake Tahoe, and yet Sorensen's might as well be a world away. This historic, 165-acre complex of cabins, owned by John and Patty Brissenden, is a kind of back-to-nature retreat that emphasizes low-impact recreation: cross-country skiing, hiking, flyfishing, birding, photography, history tours and wildflower walks. The resort, built next to the West Fork of the Carson River, was developed by Danish sheepherders in the 1920s. Situated in verdant Hope Valley, a region of meadows crisscrossed by mountain streams, Sorensen's caters to a clientele that appreciates the uniqueness of the resort, its easygoing staff and its hearty, home-cooked meals. The Brissendens, who are political and environmental advocates, have made a point of creating a learning environment, especially for children, and families have found this particularly stimulating. There is nothing humdrum about the accommodations; virtually every cabin is different—and attractive. The Chapel, with its circular staircase and loft bedroom, is a reconstructed log cabin from a theme park in Santa Cruz, California, known as Santa's Village. The Norway House is a replica of a 13th-century Norwegian building, with its hand-carved facade and sod roof; it has dormitory-style accommodations, and guests must bring their own sleeping bags. The Snowshoe, Creekside and Sheepherder log cabins, which have woodburning stoves, kitchenettes, separate bathrooms and showers, queen-size beds and sleeping lofts with twin futons, are great for small families or honeymooners. The cafe in the main lodge serves three meals a day, and is known for its beef burgundy stew, robust soups and seafood. In winter, Sorensen's is headquarters for Hope Valley Cross-Country Ski Center; in summer, the Horse Feathers Fly Fishing School holds forth. The resort is close to magnificent hiking trails and lakes in the Mokelumne Wilderness, Kirkwood downhill and cross-country ski areas, and the soothing waters of Grover Hot Springs State Park.

**Rooms:** 29 units. Cabins sleep one to eight, homes sleep six, and bed and breakfast accommodations sleep two. Some kitchens, some fireplaces with woodburning stoves, limited maid service, and complimentary drinks (cocoa, coffee, tea and wine served daily until 5 p.m.).

*Resort amenities:* Sorensen's Country Cafe (breakfast, lunch, dinner), a gift shop, a wood-fired sauna, Hope Valley Cross-Country Ski Center (rentals, lessons, wildlife and full moon tours, backcountry seminars and learn-to-ski weekends), and Horse Feathers Fly Fishing School. Programs include historic Emigrant Trail walking tours (May to October), stargazing programs (November), Bach and banjo performances (December), Sierra watercolor workshops (October), holiday wreath-making (November), flyfishing and tying classes, hiking, fishing and bicycling. Nearby are mineral hot springs, Kirkwood skiing, horseback riding, river rafting and Lake Tahoe.

*Policies:* Children under eight are free; pets are limited to log and wagon wheel cabins; two-night minimum stay on weekends (holidays and special events up to four nights).

*Rates:* Cabins are $60 to $175, homes are $150 to $300, and bed and breakfast units are $75 to $110. Group rates are available. Reservations are recommended.

*Information:* 14255 Highway 88, Hope Valley, CA 96120; (916) 694-2203 or (800) 423-9949.

## ★ Caples Lake Resort ★

An inspiring view greets new arrivals at this resort. In front of you stretches an indigo lake a mile long and filled with six species of trout. Beyond is a backdrop of dramatic volcanic peaks dominated by 10,380-foot Round Top Mountain. It doesn't matter whether you take all of this in at sunset, with the alpenglow on the mountains, or at sunrise, with Sierra reflections in the water—you will be captivated easily by this 7,800-foot alpine oasis. John Voss and his son, Joe, have created a mini-paradise here for fishing, boating, cycling, hiking and horseback riding. There's nothing pretentious about the accommodations—small rooms on the second floor of the main lodge (with bathrooms down the hall) or modest light-housekeeping cabins nearby. But everything else is truly exceptional. The restaurant, with its Nouveau California cuisine, draws aficionados from miles around, and is clearly within the upper echelon of Tahoe's fine dining establishments. Chef Bruce "Bruno" Huff is also the top fishing guide on the lake, and has been known to coax reluctant trout to the hook. You could spend hours on the lake (fortunately, waterskiing is prohibited), but there are other attractions, as well: hiking the four-mile loop from Woods Lake to Round Top Lake, mountain biking on one of several trails (with bike rentals available at the resort), horseback riding at Kirkwood Stables and, in winter, skiing at Kirkwood's downhill or cross-country ski areas. Caples Resort is particularly cozy at night, when guests can play games, read books, practice the lost art of conversation, or enjoy the warmth of a roaring blaze in the big stone fireplace.

*Rooms:* Nine lodge guest rooms (separate men's and women's restrooms and showers across the hall) sleep two per room; seven housekeeping cabins (kitchens, bathrooms, wall heaters and bedding) sleep up to six per unit.

*Resort amenities:* A lounge with a fireplace, a restaurant (breakfast, lunch, dinner), a dry sauna, a retail shop, rentals (cross-country skis, aluminum boats, mountain bikes), fishing and a marina with a boat launch. Hiking trails are available nearby. Open year-round.

*Policies:* No smoking is permitted in the lodge and cabins. A deposit equivalent to minimum stay per reservation is required (minimum two to five nights' lodging during winter and summer). Cancellations require four weeks' notice for full refund.

*Rates:* In winter, lodge rooms are $35 to $95 per night and cabins are $75 to $230 per night; in summer, rooms are $30 to $55 and cabins are $65 to $135. Weekly rates range from $240 to $810. Visa or MasterCard required.

*Information:* Highway 88 next to Kirkwood Ski Resort, P.O. Box 88, Kirkwood, CA 95646; (209) 258-8888.

## Kirkwood Ski and Summer Resort

In winter, Kirkwood bustles with thousands of skiers who enjoy the resort's high elevation, challenging slopes and usually dry powder. In summer, the crowds are gone, the wildflowers are blooming, and the meadow is lush and green. There isn't much going on here—no golf course, no bands playing, no fashionable stores. And that's just fine with guests who are looking for a quiet place to enjoy the mountains. With lower rates in summer, Kirkwood serves as a base for exploring the hiking trails, high country lakes and mountain bike routes of Eldorado National Forest. There's fishing down the road at Silver Lake, or up the road at Caples Lake. At least a dozen day hikes are possible, and Kirkwood Stables offer a four-legged ticket into the high country. Several equestrian trails wind through the box canyon that cradles the resort, including part of the historic Mormon-Emigrant Trail. Kirkwood's condominiums are comfortable and well appointed, with TVs and phones, and balconies overlook the meadows. The best units are in the Sun Meadows complex, and most condominiums have up to four bedrooms. Other units are at Edelweiss, Meadows and Red Cliff (group accommodations in summer only). Whiskey Run, a separately owned facility, has condo units with ski-in, ski-out access next to the main lodge. While dining options at Kirkwood are limited to the historic Kirkwood Inn (a great place for breakfast or a burger), there are restaurants at nearby resorts, including Kit Carson Lodge, Caples Lake, Plasse's and Sorensen's.

**Rooms:** 85 rental units. Studios and one- and two-bedroom condominiums with kitchens, phones, living rooms, TVs and private baths.

**Resort amenities:** Timber Creek Lodge, Red Cliffs Lodge, Kirkwood Inn, Cornice Cafe Restaurant and Bar (winter), a general store, tennis courts, horse stables, a downhill ski area and cross-country ski center, group and conference facilities (11,000 square feet) and underground parking (one space per condo). Winter day care (ages 3 to 6) for non-skiing children. In summer, Kirkwood Explorer's Day Camp (ages 5 to 14) offers nature studies, sports, and arts and crafts Friday through Sunday.

**Rates:** $45 to $190 in summer, $65 to $265 in winter.

**Information:** P.O. Box 1, Kirkwood, CA 95646; (209) 258-7293 or (800) 967-7500.

## Kit Carson Lodge

Perched on the eastern shores of Silver Lake, between boulders and pine trees, this rustic, wood-frame lodge feels like a 1950s kind of place, where your father or grandfather might have taken you when you were a child. You could sit on the deck overlooking the lake and talk about trivial things as you watched fishing boats trolling for trout. The richness of knotty pine envelops this place, imparting a sense of timeless antiquity to the rooms and common areas. Two types of lodging are available: the lakeshore hotel rooms, each with bedroom, bath and private sundeck, and the housekeeping cottages, which are furnished with kitchens, fireplaces, barbecues and baths with stall showers. The main lodge houses a gourmet restaurant, an art gallery and a reception desk, and next door is a general store that sells groceries, drinks and fishing tackle. The lodge is on its own access road well off Highway 88, so traffic noise is never a problem. It's clear that many of the guests are repeat visitors, who apparently do not mind the sometimes brusque demeanor of staff members or the resort's lengthy list of policies. The resort has its own dock with boat rentals and swimming lagoon.

**Rooms:** 27 units. Lakeshore motel rooms sleep one to three people; housekeeping cottages sleep two to six people and include refrigerators, gas ranges, decks, fireplaces, private baths, gas furnaces and barbecues. For the cabins, cooking utensils and bedding are supplied, but guests must bring kitchen linens, dish soap, bath towels and toiletries.

**Resort amenities:** A gourmet restaurant, an art gallery, a private beach, boat rentals, hiking trails (complimentary tour guides and slide shows available), a retail store, a gift shop and laundry facilities.

**Policies:** No pets allowed. Children ages 3 to 12 are not permitted in the cottages. Toddlers under three are allowed during the summer in designated cabins. There is a two-night minimum rental for motel rooms on weekends; deposit is required 10 days after booking reservation (balance due upon arrival). A cancellation fee of $10 is charged—no refunds. Open May to October, with one cabin open for winter.

*Rates:* $90 to $115 for hotel rooms, $115 to $170 for cabins (or $500 to $990 for weekly rentals). Off-season midweek discounts are available on daily rates.

*Information:* Highway 88 on Silver Lake, P.O. Box 1, Kit Carson, CA 95644; (209) 258-8500 or (209) 245-4760 (November to May).

### Kay's Silver Lake Resort

A rest stop has existed here since 1860, long before Highway 88 was built. Today, this place is a bit more than a stop—it has nine housekeeping cabins on a hill overlooking Silver Lake. These are rustic accommodations, with no TVs or phones, and reaching them requires a 100- to 200-yard hike (and maybe a bit of slogging on snowshoes in the winter), since there is no maintained trail. Summer is the main season, and the resort operates a small concrete launch ramp, rents 13-foot aluminum boats with 7.5-horsepower motors, and sells fuel, gas, tackle and some grocery products at its store, which is right on the highway. All parking is in front of the store. This unpretentious place offers close proximity to excellent hiking trails, horseback riding, skiing and cycling.

*Rooms:* Nine housekeeping cabins (studios and one- and two-bedroom units), with gas heat, stoves, refrigerators, dishes, cooking utensils, linen and towels. No maid service.

*Resort amenities:* A grocery store, boat rentals, a launch ramp and a beach. Fishing, swimming, waterskiing, hiking, horseback riding are available nearby. Close to Nordic and Alpine skiing and snowmobiling. Open year-round.

*Policies:* No pets, tents, RVs or visitors from local campgrounds are allowed. A deposit of a minimum night's stay (usually two nights' rental) is required and fully refundable with 14 days' notice; a cancellation fee of $5 is charged.

*Rates:* From $57 for a studio to $115 for a two-bedroom unit, depending on day of week. Weekly rates range from $320 to $610.

*Information:* 48400 Kay's Road, Pioneer, CA 95666; (209) 258-8598.

### Plasse's Resort

This idyllic hideaway on the south end of Silver Lake has a colorful history that dates back to 1853. In that year, a young French immigrant, Ramon Pierre Plasse, established a trading post on the Mormon-Emigrant Trail, located on a high ridge two miles above the lake. Later, he built a homestead on the pastoral meadow below, at an elevation of 7,200 feet, and in the 1930s his grandchildren established the resort. Today it is still owned and operated by his descendants, and the Plasses have created a unique vacation retreat that consists of a campground, an equestrian dry camp, a general store, a restaurant/bar and the original post office, which is something of a historic landmark (Plasse's granddaughter, Caraleta, is the postmistress). Behind the general store is a small library, with many scrapbooks and pieces of memorabilia from the early days. One of the treasures is a saddle used by famous trailblazer Kit Carson, who traded it to the original Plasse; it hangs from the wall in the dining room.

There are no lodge units or cabins at the resort, but the campground can accommodate up to 70 RVs and tents, and there's a central bathhouse with showers. Each site has water, a firepit and a picnic table. There's also a big playground for kids, and a pack horse station run by Kirkwood Stables. Plasse's is the start of a scenic overnight trail ride along the Mormon-Emigrant Trail to Kirkwood Ski Resort, a distance of about 18 miles. But shorter rides of a day or less also are available, and one of those can be made to the site of the old Plasse trading post. The bar is a lively watering hole (it used to be a barn), and the dining room, open Thursday through Monday, serves rib-sticking specialities such as chicken-fried steak. Doreen Plasse and her brother, John, co-own and manage the resort (with their parents), and now their children are involved as well. The resort is located well off Highway 88, yet it is within a short walk to the water's edge at Silver Lake, as well as hiking and horseback riding into Eldorado National Forest and the Mokelumne Wilderness. Open June to October.

*Accommodations:* Tent and RV sites only (with up to four persons per vehicle) include water hookups, a picnic table, fire rings, pit toilets and a central hot shower house.

*Resort amenities:* Group campsites, dry horse campsites, a general store, a dining room and bar, hiking and horseback excursions (guided tours and overnight pack trips), a children's playground, an arcade, horseshoe pits, a basketball court, a volleyball court, shower facilities, a laundromat, a propane station, a dump station and firewood. Fishing, swimming, waterskiing, sailing and jetskiing are available nearby.

*Policies:* There is a two-night minimum. A $25 deposit is required per site. Cancellation requires 14-day notice for refund, less a $3 service charge—there are no refunds for early departure.

*Rates:* Tent and RV sites are $14 to $16 per night; the dry horse camp is $15 per night.

*Information:* 30001 Plasse Road in Silver Lake, CA; P.O. Box 261, Jackson, CA 96542; (209) 258-8814.

# Lakes Basin/Feather River Country

## ★ Gray Eagle Lodge ★

Opened in 1923, Gray Eagle is the most upscale and expensive lodge on the Gold Lake Highway. After heavy snow caused the original building to collapse in 1983, a new log structure added a contemporary feeling to the place. Bleached wood, arched and beamed ceilings and an impressive rock fireplace impart a quiet elegance to the dining room, bar and salon. The restaurant, known for its gourmet cuisine (roast duck, sauteed sea bass, leg of lamb, grilled swordfish and other delicacies) is one of the most popular dinner houses in Plumas County. This giant lodge, which has a large adjoining game room with billiards, ping pong and other table games, is clearly the centerpiece of the resort. However, the cabins have their own special ambience; they are the best appointed in the region, with comfortable furnishings, firm beds and well-maintained interiors with knotty-pine walls. They are situated in an idyllic, protected forest along meandering Gray Eagle Creek, and guests can wade in the stream or swim in the 10-foot-deep natural pond at the base of Gray Eagle Falls, just a short hike away. Located on an access road off the Gold Lake Highway, just five miles south of Graeagle, the lodge does not have a lake in its front yard. But short hiking trails will take guests to Smith Lake, a rock-rimmed beauty about one mile north, or to nearby Hidden, Lily and Long lakes. Every cabin has a detailed hiking guide written by the owners. All accommodations include breakfast, dinner and daily maid service.

*Rooms:* 15 cabins, sleeping from one to four persons (some can accommodate more) with baths, comfortable beds and heaters. There are no televisions or telephones.

*Resort amenities:* A restaurant, a cocktail lounge, a lodge and a game room. Activities include hiking, fishing, horseback riding, golf, tennis and swimming nearby.

*Policies:* Pets are allowed (yo, Fido!), but at $5 per day per pet, and they must be kept on a leash. There is a three-night minimum. A minimum $300 deposit is required within seven days of making reservations. Open May to October.

*Rates:* The following rates are per cabin, per night. Cabin for one, $125; two, $155; three, $215; four, $260; each additional adult, $50. Children 10 to 16 years old are $45 per night, three to nine are $40 per night, and up to two years, $20 per night. A two-bedroom cabin is a minimum of $190 per night. Visa and MasterCard are accepted.

*Information:* Gold Lake Road, P.O. Box 38, Blairsden, CA 96103; (916) 836-2511 or (800) 635-8778 (Northern California).

## ★ Feather River Park Resort ★

This is a grand, old-fashioned resort with bigger-than-average log cabins, a fine nine-hole golf course and many recreation facilities scattered among 160 pine-studded acres in the community of Graeagle. Amid a truly serene environment, there's still plenty to do on a family vacation. The resort has two swimming pools surrounded by manicured lawns, two tennis courts and a large recreation building with ping pong, billiards, games and a snack bar. Kids can prowl the shores of the Middle Fork of the Feather River, which borders the resort, or try fishing for trout in its waters. Built in 1923, the resort is currently owned by a corporation that acquired it in the 1970s. Their goal was to prevent the resort from being torn down and the land developed, and so this large area of open space remains a crowning attraction in the heart of Graeagle. Managers Michael and June Boyd are constantly adding new things to the cabins and grounds, and the quality shows. About 90 percent of the business is repeat traffic, so it's necessary to book well in advance, except for the shoulder seasons from May 1 to mid-June, and from early September to mid-October. Located on Highway 89, the Feather River Park Resort is close to Plumas Pines and Graeagle Meadows golf courses, Plumas Eureka State Park, the hiking and equestrian trails of the Lakes Basin, and great fishing lakes from Davis to Sardine.

*Rooms:* 35 housekeeping cabins, ranging from one to three bedrooms. All have comfortable beds, kitchens, private baths, heaters, living rooms with river-stone fireplaces, and porches or decks. All linens and bedding are provided. There are no televisions or telephones. Many cabins are located along the golf course.

*Resort amenities:* A nine-hole golf course is on flat terrain with few bunkers or other hazards, and is available to guests for $10 per day or $45 per week (carts are $10 for nine holes, $15 for 18). Outside play is allowed. Other facilities include a large adult swimming pool and small children's swimming pool, two tennis courts, bike rentals ($5 per day or $25 per week), firewood (supplied to each cabin), a snack bar and refreshments, a small retail counter, river access, a game room with ping pong and billiards, and a weekly weiner roast on Fridays and bingo on Monday nights. Open from May 1 to October 15.

*Policies:* Minimum one-week rentals from June 15 to early September; two-day minimum rentals from May 1 to June 15 and September 1 to October 15.

*Rates:* A small one-bedroom, $80; a large one-bedroom, $106; two bedrooms, one bath, $120; two bedrooms, two baths, $126; and three bedrooms, $175. All rates are per night.

*Information:* P.O. Box 37, Blairsden, CA 96103; (916) 836-2328.

# Feather River Inn

With its Tudor-style façade, stone foundation and massive timbered entryway, the 100-acre Feather River Inn is one of the grand old lodges of the West. It was built in 1911 by the First Interstate Company of Chicago, a venture capital firm that also constructed the Tovar Lodge at the Grand Canyon. Originally designed as a resort, the property once rivaled the famous Ahwahnee Hotel in Yosemite in elegance. In the 1960s, it was acquired by the University of the Pacific and operated as a prep school for 17 years. In 1988, the UOP Alumni Association took it over and converted it to a conference center. Now, it once again has new management, which has reconverted it to a lodge/meeting facility. Located in Blairsden, an hour's drive north of Truckee, the inn is open to the public from March 15 to late June and from August 15 to November 15, with rooms available during and between conferences. The lodge building itself is ornately appointed, with cheerful meeting rooms. Some or all of the 37 rooms on the second and third floors may be converted back to guest rooms in the near future and, if this happens, the Inn may once again become the premier hotel in Plumas County. For now, though, overnight guests stay in alpine "chalets" and rustic log cabins, which are scattered throughout a forested hillside and connected with wooden boardwalks. These accommodations are basic and far removed from the style of the main lodge. Each room has two twin beds, simple furnishings and front porches. Most have private baths. Three meals a day are offered during conferences. From mid-May to mid-September, an elegant Sunday brunch ($12.95), open to the public, is served in the massive dining room and outside on the veranda.

***Rooms:*** 17 cabins and chalets offering 50 units, with two twin beds, most with private baths (showers or tubs). Many cabins overlook the ninth green of the golf course.

***Resort amenities:*** A nine-hole golf course (par 34) that is open for public play, a heated swimming pool, a gymnasium, basketball, tennis and volleyball courts, horseshoes, a catch-and-release fishing pond, a dance hall and two conference rooms (15 to 150 people, complimentary coffee break and catered meals). Note: Golf is optional, and green fees are $17 per person (an extra $12 for a power cart).

***Rates:*** $44 per night for cabins, depending on availability. The facility is used from July 1 to mid-August by alumni of the University of the Pacific.

***Information:*** Mr. Barry Patton, General Manager, P.O. Box 67, Blairsden, CA 96103; (916) 836-2623.

# Salmon Lake Lodge

This gorgeous, granite-rimmed lake has immediate visual appeal, and the lodge is accessible only by boat from the main access road, giving it an isolated quality that lures guests back year after year. At an elevation of 6,500 feet, the lodge is framed by rocky peaks and mixed fir and pine forest, and there's a small island where guests can take the barge to a twice-weekly barbecue. Of the 14 cabins, 10 are tent cabins with wooden floors and canvas roofs, located over a hill just out of sight from the main building. These have a double bed, two bunks, a simple kitchen with electric cooktop stove and small refrigerator; guests share a central shower house, which has dish- and clothes-washing facilities. You need to bring your own sleeping bags, towels, cooking and eating utensils. Of the other four cabins, the Hill Cabin sleeps five (two in a double bed downstairs and three in a loft). It has a fully equipped kitchen with sink, refrigerator and toaster oven, but you'll need to bring sleeping bags and towels here, as well. The Tank House Cabin, Lakeshore Cabin and Ridge Cabin sleep from six to eight, and each has a private bath with tub or shower. The most deluxe is the Ridge with all bedding provided (but not towels), three bedrooms, a living room and full kitchen. The only meals served are the twice-weekly island barbecues, which might include flank steak, zucchini casserole, rice pilaf, homemade bread and ice cream, and wine and coffee. The lake is a great swimming and boating place, and motorboats are allowed but can run only up to five miles per hour. Rowboat rentals are offered for $20 a day to the general public, but guests have free use of all rowboats, kayaks, canoes and sailboats. Built in 1929, the lodge is owned by the Christian family, and various siblings take turns running it. It is usually sold out a year in advance, with openings only in late spring and fall, if then.

*Rooms:* 14 cabins, including 10 tent cabins (with shared exterior bath facilities) that have electricity and woodburning stoves, and four regular cabins, three with private baths. All cabins include cooking facilities. All are housekeeping units, and guests must bring bedding or sleeping bags (except for the Ridge Cabin) and towels. Tent cabins are open only from mid-June to mid-September.

*Resort amenities:* Central utility house (showers, refrigerator, washing machines), barbecue, retail shop (charcoal, maps, stamps, and postcards), and non-powered boats for guests (guests can bring small boat motors and waterskiing equipment). Swimming (July to September) and boating are allowed in nearby Gold Lake. Groceries, fishing licenses, and equipment available in Sierra City. Note: There's a phone at the parking lot and dock to call the resort for barge pick-up.

*Policies:* Camping is not permitted. Guests in excess of the listed capacity will be charged $50 per person per day. A deposit, one-half of rental, is due upon reserving a cabin. It is refundable if the cabin is re-rented, less $25.

*Rates:* $400 a week for tent cabins, $500 for the Hill Cabin, $650 for the Tank House Cabin and $900 for the Lakeshore and Ridge cabins.

*Information:* P.O. Box 121, Sierra City, CA 96125; (408) 771-2622 or (916) 842-3108.

## ★ Sardine Lake Resort ★

Without a doubt, this is the most extraordinary site for a lodge in the Lakes Basin. When you stroll through the forest to the shoreline and peer up at the sweeping Sierra Buttes that frame the lake, you'll be convinced that you've been transported to the Swiss Alps. But it will take an act of Congress to get a booking at this small resort, which probably has the region's most extensive backlog of requests. Owners Dorothy and Chandler Hunt have just nine cabins, and they aren't looking for any new business, period. They don't want to discuss rates and just plain don't want to hear from anyone. However, you might have a chance at squeezing into their restaurant, known as one of the finer local gourmet dinner houses, if you reserve a few weeks in advance. Also, the resort operates a small marina where anyone can rent rowboats or boats with electric motors. The lodge was built in 1941 by Mrs. Hunt's parents, George and Audrey Browning, who first came to the area in 1936. Several generations of the family have worked here, and continue to do so. Reportedly the lake was originally named "Emerald Lake," but it was renamed in the late 1800s when a miner's mule named "Sardine" fell into the water. There is little doubt that this is the premier spot to be in the Lakes Basin; there are hiking trails to Upper Sardine Lake, Tamarack Lakes and the Sierra Buttes fire lookout. The cabins are rustic but comfortable, and are scattered on a hillside in forest above the main building. Season is from June to early October.

*Rooms:* Nine cabins, including simple one-room cabins with kitchens and baths; a two-bedroom cabin with a living room, kitchen and bath; and deluxe two-bedroom cabins. Some have bunk beds.

*Resort amenities:* A small dock with fishing boats (with trolling motor) and rowboats available for rent, ranging from $18 to $35 per day to $100 to $200 per week (1994 rates). There are extensive hiking trails nearby, including one to the summit of Sierra Buttes. Sand Pond, a Forest Service impoundment managed for swimming, is just down the access road from the Gold Lake Highway. The resort is close to Bassett's Station and Sierra City.

*Policies:* There is a $200 minimum deposit on weekly reservations.

*Rates:* From $79 to $123 per day, and from $470 to $735 per week, with $12 per day for each additional person. Rates do not include meals.

**Information:** P.O. Box 216, Sierra City, CA 96125; (916) 862-1196 in summer and (916) 645-8882 in winter.

## Gold Lake Lodge

This one-time fishing retreat was built in 1912 by Mac and Mava McCormick, who also built the White Sulphur Springs Ranch in Clio (see page 564 in Chapter 21, "Bed & Breakfasts & Other Unique Inns"). The lodge is not actually on the lake; it is one-quarter mile north of it. It is, however, at the trailhead of the most popular one-day hiking route in the Lakes Basin (the Round Lake Loop) and next to the Gold Lake Highway, making it convenient for coming and going. Owners Ann and Pete Thill have operated the lodge since 1985, and have achieved some repute with their dining room, which is open to the public as well as to guests. Accommodations are in two types of cabins: rustic and standard. The former utilize a central bath and shower facility; the latter have their own bathrooms. Most are one-room buildings, and there are no kitchenettes, since all guests are on their meal plan, called the "Modified American Plan" (breakfast and dinner) anyway. The cabins have everything furnished, including linens, and there is daily maid service. All cabins have electricity and heaters.

Guests can walk easily to any of several lakes for fishing, and the lodge offers a rowboat on Bear Lake for its guests. Recreation also includes volleyball on the premises, and there is a pack horse station nearby. Both guests and locals rave about the meals in the woodsy, knotty-pine dining room. Breakfasts include home-baked breads and cinnamon rolls, and dinners offer four to five entrees, including fresh pasta, seafood, chicken and steaks, with desserts of homemade pies and cheesecakes. The kitchen will cook your fresh-caught trout, if you wish, and will also make an optional sack lunch. Gold Lake Lodge works well for guests who like the easy highway access for exploring the sights of the area, yet want to remain close to the Lakes Basin. The lodge has been nominated to the National Register of Historic Places.

**Rooms:** 11 rustic and standard cabins, some with private baths, some with shared (outdoor) baths. New queen-size, double and twin beds are available, and two cabins have two bedrooms. Rustic, simple furnishings, electric heaters, linen and daily maid service are included. Modified American Plan (breakfast and dinner).

**Resort amenities:** A central dining hall open to lodge and outside guests for breakfast and dinner, except on Mondays. Fishing, hiking, volleyball and swimming are available, with golf, horseback riding and tennis in nearby Graeagle.

**Policies:** No pets are allowed. A $450 deposit is required per week, or two nights' rate for two or more nights' lodging (received within 10 days of reserving). Refunds are available only if cabin can be re-rented. Open June to September.

*Rates:* Per person, $80 to $140 nightly (two nights minimum on weekends) and $500 to $895 weekly; children (ages 2 to 16), $15 to $40 per night or $100 to $265 weekly. Family discounts are available.

*Information:* P.O. Box 25, Blairsden, CA 96103; (916) 836-2350 or (916) 836-2751.

## Packer Lake Lodge

Packer Lake is a four- to five-acre lake 3.5 miles off the Gold Lake Highway, on a road that is mostly paved. Its greatest assets are its esteemed restaurant and its proximity to much more scenic lakes (notably Sardine and Tamarack) and to the road that leads to the summit of the Sierra Buttes. Packer is somewhat nondescript, though it's a pleasant enough lake for fishing (trout are stocked bi-weekly). The lodge, built in 1926, has a main building and 14 housekeeping cabins—two of which are the original lakefront, one-room log cabins, with no cooking facilities or private bath. Those and four other one-room cabins share two central bath/shower facilities. Six cabins (three with two rooms and three with three rooms) have private baths and kitchens, including electric stoves and refrigerators. All cabins have electricity and linoleum floors, and linen is provided (with one exchange midweek).

The main lodge offers dinner nightly except Tuesdays, and is open to the general public with two seatings, one starting at 6 p.m., the other at 8 p.m. The chef will cook your catch, or you can sample one of six entrees such as baby-back spareribs, prime rib, honey-herb pork chops, pasta and chicken. There's a Sunday brunch and an Italian buffet night on Wednesdays. Meals are not included with accommodations. The lodge has a big stone fireplace and a full bar, along with a small retail area for fishing tackle and miscellaneous items. There's a rowboat for each cabin, as well as some rental boats, including a canoe; motors are not permitted on the lake. The lodge is near the Pacific Crest Trail, along with hiking trails to Tamarack and Deer lakes and the Sierra Buttes; the scenic Sardine Lakes are on the other side of the ridge, along with Sand Pond, the best swimming hole in the region. Located 17 miles south of Graeagle (close to Bassett's Station), the lodge has heavy advance bookings each year, and the best openings are before June 10 or after the first week of September. The season runs May to October.

*Rooms:* 14 cabins (one, two and three bedrooms), some kitchens, some bathrooms and some lakefronts.

*Resort amenities:* Free rowboats for guests, additional boat rentals, dock, limited swimming, fishing, hiking, retail area, restaurant and full bar.

*Policies:* Pets are allowed. A deposit is required within 10 days of reserving a cabin. Cancellations with eight weeks' notice receive a full refund ($5 fee for less than eight weeks).

*Rates:* $54 to $110 per day, or $355 to $735 per week. Visa and MasterCard are accepted. All meals are extra, and run $12 to $17.

*Information:* Bill Macquattie, 3901 Packer Lake Road, P.O. Box 237, Sierra City, CA 96125; (916) 862-1221 or (415) 921-5943 (off-season).

## Elwell Lakes Lodge

Built in 1920, this small lodge one-half mile off the Gold Lake Highway is operated by Sugie and John Barker, grandchildren of the original owners. Nestled in pine and fir forest, the nine small housekeeping cabins offer rustic simplicity with modern conveniences. A separate recreation building has a large fireplace with books, games and a telephone, and another building, which used to be the dining hall, is used as a lounge, two-room bed and breakfast inn and living quarters for the owners. Except for the B&B rooms, no meals are included, but there's usually a potluck among guests once a week. Anglers are in Seventh Heaven here, because they can reach as many as 23 lakes within a three-mile radius of the lodge. On Long Lake, three-quarters of a mile away, the lodge provides complimentary boats and motors for guests to use for fishing or cruising. One of the requisite activities for those staying a week or so is the three-mile hike to the top of Mount Elwell, at 7,812 feet, which has a panoramic view of the basin. Youngsters and adults alike can cool off in a creek-filled swimming pool, or at Bear and Grassy lakes, less than a quarter mile away. The lodge is open June through September, and the best availability is usually after Labor Day.

*Rooms:* Nine cabins, two B&B rooms (on the second floor of the lounge building, sharing a bath down the hall). Cabins have double and twin beds, fully-equipped kitchenettes (gas stove, refrigerators and sinks), bathrooms with showers, linen and electric heaters. The largest cabin sleeps up to six people; others vary from two to five.

*Resort amenities:* A recreation room with a fireplace, ping pong, books and games; a lounge building with second-floor views of the forest; a barbecue area; boating at Long Lake (three complimentary boat and motor rentals for guests); swimming early in the season in a pool created by Bear Creek; and seminar facilities. Fishing and hiking are available nearby.

*Policies:* No pets are allowed. A $150 deposit is due upon booking.

*Rates:* $327 to $555 per week. In September, nightly rentals are available from $55 to $93.

*Information:* Gold Lake Road, P.O. Box 68, Blairsden, CA 96103; (916) 836-2347.

# Gold Lake Beach Resort

Located on the isolated southwestern shore of Gold Lake, the largest lake in the Lakes Basin, this is a rustic lodge where people go to escape the world. Other than four-wheeling a rough road, the only way you can get there is by 10-minute ride on a shuttle boat. The resort is the essence of mountain simplicity, with accommodations in small, wood-frame cabins and tent cabins that are nestled in the forest. There are central bath and shower facilities, and a central dining hall where breakfast and dinner are served, family-style, at tables and benches. The resort has a small marina and offers a variety of water sports including fishing, canoeing and boating, and there's a gravel beach for swimming. Close proximity to the Pacific Crest Trail provides a wealth of hiking opportunities to other lakes. In the resort compound, other activities include volleyball, ping pong and horseshoes, and there's a pack station nearby. All stays include a meal plan (breakfast, lunch and dinner), and box lunches can be prepared for guests to take with them during the day. There's a large deck overlooking the lake next to the dining room that is used for relaxing. As a place for families with children, a corporate retreat, or as an isolated getaway for couples, the resort has strong appeal—and strong repeat business. Book far in advance.

*Rooms:* 10 tent and wood cabins with twin, queen-size and optional rollaways and electricity. There are two bathhouses with showers and toilets; there are no televisions or telephones. Two additional buildings, a new house and a cabin, may be available on a limited basis; check with the management.

*Resort amenities:* Complete meal service, pick-up at dock. Swimming, fishing, hiking and horseback riding opportunities are nearby.

*Policies:* There is a three-night minimum stay, but weekly stays are preferred. Groups of at least 20 may rent the entire premises. Open July 1 to September.

*Rates:* Per person, per night, starting at $95 for adults, with lower rates for children. Special family rates are available.

*Information:* 18 Quail Point Place, Carmichael, CA 95608; (916) 484-5451.

## Layman Resort

Located on a pine-studded site just 100 yards uphill from the Middle Fork of the Feather River, this rustic retreat offers tranquility and access to the river, which is one of California's most scenic waterways. The site originally was known as Camp Layman, and it was used in the late 1800s during the construction of the railroad to the Feather River Country. The 13 cabins were built in the late 1920s and early 1930s, and have kitchenettes and bathrooms with showers. Clean linen is provided weekly. The resort, situated off Highway 70/89 northwest of Graeagle, is close to the golf resorts, hiking trails, horseback riding and fishing waters of the Lakes Basin. There's a beach on the Feather River. Because it is at a relatively low elevation, 4,200 feet, the resort opens earlier (April) than other lodges.

**Rooms:** 13 rustic cabins, including nine with one bedroom, and four with two or more bedrooms. The largest is the Pine Cabin, a two-story building with two upstairs bedrooms and two hide-a-beds in the living room. All have kitchenettes and bathrooms and showers. There are no televisions or telephones.

**Resort amenities:** Swimming and fishing opportunities on the Middle Fork of the Feather River, 100 yards away; evening campfires; barbecues; horseshoes and shuffleboard.

**Policies:** A non-refundable deposit is required; a seven-day minimum is needed for long-term reservations.

**Rates:** $48 to $90 per night, $315 to $593 per week. $5 per person per night for additional persons. There is a 10-percent discount for senior citizens. Visa and MasterCard are accepted.

**Information:** Steve and June Waasdorp, P.O. Box 8, Blairsden, CA 96103; (916) 836-2356.

# Chapter 21

# Bed & Breakfasts & Other Unique Inns

## ★ Author's Choice ★

### Top 10 Unique Inns & Historic Hotels

### Top 10 Bed & Breakfast Inns

Here's what a mountain vacation is all about: It's about immersing yourself in the crispness of the air and the sweet aroma of pine needles; it's about walking from your doorstep to the edge of a lake and watching hungry trout make ripples on the surface; it's about sitting in front of a massive stone fireplace on chilly nights and sipping a glass of Cabernet; and it's about connecting with the ghosts of the past. Lake Tahoe is a place where you can revel in nature and history, with a treasure trove of unique inns, lodges and vintage hotels that are vibrant with ambience and character. They range from Victorian bed and breakfast inns to rough and tumble Gold Rush hotels and rustic lodges.

Tahoe and Carson Valley have such a wealth of unique accommodations that even the most jaded traveler can find a niche. B&Bs have amiable hosts, occasional ghosts and 100-year-old antiques. Venerable hotels that once catered to gamblers, railroad workers, miners and prostitutes are now popular retreats for honeymooners and couples looking for a distinctive experience. Outside of a handful of devoted guests who return year after year, many of these places are never advertised, and many don't even produce brochures. It may take a year's advance reservation to squeeze inside the door during high season, but the effort is amply rewarded.

Some of the outstanding properties in the region have been in the same family for generations; others are born-again lodges that were recently restored by city-weary entrepreneurs. In the last two years, in particular, the North and West shores of Lake Tahoe have experienced a boom in boutique accommodations. They include run-down motels that have been gentrified; cabins that have been rescued from near-certain oblivion; and classic rock-and-timber inns that have been lovingly restored.

For historic hotels, it's hard to beat Truckee, Virginia City and Carson City, where the mining, lumber and railroad industries created a lively traffic and sometimes extravagant wealth. The bed and breakfast inns are sprinkled liberally throughout the region. They include elegant Victorians that once served the stagecoach routes, as well as modern chalets with rustic charm but plenty of New Age comforts. And if you have an affinity for Continental style, there is a handful of European inns that conjure up visions of Switzerland, the kind of place where the owner greets you at the door and serves fresh-baked croissants in the morning.

These unique inns and lodges have a wide range of policies and amenities. Some travelers like the intimacy and personal attention of a guest house or B&B; others shy away from compulsory socializing (always necessary at breakfast) or sharing a bathroom down the hall. If peace and quiet are preeminent in your plans, you may not be happy in an old hotel next to the railroad, or in a cottage that is close to a main highway. Then again, having a convenient location to your main points of interest may require a bit of compromise. Many of these distinctive inns do not offer television or private telephones, so if you're watching the daily stock quotes you may feel positively cut off from the world. The solution to contrived entertainment is usually the lost art of conversation, or perhaps a good book pulled from a dusty shelf in the library.

The rejuvenation of so many lodgings at Lake Tahoe has been a boon to the region, because it finally reverses some of the more wretched excesses and insensitivities of the 1970s and 1980s, when nobody, it seemed, cared much about tradition and history. The prevailing decor now back in vogue is what is widely referred to as "the Old Tahoe" look. This consists of stonework and beams, knotty pine paneling, Victorian wallpaper and roaring fireplaces. Prices range from $60 to $150, and frequently the rooms come with a full or continental breakfast, as well as afternoon snacks and beverages. Of course, each of the inns offers a cozy parlor with a roaring fireplace, and lots of opportunity to meet other guests in a relaxed setting.

# Truckee/Donner

## ★ Rainbow Lodge ★
### ★ *notes Author's Choice*

It used to be a rustic stagecoach stop on the Mormon-Emigrant Trail, and later a hangout for card sharks and con men from the late 1800s through the early 1920s. When you walk into Rainbow Lodge, the character of the place virtually envelops you, with history reverberating within the granite rock and hand-hewn timber walls. The past is particularly well preserved in the bar, off the lobby. On the wall, there's a pair of wooden skis just like the ones Snowshoe Thompson wore, and at your feet there's an antique spittoon that is reportedly one of only two originals left in California. But behind the walls is a genteel lodge with elegant rooms and Victorian furnishings, as well as the regionally popular Engadine Cafe, which serves gourmet Continental cuisine and embellishes it with one of the finest wine lists in the Tahoe Sierra. Rainbow Lodge is a stone's throw from Interstate 80, yet its isolation creates a splendid aura of seclusion. Owner John Slouber, the founder of Royal Gorge Cross Country Ski Resort (see page 400), recently refurbished every one of the 32 rooms, and he's added his own unique collection of vintage ski posters from the U.S. and Europe. In winter, there are both alpine and Nordic skiers, and in summer this is a wonderful retreat for hikers and honeymooners. Rainbow is close to the Donner Summit ski areas, as well as some of the best hiking trails and alpine lakes in the region. Perched on the banks of the Yuba River, Rainbow has several rooms with river views, including a bridal suite on the ground floor. There's the obligatory stone fireplace and a guest lounge with overstuffed chairs and shelves of books. The restaurant serves three meals a day, including a choice of six breakfast items that come with the price of the room. And if the water tastes unusually good here, it's because it comes from an artesian well located behind the property. In fact, Rainbow's water is commercially bottled. The rooms range from doubles with complete baths to ones with shared baths down the hall. There's a family unit with a queen-size bed in one room and bunks in another. In every room, the interiors are individually decorated with rich reds, greens and blues, with period calico bedspreads and matching drapes, antique furnishings, brass beds and wood paneling.

*Rates:* From $69 (no bath) to $129, including full breakfast for two people. Visa and MasterCard are accepted. P.O. Box 1100, Soda Springs, CA 95728; (916) 426-3871.

## ★ Richardson House ★

Once the home of a lumber baron in the 1870s, this stately Victorian bed and breakfast inn is perched on a hill above the historic district of Truckee, and it has a commanding view of Commercial Row and the Southern Pacific Railroad station. It also has some free-roaming spirits, according to the tales of former innkeepers, who report seeing an occasional apparition or two. That would not be uncharacteristic of a home that is over 100 years old. Despite its age, the property is being carefully restored by owners Jim and Sandi Beck, investors from the San Francisco Bay Area. The inn was originally built by Warren Richardson, the owner of a Truckee lumber mill. Richardson has a page in the history books because he invented the "steam wagon" (sometimes called the "steam donkey"), which is a contraption that could move fallen trees along wooden rails to the mill. The Richardson House is surprisingly large and spacious on the inside. There are five bedrooms upstairs with shared baths and two bedrooms downstairs with an adjoining bath. Antique furnishings are in every room, and each room has a unique, period-style decor. The living room has a large picture window, and the dining room can comfortably seat every guest when there's a full house. Each morning the innkeeper prepares a sumptuous, full breakfast, which might include juices, coffee, tea, souffles, quiches, French toast, pancakes, hot cereal and fresh-baked scones. On weekends and holidays, the inn serves afternoon refreshments of wine and cheese, and to ward off Truckee's famous winter deep-freeze, there's an outdoor hot tub in the back. All of the boutiques and restaurants of historic Truckee are just a block down the hill, and Richardson House is close to major golf courses, hiking and biking trails, and ski resorts. Children 10 and over are welcome, but no pets and no smoking. Located on Spring and High streets.

*Rates:* Summer ranges from $55 to $65; winter ranges from $65 to $75. Visa and MasterCard, personal checks and cash are accepted. 10154 High Street, P.O. Box 2011, Truckee, CA 96160-2011; (916) 587-5388.

# ★ Truckee Hotel ★

In the boom years following the Gold Rush and the introduction of rail service over the crest of the Sierra Nevada, this venerable four-story hotel became virtually an institution. Located at the end of Commercial Row, which still looks much as it did 100 years ago, the hotel has had its share of ups and downs. It is rumored that it once housed a town madam, although it was never a part of the bordello trade that flourished on nearby Front Street. Mostly, it was a convenient stop for rail travelers and, eventually, for recreationists coming to Lake Tahoe. Amtrack passenger trains, as well as freight trains, still stop at the station across the street. During much of the 1980s, the Truckee Hotel had a reputation for insomnia, partly from the trains and partly from the live music in The Passage restaurant downstairs. But things are quieter now, and the Truckee has become an elegant retreat. If you stay in a south-facing room, you may hear the trains (the management provides earplugs), but the north end is relatively quiet. In 1990, Jeff and Karen Winter from the San Francisco Bay Area acquired the hotel and launched a major renovation—some might say gentrification. In fact, the hotel has become one of Tahoe's boutique bed and breakfast properties. Walk through the entrance and you are transported to the Victorian era, with old-fashioned light fixtures, polished oak and raised olive-green wallpaper. The Victorian Sitting Parlor, to the left, is furnished with antiques, and in the adjoining dining area guests enjoy a continental breakfast of muffins, bagels, cold cereal, fresh fruit, yogurt and a selection of teas and coffees. Snacks are served early evening on weekends. Evenings here are meant for reading and relaxation, although the more adventurous can roam the night haunts of downtown Truckee. Of the hotel's 36 rooms, 24 are in the European style (wash basin and shared bath down the hall), four are family rooms with shared bath, and eight are American style with full baths featuring deep clawfoot tubs. The bridal suite has a canopied bed with white lace and satin, and one of the rooms has a distinctly uncharacteristic Southwestern decor. If you're a television addict, you'll have to compete with channel surfers in the Whitney Room, a meeting and television area on the second floor. There are convenient ski lockers on the ground floor, next to the registration desk. Happily, the hotel still has lots of character, with creaks and groans, funny little depressions in the floors beneath the carpeting, and long and steep stairways that narrow by the fourth floor. One of the advantages of staying here is the proximity to North Tahoe resorts and to the boutiques and restaurants of old Truckee.

***Rates:*** Summer rates range from $60 to $105, winter rates from $75 to $115. Off-season rates are $50 to $95. Visa, MasterCard and American Express are accepted. 10007 Bridge Street, Truckee, CA 96161; (800) 659-6921 or (916) 587-4444.

## ★ Donner Country Inn ★

It's not the easiest place to find, but it's worth the effort. This unique inn, which is almost styled in the vein of a modern chalet, is across from Donner Lake and nestled in pine forest adjacent to Gregory Creek. It offers all the advantages of a B&B, including a full breakfast, but has individual rooms with private entrances and private baths (showers only) that are detached from the main building. Each of the five suites is individually decorated, with appointments such as calico drapes, queen-size brass beds and window seats. The beds have down pillows and comforters, and each room has a wood-burning stove as well as conventional heating. There are nice, homey touches including monogrammed terrycloth robes, fresh flowers and candles. What is most impressive about the inn, however, is its spacious living room/dining room, with cathedral ceiling, fireplace and earthy but elegant furnishings. Large picture windows admit plenty of sunlight for a cheerful effect, making this a place that beckons you to spend more time here. The innkeeper provides a sumptuous breakfast that can include quiche or frittata, fruit salad and fresh-baked croissants and muffins. During summer, guests can eat on a large deck with a partial view of Donner Lake. The inn was built in 1986 on the site that was used to house the Japanese team during the 1960 Winter Olympics at Squaw Valley. The inn is close to eight downhill and cross-country ski areas, three 18-hole golf courses, a large marina at Donner Lake and historic Truckee. Located at the intersection of Donner Lake Road—an exit off Interstate 80—and Donner Pass Road.

*Rates:* $95 per night, plus tax. Single or double occupancy only; no rollaway beds. Minimum two-night stay. Accepts traveler's checks, cash or personal checks, but no credit cards. Advance reservations only. 10070 Gregory Place, P.O. Box 11243, Truckee, CA 96162; (510) 938-0685 or (916) 587-5574.

## Sugar Bowl Lodge

Probably no ski area in Lake Tahoe offers as European an environment as Sugar Bowl, one of the Sierra's first dedicated ski resorts. Built in 1939, the ski area and its 28-room guest lodge have seen a parade of celebrities over the decades, including Walt Disney, who was one of the original investors, and actors such as Errol Flynn, Charlie Chaplin and James Stewart. There's a distinct Tyrolean flare in this rustic, three-story wood structure, which has a big parlor with a fireplace, The Belt Room lounge, and one of the region's best gourmet restaurants. Staying here might remind you of the Sun Valley Lodge or Yosemite's Ahwahnee Hotel—there's that Old World charm and the sense of experiencing a winter resort in its purest form. Once the skiers leave for the day, it's a cozy, uncrowded place to savor. And it's nice to step outside in the morning and be one of the first skiers to cut tracks in fresh powder. Recently, many of the rooms have been remodeled, with new furnishings, cable television, down comforters and cheerful pastels. The long, narrow hallways are lined with historic photographs, and guests must get accustomed to ascending and descending several sets of stairways. The rooms with the best panoramas are the Mountain View rooms, which overlook the ski lifts and towering Mount Lincoln (elevation 8,383 feet). There are several rooms for families, sleeping four to six people; these have queen-size beds in one room and twin beds in a loft. Mountain Family rooms have one queen-size bed and a bunk bed in an adjacent room, with a private bathtub and shower. Rooms for couples and singles have queen-size beds or twins, and there's a deluxe suite with a queen-size bed, a living room with a queen-size sofa sleeper, and a private bath with tub and shower. All guests park in a covered garage at the entrance, and must take the gondola to reach the lodge. The lodge is open only in winter, and popular holidays and weekends can be booked up a year in advance. Located on the Donner Summit, off Interstate 80 at the Soda Springs/Norden exit on Old Highway 40.

**Rates:** From $85 to $295, depending on location and size (room or suite). Open from December to March only. Bed and breakfast packages include lodging, lift tickets, parking and breakfast, and there are discounted prices for children who share a room with parents. Accepts Visa, MasterCard, American Express and Discover. P.O. Box 5, Norden, CA 95724; (916) 426-3651, ext. 542.

## Royal Gorge Wilderness Lodge

Situated in the heart of America's largest cross-country ski resort, the Wilderness Lodge is a rustic overnight retreat that has developed a reputation for its gourmet, French country-style cuisine. At the doorstep is a trail system that extends for 328 kilometers over 9,172 acres, so vast that most skiers can hope to see only a small portion of it during a week's stay. The 35 private rooms on the first and second levels of this knotty-pine lodge are small and spartan, and all share adequate but not deluxe bathrooms down the hall. Showers (along with hot tub and sauna) are in a separate building outside, so it's best to time your visit there for the end of the day. Making up for those inconveniences, however, are the spacious and posh common areas, including a huge parlor with overstuffed couches, fireplace, books, games, video and views of a frozen lake. There's a large dining room where breakfast and lunch are served buffet-style and dinner is served at your table by candlelight. The youthful employees are exceptionally courteous and helpful, and represent various nationalities. All guests arriving at night transfer to the lodge in a motorized sleigh from the Summit Day Lodge, and frequently ski out while luggage is taken separately. Open only in winter. Located on the Donner Summit, off Interstate 80 at the Soda Springs/Norden exit and one mile east of Old Highway 40.

***Rates:*** Two-night stays range from $195 to $295 per person, depending on the season and day of the week, and include all meals, skiing passes, lessons and accommodations. Open from December to early April only. Children range from $125 to $225. Toddlers are not recommended. Three-night midweek programs range from $195 to $225 for adults and $125 to $165 for children. No children under 5. Visa and MasterCard are accepted. P.O. Box 1100, Soda Springs, CA 95728; (800) 500-3871 or (916) 426-3871.

## Donner Summit Lodge

With 40 rooms, this is the largest overnight accommodation on the Donner Summit, and it's full of history, as arriving guests can ascertain from the woodsy, aging exterior and the funky interior. Currently owned by Betty Mueller, the lodge was originally built in 1914, but saw expansion after World War II. Gambling and prostitution once flourished here, and there were nooks and crannies to hide poker chips and people during police raids. If you needed to make a fast escape, you could disappear through a trap door in a telephone booth. Behind the building, there was once a silver fox farm that raised animals for the fashion industry. All of the unsavory elements are gone now, and over the years Donner Summit Lodge has become a haven for PG&E workers, highway maintenance crews and truck drivers, as well as skiers and hikers. Bedrooms are small but comfortable, with 1970s-style furnishings that won't win any interior design awards. Each room has a television but no telephone, and all rooms have indoor access. Common facilities include a coffee shop, restaurant, bar, indoor hot tub and dry sauna in the basement, and gift shop. Meals are inexpensive and filling (fresh turkey daily, barbecued beef ribs and regionally famous half-pound hamburgers), but don't look for anything gourmet. The kids will probably love this place, and you can't argue with its strategic location right off Interstate 80 (Soda Springs/Norden exit) where it's close to major skiing, hiking and boating destinations.

***Rates:*** Summer rates range from $48 to $68, winter rates from $74 to $110. Adjoining rooms with kings and doubles can accommodate families with children. MasterCard and Visa are accepted. P.O. Box 696, Soda Springs, CA 95728; (916) 426-3638.

## Donner Spitz Hutte
## (Alpine Skills International)

Here's a taste of Old World charm with the rustic ambience of the Sierra. Bela and Mimi Vadasz, who operate winter backcountry skiing and summer mountain climbing programs, own this Swiss-flavored "mountain hut" on the summit of Donner Pass along Old Highway 40, just up the road from Sugar Bowl ski area. For alpinists, this is truly an international setting, with a cozy and inviting lodge. There is plenty of opportunity to mingle around wood-burning stoves and share experiences of climbing or skiing up Mount Judah and Donner Peak. The accommodations, which are plain but comfortable, range from mini-dorms with bunks (bring your own sleeping bag and pillow) to a few private bedrooms, and represent some of the cheapest rates in the area. Everyone shares the bathrooms, which are modern and equipped with showers. Breakfast comes with each night's lodging, and features hearty, home-style cooking. On weekends and holidays, family-style dinners are served for $12 extra. Lunches, snack items, domestic and imported beer, specialty wines and espresso also are available. In summer, this is an international climbing center, with climbing courses, convenient routes next to the lodge, and an artificial climbing wall for training. But you can enjoy less rigorous activities such as wildflower hikes along the Pacific Crest Trail, mountain biking and windsurfing at Donner Lake. Incidentally, the view of the lake from here is extraordinary. Facilities include a rental/repair shop for backcountry skis in winter, and climbing shoes/boots and packs in summer. There's a plowed parking lot and dry storage for ski equipment. Mountaineering slide shows or videos are shown each Saturday night. Arrangements can be made for conferences, weddings and banquets.

***Rates:*** Bunk and breakfast, $23 a night; private room and breakfast (two-night minimum on weekends), $72 a night; family-style dinner, $12; breakfast (for non-guests), $7; day use and overnight parking (for non-guests), $5 to $10; shower after check out, $3. MasterCard, Discover or Visa are accepted for phone reservations. Take the Soda Springs/Norden exit from Interstate 80. P.O. Box 8, Norden, CA 95724; (916) 426-9108 or (916) 426-3063 (fax).

## The Sierra Club's Clair Tappaan Lodge

This is a weathered, some might say, ramshackle mountain lodge that looks as if it were built by the Swiss Family Robinson. That's not far from the truth. The lodge, located on the Donner Summit off Old Highway 40, was constructed in 1934 entirely by volunteers, and is owned and operated by the Sierra Club. While members have priority here, and use it heavily, non-members are welcome, as long as they adhere to the co-op policies of the club, such as chipping in with daily chores. That means you should be handy with a broom, a Brillo pad or a toilet plunger. Sleeping accommodations are rustic, borderline primitive. They consist of family bunk rooms, two-person cubicles and large, single-gender dorms; all require you to bring a sleeping bag or linen, along with towels and toilet kit. None of the doors has a lock, but you can store valuables in an office locker. The communal bathrooms are seedy-looking but adequate and clean. The assets of the lodge include the big sitting room with its enormous fireplace, a well-stocked library, a hot tub and a large dining area, with family-style meals provided by a professional cook. Up to 140 people can be accommodated, and things tend to get hectic with a full house. In winter, you'll need to wear snow boots to reach the front door, which is 100 yards up a steep trail from the parking lot. Bring a flashlight if you arrive after dark. Facilities here include the smaller Hutchinson Lodge that is intended for groups of up to 25 people, a cross-country trail system with 12 kilometers of groomed track, a ski rental and instructional program, and a network of four backwoods huts, each about a day's ski or hike apart. In addition, there's a warming hut, located a mile from Clair Tappaan, which is available for overnight stays, has a fireplace and an outhouse, and can accommodate up to 10 people. Clair Tappaan is close to Royal Gorge Cross Country Ski Resort (see page 400), the nation's largest, and to Sugar Bowl, Donner Ski Ranch and Boreal alpine resorts.

***Rates:*** In summer, $32 a night for adult members, $36 for non-members, $16 for children ages 4 through 12, and free for tots under 4. In winter, $32 for members and $36 for non-members midweek; weekends (requiring a two-night minimum) are $36 and $39, respectively. Children are $16 midweek and $24 on weekends and holidays in winter, and youngsters under 4 are discouraged on winter weekends. All rates are per person and include three meals a day. MasterCard and Visa are accepted, and proof of membership is required to get the Sierra Club discount. Rules require each guest to do one chore each day. Take the Soda Springs/Norden exit from Interstate 80. 19940 Donner Pass Road in Soda Springs, CA; P.O. Box 36, Norden, CA 95724; (916) 426-3632.

# North Shore
## ★ The Cottage Inn ★

Stepping into Lake Tahoe's newest born-again property is like stepping into an old hunting lodge. But beyond the deer trophy above the fireplace is a warmth that comes from the fresh-baked chocolate chip cookies, or the fresh popcorn, or the carafe of Cabernet Sauvignon that greets guests in the main lodge building every afternoon. The trademark wood and stone decor of Old Tahoe has some very contemporary touches in this lakeside haven of five duplex cottages, located just south of Tahoe City on Highway 89. In 1993, the inn was a collection of drab, aging cabins that looked like a lot of rustic properties around Tahoe. But Terry and Patti Giles, developers of boutique inns who live in Southern California, did a major overhaul, turning the cabins into upscale cottages. Each has a rich but different brick or stone (or faux stone) facade, and each has

a theme-oriented interior designed by Patti herself. There's the Western
theme suite, with knotty pine walls, decorative boots next to a gas fireplace, a steer horn above the bed and an entertainment credenza that
comes with its own library of Western videotapes, just in case you have a
craving for a John Wayne flick. Another cabin has an open, two-story
cathedral ceiling, with a queen-size bed below and another on the loft,
which is reached from a spiral staircase with branches for bannisters. A
sitting area with another gas fireplace provides warmth for any cozy
couple. Just in case you don't realize that you're in the woods, there's a
sound system that pipes in the chirping of birds. The honeymoon suite
has lavish decor and offers something you don't find in your typical lakeside cabin—a giant stone bathtub big enough for a party, complemented
by a cascading waterfall and Jacuzzi jets. There's a cathedral ceiling, a
canopied bed, a sitting area and another gas fireplace. The inn serves a
full breakfast in the morning, in the main lodge. And it maintains its own
library of video tapes to suit most any interest—or mood. This is a
couples kind of place, to be sure, and it has that feeling of intimacy that
seems to suit Lake Tahoe. Also, it's on the quiet West Shore of the lake,
close to golf and ski resorts, water sports, bicycle paths and hiking trails.

*Rates:* From $100 to $165 per unit, including full breakfast. Visa and
MasterCard are accepted. Children over 12 only. 1690 West Lake Boulevard, P.O. Box 66, Tahoe City, CA 96145; (800) 581-4073 or (916) 581-4073.

## ★ River Ranch Lodge ★

It's easy to see why this is one of the most popular small lodges in the
region. River Ranch is perched on the edge of the Truckee River, and
during normal snow years the overflow from Lake Tahoe creates frothy
rapids along the "Big Bend" next to the spacious outdoor patio. Originally called Deer Park Inn, the property dates back to 1888, when
passengers from a narrow-gauge train used to stop here on their journey
between Truckee and Tahoe City. In 1950, the old timbers were torn
down and replaced with a new building, which became a fashionable
summertime fishing lodge. Ten years later, the Winter Olympics at Squaw
Valley brought diplomats from around the world and established the 19-
room lodge as a favorite of skiers. Recently renovated, each room is now
decorated in Early American antiques. The restaurant, serving seafood,
steaks and lamb, has established a fine reputation, and the cocktail
lounge, a unique feature, is cantilevered over the rushing rapids. In summer, the lodge offers name jazz and other contemporary musical concerts
on the patio. River Ranch is close to everything; a paved bike trail that
follows the river and skirts the North and West shores of Lake Tahoe
originates here. When the river is high enough, guests can rent small rafts
in Tahoe City and float the 4.5 miles downstream to the lodge. Great

hiking in the Five Lakes area of Granite Chief Wilderness is just up the road, as are the major ski areas of Alpine Meadows and Squaw Valley.

**Rates:** $40 to $110 per room, for up to two people; additional guests are $15 more per person. No charge for children age 6 and under. Includes daily continental breakfast. Visa, MasterCard and American Express are accepted. Highway 89 at Alpine Meadows Road, P.O. Box 197, Tahoe City, CA 96145; (916) 583-4264 or, in California, (800) 535-9900.

## ★ The Olympic Village Inn ★

Constructed for the 1960 Winter Olympics and then almost completely rebuilt in 1982, this inn of 90 suites is rich with European elegance, and is without a doubt one of Lake Tahoe's finest properties. Designed in the style of a Tyrolean village, with the requisite clock tower, the lodge closely resembles some of the deluxe small inns of Vail and Beaver Creek, Colorado. In summer, the grounds have a lush garden setting, with waterfalls, a swimming pool and five hot tubs. In winter, skiers are so close to the lifts at Squaw Valley that they could walk there, but a shuttle service whisks them to the base lodge. Lots of small touches create a special ambience for guests—complimentary bicycles and sleds, guided hikes into Shirley Canyon, a videotape library and a daily morning newspaper. Each suite is sumptuously furnished, in a sort of country European style, and has modern conveniences such as a television, VCR and stereo system. There are down comforters for the beds, terrycloth robes and bathtubs with double shower heads. Each suite has a separate living room and bedroom, a small kitchenette and, on the second and third floors, a private balcony. The deluxe suites also have wood-burning fireplaces. All units are part of a time-share program, so the rental pool available to the public varies from day to day. Also, what was once the main lodge, housing the check-in desk, restaurant and cocktail lounge— the nerve center of the inn, was acquired by the ski resort in 1993 and is now, unfortunately, out of service.

**Rates:** $95 to $250. Rates are higher on holidays, and all rates are subject to an eight-percent sales tax. Visa, MasterCard and American Express are accepted. 1909 Chamonix Place, P.O. Box 2395, Olympic Valley, CA 96146; (800) 845-5243 or (916) 581-6000.

## Mayfield House

Not only is this bed and breakfast inn a classic example of the Old Tahoe style of architecture, with its stone and wood facade, but it is also centrally located to shops, restaurants and beachfront activities in Tahoe City. Built in 1932 by Norman Mayfield, a pioneer contractor in the area, the house was completely refurbished in 1979. It has five bedrooms, each decorated with down comforters, a king- or queen-size bed, antiques and a small nook where guests can have breakfast in their rooms, if they desire. Two rooms, the Den and the Study, are on the ground floor, and a third, the Guest Room, is on the first landing of the stairs. On the second floor is the Mayfield Room, which is the master suite with a large sitting area, and Julia's Room, which was once used by Julia Morgan, designer of the San Simeon castle and a personal friend of Norman Mayfield. All bedrooms share three bathrooms, two of which have tubs. A dining room and a large living room with a fireplace comprise the common areas. Innkeeper and owner Bruce Knauss, who has lived here since 1989, serves a full breakfast that might consist of Finnish pancakes, Belgian waffles, Portuguese toast or crepes. In the afternoon, there is complimentary cheese and crackers, along with wine or brandy. No smoking inside, no pets, and children by arrangement only. Located at 236 Grove Street, Tahoe City (off Highway 28), the inn is just across the road from the lake.

*Rates:* $85 to $165, plus an eight-percent room tax. All rates are for double occupancy and include a full breakfast and afternoon refreshments. Visa, MasterCard and American Express are accepted. P.O. Box 5999, Tahoe City, CA 96145; (916) 583-1001.

## Haus Bavaria

Located in Incline Village, a small community on the east shore of Lake Tahoe (and one with an idyllic shoreline of beach and rock), this modern bed and breakfast chalet, built in 1980, has charming European touches. Each of the five upstairs guest rooms opens onto a balcony, offering views of the surrounding mountains. Rooms have private baths (one with tub, the other with showers), and a combination of antique and replica furnishings. The living room has rustic wood paneling and a collection of German bric-a-brac, left over from the original owners. Innkeeper and current owner Bick Hewitt serves a full breakfast in the downstairs dining room, and the meal includes fresh baked goods, seasonal fruits and juices, fresh-ground coffee and a selection of teas. Haus Bavaria is close to two excellent golf courses at Incline, hiking trails in the Mount Rose Wilderness, several ski resorts and the beautifully manicured private beaches of Lake Tahoe that are available only to Incline residents and guests. No pets and no smoking indoors. Located at 593 North Dyer Circle, off Mount Rose Highway and Lake Tahoe Boulevard (Highway 28).

*Rates:* $90 to $125, plus room tax. Visa, MasterCard, American Express and Discover cards accepted. P.O. Box 3308, Incline Village, NV 89450; (800) 731-6222, (702) 831-6122 or (702) 831-1238 (fax).

# Christy Inn

Though not nearly as ornate as other bed and breakfasts around the Tahoe area, Christy Inn has a rich history and is marvelous close to the golf course and ski slopes of Squaw Valley. The inn was once the home of Wayne and Sandy Poulsen, Lake Tahoe's "First Family of Skiing," who founded the ski area in 1948 and raised a brood of eight children, many of whom became skiing champions and Olympians. Years ago, the Poulsens built a new family compound elsewhere in the valley, and created this small inn, which has seven bedrooms, each with private bath (most with bathtubs). The rooms have functional appointments but no particular ambience, and nothing that could be described as luxurious. On the lower level, what used to be the Poulsen's living and dining rooms is now Graham's, one of Tahoe's more celebrated gourmet dinner houses. There's a large outdoor deck and an adjacent lawn area.

*Rates:* $75 to $150, ranging from two to four people. Slightly higher during holiday periods. The entire building can be rented for $550 a night in summer, $800 a night in winter. The inn has been used for weddings and family reunions. Visa and MasterCard accepted. 1604 Christy Lane, P.O. Box 2008, Olympic Valley, CA 96146; (916) 583-3451 or (916) 583-2040 (fax).

# The Shore House

Rustic but refined, this new lakefront bed and breakfast on the North Shore of Lake Tahoe offers nine uniquely styled rooms, a half mile of white sand beach, a private pier and a full, gourmet hot breakfast each morning. Owners Barb and Marty Cohen, residents of Tahoe for 20 years, took over what was once a motel and created an intimate, romantic getaway with a main building and two cabins. Completed in spring 1995, all rooms have king- and queen-size beds, except for one room which has two doubles. Each room has a private bath, a private entrance, knotty-pine walls, custom-built log beds and Scandia down featherbeds and comforters. The Treehouse on the upper floor is decorated with a Native American motif, and has a picture window overlooking the gardens and lake. The Tallac Room features a garden and lake views from its upper floor window, two double-sized log beds and a private shower. The Pine Room on the ground floor is the largest guest room containing a king-size log bed, a private pine bath with an oversize tub and shower, garden views and a peek at the lake. The Cottage, a separate, rustic beachfront cabin, provides lake and mountain views and a bathroom with a large shower. A lawn extends to the lake, there is substantial landscaping with aspens and cottonwoods, and the main building is surrounded with decking. The Cohens prepare a hearty mountain breakfast, such as crepes, omelets and eggs Benedict; it is served in the lakeside dining room, which has a large stone fireplace. In the afternoon, they serve wine and cheese, and at bedtime there's a fresh batch of homemade cookies (courtesy of the Cohens' son, Jake). There are no television sets and no phones in the rooms (although there's a central phone in the dining room). Seven gourmet restaurants are within walking distance of the property.

*Rates:* Prices range from $100 to $140 per night for double occupancy, depending on season and the room. A two- to three-night minimum stay is required during the high season. At the time of your reservation, a deposit equal to one night's stay is required, refundable if cancelled two weeks prior to arrival. No smoking or pets allowed. Accepts Visa and MasterCard. 7170 North Lake Boulevard, Tahoe Vista, CA 96148; (800) 207-5160, (916) 546-7270 or (916) 546-7130 (fax).

## The Palmer House

With a panoramic view of Lake Tahoe, this modern, tri-level bed and breakfast retreat, located on the side of Talmont Mountain two miles south of Tahoe City, offers two luxurious guest rooms and two baths with a private keyed entrance. The Vista, which is on the highest level and has a beamed ceiling, features a master bedroom, bath with shower and tub enclosure, queen-sized bed, remote controlled television and telephone. The Heritage Room offers an antique four-poster, full-sized bed and private bath with shower. Both guest rooms open onto an oversized deck with a gas grill. The sitting room includes amenities such as a small refrigerator, microwave, coffee maker, toaster, china, glassware and television with VCR. Innkeepers Diane and Roger Palmer treat guests to an unhosted continental breakfast basket with fresh fruits, juices and bread each morning. Guests have use of the garage, which opens on the third level, as well as to a private members-only beach next to Sunnyside Lodge. In winter, it is advisable to have a four-wheel-drive vehicle to negotiate the steep and sometimes icy roads leading to the property. The home, originally built in 1959 (and featured that year in *Sunset* magazine), was enlarged in 1977 with a new wing housing the guest rooms, then renovated in 1993.

*Rates:* Prices range from $95 to $135 per room, double occupancy, or $195 a night for both rooms. Guest rooms are available on a two-night minimum basis on weekends and a one-night minimum Monday through Thursday. A deposit equal to 50 percent of the guest room fee or 100 percent of a one-night stay is required at the time of reservation. Visa, MasterCard, checks and cash are accepted. Deposits are refundable if cancelled two weeks prior to the arrival date. The Palmer House is located at 1865 Tahoe Park Heights Drive in Tahoe City. The mailing address is P.O. Box 717, Homewood, CA 96141; (800) 726-1308 or (916) 581-0187 or (916) 581-1627 (fax).

# West Shore

## ★ Norfolk Woods Inn ★
## (formerly Alpenhaus)

Here's another marvelous example of the Phoenix rising from the ashes. This West Shore inn has changed hands almost as often as a chameleon changes colors, but in 1993 Al and Patty Multon gave up their careers in Sydney, Australia (she's the Aussie, he's the Yank), and decided to put down roots as innkeepers at Lake Tahoe. They took over this seven-room, European-style lodge in Tahoma and opened up five seldom-used cabins, redecorated the place to look less like the Tyrol and more like Tahoe, and hired a top-notch chef. This is a place that makes a point of catering to families, as evidenced by the couple's own three children. There is no extra charge for kids under 12, and the Alpenhaus will even take dogs in the cabins. Four of the cabins are ideal for the small fry (each will sleep a minimum of four people), and the fifth is a honeymooner's special. Elements of that cabin have existed since the turn of the century, when evangelist Aimee Semple MacPherson lived there. The cabin has been substantially rebuilt, and it has an elegant king-size bed upstairs, a large sitting room with fireplace and a full kitchen. When Al and Patty moved here from Down Under, they brought with them a huge collection of European tapestries and Australian paintings, which adorn the restaurant. There's a small but cozy bar with stained glass panels and a selection of wines and brews (try the Buzzard's Breath from Alberta, Canada). Most of the rooms have been upgraded with antique or replica furnishings, wallpaper and other homey touches. In summer, highway noise can be distracting for guests in the east-facing rooms. Prices for the inn rooms include a full breakfast, with choice of buttermilk pancakes, French toast, omelette of the day, eggs and bacon, or hot or cold cereal with fresh fruit.

***Rates:*** $80 to $150. Visa, MasterCard and American Express accepted. 6941 West Lake Boulevard, P.O. Box 262, Tahoma, CA 96142; (916) 525-5000.

## ★ Tahoe Meadows Bed & Breakfast ★

This is one of Lake Tahoe's recent arrivals on the B&B scene, a bucolic lodge of red duplex cabins that has been lovingly refurbished by Bill and Missy Sandeman. Missy is a talented artist, and her creative watercolor paintings decorate each of the nine rooms, which have charming, country-style furnishings and cheerful colors. Some units are close to Highway 89, which can be noisy with heavy traffic in summer; others are set back in the trees. Three rooms (Lupine, Queen Anne Lace and Fox Glove) have vintage clawfoot bathtubs, great for soaking in at the end of a day of hiking, cycling or skiing. There is no television. Full breakfast, included in the rates, is served in the main lodge, with fresh juice, quiches, egg casseroles and fresh-baked goods and fresh fruit. The property also houses Stony Ridge Cafe, a new gourmet restaurant that serves breakfast and lunch. The Sandemans have a small sitting room upstairs, with a view of Lake Tahoe across the street, and guests might see Missy painting here at her easel. The inn is located in Tahoma, near Sugar Pine Point State Park and its hiking trails, the famous Ehrman Mansion, an extensive paved bike trail, Homewood Ski Area and several lakefront marinas. During winter, the ski resort will send a free shuttle to pick up guests, upon request. Located at 6821 West Lake Boulevard (Highway 89) seven miles south of Tahoe City.

*Rates:* At $65 to $75 a night, including breakfast, this is one of the most reasonably priced B&Bs anywhere. Visa and MasterCard accepted. P.O. Box 82, Homewood, CA 96141; (916) 525-1553.

## ★ Chaney House ★

If you like mingling with gregarious people who are knowledgeable about Lake Tahoe and its attractions, you'll feel right at home in Gary and Lori Chaney's mini-castle. This historic remnant of Old Tahoe is full of character, including that of the owners, who live on-site. It was built in the 1920s by Italian stone masons, and it has 18-inch-thick walls, Gothic arches and a massive stone fireplace that reaches to the top of a cathedral-like ceiling. The feeling is distinctly European, especially in the entryway and living room, and you almost expect to see a knight in armor clanking down the stairs. The four rooms, upstairs and over the garage, convey a much livelier and more contemporary impression; each is richly appointed and has a private bathroom with a shower. The Chaneys named rooms after their (now grown) children, Jeanine and Russell; one is calico feminine with a brass queen-size bed with Wendy Moon quilts made in Lake Tahoe, the other is masculine and pine-paneled, with a lake view. The Master Suite has a garden view and comes with a king-size bed. The Honeymoon Hideaway, a one-bedroom apartment over the garage, is romantically inspired, with white lace and furniture, a kitchen, an alcove with a futon couch, a queen-size bed and private bath. The house is set back from Highway 89, with a large driveway and plenty of parking. Across the road is a private beach and pier, as well as a fire pit for evening barbecues and stargazing. Rates include a full breakfast served on the patio overlooking the lake on summer days, or indoors in winter; refreshments are offered in the evenings around the fireplace. The breakfast is a buffet and consists of Lori's unique creations, dishes such as El Dorado eggs (casserole with sausage, peppers and onions, with two different cheeses); Swahili pie (similar to Dutch pancakes, but with honey and custard and covered with hot spiced apples); and crab puff (similar to a quiche with crab and eggs). There's a dog in residence, and smokers are relegated to the outdoors. Located at 4725 West Lake Boulevard (Highway 89) in Homewood, five miles south of Tahoe City.

*Rates:* $100 to $115, plus an eight-percent room tax. All rooms are double occupancy; each additional person is $20. Cash or personal checks only. P.O. Box 7852, Tahoe City, CA 96145; (916) 525-7333 or (916) 525-4413 (fax).

## ★ Rockwood Lodge ★

Here's a place for incurable romantics, wildlife aficionados or those who love the style of "Old Tahoe." Louis Reinkens and Connie Stevens, husband and wife, have operated this bed and breakfast since 1985. Located in a wooded area just off Highway 89 at Homewood, the house is a spacious mountain chalet that was built in 1939 by Carlos Rookwood, a dairyman from Northern California who used it as a summer retreat. When Louis, an aerospace consultant, and Connie, an airline flight attendant, acquired it they changed an "o" to a "c" and it became Rockwood. Among her various interests, Connie runs a non-profit organization called Wildlife Shelter Inc., and has a care facility for injured animals and birds next door. The inn has knotty pine walls, hand-hewn beams, a huge stone fireplace and a cozy sitting room with a bottle of Riesling or Cabernet just waiting to be shared. The five guest rooms, all upstairs, have names such as Secret Harbor, Rubicon Bay and Emerald Bay, which are famous sites at Lake Tahoe. Secret Harbor, the most elegant suite, features a four-poster, queen-size bed, a private bath with a double shower and Roman tub, and a partial view of the lake. All rooms have feather beds, down comforters, pedestal sinks and a sitting area for two. The interiors are richly appointed in Laura Ashley curtains and fabrics, Early American and European furniture, and brass and porcelain fixtures. Homey touches include chocolate truffles on the nightstand, a full supply of body lotions and shampoos, and a walk-in closet with terrycloth bathrobes. A modified breakfast—the specialty is Louis' Dutch Baby, a kind of fruit frittata—is served daily, on the patio when the weather permits. Between 4 p.m. and 6 p.m., hors d'oeuvres and beverages are served. The inn is a no-smoking, no-shoes environment; guests are asked to wear slippers provided by the innkeepers. Rockwood is located seven miles south of Tahoe City, on a busy stretch of Highway 89 (though it is set back from the road), and is 100 feet from the lake.

*Rates:* $90 to $200, plus an eight-percent room tax. Cash, check or money order; credit cards accepted to hold reservations only. 5295 West Lake Boulevard (Highway 89), P.O. Box 226, Homewood, CA 96141; (800) 538-2463, (916) 525-5273 or (916) 525-5949 (fax).

## Château Arbre

This new bed and breakfast , another project of the industrious Diane and Roger Palmer (see Palmer House, page 551 in this chapter), has a French country design and is located in Tahoma, on the West Shore of Lake Tahoe. Built originally in the 1930s, it includes the Château Arbre (main house) and the Maisonnette Arbre (cottage), both of which are nestled in pine trees. Completely renovated in 1995, the buildings retain the original pine walls and ceilings but have the added conveniences of modern bathrooms, kitchens and living room areas. Each of the five bedrooms in the two buildings is named for a French wine, such as Chardonnay, Cabernet Sauvignon, Champagne and Sauvignon Blanc. In the Château Arbre, guests have full use of a living room with a fireplace, a fully equipped kitchen and dining area, plus decks, a grill and a private park and beach. The cottage has a living room, a fireplace, a modern kitchen and a dining area for four people, and it has a queen-size sleeper sofa in the living room. Amenities include terrycloth robes, an extended continental breakfast in the dining area, complimentary refreshments and fruit in the kitchen refrigerator, and a bottle of wine upon arrival.

***Rates:*** Prices range from $95 to $135 per room for double occupancy, with $20 per person for each additional guest. Guest rooms are available on a two-night minimum basis on weekends and a one-night minimum Monday through Thursday. A deposit equal to 50 percent of the guest room fee or 100 percent of a one-night stay is required at the time of reservation. Visa, MasterCard, checks and cash accepted. Deposits are refundable if cancelled two weeks prior to the arrival date. Château Arbre is located at 6779 West Lake Boulevard, Tahoma, CA 96142. The mailing address is P.O. Box 717, Homewood, CA 96141; (800) 726-1308, (916) 581-0187 or (916) 581-1627 (fax).

# South Shore

## ★ Christiana Inn ★

This is one of Tahoe's most unabashedly European inns, and everything about it, from the quaint Bavarian exterior to the "après-ski" lounge with its Louis XIII cognac, brings the Alps to California. The inn is just 50 yards from the main chairlift of Heavenly Ski Area, and it's a five-minute drive (down a steep hill that can be icy in winter) to the casinos of Stateline. The "Chris" also has what is acknowledged to be one of Tahoe's finest restaurants, with intimate lighting, a superb wine list and meals prepared by graduates of the Culinary Institute. Upstairs are six suites and rooms, each meticulously appointed with antiques, wood-burning fireplaces and European decor. Each room has a private bath/shower, with furnishings such as brass and pedestal beds, lace curtains, sitting parlors and dining nooks. Three suites have two floors, allowing for even more amenities, such as a living room, wet bar, dry sauna and bathtubs with whirlpool jets. Room One and Suite Four overlook the ski runs at Heavenly. With all facilities, a continental breakfast is brought to your room every morning, and there's always a decanter of brandy to ward off the nighttime chill. In summer, the inn is blissfully quiet, surrounded by brilliant flowers and tall, fragrant pines. Located at 3819 Saddle Road, across from the Heavenly California base lodge and parking lot. It has been in operation since 1965, and is currently owned by Jerry and Maggie Mershon.

**Rates:** Summer is $50 to $125; winter is $75 to $175. Visa and MasterCard accepted. P.O. Box 18298, South Lake Tahoe, CA 96151; (916) 544-7337 or (916) 544-5342 (fax).

## ★ Strawberry Lodge ★

Built in 1858 as a stagecoach stop, this spacious and rambling old wood building is virtually an institution on US 50. One of the finest lodges of its type, Strawberry is comparable to the Rainbow Lodge, its northern neighbor on Interstate 80. Apart from ornately furnished rooms with antiques and Victorian influences, the lodge has enormous common areas. There's a large, knotty-pine dining room, a huge living room with a stone fireplace, a cocktail lounge, an outdoor gazebo and lawn, and a recreation room, featuring billiards and ping pong, that doubles as a ballroom for banquets (with weddings among the more popular functions). In summer, an ice cream parlor does a brisk business. The property has two sections—the main lodge, which adjoins the South Fork of the American River—and an annex lodge, with motel-style rooms, that is across the highway. There are 31 rooms in total (including a riverside cabin), and of the 16 rooms on the second floor of the main lodge, six require occupants to use bathrooms down the hall. All except a couple of the remaining rooms have showers, and those two have tubs. Rooms facing the river are quieter than rooms facing the highway, which is close and always busy. The management has a no-smoking policy throughout the building. Recreation options abound; there are swimming and tennis facilities on-site, and riding stables next door. A short distance up the road, at Kyburz, is one of the biggest natural attractions in the region, Horsetail Falls. The lodge also is the nearest overnight accommodation to Sierra-at-Tahoe ski area (there's a free shuttle bus for weekenders) and also offers cross-country skiing options out its back door. Furthermore, the boating/hiking mecca of Crystal Basin, full of backcountry trails to the west slopes of Desolation Wilderness, is 30 minutes northwest of here.

**Rates:** $45 to $125. Visa, MasterCard and American Express accepted. 17510 US 50, Kyburz, CA 95720; (916) 659-7200.

## Echo Creek Mountain Ranch

It would be hard to find a more idyllic venue for a corporate retreat, a vacation for three or four families, or a wedding than this custom-built, 4,000-square foot log estate, which is located not far off US 50 in South Lake Tahoe. To see this place is to immediately fall in love with it. The building is situated on 16 acres at the end of a quiet road, bordered by Eldorado National Forest and accessible to a half-mile section of Echo Creek, which has fishable trout and plunging rapids. Recently constructed of timbers and knotty pine paneling, with vaulted ceilings, this luxurious ranch has five bedrooms: three with queen-size beds, one with two bunk beds, and one with four bunks. A meandering deck partly encircles the building. There's also a bunkhouse with two bunks and a loft with four futons for sleeping bags, ideal for families with small fry. The property can sleep up to 24 people, but can accommodate 50 to 75 for banquets and conferences. Amenities include three river-rock fireplaces, handcrafted wood furniture, a full gourmet kitchen, a bar, a spacious living room with big-screen TV, three bathrooms, a multi-purpose room, a ranch-style barbecue, an indoor golf-billiards game and an outdoor hot tub. This is mountain luxury with a rustic, cozy touch that has all the comforts of home. It's close to skiing, golf, hiking and boating on Lake Tahoe, and is a 15-minute drive to Stateline.

*Rates:* $850 a night, plus tax and cleaning; weekly (seven nights) rate is $4,000, plus tax and cleaning. The cleaning fee is $250. Visa, Master-Card and American Express accepted. P.O. Box 20088, South Lake Tahoe, CA 96151. Reserve through Tahoe Keys Resort, (800) 462-5397 or (916) 544-5397.

## ★ Camino Hotel ★

This historic bed and breakfast inn is 45 minutes west of South Lake Tahoe off US 50, but is perhaps the most elegant lodging in the heart of a delightful growing region known as Apple Hill. From late August until mid-December, visitors, mostly from the Sacramento Valley, flock to the more than 60 apple growers, wineries, bakeries and fruit stands scattered throughout the Gold Country foothills of the western Sierra. Numerous festivals and weekend events, centered around delicious local produce (including apple cider and homemade pies), make the Camino Hotel a great place to stay. And the property is within a 30-minute drive of major recreation areas—the Chili Bar rafting put-in on the South Fork of the American River, and the west slope trails to Desolation Wilderness and its pristine alpine lakes. The hotel charms you the minute you walk through the door. On the ground floor, there's a spacious and elegant parlor, where a sit-down breakfast (homemade apple pancakes and rum-raisin French toast are among the specialties) is served each morning, and high tea is served in the afternoon, with desserts available into the evening. Next to the parlor is a country store and gift shop. Of the nine upstairs guest rooms, three have private baths (one with an old-fashioned clawfoot tub, the others with showers), and six share two baths. All are decorated with antiques, and each is named after a figure of local history, such as Florence Nightingale, whose descendants are from Camino. The hotel was originally built in 1888 as a boarding house for the Camino Lumber Mill, which is still operating. Years later, it became a transition house for inmates leaving Folsom Prison. Husband-and-wife innkeepers John Eddy and Paula Nobert bought it in 1980, and have created a warm, homey environment, a place for couples, families, weddings and reunions. At an extra cost, they operate wine tours in a stretch limousine during early winter and spring, an Apple Hill tour in late summer and fall, and gold panning on the Consumnes River in spring and summer. Located on 4103 Carson Road (Old US 50), off the Camino/Carson exit of US 50.

**Rates:** $65 to $95. Visa, MasterCard, Discover and American Express cards accepted. P.O. Box 1197, Camino (Apple Hill), CA 95709; (800) 200-7740 or (916) 644-7740.

# Carson Valley

## ★ Bliss Mansion Bed & Breakfast ★

Forget the budget and leave the kids at home for this dream Victorian mansion, which was in need of tender loving care for a long time until Theresa Sandrini put a fortune into it and opened the premier B&B of the region in early 1995. Not only is it in the best neighborhood of Carson City—right across from the Governor's Mansion—but it consumes an entire residential block. Cinderella would be lost here, but she'd probably find a Prince Charming in one of the corridors. Consider the four guest rooms of this truly dramatic three-story estate. Each averages over 400 square feet, and has high ceilings and a gas-fed Honduran mahogany fireplace. Three rooms have full bath with large tubs and separate showers. Each room is decorated with a combination of antiques and expensive, custom-made hardwood replicas. This house, in the historic section of Nevada's state capital, was built in 1880 by timber and railroad baron Duane L. Bliss, who left behind estates throughout the Carson Valley and Lake Tahoe areas. When it was constructed, it was the largest home in Carson Valley, but over the years it had a checkered pattern of ownership, several times facing the prospect of demolition. Mrs. Sandrini and her daughter and son-in-law, Cynthia and Patrick Houlihan, gutted the interior completely and rebuilt a truly glorious bed and breakfast inn. Just stepping inside the front door takes your breath away. You are awed by a 35-foot-long foyer with its original wallpapered ceiling and

Italian Carrara marble floor, which continues into a cavernous dining room that is decorated with porcelain chandeliers. On one side is a large stairway. To the left of the foyer is a parlor and billiards room, though the latter is now a "Media Room" with large-screen television and ample reading materials. All of the rooms are light and airy, which suited the Bliss family just fine. The acre-size property also includes a detached three-car garage with an exercise room. In the morning, a full breakfast is served, including quiche, apple fritters, fresh fruit, egg casseroles, coffee and juices, and in the afternoon there are refreshments. All guest rooms are on the second floor; the third floor, which used to be a ballroom, is now the residence of Mrs. Sandrini, her daughter and son-in-law. The innkeeper describes this inn as "Victorian with modern comforts," and those include humidifiers and instant-on hot water. No pets and no children allowed. Save this place for weddings, honeymoons and special occasions.

*Rates:* $240 and up. Visa, MasterCard, American Express and Discover cards accepted. 710 West Robinson Street, Carson City, NV 89703; (800) 320-0627, (702) 887-8988 or (702) 887-0540 (fax).

## ★ Gold Hill Hotel ★

Just down the road from one of the most important gold strikes in history is Nevada's oldest hotel, perched on the slopes of the rugged high desert east of Carson City, the state capital. Built in 1859 as Vesey's Hotel, the 13-room inn and adjacent guest house was a mainstay for Gold Hill and Virginia City, boom towns that sprang up from the discovery of the Comstock Lode. With the original stone structure still intact, and with a luxurious new addition built in 1987, guests can experience some of the opulence that characterized what was once the largest population center west of the Mississippi. Proprietors Doug and Carol McQuide have decorated all of the rooms in period furnishings, with antiques or reproductions. The four rooms in the original structure are small but quaint; two share a bathroom that is down the hallway and has an antique clawfoot tub, and two have showers. One caveat for insomniacs is that noise tends to filter up from the restaurant and Great Room below. Seven rooms in the new addition are spacious, quiet and luxurious, though they still maintain the historic ambience. Amenities include king-size beds, fireplaces, television, telephone and full bathrooms with modern tubs. Across the road, the guest house has large, family-size units, with bedroom, living room, bath and kitchen, but does not have the period furnishings of the main building. Continental breakfast of juice, coffee and muffins is provided daily in the Great Room. The Crown Point Restaurant, Bar & Lounge, added in 1987, serves dinners Wednesday through Sunday, and specializes in French cuisine. The bar stocks a vast selection of beers,

Cognacs, liqueurs, single malt scotches and restaurant. Another asset is the hotel's excellent bookstore that showcases Virginia City and Nevada history. Located one mile south of Virginia City on Highway 342.

***Rates:*** Old wing, $40 to $70, depending on the season; new wing, $60 to $135, plus room tax. Includes daily continental breakfast. MasterCard and Visa accepted. P.O. Box 710, Virginia City, NV 89440; (702) 847-0111.

## Genoa House Inn

Genoa is Nevada's oldest settlement, and it's well situated for golfers, skiers, history buffs and hot springs aficionados. With lush green pastures and rolling hills, the town snuggles against the eastern slopes of the Sierra, and is within a 20-minute drive of South Lake Tahoe, the Nevada entrance of Heavenly Ski Area and Carson City. This quaint, two-story Victorian bed and breakfast, operated by Linda and Bob Sanfilippo, was originally built in 1872 by A.C. Pratt, a newspaper publisher who printed the valley's first newspaper. Although it has been restored, the home is still listed in the National Register of Historical Places. There are three quite elegant guest rooms. Upstairs are the Rose Window, which is accented in mallard-green and burgundy, and features a handmade barnwood queen-size bed, Victorian antiques, stained glass windows, a private bath (with a tiled shower) and a private balcony. Off the same hall is the Blue Heather Room, which is decorated in soft grey-blues and features mahogany antiques, a queen-size bed and a lavish bathroom with a Jacuzzi tub and overhead shower. Downstairs is the Green Foxtail Room, which has a private entrance off the ground floor with accents of green marbling, antique furnishings and a full bathroom with clawfoot tub and shower above. Coffee is delivered to your door early in the morning, and is followed by a full breakfast either in your room or in the sunlit dining room. On the menu are items such as homemade cinnamon rolls, fresh fruit topped with yogurt, baked or coddled egg dishes and a variety of juices. The inn is 1.5 miles down the road from one of the region's newest and best 18-hole golf courses, Genoa Lakes, and is two miles from Walley's Hot Springs, the finest natural hot springs spa in the region. No pets or young children allowed, and smoking is permitted outside only. Located on Nixon Street in Genoa, next to the Genoa Community Church.

***Rates:*** $99 to $120 for double occupancy. Includes daily breakfast, refreshments on arrival and daily use of Walley's Hot Springs. Visa, MasterCard and American Express accepted. P.O. Box 141, Genoa, NV 89411; (702) 782-7075.

## The Wild Rose Inn

This recently built replica of a Queen Anne Victorian is located outside the historic Nevada town of Genoa. There is nothing rustic about this place, but its exterior charm and beautifully appointed rooms offer a romantic getaway with views over the eastern Sierra and the lush, green Carson Valley. Innkeepers Sandi and Joe Antonucci have furnished the three-story home in antiques, with strong oak influences, old toys and oak telephones. All five guest rooms come with queen-size iron or brass beds, private baths accented with brass and marble, and a tub and shower or a stall shower. The Gables, on the third floor, is a large suite with a master bedroom, day bed and trundle in another room, a cozy alcove with a single bed, wet bar and eating area, and an oversized bath. The Cameo Rose room, decorated in wedgewood blue wallpaper, is elegant and features a bath and separate dressing room with built-in wardrobe and vanity. The Garden Gate room, located on the top floor in a cupola, has five windows with panoramic views of the Carson Valley and the Sierra range, and is decorated with an iron bed and antique oak furnishings. The Cottage Corners and Stage Stop rooms capture the ambience of a romantic country inn. A full breakfast is served daily, and there is complimentary wine in the afternoon. No pets, no children under 12 and no smoking inside. Close to Genoa Lakes Golf Course and Walley's Hot Springs, and within a 25-minute drive of Lake Tahoe. Located on 2332 Main Street (Jacks Valley Road), 12 miles southwest of Carson City.

***Rates:*** $85 to $115; includes full breakfast, afternoon wine and one complimentary visit to Walley's Hot Springs. Visa, MasterCard and American Express accepted. P.O. Box 256, Genoa, NV 89411; (702) 782-5697.

## ★ Deer Run Ranch Bed and Breakfast ★

Decorated with Western and Native American artifacts, this modern, two-room bed and breakfast north of Carson City is a working alfalfa ranch in summer. It is splendidly isolated, surrounded by sagebrush and baying coyotes, and is across from Washoe Lake State Park off US 395. Owner David Vhay, an architect and builder, and his wife Muffy, a potter, have added some unique touches to the inn, including a passive solar heating/cooling system. The ranch is nestled against an earth berm on the north and east, and has sweeping views of the high desert and Sierra Nevada range on the south and west. Each of the two guest rooms has a queen-size bed with handmade quilt, and a window seat filled with pillows. Private baths are across the hall. A spacious sitting area, shared by both rooms, has a fireplace, a television with VCR, a telephone, books, games, a guest refrigerator and complimentary beverages. Navajo rugs, ranch photographs and paintings adorn the floors and walls. Full breakfast, served on a handmade table in the sitting room, includes specialities such as omelets Florentine or Provençal, Dutch Babies and home-baked breads and muffins. The meal is served on pottery plates made in Muffy's own studio. There's a welcome basket of fruit, wine and snacks upon arrival. Apart from the main house, the ranch includes a pottery studio, workshop, above-ground swimming pool, a pond that freezes over for ice skating in winter, and a large garden. Washoe Lake is a favorite spot for sailboarding and sailing, and McClellan Peak, above the ranch, is used for hang gliding and mountain biking. Located 22 miles south of Reno and eight miles north of Carson City, the ranch is 3.9 miles east of US 395 on East Lake Boulevard.

*Rates:* $80 to $95. Two-night minimum required for holidays and special events weekends. Four nights or more receives a 10-percent discount. Visa, MasterCard and American Express accepted. 5440 East Lake Boulevard, Carson City, NV 89704; (702) 882-3643.

## ★ The Nenzel Mansion ★

This lovely three-story, colonial-style home, built in 1910 by Arendt Jensen, a prominent Carson Valley banker, is located in the historic town of Gardnerville, Nevada, a 30-minute drive from Lake Tahoe. Surrounded by pastureland and stately elm trees on 1.5 acres, this recently renovated mansion, three blocks east of US 395, is now a bed and breakfast owned by Chris and Virginia Nenzel. All four guest rooms are on the second floor. The Wicker Room, furnished with white wicker and decorated in soft blue, grey and white, has a queen-size bed, while the Brass Room has a brass bed, antique dresser and soft peach and cream accents. Both of these share one bathroom that has an antique toilet and large clawfoot tub with shower. The Antique Room, decorated in mauve and blue flowers, has a queen-size bed and a private bath with shower only. The most deluxe room is the Honeymoon Suite, which is furnished with a king-size bed, sitting area and a large private bath with raspberry tile. The interior is done in white and blue with lots of flowers. Downstairs is a spacious foyer and an equally roomy parlor, where guests can gather around an impressive marble fireplace to relax, play cards or board games, or listen to music on an antique player piano. A full breakfast in the formal dining room includes coffee, juice, fresh muffins or biscuits, fresh fruit and entrees such as egg casserole or French toast. Afternoon refreshments consist of wine, soft drinks, cheese and crackers. Among the mansion's outstanding features are its three porches and a large lawn area, ideal for just lounging in the afternoon sun or for hosting weddings or receptions. Children are welcome, but no pets and no smoking inside. The mansion is close to Walley's Hot Springs and Grover Hot Springs, as well as several excellent Basque restaurants in Gardnerville.

**Rates:** $80 to $110. Visa and MasterCard accepted. 1431 Ezell Street, Gardnerville, NV 89410; (702) 782-7644.

## Adaven Inn

How do they get the name "Adaven"? Easy—it's Nevada spelled backwards. Opened in September, 1994 by Bob and Emma Reid, this born-again Victorian hotel is in the quaint town of Gardnerville, flanked by pastures on the east and the rugged peaks of the Sierra Nevada range on the west. Located in the central business district on US 395, the two-story hotel boasts nine rooms, each offering antique furnishings and a private bathroom (shower only). Four rooms have queen-size beds, two have doubles and one has two singles. Two units are two-room suites, with a queen-size bed in one and two twins in the other. The building was constructed in the late 1920s as a mercantile establishment, housing a store and a Wells Fargo Express office. In 1910, it was expanded to more than double its size and later became a hotel. In recent years, it had undergone a number of changes, until the Reids acquired it and restored it to its original elegance. Guests should be aware that the hotel is located on busy US 395 (though street noise is not intrusive), and on weekends live music from a cafe and bar downstairs filters into some of the rooms. A modified breakfast is served in the parlor downstairs, and includes fruit, pastry, cereal, espresso and juices. There's a gift shop with local knick-knacks on the ground floor. The hotel is near two good Basque restaurants: the Overland Hotel, a few doors up the street, and J & T Bar & Restaurant, a block away. Children, but not pets, are permitted. Smoking is allowed outside only.

**Rates:** $65 to $100, 10 percent less for weekdays, plus room tax. Visa, MasterCard and personal checks are accepted. 1435 US 395, Gardnerville, NV 89410; (702) 782-8720.

## St. Charles Hotel

This three-story brick hotel, across from the Nevada state capital, is one of the oldest remaining commercial buildings in Carson City, and is undergoing a gradual renovation. Completed in 1862 by George W. Remington and Daniel Plitt, the hotel catered to upscale guests and was the main stagecoach stop in town. The existing structure actually encompasses the adjacent Muller's Hotel where working class patrons, mostly French-Canadian loggers, stayed. In 1891 the two hotels were consolidated under the name of the Briggs House and, in 1901, it was the first hotel in the city to install electricity. Years later it became known as the Pony Express Hotel, and some scenes from Clint Eastwood's movie *Honky Tonk Man* were shot in the rear of the building. The 27-room hotel fell into disrepair and became a seedy hangout for transients before local realtor

Bob McFadden took it over in 1993 and began a major refurbishing. The lobby has been gentrified, and is adorned with period collectibles and old photographs. But the guest rooms vary in size and quality, and have a long way to go before they are in a league with other historic inns. Some rooms, such as the suites, have two rooms with kitchen and private bath (shower only), and a handful of antiques; other rooms are quite small, some might say cramped, with a tiny bathroom or with shared bath, and have what might be described as Spartan, thrift-store quality furniture. The best rooms are 201, 202, 207, 208, 210 and 211. The building houses a drab-looking coffee shop (Flapjack Vittles) that is under separate management, and McFadden's Bar, which is accessible only by walking outside and down to the corner. Service in the entire establishment is spotty. Located on busy South Carson Street (the business section of US 395), within walking distance of museums, state buildings and casinos.

*Rates:* Summer is $49 to $89; off-season $40 to $69. Visa, Master-Card, American Express, Discovery and Diners cards accepted. 310 South Carson Street, Carson City, NV 89701; (702) 882-1887.

# Lakes Basin/Carson Pass/Highway 88

### ★ White Sulphur Springs Ranch ★

This is one of the most elegant and charming Victorian bed and breakfast inns of the region. About a 45-minute drive north of Truckee on Highway 89, the ranch, surrounded by pastoral grazing land in the Mohawk Valley, is in relatively undiscovered, uncrowded Plumas County. It is close to three excellent 18-hole golf courses, great fishing in the Feather River, hiking in the spectacular Lakes Basin, and several historic towns. Built in the 1850s by Gould, Friend and Jamison (of the Jamison mine in Virginia City), this stately three-story home was sold in 1867 to George McClear, who ran it as a hotel for the Truckee-Quincy stagecoach line. The property has been in the family since that time, so much of the original furnishings are still there. The main house has six rooms, each individually and distinctively decorated. Two adjoining cottages, the Dairy House and the Hen House, can accommodate four to seven guests, respectively. The only downstairs room is the Fern Room, which has ferns, handcrafted antique furniture and a private bath. Upstairs, each room is like a living museum display. The Marble Room has a romantic decor with marble-top antique furniture, a velvet "fainting" couch and a rose brocade bedspread, along with a view of the picturesque Mohawk Valley. The Chestnut Room has a private balcony and a rare chestnut bedroom suite, and the Oak Room offers the regal ambience of pastel blues and greys, with a king-size bed. Upstairs rooms share two bathrooms, including one with a huge clawfoot tub. There are more period knickknacks, pictures and books in the hallways and common areas than you can properly absorb, and the attic is a virtual storehouse of history. The living room is full of scrapbooks with restaurant menus and sightseeing tips, and is a wonderful spot to enjoy tea or coffee in the morning before breakfast. Innkeepers Michael and Sheryl Cornelisen offer a sumptuous breakfast of muffins, croissants, omelets and fresh fruit, the icing on the cake for a most memorable stay. Policies include no pets and no smoking. Located on Highway 89, 40 miles north of Truckee near the town of Clio.

**Rates:** Rooms in the main house, $85 to $100; Dairy House with queen-size bed and queen-size sofabed, $120; and the Hen House with kitchen, queen-size bed, queen-size sofa and twin beds, $140. Each additional person at the Dairy or Hen House, $20. Prices include full breakfast. Visa, MasterCard and Discover accepted. P.O. Box 136, Clio, CA 96106; (800) 854-1797 or (916) 836-2387.

## ★ High Country Inn Bed and Breakfast ★

When innkeeper Marlene Cartwright greets you at the door, the first thing you notice is that she bears a striking resemblance to famous television chef Julia Child. Considering the awards and accolades she's had for her cooking, it's more than a physical resemblance. High Country Inn is a modern but woodsy bed and breakfast in Sierra City, about 45 miles northwest of Truckee on Highway 49. Nature surrounds this lovely home; on one side is the Yuba River and a grove of aspens, on another is a private pond brimming with tame trout, and on another is the awesome Sierra Buttes, a magnificent series of rocky pinnacles. There are four guest rooms, of which the Sierra Buttes Suite upstairs is the most impressive and most insistently romantic. It has cathedral windows that frame the Buttes and the pond, a private bath with antique tub and modern shower, a dressing room with a view of the river, a king-size bed and a fireplace. The Golden Pond Room has private access to a deck, a queen-size bed and a shared bath. The Howard Creek Room also has views, as well as a private bath and two double beds. A spacious living room has a telescope for viewing the buttes, and a large stone fireplace for cozy socializing; it adjoins the dining room and kitchen. Marlene and her husband Calvin, who live on the premises, offer a hearty country breakfast with various gourmet specialties. She is a fountain of knowledge about local restaurants, hiking trails and other points of interest in the nearby Lakes Basin and the rambling Gold Country towns along Highway 49. The inn also sells books and maps of the local area. No pets are permitted, and smoking is restricted. Located on Highway 49 at Bassett's, in Sierra City.

**Rates:** $80 to $120 for double occupancy. Open all year. Visa and MasterCard accepted. HCR 2, Box 7, Sierra City, CA 96125; (916) 862-1530.

## Sierra Shangri-La

One minute you're driving along winding Highway 49 west of Sierra City, and the next minute you're slamming on your brakes to see what *that* was all about. It's the place you got a brief glimpse of—an incredible high perch above the rollicking Yuba River. It takes a while to find the small access road that crosses the river, but wow! When you stand on the balcony of the main lodge, you have a breathtaking view of the river gushing rapidly over giant boulders, just below you. The lodge and its nearby cabins are nestled into verdant riparian forest, and this indeed is a Shangri-La of natural beauty. Innkeepers Fran and Frank Carter have created a truly unique property. It includes a bed and breakfast with three rooms, private baths and a common balcony, and seven housekeeping cottages, four of them ensconced on the banks of the Yuba. One, the very private "honeymoon" cottage, has a deck that overlooks the river and Jim Crow Creek. The other cottages are of varying sizes, accommodating from two to eight people; each has a full kitchen, private bath and shower, spacious deck, individual patio with barbecue, and potbellied or Franklin stove. Bed and breakfast rooms come with a deluxe continental breakfast served in your room. And there's a Great Room for meetings, seminars, reunions, weddings and retreats. The inn is close to the magnificent Sierra Buttes (hiking to the top of them is a popular outing), the Lakes Basin region and quaint Gold Country towns, and is about an hour's drive west of Truckee on Highway 49. Smoking is prohibited.

**Rates:** $60 to $85 per night; weekly rates in peak season are $315 to $725, plus a 10-percent room tax. Closed January through March. P.O. Box 285, Downieville, CA 95936; (916) 289-3455.

# Chapter 22

# Hotels, Motels & Cabins

## ★ Author's Choice ★

### *Top 10 Hotels-Lake Tahoe*
Harvey's Resort Casino—p. 574
Cal-Neva Lodge—p. 569
Embassy Suites Resort—p. 577
Hyatt Regency Lake Tahoe Resort & Casino—p. 570
Harrah's Casino Hotel—p. 576
Caesar's Tahoe—p. 575
Fantasy Inn—p. 578
Horizon Casino Resort—p. 573
Tahoe Seasons Resort—p. 578
Inn by the Lake—p. 581

### *Top 10 Hotels-Reno & Carson Valley*
Eldorado Hotel Casino—p. 585
Silver Legacy Casino Resort—p. 582
Harrah's Casino Hotel—p. 586
John Ascuaga's Nugget—p. 586
Clarion Hotel Casino—p. 584
Peppermill Hotel Casino—p. 587
Reno Hilton—p. 587
Flamingo Hilton Reno—p. 585
Circus Circus Hotel Casino—p. 584
Ormsby House Hotel—p. 588

Selecting accommodations at Lake Tahoe is like choosing from a 50-course buffet. Depending on your budget and the season, you can stay in nondescript motels or upscale hotels and condominiums. There are close to 18,000 rooms for rent in the basin, and two-thirds of them are in the south end, where Stateline's high-rise casino-hotels are surrounded by dozens of motels, most of which cater to the gambling crowds. Over the next few years, many of the older and, frankly, dilapidated properties will disappear as South Lake Tahoe redefines its motel strip along US 50 as part of a massive city redevelopment plan. The objective of the plan is to bring in quality hotels, a convention center, a transit center, new shopping areas and additional open space. The most dramatic examples of the plan, so far, have been the opening of the Embassy Suites Resort in 1991 and the Fantasy Inn a year later.

Deciding where to stay is in large part a factor of what you wish to do in Tahoe. For skiers and gamblers, US 50 offers close proximity to the casinos, restaurants and shopping, as well as regular stops for the shuttles that serve the ski resorts. It's easy to step outside of your lodging and catch a bus to Heavenly, Sierra-at-Tahoe or Kirkwood. The Stateline hotels have such a complete transportation infrastructure that guests arriving at the Reno or Tahoe airports can get along just fine without a car. You can take the Tahoe Casino Express from Reno 14 times a day directly to the front door of any of the "Big Five" properties at Stateline. In winter, the ski buses are frequent and convenient, and in summer the South Tahoe Trolley will take you to beaches, shopping and restaurants. Public transportation, with the exception of the Tahoe Casino Express, also is available for most of the other accommodations along US 50.

Getting away from the crowds and traffic at South Shore means taking to the backroads and side streets. For example, on the south side of US 50, next to Heavenly Ski Area, is the luxurious Tahoe Seasons Resort, and on the north side, next to the lake, is the boaters' paradise of the Tahoe Keys Resort. For a truly elegant setting, with a price to match, you might consider a townhouse at Glenbrook just a few miles north of Stateline. You'll need to have a car to stay at most of these places.

On the other shores of the lake, the ambience of pine forest and beaches—the natural elements of Tahoe—are decidedly more pronounced, and there are more ski resorts to choose from. Even on the East Shore, gaming is a relatively minor diversion, with only a handful of casinos. The action that most guests prefer here is not at the blackjack tables—it's outside doing something physical such as hiking, skiing, golf, boating or cycling. You'll find a lot more townhouses and rustic cabins around this section of the lake. Incline Village, for example, has only one hotel and a couple of motels, with most accommodations in condominiums. Along the California side of the North Shore, you'll find a motel strip on Highway 28, but many of these places have charming rustic cabins, cottages and beachfront rooms. There's been a whirlwind of refurbishing lately, and some of the aging properties have been revitalized. You may have to stop and look closely to find these diamonds in the rough, because the improvements are not always evident from the highway.

Perhaps the most dramatic turnaround is on the West Shore, where the mom-and-pop lodges of the 1950s and 1960s are giving way to new and younger owners whose vision is to convert them into boutique inns. Some of the nicest cabins and small lodges are here, nestled in wooded surroundings. The West Shore has wind-protected shoreline and beaches, access to the best hiking and cycling trails in the region, close proximity to major ski resorts, and a selection of fine gourmet restaurants. One drawback is that many of the accommodations front Highway 89, and the traffic in summer can be heavy and noisy. If this bothers you, ask for the room or cabin that is farthest from the road.

Keep in mind that the list here does not include all of the properties. Be sure to consult other chapters on resorts and unique inns and lodges.

## HOTELS & MAJOR PROPERTIES
## North Shore

### ★ Cal-Neva Lodge ★
#### ★ *notes Author's Choice*

If the walls could talk, what stories they would tell about this grand hotel. Let's drop a few names: Marilyn Monroe, John F. Kennedy and Frank Sinatra. In the late 1950s and early 1960s, Sinatra owned the lodge, and it was a frequent hangout for his famous "Rat Pack" and the Kennedy clan. One newsy tidbit that circulated in those days was an alleged secret rendezvous here between the former president and the glamour queen.

Certainly this stately lodge has a romantic ambience, with a lakefront view next to turquoise Crystal Bay that is the envy of Tahoe. The lodge was built in 1926 by a wealthy San Francisco developer, who coined the name "Cal-Neva" because the property straddles the California/Nevada state line. This has always been its most intriguing asset. In the California "wing," guests can marvel at the spacious Indian Room, which doubles as a museum of Washoe Indian culture and as a grand ballroom for conferences and weddings. Leave this room for the lobby and presto! You're in Nevada, with slot machines, gaming and Sinatra's pride and joy, the Celebrity Showroom. The lodge went through a succession of owners after the tenure of Ol' Blue Eyes, until it was acquired in 1985 by land developer Charles P. Bluth, who launched a major renovation that restored the "Lady of the Lake" to her original elegance.

Of all the casino-hotels in the basin, Cal-Neva is the most insistently Tahoe-esque, with its rock and wood interior and cozy lodge feel. The views from the 220 lakefront rooms and restaurants are breathtaking. The swimming pools, decks and wedding chapels are arrayed on bouldered terraces. Most of all, the environment is remarkably amiable and low-key. Bluth has wisely emphasized the "hotel" aspect of his property, rather than the "gaming," which is quite modest. He still regards the Cal-Neva as a work in progress, and continually adds new improvements and attractions. There is strong repeat business, and the clientele includes upscale couples, families and honeymooners. Rooms are decorated in French country style, and there are cottages and chalets (including the Marilyn Monroe Suite) for intimate tête-à-têtes. Cal-Neva offers history, a whiff of scandal and a splendid vista—what more could you ask for?

***Rooms:*** 220 rooms, suites, cabins and chalets with phones, televisions, in-room coffee and some fireplaces. Some are lakefront and some offer panoramic lake views.

***Amenities:*** Seven dining areas, two bars, a casino, a full-service European health spa, a sauna, a steam room, a Jacuzzi, a pool (summer only), tennis courts, a video arcade, wedding and honeymoon coordination, a florist and banquet and convention facilities (up to 400).

***Policies:*** No pets are allowed. Reservations must be accompanied by the first night's deposit or a major credit card to guarantee against late arrival. Cancellations must be made at least 72 hours in advance, and 14 days' advance notice of cancellation is required during holidays. Children under 10 are free in the same room as an adult.

***Rates:*** $69 to $189 (midweek) and $99 to $249 (weekend).

***Information:*** Cal-Neva Lodge, 2 Stateline Road, P.O. Box 368, Crystal Bay, NV 89402; (702) 832-4000 or (800) CAL-NEVA.

## ★ Hyatt Regency Lake Tahoe Resort & Casino ★

Located in woodsy Incline Village, with its multi-million-dollar lakefront mansions, the 458-room Hyatt is a born-again hotel with a nondescript facade but a dazzling interior. In recent years, a massive renovation has turned this hotel into one of the lake's star properties. Among its many assets are its excellent gourmet restaurants, its forested surroundings, its strategic location midway between South Shore and North Shore ski areas, and its special attention to families with children. Incline Village is an exclusive enclave of gated estates nestled in the pines, and guests can jog or bicycle past them on paved trails. Just up the road are two Robert Trent Jones, Jr.-designed 18-hole golf courses and Diamond Peak Ski Resort, and just across the street are several immaculate beaches. As the only large accommodation on the East Shore, the Hyatt and its environs are blissfully free of traffic congestion. Across the road from the main tower, the Hyatt has built 24 cottages with the "Old Tahoe" look, and recently opened a new restaurant, the Lone Eagle Grille, in its refurbished meeting and banquet center along the lake. The Hyatt Regency is the only casino-resort in Tahoe with a private beach, and it has a full range of water sports (including rides on the hotel's catamaran yacht). In the evening, a meal at Ciao Mien Trattoria, which combines Asian and Italian delicacies, is a memorable gourmet experience. The hotel offers unique chaperoned programs for youngsters during the winter and summer seasons.

***Rooms:*** 458 rooms and 24 lakeside cottages (one- and two-bedroom units; king-size and double beds) with phones, cable television, movie channels, stereo systems, some adjoining parlors with fireplaces and private sun decks facing the lake, some kitchens, an honor bar, a wet bar, in-room coffee, some continental breakfasts, wheelchair access and non-smoking rooms. Some are lakefront and some offer panoramic lake views.

***Amenities:*** Three restaurants, room service, grocery delivery, 24-hour casino, a sportsbook lounge, bar, lounge, shows, sauna, Jacuzzi, health and fitness club, an outdoor pool, tennis courts, a family arcade, laundry, a private beach, a volleyball net, boat rentals, a catamaran charter, parasailing, ski rentals and ski shuttles. Other amenities include the Lakeside Convention Center, a new 6,000-square-foot addition of beachfront meeting and banquet space that has been added to the pre-existing 14,000 square feet of meeting space; it now accommodates up to 1,000 people. Also, there's Camp Hyatt and Rock Hyatt adventure clubs for children with hiking, arts and crafts, beach time, volleyball, swimming, tennis, bowling, miniature golf, supervised game room activities, and movies with popcorn and soda. The fee is $35 for the entire day or $25 for an evening; reservations are required.

***Policies:*** No pets allowed.

***Rates:*** Rooms, $69 to $224; lakeside cottages, $305 to $424; one and two bedrooms, $405 to $599.

***Information:*** Hyatt Regency, 111 Country Club Drive, P.O. Box 3239, Incline Village, NV 89450; (702) 832-1234 or (800) 233-1234.

## Tahoe Biltmore Lodge and Casino

The wave of renovations that swept the North Shore properties also touched this vintage casino-hotel, which spruced up its interior and added a new restaurant. It's not the Ritz in terms of lodging (except for a few units), but it's well situated on the main highway. It's popular with senior citizens and dyed-in-the-wool gamblers, as well as young skiers on a budget, and it offers cheap eats most times of the day.

***Rooms:*** 87 economy units and cabins with phones, televisions, some lake views, wheelchair access and non-smoking rooms.

**Amenities:** 24-hour dining, 24-hour full casino, sportsbook, a bar, a lounge, free live entertainment, shows, beaches (within walking distance), an outdoor pool (summer only), a family arcade room, a recreation room, a gift shop, free parking (cars and RVs), an airport shuttle, ski shuttle route access and a 12,000-square-foot convention center.

**Policies:** No pets allowed.

**Rates:** $29 to $115.

**Location:** Tahoe Biltmore Lodge and Casino, 5 Highway 28, P.O. Box 115, Crystal Bay, NV 89402; (702) 831-0660, (800) 245-6267 or (800) 245-8667.

# Squaw Valley

## Squaw Valley Lodge

Spacious condominium accommodations, underground parking and close proximity to the ski slopes just out the door offer guests a modicum of luxury and great convenience. The units are individually owned, so the interior furnishings can vary considerably. Suites have kitchenettes, and most are comfortable, except for the occasional marshmallow mattress. There's a swimming pool in a central courtyard, and an exercise room where aerobics classes and Nautilus machines are available. The lodge operates much like a hotel, with valet service and airport shuttles.

**Rooms:** 164 studio and one-bedroom suites (all ski-in, ski-out) with phones, cable television, kitchenettes (microwave oven, dishwasher, and electric range), in-room coffee and some continental breakfasts.

**Amenities:** A sauna, a steam bath, a Jacuzzi, a pool (summer only), on-site tennis courts, a complete Nautilus room, valet ski check, ski tuning, covered parking, a shuttle to Reno-Tahoe International Airport and cable car access to the High Camp Bath and Tennis Club.

**Policies:** No pets allowed.

**Rates:** $100 to $355.

**Information:** Squaw Valley Lodge, 201 Squaw Peak Road, P.O. Box 2364, Olympic Valley, CA 96146; (916) 583-5500 or (800) 922-9970.

## Squaw Valley Inn

It's woodsy, it's low-profile and it's right next to the tram station at Squaw Valley USA's ski area. With its spacious rooms and great location, it commands high rates and strong repeat business. Owned by prominent San Francisco businessman Gordon Getty, the inn always has a lively après-ski crowd (usually over the age of 35), with local libations to match. Though it has a style that might be called "Old English," a complete interior renovation of the rooms, restaurant and lobby, scheduled for the summer of 1995, will soon exorcise anything that's old hat.

**Rooms:** 60 guest rooms (two queen-size beds in each) with phones, televisions and some kitchens.

*Amenities:* Benton's Restaurant, Slopes Fireside Bar and Grill, a Jacuzzi, a pool (summer only), 40 square miles of alpine skiing, ice skating at High Camp, two hot spas and a conference center for social functions and meetings.

*Policies:* No pets allowed.

*Rates:* $110 to $280.

*Information:* Squaw Valley Inn, 1920 Squaw Valley Road, P.O. Box 2407, Olympic Valley, CA 96146; (916) 583-1576 or (800) 323-ROOM.

### The Resort at Squaw Creek
(See page 509 in Chapter 20, "Mountain Resorts & Lodges.")

### Olympic Village Inn
(See page 548 in Chapter 21, "Bed & Breakfasts & Other Unique Inns.")

# South Shore

### Lakeside Inn & Casino

For those who can't handle throngs of people and the beehive of high-rise casinos, this small, low-profile casino-inn just east of Horizon offers something of a haven. It's built like a motel, but rooms come with amenities such as chocolates and French-milled soap, and there are nice views of Edgewood Country Club from some of the rooms. Located on US 50 at Kingsbury Grade, the inn offers a restaurant with frequent prime rib deals.

*Rooms:* 124 guest rooms with phones, televisions, in-room coffee and some lake views.

*Amenities:* A restaurant, a bar, a lounge, free live entertainment, casino, a recreation room, a pool, banquet and convention facilities, and uncovered self-parking.

*Policies:* No pets are allowed.

*Rates:* $59 to $89.

*Information:* Lakeside Inn & Casino, 168 US 50, P.O. Box 5640, Stateline, NV 89449; (702) 588-7777.

### ★ Horizon Casino Resort ★

Once a regular haunt of Elvis Presley, this aging casino/hotel has been spruced up inside and outside with new exteriors and completely remodeled rooms. The remodeling, the first in nine years, was completed in spring 1995. Out went the faded carpets, scraped-up furniture and raggedy drapes, and in came elegant lake-blue carpeting, light oak furniture, dazzling light fixtures and pastel pink and blue bedspreads. Horizon's casino is not as large or as lavish as its competitors', but the hotel attracts guests with its low prices, inexpensive buffet meals and frequent goings-on, such as country music and collectible shows outside of its front entrance. The famous Presley suite, where the King himself used to stay while he was performing here (when the hotel was called Sahara Tahoe), is available for honeymoons and special functions. For a long time, Horizon's entertainment was mostly risqué shows in its cabaret, but now it has begun to present family entertainment (magic, acrobatics and dancing), and the hotel has installed a larger children's area for video and redemption games. The signature restaurant is Josh's, and there's a buffet room with average but inexpensive meals. A covered parking garage is adjacent to the hotel, and all ski and airport shuttles stop here. Horizon is closest to the elegant Edgewood Country Club golf course, just across the street.

*Rooms:* 539 deluxe guest rooms and suites with phones, televisions, some fireplaces and some lake views.

*Amenities:* Three restaurants, bars, a lounge, a casino, showrooms, a concierge, a tour desk, a Jacuzzi, an outdoor heated pool (summer only), an Amusement Center (video and redemption games), a recreation room, a beauty salon, gift and flower shops, convention facilities (25,000 square feet), covered and uncovered valet and self-parking, and the Tahoe Casino Express luxury Reno Airport shuttle (14 departures daily; $15 per person each way).

*Policies:* No pets are allowed.

*Rates:* $69 to $99 and up.

*Information:* Horizon Casino Resort, US 50, P.O. Box C, Stateline, NV 89449; (702) 588-6211, (800) 322-7723 or (800) 648-3322.

## ★ Harvey's Resort Casino ★

With 740 rooms and suites, Harvey's is the largest hotel at Lake Tahoe. Slick, modern and very upscale, it is best described as a hotel first and a casino second. Being a good innkeeper was the philosophy of the late founder, Harvey Gross, a meat retailer from Sacramento who opened the place in 1944. Harvey's celebrated its 50th anniversary in 1994, making it Tahoe's oldest operating casino. Service here has always been top-notch, and the hotel has earned the coveted Mobil Four-Star and AAA Four Diamond ratings. The 1986 opening of the $100-million Lake Tower created a rebirth for the property, with large rooms, firm and comfortable beds, contemporary furnishings and splendid lake views. A full-service health club, the best at the Stateline casino properties, is available for guests. Of the eight restaurants, the old-timers are partial to the Sage Room, which has been a fixture since 1947 and prepares the finest steak dinners in town. A more refined restaurant on the top floor, Llewellyn's, serves excellent continental cuisine such as seafood and Viennese pastry, and has deluxe views to match. Harvey's relies on musical revues for its entertainment, plus the occasional blockbuster summer outdoor concert in its rear parking lot. The casino is the largest at Tahoe.

*Rooms:* 740 luxury rooms and suites with phones, televisions, lake views and in-room coffee.

*Amenities:* Llewellyn's, Sage Room, Seafood Grotto, El Vaquero, Garden Buffet, Carriage House, Pizzeria, Classic Burgers, bars, lounges, a casino, a concierge, a showroom, the Emerald Theater (a 285-seat lounge), retail shops, a sauna, a Jacuzzi, an outdoor lap swimming pool, a health club and spa (offering aromatherapy, massage and a tanning salon), a fitness club, a barber shop, a beauty salon, a family arcade, Kid's Day Camp (ages 6 to 13, daily activities promoting street smarts, safety and outside play), a wedding chapel, a convention center (15,000 square feet, up to 1,000 guests), a valet and a self-parking garage/lot, and the Tahoe Casino Express luxury Reno Airport shuttle (14 departures daily; $15 per person each way).

*Policies:* No pets are allowed.

*Rates:* $110 to $500.

*Information:* Harvey's Resort Casino, US 50, P.O. Box 128, Stateline, NV 89449; (702) 588-2411 or (800) 553-1022.

## ★ Caesar's Tahoe ★

Among the moderate-priced casino hotels, Caesar's has always gone after the younger crowds, as well as the young at heart. The 440 rooms were recently remodeled with contemporary mauve and green interiors, though oversized Roman tubs have remained. There are some fine restaurants here (including Primavera, a pasta place, and Pisces, a seafood place), as well as the last remaining "big name" showroom of Stateline, a lively discotheque and the always busy Planet Hollywood cafe, christened in 1994 by co-owners Arnold Schwarzenegger and Bruce Willis. The cafe is not exactly the gourmet capital of Tahoe, but it has some eye-catching Hollywood props and memorabilia on the walls. There's a large, indoor, lagoon-style swimming pool with waterfalls and, strangely enough, an elegant wedding chapel right next to it. (The tears you see flowing may be from the chlorine!) Those who crave stellar entertainment (not risqué cabarets or low-budget Broadway shows) will find a selection that ranges from country crooner Ricky Van Shelton to old-time rockers The Beach Boys. If you can wrangle a tee time, there's golf at Edgewood Country Club (one of the nation's top 100 courses) across the street. Regular shuttles from Reno and the ski resorts serve the hotel, and everything at Stateline (including the other casinos) is within walking distance.

*Rooms:* 440 newly remodeled deluxe guest rooms and suites (five theme suites: Bahama, Hollywood, Oriental, Contemporary and Roman) with phones, televisions, some wheelchair access, some non-smoking rooms, some lake views, some whirlpools or oversized Roman tubs, full service bars and dining areas.

***Amenities:*** Primavera, The Broiler Room, Empress Court, Pisces, Cafe Roma, Pompeii Cafe and Bar, Spooner's Lounge, Emperor's Lounge, Planet Hollywood, Nero's 200 Nightclub, a casino, a showroom (1,500 seats), retail shops and galleries, a health spa, massage, a sauna, a Jacuzzi, a lagoon-style indoor pool, a recreation room, a wedding chapel and facilities, a convention center (up to 1,500 people), the *Odyssey* (a yacht to entertain special guests), covered valet and self-parking, and the Tahoe Casino Express luxury Reno Airport shuttle (14 departures daily; $15 per person each way).

***Policies:*** No pets are allowed.

***Rates:*** $65 to $175.

***Information:*** Caesar's Tahoe, 55 US 50, P.O. Box 5800, Stateline, NV 89449; (702) 588-3515 or (800) 648-3353.

## ★ Harrah's Casino Hotel ★

Built in 1973, this 18-story luxury hotel is aging gracefully, and it still has plenty of spark and sophistication, thanks to constant improvements. The high-quality food and entertainment define the experience of staying at Harrah's, though the casino looks outdated and is getting a bit worn around the edges. Checking in can take some time (the bell service often seems hopelessly behind with luggage). But the rooms are spacious and comfortable (many have recently been remodeled), and there are nice touches, such as small color TVs in the bathrooms. No establishment on the South Shore can beat the daily buffet breakfast in the Forest Room on the top floor, with its panoramic, picture-window views of Tahoe and the snow-crested Sierra peaks. All of the restaurants on the upper floors, including the new Cafe Andreotti: Adventures in Pasta and Pizza, are popular and excellent. Harrah's has been experimenting with its entertainment lately, having forsaken weekly big-name (and expensive) acts for Broadway musicals, magic shows and acrobatics. But occasionally a headliner returns to the 800-seat showroom. The latest addition is a 12,000-square-foot Family Fun Center, which is filled with arcade games and the latest high-tech virtual reality mind-benders. Harrah's is fairly conservative in its management, but when it does things, it usually does them in style.

***Rooms:*** 534 deluxe rooms and suites with phones, satellite televisions, VCRs, Nintendo, two bathrooms (television and phone in each) and some lake views.

***Amenities:*** Seven restaurants, bars, a lounge with nightly live entertainment, a casino, a showroom, a concierge, bell service, 24-hour room service, laundry service, in-room ski rental and overnight ski tune-ups, retail shops, shoe shine, men's and women's health spas, massage, salons, a suntanning center, a sauna, a Jacuzzi, an indoor glass-domed swimming pool, the Family Fun Center, a pet kennel, convention space (18,000 square feet, 12 meeting rooms, 10 to 1,000 people), an uncovered valet and self-parking, rental cars (Hertz, Avis, Dollar, Budget), cabs, free ski shuttles, limousines and the Tahoe Casino Express luxury Reno Airport shuttle (14 departures daily; $15 per person each way).

*Policies:* No pets are allowed in rooms.

*Rates:* $139 to $269.

*Information:* Harrah's Casino Hotel, P.O. Box 8, Stateline, NV 89449; (702) 588-6611 or (800) 648-3773.

## ★ Embassy Suites Resort ★

This is the best large hotel for families on the South Shore. Don't want your kids hanging around slot machines? This place is blissfully quiet and free of gaming here at the newest luxury property at the lake and the largest on the California side of Stateline. If you hunger for action, you need only walk next door, into Nevada, to spin the roulette wheel or crank the one-armed bandits at Harrah's. Embassy has its trademark atrium lobby—nine floors high—and it is filled with the ambience of babbling brooks, indoor foliage and a large historic flume and waterwheel reminiscent of the Gold Rush era. All rooms are two-room suites that have two separate sleeping areas—a bedroom and a living room with sofa bed, so you can cordon off your kids and still have some privacy. The hotel has wonderful amenities for families, such as a respectable morning buffet breakfast (included in the price of the room), an afternoon happy hour with free drinks, and an indoor pool and exercise room (although the pool is a little too public—it's right next to the atrium lounge and breakfast area). Zachary's Restaurant gets mixed reviews, Pasquale's Pizza is a definite hit, and Turtle's Sports Bar and Dance Emporium always has an energetic crowd and thunderous music. There's a ski and sports shop in the lobby, underground parking and regular shuttles from the ski areas.

*Rooms:* 400 two-room suites with phones, televisions with cable hookup, VCRs, some lake views, kitchens, mini bars, full breakfasts, two-hour complimentary manager's cocktail reception, in-room coffee, wheelchair access, non-smoking rooms and room service.

*Amenities:* Zachary's, Pasquale's Pizza, Julie's Deli, Turtle's Sports Bar and Dance Emporium (big screen television and DJ music), a sauna, a Jacuzzi, an indoor pool, an outdoor sundeck, a fitness club, a family arcade, gift and sports shops (rentals, sales, repairs and accessories), a wedding chapel, convention, catering and banquet facilities (over 6,200 square feet, single-room capacity of 450), a covered valet and self-parking, car rentals, and the Tahoe Casino Express luxury Reno Airport shuttle

(14 departures daily; $15 per person each way).

*Policies:* No pets are allowed.

*Rates:* $119 to $220.

*Information:* Embassy Suites Resort, 4130 Lake Tahoe Boulevard, South Lake Tahoe, CA 96150; (916) 544-5400 or (800) EMBASSY.

## ★ Fantasy Inn ★

You can play Tarzan and Jane in the Rainforest Suite, share a bottle of bubbly in the Marie Antoinette Suite, soak in a sunken tub in the Roman Suite, or enjoy a pampered honeymoon in the elegant Romeo and Juliet Suite. This is South Lake Tahoe's most romantic small hotel, with a dozen ornate theme suites that are so creative, no one ever wants to leave them. Even the standard rooms are a cut above just about anything else at the lake, with circular beds, bathtubs built for two, ceiling-mounted swivel television sets and double-tiled showers. Owner Lonnie Mason has built a romantic, exotic, intimate retreat that is popular for weddings, honeymoons, anniversaries and other celebrations. It is a place that redefines "overnight lodging." A wedding chapel, wine or champagne upon check-in, breakfast in bed, and excellent service from an attentive staff have given Fantasy Inn strong repeat business. When the blizzard of the century is ragin', this is *the* place to cuddle up.

*Rooms:* 55 guest rooms (exotic theme rooms; king-size beds) with cable television, five-foot Jacuzzi-type bathtubs, stereos, fireplaces and in-room coffee.

*Amenities:* A wedding chapel, a minister, a ski shuttle to lifts, and room service from International House of Pancakes next door.

*Policies:* No children and no pets are allowed.

*Rates:* $110 to $210.

*Information:* Fantasy Inn, 3696 Lake Tahoe Boulevard, South Lake Tahoe, CA 96150; (916) 541-6666, (800) 367-7736 or (800) 624-3837.

## ★ Tahoe Seasons Resort ★

This is the largest and most attractive lodging on the California side of Heavenly Ski Area, with the unbeatable convenience of walking across the street to the tram and ski lifts. Large chalet suites have separate living rooms, private spas, fireplaces, VCRs, refrigerators and queen- or king-size beds. The lobby is particularly creative and spacious, and invites conversation with its big stone and brick fireplace, adjoining bar and warm ambience. Down the hallway is a cafe that serves breakfasts. Outside, the heated swimming pool is a little cloistered from its surrounding walls, but there's plenty of open space on the rooftop where tennis courts are located. Removed from the traffic of US 50 and the casinos, the resort is a quiet place much of the year, especially in summer. Its forested, residential hillside location, however, is within a brief shuttle ride of Stateline and the beaches. Also, one of the finer dinner houses at the Lake, Christiana Inn, is a short stroll down the road. There's a great concierge service here, and a tour company that offers local ski trips in winter and whitewater rafting in summer, among other outings, operates out of the hotel.

*Rooms:* 160 mountain chalet suites with direct-dial phones, two to three televisions, VCRs, refrigerators and microwaves; most have fireplaces, in-room coffee and private spas, and some have maid service.

*Amenities:* A restaurant, a lounge, a general store, room service, guest security, a concierge, billiards, video arcade games, a jukebox, two tennis courts, a Jacuzzi, a heated pool, wedding and banquet facilities and shuttle service (to and from Harrah's).

*Policies:* No pets are allowed.

*Rates:* $95 to $128.

*Information:* Tahoe Seasons Resort, 3901 Saddle Road, P.O. Box 5656, South Lake Tahoe, CA 96157; (916) 541-6700 or (800) 540-4874.

## Tahoe Beach and Ski Club

Converted from an aging motel to an upscale, time-share condominium, Tahoe Beach and Ski Club now has excellent accommodations to go with a fine beach on the shores of Lake Tahoe. All of the condos have indoor access, and some are two-story units. Beautiful polished fixtures, wood kitchen cabinets and other deluxe touches, including a completely remodeled lobby, make the place attractive, even though the wood-frame, shingled exteriors still look much the same as they have for years. There's a large grassy area behind the beach for weddings and other functions.

*Rooms:* 125 units (studio, deluxe, and standard one-bedroom condos and townhouses), with direct-dial phones, color televisions with cable hookup, VCRs, some kitchenettes and kitchens (fully equipped) and some four-person Jacuzzi tubs. Some units front the lake, and most have lake views and patios.

*Amenities:* Decks cocktail bar, a restaurant, an outdoor heated pool, a Jacuzzi and sauna (open all year), a fitness club, a ski shop and a free shuttle to Heavenly Ski Area.

*Rates:* $75 to $225.

*Information:* Tahoe Beach and Ski Club, 3601 Lake Tahoe Boulevard, South Lake Tahoe, CA 96150; (916) 541-6220 or (800) 822-5962.

## Lakeland Village

With its condominiums nudging right up to 1,000 feet of private beach, this 19-acre lakefront complex attracts families, corporate meetings, ski clubs and other groups. Operated as a condo-hotel, the village

---

units are nestled in pine forest on the north side of US 50, just one mile from Heavenly Ski Area and 1.5 miles from the Stateline casinos. The condos are woodsy and spacious, each with large living rooms, color TVs with cable, fireplaces and private decks. Walking to the water's edge on Tahoe, guests have their choice of a multitude of sports, including boating from the village's own dock. There's a terrific swimming pool with a spectacular view of the lake and its beaches. Restaurants and a major grocery store are just a few steps away.

*Rooms:* 212 units (condos with lofts; studio condos to four-bedroom townhouses sleeping up to 10 people) with phones, color televisions, HBO, kitchens, fireplaces, in-room coffee and daily maid service. Some units front the lake, and some have lake views and private decks.

*Amenities:* A restaurant, a 24-hour front desk, a cocktail lounge, tennis courts (lessons with professional available), a sauna, two Jacuzzis, two outdoor heated pools, a poolside snack bar, 1,000 feet of private beach, boat rentals, an on-site ski shop, two conference rooms (up to 75 people), catering, complimentary shuttles to casinos and local ski areas, underground lodge parking and an outdoor parking lot.

*Policies:* No pets are allowed. Full deposit is refunded if the room is cancelled 30 days or more in advance; deposit is forfeited if cancelled 29 days or less.

*Rates:* $75 to $440.

*Information:* Lakeland Village, 3535 US 50, P.O. Box 1356, South Lake Tahoe, CA 96150; (916) 544-1685, (916) 541-7711 or (800) 822-5969.

## Timber Cove Lodge Marina Resort

This 262-room Best Western property, the largest South Shore accommodation outside of the Stateline hotels, has a variety of rooms, from standard, undistinguished motel units to suites with lake views. All rooms are tastefully appointed, with air conditioning and in-room movies. Common areas are the lodge's best assets, including a private beach and marina on the lake, a spacious heated swimming pool and a hot tub. It's apparent that this property has been around for a while; the exterior is a bit weathered and some of the interiors could use sprucing up. Timber Cove is centrally located to Heavenly Ski Area and the casinos, and is served by free shuttles. There's a family restaurant and a small wedding chapel on the property.

*Rooms:* 262 rooms and suites with direct-dial phones, color televisions with cable, paid movie access, in-room coffee, some lake fronts and some lake views.

*Amenities:* A heated pool, a Jacuzzi, a sauna (open all year), a bar, a cocktail lounge, a restaurant, courtesy casino and ski shuttles, and wedding and banquet facilities.

**Policies:** No pets are allowed.

**Rates:** $60 to $165.

**Information:** Timber Cove Lodge Marina Resort, 3411 US 50, South Lake Tahoe, CA; (916) 541-6722 or (800) 972-8558 (reservations only).

## ★ Inn by the Lake ★

This is a deluxe, 100-room inn with large, beautifully furnished rooms, comfortable beds and close proximity to beaches, cycling trails and picnic areas. The rooms are more spacious than most in South Tahoe, with king- or queen-size beds, private balconies and some refrigerators and wet bars. Tucked into a forested setting just two miles from the Stateline casinos, the inn has some nice touches, such as a continental breakfast with fresh-baked breads and bagels, a year-round heated swimming pool with spa and sauna, and free transportation to casinos and ski resorts. Across the street, there's a sandy beach with a selection of water sports. The view of the lake from the upstairs rooms is one of the best along US 50. During off-season and midweek, the Inn usually offers highly discounted rates, making it a great value and a wonderful alternative to the bustle of the casinos. There's a 24-hour coffee shop, Lyon's, next door.

**Rooms:** 100 guest rooms and suites (one to three bedrooms; king- and queen-size beds) with direct-dial phones, color televisions with movie channel and cable hookup, AM/FM radios, some kitchens, in-room coffee, wet bars, continental breakfast, air conditioning, lake views, private balconies and hair dryers; 34 non-smoking rooms and one with wheel-chair access.

**Amenities:** Ski and bicycle lockers, hot cider in the lobby (in winter), a concierge, a redwood sauna, a bi-level outdoor spa, a year-round heated pool, bicycles, complimentary guest activities (children and adults), self-service laundry facilities, meeting facilities (up to 50 people with catering, equipment and secretarial support), and free casino and ski shuttles.

**Policies:** No pets are allowed.

**Rates:** $84 to $395. (No charge for children under 12 who share parents' room.)

**Information:** Inn by the Lake, 3300 Lake Tahoe Boulevard, South Lake Tahoe, CA 96157; (916) 542-0330 or (800) 877-1466.

# Reno/Sparks

Reno and the Carson Valley are in the midst of a major hotel expansion, a result of increasing convention business and the revitalization of downtown Reno. Almost every significant hotel/casino property has just completed or is engaged in adding more rooms, casino space, restaurants, parking or meeting facilities. The most important new project (opening summer, 1995) is the Silver Legacy, a 1,720-room hotel designed with a Gold Rush theme and jointly financed by Eldorado and Circus Circus. Although summer and fall can put rooms at a premium, especially during area-wide events such as Hot August Nights, winter has significant bargains—especially for skiers. With the slopes 40 to 70 minutes away, the savings on lodging and food can be substantial. Midweek rates in spring also offer deals for bargain-hunters, and sometimes they are combined with shows, meals and other perks. The Reno/Sparks area has four hotel districts: downtown along North Virginia Avenue (Eldorado, Circus Circus, Harrah's, Silver Legacy); near the convention center on South Virginia Avenue (Clarion, Peppermill); near the airport (Reno Hilton); and in Sparks, an adjoining community (Nugget). South of Reno, the Ormsby House has recently reopened in Carson City, and provides a good location for exploring Virginia City, the historic district of Carson City, and Lake Tahoe. For information on room reservations, contact the Reno-Sparks Convention & Visitors Authority, P.O. Box 837, Reno, NV 89504-0837, (800) FOR-RENO.

## ★ Silver Legacy Casino Resort ★

Reno's newest hotel is a $310 million joint venture between the Eldorado Hotel Casino and Circus Circus Enterprises. This 37-floor, 1,720-room hotel with three-tiered towers was scheduled to open in late July,1995. Its dome measures 180 feet in diameter, and encloses a 120-foot-high automated mining machine that will rise from the casino floor, moving silver ore carts and spouting silver coins. The hotel casino's exterior facade of store fronts recreates views of Reno in the 1890s and early 1900s. The hotel's interior is designed with dark woods, marble floors, the finest carpeting, gold and crystal chandeliers, various collections of art and European touches. Retail areas on the mezzanine level stretch along the skywalks and connect the Silver Legacy to the Eldorado and Circus Circus hotels.

*Rooms:* 1,720 guest rooms including 149 player spa suites and eight executive suites with telephone, television, daily maid service and front desk service.

*Amenities:* Five theme restaurants, three bars, a casino, an outdoor pool, a sun deck, theme retail outlets, 2,000 self-parking and valet spaces, and a 30,000-square-foot special events and convention center.

*Rates:* $49 to $99.

*Information:* 407 North Virginia Street, Reno, NV 89501; (702) 329-4777 or (800) MUST-SEE.

## Airport Plaza Hotel

This deluxe hotel is convenient to the airport, but not to anything else unless you have wheels. In that case, it's a short drive downtown or to the convention center. Rooms are well appointed and the restaurant is above average.

***Rooms:*** 250 guest rooms (to be expanded to 390) and 20 parlor suites, with phones, satellite televisions, AM/FM radios, some fireplaces, wheelchair access and some non-smoking units.

***Amenities:*** Plaza Court Restaurant, Library Lounge, a casino, room service, a business center, safe-deposit boxes, an outdoor pool and spa, a health club (fitness machines, spa and sauna), meeting and banquet facilities (up to 500 people), self-parking and an airport shuttle.

***Policies:*** No pets allowed.

***Rates:*** $40 to $150.

***Information:*** 1981 Terminal Way, Reno, NV 89502; (702) 348-6370 or (800) 648-3525.

## Boomtown Hotel Casino

This is a combination theme park, Middle America destination and gaming salon. Dressed up in an Old West facade, Boomtown is a booming business on Interstate 80 and pulls in the crowds largely because there's an indoor game arcade and interactive movie experience for the kids. Don't expect anything fancy in the way of accommodations.

***Rooms:*** 122 guest rooms with phones, televisions (some closed captioned), cribs and rollaways ($8.50 per night), some wheelchair access and some non-smoking units.

***Amenities:*** Two restaurants, a bar, a lounge, a casino, shows, an indoor pool, a family arcade (with more than 100 games), a prize redemption center, a Dynamic Motion Theater, an antique carousel, indoor 18-hole miniature golf, a party room, a mini mart and a gas station. RV Park amenities include 200 paved and lighted spaces, full hookups such as cable television, a message and mail center, video rentals, an outdoor swimming pool, two spas, a coin laundromat, a free casino shuttle and 24-hour security.

***Policies:*** No pets allowed. Children under 12 stay free.

***Rates:*** Guest rooms, $39 to $73; RV park, $14.60 to $15.60 (week and monthly rates available). Visa, American Express and MasterCard accepted.

***Information:*** Off Interstate 80 at the Boomtown/Garson Road exit, P.O. Box 399, Verdi, NV 89439; (702) 345-6000 or (800) 648-3790.

## ★ Circus Circus Hotel Casino ★

This is Reno's famous downtown budget hotel, with a casino that features an indoor circus. It is now interconnected with the new Silver Legacy and Eldorado hotels, so guests need never step outside to visit three of the Strip's largest casinos.

*Rooms:* 1,625 guest rooms with phones, televisions, wheelchair access and non-smoking units.

*Amenities:* Hickory Pit Steakhouse, Big Top Buffet, Three Ring Restaurant, two snack bars, five cocktail lounges, casino, shows, a midway with live circus acts and carnival games, a family arcade, a gift shop, covered valet and self-parking garage, and airport shuttle.

*Policies:* No pets allowed.

*Rates:* $25 and up.

*Information:* 500 North Sierra Street, P.O. Box 5880, Reno, NV 89503; (702) 329-0711 or (800) 648-5010.

## ★ Clarion Hotel Casino ★

With the recent opening of its new 283-room tower, the Clarion is one of the class properties near the Reno-Sparks Convention Center. Above-average rooms and superior restaurants characterize the facilities.

*Rooms:* 590 guest rooms and suites with king-size beds, direct-dial phones, message alert, wake-up service, remote control color televisions, movie channels and 24-hour room service; wheelchair access, non-smoking units, some in-room Jacuzzis, living rooms with wet bars and in-room Keno.

*Amenities:* Five restaurants, a bar, entertainment, dancing, a casino with an environment-control system providing an almost smoke-free environment, a sports and entertainment center (video and redemption games, pool tables, air hockey and a snack bar), a sauna, a spa (massage available), an outdoor pool, a sun deck, a health club, free 24-hour valet parking and self-parking lot, a 300,000-square-foot convention facility, and airport/downtown shuttle services.

*Policies:* No pets allowed.

*Rates:* $40 and up.

*Information:* Across from the Reno Convention Center; 3800 South Virginia Street, Reno, NV 89502; (702) 825-4700 or (800) 723-6500.

## Comstock Hotel Casino

This downtown hotel has several interesting touches, and is decorated to recreate the 1880s gold-mining era.

*Rooms:* 310 deluxe, Victorian-style rooms (six penthouse suites) with phones (free local calls), televisions, in-room movies, wheelchair access and non-smoking units.

*Amenities:* Three restaurants, three full-service bars, a lounge, a casino, an outdoor pool, a fitness club and spa, a full-service beauty salon, a children's arcade, dry cleaning service, a gift shop, a convention facility (5,000 square feet), free covered valet parking and complimentary airport shuttle.

*Policies:* No pets allowed.

*Rates:* $30 and up.

*Information:* 200 West Second Street, Reno, NV 89501; (702) 329-1880 or (800) 648-4866.

## ★ Eldorado Hotel Casino ★

Without question, this is downtown Reno's most deluxe property, with a beautiful marble lobby, good restaurants and above-average rooms with firm, comfortable beds.

*Rooms:* 800 guest rooms with phones, televisions, wheelchair access and non-smoking units.

*Amenities:* Seven restaurants, a bar, a lounge, a casino, cabaret shows, an outdoor pool and airport shuttle.

*Policies:* No pets allowed.

*Rates:* $60 and up.

*Information:* 345 North Virginia Street, Reno, NV 89501; (702) 786-5700 or (800) 648-5966.

## ★ Flamingo Hilton Reno ★

Much of this old warhorse in the central district has been thoroughly remodeled, including the rooms, casino and restaurants. The theater usually features an excellent and long-running show of celebrity impersonators.

*Rooms:* 604 rooms (66 suites) with phones, televisions (optional Spectravision movie service), some wheelchair access and some non-smoking units. Cribs, babysitting services and language interpreters available.

*Amenities:* Five restaurants, a bar, a lounge, a casino, shows (revues and productions), a health club, a 10,000-square-foot banquet facility serving 400 people (banquet equipment, services, and audio/visual equipment available), professional bell staff, 24-hour room service, rollaway beds, free safe-deposit boxes, message service, express mail pick-up and delivery, car rentals, free valet parking and an airport shuttle.

*Policies:* No pets allowed. No charge for children when sharing room with a parent.

*Rates:* $60 and up.

*Information:* 255 North Sierra Street, P.O. Box 1291, Reno, NV 89501; (702) 322-1111 or (800) 648-4882.

## ★ Harrah's Casino Hotel Reno ★

This dependable heavyweight on the gaming scene has deluxe rooms, some of the city's best restaurants, a line-up of big-name talent in its showroom, and now, Planet Hollywood, the movie-themed restaurant chain owned by Sylvester Stallone, Arnold Schwarzenegger and Bruce Willis.

*Rooms:* 566 guest rooms with phones, televisions, wheelchair access and non-smoking units.

*Amenities:* Four restaurants, a bar, a lounge, a casino, shows, an outdoor pool, a health club and airport shuttle.

*Policies:* Pets are not allowed, but there is a kennel on-site.

*Rates:* $40 and up.

*Information:* 206 North Virginia Street, Reno, NV 89501; (702) 786-3232 or (800) 648-3773.

## Holiday Hotel Casino

This is a fairly basic, budget-style hotel.

*Rooms:* 190 guest rooms (three deluxe suites), with direct-dial phones, color televisions, AM/FM radio, 24-hour room service, free safe-deposit boxes and a wake-up service.

*Amenities:* A 24-hour restaurant, two lounges, a bar, a casino, a barber shop, babysitting, banquet facilities and meeting rooms (seats up to 152 people), free parking and valet service and a complimentary airport shuttle.

*Policies:* No pets allowed.

*Rates:* $40 to $60.

*Information:* 111 Mill Street, P.O. Box 2700, Reno, NV 89501; (702) 329-0411 or (800) 648-5431.

## ★ John Ascuaga's Nugget ★

This outstanding property in nearby Sparks is practically a self-contained resort, with such attractive features as a large indoor pool, a showroom that features big-name entertainment, good restaurants and proximity to Victorian Square, a shopping district located across the street. The views of the railroad tracks and industrial area outside aren't much to write home about, however. Check out Bertha and Angel, the Nugget's performing elephants.

*Rooms:* 968 standard rooms and luxurious suites with phones, televisions, wheelchair access and non-smoking units.

*Amenities:* Restaurants, a bar, a lounge, an aquarium, a casino, a lower level pavilion (with sportsbook, a pub and pantry, a gift shop and a bingo parlor), shows, Jacuzzi, sun deck, indoor and outdoor pools (poolside service), a health club, a beauty salon, a barber shop, shoeshine service, an

80,000-square-foot convention center, the 30,000-square-foot Rose Ballroom (seats 2,500 people), a wedding chapel, concierge service, free 24-hour covered and uncovered valet and self-parking (1,252 spaces, a five-story parking garage with security lighting, sound system and skyway).

*Policies:* No pets allowed.

*Rates:* $60 and up.

*Information:* 1100 Nugget Avenue, Sparks, NV 89431; (702) 356-3300 or (800) 648-1177.

## ★ Peppermill Hotel Casino ★

This is one of the better hotels in Reno, with posh, oversize rooms, good restaurants and close proximity to the convention center. A 400-room addition (summer 1995) in a new tower will give the resort 1,200 rooms, 70 percent more casino space, a renovated restaurant and a new steakhouse. Peppermill is on the south side of town, away from the hustle and bustle of the Strip.

*Rooms:* 632 rooms (34 suites) with phones, remote-control color televisions, in-room movies, some Jacuzzis, wet bars, wheelchair access and some non-smoking units.

*Amenities:* Four restaurants, seven bars and lounges, a casino, free cabaret entertainment, an outdoor pool, a spa, a health club, a hair salon, a shoeshine station, laundry and dry cleaning service, a video game arcade, a gift shop, convention, banquet and catering facilities, free 24-hour valet and self-parking (covered and uncovered), and airport shuttle.

*Policies:* No pets allowed.

*Rates:* $30 and up.

*Information:* 2707 South Virginia Street, Reno, NV 89502; (702) 826-2121 or (800) 648-6992.

## ★ Reno Hilton ★

This vast hotel complex, the largest in Reno, has had a profusion of names and owners in recent years, and may be headed for yet another change. Major renovations of rooms, the addition of new restaurants, a new super arcade for kids and a substantial underground shopping mall have spruced up this property. One advantage is that it is set apart from downtown, meaning that the rowdier folks who breeze (or stumble) through North Virginia Street don't end up here. The property is close to Reno-Tahoe International Airport, and is a favorite among the convention crowd.

*Rooms:* 2,001 guest rooms with phones, televisions, wheelchair access and non-smoking units.

*Amenities:* Six restaurants, a bar, a lounge/cabaret, a casino, a sportsbook area with 400 seats and two big television screens, shows, a comedy club, an outdoor pool, a health club, a family amusement center (interactive laser tag, bumper cars, supervised soft play for toddlers, video games and a redemption center), retail shops, a 1,600-seat movie theater, a 50-lane bowling center, an outdoor golfing range, convention and meeting facilities, uncovered valet and self-parking, an RV park and an airport shuttle.

*Policies:* No pets allowed.

*Rates:* $40 to $100.

*Information:* 2500 East Second Street, Reno, NV 89595; (702) 789-2000 or (800) 648-5080.

## Sands Regency Hotel Casino

This is a large but somewhat quirky hotel, with a vastly inefficient check-in system that can take a half hour or longer. Rooms are decent, if you request the new wing, and there are acceptable restaurants on the ground floor, along with a slew of fast-food joints. It doesn't have much in the way of service, but then again it always seems to lure people in with bargain rates.

*Rooms:* 1,000 deluxe rooms (29 luxury and bridal suites) with direct-dial phones, color televisions with cable, some kitchenettes, air conditioning, wheelchair access and assistance, non-smoking units and room service.

*Amenities:* Nine restaurants, 24-hour room service, five bars and lounges, a casino, two outdoor heated pools, a penthouse health club, a salon, a video arcade, laundry and dry cleaning service, a gift shop, a 12,000-square-foot convention and meeting facility (seats 10 to 500 people), fax and copy service, safe-deposit boxes, catering, car rentals, RV parking, a 500-car parking garage and airport shuttle ($10).

*Policies:* No pets allowed.

*Rates:* $25 and up.

*Information:* 345 North Arlington Avenue, Reno, NV 89501; (702) 348-2200 or (800) 648-3553.

# Carson City

## ★ Ormsby House Hotel and Casino ★

The Ormsby House reopened under new ownership in February 1995, after spending more than $3 million in renovations since its closure in January 1993. Full casino gaming, the Mark Twain Bar and Curry Street Buffet are making their way back to this largest and most elegant of Carson City's small hotel community. Mark Twain created some of his earliest characters at the original Ormsby House, and not much has changed since then. The Ormsby House continues to offer Western elegance and old-fashioned hospitality.

**Rooms:** 200 hotel rooms, including 30 one- and two-bedroom suites with telephones, televisions, bathtubs, showers, daily maid service, wake-up service, and wheelchair access and non-smoking rooms.

**Amenities:** A coffee shop, a restaurant, two bars (both offering live entertainment), a buffet, daily room service from 6 a.m. to 11 p.m., 24-hour front desk, laundry and dry cleaning, an outdoor swimming pool, a gift shop, and free covered valet and self-parking. The 7,000 square feet of meeting and banquet facilities offer theatre-style seating for up to 750 guests.

**Policies:** No pets allowed.

**Rates:** $60 to $150.

**Information:** 600 South Carson Street, Carson City, NV 89701; (702) 882-1890.

## BEST SMALL HOTELS, MOTELS, LODGES & CABINS

Many excellent small properties (and some rather mediocre ones) surround the 72 miles of shoreline at Tahoe and neighboring communities within an hour's drive of the lake. The following is a cross section of other recommended accommodations. It is by no means all-inclusive.

# North Shore

### Mourelato's Lakeshore Resort

The first thing that catches your eye is the big white Pontiac with the Texas steer horn on the hood, which is parked in front of the office. The car was a prop used in several Hollywood movies, and Andreas and Mary Mourelato took a shine to it during an auction in Reno a few years back. Well, it gets your attention. And if it makes you stop and look closely to see what a delightful place this is, then it has served its purpose. The Mourelatos, who have owned the property since 1978, have created a kind of beachfront mini-paradise here. There are two entirely different wings, separated by a 275-foot white sand beach. The rustic wing has traditional knotty pine interiors and appointments, while the new wing has elegant furnishings (including large armoirs), white-washed walls and bleached pine ceilings—offering a hint of the Greek Islands. (That's not accidental; Andreas is from Greece, and he is an architect). These luxurious, oversized units have unusual shapes and a contemporary, cheerful feeling. The end units closest to the shoreline have sparkling views of the lake. The beach is inviting, and guests can launch their own sailing dinghies or runabouts from here. Some of the North Shore's best restaurants, including La Playa, Captain Jon's and Sweetwater, are within walking distance.

*Rooms:* 32 guest rooms and suites with televisions, some kitchens, microwaves, refrigerators, wet bars. Some units front the lake; some have lake views and balconies.

*Amenities:* A private beach with barbecues and picnic tables.

*Policies:* No pets are allowed.

*Rates:* $75 to $157.

*Information:* Mourelato's Lakeshore Resort, 6834 North Lake Boulevard (P.O. Box 77), Tahoe Vista, CA 96148; (916) 546-9500 or (800) 273-5298.

## Cedar Glen Lodge

Recently renovated, this family-run lodge, which is set in the tall trees across the highway from the lake, is meticulously maintained and far superior to the average motel. On the lower section of the hill are attractive, woodsy cottages with log facades, hand-hewn furniture and separate living rooms and bedrooms, as well as a few kitchens. On the upper side of the hill is a two-story motel unit with a roomy upper deck overlooking the lodge and the lake. In the center of the property is a large heated swimming pool, a spa, a sauna, a children's playground and a big grassy lawn that is great for relaxing in a hammock or having a barbecue. Across the road is a private beach for guests. Nice, homey touches include a newspaper at your front door each morning and a complimentary continental breakfast (rolls, fruit, juice and coffee) in the office. Owners Pat and Jodi Stone will gladly tell you about their favorite restaurants, secret beaches and hiking trails. This is a wonderfully relaxing place for families.

*Rooms:* Guest rooms with phones, televisions, some kitchens, fireplaces, lake views and continental breakfast.

*Amenities:* A spa, a sauna, a pool and a private beach. AAA-rated.

*Policies:* No pets are allowed.

*Rates:* $45 to $125.

*Information:* Cedar Glen Lodge, 6589 North Lake Boulevard (P.O. Box 188), Tahoe Vista, CA 96148; (916) 546-4281.

## Vista Shores Resort

A variety of accommodations, from lakeside beach cottages to mountainside motel-style units, gives this place something for everyone. Regular cottages are the wood-paneled, knotty-pine types of places reminiscent of the 1940s and 1950s, while the mountainside units are of '60s vintage, with sliding glass doors and painted brick walls. Units are comfortable, well furnished and spacious, and the free-standing cottages have full kitchens. There's a heated pool in summer and a private sandy beach at the lake, as well as a restaurant on the premises, with others within walking distance.

**Rooms:** Five remodeled lakeside and 22 woodside guest rooms with televisions, some with kitchens. Some units front the lake, and some have lake views.

**Amenities:** Dining, a spa, a sauna, a pool (open in summer), a private beach, a children's play area, a courtesy phone and catering for large groups and family reunions. AAA-rated.

**Policies:** No pets are allowed.

**Rates:** $50 to $175.

**Information:** Vista Shores Resort, 6731 North Lake Boulevard, P.O. Box 487, Tahoe Vista, CA 96148; (916) 546-3635.

# West Shore

## Tahoe Lake Cottages

Almost everything you could ask for in a woodsy cabin is embodied in these recently refurbished bungalows, located in Tahoma across from the lake, seven miles south of Tahoe City. Features include knotty-pine paneling on walls and ceilings; queen-size beds with firm mattresses in one- and two-bedroom units; a living room with hideaway sofa bed and television; handmade wooden furniture; a full-service kitchen with refrigerator, a gas stove and utensils; a small dining/breakfast table; and a bathroom (most with shower only). For a large family, the six-person cottage is ideal, with two bedrooms, full kitchen and a bathroom with a tub. Owner Michael Lafferty has added many nice touches, and the facility is close to state parks, the lakeshore cycling path, ski areas, marinas and hiking trails.

**Rooms:** Old Tahoe-style knotty-pine cottages with separate living rooms and bedrooms, televisions and full-service kitchens, and motel-style units with beds and bathrooms only.

**Amenities:** A swimming pool and hot tub.

**Policies:** Some pets are allowed.

**Rates:** $55 to $135. If you book six nights, the seventh night is free.

**Information:** 7030 West Lake Boulevard (Highway 89), P.O. Box 126, Tahoma, CA 96142; (916) 525-4411.

## Tahoma Lodge

Attractive from the outside and comfortable but not fancy on the inside, this property ranges from a main lodge unit next to the highway to individual cabins set back on a wooded, slightly hilly site. Cabins have mahogany paneling, full kitchens and baths with showers. Located in Tahoma, the lodge is on the West Shore Bicycle Path, and close to state parks, beaches and ski areas.

**Rooms:** Nine units, including cottages and two apartment units in the main lodge, with phones, televisions, kitchens and wood stoves or fireplaces.

**Amenities:** A Jacuzzi and pool (summer only), with access to a private beach across the road.

**Policies:** Some pets are allowed.

**Rates:** $45 to $115.

**Information:** Tahoma Lodge, 7018 West Lake Boulevard, P.O. Box 72, Tahoma, CA 96142; (916) 525-7721.

# Truckee

## Best Western Truckee Tahoe Inn

Close to the ski and golf resort of Northstar-at-Tahoe and the historic town of Truckee, this property looks much like a typical motel. But on the inside it has many personalized features that give guests extra value for their money. The walls are festooned with photographs from the Truckee Rodeo, which is held in an arena next door, and in addition to the standard rooms there are some nicely appointed two-room suites, each room with a television set (and a sofa bed in the living room). If you stay in one of these, you can borrow movie videotapes for free from the library at the front desk. There's also a free continental breakfast in the morning, with rolls, toast, cereal and juice, in an upstairs dining area. Located on Highway 267, the inn has quick access to Interstate 80, is about eight miles from Lake Tahoe, and is within a 20-minute drive of Squaw Valley and Alpine Meadows ski resorts.

**Rooms:** 100 deluxe rooms and mini-suites with phones, televisions, free movies and a free breakfast buffet.

**Amenities:** A spa, a Jacuzzi, a pool, a fitness room, sports equipment, disposable swimwear and a conference room.

**Policies:** Kids stay free; no pets are allowed.

**Rates:** $61 to $124.

**Information:** Best Western Truckee Tahoe Inn, 11331 Highway 267, Truckee, CA 96161; (916) 587-4525 or (800) 824-6385.

# Carson City

## Carson Station Best Western Hotel Casino

A well-managed and above-average small hotel, with a good restaurant across the street.

**Rooms:** 92 guest rooms and suites with phones, televisions, private balconies and some non-smoking units.

**Amenities:** A casino, a cabaret/bar lounge, a sportsbook lounge (bar and snack bar) and RV parking.

**Rates:** $40 to $60.

**Information:** 900 South Carson Street, P.O. Box 1966, Carson City, NV 89701; (702) 883-0900 or (800) 528-1234.

# Minden

## Carson Valley Inn

With its woodsy decor and extensive land holdings along US 395, this deluxe motel is a nice, out-of-the-way retreat that is popular with families and retirees, in the quiet community of Minden, south of Carson City. It's located near great Basque restaurants, quaint Victorian homes, a hot springs (outside of Markleeville), and the alpine beauty of Highway 88 and Carson Pass.

***Rooms:*** 154 rooms and spacious suites (King or Double Queen, King Deluxe, Standard Deluxe, and Spa Suites) and a 76-room motor lodge with phones, televisions, air conditioning, wheelchair access and non-smoking units.

***Amenities:*** Three restaurants, four bars, nightly live entertainment and dancing in the cabaret lounge, a casino, glass-enclosed spas, a supervised fun center (ages 4-12), a video arcade, a 60-site RV resort (full hookups, laundry, showers, a dump station and a pet area), a convenience store with fuel, a convention center (meetings, banquets and receptions), a wedding chapel, full wedding services, free valet parking and limousine transportation available.

***Rates:*** Motel, $35 to $109; hotel, $49.50 to $159; RV park, $9.25 to $16.

***Information:*** 1627 US 395, Minden, NV 89423; (702) 782-9711 or (800) 321-6983.

## MORE SMALL HOTELS, MOTELS, LODGES & CABINS
## North Shore

***Big 7:*** Tahoe-style knotty-pine rooms with phones and remote-control televisions. Dining, heated pool, picnic area and beach access. $30 to $48. Most major credit cards accepted. 8141 North Lake Boulevard, P.O. Box 759, Kings Beach, CA 96143; (916) 546-2541.

***Charmey Chalet:*** 27 standard and studio rooms with phones, televisions, some kitchens, continental breakfast, fireplaces, in-room whirlpool and lake views. Jacuzzi, pool and beach. No pets allowed. $45 to $150. 6549 North Lake Boulevard, P.O. Box 316, Tahoe Vista, CA 96148; (916) 546-2529.

***Crown Motel:*** Single and family units with phones, televisions, some kitchens, fireplaces, lake fronts and lake views. Indoor spa, heated pool and beach. No pets allowed. $65 to $165. 8200 North Lake Boulevard, P.O. Box 845, Kings Beach, CA 96143; (916) 546-3388.

***Crystal Bay Motel:*** 19 guest rooms with phones and televisions. $40-$60. 24 Highway 28, Crystal Bay, NV 89402; (702) 831-0287.

**Cottonwood Lodge:** Old Tahoe-style log cabins (king- and queen-size beds) with phones, televisions, kitchenettes, some lakefronts and lake views. Spa, sauna, heated pool, private beach and fishing/boating pier. No pets allowed. $74-$156. 6542 North Lake Boulevard, P.O. Box 86, Tahoe Vista, CA 99148; (916) 546-2220.

**Dunes Resort:** Knotty-pine cottages with televisions, some kitchens, fireplaces, lakefronts, lake views and sun decks. Private beach and barbecues. No pets allowed. $53-$186. 6780 North Lake Boulevard, P.O. Box 34, Tahoe Vista, CA 96148; (916) 546-2196.

**Falcon Lodge:** Single rooms with direct-dial phones, color televisions with HBO, some kitchens with refrigerators, some lakefronts, some lake views, continental breakfast and in-room coffee. Hot tub, heated pool, laundry and private sandy beach. No pets allowed. $39-$120. 8258 North Lake Boulevard, P.O. Box 249, Kings Beach, CA 96143; (916) 546-2583.

**Fire Lite Lodge:** 26 guest rooms with phones, televisions, some lake views and continental breakfast on weekends. A lounge with television and pool (summer only). No pets allowed. $40-$75. 7035 North Lake Boulevard, P.O. Box 135, Tahoe Vista, CA 96148; (916) 546-7222.

**Franciscan Lakeside Lodge:** Studio to two-bedroom suites with phones, televisions with cable, kitchen, some fireplaces, lakefronts and lake views. Pool, gas barbecues, private beach, volleyball, pier and buoys. No pets allowed. $70-$175. 6944 North Lake Boulevard, P.O. Box 280, Tahoe Vista, CA 96148; (916) 546-7234 or (800) 564-6754 (California only).

**Garni Motor Lodge:** 100 large guest rooms with phones and televisions. Spa facilities. $39-$109. 9937 North Lake Boulevard, P.O. Box 97, Brockway, CA 96143; (916) 546-3341 or (800) 648-2324.

**Goldcrest Motel:** Single rooms with phones, televisions, some kitchens, some lakefronts, some lake views, continental breakfast and in-room coffee. Spa, heated pool and private beach. No pets allowed. $50-$130. 8149 North Lake Boulevard, P.O. Box 579, Kings Beach, CA 96143; (916) 546-3301; (800) 852-5348.

**Holiday House:** Suites with televisions, kitchen, some lakefronts, lake views and decks. Spa, laundry, private beach and buoys. Some pets are allowed. $115-$221. 7276 North Lake Boulevard, P.O. Box 229, Tahoe Vista, CA 96148; (916) 546-2369.

**Inn at Incline and Condominiums:** Newly remodeled family resort in a secluded forest setting, featuring 50 guest rooms and condos with phones, televisions with HBO, some kitchens, fireplaces, wheelchair access and continental breakfast. Spa, sauna, indoor pool and laundry facilities. Some pets are allowed. $55-$85 and up. 1003 Tahoe Boulevard, P.O. Box 4545, Incline Village, NV 89450; (702) 831-1052 or (800) GO-TAHOE.

**Lake of the Sky Motor Inn:** 23 completely remodeled guest rooms with phones, televisions, some lake views and in-room coffee. Pool (summer only), sauna and conference room. No pets allowed. $49-$99. 955 North Lake Boulevard, P.O. Box 227, Tahoe City, CA 96145; (916) 583-3305.

**Lakeside Chalets:** Cottages and lakefront suites with televisions, kitchens, stone hearth fireplaces and some lake views. Private beach, pier, buoys, windsurfing school and rentals. Some pets are allowed. $85-$125. 5240 North Lake Boulevard, P.O. Box 270, Carnelian Bay, CA 96140; (916) 546-5857.

**North Lake Lodge:** Guest rooms with televisions, kitchens (refrigerator and microwave in all units), some fireplaces and lake views. Hot tub. Pets are allowed. 8716 North Lake Boulevard, P.O. Box 955, Kings Beach, CA 96143; (916) 546-2731.

**Rodeway Inn:** Guest rooms with phones, televisions and some lake views. Hot spa, laundry facilities and covered parking. $50-$112. 645 North Lake Boulevard, P.O. Box 29, Tahoe City, CA 96145; (916) 583-3711 or (800) 624-8590.

**Stevenson's Holiday Inn:** Spacious rooms (king- and queen-size beds) with direct-dial phones, televisions, some kitchens (refrigerators and microwaves) and fireplaces. Heated pool, spas and recreation room. 8742 North Lake Boulevard, P.O. Box 235, Kings Beach, CA 96143; (916) 546-2269.

**Sun 'N Sand Lodge:** Newly remodeled rooms with phones, televisions, some lake fronts, lake views and weekend continental breakfast. Private beach and volleyball. No pets allowed. $57-$137. 8308 North Lake Boulevard, P.O. Box 5, Kings Beach, CA 96143; (916) 546-2515.

**Tahoe City Inn:** 33 guest rooms (some waterbeds) with phones, televisions, VCRs, free movies, some lake views, in-room coffee, some private in-room spas, and wheelchair access. No pets allowed. $45-$95. 790 North Lake Boulevard, P.O. Box 634, Tahoe City, CA 96145; (916) 581-3333 or (800) 800-8246.

**Tahoe City Travelodge:** 47 non-smoking guest rooms (remodeled in 1992) with phones, remote-control televisions (free Showtime, Encore and Disney channels included), in-room coffee and some lake views. Sauna, lakeview spa and pool (summer only). No pets allowed. $44-$130. 455 North Lake Boulevard, P.O. Box 84, Tahoe City, CA 96145; (916) 583-3766 or (800) 578-7878.

**Tamarack Lodge:** 21 guest rooms and cottages with televisions, some kitchens and some lake views. No pets allowed. $35-$95. 2311 North Lake Boulevard, 2311 North Lake Boulevard, P.O. Box 859, Tahoe City, CA 96145; (916) 583-3350.

**Tatami Cottage Resort:** 18 Japanese-decorated cottages with televisions, some kitchens, fireplaces and lake views. Two acres of pine woods. Some pets are allowed. 7449 North Lake Boulevard, P.O. Box 18, Tahoe Vista, CA 96148; (916) 546-3523.

**Ta-Tel Lodge:** Nine guest rooms with phones, televisions, some kitchens and in-room coffee. Pool (summer only). No pets allowed. $30-$70. 8748 North Lake Boulevard, P.O. Box 1344, Kings Beach, CA 96143; (916) 546-2411.

**Villa Vista Resort:** One- and two-bedroom cottages with phones, televisions, some kitchens, fireplaces, lakefronts and lake views. A family resort on the lake with private beach, beach club, pool, laundry and fax service. No pets allowed. $70-$178. 6750 North Lake Boulevard, P.O. Box 47, Tahoe Vista, CA 96148; (916) 546-1550.

**Woodvista Lodge:** Large guest rooms with phones, televisions, some kitchens and some continental breakfasts. Spa, pool, children's play area, barbecues and large lawn with pine trees. $60-$140. 7699 North Lake Boulevard, P.O. Box 439, Tahoe Vista, CA 96148; (916) 546-3839.

## Squaw Valley

**Hostel at Squaw Valley:** 80 beds (dormitory-style hostel at the base of Squaw Valley) with a television and phone in common area. $18-$25. Mailing address: P.O. Box 6655, Tahoe City, CA 96145. Street address: 1900 Squaw Valley Road, P.O. Box 6655, Olympic Valley, CA 96146; (916) 581-3246.

**Squaw Tahoe Resort:** Ski-in, ski-out condos with phones, televisions, kitchens and some fireplaces. Laundry facilities, spa and sauna. $75-$190. 2000 Squaw Loop Road, P.O. Box 2612, Olympic Valley, CA 96146; (916) 583-7226.

## West Shore

**Grubstake Lodge:** Cottages with televisions, private bath, some kitchens and some fireplaces. Public phones. $38-$58. 5335 West Lake Boulevard, P.O. Box 526, Homewood, CA 96141; (916) 525-5505.

**Homeside Motel and Lodge:** Ranch-style motel rooms and two- and three-bedroom lodge rooms with televisions with cable, some fireplaces and spa. $55-$85. 5205 West Lake Boulevard, P.O. Box 1014, Homewood, CA 96141; (916) 525-9990.

**Homewood Marina Lodge:** Cottages and motel rooms with some kitchens, fireplaces, lake views and housekeeping units. Private beach, large lawn, cafe, bar and public phones. $48-$78. 5180 West Lake Boulevard, P.O. Box 526, Homewood, CA 96141; (916) 525-6728.

**Swiss Lakewood Village:** Motel rooms and deluxe housekeeping two-bedroom cabins with televisions with cable, some full-sized kitchens (fully equipped), linen, a restaurant and garden. A deposit of 25 percent of the total rental is required to hold the reservation. Refunds are given with a minimum 15 days notice prior to arrival date. $65-$145. 5055 West Lake Boulevard, P.O. Box 205, Homewood, CA 96141; (916) 525-5211.

# Truckee

**Star Hotel:** Hostel rooms with beds, private rooms, shared baths and hot showers. Laundry facilities and linen rentals. Bring your own sleeping bag. No maid service (clean up after yourself). $35-$66. 10015 West River Street, Truckee, CA 96160; (916) 587-3007.

# South Shore

**Chamonix Inn:** 32 guest rooms with direct-dial phones, remote-control color televisions and free HBO. Cafe, spa, pool, free casino shuttles and ski shuttles to local resorts. No pets allowed. $38-$85. 913 Friday Avenue, P.O. Box 5274, South Lake Tahoe, CA 96157; (916) 544-5274 or (800) 447-5353.

**Days Inn:** 42 guest rooms (some water beds) with televisions, some fireplaces and continental breakfast. Jacuzzi and pool (summer only). No pets allowed. $39-$89. 3530 Lake Tahoe Boulevard, South Lake Tahoe, CA 96150; (916) 544-3445 or (800) 350-3446.

**Elm Inn:** 102 guest rooms with phones, televisions and in-room coffee. Dining, Jacuzzi and pool (summer only). Pets are allowed. $40-$78. 4082 Lake Tahoe Boulevard, South Lake Tahoe, CA 96150; (916) 541-7900 or (800) 822-5905.

**Forest Inn Suites:** 124 one- and two-bedroom units with phones, televisions, in-room coffee and some kitchens. Sauna, Jacuzzi, pool, recreation room and ski shuttle. No pets allowed. $81-$140. 1101 Park Avenue, South Lake Tahoe, CA 96150; (916) 541-6655 or (800) 822-5950.

**Inn at Heavenly:** 14 guest rooms (weekend rentals) with televisions, some fireplaces, linen and maid service. Sauna, Jacuzzi and recreation room. Pets allowed. Deposits required. 1261 Ski Run Boulevard, P.O. Box 16584, South Lake Tahoe, CA 96151; (800) MY-CABIN or (916) 544-4244.

**Lampliter Motel:** 28 guest rooms with phones, televisions and in-room coffee. Jacuzzi, beach and boat rentals. Some pets are allowed. $35-$80. 4143 Cedar, South Lake Tahoe, CA 96150; (916) 544-2936.

**Lone Pine Lodge:** One to three beds with direct-dial phones, color televisions with cable, air conditioning, hot spa, refrigerator and in-room coffee. Free casino shuttle service. $29-$78. 864 Stateline Avenue, South Lake Tahoe, CA 96150; (916) 544-3316 or (800) 350-3316.

**Nendel's Blue Jay Lodge:** 65 guest rooms with phones, televisions, some kitchens and in-room coffee. Jacuzzi and pool (summer only). No pets allowed. $39-$89 and above. 4133 Cedar Avenue, South Lake Tahoe, CA 96150; (916) 544-5232 or (800) 258-3529.

**Secrets:** 24 rooms (waterbeds) with phones, televisions, in-room coffee and some fireplaces. Jacuzzi. No pets allowed. $58-$108. 924 Park Avenue, South Lake Tahoe, CA 96150; (916) 544-6767 or (800) 441-6610.

**Tahoe Chalet Inn:** 66 rooms and cottages with phones, televisions, some kitchens, continental breakfast and some fireplaces. Sauna, Jacuzzi, pool (summer only) and recreation room. No pets allowed. $52-$220. 3860 Lake Tahoe Boulevard, South Lake Tahoe, CA 96150; (916) 544-3311 or (800) 821-2656.

**Tahoe Tropicana:** 58 rooms (single, adjoining and penthouse suites; king, queen and some waterbeds) with direct-dial phones, color televisions with cable, some kitchenettes, air conditioning and a welcome bottle of champagne. Dining, Jacuzzi and heated pool (summer only) in gazebo, ice and vending machines, Greenhouse Restaurant, cocktail lounge, outdoor parking, free ski and casino shuttles. $30-$110. 4132 Cedar Avenue, P.O. Box 4681, South Lake Tahoe, CA 96157; (916) 541-3911 or (800) 447-0246.

**Tahoe Valley Motel:** 21 guest rooms with phones, televisions, in-room coffee and fireplace. Jacuzzi and pool (summer only). Some pets are allowed. $95-$185. 2241 Lake Tahoe Boulevard, South Lake Tahoe, CA 96150; (916) 541-0353 or (800) 669-7544.

**Tradewinds:** 68 guest rooms with phones, remote-control televisions with cable, bathtub, kitchen, in-room coffee and some Heavenly Ski resort views. Jacuzzi and pool (summer only). Pets are allowed. $30-$100. 944 Friday Avenue, South Lake Tahoe, CA 96150; (916) 544-6459 or (800) 628-1829.

**Travelodge Casino Area:** 66 guest rooms with direct-dial phones (free local calls), remote-control color televisions with HBO, AM/FM radio alarm clock, air conditioning, some non-smoking rooms and in-room coffee. Heated outdoor pool (seasonal), babysitting and shuttles (casino, ski, and airport) available. No pets allowed. $39 and up. 4003 US 50, P.O. Box 6500, South Lake Tahoe, CA 96157; (916) 541-5000 or (800) 982-2466.

**Travelodge South Tahoe:** 59 guest rooms with direct-dial phones (free local calls), remote-control color televisions with HBO, AM/FM radio alarm clock, air conditioning, some non-smoking rooms and in-room coffee. Heated outdoor pool (seasonal), babysitting and shuttle services (casino, ski and airport) available. No pets allowed. $39 and up. 3489 US 50, P.O. Box 70512, South Lake Tahoe, CA 96156; (916) 544-5266 or (800) 982-1466.

***Travelodge Stateline:*** 50 guest rooms with direct-dial phones (free local calls), remote-control color televisions with HBO, AM/FM radio alarm clocks, air conditioning, some non-smoking rooms and in-room coffee. Heated outdoor pool (seasonal), babysitting and shuttle service (casino, ski and airport) available. No pets allowed. $39 and up. 4011 US 50, P.O. Box 6600, South Lake Tahoe, CA 96157; (916) 544-6000 or (800) 982-3466.

***Value Inn:*** 62 guest rooms with phones, televisions, some continental breakfast, Jacuzzis and fireplaces. No pets allowed. $30 and up. 2659 Lake Tahoe Boulevard, South Lake Tahoe, CA 96150; (916) 544-3959.

***Viking Motor Lodge:*** 58 guest rooms with phones, remote-control color televisions, kitchenettes, continental breakfast, in-room coffee and some fireplaces. Jacuzzi, pool (summer only) and complimentary ski shuttle available. No pets allowed. $39-$80. 4083 Cedar Avenue, South Lake Tahoe, CA 96150; (916) 541-5155 or (800) 288-4083.

## Highway 88

***Alpine Inn:*** $32 and up (single-night rate with a maximum of four people); weekly rates available. Four miles from Grover Hot Springs; 14820 Highway 89 (P.O. Box 367), Markleeville, CA 96120; (916) 694-2591.

***Woodfords Inn:*** Guest rooms (single queens, some double twins) with large stall showers and color televisions with cable. Complimentary coffee, snacks and sweet rolls for sale, Jacuzzi, large yard, picnic tables, and barbecue pits. $39-$54. One-quarter of a mile south of Highway 88; 20960 Highway 89, Woodfords, CA 96120; (916) 694-2410.

## Sierra & Plumas Counties

***Bassett's Station:*** Three guest rooms (two double beds and day couch in each) with fully equipped kitchens, baths and dinettes. Cafe, mini-mart (gasoline, groceries, auto supplies, fishing tackle and camping goods), and phones in the common areas. $60 per night for two people (year-round); $3 for each additional person (room sleeps five). Highway 49 and Gold Lake Road, Sierra City, CA 96125; (916) 862-1297.

***The Buttes Resort:*** One- and two-bedroom units (motel rooms, suites, honeymoon suites and housekeeping units) with some kitchens and decks overlooking the Yuba River. Fishing boats for guests at no extra charge. $45-$125 (weekly rate is a one-day discount; stay for seven days and pay for six days). Highway 49, P.O. Box 234, Sierra City, CA 96125; (916) 862-1170 or (800) 991-1170.

***River Pines Inn:*** Standard and deluxe motel rooms (one- and two-bedroom suites with some maid service) and housekeeping cottages. Pool,

Jacuzzi, poolside cocktail bar, ping-pong and big screen televisions in the lodge. No pets allowed. $40-$190 per day (all units); $110-$475 per week (housekeeping cottages and suites). All rates are for two guests. Each additional person is $10 per day (over 16) or $5 per day (ages 3 to 16). Highway 89, P.O. Box 247, Clio, CA 96106; (916) 836-0313.

**Riverside Inn:** Guest rooms (king-, queen-size and double beds) with televisions with cable, some kitchenettes, continental breakfast and private decks overlooking the river. Patio, barbecue area and beach. Smoking permitted on patio. 24-hour cancellation notice for reservations is required. $50-$65. 206 Commercial Street, P.O. Box 176, Downieville, CA 95936; (916) 289-1000.

**Sierra Motel:** 23 guest rooms (queen-size beds) with direct-dial phones, color televisions with HBO, AM/FM radio, air conditioning, some non-smoking rooms, in-room coffee and refrigerators. No pets allowed. $38-$44. 380 East Sierra Street, P.O. Box 1265, Portola, CA 96122; (916) 832-4223.

**Sleepy Pines Motel:** 17 guest rooms with phones, color televisions, in-room coffee, continental breakfast on weekends, and some non-smoking rooms. $40-$68. 74631 Highway 70, Portola, CA 96122; (916) 832-4291.

**River Pines Resort:** 62 motel rooms and housekeeping cottages with some kitchens, air conditioning and wheelchair access. Restaurant, cocktail lounge, pool, Jacuzzi, playground, recreation room, picnic and barbecue area. $50-$75. Highway 89, one-quarter mile north of Graeagle. Mailing address: P.O. Box 249, Clio, CA 96106. Street address: 8296 Highway 89, Blairsden, CA; (916) 836-2552 or (800) 696-2551.

# Reno/Sparks

**Best Western Daniel's Motor Lodge:** 82 guest rooms with phones and televisions. No pets allowed. $60-$100. 375 North Sierra Street, Reno, NV 89501; (702) 329-1351 or (800) 528-1234.

**Blue Fountain Motel:** 60 guest rooms with phones, televisions and non-smoking units. Pets are allowed. $40-$60. 1590 Victorian Avenue, Sparks, NV 89431; (702) 359-0359 or (800) FOR-RENO.

**Bob Cashell's Horseshoe Lodge:** 48 guest rooms with phones, televisions and wheelchair access. Dining, a bar, a lounge and a casino. $30 and up. 222 North Sierra Street, Reno, NV 89501; (702) 322-2178 or (800) 843-7403.

**Crest Inn:** 46 guest rooms with phones and televisions. An outdoor pool. $40-$60. 525 West Fourth Street, Reno, NV 89503; (702) 329-0808 or (800) FOR-RENO.

**Executive Inn:** 85 guest rooms with phones, televisions, wheelchair access and non-smoking units. An outdoor pool. No pets allowed. $30

and up. 205 South Sierra Street, Reno, NV 89501; (702) 786-4050 or
(800) 648-4545.

***Fitzgerald's Casino Hotel:*** There's nothing fancy here at one of the
older downtown hotels. 351 rooms and suites with phones, televisions and
wheelchair access. Three restaurants, a bar, a lounge, a casino, credit card
and check cashing, and shows. No pets allowed. $50-$130. 255 North
Virginia Street, Reno, NV 89501; (702) 785-3300 or (800) 648-5022.

***Gatekeeper Inn:*** 28 guest rooms with phones, televisions, wheelchair
access and non-smoking units. No pets allowed. $30 and up. 221 West
Fifth Street, Reno, NV 89503; (702) 786-3500 or (800) 822-3504.

***Gateway Inn:*** 102 guest rooms with phones, televisions, wheelchair
access and non-smoking units. Dining, a bar, a lounge and an outdoor
pool. Pets are allowed. $30 and up. 1275 Stardust Street, Reno, NV
89503; (702) 747-4220.

***Holiday Inn Convention Center:*** 153 guest rooms with phones,
televisions, wheelchair access and non-smoking units. A restaurant, a bar,
a lounge, shows, a Jacuzzi, a heated outdoor pool, banquet facilities, free
parking and an airport shuttle. Small pets are allowed. Children stay free
when accompanied by an adult. $40 and up. 5851 South Virginia Street,
Reno, NV 89502; (702) 825-2940; (800) 722-7366.

***Holiday Inn Downtown:*** 286 units (guest rooms, deluxe double
accommodations and suites) with phones, televisions (free Showtime,
CNN and ESPN), wheelchair access and non-smoking units. Two restaurants, a bar, a casino, an outdoor pool, an 8,700-square-foot banquet and
convention facility (seats 20 to 400; audio/visual equipment and catering
services), parking and an airport shuttle. Pets are allowed. $40-$60. 1000
East Sixth Street, Reno, NV 89512; (702) 786-5151 or (800) 648-4877.

***Juniper Court Motel:*** 60 guest rooms with phones, televisions and
wheelchair access. No pets allowed. $40 and up. 320 Evans Avenue,
Reno, NV 89501; (702) 329-7002.

***La Quinta Inn:*** 130 guest rooms with phones, televisions, wheelchair
access and non-smoking units. Dining, an outdoor pool and an airport
shuttle. Pets are allowed. $40-$60. 4001 Market Street, Reno, NV 89502;
(702) 348-6100 or (800) 531-5900.

***Mardi Gras Motor Lodge:*** 30 guest rooms with phones, televisions
and non-smoking units. No pets allowed. $40 and up. 200 West Fourth
Street, Reno, NV 89501; (702) 329-7470.

***McCarran House Inn:*** 220 guest rooms with phones, televisions
and non-smoking units. A dining, bar, lounge, outdoor pool and airport
shuttle. No pets allowed. $40-$60. 55 East Nugget Avenue, Reno, NV
89431; (702) 358-6900 or (800) 548-5798.

***National Nine Inn:*** 32 guest rooms with phones, televisions and
wheelchair access. No pets allowed. $40. 645 South Virginia Street, Reno,

NV 89501; (702) 323-5411.

**Nevada Inn:** 43 guest rooms with phones and televisions. An outdoor pool. No pets allowed. $40-$60. 330 East Second Street, Reno, NV 89501; (702) 323-1005 or (800) 999-9686.

**Oxford Motel:** 28 guest rooms with phones and televisions. Pets are allowed. $40-$60. 111 Lake Street, Reno, NV 89501; (702) 786-3170 or (800) 648-3044.

**Pioneer Inn Hotel Casino:** 252 newly remodeled rooms and suites with phones, televisions, wheelchair access and some in-room Jacuzzis and saunas. Three restaurants, a 24-hour coffee shop, a bar, a lounge, a casino, shows and an outdoor pool. No pets allowed. $30 and up. 221 South Virginia Street, Reno, NV 89501; (702) 324-7777 or (800) 879-8879.

**Plaza Resort Club:** 100 guest rooms with phones, televisions and wheelchair access. Two restaurants, a bar, a lounge and an indoor pool. No pets allowed. $60 and up. 121 West Street, Reno, NV 89501; (702) 786-2200; (800) 648-5990.

**Reno Ramada Hotel Casino:** 233 guest rooms with phones, televisions, wheelchair access and non-smoking units. Dining, a bar, a lounge, a casino, shows and an airport shuttle. No pets allowed. $40-$60. 200 East Sixth Street, Reno, NV 89501; (702) 788-2000 or (800) 648-3600.

**Reno Spa Resort Club:** 93 guest rooms with phones, televisions, wheelchair access and non-smoking units. An indoor pool, a health club and an airport shuttle. No pets allowed. $40 and up. 140 Court Street, Reno, NV 89501; (702) 329-4251 or (800) 634-6981.

**Riverboat & Casino Hotel:** 300 guest rooms with phones, televisions, wheelchair access and non-smoking units. Two restaurants, a bar, a lounge and a casino. No pets allowed. $40-$60. 34 West Second Street, Reno, NV 89501; (702) 323-8877 or (800) 888-5525.

**Rodeway Inn:** 210 guest rooms with phones, televisions, wheelchair access and non-smoking units. An outdoor pool and airport shuttle. Pets are allowed. $60-$100. 2050 Market Street, Reno, NV 89502; (702) 786-2500 or (800) 648-3800.

**Romance Inn:** 43 guest rooms, some with themes, with phones, televisions and wheelchair access. An outdoor pool. No pets allowed. $60 and up. 2905 South Virginia Street, Reno, NV 89502; (702) 826-1515 or (800) 662-8812.

**Season's Inn:** 56 guest rooms with phones, televisions, wheelchair access and non-smoking units. No pets allowed. $40-$60. 495 West Street, Reno, NV 89503; (702) 322-6000.

**Showboat Inn:** 103 guest rooms with phones, televisions, wheelchair access and non-smoking units. No pets allowed. $40-$60. 660 North Virginia Street, Reno, NV 89501; (702) 786-7486 or (800) 648-3960.

**Silver Club Hotel Casino:** 207 guest rooms with phones, televisions, wheelchair access and non-smoking units. Three restaurants, a bar, a lounge, shows and an airport shuttle. No pets allowed. $40 and up. 1040 Victorian Avenue, Reno, NV 89431; (702) 358-4771 or (800) 648-1137.

***Stardust Lodge:*** 57 guest rooms with phones, televisions, wheelchair access and non-smoking units. An outdoor pool. No pets allowed. $40 and up. 455 North Arlington Avenue, Reno, NV 89503; (702) 322-5641.

***Sundowner Hotel Casino:*** 600 guest rooms with phones, televisions and non-smoking units. Three restaurants, a bar, a lounge, a casino, an outdoor pool and four floors of free, covered parking. No pets allowed. $40-$60. 450 North Arlington Avenue, Reno, NV 89503; (702) 786-7050 or (800) 648-5490.

***Thunderbird Resort Club:*** 132 units (studios, one- and two-bedroom townhouses) with phones, televisions with cable, VCRs, some fireplaces, some wet bars, kitchens, in-room coffee and non-smoking units. Tennis courts, an outdoor pool/spa, a recreation room, video and bicycle rentals, shuffle board, video games, laundry, a convention center (seats 50 to 500), catering, self-parking, a casino and airport shuttle. No pets allowed. $40 and up. 200 Nichols Boulevard, Sparks, NV 89431; (702) 355-4040 or (800) 821-4912.

***Town House Motor Lodge:*** 79 guest rooms with phones, televisions and non-smoking units. An outdoor pool. No pets allowed. $40 and up. 303 West Second Street, Reno, NV 89503; (702) 323-1821 or (800) 438-5660.

***Truckee River Lodge:*** 214 guest rooms with phones, televisions, wheelchair access and non-smoking units. A dining and health club. Pets are allowed. $30 and up. 501 West First Street, Reno, NV 89503; (702) 786-8888 or (800) 635-8950.

***University Inn:*** 168 guest rooms with phones, televisions, wheelchair access and non-smoking units. Dining. No pets allowed. $40 and up. 1001 North Virginia Street, Reno, NV 89557; (702) 323-0321.

***Vagabond Inn:*** 130 guest rooms with phones, televisions and non-smoking units. Dining, a bar, a lounge, an outdoor pool and airport shuttle. Pets are allowed. $30-$60. 3131 South Virginia Street, Reno, NV 89502; (702) 825-7134 or (800) 522-1555.

***Victorian Inn:*** 22 guest rooms with phones, televisions and non-smoking units. No pets allowed. $30-$60. 1555 Victorian Avenue, Sparks, NV 89431; (702) 331-3203 or (800) FOR-RENO.

***Virginian Hotel Casino:*** 118 units (rooms and suites), king-size or two double beds with phones, televisions with cable, wheelchair access, non-smoking units, an airport shuttle and free valet parking. Two restaurants (available for private parties; 20 to 80 guests), a bar, a lounge and a casino. No pets allowed. Guest rooms, $28-$56; suites, $90-$150; and penthouse suites, $90-$250. 140 North Virginia Street, Reno, NV 89501; (702) 329-4664 or (800) 874-5558

***Western Village Inn Casino:*** 280 guest rooms with phones, televisions and wheelchair access. Three restaurants, a bar, a lounge, a casino, shows, an outdoor pool and an airport shuttle. Pets are allowed. $25 and up. 815 Nichols Boulevard, Sparks, NV 89431; (702) 331-1069 or (800) 648-1170.

***Wonder Lodge:*** 63 guest rooms with phones and televisions. An outdoor pool. No pets allowed. $40-$60. 430 Lake Street, Reno, NV 89501; (702) 786-6840.

## Carson City

***City Center Carson Nugget:*** 81 guest rooms with phones and televisions. A coffee shop, a restaurant, an oyster bar, a buffet, a 24-hour casino, a theatre lounge, a gold display, free supervised kid's arcade lounge, convention facilities and RV parking in a free parking lot. $25-$60. 800 North Carson Street, Carson City, NV 89701; (702) 882-5535; (800) 338-7760.

***Days Inn:*** 62 guest rooms with phones, cable TVs with free movies, air conditioning, kitchens, some non-smoking and wheelchair facilities. An adjacent restaurant, a fax machine and RV parking. Children 12 and under stay free. $40 and up. 3103 North Carson Highway, Carson City, NV 89701; (702) 883-3343 or (800) 325-2525.

***Hardman House Motor Inn:*** 62 rooms and suites, phones, televisions, some non-smoking, some refrigerators and microwave ovens. 24-hour desk service, coffee in the lobby and parking garage. No pets allowed. $36-$90. 917 North Carson Street, Carson City, NV 89701; (702) 882-7744 or (800) 626-0793.

***Westerner Inn:*** 102 guest rooms (king, queen, two double and suites), phones and cable TVs. A restaurant and RV parking. Pets are allowed. $25-$60 (weekly rates available). 555 North Stewart Street, Carson City, NV 89701; (702) 883-6565.

# Chapter 23

# Restaurants
# & Nightlife

# RESTAURANTS

After a hard day of mountain biking, hiking, boating or skiing, nothing is more attractive than a good dinner, unless it's good company (and they should go together). One of the delights of visiting Lake Tahoe, Reno and Carson Valley is the fine quality of the dinner houses. Award-winning chefs, many of whom have decided that life in the mountains is better than in the city, have made their homes in this region, and consumers reap the rewards. Almost every type of American and ethnic cuisine is represented, from Tex-Mex to Nouveau California to French, Swiss and Asian. Typically, the casino hotels offer the most consistent high quality, at times more so than the small restaurants whose business fluctuates with the seasons. During the high seasons in summer and winter, though, the entire area shines with its delightful diversity. Even if all you want is a pizza, you'll find an outstanding place in the list below.

**Ratings:** ** Outstanding  * Recommended  No stars: Fair

## NORTH SHORE
## Carnelian Bay

### Gar Woods Grill and Pier *

With one of the longest deep-water guest piers on the lake, this well-patronized restaurant is named after Garfield Wood, the famous boat designer and builder whose elegant, mahogany power boats became a fixture of the Tahoe yachting scene from the 1920s through the 1940s. The restaurant, with its vaulted, beamed ceilings and outdoor deck, features beer-battered coconut prawns, New York steak, white chocolate Snickers cheesecake, and the "Wet Woody" tropical drink, a house specialty. The big event here is the Sunday buffet brunch, which offers a dozen entrées. A children's menu is available, and children under 4 are free for the brunch. This is a non-smoking restaurant, with wheelchair access to the restaurant and pier. Live music holds forth on Friday and Saturday, 7 p.m. to 11 p.m., and banquet facilities are available. Dinner is served from 5 p.m., and the Sunday brunch is served from 10 a.m. to 2 p.m. (summer on the deck opens at 9:30 a.m.). There is also a unique service—valet boat parking. Reservations suggested. $7-$19. MasterCard, Visa, American Express. 5000 North Lake Boulevard, Carnelian Bay, CA; (916) 546-3366.

### Old Post Office *

This locals' favorite, in a rustic, wood-frame building that used to house the U.S. Mail, makes a first-class breakfast that is based on your own imagination. Using a large selection of ingredients on the menu, you can create your own omelettes, scrambles and potatoes, which are served with fresh-ground coffee and espresso. Lunch includes Mexican tuna melt, Philly beef and lemon chicken, along with homemade chili. This is a non-smoking restaurant. Open daily 6 a.m. to 9 p.m. in summer, and 6 a.m. to 3 p.m. in winter. Breakfast is served until 2 p.m., and lunch is served from 11 a.m. $3-$7. 5245 North Lake Boulevard, Carnelian Bay, CA; (916) 546-3205.

### Other Restaurants

**C.B.'s Pizza:** Pizza, calzones, lasagna, meatball subs and chicken parmesan. $5-$15. MasterCard, Visa, American Express. 5075 North Lake Boulevard, Carnelian Bay, CA; (916) 546-4738.

# Crystal Bay

### Crystal Bay Steak and Lobster House *

The casino isn't much to write home about, but the restaurant is a diamond in the rough. It is a formally appointed room of velvet booths, crystal chandeliers and subdued music. There's an open kitchen to watch the chefs prepare your meal. Featuring steak Diane, prime rib, veal, seafood, nightly specials, tableside flambé desserts and California wines. Free covered parking. Open from 6 p.m. daily. Reservations suggested. $13-$40. American Express, Visa, MasterCard. Crystal Bay Club, Crystal Bay, NV; (702) 831-0512.

### Lakeview Dining Room *

Try for a window table for the fabulous elevated view of Tahoe at one of the lake's most romantic and historic casino hotels. Dinner features linguini primavera, veal and crab dijonaise, salmon bernaise and New York steak au poivre. Frank Sinatra used to own this place, and the rich and famous have cavorted here frequently. For small fry, there's a children's menu. Breakfast served 7 a.m. to 11:30 a.m., lunch served 11:30 a.m. to closing, and dinner served 5:30 p.m. to closing. $2-$19. American Express, Visa, MasterCard. Cal-Neva Lodge, 2 Stateline Road, Crystal Bay, NV; (702) 832-4000.

### Other Restaurants

**Last Chance Joe's Cafe:** Lunch and dinner with prime rib sandwiches, grilled Cajun hot dogs and Awful-Awful Burgers (because it's "awful big and awful good"). $2-$4. Patio of Jim Kelley's Nugget; 20 Highway 28, Crystal Bay, NV; (702) 831-0455.

# Incline Village

## Cafe 333 Restaurant and Espresso Bar **

With its Country French theme and its eclectic menu of Nouveau California cuisine combined with Southwestern, Tuscan and Pacific Rim specials, this small but successful restaurant first developed its reputation as a breakfast house. Muffins and breads are baked fresh daily, and the menu includes something called "breakfast strata," a bread pudding baked with prosciutto, spinach, tomato, basil, marscapone, parmesan cheese and cream. Dinners, recently added, include stuffed breast of chicken, parmesan herb-roasted rack of lamb and grilled filet of beef with gorgonzola butter. Most menu items are available for take-out. This is a non-smoking establishment. Open daily from 7 a.m. to 3 p.m. (breakfast and lunch) and 6 p.m. to 9:30 p.m. Thursday through Monday (dinner). Reservations accepted. $4-$20. Visa, MasterCard. 333 Village Boulevard, Incline Village, NV; (702) 832-7333.

## China Chef *

This is a mainstay of Incline Village, with tasty and piquant Cantonese and Szechuan cuisine—minus the MSG—prepared by longtime owner and chef Kwong Chiong. Menu items include sizzling wor bar (a combination of pork, chicken, shrimp and scallops with vegetables), mu shu pork and Cantonese shrimp chow mein. A full bar, take-out and delivery are available. Lunch is 11:30 a.m. to 3 p.m., and dinner is 4:30 p.m. to 10 p.m. $5-$25. Visa, MasterCard, American Express. At the Christmas Tree Shopping Center, 874 Tahoe Boulevard, Incline Village, NV; (702) 831-9090.

## Ciao Mein Trattoria **

This elegant restaurant in the Hyatt Regency is one of Lake Tahoe's finest dining experiences, combining Pacific Rim and Italian influences in a single meal. The menu features carpaccio appetizer, cappellini pasta primavera, stir-fry shiitake mushrooms, Mongolian beef and twin tournedos of beef. No cigar or pipe smoking is allowed. Reservations accepted. $4-$19. All major credit cards accepted. In the Hyatt Regency, on Country Club Drive at Lakeshore Drive in Incline Village, NV; (702) 832-1234.

## Desperado's Saloon and Grill *

It's a woodsy, funky, family place, with a Wild West ambience, which doesn't necessary meld with ritzy Incline Village. Also, the menu is a long way from basic American fare, since it has Greek salad, fettuccini and Thai pizza. Are they trying to please everyone? Well, if somebody wants smoked ribs, and somebody wants homemade lobster and crab raviolis, and somebody wants Hawaiian pizza, who cares if this is a restaurant in search of a theme? Fortunately the food is ample and delicious, and the atmosphere is casual. Desperado's serves lunch, dinner, Sunday brunch and weekend breakfasts. Open from 11 a.m. to whenever they choose to close, which is usually late. $4-$20. Visa, MasterCard, American Express, Carte Blanche, Diners Club, Discover. 570 Lakeshore at Highway 28, Incline Village, NV; (702) 832-2225.

## Hacienda de la Sierra *

Bring your appetite here. Dine in a tropical setting, with ample amounts of traditional Mexican food, featuring grilled shrimp fajitas, seafood chimichangas and deep fried ice cream. A full bar (Happy Hour includes free appetizers), take-out, a children's menu, live music, an outside deck and banquet facilities are available. Open daily with lunch from 11:30 a.m. and dinner from 5 p.m. $4-$12. American Express, MasterCard, Visa. Across the street from Raley's in Incline Village. 931 Tahoe Boulevard, Incline Village, NV; (702) 831-8300.

## La Ferme *

Country French ambience with candlelight dining create the setting for Gilles LaGourgue and Yves Gigot's specialities, including homemade smoked salmon, warm goat cheese salad, chicken pot au feu, rack of lamb, duckling leg confit and roasted chicken breast in honey and apple juice. A full non-smoking bar serves appetizers, desserts and capuccino. The cocktail bar opens at 5 p.m. and dinner is served from 5:30 p.m. to 9:30 p.m. Tuesday through Sunday. Reservations required. Entrées from $18. American Express, Visa, MasterCard. At Christmas Tree Village. 868 Tahoe Boulevard, Incline Village, NV; (702) 832-3027.

## La Fondue *

Swiss-style European charm envelopes this restaurant, and the menu features baked brie, Holstein schnitzel and 12 different Swiss fondues, including bourguignon, Alpine cheese, chocolate and ice cream. All entrées are served with soup and salad. Open 6 p.m. to 11 p.m. Wednesday through Monday. $18-$28. Visa, MasterCard, American Express. Across from the Hyatt Regency at 120 Country Club Drive #66, Incline Village, NV; (702) 831-6104.

## Le Bistro Restaurant and Bar *

This cozy French restaurant in a woodsy setting, operated by Jean-Pierre and Sylvia Doignon, usually offers four entrées a night, such as fresh grilled Pacific halibut, chausson of duck with broiled sweatbread, tournedos of Black Angus, and noisette of domestic lamb. Open 5:30 p.m. to 11:30 p.m. Wednesday through Monday. $5-$13. American Express,

Visa, MasterCard. Located across from the Hyatt Regency. 120 Country Club Drive, Suite 29, Incline Village, NV; (702) 831-0800.

## Lone Eagle Grille *

The Hyatt Regency's new lakeside restaurant (replacing Hugo's) opened in early 1995 and features barbecue salmon, New York steak, prime rib and Lake Superior whitefish. There are a few creative touches, such as an appetizer of Pacific Dungeness crab cakes with fresh red onions and sweet bell pepper. Open 11:30 a.m. to 9:15 p.m. (last seating) daily for lunch and dinner. Reservations required. $9-$19. All major credit cards accepted. In the Hyatt Regency, on Country Club Drive at Lakeshore Drive in Incline Village, NV; (702) 832-1234.

## Marie France *

Owner Marie Baudry offers romantic, fireside dining and creative, light French cuisine, such as ravioli of snails poached in a champagne sauce, onion Roquefort soup in a crust, confit of duck, stuffed salmon filet en papillotte and marinated three meat in crust au Grand Marnier. Dessert specialties include crepes suzettes and soufflés. Lunch is served from 11 a.m. to 2:30 p.m. Monday through Friday, and dinner is served from 6 p.m. daily. $17-$27. All major credit cards accepted. 907 Tahoe Boulevard, Incline Village, NV; (702) 832-3007.

## Spatz *

The panoramic view of Lake Tahoe alone is worth the drive up Ski Way to dine at Erwin Baur's elegant restaurant perched on a hill below Diamond Peak Ski Resort. With an emphasis on Northern Italian cuisine, the restaurant has a prodigious wine cellar (over 180 labels), and special entrées include chicken caprice, thrice-cooked duckling and beef Wellington. During holiday weekends, there's a fixed-price menu with a choice of four entrées. This restaurant also has a full espresso bar and an outdoor deck with more scenic vistas. Entertainment holds forth Thursday through Saturday. Dinner is served from 5 p.m. to 9 p.m. daily, lunch (summer only) from 11 a.m. to 2 p.m. daily. Happy Hour is from 5 p.m. to 7 p.m. Monday through Friday. Reservations advised. $15-$22. American Express, MasterCard, Visa. 341 Ski Way, Incline Village, NV; (702) 831-8999.

## Stanley's *

Though architecturally uninteresting—you could mistake it for a glorified coffee shop—this restaurant has been a popular tradition for over 20 years with its reasonable prices, diverse menu and well-prepared dishes. Entrées include black and blue Ahi tuna, chicken primavera, beef stroganoff à la Stanley and some of the best pastas at the lake, such as

Greek pasta, Italian pasta and Sicilian seafood pasta. Serving breakfast, lunch and dinner. Live acoustic music every Friday night. Open 8 a.m. to 2:30 p.m. (lunch) and 5:30 p.m. to 10 p.m. (dinner). Reservations recommended. $5-$18. American Express, MasterCard, Visa. Across from the Incline Village Championship Course. 941 Tahoe Boulevard, Incline Village, NV; (702) 831-9944.

## Other Restaurants

***A Country Store and Deli:*** Sandwiches, drinks and groceries. Free delivery to Hyatt Regency guests with a $20 minimum order. $2-$5. 120 Country Club Drive, Suite 28, Incline Village, NV; (702) 831-1144.

***Austin's:*** Home-cooked breakfast, lunch and dinner. $3-$16. Visa, MasterCard, American Express, Diners Club. 120 Country Club Drive #61, Incline Village, NV; (702) 832-7778.

***Azzara's:*** Complete Italian dinners, featuring pasta, poultry, veal, seafood and pizza. $8-$13. MasterCard, Visa. At Raley's in Incline Village. 930 Tahoe Boulevard, Incline Village, NV; (702) 831-0346.

***Chinese Flower Drum:*** Specializing in Mandarin cuisine. $4-$13. All major credit cards accepted. Across from the Hyatt Regency. 120 Country Club Drive #24, Incline Village, NV; (702) 831-7734.

***Las Panchitas:*** Authentic, somewhat predictable Mexican food. $7-$16. Visa, MasterCard, American Express. One of two locations at Tahoe. 930 Tahoe Boulevard, Incline Village, NV; (702) 831-4048.

***Mofo's Pizza:*** New York-style pizza. $7-$16. American Express, MasterCard, Visa, checks. At Christmas Tree Village, 868 Tahoe Boulevard #23, Incline Village, NV; (702) 831-4999.

***Newsbreak Cafe:*** Breakfast, lunch and dinner. $4-$8. MasterCard, Visa. 901 Tahoe Boulevard, Incline Village, NV; (702) 831-8599.

***Rookie's Sports Bar and Grill:*** The best burger joint in Incline, featuring half-pound heavyweight burgers with names such as Heisman, End Zone and Matador. Open 24 hours. $2-$5. Visa, MasterCard. At Raley's in Incline Village. 930 Tahoe Boulevard, Incline Village, NV; (702) 831-9008.

***Sierra Cafe:*** Open 24 hours daily. Reservations accepted. $6-$16. All major credit cards accepted. In the Hyatt Regency on Country Club Drive at Lakeshore Drive, Incline Village, NV; (702) 832-1234.

***Sierra Nevada Pizza:*** This outfit will bring your pizza to the golf course (how gauche!) or to the local beaches. $4-$17. Visa, MasterCard. In For the Good Times, 881 Tahoe Boulevard, Incline Village, NV; (702) 831-8666.

***T's Mesquite Rotisserie:*** Mesquite roasted chicken (Yucatan or soy lime marinades), sandwiches and burritos are featured. $4-$15. Cash and traveler's checks accepted. 901 Tahoe Boulevard, Incline Village, NV; (702) 831-2832.

**Uptown Cafe and Cocktail Lounge:** Dinner only. $6-$19. Visa, MasterCard. 907 Tahoe Boulevard, Incline Village, NV; (702) 831-0404.

**Wildflower Cafe:** Daily breakfast specials and lunch. Senior citizen discounts available. $3-$7. 869 Tahoe Boulevard, Incline Village, NV; (702) 831-8072.

# Kings Beach

### Bobby's Cafe *

It may look like a nondescript cafe for the Old Brockway Golf Course, but the ribs here can stand on their own anywhere. Lunch may not help you hit a hole-in-one, but it'll give you the fortitude to climb up and down the hills. The menu features Danish baby back ribs, sliced brisket of beef, lobster salad roll on a grilled bun, and hot chunks of Maine lobster meat with drawn butter. Serving breakfast, lunch and dinner. Open 7 a.m. to 10 p.m. daily. $2-$22. MasterCard, Visa, American Express. At the intersection of highways 28 and 267. 7900 North Lake Boulevard, Kings Beach, CA; (916) 546-2329.

### Cantina Los Tres Hombres *

One of two locations, this restaurant is always a hit with skiers, who need all the help they can get to warm their toes. The comfortable Mexican setting includes ample portions of fajitas grande, chile Colorado and carnitas. Open 11:30 a.m. to 10:30 p.m. daily. $5-$19. Visa, MasterCard, American Express. 8791 North Lake Boulevard, Kings Beach, CA; (916) 546-4052.

### Jason's Saloon and Grille *

Perched on the lake at Kings Beach State Recreation Area, this popular and informal haunt features American classics and regional favorites, such as giant Gulf prawns, snapper dijon, teriyaki chicken and a 12-foot-long salad bar. There are sweeping lake views from the deck, and validated parking is available. $5-$16. Visa, MasterCard, American Express. 8338 North Lake Boulevard, Kings Beach, CA; (916) 546-3315.

### Lanza's *

If you've got the whole family, a hearty appetite and no desire to dress up, this longtime Tahoe favorite will fill the bill. The traditional Italian menu includes stuffed lumaconi (beef, cheese, and spinach filling), calamari, lasagna, chicken milanese, Italian and California wines, and homemade spumoni. Full bar service (Happy Hour begins at 4:30 p.m. with free pizza slices). Dinner is served from 5 p.m. $8-$15. Visa, Master-Card. 7739 North Lake Boulevard, Kings Beach, CA; (916) 546-2434.

## Soule Domain *

This wonderfully romantic log cabin restaurant specializes in piquant sauces, yet many entrées are low in fat and calories. Try the baby bitter greens with bacon and walnut oil dressing, gorgonzola cheese, sliced pears, candied pecans and balsamic vinegar. Nouveau California cuisine is the mainstay, and the menu includes seven different fresh pastas a day. Other gourmet dishes are grilled Hawaiian ahi tuna, veal marsala picatta and fresh vegetables baked in a pastry shell with Swiss cheese, herbs, roasted garlic and tomato cream sauce. Dinner is served 6 p.m. to 10 p.m. daily. Reservations requested. $13-$22. MasterCard, Visa, American Express. Across from the Tahoe Biltmore Lodge and Casino. 9983 Cove Avenue, Kings Beach, CA; (916) 546-7529.

## Steamer's Beachside Bar and Oven

Borrowing from the Old Tahoe ambience, when elegant passenger steamships plied the lake with ladies and gents, this casual shoreside eatery specializes in hand-tossed pizzas, calzones, oven-baked Louisiana hot sausage and turnover sandwiches stuffed with a blend of cheeses, meats, tomatoes and red onions. The restaurant features upper deck dining, an outdoor heated bar and take-out service for those sultry days on the beach. Open 11 a.m. to 11 p.m. daily. $5-$19. Visa, MasterCard. 8290 North Lake Boulevard, Kings Beach, CA; (916) 546-2218.

### *Other Restaurants*

***The Char-Pit:*** Espresso drinks and croissants in the morning and salads, barbecue sandwiches, hamburgers and hot dogs in the afternoon. Happy Hour nightly. $2-$7. 8732 North Lake Boulevard, Kings Beach, CA; (916) 546-3171.

***Hiro Sushi:*** Japanese cuisine, featuring all-you-can-eat sushi dinners. $8-$19. 8159 North Lake Boulevard, Kings Beach, CA; (916) 546-HIRO.

***Las Panchitas:*** Authentic Mexican food. A children's menu (under 12) is available. $4-$16. Visa, MasterCard, American Express. One of two locations at Tahoe. 8345 North Lake Boulevard, Kings Beach, CA; (916) 546-4539.

# Tahoe City

## Bacchi's Inn

Talk about longevity—this popular place has been operated by the same family since 1932, and the menu has stayed consistent. The restaurant serves robust dishes with a rich (and sometimes overwhelming) tomato sauce and a winning, homemade minestrone soup. Don't look for calorie-savers here. The menu has 43 dinner entrées, and a banquet room is available. The bar opens at 4 p.m., the dining room at 5:30 p.m. Reservations suggested. $9-$36. MasterCard, Visa, American Express. Off Highway 28 near Dollar Point, two miles northeast of Tahoe City. 2905 Lake Forest Road, Tahoe City, CA; (916) 583-3324.

## Black Bear Tavern

Taste Old Tahoe in this 1933 building of peeled logs and antique oil lamps, complete with full bar and easy parking. And keep an eye out for old Bruin, 'cause bears have been known to come down from the woods and check out the menu. Dinner includes sizzling top sirloin steak grilled with garlic and cracked peppercorns, calamari steak, fusilli primavera, and local favorites such as Joanna's meatloaf, beef stew and chicken pot pie. The restaurant is a convenient stop on the West Shore Bike Path, a fact that is not lost to the cycling crowd. Lunch is served noon to 3 p.m. weekdays, dinner from 5 p.m. to 9:30 p.m. daily, and brunch served 9 a.m. to 2:30 p.m. on weekends. Reservations accepted. $10-$19. Visa, MasterCard. 2255 West Lake Boulevard, Tahoe City, CA; (916) 583-8626.

## Bluewater Brewing Company

This place is hard to find because it's in the back of a shopping center, but the North Shore's only microbrewery has become popular with the beer-drinking crowd. Inside you'll notice its modern, bleached pine interior, its requisite view of the tanks through oversized glass windows, and its small restaurant. The menu features handcrafted fresh ales (you can try all of them in small samplers), Hungarian goulash, chicken satay, black beans and rice, and chicken and sausage jambalaya. Try the St. Patrick's Pale Ale if you like light amber beers. This is a non-smoking establishment. Open 11 a.m. to 1:30 a.m. $5-$8. Visa, MasterCard. At Lighthouse Shopping Center. 850 North Lake Boulevard, Tahoe City, CA; (916) 581-BLUE.

## Christy Hill **

Owner and chef Matt Adams has developed a deservedly strong following at Tahoe, and this delightful lakeside dinner house serves some of the best gourmet food in the basin. You can make a meal of the appetizers alone, choosing from Maryland soft-shell crab sautéed with toasted hazelnuts, garlic and brown butter, tiger prawns sautéed with sun-dried tomato in a lemon, garlic and butter cream sauce, and three-cheese ravioli with a fresh sage, roasted garlic and sun-dried tomato demi-cream sauce. Hungry yet? Now move on to the main course, if you can. The menu features broiled, farm-raised New England elk loin with Chanterelle mushrooms, stuffed grilled eggplant, and Canadian pintelle sautéed with fresh figs in an amaretto demi-glace. This is a non-smoking establishment. Dinner is served from 5:30 p.m. (closed Monday). At Lakehouse Mall. Reservations suggested. $19-$24. Visa, MasterCard. 115 Grove Street, Tahoe City, CA; (916) 583-8551.

## Coyote's Mexican Grill *

This is a small place, with an emphasis on take-out orders, though there are a few tables inside and outside. The Mexican food is good, and is prepared without lard or preservatives. Fresh menu items include fajitas, homemade salsa, vegetarian dishes, and microbrewed beers. A children's menu is available, and phone orders are welcome. Open 10 a.m. to 10 p.m. weekly, serving lunch and dinner. $4-$7. 521 North Lake Boulevard, Tahoe City, CA; (916) 583-6653.

## Eggschange *

For a breakfast house, this place has one of the best views on the North Shore, right above the lake. Home-style cooking with a few interesting twists includes eggplant omelette, mountain mush (oats, walnuts, raisins, brown sugar and fresh fruit), fresh-baked muffins in a basket, an espresso bar and fresh-squeezed specialty juices (including honeydew, pineapple, orange and grapefruit). Great daily specials available. Open 7 a.m. to 2 p.m. daily. $4-$8. All major credit cards accepted. 120 Grove Street, Tahoe City, CA; (916) 583-2225.

## Fire Sign Cafe *

This is an unassuming place, but it's one of the locals' hangouts, particularly for breakfast. The menu also features teriyaki steak, turkey club, chicken salad sandwich and veggie potato. Open 7 a.m. to 3 p.m. daily. $4-$7. Visa, MasterCard. 1785 West Lake Boulevard, Tahoe City, CA; (916) 583-0871.

## Grazie Ristorante and Bar *

This is a large, lively, attractive and popular restaurant near the waterfront, but the place sometimes seems overwhelmed on weekends and, as a result, both service and food can be uneven. There are several dining rooms and a central kitchen that is visible to diners. The bar has a cozy fireplace and an interesting tile mural of a fish on the wall above it. The Italian menu offers creative items such as soft-shell crab, deep fried and served on house-baked focaccia with a dill-oregano tartar sauce, and house pasta such as paglia e fieno carbonara—green and white linguini, cream, peas, prosciutto, asiago cheese and fresh basil. Other entrées include osso bucco traditionale, cappelini vongole and pollo roti. Sauces are sometimes on the bland side. Dinner is served daily, and lunch is served from 11:30 a.m. Friday through Monday. $6-$18. All major credit cards accepted. At Roundhouse Mall. 700 North Lake Boulevard, Tahoe City, CA; (916) 583-0233.

## Hacienda Del Lago *

Picturesque views of Lake Tahoe with spicy Mexican entrées are the forte at this attractive restaurant. The menu features fajitas (beef, chicken, turkey and shrimp), chimichangas and 11 combination dinners, including the El Grande. The full bar has just about every flavor of frozen margaritas. Open 5 p.m. to 10 p.m. daily, Happy Hour from 4 p.m. to 6 p.m. $6-$9. Visa, MasterCard. In the Boatworks Mall. 760 North Lake Boulevard, Tahoe City, CA; (916) 583-0358.

## The Naughty Dawg Saloon and Grill *

This is a lively après-ski and après-beach hangout that is popular with twentysomethings. Decorated with a Dalmatian theme, and its walls plastered with snapshots of the owners' dogs, this high-energy bar and grill features some unique items. Try the mixed drinks served in a dog bowl. Then try the quesadilla el Naughto Dawgo, the French poodle brie sandwich, the fish tacos, the snow crab pita, the Cajun catfish sandwich, the Pit Bull bacon burger or the "dirt" dessert (crushed Oreos, Kahlua cake, whipped cream and chocolate pudding). That "dirt" alone will have you howling at the moon all night. Open 11:30 a.m. to 11 p.m. daily, with the bar open until 2 a.m. $3-$13. Visa, MasterCard, American Express. 255 North Lake Boulevard, Tahoe City, CA; (916) 581-DAWG.

## Jake's on the Lake

This is a formulaic, fairly predictable place, with its mixture of steaks, seafood and chicken. But with its reasonable prices and delightful lake views, it has endured in popularity. The menu includes prosciutto basil prawns, Hawaiian swordfish, ginger chicken, scampi and a desert called "Kimo's Original Hula Pie." Seafood specials change frequently. Breakfast, lunch, and Sunday brunch are served from 10 a.m. to 2:30 p.m., and dinner is served nightly from 5:30 p.m. to 10:30 p.m. $5-$35. American Express, Visa, MasterCard. At the Boatworks Mall. 780 North Lake Boulevard, Tahoe City, CA; (916) 583-0188.

## Pfeifer House **

Remember the 1982 movie *Forbidden Love* with Yvette Mimieux and Andrew Stevens? No? I thought not. Anyway, scenes were shot here. But that shouldn't be the reason to dine at one of Tahoe's oldest restaurants (established in 1939). The reason should be the excellence that Gold Medal winner Franz Fassbender, who moved here from Germany in the 1960s, brings to every course he serves. This is a low-light kind of place, with lots of Old European ambience. The menu includes pepper steak, leg of lamb with garlic butter, duckling with orange sauce and veal picatta. All dinners are served with soup and salad. Cocktails are served from 5 p.m., dinner from 5:30 p.m. to 10 p.m. Wednesday through Monday. Reservations advised. $12-$50. Visa, MasterCard, American Express, Carte Blanche (no personal checks accepted). One-quarter mile north of Tahoe City on Highway 89. 760 River Road, Tahoe City, CA; (916) 583-3102.

## River Ranch Lodge *

When water is released from Lake Tahoe in late spring and early summer, it comes kicking down the Truckee River like a herd of mustangs. This restaurant, part of an attractive country inn and one of the North Shore's most popular hangouts, is a warm, inviting place for dinner. There's a nice touch with the bar—it protrudes over the river, allowing you to check out the trout. The menu includes fresh fish and game, with Idaho rainbow trout, Miwok salmon, roasted fresh elk loin, flame-broiled steak and roasted free-range chicken. This is a non-smoking establishment. The riverside patio, open during the summer, often features name jazz groups and other entertainment, and also is available for private parties. River Ranch is at the end of a popular cycling and skating trail. $11-$25. Visa, MasterCard, Diners Club. On Highway 89 and Alpine Meadows Road. 2285 River Road, Tahoe City, CA; (916) 583-4264.

## Rosie's Cafe

This family-style place has rib-sticking food, and it's a longtime favorite with the locals. House specialties include Southern fried chicken, Yankee pot roast, fresh seafood and stir-fry chicken. A children's menu and full bar are available, and there's live entertainment after dinner. Open daily from 8 a.m. to 10 p.m., serving breakfast, lunch and dinner, and the bar is open until 2 a.m. $4-$18. Visa, MasterCard, American Express, Discover. 571 North Lake Boulevard, Tahoe City, CA; (916) 583-8504.

## Sunnyside Lodge Restaurant *

This is an elegant and romantic lakeside lodge with the Old Tahoe-style architecture of stone and wood-beam ceilings. Its handful of guest rooms are always full, and its restaurant is always crowded, so forget about just "dropping in." Employees have a habit of being brusque with those who do so. The menu features New York steak, Pacific king salmon, Hawaiian mahi mahi, fettuccini with seafood and ginger chicken. There's always a special dessert of the day. Open 5:30 p.m. to 9:30 p.m. daily (bar open until midnight). Don't even think about coming here without reservations. $13-$19. All major credit cards accepted. At Sunnyside Marina. 1850 West Lake Boulevard, Tahoe City, CA; (916) 583-7200.

## Tahoe House Restaurant and Backerei **

Family-owned and operated since 1977, this is not only one of the lake's best dinner houses, it's also the best bakery in Tahoe City. Heart-smart Swiss and California cuisine such as garlic linguine with applewood smoked chicken, veal Tahoe House (with marsala wine, ripe tomatoes and demi-glace), cordon bleu, wiener schnitzel and seafood risotto will whet your appetite. Save room for dessert, because chef Peter Vogt's rich creations (from homemade chocolate truffles to elegant tortes) will be irresistible. All dinners and desserts are available for take-out. The bakery (take-out only) is open daily from 8 a.m. to 10 p.m., and dinner is served from 5 p.m. to 10 p.m. Reservations advised. $7-$18. Visa, American Express, MasterCard. On Highway 89. 625 West Lake Boulevard, Tahoe City, CA; (916) 583-1377.

## Wolfdale's **

The structure that houses this restaurant is nearly a century old, having been built at Glenbrook and barged to the present location in 1901, next to the lake. Douglas Dale, the owner and chef, calls his menu "cuisine unique," because it has touches of Asian cooking and California cuisine. The menu includes light and creative fare such as Thai-barbecued chicken over kale and jasmine rice, alder-wood-roasted Columbia River sturgeon, fresh and wild mushroom pasta with broccoflower, and marinated and grilled venison loin with demi-glaze and a purée of fennel and Jerusalem artichokes. Try the spicy red pepper soup with a grilled tomatillo onion relish, or a starter of Dungeness crab cakes with a wasabi-sour cream sauce. Yum! Dinner is served from 6 p.m. Wednesday through Monday, with the bar opening at 5:30 p.m. Reservations accepted. $12-$19. MasterCard, Visa. 640 North Lake Boulevard, Tahoe City, CA; (916) 583-5700.

## Za's *

It's inexpensive, it labels itself "a simple Italian restaurant," and the locals rave about it. For nibbling, try the garlic chips, polenta with mushrooms, baked eggplant and fresh mozzarella and roma tomatoes. Main courses include smoked chicken calzone, rotini and sausage, roasted red pepper pizza and clams linguine. Anyplace that serves a gelato cannoli for dessert has got to be a hit. Dinner is served from 4:30 p.m. (closed Tuesday). $6-$10. No credit cards accepted. 395 North Lake Boulevard, Tahoe City, CA; (916) 583-1812.

## Other Restaurants

***A.J.'s Noodle Company:*** Italian deli with gourmet to-go pastas, pizzas (you bake them) and calzones. Picnic baskets available. $4-$7. In the Henrickson Building, at the entrance to the Tahoe City Golf Course. 255 North Lake Tahoe Boulevard #C, Tahoe City, CA; (916) 583-1947.

***Fast Eddie's Texas-Style BBQ:*** Family-style barbecue, with vegetarian cuisine, a salad bar, take-out and a children's menu. $2-$13. All major credit cards accepted. 690 North Lake Boulevard, Tahoe City, CA; (916) 583-0950.

***Galley Cafe:*** Breakfast, lunch and dinner. Children's half portions are available. $4-$16. Visa, MasterCard. At Roundhouse Mall. 700 North Lake Boulevard, Tahoe City, CA; (916) 581-3305.

***Lakehouse Pizza:*** A bar and grill, with a patio and take-out service. $6-$21. American Express, Visa, MasterCard. 120 Grove Street, Tahoe City, CA; (916) 583-2222.

***Willii B's:*** Specialties include seafood jambalaya, house-smoked barbecued ribs and an oyster bar. Reservations accepted. $4-$19. MasterCard, Visa, Discover. On Highway 89, south of the Lucky market on Fanny Bridge. 125 West Lake Boulevard, Tahoe City, CA; (916) 583-0346.

***Yama Sushi & Robata Grill:*** Japanese cuisine. At Lighthouse Shopping Center on Highway 28. Reservations accepted. $5-$22. Visa, MasterCard, American Express. 950 North Lake Boulevard, Tahoe City, CA; (916) 583-YAMA.

# Tahoe Vista

## Sunsets on the Lake *
### (formerly AJ's Ristorante)

Northern Italian cuisine is the mainstay at this lakeside restaurant. Main courses include Dungeness crab cannelloni, spit-roasted garlic chicken cooked over olive wood, and gourmet pizzas cooked in an olive-wood-burning oven. Happy Hour is 5 p.m. to 6:30 p.m. Dinner is served 5:30 p.m. to 9 p.m., and Sunday brunch is served 9:30 a.m. to 2 p.m. (holidays and summers only). Reservations accepted. $10-$23. Visa, MasterCard, American Express. At North Tahoe Marina, one mile west of Highway 267. 7320 North Lake Boulevard, Tahoe Vista, CA; (916) 546-3640.

## Captain Jon's *

Seafood and fireside dining with a quaint, nautical atmosphere have created strong repeat business for this restaurant. Country French seafood cuisine (fresh fish in unique delicate sauces) includes items such as salmon en croute, scampi and scallops shiitake. Starters include seafood feuille-tage—scallops, shrimp and crab baked in a Chardonnay cream sauce and served over a puff pastry shell. Open 5:30 p.m. to 9 p.m. Tuesday through Sunday. Reservations accepted. Entrées from $15. Master-Card, Visa, American Express, Discover, Carte Blanche. Full bar and private room available. 7220 North Lake Tahoe Boulevard in Tahoe Vista, CA; (916) 546-4819.

## Colonel Clair's Tahoe Grill *

Seafood, steaks, prime rib and barbecue ribs are the top choices in this Southern-style restaurant. The menu features barbecued beer shrimp, Cajun jambalaya, Creole fettuccini and hickory-smoked barbecued pork back ribs. You can order combos, such as "The Colonel's Favorite"— barbecued ribs, raspberry-glazed roast duck and spicy-hot barbecued beer shrimp. A children's menu is available. This is a non-smoking restaurant. Breakfast is served from 7:30 a.m., lunch is served from 11:30 a.m., and dinner is served from 5:30 p.m. There's also a Sunday brunch. The Sports Lounge is open daily from 10 a.m. to midnight, with Happy Hour from 4 p.m. to 6 p.m. (half-price drinks). Reservations suggested. $4-$23. 6873 North Lake Boulevard, Tahoe Vista, CA; (916) 546-7358.

## La Playa Restaurant, Bar and Grill **

With a positively inspiring and unimpeded view of the lake, famed Tahoe chef and restaurant mogul Jean Du Fau, who trained at the Bordeaux Culinary Academy in France, emphasizes fresh seafood with his trademark sauces at this establishment (one of three he owns in the area). Lakefront and deck venues are available for patrons to enjoy salmon bernaise, swordfish with beurre blanc sauce, filet mignon with blue cheese and mushroom sauce, fettucini with roasted garlic and walnuts, and specials such as sturgeon, halibut and mahi mahi. Banquets, weddings and Sunday barbecues are available. Lunch is served from 11 a.m. to 3 p.m., and dinner is served from 5 p.m. Reservations accepted. $5-$13. MasterCard, Visa, American Express, Discover. 7046 North Lake Boulevard in Tahoe Vista, CA; (916) 546-5903.

## Le Petit Pier **

Just down the road from La Playa, this is another creation of chef-proprietor Jean Du Fau, and was his first property at Tahoe. Of his three restaurants, this has the most insistently French ambience, with an elegant view of the lake and an award-winning wine list to complement the excellent meals. Appetizers alone could carry a meal here, but you can also get the works, with entrées such as medallions of veal with wild mushrooms, roast duck with blueberries, chateaubriand, medallions of venison with sauce grand veneur. Appetizers include soft-shell crab, sashimi du jour, asparagus feuilletage and paté foie gras. Desserts include baked Alaska, flambés and souflés (ordered in advance). Open 6 p.m. to midnight daily.

Reservations accepted. $17-$25. All major credit cards accepted. 7238 North Lake Boulevard (P.O. Box 48), Tahoe Vista, CA; (916) 546-4464.

## Other Restaurants

**Boulevard Cafe and Trattoria:** Traditional and creative Northern Italian cuisine. Reservations accepted. $8-$15. Visa, MasterCard. 6731 North Lake Boulevard, Tahoe Vista, CA; (916) 546-7213.

**Mustard Seed:** A natural foods market and deli. $3-$5. Visa, Master-Card. 7411 North Lake Boulevard, Tahoe Vista, CA; (916) 546-3525.

**Seedling Cafe:** A Whole Earth-type restaurant. MasterCard, Visa, Discover. 7081 North Lake Boulevard, Tahoe Vista, CA; (916) 546-3936.

# Truckee

## Basque Club Restaurant *

Who says the Basques didn't make it to Tahoe? This restaurant at Northstar resort's golf clubhouse is open in the winter months only. The weekly changing dinner menu includes two entrées, fresh baked bread, homemade soup, tossed salad, Basque beans, vegetable and dessert. Featured entrées include baked salmon with roasted red bell pepper butter, roast leg of lamb with apricot and thyme glaze, and paella (shrimp, mussels, chicken and sausage with saffron rice). Seating is family-style, so plan on interacting with your fellow diners. Children's prices are available. Open weekdays 5 p.m. to 9:30 p.m. and 5 p.m. to 10 p.m. on weekends from December to April only. Reservations suggested. $15-$17. Credit cards accepted. Bar hours are 4 p.m. to 10 p.m. At Northstar-at-Tahoe, on Highway 267 at Northstar Drive, Truckee, CA; (916) 562-2460.

## Cottonwood **

Nothing about the exterior of this place tells you that this may be the best restaurant in Truckee. Ah, but looks can be deceiving. You drive to the top of a hill, past dilapidated seasonal housing, and arrive in front of a squat, weathered building that looks as if it might blow down in the next storm. But inside is a picture of warmth and coziness, and a menu that will delight the palate. There's also a fine view of Commercial Row in Truckee below. The menu changes daily, and includes sautéed prawns with garlic, roasted pork tenderloin with maple and black pepper demi-glace, seafood stew with shellfish and boudin sausage, and starters such as a large caesar salad, grilled homemade sausage with pears and gorgonzola cheese over mixed baby greens, and roasted yellow corn polenta with wild mushrooms and garlic. Children can enjoy a cheeseburger with shoestring fries. Amenities include a funky bar, live jazz entertainment, a patio and a banquet section. Open from 5:30 p.m. daily except Monday. Reservations accepted. $13-$20. Visa, MasterCard. At Hilltop Lodge off Highway 267. 1042 Rue Hill Top, Truckee, CA; (916) 587-5711.

## Engadine Cafe **

This is simply one of the finest and most elegant restaurants in the Tahoe area, and worth the few minutes' drive west of Truckee on Interstate 80. John Slouber, the creator of Royal Gorge Cross Country Ski Resort, owns this delightful Victorian-style bed and breakfast (Rainbow Lodge), and has created an exceptional dinner house. The menu, with European influences (Slouber spent several years in France), includes one of the largest and most interesting wine lists in the region. Among the entrées are medallions of roasted zucchini, apple-glazed chicken, raspberry lamb and fettuccini arrabbiata (a vegetarian dish with mushrooms and sweet peppers in a spicy tomato sauce). Specials on the blackboard might include sole almandine with amaretto sauce and rice pilaf, as well as other seasonal seafood. Healthy heart menu items are available. Open 11 a.m. to 2 p.m. and 5:30 p.m. to 9:30 p.m. daily. $5-$19. Visa, MasterCard. No personal checks. At Royal Gorge's Rainbow Lodge, on Hampshire Rocks Road off Interstate 80, Soda Springs, CA; (916) 426-3661.

## Left Bank **

Tahoe restaurant mogul Jean Du Fau, who owns three places in the region, is usually the chef here, so you can be assured of a fabulous meal when he's in residence (call ahead to find out). This French country-style restaurant in the heart of Truckee's historic district includes salmon grille bernaise, grilled filet mignon, grilled swordfish with blueberry sauce (Du Fau uses berries in just about everything, from salad dressings to sauces and desserts), sautéed prawns Far East-style, and various wild game entrées. Desserts are sinful, and there's a wine bar available. Lunch is served 11:30 a.m. to 3 p.m. and dinner is served 5:30 p.m. to 9:30 p.m. daily except Tuesday. Reservations accepted. $6-$20. All major credit cards accepted. 10096 Commercial Row, Truckee, CA; (916) 587-4694.

## Northwoods Restaurant and Lounge

Situated off the beaten path on the road to the sprawling Tahoe Donner residential community above Truckee, this restaurant is in the rustic Tahoe Donner Clubhouse and features Oriental chicken raviolis, herb and honey roast duckling, stuffed chicken breast and steak Diane. Open from 5:30 p.m. Thursday through Sunday, with the lounge open from 4 p.m. Thursday through Monday. Reservations accepted. $6-$11. MasterCard, Visa. At Tahoe Donner Northwoods Clubhouse. 11509 Northwoods Boulevard, Truckee, CA; (916) 587-9435.

## O'B's Pub and Restaurant *

This is probably as close to the quintessential Truckee eating establishment as you can get, and has been a fixture in town for over 20 years. The place is woodsy, rustic and full of antiques, and has intimately arranged seating. The menu includes quiche of the day, grilled Cajun chicken, fresh pastas and prime rib. A children's menu and fun book are available, and there is a full bar. Open 11:30 a.m. to 3:30 p.m. for lunch and 5:30 p.m. to 10 p.m. for dinner, daily. $4-$16. Visa, MasterCard, Diners Club. There's also a Sunday brunch. 10046 Commercial Row, Truckee, CA; (916) 587-4164.

## The Passage *

This is a favorite locals' restaurant and bar on the ground level of the historic Truckee Hotel. New American and international cuisine features cioppino, jumbo sea scallops and New York Black Angus steak. Open 11:30 a.m. to 3 p.m. for lunch, and 5:30 p.m. to 9:30 p.m. for dinner. $6-$18. Visa, MasterCard. 10007 Commercial Row, Truckee, CA; (916) 587-7619.

## Squeeze In *

Literally a closet of a restaurant, Squeeze In cooks a staggering—and delicious—variety of omelettes. American-style healthy cuisine featuring 57 omelettes (try the "Racy Tracy"), Ecuadoran soup and veggie sandwiches. Open 7 a.m. to 2 p.m. daily. $3-$8. On Commercial Row. 10060 Donner Pass Road, Truckee, CA; (916) 587-9814.

## Timbercreek *

Northstar's year-round dinner house constantly experiments with new entrées, most of them winners. The ambience recreates the logging days of Tahoe and Truckee, and the atmosphere is woodsy but airy. The menu includes Thai chicken, eggplant parmesan and sun-kissed shrimp pasta. Children's menu available. Open daily for breakfast, lunch, and dinner (winter season only). $4-$17. At Northstar-at-Tahoe, on Highway 267 at Northstar Drive, Truckee, CA; (916) 587-0250.

## Truckee Trattoria *

This small but attractive restaurant has Mediterranean-style Italian cuisine that includes frutti di mare (shrimp, scallops and clams in a white wine garlic sauce), chicken fettuccini with garlic cheese sauce, pesto-filled raviolis with gorgonzola cream sauce and sun-dried tomatoes, and chocolate soufflé torte. Daily specials, espresso bar, wine and beer available Indoor dining seats 26, and the outdoor patio opens when weather permits. Open 11:30 a.m. to 9 p.m. Wednesday through Sunday. $4-$8 and up. Visa, MasterCard. At Gateway Shopping Center. 11310-1 Donner Pass Road, Truckee, CA; (916) 582-1266.

## Zena's! *

There's real history oozing from the walls of this place, which is in the vintage C.B. House (built in 1873). The Queen Anne Victorian, at the west end of Commercial Row, is the only building in Truckee to be chosen for the National Register of Historic Places. Beyond that, owner Zena Krakowsky has been called "Truckee's dessert wizard," and sweets are therefore listed at the top of the menu. Consider the possibilities—elderberry-apple pie, cranberry-banana-hazelnut torte, caramel-mocha cheesecake, triple chocolate killer cake and more. Of course, you must eat all of your meal first. The menu includes chicken turkey zauzage quiche, zourdough pancakez, and Mediterranean veggie zandwich (clever thing she does with those "z's", huh?). There's an espresso bar, bakery, cafe and catering service. Open 7 a.m. to 2 p.m. daily (breakfast and lunch), 6 p.m. to 11 p.m. on Wednesday (dinner and live music), and brunch on Saturday and Sunday. $3-$7. American Express, Visa, MasterCard, checks. 10292 Donner Pass Road, Truckee, CA; (916) 587-1771.

### Other Restaurants

**El Toro Bravo:** Mexican and seafood cuisine. $5-$14. American Express, MasterCard, Visa. 10186 Donner Pass Road, Truckee, CA; (916) 587-3557.

**Pedro's:** Open winter season only. $9-$18. At Northstar-at-Tahoe, on Highway 267 at Northstar Drive, Truckee, CA; (916) 587-0245.

**Wong's Garden:** Reservations accepted. $4-$11. MasterCard, Visa, American Express. 11430 Deerfield Drive, Truckee, CA; (916) 587-1831.

# Squaw Valley

## Alexander's *

Yes, there's a mind-boggling view of granite cliffs plunging to the valley. And, yes, it snows here a lot in the winter time. Beyond that, you may see a bungee jumper swinging past your window. Alexander's stands for Alexander Cushing, the owner of Squaw Valley ski area, who has made this his signature restaurant at the top of High Camp, where the tram ride terminates. The menu features salads, hamburgers and nightly dinner specials, such as grilled fish and chicken dishes. Open 11 a.m. to 9 p.m. daily from November to April, weather permitting. Reservations accepted, evening only. $5-$18. All major credit cards accepted. At Squaw Valley Ski Resort. 1960 Squaw Valley Road, Olympic Valley, CA; (916) 583-1742 or (916) 583-2555.

## Cascades *

Located in The Resort at Squaw Creek, this restaurant specializes in buffets for breakfast, lunch and dinner. You can choose from the cold buffet which includes dessert, or have the complete buffet. The dinner menu features pesto-flavored carved turkey with toasted pita bread, home-smoked Pacific sturgeon and blackened rib-eye steak with Cajun relish. A children's menu is available. Reservations suggested. $9-$23. Major credit cards accepted. At The Resort at Squaw Creek, 400 Squaw Creek Road, Olympic Valley, CA; (916) 581-6619 or (800) 327-3353.

## Glissandi **

Expensive, elegant and ample, this is the premier restaurant at The Resort at Squaw Creek, and one of the best on the North Shore. The menu changes seasonally, but might include New Zealand venison with plum and ginger coulis, fresh guinea hen with corn crêpes and black truffle, roast wild boar with peppercorns and chipolte chile, and a nightly selection of fresh fish. Starters, soups and salads also are creative (and pricey), and include salmon ravioli, paté of California rabbit, goat cheese soufflé tartlet, purée of roast yellow tomato with leeks and rouille, and consommé of pheasant with wild rice. If you have to look at your bill when you get it, you can't afford to eat here. Open 6 p.m. to 10 p.m. Tuesday through Saturday, dinner only. $27-$32. MasterCard, Visa, American Express, Diners Club. At The Resort at Squaw Creek, 400 Squaw Creek Road, Olympic Valley, CA; (916) 581-6621.

## Graham's **

This property was the original home of Wayne and Sandy Poulsen, the founders of Squaw Valley USA, and it still operates as a small inn. But the ground floor belongs to Graham Rock, one of Tahoe's most respected restauranteurs and the operator of Chambers Landing restaurant in the summer. Here he serves his signature entrées, known for their Mediterranean influences, and changes the menu frequently. It might include Greek leg of lamb, seafood paella, grilled Mediterranean pork loin, lamb ragout and fusilli con bucco (corkscrew-shaped pasta with fresh artichokes, morel mushrooms and prosciutto di parma in a light cream sauce). Appetizers include melanzane ripiene (grilled eggplant stuffed with zucchini, sundried tomato, basil and fresh buffalo mozzarella), and desserts include daily specials as well as regulars such as tiramisu and fruit strudel. Open 6 p.m. to 10 p.m. Wednesday through Sunday in summer, and Tuesday through Sunday in winter. The wine bar opens in winter at 4:30 p.m. $15-$19. Visa, MasterCard. 1650 Squaw Valley Road, Olympic Valley, CA; (916) 581-0454.

## Other Restaurants

***Bullwhacker's Pub and Steakhouse:*** Old West-style pub serving lunch, dinner and micro-brewed beers. $7-$28. Major credit cards accepted. At The Resort at Squaw Creek. 400 Squaw Creek Road, Olympic Valley, CA; (916) 583-6300 or (916) 581-6617.

***Ristorante Montagna:*** Italian cuisine. All major credit cards accepted. $8-$24. At The Resort at Squaw Creek. 400 Squaw Creek Road, Olympic Valley, CA; (916) 581-6618.

# WEST SHORE

## Norfolk Woods Inn (formerly Alpenhaus) *

This is a small West Shore inn with a cozy restaurant that serves breakfast and dinner in the summer. Dinner highlights include Aussie rack of lamb and peach scampi. A children's menu, wine and micro-brewed beers are available. Breakfast is served from 7:30 a.m. and dinner is served from 5:30 p.m. to 9:30 p.m. in summer. Limited schedule in winter. Reservations accepted. $4-$18. Visa, MasterCard, American Express. 6941 West Lake Boulevard, Tahoma, CA; (916) 525-5000.

## Chambers Landing **

Chef Graham Rock has a strong local following, and deservedly so, with his creative sauces and cuisine from the Mediterranean, southern Spain, southern France, Italy, Greece and Northern Africa. This summer-only restaurant features Catalan romeso (fish stew), veal saltimbocca and grilled duck breast. Open 11:30 a.m. to 2:30 p.m. for lunch, 6 p.m. to 10 p.m. for dinner, and 9:30 a.m. to 2:30 p.m. for Sunday brunch. The bar is open daily from noon to midnight. Happy hour is from 5 p.m. to 7 p.m. nightly. Reservations accepted. $16-$19. Visa, MasterCard. Seven miles south of Tahoe City. 6300 Chambers Lodge Road, Homewood, CA; (916) 525-7262.

## Swiss Lakewood **

Helga and Albert Marty have created an institution on the West Shore, and they've got a bushel of culinary awards to show for their efforts. With its European stylings, wine cellar dining nook (the special place of the house; seats 12) and cozy environs, this restaurant has a lot to recommend it. You almost expect the waiters to yodel. The menu includes roast duck with orange sauce, pepper steak flambé, beefsteak tartar, and escalopes de chevreuil (grilled escalopes of venison with glazed chestnuts and balsamic vinegar-lingonberry sauce). Desserts include cherries jubilee flambé and Grand Marnier soufflé. This is a non-smoking restaurant and bar. Open from 5:30 p.m. daily, except for Monday, and open for weekends only in winter. Open on holidays. $13-$20. MasterCard, Visa. Swiss

Lakewood Lodge, 5055 West Lake Boulevard, Homewood, CA; (916) 525-5211.

### West Side Pizza *

Small but tantalizingly good. Specializing in gourmet pizzas, pastas and chicken. Open 2 p.m. to 9 p.m. Monday through Thursday, and noon to 9 p.m. on Saturday and Sunday. Closed Tuesday. $5-$17. Across from Obexer's Marina. 5335 West Lake Boulevard, Homewood, CA; (916) 525-6464.

### *Other Restaurants*

*Old Tahoe Cafe:* Home-style cooking. $4-$7. 5335 West Lake Boulevard, Homewood, CA; (916) 525-5437.

## SOUTH SHORE

### The Beacon Restaurant *

There's always some good vibes here, including the jazz, blues and folk bands that play on the outside deck. This beachfront restaurant at Richardson's Resort, right on the shore, boasts lake and sunset views and serves lunch, dinner and brunch (Saturday and Sunday). The dinner menu features macadamia nut prawns, crab feast, scampi Italiano, fresh lake trout and fettucini primavera. This is a non-smoking establishment. Open from 11 a.m. weekdays, 10 a.m. to 3 p.m. on weekends for lunch, and 5 p.m. to 9:30 p.m. for dinner. $6-$25. Visa, MasterCard. No personal checks. At Richardson's Resort. 1900 Jameson Beach Road, South Lake Tahoe, CA; (916) 541-0630.

### The Broiler Room *

This traditional steakhouse features grilled New York steak, Jack Daniel's barbecued shrimp, Louisiana seafood gumbo, and Cajun dessert. The wine list has been honored by *Wine Spectator* magazine for the past three years. Open 6 p.m. to 11 p.m. nightly. Reservations accepted. $6-$30. Accepts all major credit cards. At Caesar's Tahoe. 55 US 50, Stateline, NV; (702) 586-2044.

### Cafe Andreotti *

This casino restaurant with a bistro-style atmosphere has a quality menu, with gourmet pizzas (Santa Fe chicken, Philly cheesesteak and backyard barbecue), spinach fettuccini and clams, and San Francisco cioppino. Party and banquet facilities are available. Open 5:30 p.m. to 10 p.m. daily except Tuesday, and 5:30 p.m. to 11 p.m. Friday and Saturday. $10-$15. Major credit cards accepted. At Harrah's Casino Hotel on US 50, Stateline, NV; (702) 588-6611.

### Cafe Fiore *

This tiny and intimate Italian restaurant has atmosphere and great cuisine such as eggplant crêpes (appetizer), scaloppine Milanese, fettuccini Alfredo and cappellini bocconcini. Outdoor dining is available (and virtually the only option if there are more than 15 people inside). This is a non-smoking establishment. Open from 5:30 p.m. daily. Reservations recommended. $13-$21. American Express, MasterCard, Visa. 1169 Ski Run Boulevard (at Tamarack), South Lake Tahoe, CA; (916) 541-2908.

### Cantina Los Tres Hombres *

Traditional Mexican ambience combines with reasonable prices at this popular restaurant. Authentic Mexican food features shrimp legumbres, chicken fajitas and veggie skewers. There's a full bar (and giant margaritas), and smoking is prohibited. Banquets and occasional entertainment are available. Open 11:30 a.m. to 10:30 p.m. daily. Reservations recommended. $5-$19. Visa, MasterCard, American Express. 765 Emerald Bay Road, South Lake Tahoe, CA; (916) 544-1233.

### Christiana Inn *

This European country inn across the street from Heavenly ski area serves elegant gourmet meals in a romantic, candlelit setting. The menu features classic beef Wellington, Long Island duck and shrimp scampi, and the staff and kitchen seem to be at their best in winter. Tahoe Sunset specials are available Sunday to Thursday, 5:30 p.m. to 7:30 p.m. The wine list falls short of expectations, but there's a large and terrific après-ski bar. This is a non-smoking establishment, and banquet facilities are available. Open 5:30 p.m. to 10 p.m. daily. Reservations suggested. $16-$25. Visa, MasterCard. 3819 Saddle Road, South Lake Tahoe, CA; (916) 544-7337.

### Dixon's

Contemporary American cuisine is combined with fresh Italian pastas and Southwestern/Mexican dishes, an unusual mix. The menu features salmon dill linguini, half chicken Santa Fe, angel-hair pasta, turkey burrito and shrimp scampi. The bar serves 13 microbreweries on tap, and there is live weekend entertainment. Open 11:30 a.m. to 3 p.m. for lunch and 5 p.m. to 9:30 p.m. for dinner daily. $6-$12. 675 Emerald Bay Road, South Lake Tahoe, CA; (916) 542-3389.

### The Dory's Oar *

This authentic Cape Cod cottage gets you in the mood for most anything fishy, including live Maine lobster and seafood from both coasts—stuffed baked whole baby salmon, charbroiled swordfish and deep fried soft-shell crabs from Chesapeake Bay. There are also four different steak selections. The Captain's Roost lounge is a full bar. Open from 5 p.m. nightly. $12-$45. All major credit cards accepted. 1041 Fremont Avenue, South Lake Tahoe, CA; (916) 541-6603.

## The Eagle's Nest Restaurant and Jazz Club

On a hill high above South Lake Tahoe, as part of a European-style time-share inn (with a requisite clock tower), this new restaurant features a slice of jazz with your dinner. Menu items include filet Torme, prawn brochette and B. B. King salmon. There's an early-bird dinner menu (5 p.m. to 7 p.m.) and live jazz performances from 8 p.m. to midnight Thursday through Saturday. Dinner is served from 4 p.m. nightly, lunch from 11 a.m. on Saturday, and Sunday brunch from 10 a.m. to 3 p.m. with free Mimosas and piano accompaniment. By the way, the views from the restaurant are terrific. Reservations accepted. $5-$15. All major credit cards. 472 Needle Peak Road, Stateline, NV; (702) 588-3245.

## Edgewood Restaurant *

Lake Tahoe's premier golf resort has an elegant clubhouse and restaurant with vaulted, beamed ceilings and sweeping views of the lake and the course. The menu includes roast rack of lamb, veal Cezanne and roast duckling. Full bar and non-smoking dining room available. Open 11:30 a.m. to 2 p.m. for lunch, 6 p.m. to 9 p.m. for dinner and 10 a.m. to 2 p.m. for Sunday brunch (summer); 6 p.m. to 9 p.m. Wednesday through Sunday in winter (dinner only). Reservations recommended. $7-$22. Visa, MasterCard, American Express. 100 Lake Parkway, Stateline, NV; (702) 588-2787.

## Evan's American Gourmet Cafe **

One of the outstanding restaurants around Lake Tahoe, Evan's is in an old-fashioned cottage. There's no waiting lobby (it's outdoors), and it's tremendously popular. Evan and Candice Williams prepare sterling dishes with entrées such as sautéed medallions of lamb, tournedos of beef and nightly fresh seafood specials. The award-winning wine list features 200 wines. Open 6 p.m to 9:30 p.m. daily except for Sunday. Reservations advised. $15-$22. Visa, MasterCard. 536 Emerald Bay Road (just north of the "Y"), South Lake Tahoe, CA; (916) 542-1990.

## Forest Room Buffet **

This is the best buffet room on the South Shore. The menu features 17 different cold salads, roast turkey, ham, roast beef and 35 varieties of special desserts, baked fresh daily by award-winning chefs. Of special note is the Friday night seafood buffet, Saturday night steak buffet and a bountiful Sunday champagne brunch buffet. Breakfast has incomparable high-rise views, with huge plate glass windows overlooking the mountains, the lake and Sierra scenery. Open 8 a.m. to 11 a.m. daily for breakfast; 11:30 a.m. to 2 p.m. for lunch, 5 p.m. to 9 p.m. for dinner (10 p.m. on weekends), and 8:30 a.m. to 2 p.m. for Sunday brunch. $8-$20. Visa, MasterCard, American Express, Diners Club, Carte Blanche. Harrah's Casino Hotel, US 50, Stateline, NV; (702) 588-6611.

### Frank's Restaurant

A fixture at South Shore since 1954, this breakfast and lunch house allows you to choose from 211 home-style menu items, featuring Frank's original hotcakes recipe and smoked salmon (served with sliced red onion, cream cheese, sliced tomatoes and bagel). Open 6 a.m. to 2 p.m. Monday through Saturday and 7 a.m. to 2 p.m. on Sunday. $3-$10. 1207 US 50, South Lake Tahoe, CA; (916) 544-3434.

### Fresh Ketch *

This is a lakeside restaurant overlooking the Tahoe Keys Marina with lunch and dinner menus featuring petrale sole parmesan, calamari steak, chicken breast piccata and tournedos bernaise or au poivre. There's a full bar (creative cocktails, extensive wine list and nearly 50 different beers), a fireside lounge and a deck. Sometimes service can be slow (you're watching the yachts come in, anyway, aren't you?) and the quality of the kitchen varies, ranging from mediocre to brilliant. Open 11:30 a.m. to 9:30 p.m. daily. Dinner reservations recommended. $14-$24. Major credit cards accepted. At Tahoe Keys Marina. 2435 Venice Drive, South Lake Tahoe, CA; (916) 541-5683.

### Friday's Station Steak and Seafood Grill *

This high-rise casino restaurant provides enough beef on your plate to feed an army. Forget the calorie counters here and be sure to have a big appetite. The house specialties include filet mignon with bernaise sauce, shrimp Louisiana and seafood mixed grill. Open 5:30 p.m. to 10 p.m. daily (until 11 p.m. Friday and Saturday). Reservations accepted. $17-$42. All major credit cards. Harrah's Casino Hotel, US 50, Stateline, NV; (702) 588-6611.

### Greenhouse Restaurant and Bar *

This popular South Shore restaurant has American continental gourmet dining, including chicken cordon bleu, roast duckling à l'orange, langouste et veau (sautéed medallions of veal and lobster), and prawns à la Cognac. There's an extensive wine list, with banquet and wedding facilities available. Open 5:30 p.m. to 10 p.m. nightly, with a full bar open 4 p.m. to 10 p.m. Reservations recommended. $12-$22. Visa, MasterCard, American Express. 4140 Cedar Avenue, South Lake Tahoe, CA; (916) 541-5800.

## Heidi's Pancake House *

One of the best breakfasts at the lake, with a quaint, Bavarian-style setting. The menu features omelettes, crepes, old-fashioned hamburgers and healthy heart items. The restaurant serves both breakfast and lunch. Open 6:30 a.m. to 2 p.m. daily. $5-$10. Visa, MasterCard. 3485 Lake Tahoe Boulevard, South Lake Tahoe, CA; (916) 544-8113.

## Josh's *

Award-winning casino restaurant with a strong Italian flavor offers Fisherman's fettuccini Bodega Bay, cannelloni romano and veal scaloppine marsala among its main courses. Open 5:30 p.m. to 10:30 p.m. nightly. $11-$20. All major credit cards accepted. At the Horizon Casino Resort on US 50 at Stateline, NV; (702) 588-6211.

## Lake Tahoe Pizza Company *

No question about it; this is *the* pizza place on the South Shore, and a great treat for families with kids. This large, woodsy restaurant serves fresh pizzas with house specialty or whole-wheat doughs that are made fresh daily per order, not pre-rolled. All meats are ground and sliced daily. You can create your own pizza or choose from gourmet treats such as Mogul Masher, Gut Buster and a spinach-garlic-shrimp combo. Hot meatball sandwiches are made from homemade wheat or white bread and are served with pasta salad and pickle. Smoking is allowed in the bar and lounge only. The full bar features local microbrewery beer on tap. $5-$15. Visa, Master-Card. South of the "Y" and north of the South Lake Tahoe Airport. 1168 Emerald Bay Road; South Lake Tahoe, CA; (916) 544-1919.

## Llewellyn's **

High-rise views of Lake Tahoe and an elegant dining environment make this restaurant one of the standouts of the South Shore. Appetizers include Thai red curry frog legs, escargot in phyllo dough and lobster bisque en croute. Dinner entrées feature lamb rack Gilroy with carmelized garlic, tournedos fromage and salmon involtini. Open 11:30 a.m. to 2:30 p.m. Wednesday through Saturday for lunch, from 6 p.m. daily except Monday and Saturday (from 5 p.m.) for dinner, and Sunday brunch is served from 10 a.m. to 2 p.m. $6-$20. Major credit cards accepted. On the 19th floor of Harvey's Resort Casino, on US 50 in Stateline, NV; (702) 588-2411.

## Midnight Mine *

This locals' favorite with a lively and casual atmosphere features prime rib, barbecued ribs, steak and shrimp, crab and lobster combination plates. Dinner includes homemade soup, salad bar, rice and honey bread. Open 5 p.m. for dinner, with the bar and lounge opening at 4 p.m. Reservations accepted. $11-$35. MasterCard, Visa. At Round Hill Center. 195 US 50, Suite 28, Zephyr Cove, NV; (702) 588-5395.

## Monument Peak *

Perched high on a mountain some 2,000 feet above South Shore, this is the main restaurant of Heavenly Ski Area. It features California-style cuisine, such as swordfish, lamb, steak and chicken; and Sunday brunch includes a wide selection of breakfast and lunch entrées, salads, fresh fruits and breads. You can dine inside or on the deck, depending on weather. Open 11 a.m. to 2 p.m. for lunch, 5 p.m. to 9 p.m. for dinner, and 10 a.m. to 2 p.m. for Sunday brunch. $6-$20. Major credit cards accepted. On the California side of Heavenly Ski Resort, at the corner of Wildwood and Saddle, South Lake Tahoe, CA; (916) 544-6263.

## M.S. Dixie II *

Lake Tahoe's newest paddlewheeler has a 3.5-hour dinner cruise that features a complete meal with your choice of New York steak or halibut, unlimited wine, live music and dancing. The lunch cruise features sandwiches and appetizers, and there's a full bar available for lunch and dinner. With a large galley and attention to detail, this cruise vessel has the best meal on the lake. Departures for the dinner cruise are made nightly at 6:30 p.m. (7:30 p.m. on Saturday only during winter); departures for the lunch cruise leave daily at noon. $5-$34. All major credit cards accepted. At Zephyr Cove Resort. 760 US 50, Zephyr Cove, NV; (702) 588-3508.

## Nephele's *

This rustic place has been around since 1977 and its forte is fresh, creative California cuisine, with daily fish, vegetable and game specialties. There's an informal dining experience, including a small back room that's a bit claustrophobic. Regular entrées include baby back ribs, Moulard duck breast, Cajun swordfish and New Zealand baby clams. Open 5 p.m. nightly, with the cocktail lounge open 2 p.m. to 2 a.m. $12-$20. MasterCard, Visa, American Express. 1169 Ski Run Boulevard, South Lake Tahoe, CA; (916) 544-8130.

## Pasquale's *

Decent snack food includes barbecued chicken calzone, shrimp pesto pizza and grilled eggplant pizza. The hand-tossed pizza is made with fresh dough and baked in a wood-burning brick oven. Open 11 a.m. to 11 p.m. daily. $7-$9. In the Turtle's Sports Bar and Dance Emporium at Embassy Suites Resort. 4130 Lake Tahoe Boulevard, South Lake Tahoe, CA; (916) 544-5400, ext. 7155.

## Passaretti's *

This family Italian restaurant serves veal parmesan, homemade ravioli and canneloni, and a complete soup and salad bar. Low-cal menus, children's menu and take-out orders are available. This is a non-smoking establishment. Open 11 a.m. to 10 p.m. daily for lunch and dinner. Reservations recommended. $4-$16. MasterCard, Visa, American Express, Diners Club. One-quarter of a mile south of the "Y" on US 50. 1181 Emerald Bay Road, South Lake Tahoe, CA; (916) 541-3433.

## Pisces *

Caesar's Mediterranean-flavored restaurant is semi-formal and expensive, but it features fresh seafood flown in daily, including daily specials. The menu includes live Maine lobster, rack of lamb Provencal, petrale sole and breast of Muscovy duck. The extensive wine list has garnered awards from *Wine Spectator Magazine*. Sunset dinner specials are available Tuesday through Friday. Reservations encouraged. $17-$34. Major credit cards accepted. At Caesar's Tahoe. 55 US 50, Stateline, NV; (702) 588-3515.

## Planet Hollywood

Opened in 1994 by Arnold Schwarzenegger and Bruce Willis, two of the chain's owners, this place is festooned with Hollywood props and memorabilia, which form the main attractions. There's the cyborg from *Terminator 2: Judgement Day*, Mel Gibson's motorcycle from *Lethal Weapon III* and a display from *Cliffhanger*. Once you get past the decorations, however, Planet Hollywood is not exactly out of this world. It's a glorified coffee shop, with basic burgers, pizzas, salads and sandwiches. You might save this place for a drink or a dessert fix, indulging in the caramel crunch pie, white chocolate bread pudding, apple strudel or butter pecan rum cake. Open 11 a.m. to 2 a.m. daily. $7-$18. American Express, MasterCard, Visa, Discover. At Caesar's Tahoe. 55 US 50, Stateline, NV; (702) 588-7828.

## Primavera *

This restaurant in Caesar's has a relaxing environment and wonderful service, even if it is next to the indoor swimming pool and has almost no view. The food is well above average, with authentic Italian specialties such as tortellini baronessa (veal-filled pasta with prosciutto, mushrooms, peas and alfredo sauce), rollatini di pollo (breast of chicken filled with prosciutto and mozzarella), and fileti con tre pepi (beef tenderloin with peppercorns, garlic, white wine and veal juice). Open 6 p.m. to 11 p.m. Reservations accepted. $11-$20. All major credit cards accepted. Thursday through Monday. At Caesar's Tahoe. 55 US 50, Stateline, NV; (702) 586-2044.

## Red Hut Waffle Shop *

Want to know where locals eat breakfast? This is the place. It's small and unassuming, but what a feast. Breakfast and lunch menus feature strawberry-banana waffles and pancakes, spinach and cheese omelettes, and "Bad Burgers" (avocado, bacon and cheese). Open 6 a.m. to 2 p.m. daily. $3-$8. 2723 Lake Tahoe Boulevard, South Lake Tahoe, CA; (916) 541-9024.

## Rojo's *

Boasting an atmosphere of "rustic old Tahoe," this restaurant is known for its friendly service and reasonably priced entrées, as well as regular live entertainment. The menu features fettucini Mediterranean, baby back pork ribs, steak Sicilian and Alaskan king crab. A full bar, appetizers and a children's menu are available. Live music and dancing are held most nights in the downstairs cabaret. Lunch served from 11:30 a.m. and dinner served from 5 p.m. $7-$16. Visa, MasterCard, American Express. At US 50 and San Francisco Avenue, South Lake Tahoe, CA; (916) 541-4960.

## Sage Room **

One of the finest steak houses anywhere, this restaurant is virtually an institution, and it's a favorite among frequent guests at Harvey's Resort Casino. It's expensive, but it has intimate lighting, a romantic ambience and exquisite service. The menu includes Black Angus one-inch thick rib-eye steak, Sage Room Steak Gilroy (garnished with garlic purée and topped with a potato crust), an appetizer of crisp raclette potatoes with pancetta and scallions, honey rabbit sausage lasagne, venison grand veneur and desserts that include Bananas Foster prepared tableside for two. Open 6 p.m. to 10 p.m. through Friday and 5:30 p.m. to 10 p.m. Reservations accepted. $19-$23. All major credit cards accepted. Saturday and Sunday. Harvey's Resort Casino, US 50, Stateline, NV; (702) 588-2411.

## Samurai Japanese Sushi Bar *

Authentic Japanese cuisine is presented by kimono-clad servers, and you can dine at tables or while seated on a tatami mat. Don't expect the kind of fresh sashimi that you get on the wharf in San Francisco, because, after all, you're in the mountains. The menu includes sushi, teriyaki chicken, sukiyaki, yakitori and tempura. Sake, beer and wine are available. Open 5 p.m. to 10 p.m. nightly. Reservations suggested. $9-$17. Visa, MasterCard, American Express. 2588 US 50, South Lake Tahoe, CA; (916) 542-0300.

## Scusa! *

This is one of the South Shore's best-loved Italian restaurants, with fresh pastas a house speciality. The atmosphere is casual, the decor is simple, and the service is usually good. The menu includes smoked chicken and ravioli, stuffed eggplant, chicken piccatta, roasted garlic bread and baked penne (smoked mozzarella, prosciutto, roasted garlic and a foccacio crust). Open 5 p.m. to 10 p.m. nightly. No cigar or pipe smoking. Reservations recommended. $7-$15. Visa, MasterCard. No checks accepted. 1142 Ski Run Boulevard, South Lake Tahoe, CA; (916) 542-0100.

## The Summit **

This is one of the South Shore's top casino restaurants, with great views from its lofty location on the top of Harrah's and an elegant dining environment. Dress up in your finest to come here. The menu features roast rack of lamb with anise crust, grilled venison and salmon with lemon couscous, and there are weekly specials. Open 5:30 p.m. to 10 p.m. Sunday through Thursday, 5:30 p.m. to 11 p.m. Friday and Saturday; closed Tuesday. Reservations suggested. $26-$50. All major credit cards accepted. Harrah's Casino Hotel, US 50, Stateline, NV; (702) 588-6611.

## Swiss Chalet *

You'll think that you stepped into Europe when you enter Kurt and Ruth Baumann's ornately appointed restaurant, which oozes Old World charm and has been a fixture of Tahoe since 1957. Don't be surprised to hear plenty of German voices, because this is where the German-speaking tourists hangout. There are the requisite Swiss clocks, cowbells, alpenhorns and other decorations on the walls. As is typical of Swiss food, everything is heavily salted, including soups and sauces. Veal dishes feature the house special, a cordon bleu, which is both crusty and tender, and other menu items include cheese fondue, curry stroganoff, German sauerbraten, a giant T-bone steak and fresh fish of the day. The restaurant's fresh pastries are spectacular, heavily loaded with chocolates. Try the chocolate cheesecake for a jolt to your system. The restaurant prohibits pipe and cigar smoking. Open from 5 p.m. daily except for Monday, with the bar opening at 4 p.m. Recommended by AAA Mobil Guide. $14-$42. Visa, MasterCard, American Express, traveler's checks. Four miles west of Stateline on US 50. 2544 Lake Tahoe Boulevard, South Lake Tahoe, CA; (916) 544-3304.

## Swiss House

A European-style restaurant with a chalet motif, Swiss House offers house specialties such as cheese fondue for two, raclettes (imported Swiss mountain cheese served with boiled potatoes and cocktail onions), wiener schnitzel and salmon en-croute. Patio, fireplace, banquet and wedding reception facilities are available. Open 11:30 a.m. to 2 p.m. for lunch, and 5 p.m. to 10 p.m. for dinner. Open daily from June through September, and Wednesday through Sunday in the winter. $6-$26. MasterCard, Visa, American Express. 787 Emerald Bay Road, South Lake Tahoe, CA; (916) 542-1717.

## Tahoe Queen

This authentic sternwheel cruise boat sails daily to Emerald Bay, serving a dinner that features prime rib, Creole chicken and charbroiled salmon, but the food is mundane and dry. If you go, go for the cruise, the live music and the dancing. The lunch cruise includes French dip sandwich, salmon and royal fruit salad platter. A full bar, wedding and banquet facilities are available. Lunch cruise, 12:30 p.m. daily; dinner cruise, 7 p.m. Sunday through Friday and 7:30 p.m. on Saturday. Reservations requested. $5-$20 (cruise extra). All major credit cards accepted. At the end of Ski Run Boulevard, South Lake Tahoe, CA; (916) 541-3364.

## Tep's Villa Roma *

This moderately priced Italian and seafood restaurant has an extensive menu that includes veal saltimbocca, shrimp scampi, veal scallopini, chicken cacciatore, seafood marinara and lobster tails. All entrées come with all-you-can-eat antipasto bar (soup and salad), and there are daily blackboard specials available. No smoking in the dining room. There is full cocktail service. Open 5 p.m. to 10:30 p.m. nightly. $9-$17. American Express, Visa, MasterCard. 3450 US 50, South Lake Tahoe, CA; (916) 541-8227.

## Water Wheel **

This is the best Chinese restaurant on the South Shore. The Water Wheel is a little hard to find, but it's great food and Polynesian atmosphere make it worth the effort. The chef's specialties include Green Jade Shrimp, Peking duck, shrimp in lobster sauce, orange peel chicken, and scallops Szechuan. The chefs use no MSG in the cooking. A full bar offers exotic cocktails. Open 4:30 p.m. to 10 p.m. daily. Reservations accepted. $6-$24. MasterCard, Visa, American Express. Two blocks away from Harrah's Casino Hotel. 1097 Park Avenue, South Lake Tahoe, CA; (916) 544-4158.

## Zackary's *

This elegant dining room in the Embassy Suites hotel has excellent service and features fresh pepper ahi, Zackary's veal saute and lobster Rolando. A children's menu is available, and cigar smoking is prohibited. Open 11 a.m. to 2 p.m. for lunch, and from 5 p.m. for dinner. Reservations advised. $14-$22. Major credit cards accepted. At Embassy Suites

Resort, 4130 Lake Tahoe Boulevard, South Lake Tahoe, CA: (916) 544-5400, ext. 7140.

## Other Restaurants

**Asia:** Regional Chinese cuisine. $6-$10. Major credit cards accepted. Harrah's, US 50, Stateline, NV; (702) 588-6611 or (800) 648-3773.

**Borselli's:** Large menu, from shrimp and scallop yakisoba to handmade pizzas and calzones. Limited schedule in winter. $8-$20. American Express and First Interstate Bank. On US 50 at 290 Kingsbury Grade, Stateline, NV; (702) 588-8521.

**The Brewery at Lake Tahoe:** The South Shore's only microbrewery, serving veggie fare and sandwiches; the best spots are on the outside deck (great people-watching), but the traffic on busy US 50 may drown out conversation. $2-$6. 3542 US 50, South Lake Tahoe, CA; (916) 544-BREW.

**Bueno Rico's:** Traditional Mexican cuisine. Reservations accepted. $4-$5. Visa, MasterCard, American Express. At Round Hill Center. 195 US 50, Round Hill, NV; (702) 588-7555.

**Cafe Chamonix:** Breakfast (served all day), lunch, daily specials and a children's menu (12 and under). Non-smoking. $3-$8. 913 Friday Avenue, South Lake Tahoe, CA; (916) 544-0439.

**Carina's:** Cafe-deli serving breakfast and lunch. At the Bijou Shopping Center. $3-$7. 3469 US 50, South Lake Tahoe, CA; (916) 541-3354.

**Carriage House:** Daily specials, a full bar, fountain items and Harvey's bakery desserts available. Open 24 hours. $5-$16. All major credit cards accepted. Harvey's Resort Casino; US 50, Stateline, NV; (702) 588-2411.

**Chart House:** You pay more for the sweeping views than for the food, which is overpriced. No cigar or pipe smoking. Reservations accepted. $15-$24. 392 Kingsbury Grade, Stateline, NV; (702) 588-6276.

**Egg Works:** Breakfast and lunch, featuring over 20 omelettes, pancakes and eggs Benedict. $4-$6. On Highway 89 north of the "Y." 868 Emerald Bay Road, South Lake Tahoe, CA; (916) 541-7360.

**Ellis Island Cafe:** Live jazz, Tuesday through Saturday nights; live comedy, Sunday. Non-smoking. $6-$8. MasterCard, Visa. 4093 US 50, South Lake Tahoe, CA; (916) 542-1142.

**El Vaquero:** Spanish cuisine. Reservations suggested. $8-$24. All major credit cards accepted. Harvey's Resort Casino, US 50, Stateline, NV; (702) 588-2411.

**Emerald Palace:** Decent, if not inspiring, Chinese food. Reservations suggested. $5-$12. Major credit cards accepted. 871 Emerald Bay Road, South Lake Tahoe, CA; (916) 544-2421.

**Empress Court:** Szechuan, Mandarin and Cantonese cuisine.

Reservations accepted. $18-$38. Major credit cards accepted. Caesar's Tahoe, 55 US 50, Stateline, NV; (702) 586-2044.

*Garden Buffet:* An above-average casino buffet, with brunches and theme night specials. Reservations accepted. $5-$17. All major credit cards. Harvey's Resort Casino, US 50, Stateline, NV; (702) 588-2411.

*Grand Central Pizza:* $5-$18. MasterCard, Visa. 2229 US 50, South Lake Tahoe, CA; (916) 544-1308.

*Hoss Hoggs:* Ribs, steak, chicken and Mexican cuisine. $3-$15. 2543 Lake Tahoe Boulevard, South Lake Tahoe, CA; (916) 541-8328.

*Le Grande Buffet:* Very inexpensive, but generally mediocre, buffet. $7-$11. All major credit cards accepted. Horizon Casino Resort, US 50, Stateline, NV; (702) 588-6211.

*La Hacienda:* Authentic Mexican cuisine. $4-$14. Visa, Master-Card. 605 US 50, Stateline, NV; (702) 588-3074.

*Lew Mar Nel's:* Creative American cuisine and a large wine list. Reservations recommended. $15-$35. MasterCard, Visa, American Express. 901 Park Avenue, South Lake Tahoe, CA; (916) 542-1072.

*Mc P's Irish Pub and Grill:* Live music nightly and free parking. $5-$17. MasterCard, Visa, American Express. Red Carpet Inn, 4090 Lake Tahoe Boulevard, South Lake Tahoe, CA; (916) 542-4435.

*The Met and Round Hill Pizzeria:* American cafe dining at a sports bar with eight televisions, two satellites and video poker games. $5-$16. All major credit cards accepted. In the Round Hill Center. 195 US 50, Suite 28, Round Hill, NV; (702) 588-8220.

*Pepe's:* An interesting combination of cuisines are served here: Filipino, Mexican and Chinese cuisine. Somehow it seems to work. $4. 4113 Cedar Avenue, South Lake Tahoe, CA; (916) 544-4486.

*Pizzeria:* On the casino floor at Harvey's, featuring brick-oven-baked pizza. Reservations accepted. $4-$7. Major credit cards accepted. Harvey's Resort Casino, US 50, Stateline, NV; (702) 588-2411.

*Sato Japanese Restaurant:* Sushi, shrimp Katsu, beef teriyaki and seafood tempura. Reservations accepted. $8-$14. MasterCard, Visa, American Express. 3436 US 50, South Lake Tahoe, CA; (916) 541-3769.

*Scott's Cafe Tahoe:* A casual breakfast and lunch place on Kingsbury Grade. $3-$5. 292-A Kingsbury Grade, Stateline, NV; (702) 588-7632.

*Seafood Grotto:* Reservations accepted. $7-$25. All major credit cards accepted. At Harvey's Resort Casino, Stateline, NV; (702) 588-2411.

*Timber House:* This coffee shop at the Lakeside Inn & Casino is open 24 hours. Reservations accepted. $3-$8. MasterCard, Visa. US 50 at Kingsbury Grade, Stateline, NV; (702) 588-7777.

*Zephyr Cove Restaurant:* Home-style meals, including steak and shrimp, fettuccini alfredo and basil chicken. $5-$16. At Zephyr Cove

Resort, four miles north of Stateline on US 50, Zephyr Cove, NV; (702) 588-6644.

# HIGHWAY 88

## Caples Lakes Resort **

This is one of the best restaurants in the Tahoe region. It's located in a rustic, weathered lodge overlooking Caples Lake, and it has fabulous views, which are a fitting complement to the creative gourmet meals. Breakfast is served daily and dinner is served nightly (except Tuesday). Featured menu items include New York steak, char-broiled chicken, scampi, fettucini alfredo, fresh catch of the day from Caples Lake and vegetable casserole. Be sure to check out weekend specials such as grilled salmon, pan-seared halibut with raspberry dill vinaigrette, and grilled lamb chops. Starters include tomato bisque soup and caesar salad, and the desserts, freshly made each day, include creative fruit pastries. Children's menu items are available. Breakfast daily from 7:30 p.m., dinner from 5 p.m. nightly except Tuesday. $13-$20. Caples Lake is a 35-minute drive from South Lake Tahoe, and is located on Highway 88 one mile east of Kirkwood Ski Resort in Kirkwood, CA; (209) 258-8888.

## Kirkwood Inn *

This historic building has plenty of character, as well as food that sticks to your ribs. The menu features barbecue beef ribs, Zack's fries (named after Zackary Kirkwood), barbecue chicken sandwich and prime rib. Nightly dinner specials and full bar are available. No smoking is permitted in the restaurant and bar. Open 6:30 a.m. to 9 p.m. Sunday through Thursday, and 6:30 a.m. to 10 p.m. Saturday and Sunday. The bar is open until 11 p.m. $6-$10. Visa, MasterCard, American Express. On Highway 88, one-quarter mile east of the Kirkwood Ski Resort exit in Kirkwood, CA; (209) 258-7304.

## Kit Carson Lodge Restaurant *

You'll find peek-a-boo views of Silver Lake at this rustic lodge in a woodsy setting. The menu features Nouveau California and French cuisine, such as rack of lamb, scampi and Cornish game hen. Offerings include a continental breakfast buffet daily, Sunday brunch and children's portions (half price for children 12 and under). Open 8 a.m. to 10 a.m. daily for the breakfast buffet, 6 p.m. to 9 p.m. Tuesday through Saturday for dinner, and 10:30 a.m. to 1:30 p.m. for Sunday brunch. The restaurant is open mid-June through late September. Reservations are recommended. $10-$17. On Highway 88 at Silver Lake, west of Kirkwood in Kit Carson, CA. 5855 Carbon Dale Road, Plymouth, CA; (209) 258-8500 (summer) or (209) 245-4760 (winter).

## Plasse's Restaurant *

Look, up on the wall, there's Kit Carson's saddle! Although there are limited hours, this is a great family dining experience in one of the historic and funky resorts of Carson Pass. The menu features beer-battered prawns, New York steak, meatloaf platter, prime rib, grilled swordfish and veal parmesan. But regulars swear by the chicken-fried steak with both white and brown homemade gravies. Yum! Open 7:30 a.m. to 11:30 a.m. for breakfast on Saturday and Sunday only, 11:30 a.m. to 2 p.m. for lunch on Saturday and Sunday only, and from 5 p.m. nightly except Wednesday for dinner. $4-$17. Visa, MasterCard. At Plasse's Resort, at Silver Lake off Highway 88. 30001 Plasse Road; (209) 258-8814.

## Sorensen's Resort *

This vintage resort in Hope Valley serves hearty and creative western California cuisine, such as Caribbean stew, grilled salmon with caper sauce, New York steak, barbecued chicken and pasta pesto linguini with clam sauce. Beer and wine are available. Open 7:30 a.m. to 4 p.m. daily for breakfast and lunch, and 5:30 p.m. to 8:30 p.m. daily for dinner. Reservations strongly suggested. $4-$19. Visa, MasterCard and personal checks accepted. 14255 Highway 88. Hope Valley, CA; (916) 694-2203 or (800) 423-9949.

### *Other Restaurants*

**Alpine Hotel Restaurant and Cutthroat Saloon**: Breakfast, lunch and dinner. $3-$13. Near Grover Hot Springs on Main and Montgomery in Markleeville; (916) 694-2150.

# Carson City

## Adele's **

Set in a Victorian house with period furnishings, this favorite continental restaurant features local lamb dishes, filet mignon (stuffed with lobster, crab, shrimp and Cognac sauce and topped with poached oysters), and Australian lobster tails stuffed with proscuitto. Dinner includes salad, vegetable and your choice of pasta, rice, or potato. Heart-healthy menu items and a full bar are available. Open 11 a.m. to 4:30 p.m. for lunch Monday through Saturday, and 5 p.m. to 10 p.m. for dinner Monday through Thursday, and 5 p.m. to 11 p.m. Friday and Saturday. Reservations recommended. $6-$35. Visa, MasterCard, American Express. 1112 North Carson Street, Carson City, NV; (702) 882-3353.

## Armio's *

The casual yet elegant Southwestern decor in this well-known dinner house complements an eclectic mix of Asian, American, Italian and Mexican dishes such as char-broiled shrimp with angel-hair pasta, chili rellenos, Thai shrimp and New York steak. The one thing that mars this otherwise delightful dining experience is the abysmally slow service. Open 11:30 a.m. to 3 p.m. daily for lunch, and 5 p.m. to 10:30 p.m. for dinner. There's a full bar with Western memorabilia on the walls. Non-smoking sections are available. Reservations recommended. $7-$19. MasterCard, Visa, American Express. On the north end of town at the Bonanza Ranch. 3700 North Carson Street, Carson City. Information: (702) 883-9696.

## Carlsbad House *

Located in the historic district, this two-story Victorian house built in 1870 features a home-style menu that includes chicken fried steak, blackened catfish and tortellini. A children's menu (12 and under) and a non-smoking section are available. Open 11 a.m. to 9 p.m. daily. Reservations suggested for large parties of eight or more. $3-$11. MasterCard, Visa, Discover, American Express. 102 North Curry Street, Carson City, NV; (702) 883-1575.

## Garibaldi's *

This old European-style restaurant, with large picture windows, vaulted ceilings, intimate seating and a solid walnut antique bar, offers northern Italian cuisine, such as lobster-filled raviolis, tiger shrimp sautéed with Thai vegetables over angel-hair pasta, and veal picatta. Non-smoking dining, a full bar and an extensive wine list are available. Reservations suggested. $6-$19. MasterCard, American Express, Visa, Discover. 301 North Carson Street, Carson City, NV; (702) 884-4574.

## Silvana Italian Cuisine *

Intimate and friendly Old World charm envelops this restaurant, which features authentic Venetian dishes. The menu includes 25 different homemade pastas, chicken marsala, pasta primavera and New York rib-eye steak. Complete dinners are served with soup or salad and garlic bread. Open 5 p.m. to 10 p.m. Tuesday through Saturday. Reservations suggested. $11-$19. MasterCard, Visa, American Express. 1301 North Carson Street, Carson City, NV; (702) 883-5100.

## Stanley's *

Continental cuisine is served in a romantic, casual San Francisco-style setting. The menu features rack of lamb, filet mignon, Greek fettucini, chicken Chardonnay and broiled salmon with lemon butter and white wine sauce. Daily specials are available. Open 11:30 a.m. to 2:30 p.m. for lunch, 5:30 p.m. to 10 p.m. for dinner Monday through Friday, and 5 p.m. to 10 p.m. on Saturday. A full bar is open Monday through Saturday from 11:30 a.m. to 10 p.m., and appetizers are available while the dining room is closed. Reservations suggested. $6-$18. American Express, MasterCard, Visa. 4239 North Carson Street, Carson City, NV; (702) 883-7826.

## The Station Grill and Rotisserie *

Modern decor, friendly service and creative presentations complement a menu that includes diverse entrées such as grilled pizza, smoked pepper tenderloins, stuffed jumbo shells, spit-roasted leg of lamb and baby back ribs, seafood crepes and turkey enchiladas. For starters, try the chicken and corn tortilla soup or the crab cakes. Open 11:30 a.m. to 2 p.m. Monday, 11:30 a.m. to 10 p.m. Tuesday through Friday, and 5 p.m. to 10 p.m. on Saturday. Reservations suggested. $4-$14. All major credit cards accepted. 1105 South Carson Street, Carson City, NV; (702) 883-8400.

## Valentino's *

The Southern Italian cuisine here is served on red-linen-clad tables beneath wall-sized Venetian murals. The menu features seafood alfredo, veal marsala and eggplant parmesan. Early-bird and children's menus, non-smoking dining and a full bar are available. Open 5 p.m. to 9 p.m. Monday through Thursday, 5 p.m. to 10 p.m. on Friday and Saturday, and 4 p.m. to 8.30 p.m. on Sunday. Reservations accepted. $5 $14. Visa, MasterCard, American Express, Discover. 2729 North Carson Street, Carson City, NV; (702) 883-7044.

## The Wild Scallion *

This cozy bistro offers "crab catcher's" sandwiches, grilled vegetable lasagne, home-style soups, pastries and desserts. Daily specials include Mexican, Italian and Chinese cuisine. Open 11 a.m. to 2 p.m. Monday through Friday (lunch only). Reservations accepted. $3-$7. Visa, American Express, MasterCard, Discover. 110 West Telegraph, Carson City, NV; (702) 883-8826.

### *Other Restaurants*

***Baron's Steak House:*** Fine dining at the Ormsby House. Reservations suggested. $10-$18. All major credit cards. 600 South Carson Street, Carson City, NV; (702) 882-1890.

***The East Ocean Restaurant:*** Chinese cuisine. $4-$9. MasterCard, Visa. 1214 North Carson Street, Carson City, NV; (702) 883-6668.

***Heiss' Steak and Seafood House:*** Early-bird and dinner-for-two menus available. $8-$13. Visa, MasterCard, American Express, Discover, Diners Club. 107 East Telegraph, Carson City, NV; (702) 882-9012.

**Mi Casa Too:** Mexican cuisine. Reservations accepted on weekdays. $5-$9. Major credit cards. 3809 North Carson Street, Carson City, NV; (702) 882-4080.

**The Panda Kitchen:** Chinese cuisine. $5-$10. MasterCard, Visa. 2416 US 50 East, Carson City, NV; (702) 882-8128.

**The Place For Pasta:** Reservations suggested. $6-$22. 1750 South Roop Street, Carson City, NV; (702) 882-1488.

## Carson Valley/Dayton

### Fiona's *

This tropical restaurant with plants and plenty of sunlight has a menu that offers soup and salad bar, sandwiches, New York steak, and nightly pasta specials. Sunday brunch features a fruit and pastry bar, crêpes, omelettes and bacon. A full bar is available. Open 11:30 a.m. to 2 p.m. for lunch Tuesday through Friday, 5 p.m. to 9 p.m. for dinner Tuesday through Sunday, and 9 a.m. to 2 p.m. for Sunday brunch. Reservations suggested. $5-$16. MasterCard, Visa, American Express, Diners Club. At the Carson Valley Inn. 1627 US 395 North, Minden, NV; (702) 782-9711 or (800) 321-6983, ext. 650.

### Mia's Swiss Restaurant *

Located in historic Odeon Hall, Mia's was the site for the filming of *The Misfits,* starring Clark Gable, Marilyn Monroe and Montgomery Clift. A beautiful ballroom and theater are located upstairs. Continental cuisine features buffalo steaks, grilled halibut, beef stroganoff, veal Oscar and wiener schnitzel. There's a full bar in an adjoining room, and nightly specials are available. Reservations accepted. $5-$24. Visa, MasterCard, American Express. 65 Pike, Dayton, NV; (702) 246-3993.

### Michael's *

This casino dinner house has chandeliers, intimate booth seating and white tablecloths for meals that include tournedos Sierra pinon, crab and angel hair pasta, and linguini creole. A non-smoking section and a full bar are available. Open 5 p.m. to 9 p.m. Wednesday through Monday. Reservations recommended. $10-$18. MasterCard, Visa, American Express, Diners Club. At the Carson Valley Inn. 1627 US 395 North, Minden, NV; (702) 782-9711 or (800) 321-6983, ext. 782.

### Other Restaurants

**Carson Valley Country Club:** Basque cuisine. Reservations suggested for parties of 10 or more. $15. 1029 Riverview Drive, Gardnerville, NV; (702) 265-3715.

***J & T Bar & Restaurant:*** Basque-style entrées. Reservations accepted. $5-$14. MasterCard, Visa. 1426 South US 395 in Gardnerville, NV; (702) 782-2074.

***Overland Hotel:*** Basque restaurant. Reservations accepted. $4-$15. MasterCard, Visa. 691 South US 395, Gardnerville, NV; (702) 782-2138.

## Virginia City
### Crown Point *

Located in Nevada's oldest hotel, this restaurant has atmosphere and a sure hand in the kitchen. The menu features New York steak, linguini with clams, daily fresh fish dishes and homemade desserts. A full bar, an extensive wine list and beer are available. Open 5:30 p.m. to 9 p.m. Wednesday through Sunday. Reservations recommended on weekends. $14-$26. Visa, MasterCard. In the Gold Hill Hotel, near Virginia City. 1540 South Main Street, Gold Hill, NV; (702) 847-0111.

### Other Restaurants

***Delta Saloon:*** Non-smoking sections, a children's menu and full bar service are available. Reservations accepted. $4-$7. Visa, MasterCard, American Express. 18 South C Street, Virginia City, NV; (702) 847-0789.

## LAKES BASIN
### Plumas Dining Room **
### (formerly Anthony's)

This truly elegant restaurant in the new clubhouse of one of the state's finest golf courses offers a wonderful menu and sterling service. The menu features beer-battered prawns, veal saltimbocca, scallops di mare, calamari steak, swordfish, chicken sauté sec and filet mignon. Children's menus and portions (age 10 and under) are available. Open from 5 p.m. in summer. Reservations suggested. $12-$18. American Express, Visa, MasterCard. Plumas Pines Country Club, 402 Poplar Valley Road, Blairsden, CA; (916) 836-1305.

### Feather River Inn

This is an elegant and historic lodge, in the vein of the Ahwahnee Hotel in Yosemite, and it is worth visiting for the Sunday brunch, the only meal served to the public. Guests can sit inside in the dining room or outside on big verandas. The menu features omelettes, a waffle bar, a California fresh fruit station, quiche, juice bar, dessert bar, champagne, coffee and tea. Open 9 a.m. to 1 p.m. Sundays in summer (closed October through June). $13. 65899 Highway 70, Blairsden, CA; (916) 836-2623.

## Iron Door **

The rustic and delightful interior—almost resembling a museum—is a warm place for one of the best meals in the Sierra. The building once housed a general store and post office for the town of Johnsville, which was founded in 1876 during the development of the Plumas Eureka gold mine. This restaurant has been around since 1961, and is the only business in what is now Plumas Eureka State Park. The place is full of character, including the bar with its old tintype photographs of the mining days. There are big, open-beamed ceilings in the main dining room, and an adjoining greenhouse-style room next to the road. The menu includes Italian calamari, Cornish game hen, pasta and seafood, lobster, pepper steak, champagne chicken, lamb chops and New York steak. Smoking is at the bar only. There's a museum, of sorts, upstairs. Open from 5 p.m. nightly April through October. Reservations are suggested; make them several days ahead of time if you're planning a weekend meal during the summer. $10-$39. Visa, MasterCard. In Plumas Eureka State Park. 5417 Main Street, Johnsville, CA; (916) 836-2376.

## Gold Lake Lodge *

This place in the heart of the Lakes Basin is rustic but popular. It serves American cuisine, including prime rib, seafood and pasta. This is a non-smoking establishment. Open 8:30 a.m. to 10 a.m. for breakfast and 5:30 p.m. to 7:30 p.m. for dinner. The lodge is closed in winter, October through June. Reservations required. $8-$15. 7 Gold Lake Road, Graeagle, CA; (916) 836-2350.

## Graeagle Meadows Clubhouse *

Above-average breakfasts, geared to get the engines running for duffers, include American and Mexican selections, such as the Greenskeeper Omelette, chicken nachos supreme and grilled turkey sandwiches. A full bar features mild or wild Bloody Marys. Open 7 a.m. to 3 p.m. daily for breakfast and lunch; closed December through March. $4-$8. Highway 89, Graeagle, CA; (916) 836-2348.

## Gray Eagle Lodge **

This woodsy but modern retreat has a large local following and strong repeat business, and is known for its gourmet meals and delectable sauces. It features American and Continental cuisine, such as grilled New York steak with rosemary butter and Cabernet sauce, rack of grilled baby back ribs and sautéed sea bass with oven-roasted tomatoes and basil. A full bar, an extensive wine list and gourmet coffees are available. Open 6 p.m. and 8 p.m. for dinner; closed November through April. Entrées from $15. 5000 Gold Lake Road, Graeagle, CA; (916) 836-2511 or (800) 635-8778.

## Olsen's Cabin *

This attractive restaurant, set in the trees off the Johnsville Road, has an inviting interior and an excellent menu. Complete dinners are served with soup, salad, baked potato or seasoned rice, fresh vegetables, bread du jour, dessert, and coffee or tea. Wine and beer are available. Featured menu items include the "captain's combo" (prawns, scallops and Alaskan king crab) and the "gourmet special"—your choice of any two items such as steak, chicken, pork chop, lamb chop, trout, scallops or prawns. A child's plate is available on selected half orders for children under 12. Open Monday through Saturday. Reservations advised. $11-$32. MasterCard, Visa. On County Road A-14 at Johnsville and Mohawk roads, Graeagle, CA; (916) 836-2801.

## Packer Lake Lodge *

This is a small restaurant in a rustic cabin next to an equally small lake. Nightly specials include New York steak, baby back pork ribs and honey-herb crusted pork chops. The chef will be happy to cook to order your catch of the day. Wednesday evening is Italian Night, featuring bingo and an Italian buffet of pizza, lasagne, pastas and eggplant parmesan. Sunday brunch includes fruit compote, eggs Benedict, fritatta, champagne and fresh juices. Open 8 a.m. to 10 a.m. for breakfast and 6 p.m. to 9 p.m. for dinner Wednesday through Monday, and 9 a.m. to noon for brunch on Sunday. The lodge is closed in winter. Reservations appreciated. $9-$15. Twenty miles southwest of Graeagle off Gold Lake Road in Sierra City, CA; (916) 862-1221.

## Sardine Lake Resort **

This delightful but rustic lodge, set on what is surely the most spectacular lake in the Lakes Basin—with a view of the majestic Sierra Buttes to match—offers a tiny, woodsy restaurant that serves New York steak, fish of the day and lamp chops. All menus include soup, salad, vegetable, potato and sourdough bread. A children's plate is available for youngsters under 12. Open from 5 p.m. Friday through Wednesday; closed in winter. Reservations requested. $14-$17. One mile south of Gold Lake Road. 990 Sardine Lake Road, Graeagle, CA; (916) 862-1196 or (916) 645-8882.

### *Other Restaurants*

***River Pines Dining Room:*** Continental and Mexican cuisine. Live dinner music holds forth on Friday and Saturday. $8-$15. 8296 Highway 89, Blairsden, CA; (916) 836-0576.

# Reno

## Atlantis Seafood Steakhouse **

A 1,100-gallon aquarium and subdued lighting create an aquatic ambience for an incredible repast. Start with appetizers—everyone does—and don't miss the flaming coconut prawns, presented at your table with a flaming pineapple crown, spiced marmalade and honey mustard. Or the bouquet of onion soup, a creamy soup with five kinds of onions that is baked in a colossal onion and crowned with Valio Swiss cheese gratinée. The entrées include seafood specialities, such as swordfish Mediterranean, seafood pan roast (Gulf prawns, scallops, clams and king crab simmered in a creamy wine sauce), seafood fettuccini and Alaskan halibut fillet. But you'll also find beef kabob, New York steak, pepper steak and double French cut lamb chops if you're not in the mood for fish. Desserts are made fresh daily and presented tableside, along with after-dinner liqueurs. Service is exceptional, and this is one of the great dining experiences in Nevada. Open 5 p.m. to 10 p.m. nightly. Free 24-hour valet and self-parking. Reservations recommended. $5-$23. All major credit cards accepted. Clarion Hotel Casino, 3800 South Virginia, Reno, NV; (702) 825-4700 or (800) 723-6500.

## Big Top Buffet *

This is the best cheap buffet in town. The buffet menu features 15 hot items, carved ham and roast beef, a wide variety of salads, fresh fruits and desserts including an ice cream bar. Special menus are offered during Friday night's seafood buffet and Saturday night's sirloin and scampi buffet. Different evenings feature Oriental, Italian, German and Mexican specials. Open 6 a.m. to 11 a.m. for breakfast; 11 a.m. to 4 p.m. for lunch, 4 p.m. to 11 p.m. for dinner, and 6 a.m. to 4 p.m. for weekend brunch. Validated covered parking available. $3-$7. No credit cards accepted. Circus Circus Hotel Casino, 500 North Sierra Street, Reno, NV; (702) 329-0711 or (800) 648-5010.

## Cafe Alfresco *

This hotel/casino restaurant features fresh, brick-oven-baked pizzas, pastas, salads, sandwiches and an espresso bar. Open 11:30 a.m. to 2 a.m. daily. $6-$11. All major credit cards accepted. Clarion Hotel Casino, 3800 South Virginia Street, Reno, NV; (702) 825-4700 or (800) 723-6500.

## Cafe Andreotti *

Excellent Italian cuisine is offered in an informal dining atmosphere, including pastas, steak and seafood. Dinner is served nightly from 5 p.m. to 10 p.m. Reservations recommended. $8-$15. All major credit cards accepted. Harrah's Casino Hotel, 219 North Center Street, Reno, NV; (702) 786-3232.

## Cafe de Thai **

This is an out-of-the-way restaurant in a nondescript shopping mall close to the airport, but it's one of the best discoveries in town. Chef Sakul is a graduate of the internationally acclaimed Culinary Institute of America in Hyde Park, New York. An extensive menu has delicious, freshly prepared Thai dishes, along with the renowned sweet and rich coffees. There's also an extensive wine and beer list. Open for lunch and dinner. In the Mira Loma Shopping Center. 3314 South McCarran, Reno, NV; (702) 829-8424.

## Christmas Tree *

High above Reno on Mount Rose Highway, this famous dinner house has long been a favorite with locals. The menu features the restaurant's trademark mountain mahogany-broiled steaks, chicken Kiev, New York steaks, vegetable fettuccini, lamb chops and combination lobster dinners. Weekly chef specials, full bar and great views of Reno and Washoe Valley are available. Live music and dancing hold forth on Friday and Saturday. Open from 5 p.m. for dinner Wednesday through Sunday; the lounge opens at 3 p.m. Reservations for parties of five or more. $9-$40. Major credit cards accepted. 20007 Mount Rose Highway, Reno, NV; (702) 849-0127.

## Galena Forest Restaurant and Bar *

Situated at the foot of Mount Rose Highway, this romantic yet casual European restaurant is far from the madding crowds of downtown Reno and within a short drive of the Mount Rose ski area. Alpine cuisine (a culmination of German, Austrian, Swiss, Northern Italian and French cooking) is the specialty here, as well as steak and fresh seafood entrées. Open from 5 p.m. for dinner Wednesday through Sunday. Reservations preferred. $14-19 MasterCard, Visa, American Express. 17025 Mount Rose Highway, Reno, NV; (702) 849-2100.

## Grand Canyon Buffet *

This new and cheery casino hotel buffet restaurant offers pasta and wok stations, carved items rotating daily (roast turkey, ham, prime rib of beef and roast top round), crab legs, peeled shrimp, salads, ice cream bar and dessert station. Open 7 a.m. to 10:30 a.m. for breakfast Monday through Saturday, 11:30 a.m. to 2 p.m. for lunch Monday through Saturday, 5 p.m. to 9 p.m. nightly for dinner, and 8:30 a.m. to 2 p.m. for Sunday brunch. $6-$12. MasterCard, Visa, American Express, Diners Club,

Carte Blanche, Discover. Reno Hilton, 2500 East Second Street, Reno, NV; (702) 789-2000.

## Great Basin Brewing Company *

Reno's only combined microbrewery and restaurant features fresh homemade beer, ale-battered fish and chips, sausages, salads and daily specials. Try the garlic French fries. There's a children's menu, and free soft drinks for designated drivers. Local musicians perform in the evening. Special group arrangements and tours are available. Open from 11:30 a.m. daily, serving lunch and dinner. $5-$10. Discover, MasterCard, Visa. 846 Victorian Avenue, Sparks, NV; (702) 355-7711.

## Harrah's Steak House **

When you're ready to pull out the stops for the best steak dinner in Reno, with accommodating waiters, flambés and rich desserts in a traditional setting, this is the place to go. Some creative touches add adventure and delight to the main fare, which includes New York pepper steak, chateaubriand, steak Diane, rack of lamb, veal piccatta, prime rib and calamari Oscar. Try starters such as crab cakes, Portobello mushrooms with fennel sauce, and grilled radicchio and Belgian endive salad. The ambience is low-light and intimate, and the service is impeccable. Open 11 a.m. to 3 p.m. Monday through Friday for lunch, and 6 p.m. to 10 p.m. nightly for dinner. Reservations required. $20-$50. Major credit cards accepted. Harrah's Casino Hotel, 219 North Center Street, Reno, NV; (702) 786-3232.

## Island Buffet *

This is a popular Polynesian luau-style feast served with prime rib, turkey, salads and desserts. Open 7:30 a.m. to 3 p.m. daily for breakfast and lunch, and 4:30 p.m. to 10 p.m. Sunday through Thursday (until 11 p.m. Friday and Saturday) for dinner. Friday night seafood buffet features clam chowder, peel-and-eat shrimp, steamed lobster and clams, and scampi. A full bar and free 24-hour valet parking are available. $4-$15. Major credit cards accepted. Peppermill Hotel Casino, 2707 South Virginia Street, Reno, NV; (702) 826-2121 or (800) 648-6992.

## La Strada *

Part of one of Reno's best casino-hotels, La Strada features Northern Italian cuisine including homemade pastas, mushroom raviolis, chicken, veal and pizza. A full bar is available. Open from 5 p.m. nightly for dinner. Reservations suggested. $12-$18. Major credit cards accepted. Eldorado Hotel Casino, 345 North Virginia Street, Reno, NV; (702) 786-5700.

## Le Moulin *

This casino-hotel restaurant has Continental cuisine featuring pasta, veal, fish and your choice of soup or salad. Open 5 p.m. to 10 p.m. nightly, with an early-bird dinner from 5 p.m. to 7 p.m. nightly, except holidays. A full bar and free 24-hour valet parking are available. Reservations suggested. $11-$30. Major credit cards accepted. Peppermill Hotel Casino, 2707 South Virginia Street, Reno, NV; (702) 826-2121 or (800) 648-6992.

## Louis' Basque Corner *

This is a town institution, even if it's not in the better part of town. Louis and Lorraine Erreguible make food that is heavy, spicy and full of character, and their place draws visitors from throughout the world. Louis, who is from the French Pyrenees, served his apprenticeship in Bordeaux. The walls in the restaurant are adorned with pictures of France, pottery from the Ciboure and famous Basque sayings. The cuisine includes paella, shrimp and tongue à la Basquaise, lamb stew, chicken with Spanish rice, rabbit in wine sauce and calamari. The menu changes daily, but family-style dinners come with soup du jour, tossed green salad, French bread, Basque beans, potatoes, ice cream and choice of wine, coffee, milk or tea. You may not want to eat anything else for the rest of the day. Waitresses dress in authentic Basque garb. A full bar and two private banquet dining rooms are available. Open 11 a.m. to 2:30 p.m. for lunch Monday through Saturday, and 5 p.m. to 9:30 p.m. nightly for dinner. Reservations accepted. $7-$15. All major credit cards accepted. 301 East Fourth Street, Reno, NV; (702) 323-7203.

## Market Place Buffet *

The Eldorado hotel's buffet house includes prime rib, homemade mushroom raviolis, salads and desserts. Open 7:45 a.m. to 11 a.m. daily for breakfast, 11 a.m. to 2 p.m. for lunch, 4 p.m. to 9 p.m. for dinner, and 7:45 a.m. to 2 p.m. for weekend brunch. A full bar, free valet and self-parking are available. Eldorado Hotel Casino, 345 North Virginia Street, Reno, NV; (702) 786-5700. $4-$10. Major credit cards accepted.

## Peppermill Food Court *

Four food stations feature Mexican, American, Italian and Chinese cuisine. The restaurant serves breakfast, lunch and dinner, and has a full bar. Free 24-hour valet parking is available. Open 8 a.m. to 10 p.m. Sunday through Thursday and 8 a.m. to midnight Friday and Saturday. $3-$8. Major credit cards accepted. Peppermill Hotel Casino, 2707 South Virginia Street, Reno, NV; (702) 826-2121 or (800) 648-6992.

## Rapscallion Seafood House and Bar *

Considered one of Reno's best seafood restaurants and a favorite with locals, this place always has 10 to 20 varieties of fresh seafood and 140 wine selections. Starters include the Cajun coconut prawns, and main courses include breaded calamari steak, Rapscallion stew (scallops, shrimp, claims and fish fillets sautéed with orange and lemon rind, leaks, tomatoes and garlic), and specials such as halibut, sea bass, snapper, king salmon, swordfish and thresher shark. Open 11 a.m. to 2 p.m. for lunch and 5 p.m. to 10 p.m. for dinner on weekdays, 5 p.m. to 10:30 p.m. for dinner on Saturday, and 10 a.m. to 2 p.m. for brunch and 5 p.m. to 10 p.m. for dinner on Sunday. $7-$28. American Express, Visa and MasterCard. 1555 South Wells Street, Reno, NV; (702) 323-1211.

## Reno Hilton Steakhouse *

The steakhouse menu features roast prime rib of beef, surf and turf, and cedar-planked salmon. Open 5:30 p.m. to 10:30 p.m. Sunday through Thursday, and 5:30 p.m. to 11 p.m. Friday and Saturday. Reservations suggested. $18-$25. MasterCard, Visa, American Express, Diners Club, Carte Blanche, Discover. Reno Hilton, 2500 East Second Street, Reno, NV; (702) 789-2000.

## Rotisserie Restaurant and Buffet *

This casino restaurant features chicken, pasta prime rib, salad bar and desserts. Open 4:30 p.m. to 10 p.m. nightly, and 8:30 a.m. to 2 p.m. for Sunday brunch. Reservations suggested. $8-$13. Major credit cards accepted. John Ascuaga's Nugget, 1100 Nugget Avenue, Sparks, NV; (702) 356-3300.

## Ruby's Diner

This authentic, '40s-style diner is set inside one of downtown's newest attractions, the National Bowling Stadium. The candy-stripe waitstaff uniforms, jukebox music, vintage memorabilia, a gift shop, a full bar tucked in the rear and neon lighting create a lively atmosphere for dining. Its private outdoor entrance allows patrons to enjoy a Peanut Butter Cup deluxe shake, a Ruby Dooby double cheeseburger, chili fries and a double hot fudge brownie during the stadium's off hours. Heart-healthy items, a children's menu, 10-percent senior discounts and non-smoking sections are available. Open seven days a week from 6 a.m. to midnight. 300 North Center Street, Reno, NV; (702) 348-7829.

## Skyway Buffet *

Harrah's always serves a good meal, and this buffet is well above average. Items include carved roast beef, turkey, prime rib, fish, salads and desserts. No smoking is permitted in the dining room. Open 8 a.m. to 10 a.m. for breakfast, 11 a.m. to 3 p.m. for lunch, and 6 p.m. to 10 p.m. for dinner. $9-$15. Major credit cards accepted. Harrah's Casino Hotel, 219 North Center, Reno, NV; (702) 786-3232.

### The Steakhouse Grill *

The menu at this casino hotel features prime rib, New York steak and 20-ounce T-bone steaks. Open 5 p.m. to 11 p.m. nightly for dinner. Reservations recommended. $17-$23. All major credit cards accepted. John Ascuaga's Nugget, 1100 Nugget Avenue, Sparks, NV; (702) 356-3300.

### Top of the Flamingo Hilton *

This is a romantic and elegant location, with bird's-eye views of downtown Reno and the surrounding mountains. The menu of continental cuisine includes caesar salad, seafood, pasta, filet mignon and desserts. There is an extensive wine list, a full bar and a dance floor. A Sunday champagne brunch is available. Open 6 p.m. to 11 p.m. nightly from Wednesday through Monday, and 9:30 a.m. to 2 p.m. for Sunday champagne brunch. Happy Hour with complimentary appetizers runs from 5 p.m. to 7 p.m. Reservations suggested. $11-$25. Major credit cards accepted. Flamingo Hilton, 255 North Sierra Street, Reno, NV; (702) 322-1111.

### Toucan Charlie's Buffet and Grille *

Buffet menus feature omelettes, Mongolian barbecue and theme nights. Open 7:30 a.m. to 10 p.m. daily, serving breakfast, lunch, dinner, Friday night seafood buffet and Sunday champagne brunch. There's free 24-hour valet and self-parking. $5-$16. Major credit cards accepted. Clarion Hotel Casino, 3800 South Virginia Street, Reno, NV; (702) 825-4700 or (800) 723-6500.

### Trader Dick's Restaurant Aquarium *

Does the name remind you of something? Oh, well, never mind. If you like aquariums, this place has a 6,000-gallon, 30-ton saltwater tank that, at 45 feet long, is one of the largest private aquariums in the West. Three pillars that support Interstate 80 above the restaurant have been integrated into the lush tropical appointments. This Polynesian-style restaurant includes Chinese stir fry, steaks, fresh fish, ribs and fried shrimp. Open 5 p.m. to 11 p.m. nightly. Reservations recommended. $10-$38. Major credit cards accepted. John Ascuaga's Nugget, 1100 Nugget Avenue, Sparks, NV; (702) 356-3300 or (800) 648-1177.

### Triple Crown Restaurant and Buffet

For inexpensive eats, this place has achieved a big reputation with locals. Just ask any cab driver. Breakfast is served from 6 a.m. to 10 a.m.

Monday through Friday; breakfast brunch is served from 6 a.m. to 8:30 a.m. Saturday and Sunday; lunch is served from 11 a.m. to 3 p.m. Monday through Friday; dinner is served from 4 p.m. to 10 p.m. Monday through Friday and 3 p.m. to 10 p.m. Saturday and Sunday; and champagne brunch is served from 9 a.m. to 3 p.m. on Sunday. $2-$5. Baldini's Sports Casino, 865 South Rock Boulevard, Sparks, NV; (702) 358-0116.

## The Vintage *
Another restaurant at Eldorado Hotel Casino offers fine continental cuisine featuring beef, veal, duckling, seafood and lamb dishes. There is a complimentary wine tasting nightly, from an award-winning and extensive wine list. Open from 5 p.m. nightly. Reservations recommended. $14-$22. Major credit cards accepted. Eldorado Hotel Casino, 345 North Virginia, Reno, NV; (702) 786-5700.

## Other Restaurants
***Bogey's Bar and Grill:*** A sports bar decorated with pennants, memorabilia and four televisions (including a giant screen). $2-$5. Wildcreek Golf Course, 3500 Sullivan Lane, Sparks, NV; (702) 673-5456.

***Boomtown Restaurant Buffet:*** $4-$9. Visa, MasterCard, American Express. Off Interstate 80, west of downtown Reno in Verdi, NV; (702) 345-6000.

***Cafe 47:*** It's on Nevada's Registry as a historic landmark. The menu includes chili cheese omelettes, hamburgers and pork chops. $3-$6. 1300 South Virginia Street, Reno, NV; (702) 329-6969.

***Caruso's:*** Italian cuisine. Reservations suggested. $12-$18. MasterCard, Visa, American Express, Diners Club, Carte Blanche, Discover. Reno Hilton, 2500 East Second Street, Reno, NV; (702) 789-2000.

***Garden Gazebo:*** Featuring a Friday night seafood buffet and a Sunday champagne brunch. $4-$9. Major credit cards accepted. Sundowner Hotel Casino, 450 North Arlington Avenue, Reno, NV; (702) 786-7050.

***Johnny Rockets:*** Burgers, fries and shakes. $3-$5. Visa, MasterCard, Discover. Reno Hilton, 2500 East Second Street, Reno, NV; (702) 789-2000.

***Limerick's:*** Reservations suggested. $7-$20. Major credit cards accepted. Fitzgeralds Casino Hotel, 255 North Virginia Street, Reno, NV; (702) 785-3300.

***Miner's Cafe:*** Open 24 hours. $2-$9. Major credit cards accepted. Comstock Hotel Casino, 200 West Second Street, Reno, NV; (702) 329-1880.

***Pancho and Willie's:*** Mexican cuisine, with American and Mexican breakfasts served daily. All lunch and dinner entrées are half price Monday through Thursday. $3-$10. Major credit cards accepted. Western Village Inn Casino, 815 Nichols Boulevard, Sparks, NV; (702) 331-1069.

***Prime Rib Company:*** $5-$11. All major credit cards accepted. Pioneer Inn Hotel Casino, 221 South Virginia Street, Reno, NV; (702) 324-7777.

## NIGHTLIFE

During every season of the year, Lake Tahoe and Reno offer a variety of nightlife, from the casino showrooms to the small clubs and restaurants. The casinos tend to vacillate on their policies regarding big-name entertainment, which is expensive and considered a loss leader for the hotel. At Lake Tahoe, Caesar's Tahoe and Harrah's are the current leaders in providing short runs and one-night stands of pop, jazz and country headliners. In Reno, John Ascuaga's Nugget, Harrah's and the Reno Hilton frequently offer celebrity singers. Several casino showrooms prefer Hollywood and Broadway-style extravaganzas, and it's hard to beat the knockout punch of the Reno Hilton for lavish shows with a myriad of special effects. For guests staying at the casino hotels, a show sometimes is offered as part of an incentive package with the room, especially during off-season midweek stays.

At Lake Tahoe, entertainment is varied and frequent during the summer, ranging from lilting jazz concerts on the patio at the River Ranch Lodge to full presentations by symphonies at the Topol Pavilion, both on the North Shore. The Tallac Historic Site has regular open-air concerts throughout the summer, featuring jazz, folk, classic and New Age music. Local weekly entertainment guides are available in both Reno and Tahoe, and they usually can be found at the airports and in most hotels.

## MAJOR SHOWROOMS
## Lake Tahoe

***Caesar's Tahoe:*** The Circus Maximus Showroom offers regular big-name entertainment. Nero's 24-hour hotline gives entertainment details at (702) 586-2000. On US 50 at Stateline, NV; (702) 588-3515 or (800) 648-3353.

***Harrah's Casino Hotel:*** Broadway and Hollywood shows are offered in the South Shore Room, with the occasional name entertainer. On US 50 at Stateline, NV; (702) 588-6606 or (800) HARRAHS.

***Harvey's Resort Casino:*** Stage and variety shows are presented in the Emerald Theater. Occasionally, a big-name summer extravaganza is offered outside in the parking lot during summer. On US 50 at Stateline, NV; (702) 588-2411 or (800) 648-3361 for show reservations.

**Horizon Casino Resort:** Variety and magic shows are held in the Grand Lake Theater. On US 50 at Stateline, NV; (702) 588-6211.

# Reno

**Flamingo Hilton:** The large theater here generally hosts impersonations of stars such as Sammy Davis, Jr., Madonna and Charlie Daniels, and they usually manage to do a better-than-average job. 255 North Sierra, Reno, NV; (702) 322-1111.

**Harrah's Casino Hotel:** Country music stars and others hold forth in Sammy's Showroom. 219 North Center, Reno, NV; (702) 788-3773 or (800) 648-3773.

**John Ascuaga's Nugget:** The Celebrity Room is a frequent venue for name acts such as Al Jarreau and various country bands. 1100 Nugget Avenue, Sparks, NV; (702) 356-3300 or (800) 648-1177.

**Reno Hilton:** Big, lavish and expensive Broadway-style stage shows in the Hilton Theater create the most impressive regular entertainment in Reno. 2500 East Second, Reno, NV; (702) 789-2285 or (800) 648-3568.

## NIGHTCLUBS
## South Shore

**Alpen Sierra Coffee House:** Live music and entertainment. 822 Emerald Bay Road, South Lake Tahoe, CA; (916) 541-7449.

**The Beacon:** Live music and entertainment on the beach, both day and night. At Richardson's Resort. 1900 Jameson Beach Road, South Lake Tahoe, CA; (916) 541-0630.

**Christiana Inn:** Live music and entertainment are held weekends in summer and several days during winter, which is high season. Across from Heavenly Ski Area. 3819 Saddle Road, South Lake Tahoe, CA; (916) 544-7337.

**Caesar's Tahoe:** Nero's 2000 offers disco dancing from 9 p.m. nightly until the wee hours of the morning. There's a cover charge that usually ranges from $4 to $8 per person. Nero's 24-hour hotline gives entertainment details at (702) 586-2000. 55 US 50, Stateline, NV; (702) 588-3515 or (800) 648-3353.

**The Eagle's Nest:** This newly reopened restaurant and jazz club is located high on the top of a peak overlooking South Shore, in a European-style lodge. Live jazz Thursday through Saturday. 472 Needle Peak Road, Stateline, NV; (702) 588-3245.

**Embassy Suites:** Live music is offered in the Atrium Bar; Turtle's Sport Bar has disco dancing and various contests. 4130 Lake Tahoe Boulevard, Stateline, NV; (702) 544-5400.

**Harrah's Casino Hotel:** There is live music in the Summit Restaurant and Casino Center Stage. On US 50 at Stateline, NV; (702) 588-6606 or (800) HARRAHS.

**Harvey's Resort Casino:** El Vaquero restaurant offers free karaoke on Fridays and Saturdays from 10 p.m. to 1 a.m. There is also live entertainment in the Emerald Party Lounge and Llewellyn's restaurant. On US 50 at Stateline, NV; (702) 588-2411 or (800) 648-3361 for show reservations.

**Horizon Casino Resort:** The Aspen Lounge usually features karaoke one night a week. The Golden Cabaret features variety stage shows with dancing, acrobatics and comedy nightly, except Monday. On US 50 at Stateline, NV; (702) 588-6211.

**Hoss Hoggs:** Live music and entertainment, with "open mike" on Monday nights. On US 50 and Sierra Boulevard, 2543 South Lake Tahoe Boulevard, South Lake Tahoe, CA; (916) 541-8328.

**Lakeside Inn & Casino:** Live music and entertainment. 168 US 50 at Stateline, NV; (702) 588-7777.

**Mc P's Irish Pub:** Live music and entertainment. 4090 Lake Tahoe Boulevard, South Lake Tahoe, CA; (916) 542-4435.

**The Met:** Live music and entertainment. At Round Hill Center. 195 US 50, Suite 28, Zephyr Cove, NV; (702) 588-8220.

**Rojo's Tavern:** Live music and entertainment. 3091 Harrison Street, South Lake Tahoe, CA; (916) 541-4960.

**Special Events:** Comedy nights on Fridays. 3051 Harrison Avenue, South Lake Tahoe, CA; (916) 542-HA HA.

**The Warehouse Nightclub:** Live music and entertainment. 128 Market Street, Kingsbury, NV; (702) 588-9535.

**Wild West:** This large C&W nightclub is one of the most happening places at the lake. Even if you can't line dance or do other smooth moves, you'll enjoy watching the action of talented amateurs. Open Wednesday through Sunday. Old-time rock 'n' roll and ladies' night are on Wednesday, with dance lessons on Thursday, Friday and Sunday beginning at 7:30 p.m. Dance contests are held on Saturdays, and there's a free fajita buffet on Sunday from 7 p.m. to 9 p.m. Cover charge: $3 per person. 40 Round Hill Center, Stateline, NV; (702) 588-2175.

## North Shore

**Bluewater Brewing Company:** Live music and entertainment. 850 North Lake Boulevard, Tahoe City, CA; (916) 581-BLUE.

**Cal-Neva Lodge:** Lounge entertainment and dancing. 2 Stateline Road, Crystal Bay, NV; (702) 832-4000.

**Captain Jon's:** Music and dancing Friday and Saturday nights. 7220 North Lake Boulevard, Tahoe Vista, CA; (916) 546-4819.

**Crystal Bay Club & Casino:** Live music and entertainment in the Lounge and Crystal Room. 14 Highway 28, Crystal Bay, NV; (702) 831-0512.

**Diamond Peak Ski Resort:** Live music and entertainment in the Diamond Peak Loft. Après-ski parties in the winter (Fridays to Sundays). 1210 Ski Way, Incline Village, NV; (702) 831-3211.

**Gar Woods Grill and Pier:** Music and dancing. 5000 North Lake Boulevard, Carnelian Bay, CA; (916) 546-3366.

**Hacienda de la Sierra:** Live music and entertainment. 931 Tahoe Boulevard, Incline Village, NV; (702) 831-8300.

**Humpty's Sports Bar & Stage:** Live music and dancing. Happy Hour daily from 4 p.m. to 9 p.m. On Highway 28. 877 North Lake Boulevard, Tahoe City, CA; (916) 583-4867.

**Hyatt Regency Lake Tahoe:** The Stage Bar offers live music and entertainment nightly except Mondays. On Lakeshore and Country Club drives, Incline Village, NV; (702) 832-1234.

**Jim Kelley's Nugget:** Live music weekend afternoons. 20 Highway 28, Crystal Bay, NV; (702) 831-0455.

**Lakehouse Pizza:** Live music and entertainment. 120 Grove Street, Tahoe City, CA; (916) 583-2222.

**Lakeview Food & Spirits:** Music and dancing. 7081 North Lake Boulevard, Tahoe Vista, CA; (916) 546-7205.

**Marie France:** Live piano nightly from 6 p.m. 907 Tahoe Boulevard, Incline Village, NV; (702) 832-3007.

**Newsbreak Cafe:** Live acoustic music on Saturday evenings. Next to Incline Cinema. 901 Tahoe Boulevard, Incline Village, NV; (702) 831-8599.

**Pameez:** Live music and entertainment. Rock and roll or blues on Fridays and Saturdays, and bluegrass on Sundays from 8 p.m. to 11 p.m. 754 Mays Boulevard, Incline Village, NV; (702) 831-1350.

**Pierce Street Annex:** Music and dancing. Latest DJ sounds Thursday to Sunday. Music of the '70s on Sundays from 8 p.m. to 2 a.m. 950 North Lake Boulevard, Tahoe City, CA; (916) 583-5800.

**Reindeer Lodge:** Music and dancing. 9000 Mount Rose Highway, Reno, NV; (702) 849-9902.

**The Resort at Squaw Creek:** Bullwhacker's Pub and Sun Plaza Deck offer live music and entertainment. 400 Squaw Creek Road, Olympic Valley, CA; (916) 583-6300.

**River Ranch Lodge:** Big-name jazz groups and other musical entertainers hold forth in the summer on the grand patio overlooking the Truckee River. On Highway 89 and Alpine Meadows Road. 2285 River Road, Tahoe City, CA; (916) 583-4264.

***Rosie's Cafe:*** Music and dancing. 571 North Lake Boulevard, Tahoe City, CA; (916) 583-8504.

***Stanley's:*** Live music. 941 Tahoe Boulevard, Incline Village, NV; (702) 831-9944.

***Tahoe Biltmore Lodge and Casino:*** Live music and dancing in the Aspen Cabaret. Comedy on Monday nights at 9:30 p.m. featuring three comedians. Cost: $5. 5 Highway 28, Crystal Bay, NV; (702) 831-0660.

***Willii B's:*** Live music every Thursday night (Ladies' Night), and acoustic music on weekends. 125 West Lake Boulevard, Tahoe City, CA; (916) 583-0346.

## West Shore

***Sunnyside Lodge:*** Live music. 1850 West Lake Boulevard, Tahoe City, CA; (916) 583-7200.

***West Shore Cafe/Topol Pavilion:*** Outdoor concerts with name jazz, popular and classical artists are held throughout the summer. 5185 West Lake Boulevard, Homewood, CA; (916) 583-8504.

## Truckee

***Bar of America:*** Music and dancing Friday and Saturday nights. 10040 Commercial Row, Truckee, CA; (916) 587-3110.

***Cottonwood:*** Music and dancing Friday and Saturday nights, with jazz offered occasionally. Off Highway 267 at Hilltop, overlooking Commercial Row. 10142 Rue Hilltop, Truckee, CA; (916) 587-5711.

***Northwoods Restaurant:*** Music and dancing. 11509 Northwoods Boulevard, Truckee, CA; (916) 587-9435.

***O'B's:*** Live band featured on the last Friday of each month, from 8 p.m. to 11 p.m. 10046 Commercial Row, Truckee, CA; (916) 587-4164.

***Zena's!:*** Live music every Wednesday night. 10292 Donner Pass Road, Truckee, CA; (916) 587-1771.

## Reno/Sparks

***Adele's at the Plaza:*** Live entertainment. 425 South Virginia Street, Reno, NV; (702) 333-6503.

***Amelia's:*** Adult disco Friday nights. 655 South Rock, Sparks, NV; (702) 858-7316.

***American Bandstand Club:*** Famed American TV rock and roll impressario Dick Clark recently opened this disco club, where the walls are a living museum festooned with rock 'n' roll posters and gold records from obscure bands such as the Beatles. Open from 8 p.m. Saturday through Thursday, from 5 p.m. on Friday, and closed Sunday and Monday October through April. The gift shop is open 10 a.m. to midnight. There's dancing to Dick Clark's favorite music from the '50s to the '90s (including disco, reggae and rock). Patrons must be 21 years old. Free validated parking. Available for private parties and special events. On the second floor of Harold's Club at 236 North Virginia Street, Reno, NV; (702) 786-2222.

*Atlantis:* Once dinner is finished, the tables are cleared away, a wall is opened and major partying begins, with disco dancing. Open from 9 p.m. Monday through Thursday, and from 10 p.m. Friday and Saturday. Cover charge ranges from free to $6. On the second floor of the Clarion Hotel Casino, 3800 South Virginia, Reno, NV; (702) 825-4700.

*Baldini's:* Live entertainment. 865 South Rock, Sparks, NV; (702) 358-0116.

*Bonanza:* 4720 North Virginia Street, Reno, NV; (702) 323-2724.

*Boots Bar & Restaurant Grill:* Dance to C&W and country rock music videos. Participate in free nightly dance lessons or Sunday night karaoke. Free six-hour validated parking is available, and there is no cover charge. Open 9 p.m. to 2 a.m. Sunday through Thursday, and 9 p.m. to 3 a.m. Friday and Saturday. On the second floor of the Horseshoe Club. 229 North Virginia Street, Reno, NV; (702) 323-7900.

*Cantina Los Tres Hombres:* Live entertainment. 7111 South Virginia Street, Reno, NV; (702) 852-0202.

*Cheers Nightclub:* Live entertainment. 567 West Fourth Street, Reno, NV; (702) 322-8181.

*Circus Circus:* 590 North Sierra Street, Reno, NV; (702) 329-0711.

*Clarion Hotel Casino:* Live entertainment. 3800 South Virginia Street, Reno, NV; (702) 825-4700.

*Dillan's Dance Hall:* Big band dancing (swing, waltz, cha-cha and tango). Admission fee is $5 per person. Open 4 p.m. to 7 p.m. Sunday. Plantation Station Casino, 2100 Victorian Avenue, Sparks, NV; (702) 358-8942.

*Dilligas Saloon:* Live country music and entertainment. 1303 East Fourth Street, Reno, NV; (702) 322-8481.

*Discopolus:* This place features a 13,000-square-foot grill, sports bar and nightclub featuring 30 beers on tap (import, domestic and micro beers) served in frosty mugs, 14 customized millennium pool tables, large satellite TVs and nightly dancing. Happy Hour buffet and lunch are served. Smoking and non-smoking areas are available. 515 South Virginia Street, Reno, NV; (702) 333-5269.

*Donna's Midnight Roper:* Live entertainment. 945 East Stillwater, Reno, NV; (702) 423-4191.

*Eldorado:* 345 North Virginia Street (at Fourth Street), Reno, NV; (702) 786-5700 or (800) 648-4597.

**Fitzgeralds:** 255 North Virginia Street, Reno, NV; (702) 786-3663.

**Flamingo Hilton:** 255 North Sierra, Reno, NV; (702) 322-1111.

**Hacienda del Sol:** Karaoke on Thursdays. 2935 South Virginia Street, Reno, NV; (702) 825-7144.

**Hangar Bar & Grill:** Live entertainment. 10603 Stead Boulevard, Reno, NV; (702) 677-0890.

**Harrah's Casino Hotel:** Entertainment is in the Rendezvous Bar. 219 North Center Street, Reno, NV; (702) 786-3232 or (800) 648-3773.

**Holiday Hotel Casino:** 111 Mill Street (at Center), Reno, NV; (702) 329-0411.

**John Ascuaga's Nugget:** Entertainment is in the Casino Cabaret. 1100 Nugget Avenue, Sparks, NV; (702) 356-3304 or (800) 648-1177.

**The Joint Venture:** Live country music. 400 South Rock Boulevard, Sparks, NV; (702) 359-7878.

**Just For Laughs:** This is a comedy club located in the Reno Hilton. 2500 East Second Street, Reno, NV; (702) 789-2285.

**Little Waldorf Saloon:** Live music and entertainment. 1661 North Virginia Street, Reno, NV; (702) 323-3682.

**Metamorphosis Lounge:** Live entertainment. 3310 South Virginia, Reno, NV; (702) 827-4044.

**Peppermill Hotel Casino:** 2707 South Virginia, Reno, NV; (702) 826-2121 or (800) 648-6992.

**Porky's:** Karaoke on Tuesdays. 3372 South McCarran Boulevard, Reno, NV; (702) 825-3777.

**Reno Hilton:** Entertainment is in the Confetti Cabaret. 2500 East Second Street, Reno, NV; (702) 789-2285.

**Reno Hotel:** 200 Lake Street, Reno, NV; (702) 788-2000.

**Rodeo Rock Cafe:** Comedy and hot country music with DJ. 1537 South Virginia Street, Reno, NV; (702) 323-1600.

**Spiro's:** Karaoke on Fridays. 310 West Fourth Street, Reno, NV; (702) 323-6000.

**Texas Longhorn Bar & Grill:** Karaoke on Wednesdays. Franktown Corners, 2325 Kietzke Lane, Reno, NV; (702) 828-3927.

**Top of the Hilton:** Live entertainment. Flamingo Hilton, 255 North Sierra Street, Reno, NV; (702) 322-1111.

**Trader Dick's:** Live entertainment. John Ascuaga's Nugget; 1100 Nugget Avenue, Sparks, NV; (702) 356-3300.

**Zephyr Bar & Grill:** Live entertainment. 1074 South Virginia Street, Reno, NV; (702) 322-8177.

# Carson City

***Carson Station:*** 900 South Carson Street, Carson City, NV; (702) 883-0900.

***Sh'Boom Saloon:*** Acoustic open microphone jam on Saturdays. 225 North US 395, Carson City, NV; (702) 849-2226.

# Virginia City

***Cabin in the Sky:*** Live entertainment. On State Route 342 at Gold Hill. 960 Sky Lane, Virginia City, NV; (702) 847-0733.

***Calamity Jane's Saloon:*** Live music and entertainment. 58 South C Street, Virginia City, NV; (702) 847-0558.

# Minden

***Carson Valley Inn:*** 1627 US 395, Minden, NV; (702) 782-9711.

# APPENDIX A: TRANSPORTATION
## LAKE TAHOE
### Airports

**Reno-Tahoe International Airport:** This is the main point of arrival for most air passengers coming to Tahoe and Reno. The airport provides more than 100 daily flights by Alaska Air, America West, American, Continental, Delta, Northwest, Reno Air, Southwest, Skywest, United/United Express and US Air. Driving time to the North Shore is 45 minutes, and to the South Shore, 75 to 90 minutes. Off US 395 at 2001 Plumb Lane in Reno, Nevada. Information: (702) 328-6400.

**Lake Tahoe Airport, South Lake Tahoe:** This airport close to the city and Stateline casinos offers commercial jet service on Reno Air from Los Angeles, and on small commuter planes on Trans World Express from San Francisco. Two miles south of the Y on US 50 at 1901 Airport Road, South Lake Tahoe. Information: (916) 542-6180 or (800) 421-9353.

**Truckee-Tahoe Airport:** Serving the North Lake Tahoe and Truckee-Donner area. On Highway 267, 10 miles north of Lake Tahoe, at 10356 Truckee Airport Road, Truckee, California. Information: Truckee-Tahoe Airport District, (916) 587-4119.

**Carson City Airport:** Serving the Carson Valley area. At 2640 East Graves Lane, Carson City, Nevada. Information: (702) 887-1234.

**Douglas County Airport:** Serving the Gardnerville-Minden area. At 1146 Airport Road, Gardnerville, Nevada. Information: (702) 782-9871.

### Railway

**Amtrak:** Daily passenger trains serve Truckee from Reno on the east and from Sacramento, Oakland and San Jose on the west. Information: (916) 587-3822; (800) USA-RAIL (872-7245).

### Bus Shuttles

**Tahoe Casino Express:** Luxury motorcoaches operate 14 times each way daily between Reno-Tahoe International Airport and hotels in South Lake Tahoe (Caesar's, Harrah's, Harvey's, Horizon and Embassy Suites). The Casino Express has its own waiting lounge near the baggage area of the airport. The trip takes 75 to 90 minutes. Cost: $15 one-way. Information: (800) 446-6128 or (702) 785-2424.

**Reno International Airport Shuttles:** Available only to flying customers. Cost: One person, $35; if more than one person, $20. Reno International Airport, Reno, Nevada. Information: (800) 824-6348.

**Greyhound Bus Lines:** Serving Truckee and South Lake Tahoe. Open daily from 8 a.m. to 5 p.m., with stations in both Truckee and South Lake Tahoe. Information and reservations: (702) 588-4645 or (916) 541-2394.

**Park and Roll:** South Shore casinos offer free shuttle service from participating South Lake Tahoe hotels and motels. Service is on demand and can be arranged in your hotel lobby. In Stateline, Nevada. Information: (702) 588-2481.

**International Good Samaritans:** If you are unsafe to drive, ask any local bartender or restauranteur to call the Good Sams for you. They will assist you in finding transportation home. Stateline, South Lake Tahoe, California. Information: (916) 542-6326.

### Public Transportation

**Nifty 50 Trolley:** San Francisco-style rubber-tire trolley provides service for the South Shore area along US 50 from Stateline to Highway 89, from July to Labor Day. There are 38 stops during the 45-minute trek. Drivers are dressed in period costumes and provide live narration. Cost: Adults, $2; seniors, $1; children under 8 are free (all day service with unlimited stops). Open 10 a.m. to 10 p.m. South Lake Tahoe, California. Information: (916) 541-6328.

**Tahoe City Trolley:** This rubber-tire trolley replica serves downtown Tahoe City and adjacent recreational centers every 20 minutes from July to Labor Day. It operates between the Lighthouse Shopping Center and 7-11 on the West Shore. It is free. Open daily from 10 a.m. to 5 p.m. except for July 4th, when it runs 10 a.m. to midnight. Special event shuttles and party reservations (10 or more) are available. Information: Trolley Hotline, (916) 581-1634.

**Truckee Trolley:** Service between Donner Lake, Tahoe Donner, Commercial Row and other points in Truckee. Open daily from 7:30 a.m. to 7:30 p.m., June to September. Cost: Adults, $1 one-way ($2 all-day); seniors (60 and over) and children (5 to 15) ride half price; children under 5 ride free. Information: (916) 581-3922.

**South Tahoe Area Ground Express (STAGE):** Bus service in the South Shore area from the Y to the casinos, with select neighborhoods in between. Cost: $1.25 each way or $2 unlimited day pass (good until midnight). South Lake Tahoe, California. Information: (916) 541-6328.

**Tahoe Area Regional Transit (TART):** This is a regular bus service along Lake Tahoe's West and North shores between Meeks Bay, Tahoe City and Incline Village to Ponderosa Ranch. It also operates between Truckee and Tahoe City. Most lodging properties are near the bus stops. TART connects with the Truckee Trolley, Truckee Bus Connections, Tahoe City Shuttle, Greyhound and Amtrak. Special schedules are available during events. Cost for one-way pass: Adults, $1; children under 5, free. All-day unlimited pass: Adults, $2.50; seniors (55 and over), $1.75. TART operates from 6:30 a.m. to 6:30 p.m., seven days a week. Information: (916) 581-6365 or (800) 736-6365.

## Ski Shuttles

**Sierra Nevada Gray Line Tours:** Daily ski shuttle service (December to April) from downtown Reno casino hotels. Information: (702) 331-1147 or (800) 222-6009.

*Tahoe Queen:* This paddlewheel cruiseboat offers a breakfast buffet and après-ski party with live music during round-trip from South Shore to North Shore at Homewood, with skiing at Homewood or Squaw Valley. Call ahead for schedules. Ski Run Marina, South Lake Tahoe, California. Information: (916) 541-3364 or (800) 238-2463.

**Royal Gorge Cross Country Ski Resort:** Free daily shuttle bus between Rainbow Lodge and Summit Station, for Rainbow guests and skiers on the Interconnect Trail. Information: (916) 426-3871.

**Alpine Meadows:** Free ski area shuttle service from Incline Village on the East Shore to Sunnyside on the West Shore. Call for schedule. Daily connections with Tahoe Area Regional Transit (TART) public transportation. Information: (916) 583-4232.

**Diamond Peak, Nevada:** Free ski area shuttle service throughout Incline Village and Crystal Bay daily. Information: (702) 832-1177.

**Heavenly:** Complimentary shuttle service at Heavenly Ski Resort. Stops near or at most lodging properties every 20 to 30 minutes (8 a.m. to 5:30 p.m. daily). Buses serve both California and Nevada entrances to Heavenly. Information: (702) 586-7000.

**Kirkwood:** Daily shuttle from various South Shore properties. Cost: Round-trip fare, $2. On Highway 88, 30 miles southwest of South Lake Tahoe, at Kirkwood. Information: (209) 258-6000.

**Mount Rose, Nevada:** Sierra Nevada Gray Line operates one daily ski shuttle package service from December to April. Package includes one half-day lift ticket and round-trip transportation from downtown Reno (John Ascuaga's Nugget, The Sands, Reno Hilton and Clarion). Cost: $29. Information: (702) 331-1147, (800) 222-6009 or, outside Nevada, (800) SKI-ROSE.

**Northstar-at-Tahoe:** Free daily ski shuttle service (December to March) between Tahoe Vista, Kings Beach, Incline Village, Truckee and Northstar. Northstar's ski shuttle connects to TART public transit for skiers from West Shore and Tahoe City. Information: (916) 587-0257.

**Sierra-at-Tahoe:** Complimentary ski shuttle bus; stops five times daily at 30 different locations in the South Shore. Information: (916) 541-7548.

**Ski Homewood:** Free ski shuttle service between North and South Lodge and downtown Homewood. Information: (916) 525-2992. (North Shore and West Shore access provided by Tahoe Area Regional Transit (TART) with connections to Reno Airport. Use TART and receive full bus fare refund towards lift ticket. Information: (916) 581-6365.)

**Squaw Valley USA:** Free daily ski area shuttle service from The Resort at Squaw Creek. Call (916) 426-3651 or (916) 583-6985.

**Sugar Bowl:** Free ski shuttle at Donner Summit; weekends and holidays only. Information: (916) 426-3651.

**Tahoe Donner at Truckee:** Tahoe Donner shuttle operates daily. Information: (916) 562-6257.

## Limousines, Tour Services and Van Shuttles

**A Aabacadadra Airport Limousine Service:** Airport shuttles, tours and wedding transportation. South Lake Tahoe, California. Information: (916) 544-2200 or (800) 334-1826.

**A-Aabel Limousine Service:** Airport service by limousine, bus or van for Tahoe and Reno. South Lake Tahoe,

California. Information: (916) 542-2277 or (800) 458-9743.

**Activities Unlimited:** Tours around Lake Tahoe, guided river rafting day trips and ski shuttles in modern stretch mini-buses. Operates out of Tahoe Seasons Resort, South Lake Tahoe. Information: (702) 588-4772.

**Aero Trans:** 24-hour daily shuttle service, including the Tahoe Basin and Reno Airport. Crystal Bay, Nevada. Information: (702) 832-7666.

**Allegro Limousine:** White luxury limousines and 19-passenger luxury tour buses available for custom-made tours, airport shuttles and weddings. South Lake Tahoe, California. Information: (916) 577-2234.

**All Season's Tahoe Limousine:** Stretch limousine for airport transfers (Reno and Tahoe), weddings, birthdays, anniversaries and tours of Tahoe. South Lake Tahoe, California. Information: (916) 577-2727 or (800) 334-1826.

**Executive Limousine:** Tours of South Lake Tahoe, Carson City and Virginia City. Free hotel pick-up and return. Reno, Nevada. Information: (702) 333-3300.

**Five Star Enterprises Transportation Services:** Full ground transportation service (buses, limousines, vans, airport service and tours). South Lake Tahoe, California. Information: (916) 587-7651 or (800) 782-4707.

**Gray Line Tours:** Lake Tahoe, Reno, Carson City and Virginia City. Reno, Nevada. Information: (702) 331-1147 or (800) 822-6009.

**Lake Tahoe Tours:** Local guides provide year-round bus tours around the lake and Virginia City. Seats up to 110 people. Airport shuttles available to Reno and South Lake Tahoe. South Lake Tahoe, California. Information: (916) 542-2277.

**Reno-Tahoe Connection:** Limo-van conversion vehicles for airport shuttles or charters in the Lake Tahoe basin, Truckee and Reno areas. Reno, Nevada. Information: (702) 825-3900.

**Royal Limousine Service:** Personalized limousine tours of Lake Tahoe, Reno and Virginia City. Truckee, California. Information: (916) 582-1300.

**Sierra West Limousine:** Serving Tahoe, Reno and surrounding areas. Airport transfers, wedding tours and lodging packages. Fleet of presidential and stretch limousines. Information: Reno Airport, (702) 329-4310; or Lake Tahoe, (702) 588-1079.

**Tahoe Limo Tours:** Emerald Bay, Lake Tahoe, Virginia City and Carson City tours. South Lake Tahoe, California. Information: (916) 577-2727 or (800) 334-1826.

**Tahoe Zephyr Enterprises:** Tours of Emerald Bay, the Lake Tahoe rim and Virginia City. South Lake Tahoe, California. Information: (916) 544-TOUR or (800) 458-9743.

**Tours Unlimited:** West Shore, Donner Party, Sierra Tours, van transportation services, nightly casino shuttle and airport transportation. Tahoe City, California. Information: (916) 546-1355.

**Truckee Tahoe Limousine and Tours:** Stretch limos and a classic 1957 Cadillac limousine. Year-round airport transportation, weddings, tours and special charters. Truckee, California. Information: (916) 587-2160 or (800) 255-2160.

## Car Rentals

**A and A Truckee Tahoe Rental:** North Tahoe and Truckee. Will meet train or bus in Truckee. Information: (916) 583-0747 or (916) 582-8282.

**Alamo Rent a Car:** At the Reno Airport. (800) 327-9633.

**All Savers:** Serving Tahoe, Reno and Carson Valley. Information: (702) 825-2050.

**Avis Rent a Car:** At South Lake Tahoe and Reno airports. Information: (800) 331-1212.

**Budget Rent a Car:** At the Reno Airport and Center Street in Reno. Information: (702) 785-2690.

**Dollar Rent a Car:** At the Reno Airport. Information: (800) 800-4000 or (702) 348-2800.

**Hertz Rent a Car:** At Incline Village, South Lake Tahoe and Reno locations. Information: (800) 654-3131.

**Incline Village Compacts Rent a Car:** Serving Incline Village and Crystal Bay. Pick-up and delivery available. Incline Village, Nevada. Information: (702) 831-3726.

**National InterRent:** At South Lake Tahoe and Reno. Information: (800) CAR-RENT or (800) 824-6348.

**Tahoe Rent a Car:** Serving South Lake Tahoe with free pick-up and delivery. Tahoe Valley Motel at US 50 at Tahoe Keys Boulevard, South Lake Tahoe, California. Information: (916) 544-4500.

**Truckee Rent a Car:** Serving the Truckee and Tahoe area. At the Truckee-Tahoe Airport, Truckee, California. Information: (916) 587-2688.

## Taxis

**Arnie's Taxi Service:** 24-hour service, serving the North and West shores from Crystal Bay to Tahoma. Tahoe City, California. Information: (916) 581-0522.

**Bus Plus:** Taxi service. South Lake Tahoe, California. Information: (916) 541-4905.

**Donner Taxi Cab:** 24-hour service in the greater Truckee area. Airport service and deliveries available. Truckee, California. Information: (916) 587-0600.

**Paradise Taxi:** 24-hour service, sightseeing tours, airport service from the South Shore, and local delivery service. South Lake Tahoe, California. Information: (916) 577-4708.

**Sierra Taxi:** 24-hour service, lake tours, charters, wake-up calls and delivery service. South Lake Tahoe, California. Information: (916) 577-8888.

**Sierra Taxi Shuttle:** 24-hour taxi service. South Lake Tahoe, California. Information: (916) 544-7000.

**South Shore Independent Taxi:** Local service and South Shore to Reno Airport shuttle service by reservation. South Lake Tahoe, California. Information: (916) 542-0999.

**Sunshine-Yellow Cab Company:** 24-hour taxi service covering the South Lake Tahoe area. South Lake Tahoe, California. Information: (702) 588-5555.

**Yellow Cab of North Lake Tahoe:** 24-hour taxi service covering the North Lake Tahoe area. Kings Beach, California. Information: (916) 546-9090.

# RENO AND CARSON VALLEY

## Air Transportation

See listings for **Reno-Tahoe International Airport, Carson City Airport** and **Douglas County Airport** on page 662.

## Public Transportation

**Citifare:** This public bus transportation serves Reno and Sparks. Wheelchair access is available on all routes; public airport transportation is available. Cost: Adults, $1; children (6 to 18), 75 cents; seniors and disabled, 50 cents; children 5 and under ride free. Free transfers are available between routes. Daily, weekly and monthly commuter books and passes are available. Discount identification cards are available for seniors and disabled persons. Daily regular service is provided, with 24-hour service on some routes. Information: Regional Transportation Commission, (702) 348-7433 (24-hour information) or (702) 348-7450 (hearing-impaired callers only).

**Citilift Paratransit Services:** Public door-to-door bus transportation in Reno and Sparks for disabled persons who cannot ride Citifare. This service is provided for people of all ages who meet the American Disabilities Act paratransit disability requirement. Hours: Pre-arranged 24-hour service daily (minimum one day notice required). Cost: 60 cents per person; authorized attendants ride free. Information: Regional Transportation Commission, (702) 348-7433 (24-hour information) or (702) 348-7450 (hearing-impaired callers only).

*Note:* There is no public bus service available in Carson Valley and Virginia City.

## Railway

**Amtrak:** Railway serving Reno through Truckee. Shuttle bus transfers are available from Sacramento to Carson City. At East Commercial Row and Lake Street, Reno, NV. Information: (702) 329-8638 or (800) 872-7245.

## Bus Shuttles

**Greyhound Lines:** Bus transportation serving Reno, Carson City and Minden. Information: Reno, (702) 322-2970; Carson City, (702) 882-3375; Minden, (702) 782-8244; or Reservations Center, (800) 231-2222.

**Reno-Tahoe International Airport Shuttles:** Available only to flying customers. Cost: One person, $35; if more than one passenger in a cab, $20. Reno-Tahoe International Airport, Reno, NV. Information: (800) 824-6348.

**Tahoe Casino Express:** Luxury motorcoach operating 14 times each way daily between Reno-Tahoe International Airport and casino hotels in South Lake Tahoe (Caesar's, Harrah's, Harvey's, Horizon and Embassy Suites). Cost: $15 one-way. Information: (800) 446-6128 or (702) 785-2424.

## Limousine and Tour Services

**Aero Trans:** Serving the Reno area. Charters and airport shuttles available.

2000 East Plumb Lane, Reno, NV. Information: (702) 786-2376.

**Airport Mini Bus:** Charters and airport shuttles serving the Reno area. 100 Sunshine Lane, Reno, NV. Information: (702) 786-3700.

**Bell Limo:** Scenic tours of northern Nevada and airport shuttle services. Featuring Cadillac and Lincoln stretch limousines. Corporate Town Cars available. Visa, MasterCard and American Express. 100 Sunshine Lane, Reno, NV. Information: (702) 786-3700 or (800) BEL-LIMO.

**Executive Limousine Service:** Open 24 hours. $49 per person for tours of Carson City and Virginia City. Free hotel pick-up and return. Most major credit cards accepted. Reno, NV. Information: (702) 333-3300 or (702) 882-7776.

**Frontier Tours:** Bus charters serving the Carson City, Reno and Sparks areas. Carson City, (702) 882-2100; Sparks, (702) 331-8687; or (800) 831-2877.

**Reno Tahoe Connection:** Limo-van conversion vehicles for airport shuttles or chartered services ($40 per hour) in Reno. Information: (702) 825-3900.

**Royal Limousine Service:** Customized limousine tours of Reno and Virginia City. Information: (916) 582-1300.

**Sierra Nevada Gray Line:** Tours of Reno, Carson City and Virginia City. Cost: $19 to $49. Information: (702) 331-1147 or (800) 822-6009.

**Sierra West Limousine:** Serving Reno and surrounding areas; 24-hour service seven days a week. Airport transfers, wedding tours and lodging packages. Fleet of presidential and stretch limousines. Information: (702) 329-4310 or (800) 258-0408.

**Tahoe Limo Tours:** Virginia and Carson City tours. $45 per hour for professional guided tours. Visa, MasterCard, American Express. Information: (916) 577-2727 or (800) 334-1826.

**Tahoe Zephyr Enterprises:** Tours of Virginia City. Information: (916) 544-TOUR or (800) 458-9743.

## Taxis

**Capitol Cab Company:** 24-hour service around the entire Carson area. Wheelchair-accessible vans available. Carson City, NV. Information: (702) 885-0300.

**De Luxe Taxi Service:** Taxi cab, courier, and delivery service to the Reno and Sparks area. Complimentary wake-up service available. Visa, American Express, MasterCard. Information: (702) 355-5555.

**D & D Vets** (Designated Drivers Vehicle Escort Transport Service): 24-hour service in Reno. Visa, MasterCard, Discover. Information: (702) 333-6700.

**Reno Sparks Cab Company:** Serving Reno and Sparks. 24-hour service and wheelchair-accessible vans available. Information: (702) 333-3333.

**Star Taxi Company:** Serving Reno and Sparks. Information: (702) 355-5555.

**Whittlesea Checker Taxi:** Serving the Reno area. Information: (702) 322-2222.

**Yellow Cab Company:** Serving the Reno and Sparks area. Information: (702) 355-5555.

## Car Rentals

**Advantage Rent a Car:** Cars, trucks and vans. At the Reno Airport. Door-to-door pick-up within service area. Information: (702) 333-6677.

**Agency Rent a Car:** Serving the Reno area. Delivery and pick-up available. Information: (702) 786-3381 or (800) 321-1972.

**Alamo Rent a Car:** At the Reno Airport. Information: (800) 327-9633.

**All Savers:** Serving Reno and Carson Valley. Specializing in long-term rentals. Information: (702) 825-2050.

**Apple Rent a Car:** Free pick-up, delivery and maps available. Information: (702) 329-2438 or (702) 329-2137; call from Reno Airport for free pick-up.

**Avis Rent a Car:** Serving the Reno area. Pick-up service available at local hotels and casinos. Information: Reno Airport, (702) 785-2727; Reno Hilton, (702) 785-2727; or (800) 831-2847.

**Budget Rent a Car:** At the Reno Airport and Center Street. Information: Reno Airport, (702) 785-2545; Center Street, (702) 785-2880; or (800) 527-0700.

**Dollar Rent a Car:** At the Reno Airport. Free hotel courtesy bus available. Information: (702) 348-2800 or (800) 800-4000.

**Enterprise:** Information: Reno Airport, (702) 329-3773; Carson City, (702) 883-7788; or (800) 325-8007.

**Hertz Rent a Car:** Information: Reno, National Guard Way, (702) 785-2554; Flamingo Hilton, (702) 348-8860; or (800) 654-3131.

**Lloyd's International Rent a Car:** Serving the Reno area. Free pick-up and return available. Information: (702) 348-4777 or (800) 654-7037.

**National InterRent:** Serving the Reno area. Information: Sands Regency Hotel, (702) 786-3757; (800) CAR-RENT or (800) 824-6348.

**Sierra Mountain Auto:** Serving the Reno area. Information: (702) 322-5993.

**Thrifty Rent a Car:** Serving the Reno area. Information: (702) 329-0096 or (800) 367-2277.

**U-Save Auto Rental:** Serving Reno, Carson City, Gardnerville and Minden. Open Monday to Saturday. Information: (702) 882-1212.

# APPENDIX B: IMPORTANT PHONE NUMBERS

## Road Conditions

**CalTrans Department of Transportation:**
(916) 445-7623, (916) 587-3563 or (800) 427-ROAD.

**Nevada State Road Condition Report:** (702) 793-1313.

**Tahoe Hotline (road conditions, weather, dining and entertainment):**
South Lake Tahoe, CA, (916) 542-INFO; North Lake Tahoe and Truckee, CA, (916) 546-LAKE; or Reno, Sparks and Carson City, NV, (702) 831-6677.

## Weather Conditions

**Local, Lake Tahoe:** (916) 541-1151.

**Lake Tahoe, Carson City and Reno:** (702) 793-1300.

**National Weather Service:** (916) 546-5253.

## Transportation Agencies

**Coast Guard:**
Lake Tahoe Station, 2500 Lake Forest Road, Lake Forest, CA 96145; (916) 583-4433.

**Federal Aviation Administration:**
**Air Traffic Control Tower,** 1701 Airport Boulevard, Lake Tahoe Airport, South Lake Tahoe, CA 96150; (916) 541-3302.

**Flight Service Station, Pilot Weather Briefing**, 601 Rock Boulevard, Reno, NV 89502; (702) 858-1300 or (800) 992-7433.

**Local Airport Weather,** 1701 Airport Boulevard, Lake Tahoe Airport, South Lake Tahoe, CA 96150; (916) 541-1151.

## Visitor Information Centers

**Alpine County Visitor Information Center:** P.O. Box 265, Markleeville, CA 96120; (916) 694-2475.

**Carson City Convention & Visitors Bureau:** 1900 South Carson Street, Suite 200, Carson City, NV 89701; (702) 687-7410 or (800) NEVADA-1.

**Incline Village/Crystal Bay Visitor & Convention Bureau:** 969 Tahoe Boulevard, Incline Village, NV 89451; (702) 832-1606 or (800) GO-TAHOE.

**Lake Tahoe Visitors Authority:** 1156 Ski Run Boulevard, P.O. Box 16299, South Lake Tahoe, CA 96151; (916) 544-5050 or (800) AT-TAHOE.

**Tahoe North Visitors & Convention Bureau:** 950 North Lake Boulevard, Suite 3, P.O. Box 5578, Tahoe City, CA 96145; (916) 546-7100, (916) 583-3494 or (800) TAHOE-4-U.

**Plumas County Visitors Bureau:** 91 Church Street, Quincy, CA 95971; (916) 283-6345 or (800) 326-2247.

**Reno-Sparks Convention & Visitors Authority:** 4590 South Virginia Avenue, P.O. Box 837, Reno, NV 89504; (702) 827-7600, (800) 752-1177 or (800) FOR-RENO.

**Tahoe Douglas Visitor Center:** 195 US 50, P.O. Box 7139, Stateline, NV 89449; (702) 588-4591.

## Chambers of Commerce

**Alpine County Chamber of Commerce:** P.O. Box 265, Markleeville, CA 96120; (916) 694-2475.

**Carson City Chamber of Commerce:** 1900 South Carson Street, Carson City, NV 89701; (702) 882-1565.

**Carson Valley Chamber of Commerce:** 1524 US 395 North, Suite 1, Gardnerville, NV 89410; (702) 782-8144.

**Dayton Area Chamber of Commerce:** P.O. Box 408, Dayton, NV 89403; (702) 246-7909 or (702) 246-3899.

**Eastern Plumas Chamber of Commerce:** P.O. Box 1379, Portola, CA 96122; (916) 832-5444 or (800) 995-6057.

**Incline Village-Crystal Bay Chamber of Commerce:** 969 Tahoe Boulevard, Incline Village, NV 89451; (702) 831-4440.

**North Lake Tahoe Chamber of Commerce:** 245 North Lake Boulevard, P.O. Box 884, Tahoe City, CA 99145; (916) 581-6900 or (916) 583-2371.

**Reno Chamber of Commerce:** 405 Marsh Avenue, Reno, NV 89505; (702) 686-3030.

**Sierra County Chamber of Commerce:** P.O. Box 222, Downieville, CA 95936; (916) 993-4190.

**South Lake Tahoe Chamber of Commerce:** 3066 Lake Tahoe Boulevard, South Lake Tahoe, CA 96150; (916) 541-5255.

**Sparks Community Chamber of Commerce:** 831 Victorian Avenue, Sparks, NV 89431; (702) 358-1976.

**Tahoe Douglas Stateline Chamber of Commerce:** Roundhill Shopping Center, 195 US 50, P.O. Box 401, Zephyr Cove, NV 89449; (702) 588-4591.

**Truckee-Donner Chamber of Commerce:** 10065 Commercial Row, P.O. Box 2757, Truckee, CA 96160; (916) 587-2757 or (800) 548-8388.

**Virginia City Chamber of Commerce:** Virginia and Truckee Railroad Car, C Street, P.O. Box 464, Virginia City, NV 89440; (702) 847-0311.

## Parks and Recreation Agencies

**California State Department of Parks and Recreation:** P.O. Box D, Tahoma, CA 96142; (916) 525-7232, (916) 653-6995 or (916) 653-8380.

**Carson City Parks and Recreation Department:** 2621 Northgate Lane, Suite 57, Carson City, NV 89706; (702) 887-2262.

**Douglas County Parks and Recreation:** P.O. Box 218, Minden, NV 89423; (702) 782-9828.

**Incline Village General Improvement District:** 900 Incline Way, Incline Village, NV 89451; (702) 832-1310.

**Nevada State Department of Parks and Recreation:** 123 West Nye Lane, Carson City, NV 89710; (702) 687-4384.

**North Tahoe Public Utility District:** 8318 North Lake Boulevard, Kings Beach, CA 96143; (916) 546-7248.

**South Lake Tahoe Parks and Recreation Department:** 1180 Rufus Allen Boulevard, South Lake Tahoe, CA 96150; (916) 542-6055.

**Tahoe City Public Utility District:** 850 North Lake Boulevard, Tahoe City, CA 96145; (916) 583-3796.

**Washoe County Parks and Recreation Department:** 2610 Plumas, Reno, NV 89509; (702) 828-6642.

## State Parks

**Auburn State Recreation Area:** P.O. Box 3266, Auburn CA 95604; (916) 885-4527.

**Burton Creek State Park:** Three miles north of Highway 89. P.O. Box 266, Tahoe City, CA 96142; (916) 525-7982.

**Dayton State Park:** On US 50, 12 miles east of Carson City, NV. P.O. Box 1478, Carson City, NV 89403; (702) 687-5678.

**Donner Memorial State Park:** On Interstate 80, 12593 Donner Pass Road, Donner, CA 96161; (916) 582-7892.

**D.L. Bliss State Park:** On Highway 89, eight miles south of Tahoma, CA. P.O. Box 266, Tahoma, CA 96142; (916) 525-7277.

**Emerald Bay State Park:** On Highway 89, eight miles north of South Lake Tahoe, CA. P.O. Box 266, Tahoma, CA 96142; (916) 525-7277.

**Grover Hot Springs State Park:** Three miles west of Highway 89 on Hot Springs Road. P.O. Box 188, Markleeville, CA 96120; (916) 694-2248.

**Lake Tahoe-Nevada State Park:** 2005 Highway 28, Incline Village, NV 89451; (702) 831-0494.

**Sierra State Parks:** P.O. Drawer D, Tahoma, CA 96142; (916) 525-7232; reserve through Mistix, (800) 444-7275.

**Sugar Pine Point State Park:** Highway 89, one mile north of Meeks Bay, CA. P.O. Box 266, Tahoma, CA 96142; (916) 525-7982.

**Washoe Lake State Park:** Three miles east of Highway 89, East Lake Boulevard, Washoe Valley, NV. P.O. Box 1478, Carson City, NV 89403; (702) 687-4319.

# Bureau of Land Management

**California State Office:**
2800 Cottage Way, Sacramento, CA 95825;(916) 978-4746.

**Nevada State Office:**
850 Harvard Way, Reno, NV 89520; (702) 785-6628 or (702) 785-6483.

**Carson City District Office:**
1535 Hot Springs Road, Carson City, NV 89706; (702) 885-6000.

# PG&E
## Recreational Facilities

**PG&E Company Campgrounds and Recreational Facilities:**
925 L Street, Suite 890, Sacramento, CA 94010; (916) 446-6616
or (916) 386-5164 (group reservations).

## Fish and Game/Wildlife Agencies

**California Department of Fish and Game:**
1701 Nimbus Road, Rancho Cordova, CA 95670; (916) 355-0978.

**Nevada Division of Wildlife:**
1100 Valley Road, Reno, NV 89520; (702) 688-1500.

**U.S. Fish and Wildlife Service:**
4600 Kietzke Lane, Building C, Room 125, Reno, NV 89502; (702) 784-5227.

# United States Forest Service

**U.S. Forest Service Visitors Center:**
870 Emerald Bay Road, South Lake Tahoe, CA 96150;
(916) 573-2600;  (916) 573-2674 (tours).

**National Forest Recreation Reservations:**
(800) 280-2267.

**El Dorado National Forest:**
Headquarters, 100 Forni Road, Placerville, CA 95667; (916) 622-5061.
Placerville Ranger District, (916) 644-2324.
Pollack Pines Ranger District, (916) 644-2349.

**Lake Tahoe Basin Management Unit:**
870 Emerald Bay Road, South Lake Tahoe, CA 96150; (916) 573-2600.

**Tahoe National Forest:**
Headquarters, P.O. Box 6003, Nevada City, CA 95959; (916) 265-4531.
Downieville Ranger District, (916) 288-3231.
Foresthill Ranger District, (916) 367-2224.
Nevada City Ranger District, (916) 265-4531.
Sierraville Ranger District, (916) 994-3401.
Truckee Ranger District, (916) 587-3558.

**Plumas National Forest:**
Headquarters, P.O. Box 11500, Quincy, CA 95971; (916) 283-2050.
Blairsden Ranger District, (916) 836-2575.
Downieville Ranger District, (916) 288-3231.
Foresthill Ranger District, (916) 367-2224.

Nevada City Ranger District, (916) 265-4531.
Sierraville Ranger District, (916) 994-3401.
Truckee Ranger District, (916) 587-3558.

**Toiyabe National Forest:**
Headquarters, 1200 Franklin Way, Sparks, NV 89431; (702) 331-6444.
Carson City Ranger District, (702) 882-2766.

## Foreign Language Assistance

**The Northern Nevada Language Bank** provides a free volunteer switchboard available 24 hours a day. 4100 Canyon Road, Reno, NV 89509; (702) 323-0500.

## Golf Association

**Sierra Nevada Chapter, PGA:** P.O. Box 5630, Sparks, NV 89432; (702) 673-GOLF.

## Historical Societies

**Carson Valley Historical Society:** P.O. Box 957, Minden, NV 89423; (702) 265-2889.

**Nevada Historical Society:** 650 North Virginia Street, Reno, NV 89503; (702) 688-1190.

**North Tahoe Historical Society:** P.O. Box 6141, Tahoe City, CA 96145; (916) 583-1762.

**Truckee-Donner Historical Society:** P.O. Box 893, Truckee, CA 96160; (916) 582-0893.

## Native American Organizations

**Bureau of Indian Affairs (Nevada):** 1677 Hot Springs Road, Carson City, NV 89706; (702) 887-3590 or (702) 887-3550.

**Pyramid Lake Tribal Council (Paiute Indians):** P.O. Box 256, Nixon, NV 89424; (702) 574-1000.

**Stewart Community Council:** 5352 Dat-So-La-Lee Way, Carson City, NV 89701; (702) 883-7767.

**Washoe Community Council:** 400 Shoshone Street, Carson City, NV 89701; (702) 883-6431.

## Nature Organizations

**California Conservation:** P.O. Box 8199, South Lake Tahoe, CA 96158; (916) 577-1061.

**League to Save Lake Tahoe:** 989 Tahoe Keys Boulevard, Suite 6, South Lake Tahoe, CA 96150; (916) 541-5388.

**Tahoe Regional Planning Agency (TRPA):** 195 US 50, Roundhill, NV 89449; (702) 588-4547.

**Tahoe Rim Trail Fund:** 298 Kingsbury Grade, P.O. Box 4647, Stateline, NV 89449; (702) 588-0686 or (702) 588-8799 (hotline).

**Wildlife Care:** P.O. Box 10577, South Lake Tahoe, CA 96158; (916) 577-2273.

# Index

*Index*

# Acknowledgments

I would like to give credit and a world of thanks to those individuals who have helped to make this project a reality. Much thanks goes to my research assistant, Sherrie Christopher of Reno, whose diligence in pursuit of accuracy has been a major asset in the completion of this book.

Grateful acknowledgment is made to Kay Williams and Tiffany Reuter of the Tahoe North Visitors & Convention Bureau; Skip Sayre, Phil Weidinger and Dawn Elliot of the Lake Tahoe Visitors Authority; Matt Bonaudi of the Reno-Sparks Convention & Visitors Authority; Bob Anderson of the Incline Village/Crystal Bay Visitors & Convention Bureau; Suzi Brakken of the Plumas County Chamber of Commerce; Candy Duncan of the Carson City Tourism Authority; and Tammy Thompson of the Truckee Chamber of Commerce.

I would also like to thank the U.S. Forest Service, particularly Tahoe National Forest and the Lake Tahoe Basin Management Unit. Special thanks to Bob Moore, Peter Soeth, Andy Steele, Cyndy Hobbs and Ann Westling of Tahoe National Forest; Don Lane of the Lake Tahoe Basin Management Unit; Buddy Antos of Toiyabe National Forest; Inez Robbins of Plumas National Forest; and Debbie Gayner of Eldorado National Forest. I would also like to thank Margaret Phillips of the Bureau of Land Management in Reno and William Sessa of PG&E.

I am deeply indebted to three biologists in the California Department of Fish and Game: Russ Wickwire, Stafford Lehr and John Hiscox. Also to fishing guides Frank Pisciotta, Judy Warren, Bruno Huff, Jim Crouse, Jack Martin of The Sportsman and Mickey Daniels. I owe a debt of gratitude to Bob Macomber of the California Department of Parks and Recreation and to the Nevada State Parks' Bill Champion and Brad Kosch. I would also like to thank Dr. Charles Goldman of the University of California at Davis.

For helping me see the aerial perspective of Lake Tahoe, I offer a big thanks to John Voss of Caples Lake Resort.

Alpine ski resort people also have been of major assistance. They include Julie Maurer, Judy Daniels, Lee Weber, John Wagnon, Monica Bandows, Stan Hansen, Jan Vandermade, John Rice, Ted Austin, Rob Kautz, Pete Bachner, Werner Schuster, Marshall Lewis, Bret Smith and Tim Cohee. And there are the "veterans" of skiing, people like Carson and Vi White of Donner Lake and Don and Norma Thompson of Reno, friends for more years than I can remember.

On the cross-county side of things, my thanks go to John Slouber, Mike Wolterbeek, Debbie Waldear, Max Jones, Steve Lannoy, Gene West and Carl Ribaudo.

Innkeepers who helped with this book include Mike Weber, Bill Parson, John Brissenden, Andreas and Mary Mourelato, Al and Patty Multon, Pete Friedricksen, Doreen Plasse, Bill and Missy Sandeman, Pat and Jodi Stone, Sandi Beck, Rachelle Pellissier, David and Muffy Vhay, Jacqui James, Patti Giles, Michael Cornelisen, Barbara Sinnott, Bob McFadden, Mike and June Boyd, and Michael Lafferty.

Also, thanks go to lodging people Lonnie Mason, Tom Davis, Chuck Bluth, Mary Jane Kolassa, Kurt Kirmayer, Patty Travins, Pat Martin, Al Goldberg, Mitchell Ostrow, Trish Walker and the management and staffs of the Inn by the Lake, Squaw Valley Lodge and the Tahoe Truckee Best Western Inn. In Reno, thanks go to Danielle Braca, Emilie Melton Williams, Beth Cooney, Ruth Whitmore, Jarre Payne, Shannon Coley and Brian Lawson.

And thanks go to those associated with local attractions, including Jim Hagan, Bill Chernock, Merle Lawrence, David Geddes, Gary Lebeck and Steven Lapkin.

I also would like to thank the following golf managers and pros: Randy Fox, Michael Kahler, Lou Eiguren, Bruce Towle, Tom Duncan, Dave Rowe, Bob Klein, Jr., John Hughes, John Clendenin, Paul Lane, Don Thompson, Gary Bushman, Don Hay, Mike Mazzaferri, Mike Mitchell, Lynn Brooks, Lane Christiansen, Lane Lewis, Al Bailey and Don Radford.

# LAKE TAHOE WILDLIFE CARE, INC.

Lake Tahoe Wildlife Care, Inc., (LTWC) is an independent, non-profit volunteer organization whose function is to raise, rehabilitate and release orphaned and injured wild birds and animals.

LTWC operates under state and federal fish and game permits. No fee is charged for any wild bird or animal brought to the center, nor is any wildlife refused care.

Since 1978, LTWC has grown from a handful of people with an idea to help wildlife in their immediate area to an organization that now serves seven counties in 30,000 square miles of California and Nevada.

In 1994, LTWC cared for nearly 1,100 wild birds and animals and 99 different species. Although some animals are so severely injured that survival is not possible, the center has an excellent rehabilitation and release rate.

Located in the High Sierras on Lake Tahoe, the area boasts a large diversity of wildlife, and numerous injuries occur throughout the year from the impact of humans and domestic pets. The number of injured wild birds and animals treated at the center increases in early spring, during particularly hard winters, and with forest fires.

In the past few years, perhaps because of their population recovery rate, the center has seen more injured bald and golden eagles, plus nu-

merous hawks and owls. The center has had particularly good success with the rehabilitation of these large raptors.

LTWC depends solely on donations and fund raisers for the operation of the center. Funds are used for the purchase of food and special formulas, medication and veterinary assistance, and to house the injured birds and animals. The staff also provides community education by presenting illustrated, informative lectures to schools and service clubs, giving children and adults alike a good start in wildlife awareness.

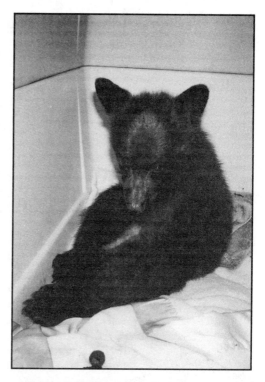

The local radio stations and newspaper provide LTWC a vehicle for distributing important information about how to co-exist with and preserve wildlife.

For more information on this organization, its needs and the services it provides to the community, please contact:

**Lake Tahoe Wildlife Care, Inc.**
P.O. Box 10557
South Lake Tahoe, CA
96158-3557
(916) 577-CARE
(577-2273)

# About the Author

Ken Castle is the former outdoors editor of the *San Francisco Chronicle* and the *San Jose Mercury News* and has enjoyed a 25-year career as a writer, photographer and editor for San Francisco Bay Area newspapers. Castle is a contributing editor of *Ski* magazine, and his articles have also appeared in *Outside, Conde Nast Traveler* and *Travel-Holiday*. His travels have taken him to six continents, from the jungles of the Amazon to the snowy peaks of the Swiss Alps, and to the depths of Lake Tahoe.

In 1979, as editor of the outdoor section of the *San Jose Mercury News*, Castle collaborated with Dr. Charles Goldman, a limnologist from the University of California at Davis, on "Project Tahoe." In the project, Castle and Goldman undertook a manned submarine expedition to explore the 10th deepest lake in the world.

Along with submarine pilot Patrick Hickey, Castle and Goldman ventured below Tahoe's surface in the *Pioneer I*, a 17-foot-long and nine-foot-high submersible originally built to inspect oil pipelines in the Gulf of Mexico. Setting off from Rubicon Point at the south end of Lake Tahoe, the *Pioneer I* dove 857 feet, over halfway to the lake's recorded depth of 1,645 feet. While submerged, Goldman and Castle examined the lake's rockfalls, outcroppings, crevasses and caves, as well as plant and fish life hundreds of feet below the depth at which surface sunlight disappears.

Project Tahoe garnered national and international media coverage and heightened public awareness of the lake and its fragile ecology. *National Geographic*, which sent underwater photographers to accompany Castle and Goldman on the expedition, ran a feature article on the project. The expedition also won the *San Jose Mercury News* a national media award for community service.

While Castle has yet to revisit the depths of Lake Tahoe in a submarine, he continues to be fascinated with the Tahoe region, returning year after year to the place that he says "feels like a second home." Castle is currently president of International Recreation Resources, a globally-oriented marketing and consulting firm in Burlingame, California. He and Kathy, his wife of 16 years, regularly enjoy a multitude of sports, including skiing, golf, flyfishing, hiking, camping and scuba diving.